Good Intentions

CENTER ON
INTERNATIONAL
COOPERATION

Studies in Multilateralism

Good Intentions

Pledges of Aid for Postconflict Recovery

edited by
Shepard Forman
Stewart Patrick

LYNNE
RIENNER
PUBLISHERS

BOULDER
LONDON

Published in the United States of America in 2000 by
Lynne Rienner Publishers, Inc.
1800 30th Street, Boulder, Colorado 80301
www.rienner.com

and in the United Kingdom by
Lynne Rienner Publishers, Inc.
3 Henrietta Street, Covent Garden, London WC2E 8LU

Library of Congress Cataloging-in-Publication Data
Good intentions : pledges of aid for postconflict recovery /
   edited by Shepard Forman and Stewart Patrick.
     p. cm. — (Center on International Cooperation studies in
   multilaterlism)
   Includes bibliographical references and index.
   ISBN 1-55587-854-7 (alk. paper)
   ISBN 1-55587-879-2 (pbk. : alk. paper)
    1. Economic assistance. 2. Economic assistance—International
cooperation. 3. Technical assistance—International cooperation.
I. Forman, Shepard, 1938– . II. Patrick, Stewart. III. Series.
HC60.G598   1999
338.91—dc21   99-38718
                                              CIP

British Cataloguing in Publication Data
A Cataloguing in Publication record for this book
is available from the British Library.

Printed and bound in the United States of America

   5 4 3 2 1

Contents

Acknowledgments

THE EDITORS OF THIS VOLUME ARE GRATEFUL TO THE SOCIAL
Science Research Council (SSRC), their partner in the Pledges of Aid project from its inception, and particularly to Ronald Kassimir, who coordinated SSRC's role in the initiative. Kenneth Prewitt and Eric Hershberg, also of SSRC, provided valuable advice and assistance in the conceptual stages.

We would also like to thank several individuals who served as advisers to the project, including Nicole Ball, Thomas Biersteker, James Boyce, Hugh Cholmondeley, Michael Doyle, Marianne Heiberg, Shijuro Ogata, and Volker Rittberger. In addition, we deeply appreciate the contributions of our colleagues at the Center on International Cooperation, especially Linda Long, Joyce Nduku, and David O'Brien.

Finally, this ambitious multinational study would have been impossible without generous grants from The Ford Foundation, the John D. and Catherine T. MacArthur Foundation, the United States Institute of Peace, and the Bellagio Conference Center of the Rockefeller Foundation. We are indebted to these institutions for their contribution to the success of our undertaking.

—Shepard Forman
Stewart Patrick

1

Introduction

Shepard Forman & Stewart Patrick

DURING THE 1990s, THE INTERNATIONAL DONOR COMMUNITY
pledged more than $100 billion in aid to three dozen countries recovering
from violent conflict.[1] From Cambodia to Bosnia, El Salvador to Rwanda,
and Tajikistan to Lebanon, multilateral and bilateral donors have supported
postconflict peace building with generous packages of grants, concessional
loans, debt forgiveness, and technical assistance. Providing a bridge
between emergency humanitarian relief and long-term development, these
financial and material resources are designed to persuade formerly warring
parties to resolve conflicts peacefully and are intended to lay the foundations for a sustainable transition to economic growth and participatory
governance. The outcome of these efforts will shape the fates of long-
suffering peoples and the future of international peace and security.

It is thus disturbing to discover that in many situations a significant
proportion of the pledged resources has either never materialized or done
so very slowly.[2] Despite ostensible good intentions, too often aid promised
has not been committed, aid committed has not been delivered, and aid
delivered has arrived too late. Moreover, the planning and implementation
of reconstruction aid has frequently suffered from inadequate preparation,
poor coordination, and lack of perseverance. In some instances the precise
amounts, sources, and contents of pledged aid have remained vague, as
have the specific conditions attached to it. At a minimum, these deficits
can be expected to produce skepticism among donors, recipients, and
publics alike about the ultimate value of the vast amounts purportedly
committed to reconstruct societies torn by conflict.

Despite the prominence of "postconflict peace building" on the international agenda, few independent empirical studies have analyzed the
composition, management, and delivery of multilateral aid packages to
countries emerging from violence. Nor have there been systematic efforts
to compare and generalize across diverse cases.

Responding to these gaps in current knowledge, the Center on International Cooperation at New York University and the Social Science Research Council in September 1997 convened an international group of scholars and practitioners to conduct a comparative study of aid delivery to postconflict societies. Employing a common methodology, teams of researchers from donor and recipient states spent eighteen months investigating the experiences of six cases: El Salvador, Mozambique, Cambodia, the West Bank and Gaza, Bosnia and Herzegovina, and South Africa. This volume contains their findings.

The book is organized into six case studies, bracketed by an overview chapter and a conclusion. This introductary chapter describes the nature of postconflict recovery and the problems of aid delivery that motivated our study. It then explains the selection of country cases and outlines the concepts and methods that framed and organized the collaborative research project. It ends by outlining the findings of the case study chapters and pointing to the value (and limitations) of the project's financial lens.

The Dimensions of the Challenge

The end of the Cold War raised hopes that the international community might employ an anticipated "peace dividend" to repair the ravages of the superpower competition in many war-torn and conflict-prone societies.[3] In fact, by the mid-1990s the world was wracked by some fifty armed conflicts, largely intrastate in nature.[4] The reinvigorated United Nations system quickly found its capacities taxed by complex humanitarian emergencies characterized by chronic violence, the breakdown of governance, the destruction of physical infrastructure, the displacement of populations, and massive human suffering. The initial international response was primarily humanitarian, so that by 1996, 10 percent of global official development assistance (ODA) and one-half of the UN aid budget were devoted to relief.

As the humanitarian tide crested and the chance for peace reemerged in many areas, the focus of international aid turned to laying the foundation for durable peace and recovery. There were many candidates for such assistance. By 1999, some forty countries were struggling to emerge from protracted civil violence (see Table 1.1).[5] Most of these ranked among the poorest in the world—and the furthest from international development goals. Just as grinding poverty helped to ignite conflict, so it promised to complicate subsequent recovery.

In addressing the international community's potential for aiding postconflict reconstruction, policymakers and members of the wider aid community have repeatedly invoked the most celebrated postwar recovery effort—the Marshall Plan.[6] Certain broad elements of the European Recovery

Table 1.1   Countries Experiencing Large-Scale Violence or Emerging from It,
            1989–1999

Africa	Europe	The Americas	The Middle East	Asia
Angola	Armenia	Colombia	Algeria	Afghanistan
Burundi	Azerbaijan	El Salvador	Iraq	Burma
Central African	Bosnia and	Guatemala	Lebanon	Cambodia
Republic	Herzegovina	Haiti	West Bank and	Indonesia
Chad	Croatia	Nicaragua	Gaza Strip	(East Timor)
Congo	Georgia	Peru	Yemen	Sri Lanka
Democratic	Yugoslavia			Tajikistan
Republic of	(Kosovo)			
Congo				
Djibouti				
Eritrea				
Ethiopia				
Guinea-Bissau				
Liberia				
Mali				
Mozambique				
Namibia				
Niger				
Rwanda				
Sierra Leone				
Somalia				
South Africa				
Sudan				
Uganda				

Sources: Carter Center, *1997–1998 State of World Conflict Report*; Brown, *International Dimensions of Internal Conflict;* Carnegie Commission, *Preventing Deadly Conflict;* and websites of World Bank, UNDP.

Program (1948–1952) might be worth incorporating in today's postconflict assistance: its emphasis on local initiative and ownership; its mixture of economic and political conditionality; its focus on modernization as well as reconstruction; its finite duration; and (where appropriate) its regional approach.

Nevertheless, fundamental differences between the present international context and that of half a century ago make unrealistic any hope of repeating the Marshall Plan model, especially the magnitude of its resources.[7] These dissimilarities include the current distribution of global power; the locus and nature of contemporary violence; the nature and absorptive capacities of today's postconflict states; and the resources and will of the donor community (see Table 1.2[8]).

In today's world, no single donor state or international organization can, by itself, address the multiple needs or bear the tremendous costs associated with reconstructing war-torn states as scattered and diverse as Bosnia and Herzegovina, Liberia, Cambodia, and Guatemala. Successful

Table 1.2   The Marshall Plan Era and the Contemporary World:
Different Contexts for Reconstruction

Marshall Plan Era	Reconstruction Today
Reconstruction followed conventional world war fought by modern armies and resulting in a clear victory for one side. War ended with unitary nation-states, separated combatants. Most borders were quickly recognized as legitimate.	Reconstruction follows localized conflict, often civil war between irregular forces of same state, with civilians as targets. The outcome of the conflict is often ambiguous and contested. Reconciliation is complicated by internal divisions and continuing, low-level violence.
Strategic concerns dominated, provided rationale for aid and "glue" for cooperation. Ideological and cultural affinity existed between donor, recipients.	No overarching threat unites donors and recipients into a common security community. Less similarity exists between donors and recipients (and more competition among donors). Humanitarian considerations are more prominent in aid decisions.
Most aid recipients were relatively wealthy democracies with advanced capitalist economies, and were economic partners and allies of donor. Recipients possessed impressive physical and human capital and high absorptive capacities. Reconstruction took place in a regional framework among contiguous countries.	Aid recipients are non- (or fragile) democracies, often failed states of marginal interest to donors. Most possess limited absorptive capacity, physical infrastructure, and social capital. War-to-peace transition is often concurrent with a transition from an authoritarian to a free polity and from a controlled to a market economy. Most recovery efforts focus on single country rather than region.
A single donor state with hegemonic power addressed the needs of sixteen recipient countries. Recipients engaged in "free-riding." International organizations were embryonic, NGOs marginal.	Multiple donor states and organizations address the needs of a single state. "Free-riding" may arise among donors. International organizations and NGOs play a prominent role and raise coordination problems.
Globalist impulses were ascendant in the United States (main donor), which possessed confidence, capabilities, and political will. Faith in state intervention, nation building was widespread.	Domestic considerations are ascendant in the donor community. Donors are skeptical about the role of the state in economic activity, the value of foreign assistance, and the prospects of nation building.

postconflict recovery thus requires multilateral cooperation among bilateral donors, UN agencies, international financial institutions (IFIs), and nongovernmental organizations (NGOs). Simultaneously, the heterogeneity of war-torn countries makes it difficult for donors to formulate consistent, harmonized policies to assist recovery efforts.

International efforts to reconstruct societies emerging from protracted violence fall under the rubric of "postconflict peace building." This concept was introduced in *An Agenda for Peace* (1991), Boutros Boutros-Ghali's vision for post–Cold War security. The UN secretary-general defined the phrase as collective "action to identify and support structures which will tend to strengthen and solidify peace in order to avoid a relapse into conflict."[9] Postconflict peace building is clearly consistent with the UN Charter's primary objective—"to save succeeding generations from the scourge of war"—and with member state commitments to "create conditions of stability and well-being" and to "promote higher standards of living." Despite painful setbacks in Somalia, Angola, and Rwanda, the concept was reaffirmed in Boutros-Ghali's *Supplement to An Agenda for Peace* (1995) and in Secretary-General Kofi Annan's UN reform package of July 1997.[10]

Multiple Transitions

Postconflict recovery commences with the signing of peace accords and lasts until some degree of political stability and self-sustaining economic growth is restored, a process likely to take several years. The end of most internal conflicts in the 1990s was accompanied by comprehensive peace accords addressing not only military settlements but also multiple political, social, and economic objectives. Although each postconflict situation (like each conflict) has unique attributes, successful recovery often involves a "triple transition": a *security* transition from war to peace; a *democratic* transition from authoritarianism (or totalitarianism) to a participatory form of government; and a *socioeconomic* transition, including both the rebuilding of economic capacities and (frequently) the movement from a controlled to a market economy.[11] The sequence and duration of these transitions can vary significantly. As a postconflict society recovers, its aid profile changes from emergency to reconstruction aid, and ultimately to development assistance.

Sustainable recovery from conflict requires laying new foundations for social peace, political stability, and economic growth in beleaguered countries. To advance these war-to-peace, political, and socioeconomic transitions, donors have supported an awesome array of essential activities. They have helped to draft and implement peace accords, plan and monitor disarmament, demobilize and reintegrate combatants, train local police, and restore human security. They have promoted efforts to reestablish the rule of law, conduct democratic elections, draft new constitutions, reform judicial systems, rebuild state structures, improve local governance, and monitor human rights.[12] And they have provided assistance to reintegrate refugees and displaced persons, provide essential services, restore transportation and communication links, rebuild social capital, replace obsolete infrastructure, jump-start industrial and agricultural production, reconstitute financial institutions, and revive commercial activity.[13] At its most ambitious, postconflict peace building resembles nation-building, as external actors seek to transform a country's "political institutions, security forces, and economic arrangements."[14] These undertakings are complex, costly, and risky. Their scope and complexity have forced donors to adapt their institutional, financial, and operational procedures and to explore new mechanisms to coordinate their separate initiatives.

As Nicole Ball observes, the phase immediately following a negotiated settlement "places the heaviest demands on donor resources."[15] Unfortunately, donors are still struggling to adjust their ample humanitarian and development capacities to meet the transitional needs of postconflict countries. Moreover, the resources available to support postconflict recovery have been restricted by budgetary retrenchment and growing disillusionment about foreign aid in wealthy donor countries.

Delayed Disbursement of Pledged Funds

Peace accords, and the aid commitments that accompany them, generate tremendous expectations within societies torn by conflict. By promising to launch economic recovery, pledges of aid can help to consolidate fragile peace agreements. The effectiveness of such incentives, however, depends on their credibility, and particularly on donors' "reputation for fulfilling pledges and a demonstrated ability to deliver the promised reward."[16] Generous promises mean little unless they can be translated promptly into accessible, flexible resources that make tangible improvements in the daily lives of long-suffering populations.[17]

It is thus of concern that much of the aid pledged by the international community arrives only after considerable delays. In the words of the World Bank, "Pledges are made, but commitment takes longer, and there is a considerable lag before actual disbursement takes place. Sustainable transitions out of conflict take several years, yet there is a tendency for donors to disengage once the conflict has receded from public attention."[18] As the case studies in this book demonstrate, unsustainable and unpredictable disbursements can wreak havoc on reconstruction and peacebuilding efforts. And by encouraging unrealistic local expectations, the donor community risks shattering these hopes entirely. A few examples will illustrate a broader pattern of problems.

Consider the case of the West Bank and Gaza Strip. In October 1993, donors responded to the Israeli-Palestinian Declaration of Principles by pledging some $2.4 billion over five years to lay the economic foundation for self-rule in the West Bank and Gaza Strip. By the end of 1994, less than 10 percent of this had been provided. By June 1997, donors to the Palestinian Authority (PA) had pledged more than $3.4 billion and committed nearly $2.8 billion, but less than half of the total pledges had been disbursed (see Table 1.3).[19] The United States, ostensibly the largest donor, had delivered on only two-fifths of its initial pledge. In justifying their performance, donors blamed rigid Palestinian centralization, local corruption,

Table 1.3   Aid Flows to the West Bank and Gaza Strip, June 1997 (U.S.$ millions)

Donor	Pledged	Committed	Disbursed
United States	500	296	207
European Union	357	357	230
European Investment Bank	300	89	n.a.
Japan	256	231	232
World Bank	230	185	66
Saudi Arabia	200	185	83
Netherlands	151	150	90
Germany	150	149	89
Arab Fund	150	149	0
Spain	123	122	31
Total for all donors	3,439	2,799	1,514

Source: Dempsey, "Palestinian Aid Faces Obstacle Course."

legal uncertainties, and Israeli intransigence (particularly periodic border closures). Meanwhile, the Palestinian Economic Council for Development and Reconstruction (PECDAR) complained of competing donor agendas, inappropriate aid conditions, and insufficient donor pressure on Israel.

Cambodia experienced similar difficulties with the uneven disbursement of approximately $3 billion promised to support its postwar recovery. The donor community pledged $880 million at the June 1992 Conference on Rehabilitation and Reconstruction of Cambodia. Only $200 million had been disbursed by September 1993 (when the new government was formed) and only $460 million by the end of 1995. According to one analyst, the "exceedingly slow" pace of aid disbursement was partly a result of donor interest in high-profile, large-scale projects requiring extensive planning. Many donor-driven projects were inappropriate for Cambodia's priority needs and development situation and barely touched rural areas outside Phnom Penh; indeed, "whole regions of Cambodia" failed to see "any tangible evidence of reconstruction." Embarrassed by their performance in disbursing aid, some donors asked the Cambodian government not to release data on aid flows after 1995.[20]

Slow delivery of pledged reconstruction assistance was also one of the major criticisms made by the Joint Evaluation of Emergency Assistance to Rwanda, an unprecedented multidonor effort to assess the aid response of the international community to a humanitarian emergency and its aftermath. Whereas emergency relief to Rwanda flowed smoothly, "financial support for national recovery [was] surprisingly slow," especially "in light of the potential social, political and economic costs of delays." Donors pledged some $700 million in response to the January 1995 Roundtable Conference for Rwandan Reconstruction (see Table 1.4), but by midyear they had disbursed only $68.1 million (less than 10 percent). Worse, only one-quarter of this aid had been received in Rwanda, and the government faced restrictions on using it to meet balance of payments difficulties or to purchase essential equipment. Moreover, much of the assistance pledged either consisted of repackaged "old money" or was needed to clear arrears to the World Bank and the African Development Bank. By the end of 1997, two United Nations Development Programme (UNDP)–organized roundtable conferences had mobilized $2.86 billion, but only $1.18 billion had been delivered to Rwanda.[21]

To some extent, these delays reflected Rwanda's limited absorptive capacity, particularly a shortage of skilled personnel in the aftermath of genocide, and reasonable donor doubts about the accountability and legitimacy of the new government. But delays were also generated by donor disagreements over the channels through which to coordinate and disburse aid; cumbersome procedures for designing and approving development projects; Rwanda's difficulties in accommodating the requirements and procedures of multiple donors; and disagreements among donors about placing explicit or implicit political conditions on the transfer of aid to the postwar government. Partly because humanitarian relief flowed more swiftly than recovery assistance, some two-thirds of the $2 billion spent during the first year of the crisis went to refugees in asylum countries rather than to tangible projects that benefited victims of violence in Rwanda. Chastising the donor community, the UNDP resident representative noted the "immense frustration . . . of recipient governments who receive large pledges of assistance but do not see all of the money arrive in the country."[22]

Similar aid complications, lags, and shortfalls have plagued other postconflict transitions, such as those in Lebanon, Mozambique, and Tajikistan.[23] The consequences are potentially grave. Insufficient external financial and other resources may exacerbate political instability and prolong economic stagnation; the two may then feed off each other to make recovery a more

Table 1.4   January 1995 Roundtable for Rwanda: Financial Tracking
(U.S.$ millions)

	Requested, January	Pledged, May	Committed, September	Disbursed, September
Financial support	189.9	186.2	111.2	50.1
Repatriation and reintegration	273.7	65.6	42.7	25.5
Rehabilitation and reconstruction	300.9	314.2	284.5	94.1
Outside Roundtable/unallocated	0.0	141.3	84.6	75.3
Total	764.5	707.3	523.1	245.1

Source: Joint Evaluation of Emergency Assistance to Rwanda.

distant prospect. Noting that any "delay in releasing pledged assistance means that much-needed resources are not available for meeting urgent reconstruction needs," the multidonor assessment of aid to Rwanda counseled donors to "suspend their normal administrative procedures in order to disburse funds." As the Swedish Ministry of Foreign Affairs notes, *"Pledges which are not honored frustrate the credibility of aid as well as of key players on the ground whose activities and mandate depend on timely access to aid resources."*[24]

Conventional explanations for unfulfilled pledges or delayed aid delivery have tended to be onesided, reflecting disproportionately either donor or recipient perspectives. In fact, both sides share responsibility for shortcomings in the design, delivery, and implementation of aid. On the "demand" side, states recovering from war often lack the capacity to absorb considerable sums of money and in-kind aid that emanate from diverse foreign sources and are intended for multiple purposes. In many cases, they do not possess the administrative structures required to design and implement comprehensive recovery plans. Insufficient human resources, immature political institutions, underdeveloped legal frameworks, limited transparency, and persistent (or resurgent) internal disputes may undermine good governance and facilitate corruption. Whether through venality, incompetence, or misfortune, some recipients fail to meet conditions established by donors such as the World Bank, the International Monetary Fund (IMF), UN agencies, or the member governments of the Organization for Economic Cooperation and Development (OECD).[25]

On the "supply" side, the generous pledges announced at multilateral conferences may in reality consist of little more than previously committed funds repackaged for political purposes. Rather than responding to urgent recovery needs, donor governments at times design aid packages to reflect their own political interests or the interests of their national service providers. Even when funds are mobilized, poor coordination among donors—and with recipient governments and NGOs—may result in duplicated or contradictory efforts, poorly allocated resources, and inappropriate projects. Delays may be exacerbated by lengthy bureaucratic formalities, protracted legislative reviews, and cumbersome procurement procedures. In some instances, multilateral peace-building initiatives have collided with structural adjustment programs set up by international financial institutions.

Case Selection and Research Methods

The apparent defects of postconflict assistance prompted us to launch a multinational, comparative study of the reconstruction experiences of six countries that have been pledged significant recovery aid. In order to explore both sides of the aid relationship, in each case we paired scholars from the recipient country and the donor community. The task of each team was to examine any financial and programmatic gaps that occurred along the chain—from pledges to disbursements to implementation. We asked the scholars to explain the causes of any apparent gaps with reference to a number of variables, including the context, composition, sources, and objectives of aid; the conditions placed on assistance; the mechanisms created to coordinate it; and the absorptive capacities and political environment of the postconflict state.

We chose to focus on Bosnia and Herzegovina, Cambodia, El Salvador, Mozambique, South Africa, and the West Bank and Gaza Strip. Several factors motivated our choices. First, each of these aid recipients has generated significant and sustained donor interest. Over the past decade, the donor community has pledged more than $25 billion to assist their emergence from conflict.[26] All six transitions have assumed symbolic importance as harbingers for the prospects of peace and security in the post–Cold War world. Second, their geographic range permits us to analyze external support for postconflict recovery across different regions, including Latin America, Europe, sub-Saharan Africa, the Middle East, and East Asia. Third, the sample includes different types of postconflict transitions following different types of conflicts: class-based civil war (El Salvador); postcolonial conflict (Mozambique); factional power struggle (Cambodia); battle for racial equality (South Africa); ethnic conflict (Bosnia and Herzegovina); and national liberation struggle (West Bank and Gaza). Fourth, the cohort represents different degrees of success, from consolidated peace (Mozambique) to fragile peace-in-progress (West Bank and Gaza). Finally, although each country has received significant attention from scholarly and policy audiences, there have been few comparative studies of recovery experiences[27] and no efforts to transcend the donor-recipient divide. In sum, the six countries constitute highly visible test cases of the international community's capacity to mobilize resources and design effective interventions for postconflict reconstruction and peace building in a variety of settings.

In adopting the comparative method, the participants in the study confronted a quandary well known to social science: the dilemma of "many variables, small sample size." One difficulty in trying to explain social outcomes is that (unlike natural phenomena) they are generally subject to multiple determinants. Moreover, these potential causes frequently exceed the modest number of available cases.[28] Recognizing such constraints, we adopted a loose version of the research method known as "structured, focused comparison." As Alexander George and Timothy McKeown describe, a research program is "focused" if scholars treat the cases selectively, concentrating on aspects relevant to the central research objectives and their data requirements. It is "structured" if researchers ask "a set of *standardized, general questions* of each case."[29] This method relies on within-case analysis of causal processes to make broad generalizations. The initial task for each country team was to establish empirically when pledges were made and whether these were fulfilled in a complete and timely manner. The researchers were then to evaluate potential explanations for any shortfalls in aid delivery. From the outset, the teams understood that gaps or delays in delivery might arise from a mixture of donor shortcomings, such as aid fatigue, free-riding, or competing interests, and recipient failings, such as political instability, absorptive incapacity, or failure to meet performance criteria or political conditions.

We asked each research team to collect and analyze data arising from four categories of questions:

1. First, researchers were to establish the *context, composition, sources, and objectives* of pledged aid. This implied a number of questions: What settlements triggered the international community's interest in assisting recovery? What amount of assistance was pledged? Which bilateral and multilateral donors offered this aid? What form did these packages take (grants, loans, debt forgiveness, etc.), and how was aid allocated by sector? Was the principal purpose peace building, economic recovery, or both? Did trade-offs exist between these objectives? Did aid reflect donor or recipient priorities?

2. Next, the teams were to examine the record on aid *conditionality, coordination, and delivery.* To begin with, did donors attach economic or political conditions to their aid? Were these appropriate, consistent, and credible? Were they enforced? Second, what mechanisms did donors create to mobilize, organize, and deliver aid? How did the donors and the recipient assign leadership (both of the overall aid effort and specific sectors)? What reporting and monitoring mechanisms existed to track aid flows? Were these transparent and effective? Last, how much aid was actually committed and disbursed? Was delivery regular and timely? Did performance vary by donor or sector?

3. Third, the researchers were to trace the *absorption, impact, and benefits* of delivered aid. Did the recipient country possess adequate institutional, human, and other resources to absorb and make effective use of external assistance? What role did the host government play in formulating a recovery plan and supervising aid delivery and implementation? Did the recipient have difficulty meeting aid conditions? What steps did donors take to build upon local capacities and to foster local "ownership" for recovery? Did assistance revitalize local political institutions, civil society, and commercial activity? Were there setbacks on the road to peace and recovery, and how did donors respond to these?

4. Finally, the teams were to assess the *causes, consequences, and lessons* of any gaps between pledges and disbursements. What explained shortfalls in aid delivery? What social, economic, and political difficulties ensued? What did donors and recipients conclude from these gaps? What do these experiences suggest for future multilateral programs of transition assistance?

These four categories promised to establish an empirical record of pledge delivery and to identify causes of delays and/or shortfalls. But the questions transcended these first-order objectives. They also probed the design, coordination, and implementation of foreign assistance and the respective roles of the donor community and the recipient in drafting reconstruction plans, mobilizing resources, establishing the terms of assistance, and executing recovery.

By pairing researchers with deep knowledge of donor and recipient countries, and by analyzing each case in detail according to a common research protocol, the project was intended to allow comparisons of different reconstruction experiences and to permit broad analytic and policy lessons. We hoped to illuminate the linkages (or broken links) between donor initiatives and local conditions in settings of complexity and unpredictable change. Such findings, by revealing the preconditions for timely and effective aid, might permit concrete policy recommendations about the design and coordination of recovery assistance.

The teams of scholars conducted extensive research within their case study countries, interviewing local officials and donor representatives and tracking aid flows through both donor and recipient country records. They also consulted widely with high officials at bilateral aid agencies and foreign ministries; international financial institutions; and the departments, programs, and agencies of the United Nations.

Given the space constraints of individual chapters, it was impossible for the case study authors to devote equivalent attention to each of the some two dozen questions outlined above. Accordingly, the project coordinators granted them considerable flexibility to focus on those questions especially pertinent to their particular case study. Nevertheless, the resulting chapters permit comparisons across the cases, allowing some important findings and policy prescriptions, as elaborated later in this introduction, in Chapter 2, and in the concluding chapter.

Definitional Issues

In carrying out this study, the research teams had to reach consensus on the usage of certain terms and concepts, including definitions of different aid flows and the term "postconflict."

Pledges, commitments, and disbursements. As used in this volume, a *pledge* denotes a public expression of donor intent to mobilize funds for which an approximate sum is given. Although aid pledges shape public and official expectations in both recipient and donor countries, donors themselves do not treat pledges as an official aid category (indeed, they often fail to keep track of them). Rather, donors begin tracking aid flows at the stage of *commitment,* defined as a firm obligation by a bilateral donor government or international organization, expressed in a contract or agreement, to furnish a recipient country with a specified amount of public assistance, under agreed financial terms and for specific purposes. Finally, a *disbursement* represents "the actual international transfer of financial resources." Depending on the type of aid flow (e.g., foreign currency funds, technical assistance, debt forgiveness), disbursements may be recorded at various stages.[30] For the purposes of this volume, the term "aid" is used broadly, to include grants, concessional loans, and harder loans also designed to advance recovery.

Postconflict. The label "postconflict" may be misleading when applied to countries where formerly warring parties have signed peace agreements. In the first place, the conflicts of power, interest, or identity that spawn civil violence do not disappear after the cessation of formal hostilities. Instead, the parties to peace accords simply consent to resolve their differences in a nonviolent manner through new procedures and institutions that may possess fragile legitimacy. In practice, violence may persist at lower levels within the society, continue unabated in certain regions, or flare sporadically during crises. Often, as in the cases of South Africa and El Salvador, conflict may transmute into random violence or criminality that threatens social stability. Consolidating fragile settlements remains a long-term process, one driven by internal dynamics and susceptible to reversals. The goal for donors is to design assistance packages that provide incentives for the nonviolent expression, management, and resolution of inevitable conflicts.

The Decentralized, Ad Hoc Nature of Reconstruction Assistance

This book's case studies show that there is no *regime*[31]—in the sense of institutionalized norms, rules, and decisionmaking procedures—governing multilateral support for reconstruction. Recently, donors have taken tentative steps to formulate common principles and best practices to inform their interventions. These include the OECD/DAC *Guidelines on Conflict, Peace, and Development Cooperation* and the UN's "Strategic Framework Approach for Response to and Recovery from Crisis." Nevertheless, external support for postconflict recovery remains a voluntary and essentially ad hoc enterprise. Bilateral donors, UN agencies, international financial institutions, and regional organizations are selective in their involvement in particular countries, and they reinvent structures of coordination from case to case.

To begin with, bilateral donors discriminate among crisis countries. The fate of any particular postconflict country is inevitably of greater interest to certain national governments than to others, so that each recovery effort attracts a unique group of bilateral donors. Their motivations and levels of engagement will reflect some combination of humanitarian, economic, diplomatic, strategic, and domestic political interests.[32]

In Bosnia and Herzegovina, for example, the "contact group" of great powers took the initiative to restore peace and to assist in the reconstruction of a country whose fate they considered pivotal for regional and perhaps international peace and security. The same donors expended much less energy in assisting conflict resolution and postwar reconstruction in (for example) Liberia or Tajikistan. In El Salvador, the United States shepherded the transition to peace and economic recovery in a country traditionally perceived to be within the U.S. sphere of influence. Likewise, Japan took the lead in Cambodian reconstruction to assert a regional role and to ensure a successful conclusion to its first foray into UN peacekeeping. (France's own heavy involvement in Cambodia, in turn, was motivated in part by desires to assert a global role and to further a cultural cause, *la francophonie*). In certain cases, domestic political dynamics may provide an initial impetus for donor commitments, shape the conditions that donors place on their aid, and determine their steadfastness in fulfilling their obligations. The Clinton administration's support for postapartheid South Africa and its attitudes toward Palestinian recovery have been influenced by important domestic constituencies.

Nor have donors agreed to a formula for burden sharing that can be applied to particular cases. This may be inevitable, given the diverse and sometimes competing objectives of multiple political actors and agencies. Frictions over burden sharing and leadership of the multilateral aid effort have been a recurrent problem, including in Bosnia and Herzegovina and in the West Bank and Gaza Strip. In both cases, disputes arose between the United States, the lead diplomatic actor, and the European Union, the lead assistance actor.

Reconstruction assistance can contribute to the goal of peace maintenance[33] in postconflict environments. Unfortunately, the frameworks to design, coordinate, and deliver such aid remain woefully underinstitutionalized. Essentially, the donor community improvises a new aid response for each country. The past decade has also revealed that donor financing for recovery efforts is uncertain and that its effectiveness is marred by inadequate coordination among multiple external actors pursuing different goals. To make optimal use of scarce resources, the donor community needs to establish more reliable institutional and financial arrangements.

Outline of the Book

Chapter 2 addresses seven challenges that bilateral and multilateral donors must confront to improve the coordination and impact of aid for postconflict recovery. To begin with, donors need to formulate a common "strategic framework" that will guide their collective effort in each crisis country. This shared vision should outline the dimensions of the task and establish principles to govern aid design and delivery. It should also facilitate the prompt assessment of recipient needs, the joint programming of aid, the designation of lead agencies, and the creation of indicators to monitor progress toward recovery and peace-building goals.

Second, donors should create new mechanisms to mobilize resources for interventions falling between humanitarian relief and traditional development assistance. Postconflict environments call for flexible, fast-disbursing funds and for multilateral pledging conferences that are more responsive to recipient needs. Third, the major bilateral and multilateral donors must pursue institutional reforms that complement these new financial instruments. Recent initiatives to address postconflict recovery undertaken within the UN system, by the Bretton Woods institutions, and among OECD/DAC member states have been tentative and have not measurably improved coordination among these autonomous actors.

Fourth, the donor community must adopt a more explicit and consistent approach to placing conditions on its reconstruction assistance. In particular, donors must reconcile their support for economic stabilization and structural adjustment with their peace-building objectives. Given the inherently *political* nature of the postconflict environment, it is futile and counterproductive to condition recovery aid strictly on narrow economic criteria. Fifth, donors need to complement better coordination at headquarters with better coordination in the field. To date, there have been as many different local structures of aid coordination as there have been cases of postconflict assistance. There has been little effort to compile the lessons of these experiences or evaluate what works best under what circumstances.

Sixth, donors need to place the capacities of societies emerging from conflict at center stage. Local authorities must be involved at all stages of the aid process and assume greater responsibilities as their potential allows. Donors can strengthen local capacities by financing important public sector expenditures, facilitating debt reduction, encouraging the mobilization of local resources, and (where appropriate) relaxing macroeconomic and fiscal rigor. Finally, the donor community must introduce greater accountability and transparency into aid delivery and implementation. An immediate step should be to create a standardized system for reporting and monitoring pledges, commitments, and disbursements. In addition, donors should sharpen the analytical tools they use to assess the *impact* of the aid that they provide.

Different Conflicts, Different Contexts for Recovery

External donors obviously need to tailor their aid interventions to specific country circumstances. Just as violent conflicts differ in their cause(s), duration, and intensity, so peace settlements differ in their terms, fragility, and economic implications. Table 1.5 (pp. 18–19) outlines the context of postconflict recovery for the six cases in this volume.

In each instance, the trigger for massive donor involvement was a peace accord or political settlement. In every case but one (South Africa), the machinery created to supervise the delivery and implementation of aid coexisted, often uneasily, with a framework to oversee the implementation of the terms of peace accords. In four countries—Cambodia, El Salvador, Mozambique, and Bosnia and Herzegovina—external assistance began in the context of a multidimensional peace operation. Although recovery assistance and peace implementation are meant to be mutually reinforcing, the mechanisms supervising these parallel tracks typically have different (if overlapping) memberships, mandates, and priorities.

Cambodia

In Chapter 3, Sorpong Peou and Kenji Yamada describe international support for the reconstruction of Cambodia following the Paris Agreements of October 1991. These accords, signed by several armed factions, ended two decades of devastating warfare. They were made possible by the exhaustion of the combatants, a decline in support from Cold War patrons, and external diplomatic pressure.

The Paris Agreements envisioned that aid would support three transitions: a shift from war to peace, including the cantonment, disarmament, and demobilization of combatants and the repatriation and reintegraton of refugees and internally displaced persons; the transformation of a socialist command economy into a free market system; and the movement from an authoritarian regime to a pluralist democracy. To prepare a neutral environment for elections, the Cambodian factions consented to a United Nations Transitional Authority in Cambodia (UNTAC). Both the Cambodian parties and external donors envisioned two recovery stages: a rehabilitation phase to meet the immediate needs of the population and to restore basic infrastructure, followed by a reconstruction phase relying heavily on the private sector.

During the years 1991–1997, the international community pledged some $3.26 billion and disbursed $2.33 billion (or 71 percent of the pledges) for Cambodian recovery. As Peou and Yamada observe, gaps between pledges and disbursements fluctuated from year to year, from donor to donor, and from sector to sector. Aid delivery was slow during the early years; multilateral donors had a lower disbursement rate than bilateral donors; and aid for infrastructure was easier to deliver than assistance for other purposes, including state building and governance.

In Peou and Yamada's view, donors contributed to aid delays and shortfalls in several ways: by reengaging the country with only a rudimentary understanding of local socioeconomic conditions and political realities; by clinging to impractical expectations about the prospects of aid itself to transform postwar (and postgenocide) Cambodia into a liberal market democracy; and by designing assistance projects that too often reflected donors' own national or institutional interests rather than objective local priorities. Donors compounded these errors by failing to create robust mechanisms of aid coordination, by declining to streamline their procedures to the context of a war-torn country, by neglecting to harmonize strategies with international NGOs, and by pursuing competing national objectives.

The Paris Agreements had mandated that the Cambodians themselves would take the lead in determining their own recovery needs. Given delays in forming a postwar government, this stipulation delayed the drafting of a national recovery plan. In addition, the consultative body created to monitor and harmonize contributions of aid, the International Committee on the Reconstruction of Cambodia (ICORC), met for the first time nearly two years after the Paris Agreements. Even then, it failed to define the roles of donors, establish priority needs, or specify a timetable for pledges and disbursements. Finally, the donor community failed to collaborate sufficiently in designing (and enforcing) aid conditions or in pressing the Cambodian government to mobilize domestic resources for recovery.

Nevertheless, Peou and Yamada emphasize, the gaps in aid delivery must be placed in the context of Cambodia's status as an extremely weak state possessing limited human, administrative, and technical capacities; minimal physical infrastructure; and a decimated civil society. The Cambodian government, permeated by a pathological combination of factional rivalries, pervasive corruption, and institutional incapacity, proved an ineffective partner to international donors, who repeatedly called for reformed structures of

Table 1.5 The Context of Postconflict Recovery

	Cambodia	El Salvador	Mozambique	West Bank and Gaza	South Africa	Bosnia-Herzegovina
Nature of Conflict	Civil war (1979–1991) involving various political factions	Class-based civil war (1979–1991) between government and FMLN guerillas	Post-colonial civil war (1975–1992) between Frelimo government, Renamo rebels	Low-intensity struggle for Palestinian sovereignty against Israel	Low-intensity struggle against *apartheid* regime	Civil war (1991–1995) among ethnic groups following dissolution of Yugoslavia
Context of Its "Resolution"	End of the Cold War and external diplomatic pressure. Cease-fire and power-sharing pending elections.	End of Cold War and exhaustion of combatants. FMLN agrees to end insurgency and contest power electorally.	End of the Cold War and exhaustion of combatants. Cease-fire pending elections.	Volatile peace process, premised on "land for peace." Final status fluid.	Capitulation of white minority regime and end of ANC armed struggle.	Contact Group imposes peace on warring factions in the context of a military stalemate.
Relevant Peace Accord or Settlement	Paris Peace Agreements, October 1991	Peace Accords, Mexico, January 1992	General Peace Agreement (GPA), Rome, October 1992	Oslo Declaration of Principles, September 1993	Conference on a Democratic South Africa (CODESA), 1990–1993	Dayton General Framework Agreement for Peace (GFAP), December 1995
Framework for Peace Implementation	*Peacekeeping:* United Nations Transitional Authority in Cambodia (UNTAC)	*Civilian Presence:* United Nations Observer Mission in El Salvador (ONUSAL)	*Peacekeeping:* United Nations Operation in Mozambique (ONUMOZ)	Rules of the game are outlined in successive interim agreements. U.S. takes lead diplomatic role	None	*Peacekeeping:* Implementation Force (IFOR); Stabilization Force (SFOR). *Civilian Presence:* Peace Implementation Council (PIC) and Office of the High Representative (OHR).

(continues)

Table 1.5 continued

	Cambodia	El Salvador	Mozambique	West Bank and Gaza	South Africa	Bosnia-Herzegovina
Nature of Transition						
Security	Transition from war to peace: disarmament and demobilization; reintegration of refugees and the internally displaced.	Transition from war to peace: disarmament, demobilization; reintegration of refugees and the internally displaced; creation of national civilian police.	Transition from war to peace, including reintegration of combatants, refugees, and the internally displaced.	End of PLO armed struggle and withdrawal of Israeli security forces. Reintegration of guerillas.	Dismantling of repressive security apparatus. End of armed struggle, reintegration of ANC soldiers.	Transition from war to tenuous peace. Demobilization of combatants, return of refugees and the internally displaced.
Political	Shift toward pluralist democracy. First elections held for a constituent assembly, May 1993.	Political reform toward a more inclusive democracy and democratic institutions. Peaceful elections held in 1994.	Shift from authoritarian regime to pluralist democracy, including first free elections, held in October 1994.	Establishment of Palestinian Authority in 1994 and the creation of quasi-state structures.	Interim Constitution is approved in May 1993. First multiracial elections held in April 1994.	Creation of decentralized, multi-ethnic state and the holding of democratic elections.
Economic	Rehabilitation (addressing basic needs) followed by reconstruction. Transition from a socialist economy to free market.	Reconstruction of the former conflict zones. Continued economic liberalization and structural adjustment.	Transition from a war to a market economy. Continued economic liberalization and structural adjustment.	Reconstruction of physical infrastructure and attempt to build a viable economy in the Palestinian Territories.	Reconstruction focuses on marginalized regions. Integration into global economy on neoliberal lines.	Reconstruction of wartime damage. Resumption of shift from command economy to free market.

Source: Compiled from the case studies discussed in this book.

governance. These shortcomings prevented the government from assuming leadership in designing a coherent recovery plan, managing the flow of external assistance, or absorbing aid in appropriate projects.

El Salvador

In Chapter 4, Herman Rosa and Michael Foley examine international assistance to El Salvador following the January 1992 peace accords between the Salvadoran government and the Farabundo Martí National Liberation Front (FMLN). The resolution of this twelve-year conflict involved three transitions: a war-to-peace transition involving the demobilization and reinsertion of rebel and government forces, the reintegration of refugees and internally displaced persons, and the restoration of basic services and infrastructure in the former conflict zones; a political transition toward a more inclusive democracy; and a continuing process of economic reform on a neoliberal model.

The United Nations, through its Observer Mission in El Salvador (ONUSAL) served as an honest broker, facilitating negotiations between the government and the FMLN, monitoring compliance with the peace accords, and mediating disputes between the parties. At critical junctures, the UN intervened to keep the peace process on track. On the aid front, the World Bank assisted the government in designing a National Reconstruction Plan (NRP), and it hosted four Consultative Group (CG) meetings in Paris to mobilize resources. UNDP played an important role in supporting demobilization, democratic transition, and reconstruction in former conflict zones.

The United States, as the dominant external political and economic actor, shepherded El Salvador's postwar transition, supervising the peace process and mobilizing impressive resources to meet reconstruction and peace-related needs. Its enormous presence in the country allowed it to jump-start Salvadoran economic recovery. It also used formal and informal conditionality to ensure the governement's compliance with some aspects of the peace process. On the other hand, as Rosa and Foley observe, its very dominance shielded El Salvador from other potential aid conditions and tempted some donors to reduce their own aid contributions.

The World Bank, El Salvador's other major patron, continued to support the government's ongoing neoliberal economic reform. This preoccupation with structural adjustment and macroeconomic stabilization gave scant attention to the special costs associated with the war-to-peace transition and the democratization of Salvadoran politics. Moreover, neoliberal orthodoxy risked undermining political reconciliation and social peace. Neither the Bank nor the United States used its leverage to induce the government to mobilize adequate national resources for peace-related needs or to address the underlying social and economic causes of the war.

Given the Salvadoran government's own impressive capacities, the donor community never established a centralized system to coordinate aid flows. Implementing an economic program blessed by both Washington and the World Bank, the government kept most economic issues off the bargaining table during peace talks. Thus the CG mechanism served mainly as a venue for mobilizing pledges and a forum for tracking aid flows. Both the Salvadoran government and the United States, which assisted it in drafting the National Reconstruction Plan, underestimated the costs of the war-to-peace and political transitions, particularly the expenses associated with ex-combatant reinsertion and democratic institutions.

Despite these shortcomings, El Salvador's "triple transition" was largely successful. The donor community mobilized impressive resources for the recovery effort. Indeed, total aid disbursements actually *exceeded* pledges during 1992–1996. Moreover, a strong macroeconomic environment facilitated the successful implementation of the peace accords and economic liberalization. The government ultimately spent more than initially planned on reinsertion and democratization, and the United States agreed to fund politically sensitive sectors like a new civilian police, judicial reform, and land transfers to ex-combatants.

Mozambique

In Chapter 5, Nicole Ball and Sam Barnes chronicle the delivery and coordination of pledges of aid to support Mozambican reconstruction following a fifteen-year civil war. As in El Salvador, the context for conflict resolution was the exhaustion of the combatants and (with the end of the Cold War) the decline in external support for the conflict. When the Frelimo government and the Renamo rebels signed the Rome General Peace Agreement of October 1992, Mozambique was by all measures the poorest country in the world. Some 30 percent of its population, more than 5 million persons, were either refugees or internally displaced. The international community would finance the vast share of its recovery.

Mozambique's war-to-peace transition required ending hostilities, demobilizing and reintegrating combatants, reforming both the national army and police, resettling refugees and the internally displaced, and repairing enormous physical devastation. The country's economic transition implied jump-starting economic activity and accelerating the shift from a controlled to a market economy. Its political transition involved creating effective institutions of governance, institutionalizing basic liberties, transforming a rebel movement into a political party, and organizing the country's first democratic elections.

By the time of the peace accords, Mozambique was already heavily aid dependent. The World Bank drafted what became the country's National Reconstruction Plan (NRP). Since the Consultative Group process focused on conventional economic development, however, donors created a parallel conference mechanism to support postconflict recovery and peace implementation. They also developed a number of forums to coordinate assistance, most prominently the United Nations Office of Humanitarian Assistance Coordination (UNOHAC). Unfortunately, coordination of assistance for peace implementation activities was complicated by disagreements among UNOHAC, the donors, UNDP, and the government.

Despite Mozambique's meager financial, technical, and human resources, the country's national ministries never ceased to function, allowing the government to shape aid priorities and to deliver some assistance itself. Still, the government was not given a central role in aid coordination, creating problems when donors abruptly handed the reins to the government at the end of UN involvement.

The envisioned national elections occurred in October 1994, after a significant delay. This achievement led donors to hail Mozambique as a "success" story of postconflict peace building. As Ball and Barnes point out, however, the credit due donors should not be exaggerated; success depended upon the commitment of Mozambique's factions to renounce violence—something that the donors could nurture but not create.

The case study reveals the difficulty in securing accurate data on aid flows in postconflict situations, given different donor procedures, incomplete reporting, and weak recipient administrative capacities. Ball and Barnes estimate that Mozambique received nearly $4 billion in grants and loans, assistance that went to a combination of objectives, including peace implementation, economic stabilization, and reconstruction. Early on, Mozambique did experience a gap between pledges and disbursements of assistance, but this narrowed after 1992. Lags that did occur in delivery of peace implementation aid typically resulted from political delays in the peace process and disagreements over the content of aid programs. The authors posit that aid gaps were less of a problem than were poorly conceived and badly executed projects. The government often differed with donors (and donors differed among themselves) about priority needs. As a result, aid pledges were "often wholly unrelated to objective need."

The Palestinian Territories

In Chapter 6, Rex Brynen, Hisham Awartani, and Clare Woodcraft describe the mobilization, organization, and delivery of assistance to the West Bank and Gaza Strip following the Oslo Declaration of Principles of September 1993. This agreement established a fluid modus vivendi between Israel, a sovereign government, and the Palestinian Authority (PA), a political entity whose final political status and territorial boundaries would be determined during the ongoing, volatile peace process. In contrast to the "asymmetry"[34] following the negotiated settlement in most civil wars, whereby the leverage of the opposition is expected to diminish or become "normalized" over time, observers anticipated that the PA's relative power would increase, culminating in the establishment of a Palestinian state.

Despite the high political profile of the aid effort and the fervent hopes of its advocates, massive international assistance did not culminate in self-sustaining economic recovery and stable political development in the West Bank and Gaza Strip. Due to setbacks in the peace process (and Israel's intermittent policy of "closure"), external aid merely kept the territories afloat, ameliorating economic crisis and forestalling the political collapse of the Palestinian Authority.

Motivated by the geopolitical salience of the Arab-Israeli conflict, international donors pledged some $4.5 billion to support the Palestinian Authority during 1994–1998. The European Union was by far the largest donor, followed by the United States. As the authors recount, these two actors clashed over the linked issues of burden sharing and aid leadership. Washington eventually triumphed, rebuffing European efforts for an enhanced political role in the peace process and ensuring that the World Bank would coordinate external assistance.

In assuming this role, the Bank introduced two successful innovations worthy of emulation in other contexts. First, after a slow start, the Bank delegated unprecedented authority to its resident representative in the field. Second, after considerable donor pressure, it created the Holst Peace Trust Fund to serve as a flexible, fast-disbursing financial vehicle. This fund played an essential role in stabilizing the political situation by financing both the recurrent costs of the PA and emergency employment-generation schemes.

The need to reconcile the objectives and responsibilities of scores of bilateral donors, international agencies, and Palestinian ministries resulted in a complicated framework to coordinate aid, including high- and low-level forums and sectoral working groups. Although membership in these distinct bodies was a source of controversy, this division of labor allowed particular sets of actors to address diplomatic issues, local aid coordination, UN coordination, bottlenecks to assistance, and sectoral initiatives. In addition, as the PA gained capacities, it gradually took on greater responsibilities for setting the aid agenda and coordinating assistance, assuming a role previously played by the World Bank and the Office of the United Nations Special Coordinator in the Occupied Territories (UNSCO). The politically charged context of Palestinian recovery made such a complex architecture unavoidable.

Donors, concerned about the transparency and accountability of Palestinian institutions, obligated the PA to commit itself to certain standards of administration and governance. In practice, however, fears about destabilizing the PA (and the peace process) and disagreements over political objectives discouraged the donor community from enforcing its aid conditions. Nor did donors make serious efforts to tie their assistance to the fulfillment of specific terms of the Oslo accords or to other peace-related actions.

Of the $4.5 billion in assistance pledged to the West Bank and Gaza, some $3.5 billion was disbursed during the time frame of the study. Although aid was initially slow to arrive, an aid pipeline was established within two years. Some donors contributed to delays in assistance (and delivery of inappropriate aid) by neglecting to streamline their standard procedures, to establish a local mission with adequate authority, or to appreciate the political realities in which they were operating. Palestinian constraints on aid delivery included low absorptive capacity, lack of technical expertise, the slow emergence of effective institutions, and lack of accountability associated with systems of political patronage.

South Africa

In Chapter 7, Michael Bratton and Chris Landsberg describe the context for external assistance in South Africa as a complex regime transition following a decades-long struggle against the racist apartheid regime. International donors provided aid to this relatively wealthy country in order to support a new, multiracial democracy. The leading edge of the "triple transition" was movement toward an inclusive democracy with equal political rights for all citizens, as embodied in the interim constitution of 1993 and the first free elections in 1994. South Africa's economic challenge was less to create a functioning capitalist economy than to integrate itself into an increasingly global market while distributing national wealth in a more socially just manner. Finally, the country faced the task of dismantling a repressive security apparatus and reintegrating former freedom fighters into productive civilian life.

Thanks to its impressive economic capacities, its well-developed state institutions, and its relative lack of dependence on external aid, South Africa was able to organize its relations with donors on a bilateral (rather than multilateral) basis and to determine, essentially, the content, terms, and conditions of international assistance. As the authors point out, South Africa was thus closer to the traditional model of development cooperation than the other five cases discussed in this book. Obviously, most postconflict countries are not in such an enviable position. Another striking feature was the South African government's conscious decision to limit involvement with (and obligations to) the Bretton Woods institutions.

Unique among the cases in this volume, South Africa was never the subject of a multilateral pledging conference. Instead, the government asked donors to devote their entire assistance to its own five-year blueprint, the 1994 Reconstruction and Development Program (RDP), replaced in 1996 by the Growth, Employment, and Redistribution plan (GEAR). Donors generally complied, designing aid that responded to the government's sectoral and geographic priorities and channeling it directly through the national budget. Rather than creating a multilateral donor forum, South Africa conducted annual bilateral consultations and (in a few cases) established binational commissions. The government's own efforts to coordinate aid were hampered by insufficient administrative capacity and cumbersome procedures for developing and approving projects.

While not aid dependent, South Africa relied upon external assistance to finance its national recovery; indeed, donors devoted twice the resources the government itself allotted to the RDP. Despite South Africa's status as a middle-income country, it became a favorite of the international community, generating pledges of approximately $6 billion. ($4.7 billion from major donors). The country's three largest donors—the United States, the European Union (EU), and Japan—accounted for 70 percent of total pledges.

Donor performance in delivering assistance was fairly positive (with the notable exception of the EU). By May 1998, South Africa had received $2.4 billion in aid—roughly half of the official development assistance (ODA) that major donors had pledged in 1993–1994, and nearly two-thirds of what they had committed. Still, there were frequent delays. These gaps tended to widen along the several phases of development cooperation: from pledge to commitment to disbursement to implementation. Indeed, the implementation of aid proved to be the most fraught aspect of aid. Although donors sometimes complicated the planning and execution of projects, most bottlenecks reflected a combination of institutional weaknesses in post-apartheid South Africa, including insufficient human, financial, and organizational capacities, and the strains of building a new state with a multitiered constitutional structure.

Bosnia and Herzegovina

As Susan Woodward, Zlatko Hurtić, and Amela Šapčanin recount in Chapter 8, postconflict assistance to Bosnia and Herzegovina took place in the context of the General Framework Agreement for Peace (GFAP), negotiated in Dayton, Ohio, in December 1995. The settlement, which ended the bloodiest war in Europe in half a century, was essentially a peace imposed by the great powers, led by the United States, on three warring communities divided (largely) along ethnic lines. The GFAP mandated a peacekeeping operation, the NATO-led Implementation Force (IFOR), subsequently replaced by a Stabilization Force (SFOR). At the political level, meanwhile, the contact group of great powers created a Peace Implementation Council (PIC). The Steering Board of the PIC designated a High Representative to oversee compliance with Dayton.

Alongside this peace implementation structure, the World Bank and the European Commission took the lead in coordinating a massive international aid effort to support a $5.1 billion Priority Reconstruction and Recovery Program (PRRP). The donor community hoped that external assistance would jump-start economic recovery and encourage the three formerly warring parties—Bosnian Muslims, Serbs, and Croats—to collaborate in the political and economic construction of a unitary, if highly decentralized, multiethnic state. As the authors describe, the envisioned "triple transition" in Bosnia and Herzegovina would require successful implementation of the peace accords and the repair of war-related destruction; the creation of political institutions and a constitutional structure appropriate to democratic governance within a federal system; and the resumption of the country's interrupted evolution from a socialist command economy to a free market system.

In the six years following the start of the war in 1992, Bosnia and Herzegovina received some $5 billion in pledges of aid from more than sixty donor countries and international agencies. The vast majority of these pledges—some $4.2 billion—were made between 1995 and 1998 at four Brussels conferences. The authors note the difficulty of assessing donor performance in delivering this aid, given the lack of uniform reporting guidelines among donors and the presence of rival, inconsistent databases. More troubling, they infer that the lack of transparency on figures of aid delivery reflects in part deliberate donor obfuscation.

The complexity of the international aid effort, involving scores of countries and international aid agencies, required recipient to coordinate closely, both among themselves and with the recipient government. The challenge of creating effective coordination mechanisms was complicated by struggles between the World Bank and the United States—respectively, the main donor responsible for the aid effort and the lead political actor responsible for peace implementation. Washington eventually triumphed in its view that the Office of the High Representative (OHR) should have a leading role in aid coordination and that delivery of assistance should be linked to the parties' implementation of the terms of the Dayton accords. The main instruments for donor coordination were the PIC Steering Board, the Economic Task Force (chaired by OHR), and several sector task forces.

Donors repeatedly declared that assistance would be dependent upon full compliance with the political terms and objectives of the Dayton GFAP. The practical effect of this political conditionality was to deny assistance to the Serb Republic. On the other hand, donors were inconsistent in their application and enforcement of these conditions vis-à-vis the various parties.

Certain donors, particularly the European Union, contributed to the slow pace of aid delivery by poor implementation capacity. Others, like the World Bank, had greater success by streamlining their standard procedures, establishing an early local presence, delegating authority to the field, and arranging the early clearance of arrears.

While Bosnia and Herzegovina had moderate absorptive capacity, the country's ability to plan and implement effective aid projects was marred by political disagreements among the several entities, particularly Bosnian Serb obstructionism; the complicated constitutional structure created by Dayton, which produced multiple bottlenecks and opportunities for gridlock; and the slow creation of functioning state institutions. On the other hand, the authors conclude, instances of actual corruption involving donor assistance have been exaggerated (Table 1.6 compares aspects of the six recovery efforts discussed in this volume).

Concluding Chapter

The findings of these six case studies suggest that even generous, well-intentioned foreign assistance provides no guarantee of sustainable recovery and lasting peace in countries emerging from civil violence. In Chapter 9, James Boyce challenges international donors to move beyond their "good intentions" to address the ramifications of external aid for peacebuilding objectives. An honest appraisal of the political impact of aid, he argues, reveals certain unavoidable policy dilemmas for external actors.

It is tempting for donors to believe that ample resources will alleviate distributional and other cleavages in conflict-prone societies. In fact, the opposite may sometimes be true. If aid is to provide an incentive for peace, Boyce argues, donors will need to consider not only "how much" assistance they should provide but also what type of aid they should give, the actors to whom they should extend it, and the conditions they should attach. To begin with, external actors must ensure that their aid tools are tailored to the conflict environment and that they strike the right balance between the short-run and long-run demands of peace. To nurture constituencies for peace, donors should use assistance to support political stability among rival factions and to foster institutionalized patterns of democratic governance. Finally, the donor community should pursue "peace

Table 1.6 The Recovery Efforts Compared

	Cambodia	El Salvador	Mozambique	West Bank and Gaza	South Africa	Bosnia-Herzegovina
Baseline Pledging and Disbursement Period	1991–1997	1992–1996	1992–1996	1993–1998	1994–1999	1995–1998
Main Pledging Conferences and Aid Initiatives	International Committee on the Reconstruction of Cambodia (ICORC): 9/93, 3/94, 3/95. CG Meetings: 1996, 1997.	CG Meetings: 5/91, 3/92, 4/93, 6/95.	CG Meetings: 12/91, 12/92, 12/93, 3/95. Peace Implementation Conferences: 12/92, 6/93.	Washington conferences: 10/93, 11/98. Multiple CG and Ad Hoc Liaison Committee (AHLC) Meetings.	Bilateral donor initiatives (multiple).	Brussels conferences to support PRRP: 12/95, 4/96, 7/97, 5/98.
Major Recovery Plan(s)	National Program to Rehabilitate and Develop Cambodia (NPRDC): 12/93. Socioeconomic Development Plan (SEDP): 1996. Public Investment Program (PIP): 1996.	National Reconstruction Plan (NRP): 2/93.	National Reconstruction Plan (PRN). National Public Investment Program.	Emergency Assistance Program (EAP): 1993. Core Investment Program: 10/95. Palestinian Public Investment Program (PPIP): 11/96. Palestinian Development Plan (PDP): 12/97.	Reconstruction and Development Program (RDP): 11/94. Growth, Employment, and Redistribution (GEAR): 3/96.	Priority Reconstruction and Recovery Program (PRRP): 12/95.
Dominant external political actor(s)	Japan, France, US	United States	Supervision and Control Commission (France, Italy, Germany, UK, US)	United States	None	Contact Group members (US, Italy, France, Germany, UK, Russia)
Lead Donors						
Bilateral	Japan (also France, US)	US (also EU)	Italy, EU	EU (also US, Japan)	EU, Japan, US	EU (also US)
Multilateral	World Bank, IMF, ADB, EU	World Bank, IDB	World Bank	World Bank	None	World Bank
Amount Pledged	$3.264 billion	$860 million initially (later increased)	Unclear	$4.18 billion	$4.7 billion by main donors ($6 billion by all donors)	$4.2 billion at Brussels ($5 billion total)
Amount Disbursed	$2.33 billion (71%)	$1,260 million (eventual)	$4–5 billion (estimated)	$2.57 billion (61%)	$2.4 billion (51%)	n.a.

Table 1.6 continued

	Cambodia	El Salvador	Mozambique	West Bank and Gaza	South Africa	Bosnia-Herzegovina
Gap (difference)	$934 million	None: Disbursements exceed pledges	Uncertain: records unavailable	$1.61 billion	$2.3 billion	Uncertain: rival databases
In-Country Aid Coordination Mechanisms	UNTAC played early role. Government created Council for the Development of Cambodia/Cambodian Rehabilitation and Development Board (CDC/CRDB), and later an In-Country Aid Coordination System (IACS).	Government coordinates international assistance. World Bank and USAID play key supporting roles. UNDP coordinates FMLN demobilization and PRODERE, CIRE-FCA programs.	Main coordination mechanisms include Office of the SRSG; United Nations Office for Humanitarian Assistance Coordination (UNOHAC); UNDP in-country coordination system; and ad hoc donor groupings.	Multiple tiers, including AHLC, Local Aid Coordination Committee (LACC), Joint Liaison Committee (JLC), and sectoral working groups. UN Special Coordinator (UNSCO) coordinates UN actors. Palestinian coordinating role in PEC-DAR, MOPIC.	Annual bilateral consultations with South African government, which coordinates assistance through RDP office, later Ministry of Finance.	Aid coordination by Steering Board of the Peace Implementation Council (PIC), chaired by OHR; by the Economic Task Force; and by sector task forces. World Bank and EC draft recovery plans, mobilize resources.
Use of "Peace Conditionality"	Inconsistent. Minimal use of any conditions before 1996.	Tensions between economic and peace conditionality.	Tensions between economic and peace conditionality.	Minimal application because of donor fears of PA collapse.	None: donors lack leverage.	Firmly stated, but inconsistently applied.
Absorptive Capacity						
Income Level ($ per capita, 1995)	Low Low: $270	Moderate Lower-Middle: $1,610	Low Very Low: $80	Low-Moderate Lower-Middle: $1,687	Moderate Middle: $3,160	Moderate Low: $500[b]
Rank, 1996 Human Development Index[a]	140 (Low)	114 (Medium)	166 (Low)	n.a.	89 (Medium)	n.a.
Foreign Aid: % GNP	29.3% (1994) (High dependence)	4.5% (1994) (Modest dependence)	89.5% (1994) (Extreme dependence)	13% (1995) (High dependence)	0.3% (1996) (Low dependence)	40% (1996) (High dependence)
per capita	$32.3 (1994)	$69.2 (1994)	$76.5 (1994)	$240 (annual avg., 1993–1997)	$9 (1996)	$380 (annual average)

Sources: Case study chapters in the book; World Bank, *World Development Report 1997*; UNDP, *Human Development Report 1996, 1998*.
Notes: a. Index ranks countries from 1 (highest) to 174 (lowest). b. Compare to prewar per capita income of approximately $2,000.

conditionality," using assistance to reward supporters of peace, to punish its opponents, and to encourage vacillators.

The Value—and Limitations—of the Financial Lens

James Boyce's conclusions usefully remind the reader (and the editors of this volume) that the financial lens has both advantages and limitations as a window on postconflict recovery.

By focusing on aid flows, researchers were able to "follow the money"—that is, to assess actual donor performance in mobilizing, designing, conditioning, delivering, and coordinating committed resources. The aid lens provided insights into the concerns and priorities of individual donors and the obstacles to collective action among them.

On the question of delivery itself, the six case studies tell a mixed story. Although precise figures were sometimes difficult to establish reliably, the donor community appears to have disbursed approximately two-thirds of its aid pledges to these six countries during the relevant baseline years. This is a fairly impressive performance. Moreover, some research teams express confidence that outstanding commitments will eventually be fulfilled.

However, the case studies document troubling delays in aid disbursements—particularly early in the recovery process, when assistance is critical to consolidate peace and bring its fruits to long-suffering populations. In Cambodia, El Salvador, and the West Bank and Gaza, for example, a year passed before an aid pipeline was up and running. Moreover, the research teams discovered that the question of aid gaps was less straightforward than initially imagined. Gaps may occur at various points in the chain between the initial offer of assistance and the implementation of projects. As a rule, gaps appear to widen as one proceeds along this chain of development cooperation. The cases also reveal frequent discrepancies between the objective needs of aid recipients, the priorities these recipients identify, and the projects the donors are willing to fund. Finally, the project calls attention to shortcomings in the manner that recovery aid is tracked, monitored, and evaluated.

The financial lens has certain limitations, however. Most significantly, aid flows themselves tell us little about the *impact* of external assistance on its intended beneficiaries. Within aid agencies and international financial institutions, performance is often evaluated according to success in transferring funds, rather than the appropriateness of the design of the aid—and its likely impact on recipient populations. Consequently, postconflict societies may receive assistance that is redundant, harmful, or squandered. This implies that in some cases a gap might even be good, if it means that less money is wasted than would have been the case otherwise. In other words, less might sometimes mean more.

At present, neither the donor community nor independent scholars possess sophisticated analytical tools to conduct longitudinal evaluations of recovery assistance. To assess the impact of postconflict aid, analysts will need to develop benchmarks for "success" (defined in terms of sustainable economic recovery and the preservation of peace) and tools to evaluate the role that aid plays in producing such outcomes.

Finally, this book's focus on *external* resources risks giving too much weight to the role of the donors in the successful recovery from violent conflict. In the end, the critical determinants of successful peace building and sustainable recovery are likely to be *internal*. The good intentions of the donor community cannot substitute for the willingness of local actors to renounce violence and to devote domestic resources to reconstruction.

Notes

We would like to thank Ronald Kassimir and Eric Hershberg of the Social Science Research Council for assistance in designing the Pledges of Aid study. We are grateful to Rex Brynen, Ronald Kassimir, and David O'Brien for reactions to earlier drafts of this introduction.

1. Members of the donor community include bilateral aid agencies of national governments, particularly the members of the Development Assistance Committee (DAC) of the Organization for Economic Cooperation and Development (OECD); the departments, programs, and specialized agencies of the United Nations; the international financial institutions (IFIs); and multiple nongovernmental organizations (NGOs) such as the International Committee of the Red Cross (ICRC) and Oxfam. According to data compiled from the OECD's *Geographical Distribution of Financial Flows to Aid Recipients 1999*, countries emerging from conflict received aid commitments of approximately $109 billion from multilateral institutions and DAC members between 1990 and 1997.

2. The World Bank, *Post-Conflict Reconstruction*, p. 21; Renner, *Budgeting for Disarmament*, pp. 26–27; Stedman, "Negotiation and Mediation," p. 375.

3. Lake, *After the Wars*, pp. 9–10.

4. Carter Center, *1997–1998 State of World Conflict Report*.

5. Other countries have obviously experienced localized violence, including India (Kashmir), Mexico (Chiapas), Russia (Chechnya), Turkey (Kurdistan), and the United Kingdom (Northern Ireland). For a classification of internal conflict in the 1990s, see Brown, "Internal Conflict: Causes and Implications," pp. 4–7.

6. See, for example, Seelye, "Crisis in the Balkans." In a more modest vein, Michael E. Brown proposes that donor states, IFIs, international development agencies, and multinational corporations cooperate "to develop 'mini-Marshall Plans' for countries in need of special economic attention." See Brown, "Internal Conflict and International Action," pp. 610, 623.

7. The limits to U.S. will and resources were apparent in early discussions of the reconstruction of the Serb province of Kosovo. See Broder, "Clinton Declares Most War Cleanup Is Europe's Task."

8. Portions of this table were inspired by Holtzman, "Post-Conflict Reconstruction," p. 29.

9. *An Agenda for Peace*, cited in Roberts and Kingsbury, p. 475; United Nations, *An Inventory of Post-Conflict Peace-Building Activities.*

10. Preamble and Chapter IX, Art. 55, of the UN Charter; United Nations, *Supplement to An Agenda for Peace,* paragraphs 47–56; United Nations, "The Secretary-General's Statement."

11. See Kumar, "The Nature and Focus of International Assistance." For a critique of the liberal assumptions behind international support for postconflict reconstruction, see Paris, "Peacebuilding and the Limits of Liberal Internationalism."

12. USAID, *From Bullets to Ballots;* Wood, "Lessons and Guidance for Donors."

13. Ball with Halevy, *Making Peace Work,* pp. 48–55; USAID, *After the War Is Over What Comes Next?*

14. Bertram, "Reinventing Governments," p. 389.

15. Ball, "The Challenge of Rebuilding War-Torn Societies," p. 613.

16. Cortright and Lopez, "Carrots, Sticks, and Cooperation," p. 127.

17. On the dangers of inflated expectations, see Rothkopf, *The Price of Peace,* pp. 63–71.

18. World Bank, *Post-Conflict Reconstruction,* p. 21.

19. Dempsey, "Palestinian Aid Faces Obstacle Course."

20. Heininger, "Cambodia: Relief, Repatriation, and Rehabilitation," pp. 127–129; Kato, "Quick Impacts, Slow Rehabilitation in Cambodia," pp. 190–194; De Soto and del Castillo, "Obstacles to Peacebuilding," p. 73; interview with Kenji Yamada, International Development Center of Japan (May 8, 1998).

21. One-third of the aid had arrived after nine months and half by the end of the year. Kumar et al., *The International Response to Conflict and Genocide,* pp. 12–15, 29–33; Reindorp, "Towards an Assistance Strategy for Rwanda," p. 3.

22. UNDP, Rwanda Mission, "Linking Relief to Development."

23. Most of the $3.2 billion pledged to Lebanon in December 1996 by international donors had "yet to materialize" by August 1997. Pearl, "Continental Divide." On Mozambique, see Economist Intelligence Unit, *EIU Country Report,* p. 13. In Tajikistan, the combination of a deteriorating security situation and a lack of donor capacities in the country hindered delivery of the $96 million pledged at the November 1997 Vienna Conference on International Support for Peace and Reconstruction. Interview with former SRSG for Tajikistan and UNDP officials (June–July 1998).

24. Kumar et al., *The International Response to Conflict and Genocide,* pp. 101–106; Swedish Ministry of Foreign Affairs, "Mobilization and Allocation of Resources," p. 4 (italics in original).

25. Postconflict Haiti, where the international community has pledged more than $2 billion for 1995–1999, may represent the starkest example. Rother, "As Leaders Bicker, Haiti Stagnates."

26. In four cases—Bosnia and Herzegovina, Cambodia, El Salvador, and Mozambique—international actors spent considerably more for multidimensional peace operations.

27. There have, of course, been valuable comparative studies on various aspects of postconflict peace building, including the War Torn Societies Project of the United Nations Research Institute for Social Development (UNRISD); the joint International Peace Academy (IPA)–Center for International Security and Cooperation (CISAC) project on postconflict peace building; the Peace Implementation Network of the Fafo Institute for Applied Social Science; and various initiatives of the Carnegie Commission on Preventing Deadly Conflict.

28. Collier, "The Comparative Method."

29. George and McKeown, "Case Studies and Theories."

30. For example, they may be recorded when placed in an earmarked account, when goods or services are provided, or when donor invoices are paid, often to a donor country contractor rather than in the recipient country itself. For DAC definitions, see OECD, *Geographical Distribution of Financial Flows.*

31. Krasner, *International Regimes.*

32. For a persuasive argument that humanitarian considerations are at the heart of the international aid regime, see Lumsdaine, *Moral Vision.*

33. For an exposition of this concept, see the special issue of *Global Governance* 4, no. 1 (1998), particularly Chopra, "Introducing Peace-Maintenance."

34. Zartman, "Dynamics and Constraints."

2

The Donor Community and the Challenge of Postconflict Recovery

Stewart Patrick

THE ROAD TO HELL, SAMUEL JOHNSON FAMOUSLY OBSERVED, is paved with good intentions. Even the noblest motivations may lead to unpleasant, unanticipated consequences. Those seeking to rebuild post-conflict countries would do well to keep in mind Johnson's aphorism, for their quests are fraught with devilish details and potential pitfalls, and the unwary risk plunging into chaos. This chapter seeks to map a smoother road by exploring new directions in the design, coordination, and implementation of recovery assistance.

The discussion here focuses on the official (rather than nongovernmental) actors involved in postconflict reconstruction. These include the agencies, programs, and departments of the United Nations; the international financial institutions; and the bilateral aid agencies. The chapter describes seven challenges these donors must overcome to support sustainable peace and reconstruction. It calls for closer collaboration in (1) designing aid interventions; (2) mobilizing resources; (3) deepening institutional reform; (4) harmonizing aid conditions; (5) coordinating assistance locally; (6) enhancing recipient capacities; and (7) ensuring accountability in aid delivery and implementation.

The first recommendation is that donors formulate an agreed framework for each postconflict situation that will lay the basis for timely collaborative action. This shared vision would define overarching aid principles, goals, and strategies and permit donors to assess needs jointly, to formulate a common assistance strategy, and to help the recovering state in drafting an initial recovery plan. Second, donors need to create flexible, fast-disbursing financing mechanisms specifically tailored to fluid postconflict environments.

35

Current institutional and budgetary divisions make it difficult to finance interventions falling between humanitarian relief and traditional development assistance, and existing pledging conferences are inadequately responsive to local needs. Third, the major external actors involved in recovery activities must strengthen and accelerate their institutional reforms to respond to the needs of countries emerging from conflict. The United Nations agencies, international financial institutions, and bilateral donors should provide greater authority and resources to their postconflict units and explore fruitful divisions of labor based on their comparative advantages. Fourth, the donor community must ensure that the various conditions it places on aid are appropriate, coherent, and consistently enforced. In particular, donors need to reconcile their support for macroeconomic stabilization and structural adjustment with their concern for peace building.

Fifth, better cooperation at headquarters must be complemented by stronger coordination in the field. Donors should establish a local presence as early as possible, delegate authority to these country missions, designate lead agencies in particular sectors, and explore multiple levels of coordination. Sixth, aid interventions must build upon and nurture local capacities for sustainable recovery. Donors should encourage local ownership of policies and programs by working with recipient governments and civil society actors at every stage, ensuring that local parties shape the aid agenda. Donors should help finance important public sector expenditures, relax insistence on macroeconomic and fiscal rigor, facilitate debt reduction, and encourage the mobilization of local resources. Finally, the donor community needs to improve accountability and transparency in the delivery and implementation of external assistance. This will require new analytic tools designed to assess not only the timely disbursement of aid but also its impact.

Adopt a Strategic Framework

Although the donor community has pledged enormous sums of external assistance over the past decade to foster the sustainable recovery from conflict in many countries, the international framework to design, coordinate, and deliver such aid remains woefully fragmented and under-institutionalized. International efforts to support postconflict recovery are ad hoc undertakings governed by few consistent principles, norms, rules, or established procedures. Such initiatives are carried out by a host of autonomous actors, including donor states, international financial institutions (IFIs), United Nations agencies, nongovernmental organizations (NGOs), and local political authorities. The resulting amalgam of interests, mandates, and capacities can stymie collective action and agreement on burden sharing, delaying early donor engagement and thwarting agreement on common approaches essential to success.

In each postconflict situation the donor community needs to formulate an agreed "entrance strategy" based on a common vision. Ideally, this strategic framework would be a comprehensive document. It would describe the causes of the conflict, articulate the rationale for external involvement, define shared aid principles, facilitate joint needs assessments, identify (and justify) aid priorities, outline a strategy to mobilize resources, encourage common programming, establish the phases of assistance, and define the responsibilities of aid providers and recipients. It would seek to reconcile the political, security, and human rights components of postconflict peace building with the accompanying humanitarian and development assistance strategies.

Although the strategic framework concept has been endorsed by the broad donor community,[1] its practical elaboration to date has been confined to the United Nations system.[2] In July 1998, the UN deputy secretary-general assumed responsibility for developing the idea.[3] As discussed below, it remains to be seen whether the UN will summon the vision and energy to transcend traditional institutional mandates and bureaucratic inertia. More significantly, the concept of a strategic framework will reach its full potential only if it is supported by *all* donors, including IFIs and national governments.

To be effective, reconstruction assistance must be prompt, coherent, and responsive to local needs. Too often it is late, fragmented, and donor driven. Donors often re-engage postconflict countries with only a rudimentary understanding of local political, social, and economic realities. To ensure adequate baseline data, donors should maintain a "watching brief" during conflicts and—as soon as local conditions permit—undertake joint needs assessments. In current practice, donors generally postpone serious efforts to plan aid interventions until they have convened a multilateral fund-raising conference (such as a donor roundtable or Consultative Group meeting). A more appropriate sequence would be for funding to follow substance. In other words, well-developed country plans would precede (and inform) efforts to mobilize resources.

Donors also need to work together in assessing the needs of each war-torn country. Too often, each donor conducts this assessment independently, using the resulting data to draft its own, self-contained assistance strategy.[4] These parallel aid efforts are then pursued through diverse pledging initiatives, variegated financing instruments, and sundry implementing partners. The result may be incoherent strategies, incompatible projects, redundant initiatives, gaps in assistance, insufficient accountability, and minimal organizational learning.

To stimulate early engagement and collaboration, the donor community should consider creating a standing triggering mechanism. Ideally, as any given conflict winds down, some impartial entity—logically, the UN secretary-general[5]—would convene a forum of key states, IFIs, UN agencies, and NGOs. This body would assist local representatives in assessing urgent needs, establishing aid priorities, and determining the appropriate sequencing of assistance. While specific country circumstances will naturally vary, recent experience points to a common set of urgent tasks. These include repatriation and resettlement; demobilization and reintegration; restoration of public safety and security (including policing and human rights); rehabilitation of basic infrastructure, including shelter, water, sanitation, and transportation; revival of agriculture and the assurance of food security; provision of basic social services, including health and education; reestablishment of governance structures, including rule of law institutions; and preparation for elections.[6]

It will not always be easy to engineer consensus among autonomous actors on the contours of a common entrance strategy, particularly in highly politicized recovery contexts, such as the West Bank and Gaza. Nevertheless, the donor community should seek the widest possible agreement on shared aid priorities and principles.

Mobilize Adequate, Appropriate Resources

Postconflict environments call for flexible, quick-disbursing funds designed for rehabilitation and reconstruction. Unfortunately, unlike funding for the UN's peacemaking and peacekeeping missions, which are based on regular budget assessments, contributions for recovery activities are entirely voluntary. Consequently, they tend to be unpredictable and subject to lengthy, competitive fund-raising campaigns. Furthermore, few donors possess financial instruments designed specifically for transitional needs falling between humanitarian and traditional development assistance.

Over the past decade, donors have realized that there is no simple continuum linking relief, recovery, and development. Rather, these three phases overlap temporally and spatially in crisis environments.[7] Moreover, although emergency aid is essential to alleviate suffering, it rarely addresses the underlying causes of poverty and conflict. (Indeed, when prolonged it may build dependency and undermine indigenous capacities.) However, when relief agencies depart too quickly, or developmental actors delay their involvement, aid ceases to flow. The challenge for donors is to build complementarity by recognizing the forward and backward linkages between these different types of interventions.[8]

Unfortunately, budgetary, institutional, and operational divisions limit cooperation between humanitarian and development actors in planning activities, mobilizing resources, and implementing projects.[9] As a rule, relief and development activities are designed by different departments or agencies; funded through distinct windows; approved through dissimilar procedures; shaped by disparate political considerations; subjected to divergent timetables; and implemented by diverse partners. Relief funds usually need to be disbursed within one year, a time horizon too short to launch sustainable recovery. Recovery thus tends to be financed by slower-disbursing development aid that may be conditioned on macroeconomic or political criteria and might not flow seamlessly when relief funding ends.

At the global level, the international community lacks a "third funding window" (between humanitarian assistance and development aid) to address postconflict recovery. In complex emergencies, resources dry up when the crisis moves into the less acute phase. Such patterns have persisted even when the United Nations incorporates rehabilitation activities into its Consolidated Inter-Agency Appeal (CAP).

The country of Georgia provides an example. In a March 1996 meeting in Tbilisi, donors included $61 million worth of postconflict, transitional programs in the CAP (in addition to $50 million for emergency relief). But by November 1996, only 40 percent of the total appeal had been funded—and only 31 percent of the early recovery programs. As the UN Department of Humanitarian Affairs (DHA) concluded, "Projects which bridge relief and development do not readily attract donor support." More broadly, DHA observed, the sudden end to many conflicts in the mid-1990s "exposed the lack of appropriate modalities among donor organizations for providing assistance that is neither 'relief' nor 'development.'"[10]

Reaching a similar verdict, the multidonor assessment of aid to post-genocide Rwanda recommended that donors create new mechanisms to "shorten the transition from emergency assistance to reconstruction aid." Echoing this suggestion, the Organization for Economic Cooperation and Development/Development Assistance Committee (OECD/DAC) Task Force on Conflict, Peace, and Development Cooperation has endorsed the creation of flexible "planning, programming, and disbursement procedures" to meet recovery needs.[11]

Expand the Consolidated Appeals Process?

Hoping to close this financing gap, the United Nations has considered creating an Expanded Consolidated Inter-Agency Appeal (ECAP). The ECAP would be designed to mobilize resources for urgent postconflict recovery activities (like the reintegration of demobilized soldiers), but at a much faster pace than conventional pledging conferences.[12] In current practice, both the (UNDP-led) roundtables (RTs) and the World Bank–chaired Consultative Group (CG) meetings occur too late to address priority rehabilitation. Moreover, the CG process requires a legitimate recipient government, a condition not always met following conflict. Unfortunately, the ECAP has never been submitted to rigorous application, and the idea remains moribund.

The United Nations Development Programme (UNDP) and the DHA undertook a preliminary study of the ECAP concept in late 1996. Despite the desultory nature of the effort,[13] the two institutions advocated including rehabilitation activities within the CAP. Such a step, they reasoned, might identify "critical funding shortfalls," make aid priorities responsive to local needs (rather than to UN agency "shopping lists"), and permit donors to monitor and manage aid flows. In July 1997, the UN secretary-general, Kofi Annan, endorsed the selective inclusion of rehabilitation activities in the appeals process, and the UN General Assembly asked member states to respond "quickly and generously" to such appeals. Lamentably, this has not occurred. As the UN's Economic and Social Council (ECOSOC) observes, donor performance "has been generally disappointing."[14]

Reform Pledging Conferences

Given the paucity of flexible, fast-disbursing resources, serious external assistance for recovery typically arrives only after the donor community convenes a multilateral pledging conference. In these gatherings (which include RTs and CG meetings),[15] donor states, UN agencies, and IFIs meet with local representatives to evaluate proposed reconstruction plans and to offer pledges to finance these.

Pledging forums have advantages for donors, recipient states, and implementing agencies. First, they provide donors with a setting to implement and mediate collective action. Inasmuch as all countries have a general interest in a pacific and prosperous international system, external support for peace building and sustainable recovery possesses attributes of a public good.[16] Accordingly, donors may confront what game theorists term a "dilemma of common interest": they may be tempted to enjoy the diffuse gains of stability and growth while letting others shoulder the burdens of peace building and economic recovery. Pledging conferences increase the prospects of equitable burden sharing by reducing temptations and opportunities to "free ride." More subtly, the practices and declarations surrounding these gatherings reinforce the notion of a "donor community" united in its normative purposes and bound by ethical obligations toward the recovering state.

On a practical level, pledging conferences allow donors to shape the recovery plans and aid priorities of war-torn states, to offer incentives that may deepen local commitments to peace, and to establish, publicize, and enforce aid conditions. By pledging jointly, donor governments also increase the likelihood of winning domestic legislative and popular support for foreign assistance, since each national effort can be placed in the context of a broader undertaking.

From the perspective of the postconflict country and implementing agencies, the conferences offer high-profile occasions to concentrate the minds of donor governments, to mobilize international resources, and to gain public assurances that at least some of their needs will be met. Occasionally, competition for prestige or pressure from peers leads donors to escalate initial pledges (Chapter 6 documents this dynamic in aid to the West Bank and Gaza).

Unfortunately, pledging conferences suffer from institutional and procedural flaws. To begin with, they possess elements of "political theater."[17] Donors exaggerate the generosity of their aid packages by "double-counting" aid previously promised or already delivered to an implementing agency (which will subsequently report the same amount). Alternatively, donors may pledge large amounts they cannot deliver soon. While this tendency to "dress up" modest pledges may generate momentum for the peace process and meet a number of political and bureaucratic needs, it also risks raising unrealistic expectations.

Apart from this problem of pledge inflation, the composition of aid packages is often driven not by objective needs but by the priorities of foreign governments or international agencies pursuing national or institutional objectives. When pledging aid, donors pick and choose among geographic regions and sectoral initiatives. They prefer to fund grand, eye-catching infrastructure projects like public buildings, bridges, or utilities, whereas more modest, less visible projects might be more appropriate and sustainable. Because donors tend to be risk averse, they generally avoid funding potentially controversial activities such as security sector reform. Certain other sectors, such as education and agriculture, are chronically underfunded. In addition, donors often earmark aid to target groups like demobilized soldiers at the expense of other vulnerable populations. Likewise, donors tend to focus heavily on urban initiatives over rural ones, creating "islands" of assistance. Finally, their frequent insistence on bilateral (and particularly "tied") aid fragments international assistance and places administrative burdens on recovering countries.

To strengthen pledging conferences, the donor community should create a monitoring system (perhaps in the OECD/DAC) to guarantee that pledges are honest, realistic, and transparent. Second, donors should develop procedures, including consultations with recipient representatives, to ensure that aid corresponds to objective needs and capacities. Third, pledging forums should be governed by formal guidelines that define relations between donors and development partners (including civil society actors), outline mechanisms to discuss recovery plans, and create robust mechanisms to coordinate and track aid delivery.

Consider a Global Reconstruction Fund

Some policymakers, seeking a holistic, high-level solution to the issue of resource mobilization, have proposed that donors pool resources to create a Global Post-Conflict Reconstruction Fund (GRF). The GRF would be similar to the Global Environment Fund administered by the World Bank, UNDP, and the United Nations Environment Programme (UNEP). The fund's core capital might be formed from donor assessments negotiated according to an agreed burden-sharing formula. A parallel trust fund window—consisting solely of concessional grants—might be filled through voluntary contributions. Donors would be represented on the GRF's governing body in proportion to their financial stake, and an interagency secretariat would manage the fund and ensure its financial probity.[18] Such a rapid-response facility could facilitate co- or parallel financing, provide a basket of resources for implementing partners, reduce the strain on postconflict governments facing multiple reporting requirements, exploit the comparative advantages of different agencies, encourage earlier local planning for recovery, and sustain multiyear recovery activities.

Establishing the facility would require much closer donor coordination. Principal multilateral stakeholders would include the World Bank, the leading institution for international development finance; UNDP, the main UN entity charged with sustainable human development; and the UN High Commissioner for Refugees (UNHCR), the primary humanitarian actor in early postconflict recovery. The greatest resistance to a GRF would doubtless come from DAC members, determined to avoid regular budgetary assessments and to retain sovereign control of their assistance in politically charged environments. Given these obstacles, a group of major donors concluded in January 1999 that a global fund was at present unrealistic.[19] Nevertheless, the concept merits further consideration.

Deepen Institutional Reforms

In order to address transitional activities falling between conventional relief and development assistance, several multilateral agencies, IFIs, and bilateral donors have recently created new functional units, budget lines, or financing windows. In 1998, some two dozen postconflict units[20] began to hold semiannual meetings to share information and resources, to establish common standards, to collect "best practices" and "lessons to be learned," and to explore joint initiatives in high-priority countries.[21] Several donors, including UNDP, UNHCR, the World Bank, the International Monetary Fund (IMF), the U.S. Agency for International Development (USAID), and the Canadian International Development Agency (CIDA), now possess financial instruments dedicated to postconflict recovery.

Some of these specialized units have shown themselves capable of flexible and innovative programming, of disbursing funds quickly, and of collaborating with one another. However, most possess modest budgets and staffs and remain marginal within their respective organizations or governments. Although such units offer valuable "venture capital," their limited resources restrict them to responding to targets of opportunity, with little coordination.[22] The following paragraphs assess recent institutional reforms taken by UN agencies, IFIs, and OECD donors.

Improve UN Coordination

The secretary-general's reform program of July 1997 elevated postconflict peace building to the top of the UN's global agenda, designating the Department of Political Affairs (DPA) as the focal point for these activities. This assignment reflected the "political nature" of the undertaking and DPA's institutional role as chair of the Executive Committee on Peace and Security. To date, there has been little practical follow-up to this designation. DPA's authority and capacity to coordinate UN interventions are limited by the department's lack of operational responsibilities and the injunction that it "fully respect . . . existing mandates, lines of authority, and funding arrangements" within the UN system.[23] Moreover, when peacekeeping is at the core of a mission, lead responsibility shifts to the Department of Peacekeeping Operations (DPKO).

The various agencies, funds, and programs of the United Nations have been prominent actors in different domains of postconflict reconstruction. Operationally, UNDP has taken a lead role in postconflict recovery. UNDP's Emergency Response Division (ERD) monitors "countries in special development circumstances," assists the Office for the Coordination of Humanitarian Affairs (OCHA) in elaborating and reviewing CAPs that include rehabilitation activities, and supports the work of UN resident coordinators in crisis countries. Aside from administering trust funds to which donors may contribute, UNDP employs its own fast-disbursing TRAC 1.1.3 resources to launch special program initiatives or to design frameworks for involvement in crisis countries. However, these funds remain modest ($50 million in 1998), and UNDP lacks the authority to coordinate effective UN responses to postconflict recovery.[24]

For its part, UNHCR has long spearheaded the resettlement of refugees. To finance its operations, UNHCR depends on core financing from donor governments and CAP appeals for emergency situations. It also administers a $20 million Voluntary Repatriation Fund. Likewise, the United Nations Children's Fund (UNICEF), the World Food Programme (WFP), the Food and Agriculture Organization (FAO), and the World Health Organization (WHO) implement extensive programs in the areas of (respectively) children in conflict, food security, agricultural rehabilitation, and health.

The United Nations has made several efforts to promote joint planning and closer coordination among the branches of its extended multilateral family.[25] Despite these and other initiatives, the United Nations has remained—in the words of its Joint Inspection Unit (JIU)—"a fragmented configuration of competing organizations." The different organs of the UN system spend inordinate time and energy jockeying for responsibilities and resources rather than judiciously assessing their relative capacities and comparative advantages and exploring fruitful divisions of labor on those bases. As the JIU complains, there "are no effective coordination mechanisms for postconflict peace building at the policy, Headquarters, or system-wide levels."[26]

It was in response to such critiques that the United Nations began to experiment with the idea of a common "strategic framework" to organize reconstruction efforts. In autumn 1997, the UN dispatched a mission to formulate a strategic framework for Afghanistan. In view of the ongoing civil war there, this choice was unfortunate. Nevertheless, the mission usefully underlined the fundamentally political nature of postconflict peace building. It also exposed certain constraints within the UN system and hinted at necessary reforms. Besides revealing that some UN organs had mandates but no resources (and vice versa), the mission demonstrated that "coordination by consensus" should yield to more forceful "coordination by management."[27] These ramifications were not welcomed at headquarters, however, where agencies, departments, and programs fought to retain their budgets and missions. They agreed only to explore limited "common programming."[28]

As a result, the strategic framework idea remains essentially an exhortation, enunciating broad principles but offering little practical guidance about how to ensure greater coordination. Moreover, the successive iterations of the concept have drifted away from a concern with politics. This contradicts the UN's own recognition that, in postconflict societies, "the overriding criterion for the selection and establishment of [aid] priorities is political."[29]

Mobilize the Bretton Woods Institutions

The Bretton Woods institutions have become important actors in supporting recovery from war and preventing the reemergence of violent conflict.[30] In September 1995, World Bank president James Wolfensohn announced that rebuilding war-torn societies would again become one of the Bank's development priorities. This decision returned the International Bank for Reconstruction and Development (IBRD) to one of its original mandates.[31]

Since 1989, World Bank lending for postconflict purposes has surged 800 percent. By spring 1998, the institution had committed $6.2 billion in loans to support 157 reconstruction operations in eighteen countries—and had provided grants worth $400 million to recovery initiatives. By 1999, one-quarter of its concessional lending to countries other than China and India went to nations either experiencing or emerging from conflict.[32] Moreover, in summer 1997 the World Bank created an internal Post-Conflict Unit (PCU) to monitor crisis countries, organize missions following conflict, develop "best practices" for donors, and coordinate with international partners. The unit has authority over an $8 million postconflict fund (generated by World Bank income) and acts as a custodian for a $16 million Japanese postconflict trust fund. The PCU has also outlined five phases of Bank involvement in recovery from crisis.[33]

The Bank can play several important roles in postconflict situations. It can mobilize resources through the CG process, arrange the clearance of arrears, facilitate macroeconomic policy coordination, foster the assessment of needs, restore physical infrastructure, and monitor aid flows. During peace negotiations, it can advise parties on the economic dimensions of possible accords. However, the Bank has yet to give sufficient operational content to its institutional guidelines on postconflict activities. In addition, an internal critique notes its procurement and disbursement procedures often create "stumbling blocks" to recovery, including "the untimely delivery of goods and the replenishment of funds." Finally, the Bank directors have yet to agree on several problematic questions, including when to re-engage crisis countries, what to do if hostilities resume, which sectors the Bank should take the lead in, and what types of trust funds (global or country specific) the Bank should pursue.[34]

The IMF has been more tentative than the Bank in adapting its procedures to postconflict needs. This reluctance reflects in part the institution's narrower mandate: to assist countries with balance of payments difficulties. Nevertheless, the Fund has expanded the scope of its existing policies on disaster assistance to include "carefully defined postconflict situations." Henceforth, the IMF will consider assisting a postconflict country experiencing severe balance of payments difficulties if the recipient government demonstrates sufficient capacity and commitment to plan and implement an acceptable economic program and if IMF support is provided in the context of a "concerted international effort."[35]

Access to Fund resources was initially limited to 25 percent of the country quota and was made contingent on the recipient's presentation of a compelling economic policy (including macroeconomic framework) and a stated intention to move as soon as possible to a normal borrowing arrangement. In April 1999, the IMF Executive Board doubled the funds available under its "emergency postconflict assistance" to 50 percent of that country's quota and introduced new terms allowing loans to be made retroactively concessional after one year.[36] Several countries have taken advantage of IMF facilities, including Albania, Bosnia and Herzegovina, Rwanda, and Tajikistan.[37] Nevertheless, the Fund's policy shift remains inadequate. Not only are the criteria for distinguishing among aid candidates vague, but the new facility also fails to address the clearance of arrears, a crushing burden for many postconflict states.

Improve Coordination Among Bilateral Donors

In parallel with these initiatives, bilateral donors have used the OECD/DAC forum to formulate *Guidelines on Conflict, Peace, and Development Cooperation*. In the words of the DAC, the ultimate goal of development cooperation should be to foster an environment of "structural stability," defined as a combination of "social peace, respect for the rule of law and human rights, social and economic development, supported by dynamic and representative political institutions capable of managing change and resolving disputes without resort to violent conflict." In order to accomplish these aims, donors must design "international responses" that are more coordinated, coherent, and integrated.[38]

Like the UN's strategic framework, these guidelines are stronger at articulating unassailable principles than at offering concrete operational advice about improving aid design and delivery. In addition, they present conflicting views about the desirable nature of coordination. On the one hand, they ask development partners to "designat[e] . . . an independent coordinating authority to monitor the donors' adherence to agreed principles." Yet elsewhere, they distinguish the "voluntary character" of aid coordination from "the concept of 'management,' which implies substantial control of the various elements present."[39]

On their own, several bilateral donors have created rapid-response functional units to assist the sustainable recovery from complex emergencies and war. In 1994, for example, the United States created an Office of Transition Initiatives (OTI) within the Bureau for Humanitarian Response in USAID. OTI is intended to serve as an agile foreign policy instrument to help conflict-stricken countries move forward rapidly toward stable, democratic forms of government. Created out of USAID's International Disaster Assistance account, OTI can make use of fast-disbursing funds without having to endure the lengthy (roughly eighteen-month) cycle of program design, congressional authorization, and implementation characteristic of a typical development initiative.[40] OTI's regular budget for 1999 is $40 million.

Canada, likewise, has pursued postconflict recovery initiatives through a Can$10 million Peacebuilding Fund within CIDA and through the smaller Peacebuilding Program of the Department of Foreign Affairs and International Trade (DFAIT).[41] Unfortunately, the budgets, staffs, and mandates of such specialized bilateral units remain modest. The units must compete for resources with bureaucratic rivals and carry out their initiatives during a time of declining political and financial support for international aid.[42]

Design Aid Conditions to Advance Peace

As a result of their diverse mandates and interests, different external actors are apt to formulate aid conditions that are incompatible, or at least exist in tension. Since postconflict recovery is a political as well as an economic undertaking, donors need to reconcile their support for peace implementation with their assistance programs for reconstruction and self-sustaining growth. In practice, this does not always occur. Rather, the two strategies may be designed, pursued, and supervised along two independent tracks. One result has been a clash between an "economic" approach to conditionality, which makes aid contingent on economic performance, and a "political" approach, which makes it contingent on peace-building objectives.[43]

The most troubling inconsistencies have arisen from the competing priorities of IFIs, which generally focus on macroeconomic stabilization and structural adjustment in isolation of wider considerations, and other external actors concerned with preventing the resumption of armed conflict. For example, peace-building imperatives collided with concerns about economic rigor in Mozambique and El Salvador. In both cases, the Bretton Woods institutions pursued neoliberal economic orthodoxy, failing to use their leverage to ensure the fulfillment of terms of the peace accords and, according to some observers, imposing conditions that aggravated social inequality and undermined political reconciliation. One widely cited article likened El Salvador to an anaesthetized patient undergoing simultaneous but disconnected operations at the hands of the IFIs and the UN.[44]

While the patient analogy is overdrawn (El Salvador was hardly a passive actor), the image of uncoordinated surgeries underlines the need to harmonize aid interventions to advance *both* recovery and peace. Postconflict assistance must be embedded in the political reality of the transition process: donors cannot afford to design aid conditions as if a conflict had never occurred. Rather than implementing conventional structural adjustment, donors should support what James Boyce terms "adjustment toward peace."[45] They can do so by tolerating larger public sector expenditures and budget deficits; by funding programs mandated by peace accords; by considering the distributional implications of their aid conditions; and by employing performance criteria and informal dialogue to ensure compliance with peace-related commitments. In El Salvador, for example, the IFIs might have used their leverage to press for lower military spending, land transfers to ex-combatants, and fiscal, judicial, and legal reform.

Recognizing the primacy of the peace-building imperative, the Carnegie Commission report *Preventing Deadly Conflict* calls on the IFIs to cooperate with the United Nations, "so that economic inducements can play a more central role in early prevention and in postconflict reconstruction." Similarly, the secretary-general's 1998 report on Africa insists that structural adjustment be "people-friendly," so as not to reignite conflict. As the document notes, the IMF's "policies of austerity have sometimes hindered reconciliation."[46]

Historically, the Fund and the Bank have resisted peace conditionality by citing their Articles of Agreement; these prohibit them from considering political criteria when making loans or from interfering in the internal affairs of any state. In the Bank's case, however, those very articles instruct the Bank to show "special regard to lightening the financial burden and expediting the . . . restoration and reconstruction" of war-torn societies.[47] This clause would seem to justify greater flexibility in applying stabilization and structural adjustment.

Moreover, despite their self-described "apolitical" status, the Bank and the Fund now condition lending on politically sensitive criteria like "financial transparency," "good governance," and "unproductive expenditures" (like high defense spending). They do so on the grounds of economic efficiency and sustainable development.[48] The IFIs have also begun to incorporate social impact analyses into their lending practices and safety nets into their stabilization and structural adjustment packages.[49] In similar fashion, they might shape their lending and nonlending activities according to country-specific analyses of the potential implications of their aid for mitigating social conflict.

The World Bank has taken tentative steps to introduce peace-building considerations into its operations. It now realizes that structural adjustment programs must be "peace-friendly" and that the actual sequence of economic policy and governance reforms should be "tailored to avoid threatening the sustainability of peace agreements."[50] Moreover, a recent internal review by the Bank's Operations Evaluation Department (OED) concedes great difficulty in "drawing the line" between economic and political issues in postconflict situations. Given "centrality of the peace objective," Bank staff are advised to question certain "conventional wisdoms." In the past, Bank procedures have sometimes threatened sustainable recovery from conflict. In the future, when confronting "deeply divided societies," the Bank may wish to use "policy and economic conditionality" to encourage "economic and distributional policies and programs that can avoid a slide into conflict."[51]

Within the donor community more broadly, the past decade has witnessed the emergence of a "second generation" of aid conditionality focused on democratic governance, human rights, administrative accountability, and excessive military expenditures. The DAC, for example, cites the "vital connection between open democratic and accountable political systems, individual rights, and the effective and equitable operation of economic systems."[52] Bilateral donors have commissioned a task force to study "Development Cooperation Incentives for Peace."[53]

Unfortunately, OECD member states rarely speak with one voice in designing or enforcing the terms of aid. Instead, they tend to stipulate irreconcilable conditions and react disjointedly when recipients fail to meet these terms. In Bosnia and Herzegovina, for example, donors sought to condition delivery of aid on progress toward a single multiethnic state, support for refugee return, and cooperation with the international war crimes tribunal. But as Hurtić, Šapčanin, and Woodward point out in Chapter 8, they did not enforce these conditions equally on the parties to conflict and, indeed, used bilateral aid channels to evade their application. Likewise, in Cambodia (Chapter 3) donors responded inconsistently following Hun Sen's coup of July 1997: the United States suspended most of its assistance, Japan chose to continue its engagement, and other donors took intermediate steps. Consequently, the divided donor community enjoyed little leverage over the new government.

If peace conditionality is to be effective, it must rest on a firmer multilateral foundation. Donors must collectively formulate clear and credible aid conditions, pursue coordinated policies toward the recipient, create joint monitoring mechanisms, and avoid selective enforcement.[54] A more rigorous approach may create uncomfortable dilemmas. Given the fragility of postconflict settings, donors may face short-term trade-offs between justice and stability. Likewise, if local parties fail to meet their commitments, donors will need to be prepared to tolerate the human and political costs of denying aid. The West Bank/Gaza case (Chapter 6) shows how difficult it is to enforce aid conditions when donors are unprepared to accept the collapse of a government.

In delineating the terms of aid, donors should be realistic about the outcomes amenable to political manipulation and social engineering from the outside. Peace conditionality cannot be purely externally driven. It can succeed only if aid recipients are willing to modify their stances in response to the incentives donors have at their disposal. It is not clear, for example, that any combination of carrots or sticks will induce the Bosnian Serbs to agree to refugee returns in Republika Srpska, particularly in the context of an imposed peace.

Improve Local Coordination

As a matter of principle, local aid coordination is a task that belongs squarely in the mandate of the recipient government. It alone has the responsibility for deciding what aid to request, from whom to request it, and how to weave external assistance into its own development strategy. However, local governance structures are often fragmentary following conflict, and the international community will by default often need to take on a disproportionate role in the coordination process, while over time orchestrating a hand-over of these tasks.

Under such circumstances, the sheer number of international actors involved in postconflict recovery has required donors in consultation with recipient authorities to create complex structures of local aid coordination. Inevitably, these mechanisms vary with the specific context, including the nature of the conflict and the degree to which peace has been consolidated; the identity, weight, and interests of the leading donors; the political status and capacities of the local authorities; and the recipient country's dependence on external assistance.

Because each bilateral donor, international agency, and IFI has its own mandate and autonomy, it is inherently difficult to formulate a common strategy for reconstruction and peace building. These tensions and inconsistencies are exacerbated by the simultaneity (or overlap) of several different transitions. A recovering country may be moving at once from war to peace, from a command to a market economy, from an authoritarian to a pluralistic political system, and from a complex emergency to a conventional development situation. Moreover, the machinery to coordinate foreign aid often coexists with a parallel framework for peace implementation. Although these twin tracks of external involvement are ostensibly complementary, the coordinating bodies established to oversee delivery of aid and compliance with peace accords typically have different members, mandates, and priorities.

The findings of the Pledges of Aid country studies suggest that donors should adopt the following general orientations.

Create local coordination mechanisms promptly. To begin with, and notwithstanding the principle of local ownership, donors should establish structures of aid coordination as soon as possible in situations where local authorities lack sufficient capacity to do so on their own. Failure to do so can delay essential recovery tasks. For example, the Paris accords of October 1991 insisted that the priorities for Cambodia's national reconstruction await the formation of that country's first democratically elected government. This postponed for two years both Cambodia's first comprehensive recovery plan and the initial meeting of the International Committee on the Reconstruction of Cambodia. Moreover, the peace agreements neglected to clarify donor roles, to specify aid targets, or to create a timetable for assistance. Donors themselves failed to create an integrated system to plan, integrate, manage, and monitor their various aid programs.[55]

Delegate authority to the field. Past experience suggests that donors should establish field-based management structures immediately. Local coordination has been particularly effective when agencies have delegated significant administrative and financial authority, including control over budgetary matters, to representatives in the field. Donors need to be able to respond flexibly in fluid situations, to act decisively, and to move funds quickly. This implies efficient institutional channels and implementation capacities and the presence of knowledgeable staff in the field. Too often, donors apply standard procedures that create delays and gaps in assistance. The World Bank's efforts in Cambodia, for example, were hindered by its lack of an early field presence and its application of cumbersome procurement rules. The Bank learned from this and similar experiences, however, and adopted a new policy devolving considerable authority to its resident representative. This delegation of authority paid dividends both in the West Bank and Gaza and in Bosnia and Herzegovina.

Anticipate and ameliorate donor rivalries. Political rivalry among donors for leadership of the aid effort and/or disagreements over the application of aid conditions can impair smooth coordination. In the West Bank and Gaza (Chapter 6), for example, the European Union (EU) sought a coordinating role commensurate with its status as the leading donor to the Occupied Territories. The United States, the leading diplomatic actor in the Middle East peace process, favored assigning this role to the World Bank. The U.S. position ultimately prevailed. Donor rivalry also occurred in Bosnia and Herzegovina (Chapter 8), as the United States clashed with the World Bank over peace conditionality and the role of the Office of the High Representative (OHR) in aid coordination. Although some clashes are inevitable, particularly in politically charged environments, donors need to anticipate and ameliorate these.

Individual bilateral donors must also improve the coherence of their national approaches toward each war-torn country. Too often, national governments fail to harmonize their political strategies and assistance strategies. Thus, a donor's development (or humanitarian) agency may be operating according to principles of "neutrality," whereas its foreign ministry will view decisions relating to recovery aid or peace implementation through a political lens, often favoring one faction over another.

Consider multiple coordination mechanisms. Experience in several postconflict environments, including the West Bank and Gaza, suggests that there may be value in creating multi-tiered coordination mechanisms, with inclusive and exclusive memberships. These might include high-level political forums to oversee progress toward peace-building goals, a committee to coordinate overall assistance, and working groups to supervise aid implementation in particular sectors. Recipients, if unable to exercise leadership from the outset, should nevertheless enjoy representation within each of these mechanisms and assume increasing responsibility for setting the agenda within them.

Strengthen the SRSG and RC/HC functions. In addition, the United Nations should redouble its current efforts to strengthen and harmonize those offices critical for effective field coordination: the position of Special Representative of the Secretary-General (SRSG) and the function of the UN Resident Coordinator/Humanitarian Coordinator (RC/HC).

Postconflict recovery often begins in the context of multidimensional peace operations under UN command.[56] For example, UN-led peacekeeping or observer missions were in place when international reconstruction efforts began in Cambodia (UNTAC), El Salvador (ONUSAL), Guatemala (MINUGUA), Mozambique (ONUMOZ), and Tajikistan (UNMOT). In such cases an SRSG is generally appointed to coordinate the activities of UN agencies on the ground and to help reconcile the UN's strategies for peace implementation and recovery assistance.

While the SRSG plays an indispensable function in postconflict countries, the position requires several urgent reforms. As pointed out in a study by the Peace Implementation Network (PIN), the UN Secretariat must provide the SRSG with a clear mandate and terms of reference, stronger administrative and policy support, and more generous and flexible financial instruments. To improve coordination within the crisis country, each SRSG should be given clear authority to speak on behalf of the various programs, departments, and agencies of the UN family. Most importantly, the SRSG should be granted direct access and supervision over the resources of those entities.[57]

Simultaneously, the United Nations should strengthen its RC system by delineating the appropriate responsibilities of different UN agencies. Several case studies in this volume (most notably that of Mozambique) document rivalries among field-based UN actors reporting to different masters at headquarters and resistant to firm management by one of their number. On the other hand, it should be recognized that the ongoing process of UN reform has begun to address some of these issues. The secretrary-general's recent innovation of a single "UN House" containing all agencies should improve local coordination. In addition, the UN's Inter-Agency Standing Committee (IASC) has made progress in reconciling the roles of the RC and the HC. The UN should further clarify the relationship between the RC/HC function and the role of the SRSG.[58]

Finally, the case studies underline that the quality of donor coordination depends on the quality of the officials chosen to fill these top positions. The United Nations must develop transparent and effective recruitment policies to ensure that the SRSG and RC/HC roles are occupied by individuals who have strong managerial skills and field experience and are attuned to local political realities.

Build on Local Capacities

Postconflict countries vary enormously in their ability to manage and absorb foreign assistance. Following extensive violence, as in Cambodia (Chapter 3), recipients may lack the human, technical, and administrative capacities required to make use of large quantities of aid or to coordinate the multiple donors and NGOs that arrive to assist their recovery. The donor community should design interventions that enable recipients to acquire these capacities as quickly as possible. Efforts to build state capacity ought to be measurable, with clear benchmarks to gauge progress in different spheres of activity.

Donors can nurture recipient capacities in several ways: by acknowledging and supporting the recipient government's central role in planning and coordinating aid; by financing important public sector expenditures; by delivering appropriate technical assistance and training; by adjusting pressure for macroeconomic stabilization; by tolerating nonconventional expenditures; by facilitating the early clearance of arrears; by insisting on the mobilization of the recipient's domestic resources; and by prolonging their engagement in the country. The following paragraphs address these points.

Acknowledge the government's central role. The donor community is often torn by its impulse to deliver assistance as quickly as possible and its desire to rely on local capacities to shape, supervise, and implement reconstruction efforts. At a rhetorical level, donors concede that "donor-driven" aid must yield to true "partnership" and local "ownership." In practice, donors preoccupied with speed frequently surrender to the temptation to design recovery programs with little recipient input—and to deliver aid through their own implementing agencies and service providers, rather than through local actors who alone can ensure the sustainability of the effort.

Donors must consult with governments and local stakeholders throughout the recovery effort. At the outset, the donor community and the government should create a standing forum to discuss the overall framework for peace building, the priorities of recovery, and the respective roles of all partners. Initially, the recipient may lack the capacity to design a workable recovery plan on its own, so that a leading donor (or donors) may need to draft the first blueprint for reconstruction in consultation with local officials. As early as practicable, though, the local governing authority should assume primary responsibility for coordinating assistance. In the West Bank and Gaza, for example, the World Bank and the United Nations Special Coordinator in the Occupied Territories (UNSCO) assisted the Palestinian Authority (PA) in 1995 in drafting its initial Core Investment Program. By 1996, the PA was able to formulate and propose to donors its own Public Investment Program.

To foster healthy political development, donor agencies need to balance their efforts to rebuild state capacities with support for private groups and institutions. Particularly in the early postconflict phase, the legitimacy of a new government may be contested by broad segments of society. To foster political reconciliation, local ownership, and indigenous capacities for recovery, donors must bolster the constructive involvement of opposition parties and civil society actors in the political and economic life of the country.

Finance important public sector expenditures. One obvious way for donors to build local capacities is to channel aid directly through the national budgets of postconflict states. Bilateral donors generally resist doing this, preferring to finance projects reflecting their own priorities, to fund service providers of their own nationality, and to procure goods from their own country. The result may be programs reflecting donor political agendas and economic interests rather than those of the local actors. On the other hand, donors often argue that there are insufficient checks and balances to justify direct budgetary support to governments whose internal standards of accountability are often considered inadequate. As a result of these tendencies, the World Bank has found it difficult to mobilize cofinancing for budgetary support in several settings, including Bosnia and Herzegovina, Cambodia, El Salvador, and Rwanda.[59] This has delayed the provision of essential public services and risked undermining popular commitments to peace.

When donors agree to provide budgetary support, the benefits can be dramatic. Perhaps the most promising precendent is the Holst Peace Trust Fund, created in 1994 to support the recurrent costs of the PA in the West Bank and Gaza. Managed by the World Bank, this revolving fund received contributions from more than two dozen bilateral donors. Because these deposits were not earmarked for particular purposes, the fund was inherently flexible. Over five years, the fund disbursed some $250 million, much to support the PA's recurrent costs and employment-generation schemes.

Deliver appropriate technical assistance and training. Most postconflict countries urgently need technical know-how on multiple matters, from fiscal policy to de-mining and public health to civil engineering. Unfortunately, too much technical assistance finances the contracts of foreign consultants (and reports of uncertain value), rather than training local individuals to deliver essential services themselves. All technical aid projects should meet the test of capacity building. One useful starting point would be to assist recovering state administrations in managing the diverse accounting and reporting requirements of donor agencies.

Adjust pressure for macroeconomic rigor. Although macroeconomic stability and structural adjustment are preconditions for sustainable growth and government revenues, in the short term they may run counter to capacity-building objectives. War-to-peace transitions are costly: Besides "normal" expenditures, postconflict governments need to deliver on specific peace commitments, finance reconstruction initiatives, and fund projects that reward loyalists and reintegrate enemies. Maintaining budgetary balance in the face of these competing demands may be impossible. Precipitate emphasis on fiscal rigor, trade liberalization, and privatization may reduce the state's capacity to deliver basic services and achieve the promise of peace accords, threatening reconciliation and undermining social peace. Consequently, external pressure for economic reform must be embedded in the political reality of the transition. This may imply tolerating larger deficits and sequencing structural adjustment differently.

On a related note, donors need to sharpen the tools they use to evaluate state budgets, including "excessive" military expenditures. Typically, aid agencies and IFIs press postconflict governments to shift spending from security to the social sector. Public order, however, is a prerequisite for peace building and sustainable recovery. In some circumstances, high defense spending may reflect ongoing pacification (as in northern Uganda or in the Khmer Rouge–dominated regions of Cambodia) or the need to preserve patronage systems that underpin political stability.[60]

Facilitate the clearance of arrears. One of the most valuable steps that the international community could take to build the capacities of countries emerging from conflict is to provide them with significant debt relief. Many such states find themselves strapped with huge financial obligations to international financial institutions—commitments often incurred by former regimes. Without early arrears clearance, these countries cannot receive new resources from either the International Development Association (IDA) or the IMF, nor can they hope to attract significant foreign investment. In current practice, the IFIs often arrange "bridging" loans from third parties, typically donor governments. For example, before the IMF could resume lending activities in Bosnia and Herzegovina, the government of the Netherlands had to agree to cover Bosnia's arrears with the Fund. Such arrangements do not affect the actual burden on the debtor country, however; the identity of the creditor merely changes. The IFIs need to reexamine the wisdom of extending aid to postconflict countries in the form of nonconcessional loans rather than grants.

In response to public pressure to reduce debt burdens on the world's poorest countries, in 1996 the World Bank and the IMF sponsored the Highly Indebted Poor Countries (or HIPC) initiative.[61] Two years later, the IFIs extended this program, partly in recognition of the "special challenge" facing war-torn countries.[62] Nevertheless, the HIPC initiative remains inadequate. To qualify, applicants must first complete two successful IMF Enhanced Structural Adjustment Facility (ESAF) arrangements, which may take six years. Second, the IMF's definition of a "sustainable" debt burden ignores that many war-torn countries cannot raise sufficient revenues or amass export earnings to service their debts. Finally, the current HIPC resources are too modest to contribute fundamentally to the reduction of poverty in these countries.[63]

Acknowledging the inadequacy of current efforts, the G7 governments announced an ambitious debt relief proposal at their June 1999 summit in Cologne, Germany. This relief, directed mainly at African countries, could amount to a $71 billion reduction in the stock of poor country debt. While the large scale of this initiative is promising, it remains to be seen whether the donors will follow through on their pledges, particularly once they address the contentious issue of burden sharing. Moreover, early projections suggest that its impact on the debt positions of highly indebted war-torn countries is likely to be variable.[64]

Mobilize local resources. Even as they provide assistance and lessen debt burdens, donors cannot afford to ignore local resources. Too often in conflict environments, foreign aid agencies and international NGOs overwhelm indigenous coping mechanisms and displace local human, financial, and material capacities. At the same time, donors frequently underestimate the value of local, "in-kind" resources, including staff, premises, facilities, transportation, and communication. To avoid fostering dependency, external actors should use explicit conditionality and policy dialogue to leverage the available and potential assets of societies emerging from conflict.[65]

The contrasting experiences of El Salvador and Guatemala may be instructive in this regard. According to Rosa and Foley (Chapter 4), the donor community failed to press the Salvadoran government to devote sufficient national resources to peace-related programs; the government's attitude was essentially that donors should fund these activities. In Guatemala, in contrast, the widespread impression that external aid would be meager led to the inclusion of a provision in the peace accords to raise the country's fiscal revenue. At the conceptual level, at least, the government accepted the principle that recovery from conflict was a joint venture.[66]

Adopt realistic time frames. Finally, in view of these formidable challenges, donors need to be more realistic about the length of their engagement. The sustainable transition from conflict requires a commitment significantly longer than the two to three years donors typically allot to reconstruction programs.[67] Where donors confront an essentially settled conflict, they may wish to negotiate an explicit timetable with the government. In cases where the "peace" is more of an uncertain truce, as in Bosnia and Herzegovina, setting firm deadlines for withdrawal may only encourage obstructionism.

Ensure Accountability

Track Aid Delivery

To ensure the efficacy and legitimacy of its efforts, the donor community must improve its capacities to monitor the delivery and implementation of postconflict assistance. Donors urgently need a standardized accounting system for reporting aid flows, one that can be applied in every circumstance. Such a comprehensive database, broken down by pledges, commitments, and disbursements, should be updated quarterly and be readily accessible to all stakeholders and interested external observers.

Despite efforts to harmonize donor reporting, it remains difficult for third parties to establish firm data on aid flows in many country settings. Although bilateral and multilateral donors alike insist that aid recipients maintain high standards of "accountability" and "transparency," their application of these principles to their own conduct is uneven at best. Too often, donors resist releasing data on the status of their pledges. Presumably, this stance is motivated by a desire to avoid embarrassing admissions of policy failure, to dodge the displeasure of their development partners, or (more charitably) to prevent the misrepresentation of their actual performance. Whatever the motivation, such opacity undermines the credibility of donors and their laudable efforts to encourage transparency among aid recipients.

Interpreting those matrices of aid flows that are made public is problematic, moreover, since it is donors themselves that usually provide the relevant data. Where parallel tracking systems exist, discrepancies sometimes arise. In Bosnia and Herzegovina, where three different actors maintain separate databases, rival estimates for aggregate aid delivery show tremendous variation—on the order of $500 million to $1 billion! As Hurtić, Šapčanin, and Woodward note in Chapter 8, the resulting impression is that the databases themselves are "a political function."

Unfortunately, global mechanisms for reporting aid flows provide no easy verification of aid delivery. The best sources available, the *Quarterly Report on Individual Aid Commitments* and the *Geographical Distribution of Aid Flows*, are published by the DAC, whose twenty-two members are responsible (ultimately) for some 99 percent of global official development assistance (ODA). Both tracking systems are muddied by the respondents' use of different reporting methods and idiosyncratic classification schemes. (Donors differ, for instance, about what counts as "relief," "reconstruction," or "development" aid.) It is also difficult to aggregate the recorded flows according to their specific purpose, to link them to individual recovery efforts, or to connect them to the relevant United Nations appeal or multilateral pledging conference. Moreover, donors tend to report their share of contributions to UN implementing agencies, which may report the same disbursement. Finally, neither the OECD nor multilateral agencies consider "pledges" an official aid category. Given the role pledges play in generating expectations, it seems essential to track them as well.

Both bilateral and multilateral donors acknowledge that current practices must change. As the OECD/DAC notes, "The large volume of resources mobilized for relief and rehabilitation makes it essential to establish an up-to-date, systematic means of tracking aid flows." Such a system would require donors to standardize their definitions of the "related nomenclature," including terms like "statement of intent, pledge, commitment, obligation and disbursement." As UNDP's Emergency Response Division observes, such terms are generally "confusing and so often used for political effect."[68]

Ideally, such a system would be maintained electronically on the World Wide Web. A useful template might be the "ReliefWeb" maintained by the UN's OCHA, particularly its Financial Tracking Database for Complex Emergencies.[69] The new tracking system could be housed and managed within the OECD secretariat, the UNDP's Emergency Response Division, or the World Bank's Post-Conflict Unit.

Making aid flows transparent would allow all stakeholders to assess progress and encourage donors to meet their obligations in timely fashion. This has certainly been the experience in the West Bank and Gaza. As Brynen, Awartani, and Woodcraft observe in Chapter 6, the accurate, accessible database maintained by the World Bank and the Palestinian Ministry of Planning and International Cooperation has spurred donors to make good on their commitments.

Encourage Local Transparency and Accountability

Reports of corruption in postconflict governments can have devastating consequences for continued donor support for their recovery.[70] Donors should thus design aid interventions in ways that maximize transparency in the use of internal and external funds and that hold local officials accountable. At the same time, donors will need to be attentive to the political realities of recovering societies and the requirements of stability.

In certain circumstances, peace-building concerns have led donors to tolerate unconventional economic instruments and to indulge recipient government policies that depart from normal standards of transparency. This is obviously a delicate issue that creates quandaries for external actors. For example, as Brynen, Awartani, and Woodcraft document in Chapter 6, Yasir Arafat and the Fateh Party have stabilized the post-Oslo political situation in the West Bank and Gaza Strip partly through a massive system of political patronage that rewards loyalists with employment in a bloated civil service and generates income through quasi-official monopolies. The problem, of course, is that such short-term expedients may prevent the reestablishment of a stable macroeconomic framework and—if unsustainable—ultimately undermine the legitimacy of the Palestinian Authority. The dilemma for donors is how long to tolerate convenient departures from economic efficiency and political accountability.

At times, donors themselves have relied on unorthodox contrivances that depart from "normal" accountability standards. As Ball and Barnes note in Chapter 5, Mozambique's smooth transition to peace was lubricated by the SRSG's creation of a $20 million discretionary fund to support Renamo's transformation into a political party. In Uganda, too, donors used cash transfers as incentives to "buy out" and reintegrate combatants.

By injecting large amounts of assistance into war-torn countries, donors unwittingly but inevitably distort local systems of production and exchange. Such an aid-driven economy alters social power balances, and rival political elites and factions may exploit foreign assistance to gain leverage over national resources (e.g., lumber in Cambodia, diamonds in Sierra Leone). Donors must be attuned to the political economy of conflict and the criminalized nature of many postconflict economies, and they should try to direct external resources to local actors who support peacebuilding goals.

Assess the Impact of Aid

Beyond creating mechanisms to gauge the delivery of promised assistance, the international community needs to develop tools to evaluate its *impact*. Within aid agencies, incentive structures generally reward the ability to "move money" rather than virtuosity in designing it appropriately. The predictable result can be too much of the wrong type of aid. There are three general reasons for the current inattention to issues of impact.

First, agencies simply lack methodologies to assess the results of recovery aid. It is difficult to apply data-hungry econometric models in many postconflict environments, where even baseline data may be lacking. In order to make capacity building a measurable activity, donors should devise benchmarks—appropriate to each country context—that will allow them to gauge progress toward economic recovery, human security, and participatory governance. In the economic sphere, these indicators would measure the reconstruction of physical infrastructure and utilities, the composition of public spending, the degree of macroeconomic balance, the appropriateness of fiscal instruments, the country's debt position, the distribution of national wealth, the reintegration of refugees and internally displaced persons (IDPs), the provision of basic social services, the rehabilitation of agriculture, and the reactivation of critical industries. In the security realm, benchmarks should assess the demobilization of former combatants, their reintegration into productive life, the reconstitution of the armed forces, the creation of a civilian police force, the disarmament of the population, and the provision of personal security. In the political arena, they should assess the strength of the rule of law and the judiciary, the protection of human rights, the progress of reconciliation panels and truth commissions, the conduct of democratic elections, the transparency of political institutions, the reestablishment of public administration, and the vigor of civil society.[71]

Second, evaluation efforts are generally assumed to be not only time consuming but also expensive. In fact, recent experience suggests that evaluation can be done rapidly and in a cost-effective manner. For example, the path-breaking multidonor evaluation of assistance to Rwanda, involving four teams and fifty-two people, lasted just a year and cost only $1.8 million dollars—a fairly modest sum given the important lessons to be derived from the study.[72] Moreover, the hidden costs of ineffective program management can far exceed the cost of even the most thorough evaluation project and have an impact that is not only monetary but also economic and political.

A final, more difficult obstacle is that there are few incentives within aid agencies to conduct self-critical evaluations of aid impact. As in most bureaucracies, officials in these institutions are likely to be constrained by concerns of self-preservation. Honest appraisals may bring unwelcome publicity, jeopardizing external credibility and funding. Moreover, they may at times offend the recipient government.

These impediments are real but not insurmountable. One approach to reduce the fear of honest appraisals would be to "multilateralize" the undertaking. Using the model of the Rwanda evaluation, in which the Danish government took the lead, one donor might convene a joint task force, including bilateral donors, IFIs, UN agencies, and prominent NGOs.[73] In the end, the feasibility of a sincere evaluation is likely to depend on the organizational culture of the institutions involved, particularly their openness to learning. Earnest evaluations will be more likely if aid agencies and their political masters hold management accountable less for the problems exposed than for the corrective actions taken in response to these appraisals.

Conclusion

Although private capital flows now dwarf ODA in this age of globalization, the vast bulk of foreign direct investment destined for the developing world focuses on a handful of dynamic emerging markets.[74] Most poor countries—and war-torn ones above all—remain marginalized from the world economy. The donor community retains an indispensable role in assisting beleaguered societies to achieve enduring political stability and sustainable economic growth.

Bilateral and multilateral donors have committed themselves rhetorically to support postconflict recovery, and they have reaffirmed this objective repeatedly in pledging conferences and other venues by offering generous support for these purposes. Good intentions notwithstanding, the external interventions to support reconstruction have been hindered by insufficient collaboration in the design and execution of assistance; inadequate financial mechanisms to meet transitional needs falling between relief and development; misleading pledging conferences; incompatible aid conditions; inattention to local capacities; unreliable databases; and weak tools to gauge the impact of assistance.

Improving international assistance is not simply a technical exercise. It requires political will. Still, the findings above point to several concrete reforms. This chapter proposes that donors:

Formulate an agreed "strategic framework" for each postconflict country. Each framework document should lay out the principles and objectives of collective action, facilitate joint needs assessment, and permit a rational division of labor.

Establish additional mechanisms to mobilize resources rapidly for transitional situations. Individual donors should either designate new budget lines for reconstruction activities or streamline such assistance within their humanitarian or development budgets. Collectively, donors should consider the value of an expanded consolidated appeals process and a global reconstruction fund.

Reform current pledging conferences. Donors should ensure that pledges made at Consultative Group meetings and roundtables correspond to realistic needs assessments and recipient priorities.

Deepen tentative steps toward institutional reform. The United Nations agencies, the international financial institutions, and bilateral donors should provide greater authority and resources to their functional postconflict units and explore fruitful divisions of labor based on their respective comparative advantages.

Harmonize the conditions donors place on their assistance. To the degree that their interests and mandates allow, donors need to reconcile the terms of their assistance. The overriding goal must be to prevent the resumption of violent conflict.

Improve coordination in the field. External actors should create local mechanisms of aid coordination quickly, make them compatible with parallel peace implementation structures, delegate authority to the field, moderate national and institutional rivalries, and consider multitiered frameworks for coordination.

Nurture the indigenous capacities of postconflict countries. Besides consulting with local officials and broader elements of civil society at every stage of recovery, donors should finance important public sector expenditures, relax insistence on macroeconomic and fiscal rigor, facilitate debt reduction, and mobilize local resources.

Create a standardized, transparent system for reporting, tracking, and monitoring aid flows. Such a database would track pledges, commitments, and disbursements to countries under reconstruction.

Sharpen tools to assess the impact of aid. Finally, while monitoring aid delivery is imperative to sustain the legitimacy of the international community's efforts, it is only a first step. Donors need better tools to evaluate the effectiveness of these disbursements.

Notes

I would like to thank James Boyce, Michael Foley, Shepard Forman, David O'Brien, and Ron Kassimir for comments on earlier versions of this chapter. I am also grateful to Nicole Ball, John Eriksson, Johanna Mendelson Forman, Steve Holtzman, and Dirk Salomons for helpful advice.

1. In May 1997, the umbrella group of major bilateral donors, the Development Assistance Committee (DAC) of the Organization for Economic Cooperation and Development (OECD) formally endorsed the concept. OECD/DAC, *Conflict, Peace, and Development Cooperation*, pp. 33, 48.

2. Cholmondeley, "The Role of the UN System"; UNDP/ERD, "Informal Briefing Note."

3. UN, Deputy Secretary-General, "Draft Generic Guidelines," and "Strategic Framework for Afghanistan."

4. World Bank, "Partnership for Development," pp. 11–20, 48.

5. Conferring authority on an impartial actor like the secretary-general would reduce fears of a power grab; it need not imply UN leadership in coordinating the subsequent aid effort.

6. Center on International Cooperation, "Meeting Essential Needs in Societies Emerging from Conflict."

7. United Nations, General Assembly, "Strengthening of the Coordination of Emergency Humanitarian Assistance"; Macrae, "Linking Relief, Rehabilitation, and Development," pp. 17–18; Duffield, "Complex Emergencies," p. 40.

8. UNDP, Rwanda Mission, "Linking Relief to Development"; European Commission, "Linking Relief, Rehabilitation, and Development."

9. Speth, "Linking Relief to Development," p. 4.

10. United Nations, DHA, *Humanitarian Report 1997*, pp. 103–106.

11. OECD/DAC, *Conflict, Peace, and Development Cooperation,* p. 34; Joint Evaluation of Emergency Assistance to Rwanda, *The International Response to Conflict and Genocide*, pp. 32–35, 101–106.

12. UNDP/ERD, "One-Page Rationale."

13. UNDP and DHA failed to agree on their respective responsibilities and the ECAP's relationship with other resource mobilization mechanisms.

14. United Nations, "Second Report to the Secretary-General," p. 13; United Nations, DHA-UNDP, "Building Bridges"; United Nations, "Report of the Secretary-General"; United Nations, ECOSOC, "Strengthening of the Coordination of Emergency Humanitarian Assistance."

15. Among the cases in this volume, only South Africa has never been the subject of a pledging conference.

16. Boyce, "External Assistance," p. 2106.

17. The expression, in this context, is Rex Brynen's.

18. Lake, *After the Wars*, p. 23; Fahlen, "Post-Conflict Reconstruction"; World Bank, *Post-Conflict Reconstruction,* p. 48.

19. UNHCR and World Bank, "Roundtable on the Gap"; Ogata and Wolfensohn, "The Transition to Peace."

20. Bilateral participants have included, among others, Canada (CIDA and DFAIT), Germany (GTZ), the Netherlands (Ministry of Foreign Affairs), Sweden (SIDA), United Kingdom (DFID), and the United States (USAID/OTI). Multilateral organizations involved in the initiative include FAO, IOM, UNICEF, UNDP, UNHCR, UNHCHR, UN OCHA, UNOPS, UNRISD, WFP, WHO, IMF, World Bank, and ECHO. World Bank, "'Conflict Prevention and Post-Conflict Reconstruction," p. 26.

21. The postconflict units have formed working groups on children in conflict, de-mining, demobilization and reintegration, early warning, gender and conflict, refugees, security sector reform, human rights, small arms, good governance and transparency, social and cultural rehabilitation, and tools for evaluation.

22. Moreover, some important agencies, including UNICEF and FAO, possess no core funding for postconflict recovery activities as such.

23. United Nations, "Comments of the Secretary-General."

24. "TRAC" stands for "Target for Resource Assignments from the Core." TRAC 1.1.3 initiatives have included demobilization in Angola and Mali; mine action in Cambodia and Laos; election preparation in Cambodia and Haiti; socio-economic rehabilitation in Lebanon; government capacity building in Rwanda; peace building in El Salvador; and area rehabilitation in Afghanistan, Azerbaijan, Bosnia and Herzegovina, Georgia, Guatemala, Somalia, and the Palestinian territories. UNDP/ERD, "TRAC 1.1.3 Crisis Committee Approvals"; UNDP/ERD, "Working for Solutions to Crisis."

25. Initiatives have been launched, for example, by the Executive Committees on Peace and Security and Humanitarian Assistance, by the United Nations Development Group, by the Inter-Agency Standing Committee (IASC) Reference Groups on Post-Conflict Reintegration, by the ECOSOC humanitarian segment, and by the Deputy Secretary-General. The Executive Heads of the UN system organizations, meeting in the Administrative Committee on Coordination (ACC), have similarly tried to harmonize their actions at the country level through the resident coordinator system. In addition, the World Bank and the UNHCR have signed a "Framework for Cooperation" to foster the sustainable reintegration of refugees and have inaugurated a multidonor evaluation of financing instruments and institutional responsibilities needed to bridge the gap between relief and development.

26. United Nations, Joint Inspection Unit, "Coordination at Headquarters and Field Level."

27. United Nations, "Draft Strategic Framework for International Assistance in Afghanistan"; Donini, *The Politics of Mercy.*

28. United Nations, Deputy Secretary-General, "Draft Generic Guidelines" and "Strategic Framework for Afghanistan."

29. United Nations, *An Inventory of Post-Conflict Peace-Building Activities,* p. 1.

30. See Marshall, "Emerging from Conflict."

31. Established in 1944, the IBRD was "to assist in the reconstruction and development of territories of members . . . including the restoration of economies destroyed or disrupted by war." In fact, for decades the IBRD and its concessional window, the International Development Association (IDA), focused their portfolios overwhelmingly on "normal" development activities. Blustein, "A Loan Amid the Ruins"; World Bank, *Post-Conflict Reconstruction,* pp. v, 6–10; World Bank, Articles of Agreement, I (i).

32. World Bank, *The World Bank's Experience with Post-conflict Reconstruction,* pp. 14–15.

33. These include a "watching brief"; a "transitional support strategy"; "early reconstruction activities"; "postconflict reconstruction" properly speaking; and

(eventually) "normal lending operations." See World Bank, *Post-Conflict Reconstruction*, pp. 40–48.

34. World Bank, *The World Bank's Experience with Post-conflict Reconstruction*, pp. 7–8.

35. IMF, "A Macroeconomic Framework"; IMF, *Annual Report* (1996), pp. 124–126; IMF, "Adaptations of IMF Policies and Procedures."

36. The country would be eligible for an Enhanced Structural Adjustment Facility, or ESAF.

37. Other postconflict states have used standard facilities. www.imf.org/external/np/exr/facts/confl.htm.

38. OECD/DAC, *Conflict, Peace, and Development Cooperation*, pp. 5–9, 17.

39. "Good coordination should not be confused as forcing activities into a single mold." OECD/DAC, *Conflict, Peace, and Development Cooperation*, pp. 29–35. This view can be contrasted with the UN conclusion that "coordination by consensus" is inferior to "coordination by management." United Nations, DHA, "Afghanistan: Coordination in a Fragmented State."

40. In the past several years OTI has launched initiatives to advance human security, civil society, and good governance in more than a dozen countries, including Angola, Haiti, Guatemala, Bosnia and Herzegovina, and Rwanda. Natsios, *US Foreign Policy;* USAID/OTI, "Operational Challenges," pp. 8, 14.

41. Some other bilateral donors, like Sweden, do not possess dedicated postconflict units or budget lines, but instead streamline reconstruction assistance through development agencies.

42. Ball with Halevy, *Making Peace Work,* p. 56.

43. Following complex emergencies, one encounters a third, humanitarian paradigm that calls for aid to be delivered impartially on a basis of universality and nondiscrimination—that is, without conditions.

44. De Soto and del Castillo, "Obstacles to Peacebuilding," pp. 70–72. Similar tensions between stabilization and peace building have plagued Mozambique. See Hanlon, *Peace Without Profit.*

45. Boyce, "Adjustment Towards Peace"; Boyce and Pastor, "Aid for Peace."

46. Carnegie Commission, *Preventing Deadly Conflict,* p. 146; United Nations, "Africa: Secretary-General's Report," p. 2.

47. World Bank Articles of Agreement, Art. IV, Sec. 10; and Article II, Sec. I, part (b).

48. Boyce, "External Assistance," pp. 2111–2113.

49. Graham, *Safety Nets.*

50. World Bank, *World Development Report 1997,* p. 161.

51. The OED reviewed the Bank's role in Bosnia and Herzegovina, El Salvador, Uganda, Cambodia, Eritrea, Haiti, Lebanon, Sri Lanka, and Rwanda. In some African countries, the authors note, insistence on structural adjustment "undermined the peace process by forcing too many budget cuts." Similarly, the Bank's pressure to downsize the Cambodian civil service "was not politically realistic from the outset," since it ran counter to compromises made to forge a governing coalition. Likewise, efforts to improve government tax collection in Uganda turned out to have "a chilling effect" on foreign investment. The OED recommends that Bank staff develop "Good Practices" that are "sensitive to predatory and exclusionary behavior." World Bank, *The World Bank's Experience,* vol. 1, pp. x, 24–26; World Bank, "Conflict Prevention and Post-Conflict Reconstruction," p. 5.

52. Stokke, *Aid and Political Conditionality*, pp. 21–24, 80; OECD/DAC, *Conflict, Peace, and Development Cooperation.*

53. This initiative focuses on Sri Lanka, Bosnia, Afghanistan, and Rwanda.

54. Hovi, *Games, Threats, and Treaties,* pp. 4–5.

55. Chapter 3 describes the Cambodian government's belated—and troubled— efforts to create its own machinery for aid coordination.

56. Bosnia and Herzegovina, where the Contact Group created an Office of the High Representative (OHR), is an exception in this regard.

57. Peace Implementation Network, *Command from the Saddle.*

58. United Nations, OCHA, "Relations Between Representatives of the Emergency Relief Coordinator and Special Representatives of the Secretary-General."

59. World Bank, *The World Bank's Experience,* vol. 1, p. 27.

60. When donors pressed the government in Sierra Leone to reduce subsidies to soldiers, for example, some 8,000 defected to the rebel opposition.

61. Africa's debt burden is especially onerous, with sovereign debt exceeding 80 percent of the continent's GDP. Mozambique's plight has been particularly compelling. See "Bending the Rules" and "Help for a Self-Helper."

62. IMF document cited in Chote, "Finally, Relief in Sight"; Muscat, "Conflict and Reconstruction," p. 39; World Bank, *The World Bank's Experience,* vol. 1, p. 9.

63. Oxfam, "Oxfam International Submission."

64. Cohen, "An Agreement on Debt Relief for Poor Lands"; "Debt Rhetoric Has to Face Reality Test."

65. Boyce, "Adjustment Towards Peace" and "External Assistance."

66. Carothers and Fuentes, "La Cooperación Internacional en Guatemala." Contrary to expectations, Guatemala garnered significant pledges of aid from the donor community. However, there has been significant political resistance to the implementation of even this modest provision. As a result, the country depends heavily on international assistance for much of its discretionary budget.

67. Paris, "Peacebuilding and the Limits of Liberal Internationalism," p. 58.

68. OECD/DAC, *Conflict, Peace, and Development Cooperation,* p. 36; UNDP/ERD, "Building Bridges Between Relief and Development."

69. The database is available at www.reliefweb.int/fts/index.html.

70. Hedges, "Leaders in Bosnia Are Said to Steal up to $1 Billion."

71. On typical transition needs in these three spheres, see Ball with Halevy, *Making Peace Work,* pp. 52–54.

72. Niels Dabelstein, Danida, personal communication, February 1999; Joint Evaluation, *The International Response.*

73. Alternatively, an OECD/DAC task force could be assembled for this purpose.

74. Garten, *The Big Ten.*

3

Cambodia

Sorpong Peou, with Kenji Yamada

THIS CHAPTER ANALYZES THE RELATIONSHIP BETWEEN PLEDGES and disbursements of assistance to war-torn Cambodia since 1992. It seeks to determine the nature of the gaps between pledge and delivery and to evaluate possible causes of these gaps.[1] This is a very important topic because Cambodia has been heavily aid dependent. During the 1980s, the Soviet Union alone was believed to have given the country aid worth $2 billion. Between 1991 and 1997, the international community spent more than $4 billion on Cambodia.

Until now, evidence on this matter has relied on a few unpublished reports on the massive infusion of foreign aid in Cambodia. None of these accounts provides a systematic analysis of gaps between pledges and disbursements.[2] We seek to answer two fundamental questions: Were donors as good as their word in fulfilling pledges of aid? If not, why was aid slow in arriving?

This chapter examines the domestic obstacles to the delivery and implementation of foreign aid, stressing Cambodia's limited absorptive capacity, the leadership's lack of aid coordination skills, and endemic factional conflict. The chapter also identifies important external constraints on aid disbursements, including the donors' primitive knowledge of Cambodian needs, competing donor interests and policies, misplaced optimism concerning early Cambodian recovery, the intrusion of values-driven expectations, and the lack of donor coordination.

The study is divided into three sections. In the first part, we describe Cambodia's "triple transition": the evolution from war to peace, the initial steps toward political liberalization, and the adoption of a neoliberal model of economic development. We outline the pledging mechanisms and processes established by the donor community and document the percentage of aid pledges converted into disbursements. We reveal certain patterns and classify pledge-disbursement gaps by year, donor, and type of aid.

This typology provides a useful starting point to address the relative role of domestic and donor factors in influencing timely aid delivery. In the second part, we examine the hypothesis that Cambodia's domestic constraints were serious obstacles to aid disbursements in the first few years of the triple transition. Finally, in the last part, we evaluate the hypothesis that a combination of donor shortcomings—including low levels of awareness about Cambodian needs, high expectations, national approaches to peace and democracy, and competing economic and politico-strategic interests—may also have determined the varying levels of aid disbursement.

We contend that although donors' overall performance in terms of disbursement rate was generally good, disbursements still lagged. To some degree, a pledge-disbursement gap is inevitable whenever donors attempt to disburse aid to a weak state like Cambodia. A weak state is defined in terms of its inability to absorb fully the amount that has been pledged, due in part to the lack of implementing capacities (human, financial, and administrative) and in part to factional politics that perpetuates political instability. As Cambodia improved its mechanisms for national economic planning and aid coordination, disbursement rates increased. However, persistent factional fighting tended to have the opposite effect, counterbalancing these managerial improvements and reducing aid delivery, particularly in 1992 and 1997. These conflicts eventually culminated in a violent coup in July 1997, causing aid to decline by 27.54 percent (from $518,082,000 in 1996 to $375,404,000 in 1997).

On the supply side of aid, donors had problems of their own that contributed to slow aid disbursement. They lacked an understanding of Cambodia's socioeconomic and political needs during the triple transition; their expectations for Cambodian recovery were often inflated by their own values; and they lacked coherent mechanisms to coordinate their efforts. Moreover, their competing economic and political interests were a crucial variable. Finally, much donor aid was channeled through nongovernmental organizations (NGOs) to avoid government corruption and to meet basic social needs, but this in turn created other problems that often hindered effective aid disbursements.

Cambodia's Triple Transition, Pledges of Aid, and Disbursements

In this section, we describe Cambodia's "triple transition," examine donors' pledges of aid and the pledging process, and seek to identify trends and patterns of aid delivery.

Cambodia's Triple Transition

From 1970 to 1975, Cambodia was engulfed in a civil war that led to the victory of a revolutionary movement, the Khmer Rouge. Under the leadership of Pol Pot, the Khmer Rouge conducted a reign of terror that brought death to more than a million Cambodians. The entire country was turned into a labor camp and a killing field. State institutions broke down as the new leadership sought to build a new, egalitarian society. When Vietnam invaded Cambodia on Christmas Eve 1978, the Pol Pot regime quickly crumbled. The Vietnamese armed forces ousted the Pol Pot leadership and installed a new regime. The People's Republic of Kampuchea (PRK) began its rule in the midst of intense warfare with regrouped Khmer Rouge forces.

Other armed Cambodian resistance groups, particularly the royalists loyal to Prince Norodom Sihanouk (a group known as Funcinpec) and the Khmer People's National Liberation Front (KPNLF), joined the Khmer Rouge to create the Coalition Government of Democratic Kampuchea (CGDK). The CGDK continued its armed resistance against the PRK (later changed to State of Cambodia or SOC) and the Vietnamese army throughout the 1980s.

During this period, the PRK enjoyed only limited international support. In a concerted effort to punish Vietnam's aggression against Cambodia, Western states and their Asian allies, especially China and members of the Association of Southeast Asian Nations (ASEAN), banded together to counterbalance the Soviet-supported states of communist Indochina. This former bloc supported the CGDK and sought to isolate the Vietnamese and Soviet-backed PRK.[3] Throughout the 1980s, Cambodia remained effectively isolated from the West.

Following the end of the Cold War, the permanent members of the UN Security Council hammered out their differences over Cambodia during eight months of negotiations. The resulting permanent-member framework was essentially a peace settlement among great powers, with no involvement from either the Cambodian factions or any other states.[4] Significantly, the permanent members urged the Cambodian factions and the involved foreign states to accept a UN intervention. On October 23, 1991, the factions signed the Paris Agreements. This peace accord envisioned three transitions: from war to peace, from authoritarianism to liberal democracy, and from a socialist command economy to a market-oriented system.

To begin the war-to-peace transition, the factions committed themselves in principle to a cease-fire and to the cantonment, disarmament, and demobilization of their troops. By Article 8 of the agreements, foreign forces would withdraw from the country under international verification. Article 9 mandated that "[all] forces shall immediately disengage and refrain from all hostilities and from any deployment, movement or action." In order "to stabilize the security situation and build confidence among the parties to the conflict," Article 10 required the immediate cessation of "all outside military assistance to all Cambodian parties."

As far as the political transition was concerned, the Paris Agreements committed the Cambodian signatories to compete for political power through the ballot box rather than through armed conflict. The United Nations Transitional Authority in Cambodia (UNTAC) would attempt to create a neutral political environment for free and fair elections.

The Paris Agreements embraced a neoliberal economic agenda, envisioning the transition from a centrally planned to a market-based economy. Reconstruction and development were deemed essential to lasting peace— and vice versa. The accords envisioned two consecutive steps to facilitate sustained economic recovery. During the first ("rehabilitation") phase, Cambodia and its donors would give particular attention to key areas of basic needs such as food, security, health, housing, training, education, the transport network, and the restoration of basic infrastructure and public utilities. The subsequent reconstruction phase would aim to promote local entrepreneurship and the private sector generally.[5]

The Paris Agreements made it clear that the donor community would not be held responsible for determining Cambodia's recovery needs, priorities, and plans. These responsibilities would rest with the Cambodian people. Article 11 of the agreements stated that the "implementation of a longer-term international development plan for reconstruction should await the formation of a government following the elections and the determination and adoption of its own policies and priorities."[6]

Moreover, foreign donors were instructed not to impose a development strategy on the country. Rather, they should provide assistance to "complement and supplement local resources," making this aid "available impartially with full regard for Cambodia's sovereignty, priorities, institutional means and absorptive capacity." To harmonize and monitor contributions to Cambodian recovery, the donor community would establish a consultative body, the International Committee on the Reconstruction of Cambodia (ICORC). The United Nations would be asked "to support ICORC in its work, notably in ensuring a smooth transition from the rehabilitation to reconstruction phases."[7] However, the agreements did not define the donors' role clearly, nor did they specify when foreign aid should be pledged or disbursed, or which needs would be targeted.

In principle, international assistance to Cambodia was not to be directed at supporting any particular political party or regime but rather at rehabilitating the country in preparation for a smooth transition toward a market-based economy and sustainable economic growth. The Paris Agreements stipulated that "economic aid should benefit all areas of Cambodia, especially the more disadvantaged, and reach all levels of society."[8]

Donors, Pledges of Aid, and the Pledging Process

In June 1992, the Japanese hosted the Ministerial Conference on Rehabilitation and Reconstruction of Cambodia. The resulting Tokyo Declaration established ICORC, composed of bilateral and multilateral donors. Japan and France, as cochairs of ICORC, would convene annual meetings of donors, with the participation of the Special Representative of the Secretary-General (SRSG) for Cambodia. The United Nations Development Programme (UNDP), in cooperation with UNTAC and other relevant international agencies, would provide ICORC with technical and administrative support. Representatives of NGOs active in Cambodia (and nominated by the NGO Cooperation Committee for Cambodia known as CCC) would also be welcome to present their views as observers at ICORC meetings. Cambodia itself would be represented by a national delegation representing the SNC (the Supreme National Council, made up of representatives of the four Cambodian signatories of the Paris Agreements and headed by Prince Norodom Sihanouk) and, after the election, by the new government.

ICORC was to serve as an international conference mechanism for coordinating, in consultation with a future government, the medium- and long-term assistance for Cambodian reconstruction. According to its founding document:

> 1. ICORC will be a long-term consultative body, which will provide a forum through which contributors can exchange views and information with the Cambodian authorities, with the objective of better coordinating international assistance for the reconstruction of Cambodia.
> 2. ICORC is expected to enable the Government of Cambodia . . . to put its view before the contributors and to facilitate its planning with advance notice of aid levels and aid priorities to be provided by the contributors. It is also expected to enable the contributors to consult with and advise the Cambodian authorities on development requirements, which would be helpful for the contributors in setting their own aid levels and priorities for the benefit of Cambodia.
> 3. An important role of ICORC will be to provide an occasion for the coordination of assistance to Cambodia to develop an institutional economic and social planning and aid management capacity necessary for the successful implementation of the reconstruction program.[9]

Three ICORC conferences were held: in September 1993, March 1994, and March 1995. At ICORC III, participants agreed to replace this framework with Consultative Group (CG) meetings led by the World Bank and the host government. This shift indicated the donor community's desire to move away from its "soft" position on Cambodia, dominant during the rehabilitation phase, toward greater emphasis on development assistance. This shift would require the Cambodian government to develop action plans and to submit progress reports to the donor community. By late 1998, two CG meetings had taken place (in 1996 and 1997). A third such meeting scheduled for July 1998 was canceled (for reasons to be explained below).

Membership of ICORC and the CG mechanism was open to all countries and international organizations interested in contributing to the long-term reconstruction of Cambodia. More than a dozen international agencies and financial institutions[10] and more than thirty states[11] chose to participate. (It should be noted that not all participants were donors.)

The donor community showed commendable generosity in pledging aid for Cambodian recovery. In May 1992, the UN secretary-general issued a *Consolidated Appeal for Cambodia's Immediate Needs and National Rehabilitation*, requesting a total of $595 million. The first wave of aid pledges arrived the following month at the Tokyo conference, where donors pledged $880 million, or almost $300 million more than the secretary-general had requested.

Between 1992 and 1997, total aid pledges for Cambodia climbed to $3,264 million. At the last CG meeting, in 1997, donors pledged $475 million. After the cancellation of the third CG meeting, few donor missions visited the country, and their main goal was fact-finding, rather than reviewing new projects. Only France indicated that it might proceed with new projects.[12]

Preoccupied with giving Cambodia a new lease on life, most donors initially attached few conditions to their aid pledges. According to Prime Minister Norodom Ranariddh, there "were no conditions to the aid, no pressure. Donors asked for clarification and we showed our determination [to enact the reforms]."[13] This attitude changed when ICORC yielded to the Consultative Group mechanism in 1996. In the words of one top Council for the Development of Cambodia (CDC) adviser, Cambodia's "honeymoon ended." Henceforth, the donor community insisted that the government adopt stricter accountability and reporting standards and develop long-term development plans that went beyond emergency and humanitarian activities. Still, donors generally believed that it would be ineffective to attach conditions to their aid.[14] The bulk of aid continued to be channeled through donor agencies and NGOs, rather than flowing directly to the government.[15]

Disbursements: Trends and Patterns in Aid Delivery

The delivery of international pledges from 1992 to 1997 did not go according to plan. This section describes trends and patterns in aid delivery during the period.

From a baseline of $250 million in 1992, disbursements surged to more than $513 million in 1995, leveled off to $518 million in 1996, and declined noticeably to $375 million in 1997. By the end of 1997, the donor community had disbursed some $2.33 billion to Cambodia out of total pledges worth $3.26 billion.[16] Consequently, the overall pledge-disbursement gap was quite significant—close to $1 billion ($934 million).

For the 1992–1997 period, delivery of pledges averaged 71 percent. Dividing the aid effort into two subperiods, 1992–1995 and 1996–1997, we find a fairly low disbursement ratio of 58.9 percent in the first period and a more successful ratio of 91 percent in the second. Looking more closely at the latter period, we discover that deliveries reached 103 percent of pledges in 1996 but that these declined to 78 percent the following year. Thus, donors had more difficulty disbursing aid in the first four years— and more difficulty disbursing aid in 1997 than in 1996.

Although it is difficult to measure the gap *by donor* from year to year, the average rate of pledge disbursement in 1992–1995 is 74 percent for bilateral donors, but only 39 percent for multilateral donors.[17] From 1992 to 1996, bilateral sources accounted for 65.88 percent ($1.29 billion) of total disbursements ($1.961 billion), compared to 29.93 percent ($578.66 million) for multilateral sources and 4.1 percent ($81.24 million) for NGO "core resources."

Individual bilateral donors also varied considerably in their delivery performance. Table 3.1, covering the period 1992–1995, shows that Japan led all bilateral donors, disbursing 123.2 percent ($395,854,000) of its total pledge ($321,400,000) during 1992–1995. Other bilateral donors with strong disbursement-to-pledge ratios include Russia (117.3 percent), the Netherlands (101.6 percent), Sweden (81.3 percent), and Australia (70.25 percent). The United States (63.2 percent), the United Kingdom (55.4 percent), and Germany (54.1 percent) each delivered on more than half of their pledges. Bilateral donors with larger gaps included France (42.4 percent), Denmark (31.0 percent), Thailand (12.3 percent), Belgium (6.5 percent), and Norway (2.0 percent).

Multilateral donors showed similar variation in the percentage of disbursement during the 1992–1995 period. The European Union (EU) led, disbursing 76.0 percent ($92,979,000) of total pledges ($122,346,000). The UN agencies disbursed 54.3 percent ($92,088,000 of $169,435,000 pledged). Donors disbursing less than 50 percent included the International Monetary Fund (IMF) (44 percent), the World Bank (26.4 percent), and the Asian Development Bank (ADB) (24 percent).

The year 1997 presented a grimmer picture, as total disbursements declined dramatically. Aid from Japan and France fell off badly. A few donors, including the United States, Australia, and Germany, actually increased their aid marginally (see Table 3.2, pp. 76–77). The World Bank, ADB, UN agencies, and EU all cut their aid significantly.

Table 3.1   Summary of Pledges and Disbursements, 1992–1995

Donors	Pledges (U.S.$ thousands)	Disbursements (U.S.$ thousands)	Disbursement Rate (%)
Multilateral organizations			
ADB	280,100	67,235	24.00
World Bank	285,000	75,249	26.40
European Union	122,346	92,979	75.99
IMF	120,000	52,750	43.95
UN agencies	169,435	92,088	54.35
Total for multilaterals	976,881	380,301	38.93
Bilateral Agencies			
Australia	81,259	57,087	70.25
Belgium	8,329	541	6.50
Canada	26,557	18,849	70.97
Denmark	61,000	18,971	31
France	208,570	88,478	42.42
Germany	57,024	30,823	54.05
Ireland	13,000	0	0
Japan	321,400	395,854	123.16
Netherlands	42,000	42,668	101.63
Norway	10,500	212	2.02
Russian Federation	10,400	12,200	117.30
Thailand	1,200	147	12.25
Sweden	67,500	54,851	81.26
United Kingdom	48,600	26,913	55.37
United States	244,800	154,685	63.18
Other bilateral donors	121,387	64,390	53.04
Total for bilaterals	1,311,826	966,669	73.69
Totals	2,288,707	1,342,664	58.66

Source: CDC/CRDB, Development Cooperation Report (1994/95).
Notes: ADB: Asian Development Bank.
IMF: International Monetary Fund.

In short, multilateral sources decreased from $197,976,000 in 1996 to $123,069,000 in 1997, while bilateral sources went from $284,281,000 to $202,459,000. The 27.5 percent reduction in total aid—a loss to Cambodia of $142,678,000—made 1997 a tragic year for the country.

Levels of aid disbursement also varied across sectors. As Tables 3.3–3.9 (pp. 78–82) show, donors have pledged several types of aid to Cambodia: free-standing technical cooperation (FSTC); investment-related technical cooperation (ITC); investment project assistance; budgetary and balance of payments support; food aid; and emergency assistance.[18] During the period 1992–1997, FSTC accounted for 32.49 percent of all aid to Cambodia, followed by investment project assistance (29.40 percent), emergency relief (12.46 percent), and budgetary and balance of payments support (16.01 percent). Assistance for food aid and emergency relief declined by 36 percent annually during 1992–1996, while FSTC increased by 51 percent and ITC by 66 percent annually.

Table 3.6 shows how aid allocations in different sectors changed from year to year. Over time, aid for rehabilitation purposes (especially emergency relief) declined, whereas aid for reconstruction efforts rose. Humanitarian aid and emergency relief declined abruptly from $141 million in 1992 to $53 million in 1993, ultimately falling to $12 million in 1996. Aid for economic reconstruction rose dramatically. As for disbursements by type (Table 3.3), in the case of free-standing technical cooperation, disbursements increased from $39 million (1992) to about $187 million (1996), before declining slightly to $176 million (1997). Aid for investment-related technical cooperation also increased from $7 million (1993) to $50 million (1996). Likewise, investment project assistance surged from $32 million (1992) to $174 million (1995)—then declined to $130 million (1997). Clearly, donor emphasis shifted over time from providing relief to permitting reconstruction and building Cambodia's capacity to formulate development policies and launch investment projects.

Budgetary and balance of payments support rose dramatically in 1992, thereafter averaging some $70 million annually through 1996. This support plummeted in 1997, however, as grants fell almost 97 percent and loans declined to zero. This total reduction (of $63,846,000) accounted for half of all aid losses in that year. Foreign assistance for other purposes fell too, though not so dramatically. For instance, grants for ITC dropped almost 50 percent, and emergency/relief assistance also declined from $54.78 million to just under $40 million.

Overall, we can make the following general observations. First, aid disbursements rose smartly in 1995, went up slightly in 1996 (0.93 percent), but dropped noticeably in 1997 (by 27.54 percent). Second, the gap between pledges and disbursements was much narrower in 1996–1997 than during the period 1992–1995, but the total amount of aid disbursed in 1997 was less than during 1995 and 1996. The most dramatic decline in aid disbursements came in 1997, and it fell most heavily in the area of budgetary and balance of payments support. Third, the bilateral donors disbursed a far higher proportion of their pledges than did multilateral donors. Fourth, international financial institutions (IFIs) delivered a far lower percentage of their pledged aid than did other international organizations like the UN agencies or the EU. Fifth, there was no consistent pattern between the size of pledges by bilateral donors and the resulting gaps in delivery. Japan, for instance, pledged the largest amount of aid but delivered more than it had pledged (123 percent). In contrast, the United States made the second largest pledge but delivered on only 63 percent of its promise. Nor is there any consistent correlation between small pledges and small gaps. Norway, for instance, pledged only $10,500,000, but it delivered only 0.2 percent of this sum. Finally, aid for emergency relief purposes declined over the 1992–1997 period, while aid aimed at promoting economic development increased noticeably.

Table 3.2 Summary of External Assistance Disbursements by Donor, 1992–1997 (U.S.$ thousands)

Major Donors	1992	1993	1994	1995	1996	1997	Total 1992–1997
Multilateral donors							
UN Agencies	13,276	30,977	26,154	30,968	50,315	39,771	191,461
World Bank	0	68	40,009	29,601	40,401	28,115	138,194
IMF	0	8,800	21,238	42,290	400	0	72,728
Asian Development Bank	0	12,297	12,388	37,860	49,238	18,390	130,173
European Union/EEC	32,118	19,068	9,163	28,886	57,622	36,793	183,650
Subtotal for multilateral agencies	45,394	71,210	108,952	164,105	197,976	123,069	710,706
Bilateral donors							
Australia	10,511	15,917	13,792	27,508	20,172	27,296	115,196
Austria	809	10	0	24	0	0	843
Belgium	1,941	2,184	971	2,695	1,986	1,672	11,449
Brunei Darussalam	50	0	0	0	0	0	50
Canada	5,821	6,584	4,512	4,261	3,179	4,179	28,536
China	912	871	7,089	3,129	10,850	9,496	32,347
Denmark	3,997	5,880	5,844	5,129	20,813	5,076	46,739
Finland	1,696	679	575	0	0	0	2,950
France	5,797	32,260	35,807	62,237	42,887	26,492	205,480
Germany	2,637	2,483	3,349	13,896	9,607	10,082	42,054
Hungary	0	100	0	0	0	0	100
India	1,103	570	113	565	0	0	2,351
Indonesia	0	0	78	550	0	0	628
Ireland	108	0	0	1,962	0	37	2,107
Italy	5,281	1,483	560	919	0	0	8,244
Japan	66,897	102,025	95,606	117,902	111,000	59,843	553,273
Republic of Korea	0	30	0	0	252	0	282
Luxembourg	157	18	0	0	0	0	175
Malaysia	197	204	376	0	0	0	777
Netherlands	17,159	11,147	9,980	3,447	11,542	3,257	56,532

(continues)

Table 3.2 continued

Major Donors	1992	1993	1994	1995	1996	1997	Total 1992–1997
New Zealand	0	0	243	254	209	43	749
Norway	7,876	3,105	806	924	1,441	2,149	16,301
Russian Federation	5,100	3,700	2,100	1,040	280	262	12,482
Singapore	0	0	150	10	0	0	160
Sweden	13,368	14,994	10,098	25,314	16,079	17,413	97,266
Switzerland	2,122	2,001	291	353	0	67	4,834
Thailand	7,598	229	4	147	1,089	2,224	11,291
United Kingdom	7,032	5,075	7,099	10,700	4,134	2,250	36,290
United States	35,551	33,809	31,701	45,149	28,761	30,509	205,480
Subtotal for bilaterals	203,720	245,359	231,144	328,115	284,281	202,459	1,495,078
NGOs (core resources only)	1,069	5,322	17,949	21,100	35,800	49,876	131,116
Total disbursements	250,183	321,891	358,045	513,320	518,082	375,404	2,336,925

Source: CDC/CRDB, *Development Cooperation Report (1997/98).*

Table 3.3 Summary of External Disbursements by Type, 1992–1997 (U.S.$ thousands)

Type of Assistance	1992	1993	1994	1995	1996	1997	Total (1992–1997)	Allocation (%)
Free-standing technical cooperation	39,434	77,995	106,197	172,762	186,973	176,006	759,369	32.49
Investment-related technical cooperation	8,855	7,305	16,018	34,550	50,652	25,555	142,935	6.12
Investment project assistance	32,758	67,471	122,510	174,447	159,184	130,614	686,984	29.40
Budgetary aid/balance of payments support	1,410	73,486	69,170	77,887	66,493	2,647	291,093	12.46
Food aid	39,227	26,034	12,394	4,001	0	632	82,288	3.52
Emergency and relief assistance	128,499	69,600	31,756	49,673	54,780	39,948	374,256	16.01
Total disbursements	250,183	321,891	358,045	513,320	518,082	375,404	2,336,925	

Source: CDC/CRDB, *Development Cooperation Report* (1997/98).

Table 3.4 Percentage Increases in External Assistance Disbursements by Type, 1992–1997

Type of assistance	1992 (U.S.$ thousands)	Change 1992–1993 (%)	1993 (U.S.$ thousands)	Change 1993–1994 (%)	1995 (U.S.$ thousands)	Change 1995–1996 (%)	1996 (U.S.$ thousands)	Change 1996–1997 (%)	1997 (U.S.$ thousands)	Average Change 1992–1997 (%)
Free-standing technical cooperation	39,434	97.79	77,995	36.16	172,762	8.27	186,973	–8.35	176,008	39.80
Investment-related technical cooperation	8,855	–17.50	7,305	119.27	34,550	46.60	50,652	–49.55	25,555	42.90
Investment project assistance	32,758	105.97	67,471	81.57	174,447	–8.75	159,184	–18.08	130,614	40.65
Budgetary aid/balance of payments support	1,410	5,111.77	73,486	–5.875	77,887	–14.63	66,493	–96.02	2,647	1,001
Food aid	39,227	–33.63	26,034	–52.39	4,001	–100	0		632	–50.75
Emergency and relief assistance	128,499	–45.84	69,600	–54.37	49,673	10.28	54,780	–27.08	39,948	–12.12
Totals	250,183	28.66	321,891	11.23	513,320	0.94	518,082	–27.54	375,404	11.32

Source: CDC/CRDB, *Development Cooperation Report* (1997/98).

Table 3.5 Percentage Increases/Decreases in External Disbursements by Type and Terms, 1994–1997

Type of Assistance	Terms	1994 (U.S.$ thousands)	Change 1994–1995 (%)	1995 (U.S.$ thousands)	Change 1995–1996 (%)	1996 (U.S.$ thousands)	Change 1996–1997 (%)	1997
Free-standing technical cooperation	Grants	105,859	61.27	170,717	8.16	184,651	-6.85	171,995
	Loans	338	504.73	2,044	13.60	2,322	72.83	4,013
Invetment–related technical cooperation	Grants	15,402	121.13	34,058	46.14	49,773	-49.55	25,555
	Loans	616	-20.13	492	78.66	879	0	0
Investment project assistance	Grants	110,610	16.55	128,920	-15.96	108,339	-9.60	97,936
	Loans	11,900	282.59	45,528	11.68	50,845	-35.73	32,678
Budgetary aid/balance of payments support	Grants	10,732	94.78	20,904	98.77	41,550	-93.63	2,647
	Loans	58,438	-2.49	56,983	-56.23	24,943	0	0
Food aid	Grants	12,394	-67.72	4,001	-100	0		632
Emergency and relief assistance	Grants	31,756	56.42	49,673	10.28	54,780	-27.08	39,948
Subtotals	Grants	286,753	42.38	408,273	7.55	439,093	-22.86	338,713
Loans		71,292	47.35	105,047	-24.81	78,989	-53.55	36,691
Totals		358,045	43.37	513,320	0.93	518,082	-27.54	375,404

Source: CDC/CRDB, Development Cooperation Report (1997/98).

Table 3.6 Summary of External Assistance Disbursements Provided to each Sector, 1992–1997 (U.S.$ thousands)

Sectors	1992	1993	1994	1995	1996	1997	1992–1997	Distribution (%)
Economic management	574	53,866	73,186	83,196	73,182	10,947	294,951	12.62
Development administration	6,051	14,644	28,303	64,236	88,185	78,732	280,151	11.99
Natural resources	315	1,236	1,541	1,072	3,349	5,844	13,357	0.57
Education/human resource development	15,763	28,520	28,884	42,336	34,738	48,269	198,510	8.49
Agriculture, forestry, fisheries	16,875	27,528	24,269	36,650	64,559	18,012	187,893	8.04
Area /rural development	35,103	43,548	28,542	70,191	78,097	67,918	323,399	13.84
Industry	132	10	7	0	600	0	749	0.03
Energy	1,057	7,498	23,702	38,972	13,772	17,335	102,336	4.38
International trade	0	0		58	168	50	276	0.01
Domestic trade	300	0	297	273	2,016	7,448	10,334	0.44
Transport	8,682	45,126	57,743	78,299	60,249	37,236	287,335	12.30
Communications	860	1,350	2,086	3,936	22,344	16,761	47,337	2.03
Social development	5,571	15,802	27,095	41,147	20,828	18,833	129,276	5.53
Health	15,483	28,867	20,788	24,877	43,696	32,027	165,738	7.09
Disaster preparedness	2,359	220	0	0	0	164	2,743	0.12
Humanitarian aid and relief	141,058	53,676	41,602	28,077	12,299	15,829	292,541	12.52
Totals	250,183	321,891	358,045	513,320	518,082	375,404	2,339,925	

Source: CDC/CRDB, Development Cooperation Report (1997/98).

Table 3.7   Donors' Disbursement Rate as a Percentage of Commitments

ADB	76.3
IBRD	97.4
EU	89.5
FAO	64.9
UNDP	91.8
Average of multilateral donors	87.2
Australia	80.9
China	100
Denmark	100
France	84.7
Germany	40.3
Japan	74.4
Korea	100
Netherlands	99.8
Sweden	90.8
United Kingdom	62.3
Average of bilateral donors	75.6
Average of multi/bilateral donors	80.2

Source: CDC/CRDB, Development Cooperation Report (1996/97).
Notes: ADB: Asian Development Bank.
IBRD: International Bank for Reconstruction and Development.
EU: European Union.
FAO: Food and Agriculture Organization.
UNDP: United Nations Development Programme.

Domestic Constraints on Aid Delivery

During 1992–1995, donors delivered only 58.9 percent of the aid they had pledged. This section identifies three important domestic constraints on aid delivery: Cambodia's extremely low absorptive capacity; the government's weak leadership in aid coordination; and the persistent political instability generated by factional conflict. Indeed, the record shows that when these domestic impediments declined, the gap between pledges and disbursements narrowed.

Cambodia's Limited Absorptive Capacity

Although there is no way to correlate aid gaps definitively with Cambodia's limited absorptive capacity, donors certainly considered the country's weak infrastructure, human resources, and administrative and financial capacities to be daunting obstacles to postwar recovery efforts. In report after report, donors expressed misgivings about giving Cambodia too much aid, too fast.

An interagency humanitarian mission that visited the country during the period October 31–November 13, 1991, took note of the "considerable concern expressed from a number of quarters in Phnom Penh that the

Table 3.8 Disbursement Rate by Sector (percentages)

Development administration	79.2
Agriculture, forestry, fisheries	72.1
Area/rural development	59.1
Economic management	98.3
Health	68.6
Human resource development	76.9
Social development	83.8
Transport	81.4

Source: CDC/CRDB, Development Cooperation Report (1996/97).

Table 3.9 Disbursement Rate by Type (percentages)

Free-standing technical cooperation	74.8
Investment-related technical cooperation	81.8
Investment project assistance	76.3

Source: CDC/CRDB, Development Cooperation Report (1996/97).

current capacity within the country, both national and international, to receive, deliver and monitor increased assistance effectively, was overloaded."[19] Similarly, in their joint report of August 1993, the ADB, IMF, UNDP, UNTAC, and World Bank warned publicly that "assistance should be provided in a manner which realistically takes into account absorptive capacity" and that donors should "seek to develop that capacity."[20]

Donors registered their deep worries about Cambodia's limited absorptive capacity repeatedly during the transitional period, particularly at ICORC meetings. At ICORC II, the Finnish representative stated that "capacity building in Cambodia is of paramount importance for improving aid absorption capability. Too much aid in an uncoordinated manner might suffocate or slow down natural development."[21] Callisto Madavo, the representative of the World Bank, pressed the Cambodian leadership to step up its capacity-building efforts. A confidential report by UNTAC, circulated after the 1993 elections, noted that the country's poor communications and lack of an operational banking system complicated simple logistical tasks.[22]

As UNTAC informed donors before a February 1993 meeting, Cambodia's infrastructure had "fallen into a serious state of disrepair."[23] The infrastructure was indeed appalling. Ports were unable to off-load goods, and the country's meager road system (including 3,000 km of national, 3,100 km of provincial/secondary, and 28,000 km of local/tertiary roads) had received little or no maintenance during the 1970s and 1980s. As for utilities, donors reported that "most of the telecommunications network has been destroyed or the equipment is so obsolete that spare parts cannot be obtained. Cambodia's electric power system is one of the least developed in the world, and rural areas have no service at all."[24]

In addition, donors were appropriately concerned about the lack of *suitably qualified personnel* in Cambodia who could plan and implement a program of national reconstruction. Two deadly wars and the horror of genocide had decimated the country's human capital. The Khmer Rouge reign of terror, which cost more than a million lives, had fallen disproportionately on the educated and professional segments of the population. As a result, Cambodia faced chronic shortages of skilled persons. In early 1990, the country had only 3,000 individuals with a postsecondary education. Only 360 individuals had some degree of managerial skill. One long-time observer of Indochina predicted that "[this] dramatic shortage of skilled manpower means that Cambodia can absorb very little economic aid—perhaps not more than $200 million a year."[25]

It may be helpful to recall that foreign aid throughout the 1980s was apparently well absorbed. The disbursements in this period included $126.2 million in 1983, $109 million in 1984, $122 million in 1985, $188.2 million in 1986, $196.5 million in 1987, $210 million in 1988, and $24.8 million in 1989.[26] These figures should be treated with care, however. The bulk of this aid came from the socialist bloc, whose objectives were politically rather than economically motivated. Because Cambodia was at war, most socialist assistance was directed at influencing the armed struggle and could easily be absorbed.

Complicating recovery efforts, the Cambodian government made no serious effort to anticipate its future skill requirements.[27] This may have been understandable, given decades of warfare. As late as the 1996 CG meeting, a Cambodian leader admitted that "our ministries have limited technical capability and qualified human resources ideally necessary to effectively plan, prioritize, and implement programs and assistance activities and delivery of services."[28] The World Bank concluded that this shortage of skilled personnel "caused rehabilitation efforts to proceed more slowly than expected" and "slowed the disbursement in the country of funds provided by donors."[29] (As shall be discussed later, these administrative inefficiencies were also perpetuated by factional politics.)

Cambodia lacked not only human resources but also *administrative capacity*. The state administration was poorly staffed, technically ill equipped, and loosely regulated. Despite its large size—between 200,000 and 215,000 people in 1990—the civil service remained underinstitutionalized. No public service commission existed to conduct entrance examinations, to determine promotions, or to carry out disciplinary measures. Appointments were based purely on political considerations rather than on the candidate's level of education or other appropriate qualifications. As a confidential UN report noted, "There exists no single compilation of rules and regulations on personnel management for the civil service, including for appointment and promotion, transfer, disciplinary measures and appeals."[30] In their August 1993 report, the ADB, IMF, UNDP, UNTAC, and World Bank complained that "the administration structures currently in place cannot effectively enable the future government to deal with the growing needs of the population and of a market-oriented economy."[31]

The Cambodian government failed to convince donors that it had met their requirements regarding administrative reform. At a meeting on January 16, 1997, UNDP resident representative (and UN system resident coordinator) Paul Matthews urged the government to develop a "clear vision of and commitment to a new, appropriate administration."[32] Cambodia must conduct a thorough reappraisal of its civil service, including guidelines for selecting and paying public servants. Donors remained unconvinced that the Executive Committee (or COMEX) was the appropriate instrument to lead the administrative reform program, given the full-time attention that this contentious issue would require. The government had presented no more than a simple list of projects lacking any serious rationale or vision. During the second CG meeting, July 1-2, 1997, donors again raised the lack of real progress in administrative reform. One UNDP official described this as "Cambodia's greatest failure."[33]

Cambodia's severe lack of human and administrative capacity facilitated *rampant corruption*, which reached levels that appalled donors. Moreover, government officials gave the strong impression that they had no capacity to control this problem.[34] In certain cases, corruption hindered the flow of international aid. At the second CG meeting, the IMF representative complained that continual governance problems threatened the country's economic future. Soon afterward, the IMF postponed its midterm review of Cambodia's second annual Enhanced Structural Adjustment Facility (ESAF), originally scheduled for completion by December 1996. This step delayed the anticipated delivery of approximately $20 million. Subsequently, the IMF responded to Cambodia's failure to prevent illegal timber exports or to improve fiscal administration by suspending balance of payments support for 1997. These losses cost Cambodia another $60 million. It is reasonable to assume that the suspension of IMF aid negatively influenced disbursements for other projects. Cambodian Finance Minister Keat Chhon certainly feared this, warning that "the collapse of the ESAF program could prevent the [government] from mobilizing the $500 million pledged during the 2nd CG meeting."[35]

Another domestic cause of slow aid delivery was Cambodia's *lack of financial resources*. The country emerged from decades of war with considerable arrears to the IMF. In 1992, it owed the Fund $57.9 million, compared to its resources of $11.3 million.[36] Since Cambodia's reserve tranche of up to $8.8 million could be made available only after the country repaid its overdue obligations, Cambodia needed $37.8 million to clear its arrears. No IMF or World Bank financial assistance could be pledged or dis-

bursed—nor any loan programs considered—until these arrears were settled. This dilemma was not resolved until October 1993 (one month after
the coalition government was established), when bilateral donors—led by
Japan and France—gave Cambodia $53 million to clear its arrears to the
IMF. This allowed the country to borrow $9 million under the Fund's Sys-
temic Transformation Facility (STF).

Donors, who were covering almost half of the government's expenditures,[37] pressed Phnom Penh to improve its financial situation. They
insisted that Cambodia reduce spending on defense and security—which
accounted for 60 percent of total recurrent expenditure (salaries and running costs)—and increase its tax revenue to sustain individual aid projects.

The donors also expressed serious concern about the country's persistent inability to meet 10–20 percent of total project costs through counterpart funding from its own resources. (That is, donors were to fund between
80 and 90 percent of the cost of a project; Cambodia was to cover the rest.)
In April 1996, the government approved two documents: the *First Socioeconomic Development Plan, 1996–2000* (SEDP) and the *Public Investment Program* (PIP) for the three-year period 1996–1998. The SEDP was
designed to reduce and ultimately eradicate Cambodian poverty; the PIP
was an investment management tool designed to maintain discipline over
the level and allocation of resources for the different sectors of the economy. As envisioned, it was to be funded by $1.7 billion in official devel-
opment assistance (ODA). Donors and foreign investors would provide
equipment, construct buildings, and train Cambodian staff, but the Cambodian government would be required to provide essential services supporting such donor activities. In other words, Cambodia itself would provide counterpart funds to support donor activities and would prepare to
assume the costs of services and to run the established facilities.

By 1996, however, Cambodia's commitment of counterpart funds to
the PIP remained insignificant: only 3.5 percent of $1.5 billion. The gov-
ernment continued to have difficulty paying recurrent costs. According to
one top CDC official, Cambodia could afford neither the 20 percent counterpart fund required by the ADB nor the 15 percent counterpart fund
required by the World Bank: this failure "is the reason why these two
donors experienced the largest pledging gap."[38] The ADB complained that
"the PIP does not accurately capture the domestic counterpart fund
requirements for externally-assisted projects." The World Bank, similarly,
demanded that Cambodia include counterpart financial obligations in its
national budget.[39]

Thus the lack of Cambodian counterpart funds contributed to the IFI's
low disbursement rate. These multilateral donors provided loans through
government institutions, whereas bilateral donors tended to provide
grants—and often to disburse these through NGOs. Thus, donors whose

aid was in the form of loans tended to have more problems with Cambodia's limited absorptive capacity. Moreover, multilateral donors were generally less flexible than bilateral ones, which were more willing to provide counterpart funds for their own projects in Cambodia.

The precise extent to which Cambodia's limited absorptive capacity impeded the flow of aid may be never known, but the country's human, financial, and administrative weaknesses clearly created difficulties for donors. One example is the EU's Rehabilitation and Support Program for the Agricultural Sector of Cambodia (PRASAC). Initially scheduled to run from January 1995 to June 1997, this $44 million project suffered from unrealistic planning, an insufficient time frame, and inadequate personnel and equipment. Although the EU hoped that the project's "rapid implementation" would have "rapid impact," the project's "design had little detailed analysis of the capacities, constraints, and prospects of provincial and local government and society in Cambodia." The strategy of on-the-job training of government staff, based on the principle of "learning by doing," proved inadequate to the challenge.[40]

Cambodia's limited absorptive capacity not only slowed the disbursement of aid; it also reduced the effectiveness of aid that was delivered. Donors apparently realized that the rehabilitation process was bound to be slow because the country's conditions were unfavorable to quick economic development. One can also argue that relief efforts primarily concerned with meeting basic human needs (noted earlier) contributed to the slow disbursements of aid. During the first few years of any economic transition, when rehabilitation efforts begin, there is bound to be a wide gap between aid pledged and delivered.

In-Country Aid Coordination and Problems of Corruption

Cambodia's low absorptive capacity was but one domestic obstacle to postwar rehabilitation and reconstruction efforts. The government's failure to coordinate ODA proved to be a second impediment to the timely delivery of international assistance. Conversely, the rise in aid disbursement (from $250 million in 1992 to $513 million in 1995) appeared to coincide, at least in part, with gradual if limited improvements in Cambodia's coordinating role.

Having been isolated from the international community throughout the 1975–1991 period, Cambodia initially lacked any familiarity with the pledging conference framework and its associated aid coordination mechanisms. During the transitional period, when UNTAC played the role of Cambodia's legitimate authority, its Rehabilitation Component was given the tasks of designing a plan for Cambodia's rehabilitation and reconstruction and for setting priorities to meet the country's immediate needs.

Moreover, the Rehabilitation Component was to mobilize funds and then coordinate rehabilitation activities during the transitional period. After UNTAC departed in September 1993, Cambodia seemed to have no clear idea of what needed to be done.[41]

Certainly, the establishment of a coalition government after the elections in May 1993 made it less difficult for donors to begin disbursing their aid. But it would be misleading to suggest that—with a legitimate government now in place—obstacles to aid disbursements no longer existed. Indeed, the newly elected government possessed little experience in aid coordination. During the transitional period, the SNC depended on UNTAC and did not set priorities for economic development, nor did it have sophisticated plans of action. Instead, it rushed to approve a large number of aid projects. In general, the council was in no position to do anything beyond getting the Cambodian factions to agree on election-related matters. At the March 30–31, 1992, preparatory meeting in Tokyo of the Ministerial Conference on Rehabilitation and Reconstruction of Cambodia, the SNC delegation presented a short statement, which briefly identified four areas of need: rural development, infrastructure, forestation and environmental protection, and reintegration of demobilized soldiers. However, the SNC delegation presented no action plans to address these issues at all.[42]

After UNTAC departed, Cambodia desperately needed a formal mechanism to address the day-to-day planning of international assistance, screening of projects, and coordination of aid. Ideally, such a mechanism would permit close collaboration among the government, bilateral donors, international organizations, and NGOs. In particular, it would help to identify priorities for international assistance. Unfortunately, not until December 1993 did the newly elected government begin to prepare a comprehensive program for Cambodian recovery.

In February 1994, the Cambodian government formulated the National Program to Rehabilitate and Develop Cambodia (NPRDC). Based on the political program of the coalition government, the NPRDC was subsequently submitted to ICORC II (held in Tokyo on March 10–11, 1994) for endorsement and was finally ratified by the National Assembly in May 1994.[43] As Phnom Penh took steps to establish coordination mechanisms, actual deliveries of foreign assistance increased modestly, from $321 million (in 1993) to $358 million (in 1994). Donors may have been reassured by the establishment in 1994 of the Council for the Development of Cambodia and the Cambodian Rehabilitation and Development Board (CDC/CRDB) to coordinate joint endeavors with the donor community.[44]

Still, the small magnitude of this aid increase during 1993–1994—some 11.23 percent—suggests that donors still lacked confidence in Cambodia's future economic performance. At the ICORC II meetings in March

1994, they expressed doubt about CDC/CRDB's ability to monitor and coordinate foreign aid effectively. The Cambodian minister of the economy acknowledged the donors' concerns, conceding that his country still needed to delineate an effective division of labor and operational responsibilities between the CDC/CRDB and individual ministries. Although a local area network (LAN) system was set up for the PIP within the Ministry of Planning, there remained no comprehensive and accurate database to monitor flows of aid for the PIP. Donors encouraged Cambodian line ministries to pursue a program approach to investment packages rather than pursuing individual projects that might not be consistent with overall sector policies.

Donor confidence seemed to increase in late 1994 and 1995, as aid disbursements jumped from $358 million to $513 million. Several factors explain increased donor optimism. First, the government had made an effort to improve aid coordination. Second, the Cambodian leadership made progress in formulating concrete plans for development. In particular, on February 11, 1995, the government released a comprehensive document, *Implementing the National Program to Rehabilitate and Develop Cambodia.* Third, in mid-1995 the government established the In-Country Aid Coordination System (IACS), intended to promote dialogue among government and donors and to monitor the progress of the assistance effort. The IACS would allow development partners to identify and to resolve operational constraints encountered in program implementation. "Most importantly," according to UNDP, "it would facilitate effective conversion of pledges made at external forums into detailed and coordinated commitments, as well as joint monitoring of programs being implemented."[45] Fourth, and finally, in late 1995 the Cambodian government finalized the development plan for 1996–2000, designed to build upon the objectives of the NPRDC.

Despite these Cambodian measures to bolster donor confidence during 1995–1996, donor perceptions of Cambodia's aid coordination system did not improve significantly. The CDC/CRDB's early attempt to set up an operational organization proved unsuccessful. Staff recruitment proceeded at a very slow pace, largely because of the shortage of qualified personnel. The Australian representative to the July 1996 CG meeting expressed concern that the CDC lacked "a clear policy on aid coordination." Moreover, "[If] the CDC is to perform an effective job, its role must be clear and line ministries must work within a coordinated framework."[46] "There is total anarchy in CDC," one Cambodian official conceded.[47]

Despite considerable efforts, a UNDP report of 1996 noted that "projects and programs initiated so far have been embarked on in an ad hoc manner." Reconstruction efforts to date had been marred by "lack of cohesion among different activities, lack of an overview of human resource needs and lack of a clear policy framework." The Cambodian government had failed to clarify its priorities or to coordinate "different activities to achieve common objectives."[48] In response to the CRDB's inability to coordinate recovery, donors often initiated operational practices—condoned by government departments—seen as expedient in the short run but undesirable in the long term. Examples of these practices were the establishment of Program Implementation Units (PIUs) and Project Management Units (PMUs). Independent of any national or even similar donor structure, these were designed to "get the job done" by bypassing the government.

Keat Chhon, senior minister in charge of rehabilitation and development (and minister of economy and finance), acknowledged that the Cambodian government was "increasingly aware of the institutional and technical complexities and requirements involved in improving the prioritization, mobilization, coordination, absorption and management of externally-provided development resources." Unfortunately, he added, "in the past, our lack of experience in these areas, and of a clearly defined management system have caused implementation delays for development and investment projects."[49]

The CRDB thus remained ineffective as aid coordination machinery. Cambodian officials pleaded with donors that the CDC/CRDB was "still in its early stages" and that they were still learning the complexities of prioritizing proposals, negotiating and mobilizing aid, and managing programs and projects of external assistance. However, the effectiveness of the CDC/CRDB in coordinating the reconstruction was reduced by the fragmented structure of assistance. The government possessed no integrated system to plan, implement, manage, and monitor projects. Instead, each of the central agencies and line ministries dealt directly with donors, through a PIU, and none reported directly to the CRDB.

Moreover, each donor used its own unique methodology. Concerned that the Cambodian state was being marginalized, finance minister Keat Chhon proposed that the government and international donor or agency representatives set up joint monitoring committees to periodically review progress in the implementation of aid programs.[50]

Donors were understandably disappointed in the inadequate skills of CDC/CRDB officials, who tended to be "political appointees" rather than "technocrats." A development consultant based in Phnom Penh, for instance, complained that Cambodian ministers "do not know what they are supposed to know." They "don't read reports presented to them; they don't even know when loan agreements were signed and who signed them." They "certainly don't have a clue about the big picture. No contingency plans. It's frightening."[51]

Donors' reluctance to disburse aid fully also appeared to be influenced by their legitimate concern about corruption in Cambodia. The problem of "rent seeking" was prevalent, as government officials sought to benefit personally from external and public resources. Although corruption was a typical form of rent seeking, it also took official forms due to the limited capacity of the government to plan, implement, and supervise projects and programs initiated by donors. Although it is unclear to what extent corruption slowed aid disbursements, most donors took precautions when delivering aid. UNTAC reported such concerns in early 1993, noting that the aid system was "cumbersome and subject to abuse" at all levels. This report identified corruption as one of the reasons for delays in aid delivery and noted that UNTAC had "examined the problem and proposed a series of reforms in the public sector that aims at simplifying rules and procedures and eliminating the most blatant forms of corruption."[52]

The problem of corruption remained unresolved, partly because the salaries of civil servants were extremely low (not more than $20 per month). That said, the root cause of corruption was the state's inability to meet social needs and to regulate social behavior. The ad hoc system of salary supplementation that donors have allowed to develop presented big obstacles to administrative reform.[53]

Cambodia's limited absorptive capacity and the obvious lack of effective aid coordination—compounded by the rampant corruption—exacerbated donor fears that rapid aid disbursement would do more harm than good. As Cambodia's absorptive and coordination capacities improved, however slowly, aid began to flow more quickly. However, factional politics also perpetuated the country's limited absorptive capacity.

Factional Conflict and Political Instability

As noted earlier, aggregate disbursements surged in 1995, peaked in 1996, but then dropped dramatically in 1997 (despite reaching 78 percent of pledges for that year). Given the gradual improvements in both absorptive capacity and coordination ability by 1997, neither of these factors is likely to explain this shortfall in aid delivery. Rather, it reflects a third domestic factor: the intensification of factional conflict. As the economist Mya Than has noted, "[Without] peace and political stability in Cambodia, no rehabilitation and reconstruction programs, however brilliantly conceived, can be implemented."[54]

Factional politics in Cambodia slowed aid distribution from the outset of the recovery effort. The Cambodian signatories of the 1991 Paris Agreements, having fought one another for more than a decade, distrusted one another deeply. Accordingly, UNTAC faced enormous challenges in keeping the peace, particularly given the repeated and escalatory violations of the cease-fire and of human rights. The Khmer Rouge was the main culprit.

Since the SOC (led at the time by Prime Minister Hun Sen) controlled about 90 percent of Cambodian territory, resistance leaders viewed any aid disbursed to Cambodia as bolstering their enemy's political legitimacy. This was particularly true in the area of budgetary support.

Factional obstacles to aid disbursement became less acute, however, as it became clear that the Khmer Rouge would not participate in the election of May 1993. The election resulted in the formation of a coalition government among Funcinpec, KPNLF, and SOC.[55] Pleased by the success of Cambodia's first democratic elections in recent decades, donors accelerated the disbursement of budgetary and balance of payments support. From $1,410,000 in 1992, aid for this sector shot to $73,486,000 in 1993 and remained fairly steady for the next two years (at $69,170,000 in 1994 and $77,887,000 in 1995). In short, factional politics slowed initial aid disbursement as donors adopted a wait-and-see policy.

Still, recurrent political factionalism continued to delay the delivery and implementation of donor aid throughout the 1990s. In the post-UNTAC period, the parties' power struggles and rent-seeking gambits delayed the implementation of a power project. Six months were lost during the procurement stage because "Funcinpec and CPP [Cambodian People's Party] officials remained deadlocked, anticipating kickbacks from one or the other of the final bidders." The problem "was finally resolved by selecting the third bidder instead."[56]

The noticeable decline in aid disbursement in 1997 can be explained by renewed factional bickering. During 1996, the first prime minister, Norodom Ranariddh, began to take an aggressive stand against Funcinpec's coalition partner, the CPP; these provocations included particularly harsh statements at the March 21–22 Funcinpec party congress. The parties' mutual resentment intensified, as each sought to woo Khmer Rouge defectors in the hopes of strengthening its politico-military power base.[57] Conflict escalated rapidly in 1997, culminating in a violent coup by the second prime minister, Hun Sen, against Prime Minister Ranariddh.[58]

The growing political instability during 1996–1997 resulted in decreased donor disbursements of budgetary and balance of payments support, which declined from $77,887,000 (1995) to $66,493,000 (1996), and then to $2,647,000 (1997).[59] As of late 1998, the IMF continued to withhold loans for budgetary support. Bilateral donors, including Sweden, likewise suspended balance of payments support.[60] According to Keat Chhon, 1997 was "the first year in which we have not received any direct budgetary support, other than support previously earmarked."[61]

The July coup also discouraged any new initiatives to reestablish Cambodian-donor dialogue through the In-Country Aid Coordination System. No pledging conferences for Cambodia took place following the coup. Factional politics have caused the "death of administrative reform and demobilization," notes one CDC official. In such a context, "there is no reason for multilateral meetings to take place in the near future."[62]

Donors had registered their displeasure with continued internal conflict and poor aid management. In 1996–1997, the IMF first postponed and then canceled two scheduled loans of $20 million, and ultimately (in mid-1997) terminated its loan agreement with Cambodia. Exasperated by persistent conflict and high levels of military spending, donors pressed the government to pay more attention to productive, nonmilitary needs. At the CG meeting in 1997, the World Bank objected that Cambodia's "nondefense current expenditure is half the [desired] target." The Bank insisted that the budget's composition "be changed to support development priorities," in particular, by shifting "from defense towards the social sectors and economic infrastructure."[63] The special representative of the UN secretary-general registered similar complaints.[64]

Still, the situation was a complicated one. As an ADB official acknowledged at the same CG meeting, "Cambodia's major economic challenges are all ultimately traceable to political concerns."[65] Other donors concurred. The greatest obstacle to Cambodian recovery was "a stable political framework," observed Australian aid official Peter McCawley. He warned that the "willingness of aid donors . . . to work in Cambodia will weaken unless the coalition partners are able to resolve tension between them, ensure stability, and maintain an apolitical public sector during the period leading up to the [next] elections."[66]

While it is fairly early to assess the impact of the July 1997 coup on donor decisions to disburse other types of aid to Cambodia, some patterns are apparent. Disbursements in budgetary aid/balance of payments support for 1997 amounted to only $2.647 million (a 96.02 percent decrease from 1996). From 1996 to 1997, France reduced its aid for this sector from $42.88 million to $26.49 million; Japan from $111 million to $59.84 million; and Great Britain from $4.13 million to $2.25 million.

The negative impact of the coup on aid disbursements in 1997 should not be exaggerated, however. Germany did not reduce its budgetary aid and balance of payments support but instead increased it slightly. At first glance, it appeared that the United States had suspended all new bilateral aid (and two-thirds of its total $38 million in foreign aid to Cambodia).[67] In reality—at least based on current aid figures—U.S. aid in 1997 amounted to $30.50 million, even larger than the 1996 amount ($28.76 million). Similiarly, Australia actually increased its aid in 1997 (from $20 million to $27.29 million).

In late 1997, donors conditioned aid disbursements worth $21 million on the conduct of free, fair, and credible elections, scheduled for July 26, 1998. In order to receive this assistance, the government would need to pass legislation ensuring free and fair polls; allow international observers to monitor the elections; take steps to neutralize the armed forces; reduce the number of bodyguards used by politicians; and repeal laws extending impunity to government employees. On February 15, 1998, a multilateral group called Friends of Cambodia (including Canada, Australia, France, Germany, Japan, New Zealand, South Korea, the United Kingdom, and the United States) met with the ASEAN troika to discuss Cambodia. The participants agreed that the country needed to develop a climate for free, fair, and credible elections. While Russia objected that the Paris Agreements had been "imposed" on Cambodia and that it did not wish to interfere in Cambodia's domestic affairs, other Western donors adopted a harder line. Several members of the EU (such as France, Great Britain, and Germany) reserved the right to withdraw aid if the warring factions did not end their hostilities, if human rights were not respected, and if all parties were not allowed to participate in the elections. Japan, which committed $7.68 million for the elections, and Australia, which committed another $400,000, linked their disbursements to free and fair elections. The United States came down particularly hard on Hun Sen, arguing that if "conditions for free and fair elections do not exist," donors should provide no technical and financial support for Cambodia.[68]

As the paragraphs above document, Cambodia's limited capacity to absorb and coordinate aid and its persistent factional fighting created real problems for timely delivery and successful implementation of assistance. Still, these shortcomings tell only part of the story. In the words of one UNTAC report, dated February 23, 1993, "the lack of absorptive capacity should not be created or excused for limited disbursement."[69] Moreover, as Khalid Ikram of the World Bank noted, some "skills do exist in the administration to carry out much of the rehabilitation exercise"; indeed "one also has evidence from the development efforts since 1980 that Cambodians can deliver."[70] Japan, which delivered more than what it had pledged in the 1992–1995 period, showed a clear ability to overcome the numerous difficulties still facing Cambodia.

External Constraints on Aid Disbursements

This section examines why some donors were more successful than others in disbursing pledges. Cambodia's absorptive weaknesses, inadequate coordination, and factional fighting alone do not account for variations in donor performance. Gaps in aid disbursement and the less-than-desirable quality of aid delivered owed much to the donors' lack of baseline knowledge about Cambodia's socioeconomic and political needs, their unrealistic values and expectations, and their competing economic and political interests.

It may be worth pointing out that Cambodia has not developed a proper national statistical system; every government ministry produces its own data. Although the National Institute of Statistics should serve as the sole source of recognized national statistics, it hardly has any budget and carries out ad hoc surveys only when donors provide funding.[71] Moreover, NGOs, an important aid channel, have lacked the capacity to implement many donor projects and have failed to coordinate their actions.

Lack of Baseline Knowledge and Inappropriate Aid Initiatives

Although early donor missions found the Cambodian economy near collapse, they offered little guidance about how to respond to the crisis. In general, the lack of accurate data on the country's needs hindered the delivery of foreign aid throughout the early 1990s. It may also have encouraged inappropriate donor policies.

After a decade and a half of international isolation, from 1975 to 1990, the socioeconomic developments inside Cambodia remained largely unknown to Western donors. Major international financial institutions and Western donors had no formal relations with the country until the signing of the October 1991 agreements. World Bank relations with Cambodia, dating from July 1970, had been interrupted in 1975; these resumed only in September 1992. Meanwhile, by spring 1992, the IMF had done no more than to express a desire to normalize bilateral relations that had been terminated by the Khmer Rouge victory in 1975.

A preliminary UN survey in 1990, aimed at "gathering data pertinent to a possible United Nations role in the settlement of the Cambodian problem," reveals just how little the world knew about the country and the challenges of its recovery.[72] The mission spent only two weeks in Cambodia, clearly insufficient to provide a detailed picture of the country's problems. Moreover, it contained no Cambodians and conducted interviews in English, French, and Khmer, relying on interpreters "who were without exception diligent but sometimes not familiar with technical terminology and concepts." As its own report concluded, the "mission . . . fears that some of the information and nuances which were being communicated may have been lost. Indeed, this may be the cause of some of the apparent inconsistencies or lacunae."[73]

Preparatory meetings prior to the ICORC indicated how difficult it was for donors to make pledges and to disburse their aid promptly. At the Tokyo meeting on March 30–31, 1992, officials from UNICEF, the World Bank, the IMF, and other agencies cautioned participants about the difficulty of getting accurate or reliable statistical data on Cambodia.[74] As the ADB representative put it, "National income accounts based on the UN system of national accounts have not been available since 1968. Prices were collected in Phnom Penh since 1991, but no price indices had been computed. Budgetary figures are not readily available. Employment statistics outside of the public sector are not collected and compiled."[75] Problems associated with statistical reliability continued to plague donor efforts. The issue reemerged repeatedly at ICORC meetings.[76]

Inadequate understanding of the local context undermined the international community's efforts to moderate factional hostility, which in turn impeded effective project implementation. Although UNTAC was tasked with coordinating aid, its ability to do so was constrained by the overarching goal of achieving national reconciliation among the Cambodian factions. In keeping with the Paris Agreements, UNTAC insisted that assistance could not benefit one faction at the expense of another; this UN principle of strict impartiality was fundamental to reconciliation. Nevertheless, UNTAC and other donor countries could have done more to resolve the political problems first. Even after the 1993 election, for example, all donors disapproved of any peace deal with the Khmer Rouge rebels. While this stance appealed to the donor sense of justice, it also forced Cambodia to continue spending huge amounts of its budget on defense, reducing the funds available for nonmilitary development purposes.

Moreover, while the war was still raging, donors prematurely bypassed critical rehabilitation needs to embrace projects of economic reconstruction. This was true for the World Bank, for example, even though it possessed no comparative advantage in sociocultural analysis and ignored the dynamics of Cambodian society. The Bank did not draw on Cambodian scholars, nor did it promote the development of independent local capacities in social science research. Although in theory there was a distinction between rehabilitation and reconstruction, in practice donor programs "were already evolving prematurely toward 'immediate reconstruction cum expansion bypassing rehabilitation.'"[77] The failure to distinguish rehabilitation and reconstruction may have contributed to slow disbursements of aid because Cambodia's absorptive capacity was limited and still in need of rehabilitation.

Insufficient awareness of Cambodia's basic problems and real needs apparently delayed the implementation of specific projects. For example, in the mid-1990s, the ADB made little progress in improving rural infrastructure because of delays in recruiting a project implementation consultant. The project continued to suffer from limited administrative capacity (in its Project Management Office, its six provincial Project Implementation Units, as well as in its counterpart facilities). The existing ADB executing agency failed to realize that the implementation of such a large project required a proportionally large input of administrative personnel and supporting facilities (including office space, equipment, and vehicles). Another ADB basic skills project—involving such components as contract awards, civil works, procurement of equipment/facilities, staff development, and consultant services—progressed slowly because of delays in the procurement of equipment and furniture.

The disbursement of aid may have been slowed by donors adopting a "Khmerization policy," intended to ensure that Cambodians themselves could implement aid projects. While the policy was good from the point of view of project sustainability, it was problematic in terms of aid disbursement. It was difficult to find competent Cambodians who were not already politicized. Donors therefore adopted a wait-and-see attitude, slowing aid flows.[78] According to one European diplomat, the principle of "partnership" required a German aid agency to find "counterpart people" to implement projects at the provincial and district levels; unfortunately, it was difficult to find competent Cambodians willing to work for the low salary of $20 per month. The policy of partnership thus "prolonged aid implementation."[79] Meanwhile, donors missed out on the talents of Cambodian expatriates, who could have been of great help to donor projects. In a review of its experiences in postconflict recovery, the World Bank observes that "the ICORC group, as a whole, including the World Bank, has made inadequate use of the diaspora's potential as a medium-term solution of the absorptive capacity problem."[80] However, employing Cambodian expatriates would raise complications of its own, since most of them are part of the international labor market and require international salaries.

Although donors recognized Cambodia's "unique situation," Douglas Grube observes, they still relied on traditional approaches and were not willing to take risks to adapt aid to the specific country context. This stance "affected [and] limited the effectiveness of aid."[81]

Donors' Problems: Insufficient Coordination,
Unrealistic Expectations, and Inappropriate Aid

Several other "external" factors may also have contributed to gaps and delays between aid pledges and deliveries. Potential causes include the political considerations of bilateral donors; the institutional shortcomings of multilateral organizations and multilateral pledging mechanisms; the unrealistic expectations of various donors; and the inappropriate composition of some donor assistance. The following paragraphs assess the role that these factors may have played in slowing aid delivery.

For the most part, domestic political considerations seemed insignificant in determining the provision of aid to Cambodia. Given the potential role of domestic interest groups and activist legislatures in the formulation of foreign policy within liberal democracies, one might have imagined that domestic forces would present a major obstacle to effective aid disbursement. In fact, there is little evidence that internal political considerations played a critical role in either slowing or increasing aid disbursement to Cambodia. During the 1980s, the United States continued to provide assistance to the Cambodian resistance forces, to the benefit of the Khmer Rouge, even though U.S. law banned any aid to groups violating human rights.[82] Nor, likewise, did human rights violations and factional politics during 1997 seriously affect the overall level of aid disbursements by many Western liberal democracies. Indeed, these actually increased in some cases; but it is clear that political considerations have influenced the targeting of the aid sent to Cambodia. Thus, the decline in the proportion of pledged aid actually delivered during 1997 reflected (in large part) reduced budgetary support, aimed at forcing Hun Sen to hold a free, fair, and credible election.

In some cases, political considerations led donors to make pledges that could not be fully fulfilled because of the unfavorable conditions in Cambodia. For instance, in 1994 the EU replaced the EC/Cambodia Rehabilitation Program with the European Rehabilitation Program in Cambodia (PERC), primarily to demonstrate that the new Cambodian government was effective in delivering services. Around $80 million was allocated under PERC to several programs, the largest of which was PRASAC. But its "rapid implementation" framework turned out to be unrealistic, being both politically driven and not taking account of Cambodia's limited absorptive capacity.

Organizational constraints may also help to explain why multilateral donors such as the World Bank and the ADB experienced the widest gaps. The World Bank managed to process a $63 million Emergency Rehabilitation Project (ERP) for Cambodia within eight months—a reasonable time period for negotiations with a borrower. Unfortunately, two years lapsed between the conception and the implementation of this project.[83] Although the Bank was understandably apprehensive about Cambodia's limited absorptive capacity, its inability to coordinate aid, and its continuing factional politics, the delay also reflected internal Bank constraints. One procurement consultant complained that "the Bank's standard procedures were inappropriate." Likewise, a Bank report concluded, "Under the ERP, Bank procedures were simplified but still proved to be too cumbersome."[84] The Bank was not alone in its shortcomings. One top CDC official complained that "the IMF calendar is too rigid and not realistic."[85] The Fund did not take into account Cambodia's domestic problems, which made it extremely difficult to comply with the IMF's demands.

As a lead agency, the World Bank could have made a greater effort to facilitate aid coordination in Cambodia. Not until the end of 1995 did the Bank decide to establish a "liaison" office in Phnom Penh, and political instability prevented its formal representation from being established until January 1997. To date, no Bank resident mission has been created to facilitate coordination and local operations.

Although donors created pledging mechanisms to coordinate their approach to Cambodian reconstruction, they established no multilateral mechanism to ensure follow-through on the promises made in these public forums. The lack of collective aid coordination persisted even though donors knew that Cambodia was in no position to coordinate assistance on its own. Donors seemed to lack the will to help perform some urgent functions the government could not do on its own. One close observer of the ICORC and CG meetings, who worked at the CDC, concluded that "when donors got together, they just wanted to show their united stance and presented a united voice vis-à-vis Cambodia. It's just a public show, which became irrelevant to what they actually do on the ground."[86]

Although donors understandably pushed Cambodia to improve transparency, they did not set a particularly good example themselves. Bilateral donors, in particular, were not forthcoming with reports of their own aid flows; moreover, they reported to the Cambodian government according to idiosyncratic procedures, making it harder for the CDC to do its job. In the absence of a central body to monitor aid flows, there was little assurance that donors would deliver on the amounts that they had pledged. Thus, pledging appeared to be easier than disbursement, especially since donors could not be held accountable.

Third, donor *expectations* constrained aid disbursements. Whereas some aid recipients (like South Africa) enjoyed the capacity to resist donor conditions, Cambodia remained heavily aid dependent. Indeed, UNDP and the World Bank essentially set the recovery agenda for Cambodia, preparing documents and position papers in the absence of Cambodia's capacity to coordinate and administer aid. In effect, the Bank and the donor hosting the pledging conferences (either France or Japan) "dictated the agenda" of these gatherings, with little input from the Cambodians. The Bank and lead donors spent one and a half days focusing on only a "few key issues" that concerned them particularly.[87] As a result, Cambodia was vulnerable to demands from donors, who anticipated rapid progress toward recovery. As one aid official explained, "Donor agencies are basically 'result-oriented'; they emphasize 'quick impact.' Because of their high expectations, they ended up stopping taking things seriously after one year or two, after they saw no 'quick impact.'"[88]

From one perspective, one might see the IMF's suspension (and cancellation) of loans and termination of its agreement with Cambodia as perfectly justified, since Cambodia failed to meet explicit aid conditions. But one could also argue that the Fund's expectations—particularly in the areas of economic and fiscal management—were too high for a war-decimated country. The pressure that the IMF and World Bank placed on Cambodian leaders to "get their house in order"—a strategy based on short- and medium-term market-oriented preferences—may even have exacerbated the political crisis of 1997.[89] The IMF's withdrawal of support in July 1997 encouraged other donors, including the World Bank, to make no new pledges.[90]

Still, notwithstanding the tradition that donor assistance depends on a country's de facto certification by the IMF, there is no conclusive evidence that the Fund's action itself caused other donors to suspend or cancel their existing aid projects in Cambodia. The IMF's aid in 1996 had amounted to only $400,000; in 1997, the amount was reduced to zero. While donors suspended budgetary aid and balance of payments support, it is not clear that IMF actions induced this response. Moreover, only a few aid projects have been suspended since late 1996. Because the Fund's aid package was generally seen as "prestructural adjustment," donors could still go their ways without having to follow the Fund strictly.[91]

The *types of aid* donors provided and their preferences also played a role in determining why some donors' disbursement gaps were narrower than others. As noted earlier, Japan delivered more aid than it had pledged. Available data show that, during March 1991–February 1994, Japan provided most of its assistance to Cambodia in the form of infrastructure, concentrating on bridge building, medical equipment, electricity generation, water supply facilities, national roads, road construction, and structural adjustment support.[92]

Donors with disbursement percentages lower than 70 percent appear to have been more closely involved in administrative capacity building. The United States (with 63.3 percent delivery) not only funded projects to improve the health and economic well-being of vulnerable groups and to develop the country's infrastructure, but also financed to build democracy, political institutions, and free market mechanisms. France (which delivered only 42.4 percent) focused more on projects to promote the rule of law and to provide human resource training. Time-consuming projects may have slowed aid disbursements.

By way of generalization, the disbursement gaps among donors varied according to national approaches, which may have been driven by self-interest and ideological preferences. Donors like Japan, which viewed infrastructure development as a priority and had a strong and long-term economic interest in the country, tended to disburse aid more quickly. Those such as the United States, which viewed democracy building as imperative to peace and advocated recovery at the grassroots level, faced more difficulty disbursing aid. For donors involved in the process of rebuilding state capacities, like France, the challenges were even greater.[93]

NGOs and Problems of Implementation

Donors channeled some of their aid to Cambodia directly to NGOs, which then implemented projects. In Cambodia, NGOs have been able to attract funding from all major sources: multilateral, bilateral, and independent. In

1996, bilateral and multilateral resources disbursed through NGOs were $64 million, of which $35.8 million (about 56 percent) came from NGOs' "core or own" resources. In 1997, the total disbursement increased to $72 million, of which $49.87 million (about 70 percent) came from NGOs' core or own resources; multilateral and bilateral donors contributed about 11 and 19 percent, respectively.[94] Seen in this context, NGOs are both donors and implementing agencies of projects funded by bilateral donors.

Clearly, levels of aid disbursement would have been lower in the absence of these NGOs. Many donors unfamiliar with Cambodia hoped to employ them as implementation agencies. Generally speaking, NGOs had a comparative advantage in executing projects at the community level, especially during the rehabilitation phase. One reason that bilateral donors had a higher rate of aid disbursement than multilateral ones was that they used NGOs to help implement some of their aid projects.

Unfortunately, donors were bound to encounter some problems when depending on NGOs to implement their projects, at times slowing the disbursement of international assistance. Pledged assistance was sometimes not fully disbursed because agencies, like the U.S. Agency for International Development (USAID), subcontracted their programs with NGOs. Subcontracting created problems when the quarterly payments extended by donor agencies to NGOs were less than anticipated; this situation arose, for example, when interim financial reports indicated that NGOs had significantly underspent their previous installment of grant funds. (In 1995, for example, some seventy NGOs received financing worth $47 million, whereas their total expenditure was slightly over $35 million.) The overall effect was to increase the gap between donor pledges and actual disbursements. Still, the problem of NGO underspending should not be exaggerated. In 1994, 130 of the more than 200 NGOs reported a total expenditure of $70 million on 297 projects. In 1996 and 1997, the total expenditures were about $65 million and $71 million, respectively.

In addition, NGOs often *worked at cross-purposes,* hindering the timely disbursement and effective coordination and implementation of projects. Following the Paris Agreements of 1991, the NGO community became increasingly active in public advocacy. The CCC, a coordinating committee for Cambodia founded in April 1990 by an umbrella group of forty-one NGOs, was invited to the Donor Consultative Group meetings in Phnom Penh and to the Ministerial Conference on Rehabilitation and Reconstruction of Cambodia in June 1992. The CCC had two objectives: to serve as a mechanism for improving communications between NGOs and international organizations and to strengthen communications between agencies and the government.

NGOs often competed with each other, both to secure donor funds and to create their own programmatic "niches." These conflicts of interest prevented them from ever putting out a common position paper.[95] One donor agency worker blamed NGOs for not sharing information with one another, despite the existing CCC network. Dissatisfied, many NGOs withdrew from the CCC and refused to return.[96] The creation of a so-called aid market prevented the NGO community from speaking with a single, forceful voice and may have contributed to slow aid disbursements.

Other sources of delayed aid disbursements included the lack of NGO capacity to implement either "quick-impact" or longer-term donor-funded projects, and the frequent clash between NGO and donor development philosophies.

The first question is how effective NGOs were in implementing development aid projects. During the 1980s, NGOs had difficulty recruiting expatriate personnel, primarily because of the Cambodian system of visas, which regulated the entrance of foreigners on the basis of an NGO's budget, past track record, and ideological persuasion. Until the mid-1980s, Western agencies were not allowed to field technical staff, because the Soviet bloc provided all of Cambodia's technical assistance. Although visa restrictions were eased slightly after the mid-1980s, the number of aid workers remained small, increasing from thirty-four in 1982 to around 100 by the end of 1986. By mid-1992, as a big wave of new international NGOs arrived and older ones expanded their staffs, the number jumped to several hundreds.[97]

From 1979 to 1990, NGOs in Cambodia were preoccupied with urgent humanitarian and relief issues rather than development. The bulk of multilateral assistance given to refugees and displaced persons at the Thai-Cambodian border was food related. From 1985 to 1991, about half the total budget of the United Nations Border Relief Operation (UNBRO)[98] was allocated to food, with health and sanitation taking up one-third of the total. From around 1989, Western assistance began to flow into Cambodia through NGOs, reaching an estimated $20 million in that initial year, $28 million in 1990, and $40 million in 1991. Although NGOs became involved in providing emergence assistance to Cambodia in late 1979, "NGO involvement in the industrial sector declined after the emergency phase and was further reduced in 1989."[99]

After the signing of the 1991 Paris Agreements, the capacity of NGOs to implement aid projects improved (especially as Western NGOs got involved), but not as much as one might have imagined. Ostensibly, foreign experts gave NGOs a comparative advantage in executing projects at the community level. In reality, as one UNTAC report noted, "longer-term development programs requiring more fundamental restructuring and the coordinated inputs of different organizations . . . are often beyond the capacity of most NGOs."[100]

These difficulties in implementing projects persisted. An inherent weakness of NGOs lies in weak managerial capacity and inadequate "collective capacity to analyze their experiences and to articulate those analyses for policy formulation."[101] In addition, long-term development programs required fundamental restructuring and coordination among multiple organizations. Most NGOs in Cambodia lacked this sort of *implementation capacity.*

It is difficult to assess the NGO record in implementing recovery projects in Cambodia; there exists no serious study on this topic. Still, it is clear that the proliferation of NGOs during the 1990s far outpaced the spread of technical expertise within the NGO community. NGOs absorbed a considerable proportion of aid, but they were often unable to carry out all the projects that donors proposed or financed. For instance, the Cambodian Mine Action Center (CMAC) had adequate money for 1998 and 1999, but (according to one Canadian officer) it lacked the management capacity to run more than twenty projects at a time.[102]

In the words of one donor agency official, "Few NGOs have the skills necessary for long-term development projects and [thus they] couldn't even develop any long-term vision."[103] Another NGO worker complained that NGOs "sent in incompetent people who did not have the faintest idea of what they were supposed to do, who agreed to short-term commitments, and who had advanced academic backgrounds" (especially in economic development).[104] While this statement seems exaggerated, most NGOs were not interested in working at the national level but wanted to go straight to the community; this often conflicted with donors' "political" agendas.

In some cases, NGOs could not implement the donors' quick-impact projects. In 1995, an NGO forum, "Differing Approaches to Development Assistance in Cambodia: NGOs and the European Community," debated the European Commission's PRASAC initiative.[105] NGOs complained its "fast-track" approach would overwhelm NGO projects on the ground, weaken local NGOs by recruiting their local staffs, and disrupt support for earlier EC programs. Clearly, there was a conflict of goals: whereas the EC's primary motive was to support the newly elected government in Phnom Penh, NGOs had humanitarian concerns and could not rush to meet targets. According to one report, most NGOs "would not be in a position to use rapid impact higher technology options even if they believed them appropriate."[106]

The NGO community urged donors to be sensitive to Cambodia's short-term needs and priorities, whereas donors preferred to focus on reconstruction and economic development. NGOs generally advocated a micro development approach—one that directed aid not to central government institutions but toward activities at the provincial, district, and village level—but donors viewed NGOs as convenient tools to implement projects often directed at higher levels. In general, one analyst writes, NGOs were "peripheral to determining development strategies."

A number of recent developments signal a disturbing trend in certain bilateral assistance programs. A number of donors have chosen to ignore the long-established programs of NGOs in particular areas and are designing large-scale projects that may completely wipe out 10 years of NGO and Cambodian efforts and investment.[107]

Although they should not be exaggerated, differences between the NGOs' microeconomic and the donors' macroeconomic approach to development persisted. At the CG meeting in 1996, the NGO Forum on Cambodia outlined a long-term commitment to development through capacity building and sustainable management of natural resources for the purpose of alleviating poverty and of ensuring environmental sustainability. The forum argued that the donors' programs for demobilization and administrative reform were too ambitious and would carry a high social cost.[108] Because of a central focus on rural development and agricultural development, NGOs did not receive the same kind of relative attention from bilateral and multilateral agencies. This reflected the donors' open-market strategy, which was driven by the need to concentrate on infrastructure development with the aim of attracting private investment for long-term development.

Conclusion

Aid for peace building in Cambodia has offered some valuable lessons for donors. No doubt, the donor community has demonstrated much goodwill in its determination to help ease up the complex triple transition in this war-torn country. Our findings, however, show that a gap between pledges and disbursements did exist. This gap fluctuated from year to year and varied from donor to donor as well as across aid types.

To begin with, we suggest that gaps between pledges and disbursements must be placed in the broad context of Cambodia's condition as a weak state—one possessing extremely limited capacity to absorb and coordinate aid and wracked by perennial factional politics. The evidence presented suggests that Cambodia's meager capacities to absorb and coordinate assistance slowed aid delivery (although disbursements increased steadily from 1992 to 1995, as the local situation improved). The low disbursement percentage in 1992, 1996, and 1997 resulted in large part from acute factional conflict. After the coup of July 1997, no new aid pledges were made. Of the several domestic obstacles, then, factional conflict appears to be the most powerful variable explaining slow disbursements.

The mediocre record of aid delivery from 1993 to 1995 (58.9 percent overall) was influenced by external factors, too. Donors approached the recovery of Cambodia with a limited knowledge of the country's problems, unrealistic expectations, and narrow, national approaches to peace and

recovery. Uncertain of what to do in Cambodia, donors adopted inappropriate policies that prevented them from delivering on their pledges. Too
often, large pledges were built on overly optimistic scenarios. In addition,
while NGOs generally helped donors in the process of disbursing aid, they
also hindered aid deliveries because of their limited expertise and their
conflicts with donors over rival philosophies of development.

In general, multilateral donors tended to have more difficulty disbursing pledged aid than did their bilateral counterparts. The evidence in
this case reaffirms that international financial institutions are less politically (and more economically) inclined than bilateral donors. The case
study also shows that donor success at delivering on aid pledges tends to
vary across types of aid. Projects related to administrative capacity building, especially at the state level, and long-term reconstruction projects
were more difficult to implement than those related to infrastructure
development and humanitarian relief. It should not be surprising, in this
light, that Japan gained a reputation as Cambodia's largest and most
effective donor.

Despite the evident gaps between pledges and deliveries, foreign aid
benefited Cambodia's socioeconomic and political development. Without
aid, Cambodia would not have experienced significant economic growth
and, indeed, its government might have collapsed. Thanks to the presence
of more than 200 international NGOs and a smaller number of local
NGOs, the rudiments of a civil society have emerged in Cambodia. Nevertheless, foreign assistance has not laid a solid foundation for a sustainable triple transition. Institutional capacity has remained fragile, as manifested by the ongoing violence and military conflict. The process of
democratization has also come under attack, as Second Prime Minister
Hun Sen staged a violent coup against Ranariddh and solidified his grip on
political power.[109]

What valuable lessons can we draw from the Cambodian experience?
First, one must distinguish between recipient countries suffering from inter-
state conflict and those suffering from civil wars. Domestic conflict tends
to be protracted. Even after it ends, the problems of project implementation
are enormous, given the country's severely limited infrastructural, human,
administrative, and financial capacities. Weak states in transition from war
to peace pose daunting obstacles to long-term development projects.

One implication of the Cambodian case is that donors must adopt a
bolder and more far-sighted attitude toward those in need of their assistance, but that their policies must be tempered by realistic expectations.
Donors need to set more concrete conditions for aid disbursement, but
these must be both appropriate and practical. Donors cannot fulfill all of
their wishes at once; they must confront the need to make hard choices.
For example, donors resented Cambodia's high defense spending and

military efforts; at the same time, they objected initially to any efforts at national reconciliation with the Khmer Rouge. Similarly, donors disliked factionalism and pushed for political stability, but their attitude may have prompted Hun Sen to oust his copremier—an event contrary to donors' liberal political agendas. Until 1995, aid to Cambodia was pledged with no strings attached. When the political and security situation in Cambodia deteriorated, beginning in 1996, the donor community reacted by demanding that the government restore stability. Although the demand seemed quite reasonable at the time, it did not lead to stability. Hun Sen justified the coup in July 1997, a few days after the second CG meeting, on the grounds that the country needed better stability. Thus, it is important that aid be pledged and disbursed with the following logic in mind: while the transition from war to peace must be encouraged, some sort of "democratic conditionality" needs to be attached to aid.[110]

As far as aid coordination is concerned, even though the recipient country must take primary responsibility, it would be helpful for donors to coordinate their aid projects more effectively, at least during the initial period of rehabilitation and reconstruction. Recipient countries should bear in mind that donors and implementing agencies cannot do everything for them. Competition among donors or among NGOs tends to create supply-driven aid projects and programs that may not be responsive to real needs. Donor agencies and NGOs tend to compete for resources; to be bound by mandates, conventions, rules, and constituencies; and to be preoccupied with their own survival and growth. These facts are likely to remain unchanged in the future.

A systematic approach to peace is absolutely necessary. In an extremely weak state like Cambodia, racked by violence and war, the transitions from war to peace and from authoritarianism to liberal democracy must be given top priority; otherwise, failure in these efforts may jeopardize the economic transition. It must be borne in mind that the three elements of the triple transition rarely occur as simultaneous phases. Unless the war-to-peace transition succeeds first, the economic transition may be interrupted or even stopped. By devoting resources at hand to winning a war, weak states may be unable to meet the challenges of sustainable economic development. By wrongly assuming that economic development in the midst of warfare will lead to peace and democracy, donors may ignore the fact that aid infusions alone may not enable them to achieve these goals. Indeed, it is unclear whether economic development always promotes liberal democracy.[111] Donors will also need to play a more proactive role, keeping in mind that weak states like Cambodia are deeply in need of their leadership, despite the recipient's usual rhetoric about the need to defend state sovereignty and political independence.

Notes

We would like to thank the following individuals for their thoughtful and helpful comments on the different drafts of this paper: Michael Doyle (professor Princeton University), Douglas Grube (consultant in management and organization development), Joanna Macrae (research fellow, Overseas Development Institute), and Martin Godfrey (Cambodia Development Resource Institute).

1. The study is based on more than 100 interviews conducted in Cambodia, public documentation, confidential reports, and important secondary sources. Given the difficulties of conducting empirical research and extracting reliable economic data in Cambodia, the findings here must be regarded as tentative. As Douglas I. Grube, a consultant in management and organization development, admits, "nobody really knows the distinction between pledge and disbursement. People just don't know. Donors' transparency is questionable; they exaggerate the amounts pledged and disbursed. The Cambodian government does not even have the capacity to get the correct answers from donors. This is an 'accounting game.' What is worth understanding is the 'game.' So to get a comprehensive picture is impossible." Interview, May 1998.

2. See Grube, "Donors in Disarray," and McAndrew, *Aid Infusions.*

3. Mysliewiec, *Punishing the Poor.*

4. Peou, *Conflict Neutralization in the Cambodia War.*

5. UN Document, A/46/608; S/23177, October 30, 1991, p. 56.

6. Ibid.

7. Ibid., p. 57.

8. Ibid., p. 55.

9. Tokyo Declaration on Rehabilitation and Reconstruction of Cambodia, Annex: Framework of ICORC (June 22, 1992).

10. Organizations involved included the EU, UNTAC, UNDP, UNICEF, WFP, UNHCR, ILO, FAO, UNESCO, WHO, the World Bank, the IMF, and the ADB.

11. Australia, Austria, Belgium, Brunei, Cambodia, Canada, China, Denmark, Finland, France, Germany, India, Indonesia, Ireland, Italy, Japan, Laos, Malaysia, the Netherlands, New Zealand, Norway, the Philippines, Russia, Singapore, Spain, Sweden, Switzerland, Thailand, the United Kingdom, the United States, and Vietnam.

12. Grube, "Donors in Disarray," p. 3; interviews, May 1998.

13. Cited in Ear, "Cambodia and the 'Washington Consensus,'" p. 75.

14. Many interviews with donors indicate that they did not believe that conditions would work.

15. Interviews, May 1998.

16. CDC/CRDB, *Development Cooperation Report (1997/98),* p. 6.

17. McAndrew, *Aid Infusions,* p. 3.

18. Normally, humanitarian assistance is not related to national development efforts (nor to capacity building) but aims to relieve distress and improve the well-being of the most needy. Free-standing technical cooperation aims to transfer technical and managerial skills and technology to permit Cambodia to undertake future development activities. This assistance includes feasibility studies. Food aid includes grants and loans for the purchase of food and associated costs like transport, storage, and distribution. Program/budgetary aid or balance of payments support is provided to ensure broader development programs, to help pay for commodity inputs, to support Cambodia's current account balance, and to make foreign exchange available. Investment-related technical cooperation is directed toward strengthening Cambodia's capacity to execute specific investment projects.

19. Report of the UN Inter-Agency Humanitarian Mission to Cambodia (October 31–November 13, 1991), pp. 3, 4.

20. ADB et al., *Cambodia: Short-Term Needs,* p. 20.

21. A statement by the representative of Finland, ICORC II, Tokyo, March 10–11, 1994.

22. UNTAC Control of Budgetary Disbursements (undated).

23. UNTAC, *Rehabilitation and Development in Cambodia,* p. 3.

24. ADB et al., *Cambodia: Socio-Economic Situation and Immediate Needs,* p. 10. See also UNDP, *Comprehensive Paper on Cambodia,* pp. 37–53.

25. Than, "Rehabilitation and Economic Reconstruction in Cambodia," p. 281.

26. The amounts of aid from the socialist bloc include: $85 million in 1982, $92 million in 1984, $112 million in 1985, $117 million in 1986, $183.1 million in 1987, $192 million in 1988. We are grateful to Joanna Macrae for providing this information.

27. UNDP, "Capacity Building and Coordination of External Cooperation," discussion paper presented at the first Consultative Group meeting (CGM I), July 11-12, 1996), p. 4.

28. Statement of senior minister-in-charge of rehabilitation and development and minister of economy and finance, and vice-chairman of CDC, "Capacity Building and Aid Coordination Issues," CGM I, July 11, 1996, p. 1.

29. Statement by Callisto Madavo, ICORC, Tokyo, March 10–11, 1994, p. 3.

30. United Nations, *Report of the United Nations Fact-Finding Mission,* p. 74.

31. ADB, et. al., *Cambodia: Short-Term Needs,* p. 11.

32. Statement by Paul Matthews, January 16, 1997.

33. Interview, December 7, 1997.

34. They argued that the IMF did not understand that there was "total anarchy in the logging industry." As one official emphasized, "There is a logging movement in Cambodia; that is, the military and ordinary people and the Khmer Rouge—they all are involved in the business. It's beyond the government's control." Interviews, November 1996.

35. *Cambodian Business,* January 1998, p. 14.

36. Cambodia had never borrowed from the World Bank.

37. It should be borne in mind that most aid has not been included in the government budget. Projects in rural development, health, education, etc., have effectively taken over what should properly be government functions.

38. Interview, May 1998. Before July 1997, the World Bank and the ADB had pledged $80 million and $75 million, respectively. Cambodia was supposed to provide $30 million, but it could not meet this requirement. In addition to this strict financial requirement, Cambodia must stand ready at any time to release its counterpart fund on a monthly basis. Under severe financial constraints, the government was never ready for this kind of commitment.

39. ADB Issues Paper on the Government's Public Investment Program (presented at CGM, Tokyo, July 11–12, 1996), p. 3.

40. Intrac, *Differing Approaches to Development Assistance in Cambodia.*

41. During the transitional period, UNTAC helped coordinate foreign aid to Cambodia. A Donor Consultative Group (DCG) established in 1991 was given the responsibility to coordinate rehabilitation and humanitarian assistance. Apparently, potential donors were very concerned about the way in which their aid would be coordinated and managed.

42. Statement of the Delegation of the SNC, presented at the preparatory meeting of the Ministerial Conference on Reconstruction of Cambodia, Tokyo, March 30, 1992.

43. Government of Cambodia, *National Programme to Rehabilitate and Develop Cambodia*. International aid coordination meetings in a number of sectors have been held since 1994: energy (October 1994), agriculture (November 1994), education (December 1994), women in development (April 1995), transport (May 1995), urban development (August 1995), water supply and sanitation (July 1996), and so on. Such meetings were expected to help the government implement its policies and strategies in each sector.

44. The National Program to Rehabilitate and Develop Cambodia recognized the benefits of effective aid coordination and pointed to the importance the government placed on this particular effort. The CDC was a committee of ministers (initially headed by First Prime Minister Ranariddh) responsible for orientation; necessary, strategic decisions and approaches; and overall coordination and management. Directly responsible for aid coordination and management is the National Committee for Rehabilitation and Development (NCRD), the operating arm of the CDC. The CDC/NCRD works closely with the ministries involved. At this point, however, the body still did not function. The CRDB, the In-Country Aid Coordination System, consults and collaborates with central ministries and agencies such as the Ministry of Planning, the Ministry of Economy and Finance, the Ministry of Foreign Affairs, and other relevant line ministries. It is intended to forge consensus on priorities; ensure coordinated effort; strengthen aid management; and provide an in-country coordination mechanism that involves interministerial consultations, government-donor consultations, and consensus-building meetings on reports, documents, and programs to be presented by the government at the CG meetings. The CRDB set up the National Public Investment Management System (NPIMS), a development assistance database for all external assistance flows, and annually prepares the Development Cooperation Report, which analyzes disbursements of international assistance.

45. UNDP, "Aid Coordination in Cambodia," discussion paper, CGM II, July 1–2, 1997, p. 4.

46. Australian Statement: Session III: Capacity Building and Aid Coordination Issues, CGM I, July 11–12, 1996.

47. Interview, November 1996.

48. UNDP, "Capacity Building and Coordination of External Cooperation," discussion paper, CGM I, Tokyo, July 11–12, 1996, p. 2.

49. Statement of senior minister-in-charge of rehabilitation and development and minister of economy and finance, and vice-chairman of CDC, "Capacity Building and Aid Coordination Issues," CGM I, Tokyo, July 11, 1996, p. 2.

50. Agenda Item 3: Aid Coordination Issues, statement by Keat Chhon, CGM II, July 1–2, 1997, p. 3.

51. Interview, May 1998.

52. UNTAC, *Rehabilitation and Development in Cambodia*, p. 31.

53. We would like to thank Martin Godfrey of the Cambodia Development Resource Institute (based in Phnom Penh) for raising this point.

54. Than, "Rehabilitation and Economic Reconstruction in Cambodia," p. 279.

55. Funcinpec emerged as the winner, collecting fifty-eight of the 120 seats in the constituent assembly. The SOC, whose political party was named the Cambodian People's Party, or CPP, received the second largest number of votes with fifty-one seats. The KPNLF was third with ten seats. Another obscure party (Moulinaka) managed to get one. Together they formed a coalition government, which ruled the country.

56. World Bank, *The World Bank's Experience with Post-conflict Reconstruction*, vol. 5, p. 25.

57. Peou, "Cambodia: A New Glimpse of Hope?" pp. 83–103.

58. Peou, "Hun Sen's Preemptive Coup," pp. 86–102.

59. CDC/CRDB, *Development Cooperation Report (1996/97)*, p. 6.

60. Correspondence with Magnus Cedergren, Asia Department, SIDA, Sweden, April 7, 1998.

61. *Cambodian Business,* January 1998, p. 16.

62. Interview, May 1998.

63. Kyle Peters, "Statement on Recent Economic Developments," CGM II, July 1–2, 1997, p. 2.

64. Joint Statement of UN Representatives to Cambodia, CGM II, July 1–2, 1998.

65. ADB's Statement on Macroeconomic Management, CGM II, July 1–2, 1998, p. 2.

66. Peter McCawley's statement, CGM II, July 1–2, 1997, p. 5.

67. See Stanley O. Roth, assistant secretary for East Asian and Pacific Affairs, statement before the House International Relations Committee, Asia and the Pacific Committee, Washington, D.C., February 1998. See also International Republican Institute and National Democratic Institute for International Affairs, *The Continuing Crisis in Cambodia,* p. 4.

68. Interviews, February 1998.

69. UNTAC, *Rehabilitation and Development in Cambodia,* p. 31.

70. Khalid Ikram, "An Approach to the Economic Development of Cambodia," paper presented at the preparatory meeting of the Ministerial Conference on Reconstruction of Cambodia, Tokyo, March 30, 1992, p. 4.

71. We would like to thank Martin Godfrey for raising this point.

72. United Nations, *Report of the United Nations Fact-Finding Mission,* p. 1.

73. Ibid., p. 4.

74. Statement by Anne Bruzelius, UNICEF representative in Cambodia, paper presented at the Preparatory Meeting of the Ministerial Conference on Reconstruction of Cambodia, Tokyo, March 30–31, 1992, p. 1. Khalid Ikram, "An Approach to the Economic Development of Cambodia," paper presented at the Preparatory Meeting of the Ministerial Conference on Reconstruction of Cambodia, Tokyo, March 30–31, 1992, p. 1. Statement by the IMF, paper presented at the Preparatory Meeting of the Ministerial Conference on Reconstruction of Cambodia, Tokyo, March 30–31, 1992.

75. Statement by representative of the ADB, paper presented at the Preparatory Meeting of the Ministerial Conference on Reconstruction of Cambodia, Tokyo, March 30–31, 1992, p. 5.

76. At ICORC II, UNICEF put out a statement indicating that "reliable statistical data for Cambodia as a whole do not exist, due to the weakness of data collection systems," and that "the lack of reliable data on a national scale is the most visible result of the weakness of data collection systems in the social sector." UNICEF, "Summary of UNICEF Program of Cooperation in Cambodia: 1992–1995," p. 2.

77. World Bank, *The World Bank's Experience with Post-conflict Reconstruction,* vol. 5, p. 23.

78. Interview, May 1998.

79. Ibid.

80. Although some expatriates lacked the interpersonal skills to work effectively with local Cambodians, "the expatriates have the greatest advantage of language and generally have been willing to work for concessional remuneration." World Bank, *The World Bank's Experience with Post-conflict Reconstruction,* vol. 5, p. 26.

81. Douglas Grube's comments on an early draft of this paper.

82. Drachman, "The War in Cambodia," pp. 661–695.

83. *The World Bank's Experience with Post-conflict Reconstruction,* vol. 5, p. 23.

84. Ibid., p. 25.

85. Interview, May 1998.

86. Ibid.

87. Ibid.

88. Ibid.

89. Peou, "Hun Sen's Preemptive Coup," pp. 86–102.

90. Although the Bank signed an agreement on a water sanitation project after July 1997, this project had either been previously agreed or was simply based on "special consideration."

91. Interview, May 1998.

92. Japan's Assistance to Cambodia from March 1991 to February 1994, presented at ICORC II, March 10–11, 1994.

93. France's state-centric approach stood in sharp contrast to the "civil society" approach adopted by the United States. Interview with a French diplomat, May 1998.

94. CDC/CRDB, *Development Cooperation Report (1997/98),* p. 19.

95. Interview, May 1998.

96. Ibid.

97. Benson, *The Changing Role of NGOs,* p. 82.

98. UNBRO was established in 1982 to provide material assistance and protection to Cambodian displaced persons and affected Thai villagers at the Thai-Cambodian border.

99. Benson, *The Changing Role of NGOs,* p. 79.

100. UNTAC, *Rehabilitation and Development in Cambodia,* p. 3.

101. Mysliwiec, "Cambodia: NGOs in Transition," p. 113.

102. Information provided by Lt. Col. Chip Bowness of the CMAC, April 2, 1998.

103. Interview, May 1998.

104. Ibid.

105. Intrac, *Differing Approaches to Development Assistance in Cambodia.*

106. Ibid., p. 47.

107. Mysliwiec, "Camboida: NGO in Transition," p. 122.

108. NGO Forum on Cambodia Statement to CGM I, Tokyo, July 11–12, 1996.

109. Peou, "The Cambodian Elections of 1998," pp. 279–297.

110. James K. Boyce and Manuel Pastor have developed the idea of aid for peace. They argue for political conditionality in their advocacy for the need to establish links between aid and peace. See their "Aid for Peace." The crux of the matter is how to achieve peace. As demonstrated by this study, donors were not interested in peace through national reconciliation with the Khmer Rouge. The push for peace through violent means to defeat the rebels and for political stability seemed to perpetuate violence and armed conflict. "Democratic conditionality" may not succeed, however, when the recipient country's power structure remains hegemonic. See Peou, *Foreign Intervention and Anti-Democratic Regimes in Cambodia.* Democratic conditionality may help political leaders in recipient countries to be more aware of the need to make democratic compromises rather than to take violent action to restore peace and stability, often with the aim of monopolizing

power for themselves. Despite the rhetoric about "building democracy" through foreign aid, argues Steven W. Hook, the U.S. aid policy has not given priority to democratic and democratizing states. Security concerns and economic self-interests have been forces stronger than the policy of "building democracy." See Hook, "Building Democracy Through Foreign Aid."

111. For alternative views, see Hewison, Robison, and Rodan, *Southeast Asia in the 1990s,* and Przeworski and Limongi, "Modernization: Theories and Facts," p. 177.

4

El Salvador

Herman Rosa & Michael Foley

EL SALVADOR'S TRANSITION FROM WAR TO PEACE IN THE
1990s, perhaps more sharply than others in this volume, was a "triple transition." It encompassed far-reaching economic reform; the demobilization
and reinsertion into civilian life of both the rebel Farabundo Martí
National Liberation Front (FMLN)[1] and a significant portion of the
nation's security forces; and political reform. The latter process, geared
toward democratization, included the reform of existing institutions and
the creation of new ones as mandated by the 1992 Peace Accords between
the FMLN and the government of El Salvador, led by the right-wing
National Republican Alliance (ARENA)[2] party. The war-to-peace transition also demanded the permanent resettlement of refugees and displaced
persons affected by the war, extensive reconstruction of damaged infrastructure, and the restoration and restructuring of social services in former
conflict zones.

The implementation of the Peace Accords and postwar reconstruction
required significant funding. Yet, with the exception of physical reconstruction needs, the Salvadoran government was slow to recognize both the
extent of its obligations and the level of funding required. The government's overriding commitment to the economic reform model preached by
the Bretton Woods institutions and backed by the United States contributed
to the view that funding for peace and reconstruction should come from
sources other than ordinary government revenue. Indeed, as we will see
below, both the government of El Salvador (GOES) and the World Bank
maintained that the bulk of funding should be sought from international
donors. The international community responded generously to El Salvador's aid requests. We find, in fact, that there was no significant "pledging gap" in the Salvadoran case; on the whole, international donors provided more than they had initially pledged and, in some areas of need,
more than the government requested. Nevertheless, delays in funding, gaps

in the sorts of things the international community was willing to fund, and the government's own reluctance to back certain programs meant that the process was marked by periodic crises and that components key to the Peace Accords, notably the reinsertion of ex-combatants and the deployment of the new National Civilian Police, suffered long and costly delays.

How do we explain the notable successes and significant shortcomings of this process? The El Salvador case differs sharply in two important respects from most of the other cases in this book. First, the economic "transition" was solidly under way before the peace process had yielded significant fruits, putting the Salvadoran government in a strong position vis-à-vis foreign donors and limiting, to some extent, their ability to apply conditionality. Backed by the World Bank, the government was able to resist pressures to increase levels of taxation and managed, though to a lesser degree, to impress its own limited vision on reinsertion programs and the development of a civilian police force. Second, donor response, though at times tardy, eventually matched government estimates of need, at least as these were enunciated at the beginning and end of the process. The lack of significant pledging gaps points to both the considerable willingness of international donors to support the peace process in El Salvador and the reasonableness of demands formulated by the Salvadoran government. But it also suggests that donors were willing to settle for an expeditious end to large-scale monitoring and funding once basic issues had been settled and the electoral process was more or less on track. Economic orthodoxy, meanwhile, and the funding program adopted by the World Bank did little to alleviate poverty in the former conflict zones and much to exacerbate it.

Despite the relative strength of the incumbent administration, the government of El Salvador ended up spending far more for certain programs—particularly democratic institutions and reinsertion programs—and the international community far less for these same programs than initially proposed. Although economic orthodoxy prevailed and few steps were taken to address the grinding poverty that afflicts most of the population affected by the war, the government found the money to meet its fundamental obligations under the terms of the Peace Accords, thanks largely to international scrutiny and pressure from the FMLN and the United Nations Observer Mission in El Salvador (ONUSAL). Thus, despite the failure of the few efforts made to openly apply "peace conditionality"[3] in the pledging and disbursal of funds, the process yielded a relatively successful transition from war to peace and significant steps toward the democratization of Salvadoran politics.

In the following sections we lay out the trends in external funding and economic growth both during and after the war. After reviewing this background, we turn to patterns of funding, reserving for the last section a discussion of the politics of postwar reconstruction, the roles of significant actors in the process, and the impact of international aid on the process.

Trends in External Funding and Economic Growth During and After the War

External funding provided crucial support to the government of El Salvador during the twelve-year civil war; it has also been a key element in the postwar recovery effort. The continuing supply of funding meant that El Salvador approached the war-to-peace transition from a position of economic strength, despite the high cost of the war.

Official funding grew rapidly during the 1980s (see Figure 4.1) and rose again in the first three years of the postwar period (1992–1994).[4] U.S. economic assistance was crucial in sustaining the Salvadoran government throughout the war and played an important role in "front-loading" the postwar reconstruction effort. Whereas the World Bank and the International Monetary Fund (IMF) were largely absent from El Salvador during the 1980s,[5] the United States government disbursed $2.5 billion in direct economic assistance, in addition to considerable military aid. U.S. funding represented 88 percent of total official funding during 1984–1987 and was still 70 percent in 1988–1991 (Table 4.1). In the postwar period of 1992–1995, funding from other sources increased significantly, and the U.S. government's share of total funding dropped to 46 percent. Still, the United States was responsible for 71 percent of all grants, making it the dominant donor until 1995.[6]

The Pattern of Postwar Economic Growth Under Orthodox Economic Reform

Strong growth accounts for much of the Salvadoran government's ability to manage the implementation of the Peace Accords in the 1990s. At the same time, the peculiarities of the pattern of growth have had an impact on the peace process and on the sorts of measures emphasized.

The relative strength of the economy after 1991 is explained in part by economic reforms begun in 1989 but also by the large flow of remittances generated by Salvadorans who had fled the country in the late 1970s and throughout the war.[7] Official funding and significant debt forgiveness,[8] principally on the part of the United States, also contributed to the government's ability to manage the costs of postwar reconstruction. In addition, these years witnessed large inflows of private capital, as confidence returned and the exchange rate risk was almost eliminated when the

Figure 4.1   El Salvador: Trends in Official Funding, 1979–1997
(grants and net loan disbursements in U.S.$ mllions)

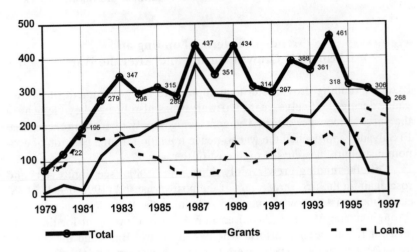

Source: Based on Central Bank data.
Note: Totals are exclusive of military aid.

Table 4.1   El Salvador: Importance of U.S. Government Economic Aid, 1984–1995
(total funding for the period in U.S.$ millions, and percentages)

Economic Aid	1984–1987	1988–1991	1992–1995	1996–1997
Total funding	1,337	1,396	1,528	564
United States	1,174	983	697	83
U.S. funding/total funding	88%	70%	46%	15%
Grants	991	978	925	102
United States	922	839	653	64
U.S. grants/total grants	93%	86%	71%	63%

Source: Based on Central Bank data.
Note: "Economic aid" here includes both grants and loans in the forms of balance of payments (or Economic Support Fund–ESF) assistance, P.L. 480 food aid, and development assistance. The first two released local currency for government use. These figures exclude direct military assistance.

monetary authorities adopted, for all intents and purposes, a fixed exchange rate system.

The resultant foreign exchange abundance provided the context in which economic liberalization was adopted in the 1990s, and it fostered both the relative robustness of the economy and the new pattern of economic growth established in this decade. Indeed, during the 1990s, the Salvadoran economy began to achieve gross domestic product (GDP) growth rates similar to the ones prevailing during the pre-war years of the 1970s (see Figure 4.2). At the same time, the flow of remittances and other sources of foreign exchange put significant pressure on the economy, prompting fears of a "Dutch disease" effect—inflationary pressures resulting from the sudden infusion into an economy of large quantities of fresh capital.

The pattern of economic growth of the 1990s, for just these reasons, has been completely different from the one prevailing before the war. This reflects a major change in the way the economy is functioning and in the sources of its dynamism. As shown in Figure 4.3, from 1994 through 1997, GDP grew at an average yearly rate of 4.6 percent. Yet, the average growth rate of the agricultural sector was only 0.9 percent. In contrast, the financial sector grew at an average rate of 14.6 percent. This pattern of economic growth, which combines the economic dynamism of urban economic activities with a deep crisis in the agricultural sector (and hence in rural areas, where much of the conflict took place), was consolidated during the 1990s as the economy was liberalized.

Another distinguishing aspect of the pattern of growth of the 1990s is the smaller role of the public sector. This reflects both the shrinking and the impoverishment of the state that resulted from an economic reform program that did not include the strengthening of public sector finances on the income side as one of its key components. As a result, the tax ratio of revenue to GDP during the 1990s has been below 12 percent, much lower than in the 1970s and most of the 1980s. Low tax receipts have limited enormously state capacity to respond to many of the demands of postwar reinsertion and reactivation, particularly of the agricultural sector.

Figure 4.2   El Salvador: GDP Growth, 1972–1997 (annual percentage rates)

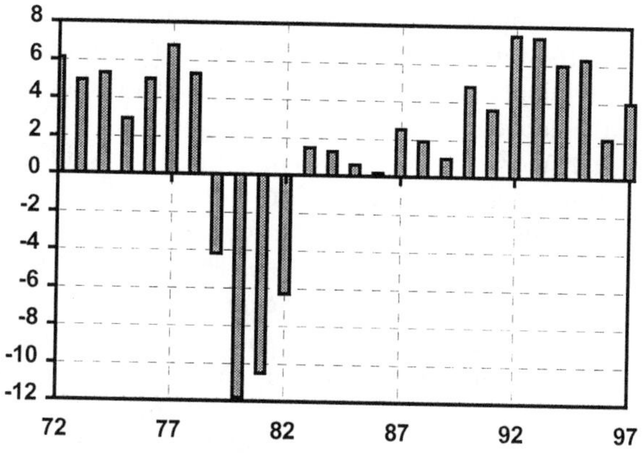

Source: Central Bank.

**Figure 4.3   El Salvador: Sectoral Growth, 1971–1978 Versus 1994–1997
(average annual percentage rates)**

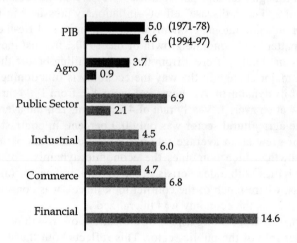

Source: Central Bank.

These results were achieved while the Bretton Woods institutions had become heavily involved in Salvadoran economic reform. A standby agreement with the IMF was approved in August 1990—the first since 1982—and precautionary agreements have been in force almost without interruption since then.[9] The World Bank's first structural adjustment loan (SAL I) was approved in February 1991. With SAL I, economic reform renewed its pace. Import tariffs were lowered further, the banks (nationalized under the reformist military junta in 1980) were privatized, and additional measures to deregulate the economy were taken.

By 1992, the World Bank had assumed the leadership in guiding the economic reform process in El Salvador, with the IMF, the U.S. Agency for International Development (USAID), and the Inter-American Development Bank (IDB) playing a supporting role. The World Bank's portfolio of loans to El Salvador expanded significantly, with twelve loans worth $451.5 million approved between 1991 and 1997.[10] The loan portfolio of the IDB also became quite large, as twenty loans worth almost $1.4 billion were approved during 1990–1997.[11] In contrast to the World Bank portfolio, which had little direct connection with the peace and reconstruction process that got seriously under way in 1992, the IDB portfolio included loans for a Social Investment Fund, education, the environment, and judicial reform. These did address, at least in part, postwar reconstruction needs.

Indeed, some have argued that the World Bank's preoccupation with orthodox economic reform at times came into conflict with the need to raise funds for reconstruction and to develop policies that would further a genuine reinsertion of ex-combatants and affected civilians into a transformed national economy. We generally concur in this assessment. The major omissions have been in the areas of fiscal and agricultural policies. The fiscal policy supported by the World Bank has resulted in a very low tax burden that has limited state capacity. Equally important, the World Bank has been slow to recognize the depth of the crisis in the agricultural sector and to connect that crisis to Bank-supported government policies that reflect a strong antiagricultural bias.

The World Bank's recent review of the El Salvador experience is disingenuous on these points at best.[12] While the synthesis report for the series of case studies includes among Bank programs in support of post-conflict reconstruction such activities as "jump-starting the economy, resettlement and investment in war-affected regions, repair of war-damaged infrastructure, reform of a nonfunctioning or currupt civil service and public administration, and targeted programs for veterans and vulnerable groups,"[13] the El Salvador report treats the economic reform package itself as the Bank's major contribution to postwar reconstruction, ignoring both its costs and limitations and the Bank's absence from most other activities relevant to postwar reconstruction. We discuss these points at greater length below.

Postwar Reconstruction, Reinsertion, and Political Reform

Initial Planning for the Postwar Period and the 1991 Consultative Group Meeting

In contrast to the economic reform process, which had the highest priority for the government and the leading donor (the U.S. government, through USAID), the postwar reconstruction and political reform process that unfolded after the January 1992 Peace Accords caught the government and its sponsors much less prepared. USAID began its own planning for postwar reconstruction early in 1991, but at that time the focus was still on economic reform.

The continuing preoccupation with economic reform, shared by both the Salvadoran government and the World Bank, was apparent at the first Consultative Group (CG) meeting for El Salvador in May 1991. USAID had planned this meeting some two years before, hoping to attract other donors to El Salvador on the basis of what USAID expected would be significant advances on the economic reform front. This was still the prevailing logic during the first CG meeting, held in Paris. Indeed, the chairman, from the World Bank, presented the gathering as primarily "an opportunity for the donor community to learn first-hand about the Government's economic and social program and public investment priorities," and only secondarily as a venue to review the needs of postwar reconstruction. This emphasis accurately reflected the government's presentation as well.[14] With negotiations to end the war advancing by then, the emphasis on successful economic reform did not strike a chord with most bilateral donors. With the exception of the United States, which pledged an aid package in excess of $200 million, donors responded coolly. The government itself requested external support in only general terms, presenting no estimate whatsoever of funding requirements to meet postwar needs. The only specific GOES request was for a $9.1 million technical assistance package that included a request for $1.44 million to prepare the National Reconstruction Plan (NRP).[15]

The NRP began with a very narrow focus, emphasizing the reconstruction of infrastructure. A glaring omission was the NRP's failure to address the needs and costs of strengthening democratic institutions, in accord with agreements already reached between the government and the FMLN in the ongoing peace talks. The only person to mention this issue at the first Consultative Group meeting was the resident representative of the United Nations Development Programme (UNDP) for El Salvador, whose official statement noted that "international technical cooperation would be useful in the Government's efforts to comply with negotiated agreements, to sustain the peace process, and to achieve national reconciliation."[16] However, this suggestion was not even noted in the chairman's report of the meetings proceedings, suggesting the low priority such considerations merited in the eyes of Bank officials.

Defining Funding Priorities for the Postwar Period:
The Formulation of the National Reconstruction Plan

After the rather muted response from donors at the May 1991 CG meeting, the GOES began to work in earnest to develop the NRP, with the help of UNDP and USAID. UNDP funded the National Reconstruction Committee, established within the Ministry of Planning in July 1991 to develop the NRP. In 1991, UNDP also initiated dialogues with the FMLN leadership regarding the NRP. Nevertheless, the FMLN maintained grave doubts about the NRP's priorities and plan of implementation right up through the Consultative Group meeting of 1992, as we shall see below.

USAID began its own planning for the postwar period at this time and supported the formulation of the NRP, commissioning two studies to assess alternative programs for reintegrating ex-combatants into civilian society and needs in the area of infrastructure restoration and reconstruction. In addition, the U.S. Military Group and USAID collaborated in the preparation of an ex-combatant assistance strategy designed to reintegrate soldiers from both sides of the conflict.[17] Both planning efforts seriously underestimated the costs of these programs as well as the amount of time required to implement them, primarily because of two assumptions adopted by USAID in planning its assistance strategy for the NRP: (1) that ex-combatants would be dealt with on an individual basis; and (2) that they should be reintegrated into society as quickly as possible, that is, that they lose their identity as ex-combatants and receive benefits along with others who had suffered from the war. Neither assumption proved feasible given the insistence of the FMLN on a role in the process and established practices of collective decisionmaking and management among many partisans of the rebel forces.

Based on these assumptions, USAID planners initially allocated only $7.5 million for direct assistance to ex-combatants in its $250 million Peace and Recovery project. The proposal was rejected by both the armed forces and the FMLN. USAID responded by increasing the allocation for direct assistance to ex-combatants, which reached $124 million by the beginning of 1996, and by reducing funds for infrastructure and other activities.[18] Nevertheless, the vision that ex-combatants should be provided with only very limited, specifically targeted assistance influenced the NRP's overall design. Thus, the preliminary version of the NRP of September 1991, with total funding requirements of $560 million, allocated only $88 million for direct assistance to ex-combatants. It allocated another $92 million for general programs for a target population of about 700,000 individuals affected by the conflict.[19] On the other hand, this plan allocated $325 million, or 58 percent of the total, for infrastructure.

The government's revised, November 1991 version of the NRP foresaw higher total requirements, of $930 million, but followed the same logic as before.[20] The allocation for infrastructure reached $626 million or 68 percent of the total. As in the first version, there were no provisions for the costs of demobilizing the National Police, for establishing the new National Police Academy and the National Civilian Police, or for other programs related to the democracy-building aspects of the accords. Government estimates for this area were not revealed publicly until the second Consultative Group meeting, in March 1992, when they were presented as part of a supplemental document. Nevertheless, they received prime billing, thanks in large part to pressure exerted by the FMLN, UNDP, and concerned donors.

In fulfillment of a provision of the Peace Accords, the government formally presented the NRP to the FMLN in mid-February 1992.[21] Over the next month, the government and the FMLN held a series of meetings to discuss the NRP, in the presence of representatives of UNDP and the European Community (EC). The FMLN criticized the plan's overemphasis on infrastructure and demanded an expansion of the land program for ex-combatants (mandated by the accords) and more comprehensive reinsertion programs.[22] The FMLN considered these programs indispensable for the successful demobilization of its forces. The FMLN also won an agreement, subsequently left largely unimplemented, to permit greater involvement of nongovernmental organizations (NGOs) in the implementation of the NRP. Although the government and the FMLN reached only partial agreement on the above issues, they did agree to include as part of the NRP a program for strengthening the democratic institutions created by the Peace Accords.

The version of the NRP that the government presented at the March 1992 CG meeting had funding requirements of $1,528 million. The GOES requested donor support for a priority package of projects worth $1,008 million (Table 4.2). Infrastructure was still the big-ticket item in this priority package, absorbing 46 percent of the total, whereas funds allocated to direct assistance to the demobilized and general programs for the target population represented together 25 percent of total requirements. The priority package also included a request for external support for democratic institutions ($228.1 million) and a technical assistance package ($33.9 million).

Reinsertion needs, including funds for purchase of land promised ex-combatants of both sides and civilians identified with the FMLN, agricultural and small enterprise credit, education and training programs, and rehabilitation of the disabled, were still being underestimated at this time. It was only at the next CG meeting in April 1993 that reinsertion needs, together with the needs for democratic institutions, were put in the center of the table. This followed an agreement in late 1992 between the GOES and the FMLN on an acceptable reinsertion package (an accord provoked by a breakdown in the timetable for demobilization and brokered and endorsed by the UN). The reinsertion package, which entailed $316.8 million in spending for the period 1993–1996, was included in the priority program presented to donors in the April 1993 CG meeting (see Table 4.3). The estimated requirements for democratic institutions also increased in this priority program, while infrastructure was moved to the sidelines and excluded from the priority needs.

Pledges and Commitments: The Donor Response

The March 1992 Consultative Group meeting, held sixty-seven days after the signing of the Peace Accords, drew substantial donor response—

Table 4.2   National Reconstruction Program, March 1992 Version, Medium-Term
Phase Estimated Needs for 1992–1996 and Priority Program
(U.S.$ millions)

	Estimated Needs	Priority Program	
Infrastructure	554.9	468.0	46.4%
Specific programs for demobilized	90.6	64.3	6.4%
General programs for target population	380.0	185.7	18.4%
Democratic strengthening programs	392.8	228.1	22.6%
Technical assistance	33.9	33.9	3.4%
Other programs	75.8	27.6	2.7%
Total	1,528.1	1,007.7	100.0%

Source: Author, based on MIPLAN, *National Reconstruction Plan* (1992).

Table 4.3   National Reconstruction Program, April 1993, Revised Needs for
1993–1996 and Priority Program (U.S.$ millions)

	Estimated Needs	Priority Program	
1. Infrastructure	647.9	117.8	9.9%
2. Specific programs for demobilized	342.2	316.8	26.8%
Physical disability rehabilitation	8.9		
Pensions for disabled	8.2	8.2	
Scholarships for demobilized	16.5	0	
Agricultural credit	62.0	62.0	
Microenterprise credit	27.0	27.0	
Housing	77.1	77.1	
Land acquisition	142.5	142.5	
3. General programs for target population	272.4	192.4	16.3%
4. Other programs	30.9		
Total 1–4	1,293.4		
5. Democratic strengthening programs		534.3	45.2%
National Public Security Academy		104.7	
National Civilian Police		173.0	
Human Rights Ombudsman's Office		16.8	
Justice system strengthening		207.8	
National Council of Judiciary and Judicial School		12.0	
Elections tribunal		20.0	
6. Technical assistance		21.5	1.8%
Support for democratic institutions		16.7	
Poverty alleviation including support for the demobilized		3.4	
Support for NGOs, monitoring system, preinvestment		1.4	
Total NRP priority program (1–6)		1,182.8	100.0%

Source: Author, based on MIPLAN, *Consolidating the Peace* (1993).

around $800 million in pledges for the first two years.[23] The United States
made the largest pledge, $250 million. The Japanese representative said that
Japan's contribution would be "comparable to any of the biggest donor
countries," adding that in the first year $100 million could be used as a
guideline.[24] Other large donors included Germany ($30 million for 1992),
Sweden ($30 million over three years), and the European Community ($63

million in the form of grants for 1992, with a similar figure promised for 1993). The IDB offered, in addition to its planned lending program, $150 million in emergency loans to support the NRP. The World Bank pledged $50 million for a second structural adjustment loan (Table 4.4).

Initially, the GOES was enthusiastic about this donor response, which went beyond its own expectations.[25] However, at the next Consultative Group meeting, in April 1993, the government complained that "many pledges made by donors in the last CG meeting have taken a long time to materialize."[26] Indeed, the GOES reported that by February 1993 the grants and loans that donors had committed had reached only $342 million, with another $333 million still under negotiation.[27] Moreover, government estimates of needs had grown, in large part as a result of pressures exerted by the FMLN and ONUSAL to attend to the problem of reinserting ex-combatants. In the GOES report presented at the April 1993 CG meeting, the total estimated funding needs of the NRP for 1993–1996 were

Table 4.4   Pledges at the March 1992 Consultative Group Meeting for El Salvador (U.S.$ millions)

	Amount	Comments
Bilateral	441.8	
United States	250.0	
Japan	100.0	Does not include $5 million in emergency support package.
Germany	30.0	
Sweden	20.0	Amount for 1992–1993; an additional $10 million was pledged for 1994.
Canada	10.0	
Spain	8.0	
Norway	6.0	
Switzerland	6.6	
Other bilateral	11.2	
Multilateral	358.0	
IDB	150.0	Emergency loan program
EC	63.0	Grants
CABEI	77.0	Loans
World Bank	50.0	Loan
IFAD	10.0	Loan
WFP	8.0	Grant
Total	799.8	

Source: Based on MIPLAN, Resumen Promesas (1992).
Notes: When a range was given we took the low figure. Italy is not included because it made no specific pledge.
CABEI: Central American Bank for Economic Integration.
EC: European Community.
IDB: Inter-American Development Book.
IFAD: International Fund for Agricultural Development.
WFP: World Food Programme.

$1,828 million, excluding technical assistance. With expected external funding of $601 million and government commitments of $407 million, the government projected a financing gap of $820 million (Table 4.5).[28]

As seen in Table 4.5, the largest proportion of external funds was directed to infrastructure ($365 million, or 61 percent of the total), leaving large financing gaps in the programs more critical for the peace process. For these programs—namely, democratic institutions and programs for the demobilized—anticipated external funding was only $36 million and $104 million, respectively. The government's own priorities contributed to severe funding gaps, particularly for the training and deployment of the civilian police and the programs for reinsertion among the rural population (land purchase and agricultural credit programs).

These emerging funding gaps, coupled with the government's continuing reluctance to fund programs, like reinsertion and the new civilian police, which the FMLN, the UN, and some donors considered high priorities, gave a sense of urgency to the GOES presentation before the CG meeting of April 1993. The government decided to adopt a new strategy

Table 4.5   National Reconstruction Program, Revised Needs for 1993–1996, Expected Funding and Financing Gap (U.S.$ millions)

	Estimated Needs	GOES Commitments	Expected External Funding	Financing Gap
1. Democratic strengthening programs	534.3	232.7	36.0	265.6
National Public Security Academy	104.7	28.0	9.9	66.8
National Civilian Police	173.0	35.4	6.0	131.6
Human Rights Ombudsman's Office	16.8	6.4	1.1	9.3
Justice system strengthening[a]	219.8	162.3	15.0	42.5
Elections tribunal	20.0	0.6	4.0	15.4
2. Specific programs for demobilized	342.2	28.6	103.9	209.7
Physical disability rehabilitation	8.9	0.5	8.9	–0.5
Pensions for disabled	8.2	0.7		7.5
Scholarships for demobilized	16.5	1.5	15.0	
Agricultural credit	62.0		10.0	52.0
Microenterprise credit	27.0		10.0	17.0
Housing	77.1	2.6	12.5	62.0
Land acquisition	142.5	23.3	47.5	71.7
Subtotal (1+2)	876.5	261.3	139.9	475.3
3. Infrastructure	647.9	83.1	365.1	199.7
4. General programs for target population	272.4	59.1	95.7	117.6
5. Other programs	30.9	3.3	0.0	27.6
Subtotal (3+4+5)	951.2	145.5	460.8	344.9
Total (1–5)	1,827.7	406.8	600.7	820.2

Source: Author, based on MIPLAN, *Consolidating the Peace* (1993), annex 3.
Note: a. Includes National Council of Judiciary and Judicial School.

at that meeting, requesting that donor assistance be channeled through fast-disbursing vehicles, such as the upcoming World Bank's second structural adjustment loan (SAL II). The government rationale was that previous pledges were taking too long to materialize, that earmarking of external funding gave the government little flexibility to reassign resources to priority areas, and that it faced tight fiscal constraints.[29] The World Bank strongly supported the government stand and proposal.

The Nordic Statement, presented on behalf of Denmark, Finland, Norway, and Sweden, tackled head on this request for fast-disbursing aid. Responding to the suggestion that cofinancing of SAL II would expedite the funding process, the Nordic countries replied that the primary purpose of aid was to support peace and reconciliation and that this "should have some implications on the structure and conditions related to structural adjustment loans." Yet, SAL II, as it was then being considered, bypassed "some of the most critical issues related to the peace process."[30] The Nordic Statement went on to request that the World Bank include loan conditionality in the upcoming SAL II to guarantee (1) that additional external and internal funds would be set aside to finance what was agreed in the Peace Accords, such as transfer of land and the construction of democratic institutions; (2) that the modernization of the public sector would include efforts to find an appropriate role for the military in a modern, democratic, and peaceful society; and (3) that extraordinary efforts would be undertaken to increase tax revenues within El Salvador. A separate Swedish Statement reiterated these points and noted that Sweden would consider cofinancing SAL II only if these issues were clearly addressed. In this case, funds for the SAL loan would come over and above funds already committed to El Salvador.[31]

In the end, none of these issues were taken up in the $50 million SAL program approved by the World Bank in September 1993, thus confirming a scheme in which economic and political reform would continue on separate tracks. On the one hand, the GOES preferred the greater "flexibility" provided by an unencumbered balance of payments support package. On the other hand, the World Bank had its own, strictly economic, "triggers" and conditions governing disbursement of structural adjustment funds. Neither the GOES nor the World Bank, accordingly, proved amenable to the demand for peace conditionality emanating from the Nordic countries. Germany was the only donor to respond to the GOES request, providing $12.5 (DM 20 million) in cofinancing for SAL II. Apart from this support (which was not pledged until after the meeting), the GOES–World Bank strategy backfired: no new pledges were forthcoming at the April 1993 CG meeting. Instead, donors simply reaffirmed previous pledges.[32] Nevertheless, the gap between funds committed by donors and pledges narrowed over time, so that by May 1994, amounts already committed ($793 million) approximated the $800 million pledged in 1992 (see Table 4.6).

Table 4.6   External Funding Approved by Donors for the NRP, 1993–1995
(U.S.$ millions)

	Feb. 1993	May 1993	Aug. 1993	Sept. 1993	May 1994	July 1995
Grants	321.9	337.3	340.5	367.4	432.3	517.4
Investment projects		264.4	266.0	291.0	330.3	376.2
Democratic institutions		51.5	52.8	54.7	58.2	54.9
Technical cooperation		21.4	21.7	21.7	43.8	86.3
Loans for investment projects	20.5	126.6	265.3	265.3	360.8	442.5
Total grants and loans	342.4	463.9	605.8	632.7	793.1	960.0

Source: MIPLAN, *Financiamiento Contratado,* February 1993; May 1993; August 1993; September 1993; May 1994; July 1995.

Note: Funding for "democratic institutions" decreases from May 1994 to July 1995 because until May 1994 this rubric erroneously includes some reinsertion programs. In the July 1995 report, these programs move to "technical cooperation."

A UN summary report presents similar figures: at the beginning of 1994, pledges of assistance amounted to $994.3 million, including pledges made before the completion of the NRP.[33] By July 1995, as Table 4.6 shows, $960 million had already been committed and negotiated with donors. If we include funding under negotiation, total NRP external funding as of July 1995 reaches $1,010 million, or just over the $1,008 million requested at the 1992 CG meeting, and substantially more than the roughly $800 million pledged at that time. In brief, *no gap between pledges and commitments is apparent in this case, taking the pledges of the international community as a whole.*

Table 4.7, with the breakdown by donor, shows that by July 1995 most donors had committed funds beyond their 1992 pledges. The four biggest donors—the United States, Japan, the IDB, and the European Community—accounted for 81 percent of total funding reported for the NRP. The United States, the biggest donor overall, also provided the largest amount of grant aid. In contrast, Japan, the second biggest donor overall, provided most of its aid as loans. The European Community, the fourth largest donor overall, provided all of its aid in the form of grants, triple the level provided by Japan. The IDB, as a multilateral bank, provided all of its aid in the form of loans.

This table greatly underreports the contribution of the Nordic countries, which channeled most of their aid through NGOs and UNDP. According to the UN, during 1992–1996 the Nordics contributed $26 million; Japan $207 million; the European Union $196 million; the IDB $167 million; Germany $29 million; and Spain $17 million. The United States approved $276 million for reconstruction and the strengthening of democratic institutions.[34] Taking the 1992 pledges as a baseline, whether we rely on the government's own figures or those of the United Nations, it appears that *there were no pledging gaps at the individual donor level.*[35]

Table 4.7   NRP External Funding Approved by Donors and Under Negotiation as Reported by the Government of El Salvador, July 1995 (U.S.$ millions)

Donor/Creditor	March 1992 Pledge	Grants Approved	Loans Approved	Total	% of Total	Under Negotiation
United States	250.0	256.5	7.2	263.7	27	
Japan	100.0	34.8	175.3	210.1	22	8.8
IDB	150.0		204.9	204.9	21	
European Community	63.0	103.7		103.7	11	
Germany	30.0	13.7	22.1	35.8	4	8.0
China (Taiwan)		30.0		30.0	3	
Canada	10.0	21.9		21.9	2	
CABEI	77.0		20.0	20.0	2	
Spain	8.0	14.8		14.8	1.5	18.7
IFAD	10.0		13.0	13.0	1	0.5
UNDP		11.0		11.0	1	0.1
WFP	8.0	9.2		9.2	1	
Switzerland	6.6	7.2		7.2	<1	
Sweden (three years)	30.0	4.5		4.5	<1	
Norway	6.0	3.5		3.5	<1	1.1
Other bilateral	11.2	6.8		6.8	<1	12.9
World Bank	50.0					
FAO						0.3
Total	809.8	517.4	442.5	960.0	100	

Source: MIPLAN, *Financiamiento Contratado* (1995a).
Note: World bank loans are not included in GOES reports on funding for NRP.
CABEI: Central American Bank for Economic Integration.
FAO: Food and Agriculture Organization.
IDB: Inter-American Development Bank.
IFAD: International Fund for Agricultural Development.
UNDP: United Nations Development Programme.
WFP: World Food Programme.

Funding Priorities

For the final CG meeting, held in Paris in June 1995, the GOES prepared tables on external and government funding by NRP program to March 1995. These tables were later updated to April 1996 and presented in a government report on compliance with the Peace Accords.[36] When combined with the tables on commitments and expected funding presented at the 1993 CG meeting, these figures on actual funding give a fairly clear picture (despite some inconsistencies) of the evolution of donor and government priorities.

Funding for Democratic Institutions and Reinsertion

External funding for democratic institutions was quite low, only $57 million by March 1995. Given this meager donor response, the government increased significantly its overall funding for this area. At the same time, the GOES concentrated its efforts on the public security system (police academy and national civilian police). As shown in Table 4.8, Salvadoran funding for public security increased from commitments of $64 million in 1993 to $189 million by March 1995, a threefold increase, and to $373 million by April 1996.[37] Other areas under this general rubric showed small financing gaps, with the government providing overall 89 percent of financing. External donors also concentrated most of their funding for democratic institutions on the new public security system, though to a lesser extent than the government. By April 1996, public security had absorbed $42 million of external funds, or 52 percent of total external contributions for democratic institutions.

In the area of reinsertion of ex-combatants,[38] one of the most difficult and critical challenges in the war-to-peace transition, the willingness of some donors to increase their funding played a critical role. By March 1995, actual external funding was $238 million, more than double the amount expected in 1993. The government also increased its funding from a very low 1993 commitment of $29 million to $119 million in 1995; most of this increase covered indemnity payments to demobilized members of the army and former security bodies, which donors had declined to finance. The government also increased its funding for agricultural credit and programs for the war-disabled (Table 4.8).

Despite this upward trend, the government reported a significant funding gap in reinsertion programs up to the formal end of the war-to-peace transition in 1995. The government was reluctant to fill this gap itself, as was apparent in the June 1995 CG meeting, held two months after a UN-brokered agreement between the government and the FMLN designed to extend the deadline for completing the Peace Accords to October 1995. At this meeting, the GOES requested modest and highly targeted financial support of $118 million to cover a "financing gap" in reinsertion programs, along with $10 million in technical assistance for reinsertion and democratic institutions. Remarkably, GOES estimates of final needs for other programs were reduced with respect to the figures presented in 1993 and represented as basically fulfilled (see discussion below).

The GOES report warned donors: "Where pledges fall short of these requirements, the Government would be forced to cut back or eliminate some programs, risking a breakdown in the peace process."[39] Apparently, donors did not respond to this warning: as of April 1996, reported external funding was just $2 million higher than the March 1995 figure (see Table 4.8). By contrast, the government reported that its own funding had increased by almost $20 million, although the GOES did not specify which of the programs benefited. In addition, the 1996 government report mentions that the GOES intended to spend an additional $86 million during 1996–1997.[40] The research team was unable to determine whether this

Table 4.8 External Funding for Democratic Institutions and Reinsertion, 1993, 1995, 1996 (U.S.$ millions)

	Estimated Needs 1993–1996	External Funding			Government Funding		
		Expected CG 1993	Actual March 1995	Actual April 1996	Commitments CG 1993	Actual March 1995	Actual April 1996
Democratic institutions	534.3	36.0	58.7	80.5	232.7	343.4	673.3
National Public Security Academy	104.7	9.9	18.2	16.3	28.0	41.4	57.4
National Civilian Police	173.0	6.0	6.8	25.5	35.4	147.4	373.4
Justice system strengthening	219.8	15.0	14.9	15.8	162.3	102.8	196.5
Elections tribunal	20.0	4.0	11.6	14.9	0.6	1.2	1.2
Human Rights Ombudsman's Office	16.8	1.1	1.7	2.4	6.4	7.9	11.3
Legislative body strengthening			1.3	1.3		2.1	2.9
COPAZ[a]		n.r.[b]	1.5	1.5		1.4	n.r.
Truth Commission		n.r.	2.2	2.2		0.0	0.0
Ad Hoc Commission		n.r.	0.6	0.6		0.0	0.0
Other[c]						39.2	n.r.
Programs for demobilized	342.2	103.9	237.9	239.6	28.6	118.9	138.4
Programs for war-disabled	17.1	8.9	9.6		1.2	11.1	
Scholarships for demobilized	16.5	15.0	18.7		1.5		
Agricultural credit	62.0	10.0	10.3			20.0	
Microenterprise credit	27.0	10.0	8.1				
Housing	77.1	12.5	18.1		2.6		
Land acquisition	142.5	47.5	91.2		23.3	30.0	
General attention			32.3				
Vocational/administrative training			10.5				
Agricultural training/technical assistance			7.0			0.6	
Reinsertion/enterprise development			6.5				
Production/housing support (Usulután)			20.6			4.9	
FMLN leaders/middle cadres program			5.0			3.4	
Indemnization to demobilized from army and former security bodies						48.9	

Source: Author, based on MIPLAN, *Consolidating the Peace*; MIPLAN, *Financing Needs*; and GOES, *Los Acuerdos de Paz.*
Notes: a. COPAZ was the multipartisan National Commission for the Consolidation of Peace, established to oversee implementatin of the accords. COPAZ, the Ad Hoc Commission (to purge the armed forces), and the Truth Commission were all mandated by the Peace Accords, as were the Human Rights Ombudsman's Office and the new National Civilian Police.
b. Active program at the time but not reported.
c. General attorney's office (fiscalía general), general ombudsman (procuraduría general), general attorney (procuraduría general), state intelligence body, vice-ministry of public security, and financial support to peace agreement bodies.

additional funding was forthcoming; had it been allocated, it would have taken government funding for democratic institutions and reinsertion to $224 million.

Table 4.9 gives the breakdown of external funding for democratic institutions by donor as of March 1995. Note that the United States is by far the biggest donor, providing 69 percent of funding. Most U.S. aid was divided among public security, judicial sector reform, and support for the elections tribunal. Spain, in contrast, concentrated its contributions almost exclusively in public security. Although the Nordic countries provided only 11 percent of external funding for democratic institutions, they financed the highly sensitive Ad Hoc Commission in charge of purging the army and, together with the United States, provided most of the financing for the Truth Commission. All of the external funding for democratic institutions took the form of grants.

The breakdown by donor for the area of reinsertion (Table 4.10, p. 133) shows that the three biggest donors provided 88 percent of external funding. Again, the United States was the dominant actor, providing 57 percent of total external funding, followed by the European Union (EU) with 20 percent and Germany with 11 percent. The United States and Germany provided some of their funding in the form of loans; nevertheless, loans account for only 15 percent of the external funding provided for this area.

Table 4.9   External Funding for Democratic Institutions, Breakdown by Donor as of March 1995 (U.S.$ millions)

	United States	Spain	Nordic Countries[a]	European Union	Other Bilateral	UNDP	Total
As of March 1995	40.3	5.8	6.6	2.8	2.8	0.4	58.7
National Public Security Academy	10.0	5.7	1.2	1.3			18.2
National Civilian Police	6.0		0.7				6.7
Justice system strengthening	14.9						14.9
Elections tribunal	7.3		2.7		1.5	0.1	11.6
Human Rights Ombudsman[b]		0.1		0.7	0.7	0.2	1.7
Legislative body strengthening	1.1			0.2			1.3
COPAZ[c]			0.4	0.4	0.6	0.1	1.5
Truth Commission	1.0		1.0	0.2			2.2
Ad Hoc Commission			0.6				0.6

Source: MIPLAN, *Financiamiento Contratado* (July 1995); MIPLAN, *Financing Needs.*
Notes: a. Sweden, Norway, and Denmark.
   b. The $4.2 million total for Human Rights Ombudsman as of July 1995 derived from this table exceeds by nearly $2 million the total external funding by April 1996 under this rubric in the preceding table. The April 1996 figure is most likely the erroneous one.
   c. National Commission for the Consolidation of Peace.

Funding for Infrastructure

Of all categories, infrastructure had the highest priority for the government. Some donors responded to El Salvador's requests in a substantial fashion, especially in support of the rehabilitation and expansion of the electrical energy system, which absorbed slightly more than half of the external funding for this area by March 1995. The size of external funding for infrastructure relative to other categories is worth noting. Taking the March 1995 figure as a reference, we find that the international community provided more than five times the funding for infrastructure than they contributed to building and strengthening democratic institutions, and close to twice what they devoted to the reinsertion of ex-combatants (see Table 4.11). There are several likely reasons for this pattern, including the reluctance of some governments to fund public security measures, unfamiliarity with the new "peace-building" projects, and existing donor capacity to generate large and small infrastructure projects under the traditional rubric of "development."

Nevertheless, the breakdown by donor for March 1995 reveals considerable variation among donors in their eagerness to fund infrastructure projects (see Table 4.12). Japan was the leading funder in this area, followed by the IDB, then the United States. Ninety-five percent of Japan's support for infrastructure projects and 100 percent of the IDB's was in the form of loans, whereas U.S. aid was basically in the form of grants. Interestingly, most of the donors who played a major role in funding democratic institutions and reinsertion programs are absent here. Moreover, the United States' $52 million contribution under this rubric constituted just 38 percent of its spending on programs for the demobilized, and it was only one-sixth of its total $300 million contribution to the peace and reconstruction process. Japan, on the other hand, apart from a small contribution for the emergency phase of the NRP, played no role in funding Peace Accords–related programs, concentrating the overwhelming bulk of its financing in infrastructure projects. For the IDB, similarly, infrastructure funding represented some 70 percent of its contribution to postwar reconstruction. At the individual donor level, then, *international financing for infrastructure was a low priority for the vast majority of donors but a major component of funding for a few, large contributors.*

Funding Patterns, Processes, and Key Actors

As we have seen, no significant pledging gap appeared in the case of El Salvador. Indeed, the international community more than fulfilled the pledges made at the first post–civil war Consultative Group meeting, as well as at subsequent meetings. Nevertheless, significant funding gaps

Table 4.10 External Funding for Programs for Demobilization, Breakdown by Donor, March 1995 (U.S.$ millions)

	United States	European Union	Germany	Taiwan	Nordic Countries[a]	UNDP	Other[b]	Total
Programs for demobilized	135.7	47.4	25.8	15.0	4.9	6.0	3.1	237.9
Programs for war-disabled	5.7	3.7					0.2	9.6
Scholarships for demobilized	13.2		5.5					18.7
Agricultural credit	10.3							10.3
Microenterprise credit	8.1							8.1
Housing	1.1		13.8		2.2		1.0	18.1
Land acquisition	64.8	11.4		15.0				91.2
General attention	13.3	11.7			2.7	2.7	1.9	32.3
Vocational/administrative training	10.5							10.5
Agricultural training/technical assistance	3.7					3.3		7.0
Reinsertion/enterprise development			6.5					6.5
Production/housing support (Usulután)		20.6						20.6
FMLN leaders/middle cadres program	5.0							5.0
Grants	119.5	47.4	20.3		4.9	6.0	3.1	201.2
Loans	16.2		5.5	15.0				36.7

Source: MIPLAN, *Financing Needs.*
Notes: a. Sweden ($1.7 million), Norway ($2.6 million) and Denmark ($0.6 million).
b. Japan ($1.0 million), Switzerland ($1.0 million), Holland ($0.5 million), Canada ($0.4 million), France ($0.2 million).

Table 4.11 External and Domestic Government Funding for the National Reconstruction Program, 1993, 1995 and 1996 (U.S.$ millions)

	Estimated Needs 1993–1996	External Funding			Government Funding		
		Expected CG 1993	Actual March 1995	Actual April 1996	Commitments CG 1993	Actual March 1995	Actual April 1996
Democratic institutions	534.3	36.0	56.8	80.5	232.7	343.4	673.3
Programs for demobilized	342.2	103.9	237.6	239.6	28.6	118.9	138.4
Infrastructure	647.9	365.1	422.5	315.8	83.1	0.0	126.7
Programs for target population	272.4	95.7	97.2	523.1	59.1	19.0	26.0
Other programs	30.9	0.0	112.1	i11.1	3.3	144.7	144.7
Total	1,827.7	600.7	926.2	1,269.5	406.8	626.0	1,109.1

Source: Author, based on MIPLAN, *Consolidating the Peace*; MIPLAN, *Financing Needs*; GOES, *Los Acuerdos de Paz*.

Table 4.12 External Funding for Infrastructure, Breakdown by Donor, March 1995 (U.S.$ millions)

	Japan	IDB	United States	CABEI	Other	Total
Infrastructure	204.1	144.1	52.1	19.9	2.3	422.5
Electrical system rehabilitation	70.1	125.2	1.4	19.9		216.6
Major bridges reconstruction	94.6					94.6
Water and sanitation	28.5	18.9			0.4	47.8
Basic social infrastructure	10.9		39.6			50.5
Public service improvement			5.5			5.5
Rural roads			4.6			4.6
Other			1.0		1.9	2.9
Grants	10.9		51.0		2.3	64.2
Loans	193.2	144.1	1.1	19.9		358.3

Source: MIPLAN, *Financing Needs*.
Notes: CABEI: Central American Bank for Economic Integration.
IDB: Inter-American Development Bank.

appeared during the course of the peace process. Most of these were resolved by significant increases in the commitments of the Salvadoran government itself. Remarkably, as we have seen, the government saw itself forced to increase spending in precisely those programs where it had most counted on external funding: reinsertion and democratic institutions.[41] Why this was so—and why the international community did not fund more vigorously those programs most favored by the rhetoric of postwar transition and democratization—is a puzzle we pursue in the analysis that follows. Though no clear answer emerges, the discussion illustrates some of the pitfalls that can accompany external funding in transitional societies and some of the differences that may divide, and at times discourage, donors.

The Godfathers:
The Role of the United States and the World Bank

As foreseen by USAID in 1989, the World Bank played host to efforts to raise additional funds for El Salvador from the international community during the first Consultative Group, held in Paris in May 1991. Throughout that meeting, the Bank praised the government's economic program and endorsed the GOES position that the expenses for postwar reconstruction should be borne by the international community, so that the already-established goals and methods of the economic stabilization and structural adjustment program would not be jeopardized. As we suggested at the outset, the World Bank's own funding priorities continued to stress economic and administrative reform, with little in the way of direct support for peace and reconstruction-related spending, and they appeared to take little account of the special circumstances and special demands generated by the war-to-peace transition.[42]

In the three subsequent Consultative Group meetings, World Bank representatives, seconded by the IMF, continued to stress their confidence in the government's overall economic program, the progress on reforms undertaken in that context, and the necessity for external financing to cover costs derived from the Peace Accords. At no time did the World Bank question the government's contention that it lacked the ability to meet a larger share of the financing demands, condition World Bank lending on government compliance with any aspect of the Peace Accords, or take into account in any significant way the special circumstances generated by the peace process in pursuing its program of economic and policy reform.[43] The Bank clung to this stance despite significant pressure from some member countries, the Nordics in particular, to push the government to increase tax revenues and to take Peace Accords–related obligations into account in formulating loan packages. The World Bank's behavior in the case of the Guatemalan accords provides a useful counterpoint to this record.[44] Our research, accordingly, supports the contention of Alvaro de Soto and Graciana del Castillo that the internationally supported peace process and the work of the international financial institutions directed toward economic and state reform were essentially on "two tracks," with the World Bank in particular giving little consideration to the impact of its policies on the peace process.[45]

The United States had assumed the role of sponsor of the Salvadoran government in its relations with the international financial institutions and the international community generally well before the onset of the peace process. The United States continued to play a leading role through much of the postwar reconstruction process. In the course of 1991, for example, USAID provided the government with significant help in preparing the National Reconstruction Plan.[46] As the GOES considered the design of an agency for implementing the National Reconstruction Plan, USAID supported a proposal to use an institution already developed for the counterinsurgency program, the National Commission for the Restoration of Areas (CONARA), and its linked Municipalities in Action program. Because of its counterinsurgency connections, the GOES abolished CONARA and replaced it with the Secretariat for National Reconstruction (SRN), which simply incorporated the former agency's personnel and equipment under the new name.[47] This naturally failed to appease critics, including potential donors in the European Community. For the first two years of its existence, the SRN was supported almost wholly by U.S. funding.

In other areas, too, the United States faced an international community that was unable to provide sufficient levels of funding quickly enough, or was reluctant to fund aspects of the accords that Washington regarded as crucial. The U.S. government initially provided some 90 percent of the start-up costs for the new National Civilian Police. Spain and the Scandinavian countries eventually provided additional funding, reducing the U.S. share to 45 percent. In the case of the National Police Academy, similarly, the United States was an important donor, alone accounting for 55 percent of the total. Both donor wariness over funding policing programs and concerns about the government's seriousness in implementing reform in this area held back other donors.[48]

In the area of judicial reform, even more pronouncedly, the United States (which had carried on largely fruitless efforts in this respect before the war's end) shouldered the bulk of the burden, eventually providing some $17.9 million of a $20.5 million program.[49] But the United States did not support financially the Human Rights Ombudsman's Office or the Ad Hoc Commission (to purge the armed forces); funding for these efforts was carried largely by the Scandinavian countries and the EU, with a few others.

In the area of programs for the demobilized, the United States provided the bulk of the funding for the land transfer program, some $64.8 million out of a total of $91.2 committed as of March 1995, or 71 percent, according to government figures. By August 1996, USAID had committed almost one and a half times its original budget for land transfer, in part because of increases in land prices as the program dragged on and in part because other donors, with the exception of the EU, did not join the effort.[50]

In many of these cases, the United States' enormous, early presence in the country allowed USAID to mobilize funds rapidly, while awaiting support from other donors. Indeed, USAID's stated intention was to "front-load" the funding process, drawing on existing resources and programs and programming new money, in anticipation that other donors would eventually join the effort. In at least one case, however, significant new U.S. funding resulted from a congressional initiative. In the drive to register voters and ready the electoral mechanisms for the historic 1994 elections—the first time in Salvadoran history that a full spectrum of parties would present candidates in simultaneous presidential, legislative, and municipal elections—NGO and opposition party complaints that the electoral tribunal in charge of preparations was dragging its feet prompted the U.S. Congress to intervene with fresh funds to meet deadlines and involve civil society in the process.

Finally, the United States played a significant role in conditioning aid disbursements on compliance with specific requirements (not always tied to postconflict reconstruction) and in earmarking funds for specified projects. In a clear case of "political conditionality," the United States briefly threatened to withhold military aid if the Salvadoran High Command did not resign as the Truth Commission had recommended.[51] Moreover, in practice, U.S. approval for the disbursement of local currency funds regularly involved informal conditionality, according to one highly placed USAID official. Furthermore, the earmarking of funds for purposes like land purchases was often greeted with dismay by Salvadoran officials, who desired the sort of "flexibility" that the cofinancing arrangement proposed for SAL II had been designed to give them.[52] In this respect, USAID policy contrasts favorably with that of the World Bank where "peace conditionality" is concerned.[53]

Despite the advantages of the U.S. presence, the preponderance of U.S. funding in the process of national reconstruction and the "double transition" to peace and a democratic system appear to have had contradictory impacts on other actors. The high priority the United States gave to the government's program of economic liberalization, like similar support on the part of the World Bank and IMF, reinforced the Salvadoran authorities' refusal to negotiate on the economic framework or to adopt policies at variance with prevailing economic orthodoxy in dealing with postwar reconstruction. It also strengthened the GOES' determination to seek funding for Peace Accords–related programs from international donors.

For example, although USAID planners noted that funding gaps persisted for the National Civilian Police, land transfers, assistance to ex-combatants, and the implementation of democratic reforms, its 1993 Economic Support Fund program for El Salvador focused aid conditionality on economic and administrative reform measures; AID set just three conditions under the rubric of "strengthening democratic institutions, including specific measures on judicial reform, the electoral tribunal, and a new labor code" (the last the result of pressures from U.S. labor unions and their congressional supporters).[54]

Similarly, although the same USAID report notes the need for donor coordination, U.S. support for the Salvadoran government position on a number of disputed issues surrounding implementation of the NRP—coupled with USAID distrust of the capacity of the UNDP to coordinate and administer programs—proved an obstacle to such coordination. Indeed, many donors initially supported the idea of a UNDP or multilateral donor-administered fund to implement the NRP.[55] Moreover, some donors reportedly decided to leave to the United States "highly visible and politically risky projects, such as public security and land redistribution."[56] In this light, we would risk the hypothesis that U.S. "front-loading" of financing for the NRP forestalled politically embarrassing or economically unacceptable conditionality on the part of other donors. At the same time, the U.S. presence reduced the likelihood that other members of the international community would come forward to fund crucial aspects of the peace and reconstruction process. A look at key policy disputes in the course of the peace and reconstruction process tends to support this hypothesis.

Implementation: The Struggle to Control Postwar Reconstruction

The Peace Accords provided for FMLN participation and that of "other sectors of the nation" in the development of the National Reconstruction Plan. After the FMLN lodged complaints with UNDP about noncompliance with these agreements, FMLN representatives were invited to meet with government representatives, starting on February 14, 1992, to discuss the GOES draft document. When talks broke down, however, the government finalized its plan without significant concessions to the FMLN or its associated NGOs. Although later talks narrowed differences between the two sides, the initial disagreements, publicized by NGOs and solidarity groups sympathetic to the FMLN, sparked concerns among some donors.

In particular, the FMLN and its supporters argued that NGOs (most, but not all, of which had been linked to the FMLN) had had long experience in the former conflict zones that were the chief target of the reconstruction program. Accordingly, they should be given not only a major implementing role, but also some voice in decisionmaking on aid to these areas of the country and to the portion of the population tied to the FMLN. The government rejected this position, which it saw as an attempt to fortify the political power of the FMLN in the countryside. The GOES was seconded by USAID, the bulk of whose personnel consisted until 1994 of carryovers from the period of the war and who continued to regard the FMLN and the civilian organizations associated with it from a counterinsurgency perspective.[57]

Other donors, many of which had supported the NGOs in question either directly or indirectly during the war, shared the FMLN position to one degree or another. Such concerns, together with doubts about the government's capacity and honesty in administering funds, played a role in another major controversy about mechanisms for the administration of funds. As noted above, the United States supported the government's decision to channel funds for the NRP through the Secretariat for National Reconstruction, formerly CONARA, a counterinsurgency development agency. The FMLN, quietly supported by some donors and the UNDP, insisted that the accords called for the UNDP to carry out this role.[58]

While the governments of El Salvador and the United States insisted that the UNDP role should be strictly complementary and that the FMLN could not, under Salvadoran law, play a decisionmaking role without provoking an unprecedented situation of "cogovernment," UNDP officials attempted to provide forums for "concertation" among the GOES, FMLN, and NGOs in the further development and implementation of the NRP. UNDP officials and European states, moreover, noted that donors had funded projects outside government channels for years; some donors worried about the ability of the government to manage funds transparently.[59] In the end, many donors found alternative channels for funding, but an important opportunity for coordination was lost, as was perhaps a certain level of donor willingness to fund programs over which they would have no control.

In fact, certain donors, notably the Netherlands, Norway, Sweden, Canada, and Spain, apparently preferred to channel funding outside the government. A rough estimate, based on the UNDP's 1997 report on external assistance for El Salvador, suggests that Canada, the Netherlands, Norway, and Sweden channeled between 60 and 75 percent of their funding through NGOs, their own agencies, or multilateral projects; in contrast, the United States, the European Union, and Germany delivered only about 10 percent of their funding through such outlets, channeling the rest directly through the Salvadoran government.[60] Differences in the overall size of donor contributions no doubt contributed to this division, since there were undoubtedly limits to the absorptive capacity of NGOs and UN agencies carrying out projects in El Salvador. Nevertheless, it is striking that some of the very donors that had been most critical of the government's conduct, both during the war and in the postwar peace and reconstruction process, chose so consistently to fund through alternative channels.

Some donors, the United States included, at times sought close control over certain projects. When it appeared impossible to achieve U.S. objectives through a given Salvadoran government agency, the United States occasionally contracted out projects with large U.S. consulting firms or NGOs that could meet rigid U.S. government accounting requirements.[61] Likewise, the European Union managed its own program for the support of ex-combatants in the department of Usulután, winning USAID cooperation in wrapping up land titling issues, setting conditions for access to land, and launching an ambitious program for the recovery of salt flats, coffee plantings, and agricultural lands in the hands of resettled ex-combatants and civilians in the area. Even before the initiation of reconstruction, Italy had supported the Programme for Displaced Persons, Refugees and Returnees (PRODERE), the UNDP's program of development support for refugees, repatriate communities, and other residents of the conflictive zones.

Caught in the Middle:
The Role of the United Nations Development Programme

The UNDP played an important role in programs for the demobilized and democratic institutions and support for reconstruction and development efforts in the former conflict zones. It both mobilized funding and channeled it either directly to the government or into programs that UNDP administered. Following its work with the government (and NGOs) on the NRP, the UNDP coordinated the emergency program for the demobilization of the FMLN, from March through November 1992.[62]

The UNDP also coordinated talks between the government and the FMLN to settle the issue of training for FMLN ex-combatants, which was needed to facilitate their effective reinsertion into civilian life. Subsequently, the agency directed an emergency agricultural training program for ex-combatants put into place when it became evident that demobilized ex-combatants who had chosen to accept a parcel would have no source of income during the several months after demobilization because planting season had passed.[63] The UNDP coordinated all three of the training programs designed for ex-combatants of the FMLN.[64] Each component was to be accompanied by appropriate credit programs, whose design and implementation, however, were left in the hands of the government.

The UNDP had played a central role before the war's end in working with refugee populations in and around the conflict zones and with the NGOs that served them. Through the International Conference on Central American Refugees (CIREFCA), UNDP began promoting negotiations on repatriation and resettlement between the reluctant government of El Salvador and Salvadoran NGOs and refugees' organizations, in order to facilitate the return of refugees and to ensure the survival of their communities. With the end of the war, UNDP continued to press for concerted action between the government and NGOs. Nevertheless, UN efforts were little rewarded, as the government continued a policy of stalling legal recognition, refusing project proposals, and avoiding discussions with "opposition" NGOs through much of the reconstruction period. Conflict on the issue came to a head early in the process, in February 1992, when a UNDP-directed interagency mission of fifty United Nations experts was rebuffed by President Cristiani himself when it attempted to reconcile NGO reconstruction proposals with the emerging NRP.[65]

Despite these conflicts, UNDP continued to provide technical assistance to the government in the development of the National Reconstruction Plan, preparations for successive Consultative Group meetings, and the deployment of SRN resources. In addition, UNDP worked with governmental, multilateral, and nongovernmental agencies to support the integration of repatriated communities within the CIREFCA framework, and it provided technical support for the International Fund for Agricultural Development (IFAD) in the development of a major multilateral development project (PROCHALETE) for the department of Chalatenango. The PRODERE program, also focused largely in former conflict zones, continued under UNDP auspices, with $17.6 million in funding from Italy. Finally, UNDP was a key channel for international support for the Human Rights Ombudsman's Office, the National Council of the Judiciary, the Judicial Training School, the National Public Security Academy, and the Supreme Electoral Tribunal.

Overseeing the Peace Process: The Critical Role of ONUSAL

While UNDP efforts were tied directly to international funding, ONUSAL played a pivotal role in the peace process overall and, at least indirectly, helped assure donors that their contributions were well spent. Indeed, the massive UN presence arguably provided, in the eyes of some donors, a substitute for the sort of "peace conditionality" that some have argued ought to have been applied as the peace process stalled or seemed to be in trouble. [66] The United Nations played a key—and unprecedented—role in the evolution of the Peace Accords themselves, agreeing in July 1990 to post an observer mission to verify compliance with agreements on human rights. As the accords took shape, UN responsibility for verification grew accordingly; but alongside that, the secretary-general's office assumed increasing responsibility as mediator between the sides.

From the beginning of the process of demobilization and disarmament, ONUSAL was called in to settle disputes between the government and the FMLN. The accords, for example, provided a detailed calendar for the dissolution of the government's security forces and rapid-reaction battalions parallel to the concentration of FMLN forces into camps and their staged disarmament and demobilization. Disputes erupted almost immediately over the army's folding security units that were slated for dissolution into the regular forces. ONUSAL objections forced the government to change

course, though in the end, the National Police—also scheduled for dissolution—was swollen with new members transferred from these units.[67]
Several times, FMLN commanders in the field slowed movement into the
camps to protest government efforts to dislodge peasants occupying land
in anticipation of the land transfer program. Negotiations over the latter
issue collapsed in mid-1992, and the FMLN again suspended demobilization. A UN team of agrarian specialists evaluated the situation, and
ONUSAL offered the parties a take-it-or-leave-it proposal, to which both
parties agreed.[68]

Similarly, in late August 1993, with the approach of the March 1994
elections (in which the FMLN was to participate for the first time in simultaneous presidential, legislative, and municipal elections), ONUSAL brokered an agreement among the parties to deal with delays in implementing the accords on the training and deployment of the new National
Civilian Police and to recover arms distributed by the armed forces to
civilians. A timetable was worked out for implementation of agreements
on regulating the private use of arms, phasing out the old police force,
ensuring the autonomy of the new police from the army, and accelerating
the transfer of land and reinsertion programs. In December 1993, the
assassination of two senior FMLN officials and others, on both sides,
brought UN Under-Secretary-General Marrack Goulding to San Salvador; he
pressured the government to pursue the cases and to establish a Joint Group
for the Investigation of Illegal Armed Groups with Political Motivations to
look into the continued existence of "death squads" in the country.[69]

Throughout the peace process, the FMLN relied to a significant degree
on the United Nations, and to a lesser degree on donor countries, to force
government compliance with the agreements reached and to help work out
new agreements favorable to the former rebels. In part, this stemmed from
the structural weakness of the FMLN, which reflected what William Zartman calls the inevitable "asymmetry" in the bargaining relationship between an incumbent government and rebels.[70]

With each step in the demobilization process, the rebels lost more of
their power to coerce compliance with the Peace Accords or to win new
agreements on issues not settled in the accords. The January 1993 surrender of antiaircraft missiles—which the FMLN had secretly held back in the
course of disarmament as a possible bargaining chip to persuade the government to carry out the agreed-upon purge of the armed forces—and the
revelation of significant FMLN arms caches in May 1993, which momen-
tarily threatened the peace once again, ultimately deprived the FMLN of
the arms that had brought it a place at the bargaining table to begin with.
The FMLN coalition, moreover, split apart in the course of 1993 and 1994.
Neither of the resulting factions was inclined to use the tools of mass mobilization to press its case when locked in disagreements with the government,

thanks in part to a domestic political atmosphere in which demonstrations and marches were consistently labeled "attacks on the peace process" and on the promise of "reconciliation." In these circumstances, the FMLN was almost forced to rely on the international community to ensure compliance with the accords and to advance its point of view on disputed issues. Its relatively poor showing in the 1994 elections only reinforced this situation.

Thus, ONUSAL and, when needed, the secretary-general's office played an indispensable role in bringing the parties to the bargaining table, mediating disputes, and, at times, brokering agreements based on UN proposals. Though the FMLN relied on the support of donor countries to gain the right to speak before the Consultative Group meetings and in disputes over the shape and implementation of the NRP, by and large the former rebels turned to the United Nations, not the donors, in their search for leverage with the government.

Seeking Closure

The 1994 elections brought to power a less conciliatory faction of the ARENA party that had negotiated for peace starting in 1990, at times in the teeth of opposition from its hard-line elements. Under the presidency of Armando Calderón Sol, several of these hard-liners gained important positions in government. They were determined to end as soon as possible what they saw as unwonted international interference in the internal affairs of the country. At the same time, both they and more moderate forces within ARENA understood that they would have to do so without alienating the international community.

A new consensus was emerging, moreover, on one of the more controversial aspects of the Peace Accords, the installation of the new National Civilian Police. The armed forces and hard-liners within the government had blocked the rapid development of the new police force under President Cristiani, whose administration had not only maintained the old force (implicated in death squad violence during the war) in the field well beyond the stipulated period for its demobilization, but also continued recruitment and training. With the Calderón Sol administration, a new awareness dawned that the National Civilian Police, who were widely praised early in their development for their professionalism, were a necessary ingredient in the postwar order. The new administration apparently decided that it would be more desirable to seek to control them than to block their deployment any further.

Accordingly, the Calderón Sol government proclaimed its devotion to fulfilling the accords and actively sought ways to win agreement that the peace process was indeed coming to an end, to give way to normal politics in a postwar, democratic El Salvador. Nevertheless, a good deal was left incomplete even by the fall of 1994: the land transfer process—on which credit and housing programs for ex-combatants in most cases depended— was nowhere near completion; the National Civilian Police had not yet been fully deployed, and there were increasing disputes about the incorporation, without screening or human rights training, of members of specialized units of the old National Police; and several legal reforms, including those affecting police conduct and judicial process, remained outstanding.

In October 1994, in a UN-sponsored effort to make advances on outstanding issues, the government agreed to "strict and active cooperation to assure the complete fulfillment of all the Peace Accords remaining or in execution." In April 1995, the UN, FMLN, and GOES agreed to a detailed work plan, which included provision for high-level "trilateral" sessions whenever special difficulties arose. The work plan included a final calendar for compliance with outstanding agreements or settlement on disputed issues. The land transfer program, for instance, was to be completed by July 3, 1995; the microenterprise credit program was to extend credits to ex-combatants by May 30 (a full two and a half years after demobilization!); and remaining disputes about the police force and the National Public Security Academy were to be resolved between April and December 1995. In the event, the land transfer program, though 99 percent complete, continued unfinished past the (thrice revised) December 1996 deadline.[71] Disputes over the government's handling of the police continued to concern those following the issue well after the peace process was officially declared completed.[72]

Nevertheless, by 1995, both the United Nations and major international donors were also anxious to declare the process completed and successful. The FMLN had been incorporated into the nation's political life, despite continuing tensions. The major institutional changes advanced by the accords were complete or well under way, including the downsizing of the armed forces, the creation and deployment of the National Civilian Police, the establishment and strengthening of an independent Human Rights Ombudsman's Office, the renewal of the Supreme Court and the judiciary more generally, and the reform (still in process) of the electoral organs.

Despite the crime wave that seized the country with the end of the war and worries that former combatants and ex-members of the security forces were banding together to demand greater attention, El Salvador had not experienced the sort of civil chaos and armed confrontation that accompanied the end of the contra war in Nicaragua. Although there had been questions about the conduct of the 1994 elections, ONUSAL had declared the process basically free and fair, and the FMLN had accepted the results and regrouped for the next round. The United Nations, moreover, had by this time taken on more difficult peacekeeping and peace-building tasks elsewhere, and it was anxious to point to El Salvador as an example of how much could be accomplished. The downsizing of ONUSAL, which had been going on since it reached its peak deployment for the March 1994 elections, was constant through the rest of the year, despite delays in closing the mission definitively. El Salvador had cost the United Nations more that $100 million for ONUSAL alone.[73] With the rising costs associated with its suddenly expanded efforts around the world, the UN was anxious to move on.

In this setting, the government prepared for the Consultative Group meeting of June 1995. Just prior to this meeting, representatives of GOES and the FMLN traveled to Brussels to try to raise money from the European Community for the land program. But in contrast to earlier meetings, the FMLN were treated now as "part of the establishment."[74] Moreover, in contrast to previous years, when the FMLN viewed government requests as inflated and designed to fund existing programs as much as new ones, the government's presentation before the Consultative Group targeted just the handful of programs specifically mentioned in UN-brokered agreements for completion of the peace process. Thus, as mentioned above, estimated expenses for the peace and reconstruction process were scaled back in most areas from 1993 CG estimates.[75]

Conclusion

El Salvador faced its "triple transition" with significant advantages when compared with many of the cases analyzed in this project, but *also with the disadvantages of some of those same advantages*. El Salvador also represented a "first" in the extent to which the United Nations played an active role in mediating an internal conflict and overseeing the implementation of the subsequent accords between the rebels and the sitting government.[76]

Strong Patrons, Skewed Incentives, Failed Planning

El Salvador began the process enjoying strong political and financial support from the United States, as well as the wholehearted backing of the World Bank. Such powerful patronage had its costs. It meant that the Salvadoran government entered both the peace talks and the Consultative Group framework from a position of strength regarding its economic program. Thus, the government was able to keep most issues touching on the economy off the bargaining table throughout the peace talks. At the same time, in the design of postwar reinsertion and reconstruction programs, the prevailing orthodoxy meant that both income support and productive investment for the tens of thousands of ex-combatants and civilians in the conflict zones would be shortchanged in favor of ameliorative programs such as the restoration of infrastructure and the rehabilitation of public services. Credit programs, small enterprise development, and even productive sector rehabilitation for the new landholders of the land transfer program were either grossly underfunded and limited in scope or seriously delayed pending final titling of the new properties.

While it was possible for individual donors to launch such programs on their own, the overall policy environment was not conducive to promoting self-sustaining new enterprises, particularly in agriculture, where trade liberalization has had a devastating impact even on well-financed commercial growers, and particularly among those most affected by the conflict, who faced credit markets skewed against them both by traditional practice and by the high real interest rates prevailing in the wake of structural adjustment. The World Bank's economic package did nothing to mitigate these effects and much to exacerbate them. The Bank's agricultural sector reforms concentrated on dismantling or privatizing supporting institutions, reducing the size of the Ministry of Agriculture, and, later, promoting land titling, with the express aim of enabling weaker producers to sell to the more fortunate. The IDB's Social Investment Fund, touted as a "social safety net" measure, was nothing of the sort, as it concentrated on small infrastructure projects to the exclusion of income support or productive investment.

U.S. sponsorship also enabled the Salvadoran government to drag its feet on full implementation of certain of the Peace Accords. Even where the U.S. government had major investments in specific programs, such as land transfer and the new civilian police (where the United States was by far the major donor), the United States did not always exercise the leverage it might have to push forward compliance. When the military balked, for example, at transferring properties of the outgoing National Police to the new police force for its police academy and for posts around the country, the United States went along, footing the bill for a drawn-out search for suitable property that delayed significantly deployment of the new force and drove up the cost of the program.[77]

The United States, moreover, backed the government on a number of issues that troubled other donors. Well into 1993, the USAID mission in El Salvador was composed largely of individuals who had been closely associated with the counterinsurgency program of the war years. The mission's suspicion of the FMLN and the civilian organizations associated with it and with the peace movement in El Salvador, its backing of the government in its refusal to give the FMLN and associated NGOs a greater role in the development of the National Reconstruction Plan, and its consistent support for the Secretariat for National Reconstruction over other channels of coordination created significant discomfort for other donors. This was particularly true for those—like the Netherlands, the Nordics, Canada, and, to a lesser extent, Spain—that had provided funding for opposition NGOs and community organizations during the war. These donors, though representing a relatively small percentage of total funding for El Salvador, contributed much of their aid through nongovernmental and multilateral channels and gave significantly for democracy-building and reinsertion initiatives. They supported temporarily underfunded activities and those neglected by larger donors, such as the Ad Hoc Commission (to purge the Salvadoran armed forces), the Human Rights Ombudsman's Office, documentation services for uprooted civilians (under the UN High Commissioner for Refugees), resettlement of refugees and internally displaced persons both during and after the war, and agricultural and microindustrial development projects in the ex-conflict zones. It is significant that Sweden, the country closest to the controversies outlined above, was the only donor that did not fulfill its 1992 pledge.

Overall, the general "umbrella" the United States initially provided for the GOES to pursue its preferences on a variety of issues simultaneously shielded the government from unwanted conditionality on the part of other donors and discouraged certain of them, chiefly the Nordics but perhaps others, from participating more fully. At the same time, the United States provided a guarantee that key programs would be funded even when the international community did not contribute to the degree desired by both Washington and the Salvadoran government. There is considerable evidence, however, that the United States learned significant lessons from its experience in El Salvador. With the change in personnel that accelerated in 1994, the USAID mission began to work seriously with elements of civil society that it had rejected earlier.[78] Its strategy document for 1997–2002 focuses USAID efforts almost wholly on addressing the pressing problems of rural poverty, which it views as a continuing threat to the viability of the achievements of the peace process.[79]

The World Bank, by contrast, has continued largely along its original course of support for "economic reform" conceived along neoliberal lines. Despite a growing recognition within El Salvador that trade liberalization and current monetary policy have proven disastrous for agriculture and the countryside generally, the Bank has provided little more than the nostrum that farmers faced with ruin will have to seek employment elsewhere. Not a single Bank project addresses the question of how such employment might be developed. The major Bank initiative for rural areas, the Land Registration Project, has as its express purpose the "freeing up of land markets," and Bank officials have pressed the government to find ways to encourage the breakup of the land reform cooperatives to this end.[80] Privately, Bank officials cite the "success" of the Chilean counterreform as an example of what they have in mind.[81] But the latter, though it did not return land to former owners, resulted in the widespread displacement of peasant producers, while agricultural wages still had not returned to their 1970s levels well into the 1990s.

Economic liberalization, not the social, economic, and political require-ments of postconflict reconstruction, was what has preoccupied Bank plan-ners in the case of El Salvador. While it is evident from other cases reviewed in this volume that the Bank has performed better elsewhere, the recent reorganization of the Bank, which gives significant new power to country representatives in the choice and design of projects and the inter-pretation of Bank policies on participation, NGOs, and poverty alleviation, suggests that who is in place when will continue to play a large role in the World Bank's efforts in postconflict situations. In their own way, and with-out the sort of self-criticism that might give force to the observation, the Bank's own reviewers second this view.[82]

One negative consequence of the strong position the government of El Salvador enjoyed with respect to the United States and the international financial institutions was the failure of planning documented in this chap-ter. On the one hand, the prevailing economic orthodoxy provided scant room for the sorts of measures that would have to be taken to ensure that the social and economic causes of the civil war were removed, or even that the government would meet its immediate obligations under the Peace Accords to provide for the effective reintegration of the FMLN and its civilian supporters in the countryside. On the other hand, both the economic model and the strength of external support apparently blinded government planners to the true costs of postwar reconstruction. They were not alone, however, as even the United States failed to anticipate the escalating costs of reinsertion. Pretransition planning failed to recognize the bargaining strength of the FMLN or to anticipate the true costs of reintegrating sectors of society and regions of the country formerly at war. Both factors merited greater attention in the period leading up to the final accords.

Monitoring, Coordination, and Conditionality

The high profile role of the United Nations in El Salvador contributed in significant and complex ways to funding for postwar peace, democratiza-tion, and reconstruction. Though UNDP was blocked from playing the coordinating (and monitoring) role that was initially proposed for it in funding and implementing the Peace Accords and the National Recon-struction Plan, the secretary-general's office, through ONUSAL, played a critical role in monitoring compliance with the accords and mediating dis-putes between the FMLN and the government. In the Salvadoran case, the United Nations was able to exercise significant leverage for compliance toward both parties to the accords.

The UN role, and its relative strength, had two effects for donors. First, it meant that donor countries with a specific interest in the peace process could rely on the United Nations to oversee and help advance the process. Despite concerns about government compliance on the part of some donors, it was possible to leave to the UN matters that might otherwise have been the subject of conditionality. At the same time, the UN's role arguably lowered the incentives among donors to apply peace conditionality. The United Nations presence provided a guarantee of at least limited compliance, but also a disincentive to closer monitoring and conditionality on the part of individual donors or groups of donors interested in the peace process.

The character of the UN presence—and specifically that it was vested most potently in the political arm of the United Nations (ONUSAL) rather than in UNDP—also shaped the situation facing donors. ONUSAL's focus was on implementation of the Peace Accords, not reconstruction or even the funding of accords-related activities. It responded to crises in implementation and not, generally speaking, to complaints about the adequacy of funding or the character of implementing institutions. The result was that the UN focused on specifically political questions about the pace of implementation and the seriousness of the parties' compliance rather than on the quantity of financing or the quality of the use of funds for postwar reconstruction, reinsertion, and institution building.

Though ONUSAL concerned itself with the slow pace of purchases and title transfer in the land program, the lack of production credit, and the often despairing situation of ex-combatants and civilians on the land, it was unable to mobilize funds or mount programs to address these issues. UNDP was well positioned to do the latter and had acted effectively in this respect in dealing with the demobilization of the FMLN. But the U.S.-backed decision to leave much of the funding for postwar transition in the hands of the SRN meant that international donors either settled for that agency, with all its failings, or found alternative channels of their own. The result was a profound lack of coordination, particularly when it came to development assistance for rural areas.[83] Such lack of coordination, however, might also have contributed to the significant shortfalls noted above in international funding for crucial programs for the demobilized and for building and strengthening democratic institutions.

The World Bank's role in coordinating international aid through the Consultative Group process, moreover, is seriously overstated in its recent self-evaluation,[84] as the major forces promoting attention to peace and reconstruction issues operated well outside the Consultative Group process (the FMLN and ONUSAL) or were thwarted in their efforts (UNDP, the Nordics). The CG process, while significant for the initial mobilization of funds ("pledging"), proved more important in 1993 and 1995 as a forum in which donors could track progress and voice their concerns. There was little "coordination" involved at this level, and indeed, as we saw, significant opportunities for coordination were lost in disputes among the FMLN, smaller donors, the United States, and the GOES early in the process.

Both the Bank and the United States, moreover, apparently made overt conditionality difficult to apply. The Scandinavian countries' effort to link compliance with the Peace Accords and greater commitment on the part of the Salvadoran government to SAL II failed in the face of Bank and GOES intransigence. Without the support of the Bank or of the United States, it could hardly have been otherwise. As Thomas Carothers and Juan Alberto Fuentes note with regard to the Guatemalan case, peace conditionality can be extraordinarily difficult to apply where major donors refuse to cooperate and where the recipient country is otherwise relatively independent of international aid. This is particularly so to the extent that donors are unwilling to withhold not only aid but trading privileges as well.[85] Nevertheless, the United States used both formal and informal means to apply conditionality on a wide variety of questions.

Ironically, finally, the Salvadoran government ultimately expended far more on building new, more democratic institutions and on the reinsertion of ex-combatants than originally planned. In part, this was owing to the considerable pressure put on the government throughout the process by the FMLN and ONUSAL. It seems clear that it was due partly to continued international attention to the issues of postwar reconstruction and peace building in El Salvador, even when the latter did not involve significant new funding or publicly visible conditionality. The informal conditions attached to disbursements of U.S. funds undoubtedly contributed to this. But so did the international spotlight provided by the Consultative Group meetings, which, though they did not succeed in raising significant new funds after 1992, provided an opportunity for the government to prove its seriousness to the international community and for the donors to raise their concerns.

Despite the shortcomings of the international effort and of resultant measures, particularly those affecting the rural population most affected by the war, it is clear that the Salvadoran process was largely successful, in both the deployment of the international system in the pursuit of a peaceful settlement and democratic transition and the mobilization of large sums of money to facilitate fulfillment of the Peace Accords and to carry out postwar reconstruction. Though one might argue over the degree to which democracy is indeed "consolidated" in El Salvador today, and though a significant proportion of the affected population remains "at risk" in the current economic situation, the peace and reconstruction process accomplished a great deal—from the successful demobilization of the FMLN and a portion of the security forces, to the creation of a strong Human Rights Ombudsman's Office, to important steps in police and judicial reform. Generally free and fair elections were held in 1994, with the open participation, for the first time in Salvadoran history, of the left. Moreover, municipal elections in March 1997 returned a large portion of urban El Salvador for the FMLN and its allies, marking the beginning, it is hoped, of significant alternation in power in a democratic framework.

The process by which all this was accomplished combined international pressure to comply with the negotiated accords and government efforts to maintain control of the process with control of funding at the center of a significant part of that struggle. In this picture, the FMLN played only an ancillary role, particularly after the demobilization of its forces, depending more on international pressures than on legislative clout or popular mobilization to achieve its goals. The United Nations, the international donor community, and (equally, if at times more ambiguously) the United States played key roles in maintaining the balance between a government newly possessed of its "monopoly of armed force" and not always disposed to comply with agreements that could threaten its future hold on power and a civilian (and newly civilianized) opposition weary of war and eager to put the past behind them.

International donors pledged significant support for this process at its inception and backed those pledges (eventually) with firm commitments and actual disbursements of funds. The shortfalls and delays documented here undoubtedly affected the process and, to some extent, the outcome; but they did not endanger its generally positive content. Problems of coordination undoubtedly contributed to uneven coverage, particularly where support for local resettlement and development efforts were concerned. Nevertheless, international funding was crucial both to move the process forward and to ensure greater participation by the Salvadoran government itself than either government officials or their backers in the World Bank at first deemed necessary.

Notes

1. Frente Farabundo Martí para la Liberación Nacional (FMLN).
2. Alianza Republicana Nacionalista (ARENA).
3. The issue was aired most thoroughly by James Boyce and others in their review of the economic concomitants of the peace process in El Salvador. See Boyce, "External Resource Mobilization." It has arisen repeatedly in subsequent international aid efforts, but particularly in the Bosnian case (described in this book), where it has, however, played out quite differently than in El Salvador. The World Bank's Operations Evaluation Department, which recently reviewed the Bank's experiences with postconflict reconstruction, devotes considerable attention

to the question with regard to the El Salvador case. See World Bank, *The World Bank's Experience,* vol. 3.

4. Nevertheless, assistance during the first five years of the postwar period (1992–1996) came to just 84 percent of that provided during the last five years of the civil war (1987–1991). In terms of the composition of aid, grants represented 70 percent of total funding during the period 1984–1995. By 1996–1997, however, grants made up only 20 percent of total funding.

5. The only World Bank operation was a $65 million reconstruction loan after the 1986 earthquake. The IMF provided $87 million in 1982 under the framework of a one-year standby agreement. Rosa, *El Banco Mundial y el Futuro del Ajuste Estructural en El Salvador.*

6. The era of highly concessional funding ended in 1995; since 1996, loans have been the dominant form of external official funding (see Table 4.1). U.S. funding dropped sharply in 1996–1997, and the U.S. share of total aid to El Salvador fell to just 15 percent.

7. During the 1980s, there was a massive emigration of Salvadorans, mostly to the United States. As a result, private remittances grew significantly, from a mere $45 million—or less than 1 percent of GDP in 1979—to $824 million, or almost 11 percent of GDP in 1993. As a primary source of foreign exchange, remittances became far more important than agro-exports. Whereas in 1978 traditional agro-exports (coffee, cotton, sugar) provided 80 percent of foreign exchange, by 1996 remittances provided 59 percent of foreign exchange and traditional agro-exports only 21 percent. From the late 1980s, this flow of private remittance from Salvadorans living outside the country contributed (and continues to contribute) significantly to the strength of the Salvadoran economy.

8. El Salvador entered the civil war with low levels of public external debt: $405 million in 1979 (World Bank, *El Salvador. Updating Economic Memorandum*). By 1992, external debt had risen to $2,338 million, with U.S. loans representing 34 percent of total public external debt in that year. At the end of 1992, Washington and San Salvador signed an agreement to reduce this bilateral debt by $464 million. In addition, the GOES achieved further debt reductions of $81 million during 1990–1993. This includes $32.4 million with Mexico, $36.7 million with other bilateral Latin American governments, $7.7 million with Canada, and $3.8 million with CABEI (MIPLAN, *Memoria de Labores,* 1994). Debt rescheduling also provided some debt service relief. According to MIPLAN (*Memoria de Labores,* 1994), $382.5 million were rescheduled during 1990–1993, allowing for debt service savings of $133.7 million—reducing total external debt to $1,985 million by the end of 1993. During 1994–1996, a sharp increase in multilateral lending raised the country's total external debt by 26 percent, to $2,497 million. Nevertheless, this level of debt represented only 24 percent of GDP, moderate by international standards. In 1996, four creditors accounted for almost 80 percent of the debt: the Inter-American Development Bank (IDB) was by far the most important, accounting for 42 percent of total debt; the United States, the World Bank, and the Central American Bank for Economic Integration (CABEI) together held 37 percent.

9. No use was made of IMF funds under this agreement, nor under subsequent agreements, as the main objective of these agreements has been to improve the image of El Salvador with external creditors, donors, and foreign investors through the IMF rubber stamp of approval on the GOES economic program. Thus, the August 1990 agreement with the IMF, the first since July 1982, allowed a Paris Club agreement to reschedule some bilateral debt in September 1990 and opened the doors for new loans from the World Bank and IDB in support of economic reform.

10. A second structural adjustment loan (SAL II) to deepen the economic reform was approved in September 1993, and most of the other loans that followed also supported the economic reform process that stressed privatization, public sector reforms, and sectoral reforms in the energy and agricultural sector. In the social sector, there were only three loans from the World Bank during that period: a general loan in 1991 for social sector rehabilitation for $26 million and two loans for education in 1995 and 1997 for $34 million and $92 million, respectively.

11. Six infrastructure loans absorbed the largest portion ($748.9 million). There were also four loans for education, the environment, and judicial reform, which absorbed only $105.5 million; and three loans worth $153 million for the Social Investment Fund, which was originally designed as a compensatory mechanism for the impact of economic reform on the poor. The global economic reform was supported with three loans: a $90 million Investment Sector loan in 1992, a $19.7 million loan for Fiscal Administration Modernization in 1995, and a $70 million Modernization of the Public Sector loan in 1997.

12. World Bank, *The World Bank's Experience,* vol. 3.

13. World Bank, *The World Bank's Experience,* vol. 1, p. 11.

14. World Bank, *Consultative Group for El Salvador, Paris, May 15 and 16, 1991.* Again, the Bank's recent evaluation of the process, in claiming a major role for the Bank in aid coordination, overstates the case when it argues that "a main purpose of the first CG meeting was to garner donor support for the preparation and implementation of a national reconstruction program." *The World Bank's Experience,* vol. 3, p. 21. If so, this intention was scarcely made clear in the chairman's remarks; and it was almost entirely a failure.

15. MIPLAN, *Economic and Social Program.*

16. World Bank, *Consultative Group for El Salvador, Paris, May 15 and 16, 1991,* Annex IX. He noted that recent accords had mandated the creation of an Office of the Attorney General for Human Rights and a Supreme Electoral Council, and the reform of the judicial system.

17. Development Associates, *Evaluation,* II-8.

18. Management Systems International, *Assistance to the Transition,* p. 95.

19. This total included, besides ex-combatants, 12,000 displaced families, 30,000 persons to be repatriated that had been living in camps outside the country, and 550,000 poor persons living in the eighty-three municipalities most affected by the conflict; MIPLAN, *National Reconstruction Plan Preliminary Version.*

20. MIPLAN, *National Reconstruction Plan, Revised Version.* The target territory was expanded to ninety-nine municipalities in this version and the target population to 800,000.

21. The Peace Accords committed the government to submit the NRP to the FMLN within thirty days of the signing of those accords (January 16, 1992), so that its suggestions could be taken into account. The government formally presented the NRP to the FMLN on February 14.

22. MIPLAN-SRN-FMLN, *Actas de Reuniones.*

23. World Bank, news release no. 92.

24. Urabe, *Statement by the Japanese Representative.*

25. MIPLAN, *Memoria de Labores 1991–1992,* p. 3.

26. MIPLAN, *Consolidating the Peace,* p. 22.

27. MIPLAN, *Financiamiento Contratado,* February 1993.

28. MIPLAN, *Consolidating the Peace,* Annex 3. "Expected external funding" here apparently represents funds committed or under negotiation, hence the gap between the 1992 pledges and this figure. But it is still well below that announced

early in the year when MIPLAN recorded $342 million committed and another $333 million under negotiation.

29. MIPLAN, *Consolidating the Peace,* p. 22.

30. Nordic Statement.

31. Swedish Statement.

32. MIPLAN, *Los Grupos Consultivos.*

33. United Nations, General Assembly, *Assistance.*

34. Ibid.

35. The one exception is Sweden, whose dissatisfaction with progress on Peace Accords–related agreements and with the negative response to its initiative at the 1993 CG meeting certainly must have contributed to this outcome.

36. GOES, *Los Acuerdos de Paz.*

37. The latter figure apparently includes operational expenses, which, at this stage in the process, ought to have come under the government's purview in any case.

38. It is important to recall that this rubric included programs for ex-combatants of both the armed forces and the FMLN, as well as for those civilians eligible for land and agricultural credit under the Land Transfer Program, which was intended to settle the rural civilian population most closely tied to the FMLN in former combat areas.

39. MIPLAN, *Financing Needs.*

40. GOES, *Los Acuerdos de Paz,* p. 57.

41. One government official reportedly told members of a USAID evaluation team that if the government had known the actual costs in advance, it would have refused to sign the Peace Accords. Management Systems International, *Assistance,* p. 2.

42. Nevertheless, according to a draft report prepared for the U.S. General Accounting Office on postwar reconstruction, World Bank officials claimed that they had urged the government to seek a genuine consensus with the FMLN over the terms of reconstruction and warned the government that without such a consensus, it would be difficult to persuade international donors to support the NRP. The same study reported that World Bank and IDB officials had serious doubts about El Salvador's capacity to program and disburse the large amounts of funds contemplated in the NRP. See Lawrence, *Postwar El Salvador,* pp. 8, 38. The World Bank's recent self-evaluation, quoted earlier, also claims a larger role for World Bank officials in addressing the agenda of reconstruction, though the documentary evidence is less than supportive on this point.

43. One exception might be in the area of agricultural policy, where the Bank's declared list of priorities included completion of the land transfer program for ex-combatants and civilians affected by the war. A strong argument can be made, however, that precisely in this realm the policies favored by the Bank, and acquiesced in by the government, tended to undermine the intent of that program. Foley et al., *Land, Peace and Participation.* See below.

44. There the Bank participated in agreements that would have the government raise some $700 million (or 27 percent) of the estimated $2.6 billion cost of financing the Peace Accords. Included in the agreement was a government commitment to raise tax revenues from 8 percent of GDP to 12 percent by the year 2000. By contrast, at its highest estimates, in 1993, the Salvadoran government projected spending just $407 million of the $1.8 billion needed for postwar reconstruction, or less than 23 percent of the total. The incidence of taxation in El Salvador was (and is) among the lowest in the region, at just 7.6 percent of GDP in 1989, rising to 9.7 percent in 1994 with an increase in the regressive value-added tax (Segovia,

"Domestic Resource Mobilization," p. 115). Boyce and Segovia have both argued that such figures account for the persistent fiscal constraints the country suffered during the postwar period, and that such constraints might have been remedied by a policy of "peace conditionality" on the part of the Bank directed at, among other things, raising government revenues. Segovia, "Domestic Resource Mobilization"; Boyce, "External Resource Mobilization."

45. De Soto and del Castillo, "Obstacles to Peacebuilding."

46. The agency also set aside $13.5 million in local currency generated through its balance of payments support (ESF) and food aid programs (PL-480) for immediate disbursement by the government of El Salvador once the Peace Accords were signed. Finally, USAID worked out a project agreement with GOES for national reconstruction, promising a total of $250 million in new and previously programmed aid for the effort, to which the United States eventually added another $50 million.

47. WOLA, *Reluctant Reforms.*

48. GAO, *Aid to El Salvador,* p. 7. That donor concerns about the government's seriousness in implementing reforms were well founded is documented in the assessment made by Gino Costa, the UN's chief adviser for public security matters in El Salvador. See Costa, "La Reforma Policial."

49. UNDP, *Technical and Financial Cooperation,* pp. 173–174. These figures are through 1996, hence the discrepancy with those presented in Table 4.9 above. Here, too, international concerns were supported by ample evidence, through 1994, that the Salvadoran system would resist reform. See Costa, "La Reforma Policial," and Popkin et al., *Justice Delayed.*

50. Management Systems International, *Assistance,* Annex G.

51. Stahler-Sholk, "El Salvador's Negotiated Transition," p. 40.

52. Interview, Washington, D.C., July 25, 1998.

53. The World Bank's defense of its conduct with regard to peace conditionality is curious. After noting that the Bank funded direct costs for the Social Sector Rehabilitation Project (indirectly related to postconflict reconstruction), the report goes on to argue that "a basic rationale for SAL II was to provide *fiscal flexibility* to the GOES to help it meet the unprecedented fiscal demands of the Peace Accord–mandated programs. While the link to the Peace Accords components is not stated in the SAL documents as such, both the GOES and the Bank shared the understanding that the fungible counterpart resources provided by SAL II would be very timely in this regard." World Bank, *The World Bank's Experience,* vol. 3, p. 42. Flexibility, however, is not conditionality.

54. USAID/El Salvador, *FY 1993 ESF,* p. 4. Similarly, the 1994 ESF program raised several concerns about implementation of the Peace Accords, but included little in the way of direct conditionality. USAID/El Salvador, *FY 1994 ESF.*

55. Lawrence, *Postwar El Salvador.*

56. GAO, *El Salvador,* p. 11.

57. Foley, "Laying the Groundwork."

58. Indeed, Article 9 of the accords stated, "Given the large amount of additional resources that will be required to implement the aforementioned plan, both parties will call upon the international community to lend the greatest support possible to this drive. A national reconstruction fund will be created for this purpose by the U.N. Development Programme." The same article defined the role of the UNDP to include: "counseling the government in everything that pertains to mobilizing foreign support, contributing to the preparation of projects and programs that receive such support, expediting arrangements with official organizations of a

bilateral and multilateral nature, mobilizing technical assistance, and cooperating with the government in making its plan compatible with the activities of nongovernmental organizations at the local and regional level."

59. Lawrence, *Postwar El Salvador.*

60. UNDP, *Technical and Financial Cooperation.* Unfortunately, the UNDP report does not utilize the categories adopted by the government in classifying aid projects and does not classify funding according to its relevance to the peace and reconstruction process. For this reason, the figures presented by the UNDP allow only a rough estimate of the proportion of funds for peace and reconstruction channeled through nongovernmental outlets.

61. A major maternal and infant health program, with significant influence in the NRP area, was carried out in this way, utilizing a U.S. consulting firm to serve as an "umbrella" for numerous Salvadoran NGOs.

62. Because the Salvadoran government had not budgeted explicitly for this phase of the peace process, UNDP put out an appeal in March 1992 for contributions to a trust fund for support of ex-combatants of the FMLN while concentrated in camps around the country preparing for demobilization. Only two donors, Canada and Norway, responded immediately; Japan disbursed $300,000 in mid-April, followed by Sweden, Denmark, and Switzerland in May. The United States added a final $500,000 in June. The European Union funded Doctors Without Borders to set up basic infrastructure for the camps and CARITAS to provide a portion of the food aid. Because of the delay in funding, UNDP raised temporary funds from within the United Nations system to meet the immediate needs of the program. UNDP, *Final Progress Report;* interview with UNDP official, January 11, 1993.

63. The World Food Programme, the Food and Agriculture Organization, and the International Labour Organization all participated in the effort, with funding from Denmark, France, the Netherlands, Norway, Sweden, Switzerland, and the United States.

64. Agricultural training for approximately 6,500 ex-combatants; technical and vocational training (with an orientation toward creating "microenterprises") for another 2,500; and management training for 600 "midlevel" commanders and leaders of the FMLN.

65. Lawrence, *Postwar El Salvador,* pp. 8–9.

66. The argument is not that donors saw no need for conditionality, but rather that faced with the intransigence of the World Bank on this issue, or of the United States with regard to specific matters pertaining to the Peace Accords, concerned donors could continue to rely on the United Nations to press home significant issues. This did not prevent some donors, as we have seen, from channeling their funding through alternative agencies or even, as in the case of Sweden, withholding funding that had been pledged.

67. Costa, "La Reforma Policial."

68. Wood, "The Peace Accords," p. 89.

69. United Nations Security Council, *Further Report.*

70. Zartman, "Dynamics and Constraints," p. 3.

71. Spence et al., *Chapultepec: Five Years Later.*

72. See, for example, Stanley et al., *Protectors or Perpetrators?*

73. According to the government report presented at the June 1995 CG meeting, the cost of the ONUSAL mission at that time was $110.9 million. MIPLAN, *Financing Needs.*

74. Interview with Salvador Cortés, former FMLN representative at the 1992,

1993, and 1995 Consultative Group meetings, February 11, 1998.

75. The most plausible explanation for these changes was that in 1995, as we have seen, the Calderón Sol administration was seeking closure on the Peace Accords and, implicitly, on international monitoring and interference in Salvadoran affairs. With the help of the United Nations, the government and the FMLN came to a series of agreements meant to close out the process. Out of those agreements came a handful of discrete funding proposals put forward at the 1995 meeting. Overall, however, the government was anxious to present the process as essentially closed, and the estimated costs of peace and reconstruction efforts were lowered accordingly.

This interpretation raises questions about the character of the higher estimates of need presented in 1993 and, indeed, about the methods by which any such estimates are generated. Government estimates were undoubtedly inflated. At the same time, however, the 1993 presentation more accurately represented needs in the areas of democracy building and reinsertion, a fact attributable to the pressure put on the GOES by the FMLN, ONUSAL, and allied donor countries.

76. The only comparable deployment of UN personnel with significant powers of oversight and implementation was the UN mission in Namibia, 1986–1990, where the United Nations carried out a far-reaching plan to mount the first free and fair elections in the former trusteeship territory. Namibia, however, was a non-self-governing territory, not a member state, and the UN mission was carried out under the authority of the United Nations Decolonization Committee.

77. Costa, "La Reforma Policial."

78. Even before this, USAID had quietly dropped its insistence that most local reconstruction aid flow through the Municipalities in Action (MEA) program, to which FMLN-related NGOs had raised important objections. Money from the MEA program, as it was called, was rechanneled to land purchase and other reinsertion projects, democratic institutions, and infrastructure projects carried out by the Ministry of Public Works and other agencies less politicized than the municipalities. Interview with former USAID/El Salvador official, July 25, 1998.

79. USAID/El Salvador, *Sustainable Development and Democracy.*

80. Foley et al., *Land, Peace and Participation.*

81. Interview with World Bank official, Washington, D.C., December 3, 1996.

82. World Bank, *The World Bank's Experience,* vol. 1, p. 3.

83. A survey of development NGOs carried out by one of the authors in 1995 found a pattern of intense competition, overlap of services in some parts of the country, and accompanying neglect of other areas, fueled by lack of coordination and short-term "project orientation" among donors. See Foley et al., *Land, Peace and Participation.*

84. World Bank, *The World Bank's Experience,* vol. 3.

85. Carothers and Fuentes, "La Cooperación Internacional," p. 17.

5

Mozambique

Nicole Ball & Sam Barnes

IN THE 1990s, AFTER FOUR DECADES OF ATTEMPTING TO DELINK development assistance from politics, donor agencies increasingly found themselves being drawn into one of the most political activities of all—assisting countries to make the transition from civil war to peace. Peace building involves not only "traditional" humanitarian and development tasks such as resettling war-affected populations, repairing and building economic and social infrastructure, and restoring and strengthening economic activity. It also entails helping to create safe and secure environments and supporting efforts to replace exclusionary political systems with more participatory structures.

One of the earliest peace-building efforts occurred in Mozambique, where the government and the Mozambique National Resistance (Renamo) signed the General Peace Agreement (GPA) on October 4, 1992, nearly ending fifteen years of war.[1] At the time of independence, in June 1975, Mozambique was one of the world's poorest countries. It possessed an extremely weak human capital base and a poorly developed infrastructure dependent on Portuguese settlers—who departed in large numbers in 1974 and 1975, effectively crippling the economy. The lengthy, often brutal war against Renamo, faltering economic policies, and severe, extended drought conditions left Mozambique heavily dependent on the international community for its survival.

Consequently, international assistance financed the vast majority of the costs associated with Mozambique's war-to-peace transition. Bilateral and multilateral assistance supported humanitarian activities, aided the implementation of the peace agreement, and set in motion medium- and longer-term development efforts. Mozambique's needs ran the gamut from refugee resettlement, economic revitalization, and infrastructure repair to the demobilization and reintegration of government and Renamo soldiers, the organization of the first national election, the transformation of

159

Renamo into a political party, and the reform of both the national army and the police.

Diplomatic support and assistance also underpinned the successful outcome of the peace process, as external actors facilitated negotiations and supported the first multiparty elections. Peacekeeping forces not only undertook traditional postconflict activities, such as supervising the separation of forces and the cease-fire; they also provided logistical support for the electoral process—for example, by distributing voter education and election materials throughout the country. While the determining factor in making and consolidating peace was the political will of the warring parties to conclude and implement the GPA, external support was also critical to the successful transition.

We begin this chapter by reviewing briefly the causes of the conflict in Mozambique. We then outline how external financial assistance in the years between independence and the signing of the GPA, particularly during 1987–1992, set the stage for the international community's subsequent response to the Mozambican peace process.

In the remainder of the chapter, we focus on donor support for the peace process during 1992–1994. After examining a series of conceptual issues relating to the assessment of pledges, commitments, and disbursements, we describe and analyze the mechanisms through which donors pledged resources to support the peace process and coordinated the implementation of the peace agreement. Next, we review the financial resources the donor community allocated to peace implementation and evaluate donor performance in delivering on pledges. This discussion highlights two other important gaps in donor financing: an "implementation gap" and a "conceptual gap." We substantiate our arguments with sectoral examples, reviewing donor assistance for demobilization and reintegration, national elections, and mine clearance. We conclude by offering some observations about the appropriate design and delivery of assistance intended to consolidate peace.

Laying the Groundwork:
External Assistance to Mozambique Prior to 1992

Sources of External Assistance

Since attaining independence in 1975, after more than ten years of war, Mozambique has received significant amounts of external assistance from a wide variety of sources. During the Cold War, the country enjoyed a high degree of political legitimacy in the eyes of donors that endorsed its declared commitment to socialist development. In 1975, land, education, health, legal practice, and rented property were nationalized. In 1977, the ruling party, the Mozambique Liberation Front (Frelimo), enunciated a socialist strategy based on state ownership of key productive assets, including the centralization of agricultural production through state farms, cooperatives, and communal villages. Mozambique's international political legitimacy was enhanced by its position as one of the "frontline states" in the struggle against both white minority rule in Rhodesia (before 1980) and the apartheid regime in South Africa. As a result, from 1975 through 1985, Mozambique received substantial financial aid and technical assistance from the Soviet Union, Cuba, Eastern European countries, the Nordic countries, members of the European Community, and Canada.[2] In the late 1980s, following alterations in its economic and political policies, Mozambique began to receive significant assistance from the United States, the World Bank, and the International Monetary Fund (IMF). Meanwhile, financial flows from the East Bloc countries dried up in the years preceding the collapse of the Soviet Union.

The Causes of War

Ironically, the same factors that led Mozambique to receive substantial external assistance in the immediate postliberation period also produced the conditions that drew Mozambique back into war. The conflict that began in 1976 had its roots primarily in the regional political environment. Following independence in 1975, Mozambique entered the struggle against white minority rule in southern Africa. It provided the guerrillas of the Zimbabwean African National Union (ZANU) free access to its territory, applied UN sanctions to Rhodesia, and closed its border with that country in 1976. The Rhodesian security forces countered by creating Renamo.[3]

Renamo's members were initially Portuguese settlers and former colonial security force members who had emigrated to Rhodesia following Mozambican independence; they also included black Mozambicans who had fought with the settlers against Frelimo since the early 1970s, primarily of the N'dau ethnic group. During the period of Rhodesian sponsorship, 1975–1979, Renamo both supported the Rhodesian security forces in conducting operations inside Mozambique against ZANU's military wing, the Zimbabwean African National Liberation Army (ZAPLA), and sought to overthrow the Frelimo government. In the early 1980s, the South African Military Intelligence Directorate assumed responsibility for Renamo and sponsored an intensified program of economic destabilization and a war of terror against the civilian population. This campaign was designed to destabilize the entire southern African region and deny the African National Congress (ANC) bases in Mozambique and other frontline counties.[4]

In the absence of external support, it is highly unlikely that an internal opposition to the Frelimo government would have become sufficiently organized and equipped to pursue a civil war. In the first years following independence, the Frelimo government achieved some notable economic and social achievements—for example, by dramatically expanding access to health and educational facilities between 1976 and 1981.

Still, Mozambique's internal economic policies and resulting political dynamics also contributed to the strength of the armed opposition. Over time, support for Renamo came to reflect a genuine and not insignificant domestic discontent with the government's internal economic policies.[5] A growing proportion of the population became disillusioned by Frelimo's centralism, lack of concern for regional equity, and failure to support the interests of peasant farmers in some parts of the country. The authorities alienated segments of the population by centralizing the agricultural sector, forcibly removing peasants to communal villages, reducing the power and authority of traditional leaders, allowing the Shangane of southern Mozambique to dominate the government, and giving the southern part of the country preferential access to government resources. In addition, the Mozambican economy suffered from built-in distortions and rigidities characteristic of centrally planned systems. Public investments were frequently made on noneconomic criteria; the managers of state enterprises were untrained and inexperienced; and price controls and administrative regulations hampered efficient production and resource allocation.[6] Discontent was particularly severe in Manica and Sofala provinces where the N'dau, the backbone of Renamo, were the dominant ethnic group.

Periods of severe drought in 1986 and 1992, which contributed to major crop failures in an already weakened agricultural sector, intensified the economic decline engendered by persistent warfare and poorly conceived economic and social policies. The centralization of political power and the lack of democratic channels to express opposition or to influence government policies further fueled popular discontent. In sum, although external support for Renamo had to be terminated to bring the civil war to an end, achieving a durable peace would require addressing a number of critical domestic factors.

Aid to Mozambique, 1987–1992

Much of the aid received by Mozambique in the decade following independence was intended to support the government's economic and political policies, but the massive impoverishment and displacement created by war, drought, and economic policy failure meant that by the late 1980s, external assistance was increasingly oriented toward relief and economic restructuring.

Economic restructuring. Following severe criticism of its economic policies at the Fourth Frelimo Party Congress in 1983, the Mozambican government developed the Economic Action Program, 1984–1986 (PAE). The PAE focused on increasing agriculture production and trade, improving the supply of inputs and basic consumer goods to smallholder farmers, providing price supports, and improving the financial situation of enterprises. It also foresaw the introduction of tighter credit policy, changes in interest rates, and a review of the exchange rate policy. Mozambique complemented the PAE by joining the World Bank in September 1984 and, that same year, rescheduling its debt through the Paris Club.[7] The PAE was partially financed by the World Bank's first rehabilitation credit, which carried no formal conditionality but was viewed as demonstrating to the Mozambican government the usefulness of recovery-cum-adjustment loans and establishing a relationship between the Bank and the government. In the view of the Bank, the first rehabilitation credit laid the basis for the policy-based credits that followed.

The economic environment began to improve in 1986 as, for example, fruit and vegetable production responded positively to the elimination of price controls and other reforms began to take hold. In January 1987, the government announced an Economic Rehabilitation Program (PRE), launching the country into an IMF-supported structural adjustment program. Financed by a second World Bank rehabilitation credit valued at $70 million, the PRE initiated reforms of Mozambique's trade regime, foreign exchange allocation system, pricing and distribution policies, fiscal policy, agricultural marketing and producer prices, industrial pricing, and transport sector.[8] The government complemented these economic reforms after the Fifth Frelimo Party Congress by introducing important political reforms in 1990 and 1991. These included a new constitution to provide for a multiparty democracy, as well as legislation protecting freedom of association and the press and establishing an independent judiciary.[9]

The first World Bank–sponsored Consultative Group (CG) meeting was held in April 1987. However, the CG process and the peace process did not intersect until 1991, after the first three protocols of what became the General Peace Agreement had been signed. At the December 1991 CG meeting, a number of donors commented on the links between the transition from war to peace and the transformation of the Mozambican economy. Several donors, including the World Bank chair of the meeting, stressed the importance of donor flexibility once Mozambique entered the war-to-peace transition.[10] At a side session, the government put forward a draft plan for demobilization of 45,000 government troops. Although the donors were pleased with this effort to reduce military spending even as the war continued, they were unwilling at that point to provide funds, reportedly out of concern for potential impact on the ongoing peace negotiations.

The paper presented by the World Bank and the government to the 1991 CG meeting outlined the four main pillars of what became Mozambique's National Reconstruction Plan (PRN): first, reestablishment of security through disarmament, demobilization, and road repair; second, reactivation and expansion of production, especially in rural areas and among the war-affected (including demobilized soldiers); third, resettlement of the internally displaced and refugees and the prompt shift of resources from emergency assistance to supporting livelihoods; and fourth, reintegration of former combatants.[11] The paper envisioned a two-pronged strategy for reconstruction. To begin with, donors would provide assistance to areas securely under the control of the government; but if the peace negotiations concluded successfully, the country would need additional aid to support recovery in the rebel-held and former conflict zones. According to the CG document, the PRN would be funded by a combination of national resources freed by ending the war and significant external funding.

Despite the attention to postconflict issues and planning for the post-war period, most of the discussion at the Consultative Group meeting focused on traditional economic development issues, such as structural adjustment, economic management, accountability and transparency, and consolidation of the reform process. The Bank in particular was unwilling to depart significantly from "business as usual" and shift resources into peace implementation or reconstruction activities.[12] Although donors expressed willingness to support war-to-peace transition programs once peace was achieved, in general

> [t]here was . . . no indication that there would be any modification in the pace of reform measures or the macroeconomic stabilization targets. Indeed, improved . . . initiatives linked to improved economic management and the consolidation of economic reforms were considered two key elements in minimizing the risks inherent in the "rough passage in the transition period."[13]

Emergency assistance for the war- and drought-affected. During the second half of the 1980s, the government had sought greater humanitarian assistance from donors, both to increase its legitimacy vis-à-vis Renamo and to improve the economic situation for its people. Intensified military activities in the Zambezi Valley in 1985–1986 nearly doubled the number of war-affected and internally displaced, which rose from 1.8 million to 3.2 million. In addition, the major crop failure in 1986 threatened famine. In these desperate circumstances, Maputo asked the United Nations to launch an emergency appeal. The UN secretary-general responded in February 1987 by alerting the donor community to the looming crisis. The following month, at a United Nations–sponsored conference in Geneva, donors pledged $330 million for emergency relief, including 625,000 tons of food. For the next decade, Mozambique would receive one of the highest levels of per capita humanitarian assistance through the emergency appeals process (see Table 5.1).

Table 5.1   Mozambique Emergency Appeals, 1987–1992 (U.S.$)

Appeal Year	Total Requirements	Total Pledges
1987/88	n.a.[a]	337,442,000
1988/89	380,406,000	363,565,820
1989/90	361,790,640	323,790,640
1990/91[b]	135,789,026	122,262,877
1991/92	262,522,468	168,494,735
1992/93	447,179,020	315,410,078
Total	1,587,687,154	1,630,966,150

Source: UNSCERO, Closing Reports (1987–1993).
Notes: a. Requirements were not given a dollar value.
b. 1990/91 appeal did not include market food aid.

To supervise this humanitarian initiative, the UN secretary-general appointed a Special Coordinator for Emergency Relief Operations (UNSCERO). To assist the UN special coordinator, who also served as United Nations Development Programme (UNDP) resident representative, an Emergency Unit was established within the UNDP country mission in late 1987. This unit was mandated to support the government's efforts in coordinating aid, assessing needs, consulting with donors, and disseminating information about the emergency program. Unfortunately, the decision to finance and staff the unit exclusively through UNDP limited the unit's credibility with other UN agencies that had more extensive operational experience, notably the United Nations Children's Fund (UNICEF), the World Food Programme (WFP), and the United Nations High Commissioner for Refugees (UNHCR). To make things worse, UNDP also consistently named unit heads with no previous emergency experience.[14] Under these conditions, the other UN agencies had little incentive to collaborate with UNSCERO.

The emergency appeal process continued until the signing of the GPA in 1992. Thereafter, emergency needs were integrated into the Consolidated Humanitarian Assistance Program of the United Nations Operation in Mozambique (ONUMOZ). From 1987 to 1992, Mozambique received pledges worth more than $1.6 billion through its emergency appeal. The UNSCERO office produced monthly statements of pledges that it anticipated would materialize into concrete assistance. However, neither the donors nor the government tracked actual disbursements or obligated funds against pledges.

The emergency appeal process in Mozambique was a collaborative effort of the government of Mozambique and the United Nations. Each year a joint mission, including headquarters staff from relevant UN agencies, traveled to the provinces to identify needs. These missions adopted a multisector approach, assessing broad categories of needs in sectors such as food aid, logistics, relief and survival items, agriculture, health, social welfare, water, education, returnees, and institutional support. This enabled the missions to anticipate development initiatives usually associated with postconflict reconstruction, including the rehabilitation of health centers, schools, and water sources and the distribution of seeds and tools. Personnel from the Mozambican line ministries collaborated with officials from UN agencies to define priority needs; these were then included in the Emergency appeal that UNSCERO prepared with the Mozambican National Executive Commission on the Emergency (CENE). The Mozambique appeal was an assessment of priority needs from the perspective of the affected country. As such, it differed from the UN agency–generated Consolidated Inter-Agency Appeals (CAPS) conducted by the Department of Humanitarian Affairs (DHA) (and later the Office for the Coordination of Humanitarian Affairs, OCHA) in the 1990s, which often reflected agency priorities.

The success of the Mozambican appeal over more than seven years reflected in part donor willingness to treat it not as a UN fund-raising exercise, but rather as an assessment of the country's genuine needs worthy of support by UN agencies, bilateral donors, or nongovernmental organizations (NGOs). The implementing entities were not defined in the appeal, leaving it open for donors to negotiate specific terms with the government.[15] This framework was advantageous to the government, since Maputo could maintain its legitimacy with donors, ensure services in health and education, and direct all emergency relief to government-controlled areas, even as Renamo's control over national territory was increasing. This approach helped support the government during the war, so that Mozambique never fell into the category of a "failed state." This fact assisted the country's postconflict reconstruction.

In 1986, the International Committee of the Red Cross (ICRC) negotiated with the Mozambican government and Renamo to provide humanitarian assistance in Renamo areas. Food aid was limited (since it was not necessary), with most interventions concentrating on relief items, medical support, and distribution of seeds and tools to promote agricultural production. Still, there was no donor effort to include support for Renamo areas within the UN appeal process.[16] In late 1991, when it became evident that Mozambique would suffer greatly from the southern African drought, the ICRC requested that the UN and bilateral donors consider providing emergency food aid to Renamo-controlled areas. The ICRC collaborated with the donor community to obtain information on needs in those areas, hoping to pressure the government and Renamo to permit access to all Mozambicans in need—or at least to create humanitarian corridors. The government and Renamo disagreed strongly about the appropriate logistical arrangements to gain access to the vulnerable Renamo populations. Renamo preferred costly airlifts or cross-border operations, hoping to forestall the resumption of road access to the areas they controlled. The government, which hoped to open up previously accessible areas, and the donors, which hoped to reduce the costs of the operation, backed overland routes.

A UN Drought Appeal for Southern Africa (DESA) was launched in Geneva in June 1992. Although this appeal called on both sides to permit humanitarian access to all Mozambicans and a cease-fire, the UN did not invite Renamo to participate in the conference. This fact underscored both Renamo's lack of international legitimacy as an accepted opposition group and its lack of the political savvy required to pressure donors for a seat at the table.

The DESA experience witnessed a divergence between the UN's recently created DHA and the Mozambican government over the shape of the humanitarian agenda. DHA sought to integrate DESA, its first foray into the emergency appeal business, into the framework of the agency-driven consolidated appeals process. Mozambique, following past practice, had written its own drought appeal with the help of UNSCERO. As the DESA appeal was being assembled in Geneva, UNSCERO backed Mozambique's view and insisted that the Mozambique portion of the appeal should be consistent with field-determined needs, rather than being driven by agendas from UN agency headquarters. The ultimate choice of a field-based approach was made possible by the five-year history of UNSCERO-supported emergency appeals.

Jump-Starting Postwar Planning

One important reason that Mozambique was able to mobilize international support was that it never fell into the category of "failed state." All central line ministries and provincial governments continued to function, though with reduced capacity and coverage. The state played a major role in identifying emergency priorities. Additionally, planning for postwar reconstruction was placed on the political agenda as early as 1989. Provincial governors were asked to carry out surveys of war damage to social infrastructure (schools, health posts, water sources) so that the government could begin determining the costs of reconstruction and prioritizing needs in the event of a peace agreement. Such activities helped build internal and external political constituencies for peace.

The Ministry of Finance began planning for demobilization in 1990, as negotiations with Renamo got under way. The challenge was to reduce military expenditures, which accounted for a large portion of the state budget and hampered the government's ability to apply resources to other areas. This effort won applause from the donor community for promoting fiscal transparency and confronting the previously "untouchable" status of the military in justifying public expenditure. This initial planning process, financed by technical assistance from Switzerland, gave the government a two-year lead before the GPA was signed. In early 1991, the Ministry of Finance established a Reintegration Unit. This unit collaborated with the Ministry of Defense to determine which soldiers should be demobilized and cooperated with civilian ministries (agriculture, health, labor, education) to prepare their reintegration into civilian life.

At the December 1991 Consultative Group meeting, the government presented a plan to demobilize 45,000 government troops. Donors did not support this initiative, considering it too costly and fearing that it might upset the ongoing, delicate peace negotiations. However, the presentation and discussion of the plan helped to build a base for future support among donor agencies, who possessed little or no prior experience with the demobilization and reintegration of ex-combatants.

Donor Coordination

The mechanisms of donor coordination in Mozambique corresponded to the two separate paths of donor involvement in that country: emergency relief and development assistance. With UN support, the government established a commission (CENE) to coordinate humanitarian assistance. The government chaired weekly meetings of the Emergency Operations Group (EOG), attended by representatives of UNSCERO, UN agencies, bilateral donors, and NGOs. UNSCERO and the UNDP Emergency Unit provided institutional support to the government's coordination effort and (in its first years) served as its secretariat, enhancing credibility with donors. UNDP provided more than $2 million to allow CENE to establish its own monitoring and coordination capacities, including Provincial Emergency Commissions (CPEs) that, with the assistance of UN advisers, assessed needs and coordinated response in the provinces. The CPEs worked with Provincial Planning Commissions to gather information for the PRN. In six key provinces, the UN advisers helped coordinate humanitarian assistance to Renamo-controlled areas in the critical period after the GPA and before the UN peacekeeping mission had been put into place.

Donor coordination was complicated by the nearly complete separation of emergency and development programs within both bilateral and UN agencies. The minimal information flow and consultation between the two groupings prevented joint planning that might have smoothed Mozambique's transition between relief and development.

Prior to the introduction of the CG process in 1987, cooperation among development partners occurred through bilateral negotiations with the government and was driven by political groupings. The most prominent of these was the "Like-Minded Group" of bilateral donors, including Norway, Sweden, the Netherlands, Switzerland, Denmark, and Canada. Assistance from the United States, which had been prohibited before the mid-1980s, began to emerge in the relief field in the 1980s and in the development area in the 1990s. Still, the United States was never included in discussions with the Like-Minded Group since it had not been a historical ally of the Frelimo government, and its approach to aid delivery and implementation was to bypass the government. The Like-Minded Group exercised a strong influence over emerging Mozambican policies on economic liberalization, postwar planning and reconstruction, and coordination and rationalization of external assistance.

Mobilizing External Resources
for Peace Implementation, 1992–1994

By the time the General Peace Agreement was signed in Rome on October 4, 1992, Mozambique had established itself as a major recipient of external financial assistance from a broad range of bilateral and multilateral donors. The government continued to function throughout the war, had been actively involved in defining war- and drought-related needs, and possessed some capacity to deliver assistance itself through national and provincial structures. Also, a large number of NGOs already operating in Mozambique were available to implement donor programs. Effective donor coordination and aid pledging mechanisms for both relief and development assistance were also already in place. To its credit, the government had the foresight to begin to plan for postconflict reconstruction while the peace accord was being negotiated, and it had already demonstrated a commitment to significant economic and political reforms in the preceding years that could form the basis of a durable peace.

Nonetheless, significant problems impaired the design and delivery of external assistance for peace implementation in Mozambique. Despite extensive planning and preparation for postwar reconstruction, demobilization, and reintegration, neither the government nor the international agencies operating in Mozambique were prepared for the speed with which the population moved to resettle in their home areas after October 1992. In addition, many agencies (and their donors) could not break out of their narrow, one-year time frame for emergency assistance to support resettlement and initial reintegration over a more viable three-to-five-year period. Political jockeying between Renamo and the government delayed the peace process, exacerbating the difficulties associated with short donor time frames.

Objectively, the country needed a mechanism to help define and coordinate external support for peace implementation activities. However, the entity that the United Nations Operation in Mozambique (ONUMOZ) established for this purpose, the UN Office of Humanitarian Assistance Coordination (UNOHAC), was compelled to maintain the neutrality of the peacekeeping operation in relation to both the government and Renamo. Shortly after the negotiation of the GPA, a DHA mission consulted with all UN agencies in Mozambique on a new structure of coordination. Because UNSCERO did not represent all UN agencies and was closely tied to the government's wartime aid coordination mechanisms, the agencies agreed to the creation of a new structure—UNOHAC. Unfortunately, this agreement was short-lived, and there were significant tensions for at least the first year of the peace process between the new entity and UNDP, other UN operational agencies, and the bilateral donors.

Meanwhile, the peace agreement generated tensions between the Frelimo government and the representatives of the donor community. Although the government had ceded some of its sovereignty and authority voluntarily to the United Nations in signing the GPA, it nonetheless felt that the international community should be more sensitive to its views and positions.

For their part, donor governments were eager to keep the peace process moving forward, even though they recognized that the one-year time frame envisioned by the GPA was too short. Their attitude derived at least in part from the financial burden of the ONUMOZ mission and the associated peace implementation programs, some of which—such as demobilization—became more costly the longer the peace process continued. Donors thus sought to overcome all delays, whether caused by political tensions between Renamo and the government, by slow decisionmaking within the government, or by disagreements over program content. Consequently, the donors and their governments became quite involved in planning and overseeing critical peace implementation programs, in many cases effectively bypassing the government, the Commission on Reintegration, and/or UNOHAC.

The democratic elections envisioned in the GPA were finally held in October 1994, after a one-year delay and a last-minute boycott threat by Renamo. They were declared to have been "free and fair" by the Special Representative of the Secretary-General (SRSG). Despite the problems associated with peace implementation, Renamo's acceptance of the outcome led donors—and particularly the United Nations—to tout Mozambique as a major success story for the international community. "Success," of course, is a relative term. In contrast to Angola and other ostensibly "postconflict" countries, Mozambique has not returned to war, the armed opposition was demobilized and disarmed, and refugees and the internally displaced were able to return home.

These achievements are indisputable. It is uncertain, however, how much credit the United Nations deserves for these outcomes. As a rule, *the* critical element in the successful implementation of any peace process is the political will of the parties to the conflict to make peace and to sustain the peace process. The Mozambique experience demonstrates that external support can nurture fragile local political will, but it also suggests that external actors cannot *create* it. In Mozambique, as in Namibia and El Salvador, the international community encountered societies weary of armed conflict and warring parties willing—to varying degrees—to stop the killing. This fact distinguishes those "success stories" from the cases of Angola, Bosnia, Palestine, Sierra Leone, or Sudan.

Nurturing political will requires political, security, and financial resources. The international community continued to be generous with political and financial resources in Mozambique, and fortunately, given its track record regarding the use of force to support peace implementation, it did not face a situation in which it was necessary to decide whether or not to use its security resources for military purposes.[17] As Table 5.2 shows, Mozambique received an annual average of $995 million in grants and loans between 1993 and 1996. Direct peace implementation costs, such as demobilization and reintegration of soldiers, de-mining, refugee repatriation, resettlement, and national elections accounted for less than one-third of this over the two and one-half year life of the peace operation.[18] The remainder was allocated to economic stabilization and reactivation. Clearly, a stable macroeconomic environment is a precondition to successful recovery from violence. However, the effort to create a viable economic framework must not undermine the implementation of peace agreements or the consolidation of peace. As we discuss below, this seems to have been less of a problem in Mozambique than in some other countries. The Bretton Woods institutions have been criticized for economic conditionalities imposed on Mozambique.[19] During the peace process, however, these issues were more muted, probably because so much attention was focused on implementing the Rome Agreement and concerns that

Table 5.2 **Mozambique External Assistance Flows, 1990–1997 (U.S.$ millions)**

	1990	1991	1992	1993	1994	1995	1996	1997
Gross disbursements	1,066	991	927	841	1,048	1,082	978	814
Grants	873	749	788	692	820	852	678	544
Loans	193	241	139	149	228	230	300	270
External debt service	9	14	19	32	25	187	59	33
Principal	3	5	6	27	11			
Interest	6	9	13	5	14			
Net disbursements	1,063	986	921	814	1,037			
Net transfers	1,057	977	908	809	1,023			

Source: 1990–1994 UN Development Cooperation Report; World Bank Debt Tables, 1995–1997; Ministry of Planning and Finance, Maputo.

the peace might not hold. Other countries have had quite different experiences with the international financial institutions (IFIs) during the peace implementation period.[20]

Each of the case studies in this book explores whether donor agencies give the appearance of being more generous than they actually are. Specifically, do donor agencies promise more to countries undergoing war-to-peace transitions than they ultimately deliver? An examination of the aid for peace implementation provided to Mozambique suggests that the problem was less a gap between pledges and disbursement than it was a "gap" in implementation or conceptualization.

Before turning to issues of delivery and possible "implementation" and "conceptual" gaps, we need to clarify the distinctions between different types of aid flows. We also need to review the different mechanisms through which donors provided funds to Mozambique for peace implementation and coordinated their assistance strategies.

Conceptual Issues Concerning External Financial Assistance

One of the greatest obstacles to compiling accurate information on external financial assistance is that there is no common terminology or definitions among the various entities tracking assistance (such as UN agencies, the World Bank, the Organization for Economic Cooperation and Development [OECD], or the recipient government). In the Mozambique case, different entities tracked assistance at different periods of time, making it impossible to develop a consistent data set over time. In addition, the government and donors often tracked assistance over different time frames and fiscal years. Sometimes, as was the case for emergency appeals in Mozambique, planting seasons defined the pledging and delivery periods. In short, any financial figures must be viewed skeptically and as indicative rather than completely accurate.

Most donors pledged assistance against defined needs. The question of *who* defined those needs—and how pledges corresponded to these—is the subject of great debate. During the war years, Mozambique's emergency needs were defined by joint missions, and the government and the UN agreed on several categories of need (including food aid, logistics, relief and survival items, agriculture, water and sanitation, health, roads and bridges, returning refugees, education, social welfare, and institutional support). There was considerable debate concerning what should be considered "emergency" aid and what should be left to development programming. From the early emergency appeals, the Mozambique government argued strongly for linking relief to longer-term development. As a result, these emergency appeals included the distribution of seeds and tools to displaced families, the provision of educational materials to primary schools in war-affected areas, and the rebuilding of rural health posts attacked during the war.

Once the GPA was signed, the appeals were expanded to include specific "peace-building" sectors such as mine clearance, demobilization, reintegration of demobilized soldiers, and support for elections and the political process. As the responsibility for defining humanitarian needs shifted from UNSCERO (and the government) to UNOHAC (in consultation with the government, Renamo, and the donors), donors did not always agree on some of the particulars of the needs and programs presented.

The time frame of the emergency appeals usually followed the agricultural year (May to April). This did not coincide with the Consultative Group delivery period, which used the calendar year. In the postpeace agreement period, the government presented its humanitarian needs to donors on four different occasions. The first was at the Rome Conference in December 1992, which covered a one-year period (the initial time frame of the GPA). In May 1993, UNOHAC revised estimates of humanitarian needs (excluding elections and the political process) for the one-year period from May 1993 to April 1994 (following the UNSCERO practice of employing the agricultural year). UNOHAC produced an update in November 1993 and, in April 1994, conducted an additional needs assessment to cover the revised program for demobilization and reintegration and to carry the humanitarian program through the end of ONUMOZ's mandate (which had been extended until December 1994). ONUMOZ defined electoral needs, in cooperation with the two parties.

When tracking pledges against needs, donors (to inflate their pledges) often tried to claim that a particular contribution was against a need. In fact, pledges were often wholly unrelated to any stated need. In the 1987–1992 period, pledges were made public at the annual appeal meetings. This was problematic, since many countries would repledge the same funds that they had not yet delivered on from the previous year. UNSCERO tracked the pledges through the year, but inevitably many pledges reappeared year after year.

The UN never attempted to track disbursements comprehensively, in part because donors had different aid definitions and accounting practices. The UN did track delivery of relief aid, both food and nonfood, but it restricted its tracking of nonfood project assistance to *obligations*— defined as having a contract signed with a particular implementer. UNOHAC, recognizing that the "pledging year" was not always consistent with the disbursement year, avoided double counting by carrying over undisbursed pledges into the following year.

The Mozambique government did not track pledges, but it did track actual *disbursements* in a given calendar year. In 1995, the government, with World Bank help, upgraded its efforts to track aid flows. At that point, the UN ceased monitoring humanitarian aid flows, so that henceforth the annual UNDP Development Cooperation Report was limited to data provided by bilateral donor responses to UNDP questionnaires. Unfortunately, these data are unreliable, since donor government ministries did not always communicate information on aid flows to their country's embassy in Maputo. Nor did donors or the government create mechanisms to track private sector investment—an important indicator of postconflict economic revitalization.

Pledging and Donor Coordination Mechanisms

At the time the General Peace Agreement was signed, Mozambique had two major pledging mechanisms: the Consultative Group and the UN emergency appeals processes. In addition, smaller, parallel pledging processes were conducted by agencies such as UNICEF, UNHCR, the ICRC, and Oxfam. When the GPA entered into force, donors created a third major pledging mechanism: a conference specifically intended to attract external support for peace implementation. Such a conference had been promised in the Agreed Agenda of the Rome negotiations of May 28, 1991. Donors anticipated that such a gathering would serve as an incentive, encouraging the parties to conclude a peace agreement. Therefore, the GPA included a formal request to the Italian government to host such a meeting.[21]

In the end, two conferences dealing with assistance for peace implementation were held. The first was convened in Rome by the Italian government on December 15–16, 1992, a week after the first postwar Consultative Group meeting was held in Paris. The second, cochaired by Italy and the United Nations, took place in Maputo on June 8–9, 1993.

The donor community also created multiple forums to coordinate its assistance to Mozambique. The major multidonor coordination groups were UNOHAC, the World Bank–led Consultative Group process, and UNDP's in-country coordination mechanism, led by the UN resident coordinator. In addition, the Like-Minded Group (Canada, Denmark, the Netherlands, Norway, Sweden, and Switzerland) maintained their own caucus, at times playing an important role in developing programs and influencing aid policies regarding peace implementation. The special representative of the secretary-general, Aldo Ajello, also held weekly meetings with two groups of ambassadors. One of these gathered the Like-Minded Group. The other group consisted of ambassadors from the six countries designated as members of the high-level politico-military commissions mandated by the peace accords: Britain, France, Germany, Italy, Portugal, and the United States. Within both of these informal political forums, discussions touched on important topics affecting the provision of aid, including the timing of the elections and decisions to create a special fund for Renamo.

The political framework for peace implementation. The General Peace Agreement was negotiated by the Catholic lay organization Communita de Sant'Egidio, which had maintained contacts with both Renamo and the government during the conflict. A number of countries played important facilitating roles during the discussions in Rome between July 1990 and the signing of the accord in October 1992. These included Botswana, Great Britain, Congo, France, Kenya, Portugal, the USSR, the United States, Zambia, and Zimbabwe. The United Nations sent observers only in June 1992 when it became evident that it would be helpful to have the UN supervise the implementation of the agreement.

However, at the field level, the humanitarian issues and the need for corridors and access to populations in Renamo areas were a major concern for UNSCERO, the UN agencies, and the ICRC. The latter was the only international organization working in Renamo areas at that time. Given the widespread drought in southern Africa, more than 3 million Mozambicans needed food relief. Providing this assistance would have been impossible without agreement from Renamo and the government to allow access. In early July 1992, delegations from the government, Renamo, and UN agencies in the field (WFP and UNICEF)—led by UNSCERO and the UNDP resident representative[22]—met in Rome to work out a practical approach to humanitarian corridors. The Declaration of the Republic of Mozambique and Renamo on the Guiding Principles for Humanitarian Assistance, signed by the two parties on July 16, named the UN to preside over a commission to coordinate and supervise all humanitarian assistance operations. This declaration signified that any peacekeeping mission in Mozambique would have a major humanitarian component.

The GPA contained provisions governing the formation and recognition of political parties, the press, and other political freedoms; the election of a new parliament and president; the creation of a new national defense force; the future role of the National Service for People's Security; the reform of the police; the cessation of hostilities and separation of forces; and the reintegration of demobilized soldiers.

The accord also asked the government of Italy to convene a donor conference to discuss financing activities associated with implementing a number of these provisions, particularly the electoral process, emergency programs, political parties, and the reintegration of war-affected persons, including demobilized soldiers. This request implicitly recognized that Mozambique urgently needed financial assistance to implement key peace-related programs. Unless the country's development cooperation partners supported this process, economic and social development would continue to languish.

The United Nations supervised and monitored the overall implementation of the peace agreement through its senior diplomat in Mozambique, the SRSG. To assist the SRSG, the GPA set up a Supervisory and Monitoring

Commission (CSC) and three subsidiary commissions: the Cease-Fire Commission (CCF), the Joint Commission for the Formation of the Mozambican Defense Force (CCFADM), and the Commission on Reintegration (CORE). Only CORE was directly relevant to the funding and coordination of donor assistance for peace implementation. It had responsibility for planning, organizing, supervising, and monitoring the economic and social reintegration of military personnel. The membership of CORE included representatives of the government, Renamo, the United Nations (as chair), and "invited countries."[23] In practice, virtually all demobilization and reintegration programs would be planned and organized by the donors and implemented by nongovernmental actors. The activities of other commissions impinged upon donor activities only insofar as the work they carried out influenced the pace of peace implementation.

Pledging. Because the peace process called for a separate donor conference to address funding peace-related programs, specific peace implementation activities were not the focus of the two Consultative Group meetings held between the peace agreement of October 1992 and the elections of October 1994. Instead, the CG meetings (held in December 1992 and December 1993) concentrated on issues of economic management and reform, including the country's foreign exchange allocation system, its financial sector, public enterprise restructuring, and the development of institutional capacity to implement ongoing economic and social reforms.

Although traditional economic issues dominated these meetings, the background documents prepared for them did incorporate information about the National Reconstruction Plan, its costs, and its implications for external financing. Pledging at the CG conferences also included all emergency and commercial food aid, even that intended for specific peace implementation programs. These documents clearly assumed that money pledged for PRN-related programs would be in addition to (and thus not reduce) funding for the regular economic program. The World Bank was particularly concerned that, given "Mozambique's limited budgetary resources, this assistance should not come at the expense of balance of payments support."[24] Documents prepared for the 1993 CG meeting suggested a desire to integrate the PRN with the National Public Investment Program, in order to "ensure future sustainability in terms of recurrent costs and implementation capacity"[25] In sum, the CG process did not occur in isolation from Mozambique's postconflict recovery and peace implementation needs, although it did not delve deeply into these issues, either.

At the December 1992 donors meeting on postconflict recovery and peace implementation, Mozambique requested $402 million for the first phase of postwar reconstruction activities. Major program areas included demobilization and reintegration of ex-combatants, repatriation of refugees, resettlement of refugees and internally displaced persons (IDPs), and preparation for elections. Although the specific programs under each heading would require further elaboration, donor representatives worked with the government and the UN agencies in Mozambique to provide preliminary cost estimates and an indication of the types of programs that would be carried out in each of these areas.[26] In the case of demobilization and reintegration of ex-combatants, for example, a working group of UN agencies convened by the Reintegration Unit in the Ministry of Finance designed a $61 million program covering civilian services in the assembly areas, as well as postdemobilization programs.[27] (Table 5.3 classifies the funding requested for peace implementation by program area.)

By the end of the Rome meeting, donors had pledged some $318 million against the $402 million requested.[28] (See Table 5.4.) They also sent a strong signal about the shape they wanted reintegration programs to take, indicating that "international cooperation should address the needs of all vulnerable groups in priority areas, without discrimination. There should be integration of programs for the demobilized (after they have left assembly points), returning refugees, displaced persons and locally affected populations." In short, reintegration programs targeting demobilized soldiers were not acceptable to donors at that time. The donors also contemplated proposing a change in CORE's mandate to include reintegration activities for all war-affected populations, not just demobilized soldiers. This idea, however, was dropped.[29]

By the time the United Nations and the government of Italy convened a follow-up meeting of donors in early June 1993, a total of $450 million had been pledged. At that meeting, donors promised another $70 million worth of assistance. In addition, UNOHAC presented its plans for a $559.6 million humanitarian assistance program. This proved to be controversial, however, as some donors rejected the plan's developmental, medium-term approach to the restoration of basic services and reintegration of war-affected populations. The United Nations also created two trust funds, supervised by SRSG Ajello and the Italian ambassador to Mozambique. One was intended to facilitate Renamo's transformation into a political party; the other provided funds for all registered political parties participating in the electoral campaign. The Renamo trust fund ultimately received $13.6 million in contributions; the all-party trust fund received $1.88 million.

In addition to these multilateral mechanisms to mobilize resources, UNICEF, UNHCR, ICRC, and some NGOs launched separate appeals to support their own work in Mozambique. By and large, these were driven by institutional needs rather than sectoral priorities. In some cases, the content of these appeals reflected the broader humanitarian program, which did not specify implementing partners. Usually, however, these parallel appeals were launched from headquarters as part of the institutional fund-raising strategy.

Table 5.3   Rome Conference Peace Implementation Program[a] (U.S.$ millions)

Program Components	Estimated Cost
Electoral process[b]	
Operating costs, electoral organization	8.1
Electoral material	21.6
Air transport	12.0
Surface transport	9.8
Civic education	3.9
Training of electoral personnel	2.0
Equipment	1.3
Constituency identification	0.7
Technical assistance	2.9
Food rations, tents, etc.	4.6
Contingencies	10.0
Total	76.9
Emergency and reintegration program for displaced persons and returnees	
Selected seeds and tools and first assistance packages	105.0
Logistics	70.0
Primary health care and nutrition	15.0
Education	2.0
Water supply	20.0
Vulnerable groups	2.0
Repair of roads and bridges	20.0
Social and productive activities	45.0
Institutional support	2.0
Total	265.0
Reintegration of demobilized soldiers	
Assembly area operating costs	10.0
Transition to civilian life[c]	
Distribution of clothing	1.5
Transportion	24.0
Management costs of Reintegration Commission	1.5
Technical unit management costs	0.5
Social and economic reintegration	
Technical and professional training	6.5
Equipment and distribution of kits	9.0
Scholarships	4.2
Disabled soldiers	2.1
Vulnerable groups	1.7
Total	61.0
Total	402.9

Sources: Government of Italy, "Letter Dated 30 December 1992 Transmitting the Conclusions of the Donors Conference for Mozambique, Held in Rome on 15 and 16 December 1992," Document 28, in *The United Nations and Mozambique, 1992–1995*, pp. 152–163, 165, 169.

Notes: a. Excludes all emergency and commercial food aid.

b. Excludes support for political parties mandated by GPA.

c. Excludes demobilization indemnities ($22.5 m.) to be paid by the Government of Mozambique.

Coordination mechanisms.   The UN secretary-general gave the SRSG responsibility for coordinating humanitarian assistance. To support this task, the United Nations created UNOHAC to coordinate humanitarian assistance within the peacekeeping mission. Although UNOHAC was under the

Table 5.4   Pledges Registered at Rome Conference (U.S.$ millions)

	Non-Food Aid	Food Aid[a]
Australia[b, e]	1.13	4.52
Austria[d]	2.00	
Belgium	0.16	
Commonwealth secretariat	0.20	
Canada[b]		15.66
Denmark	8.00	
European Community	71.09	25.96
Finland	1.56	
France	6.00	1.87
Germany	16.60	
Italy	107.53	6.65
Japan[b]	1.00	
Luxembourg	0.19	
Netherlands	13.59	
Norway[b]	8.00	
Portugal	5.23	
South Africa[c]	3.44	
Spain	3.20	
Sweden	22.00	
Switzerland[b]	12.00	
United Kingdom[b]	4.71	
United States	20.00	25.00
Subtotal	307.63	
ONUMOZ	11.05	
Total	318.68	79.66

Sources: Government of Italy, "Letter Dated 30 December 1992, Transmitting the Conclusion of the Donors Conference for Mozambique, Held in Rome on 15 and 16 December 1992," Document 28, in *The United Nations and Mozambique, 1992–1995,* p. 170.

Notes: a. Several donors confirmed food aid pledges from the CG meeting that are included here for informational purposes only.

b. Countries that expressed the willingness to increase their commitments and communicate their pledges once their 1993 budget lines are approved.

c. Estimates only.

d. Through UNICEF.

e. Already pledged at CG meeting.

overall authority of the SRSG, the humanitarian coordinator also reported to the DHA in New York. This dual reporting arrangement, as well as the decision not to appoint the UNDP resident coordinator as humanitarian coordinator, created tensions between the latter and the SRSG. This was particularly acute in the case of the first humanitarian coordinator, who differed with the SRSG about the proper approach toward humanitarian assistance in a postconflict environment. These differences were characterized by SRSG Ajello as the clash between the culture of peacekeeping and the culture of development. Ajello was strongly opposed to the introduction of long-term perspectives into peace implementation activities. To complicate matters, some organizations that seconded staff to UNOHAC were unwilling to allow those staff to report solely to the humanitarian co-ordinator and not to their own headquarters.[30] Two major humanitarian assistance organizations, UNHCR and WFP, were slow to develop links with UNOHAC, viewing it "as an unnecessary interference with their work."[31]

UNDP had been coordinating emergency assistance to Mozambique for some years, and it had a special unit, UNSCERO, already in place. The UN merged the UNSCERO unit into UNOHAC. UNOHAC's staff, drawn initially from UNSCERO or UN agencies in the field, possessed a deep knowledge of the country. This permitted the humanitarian component to start up before the other components of the operation. However, tensions developed because the resident coordinator/UNDP resident representative was not given the responsibility of coordinating humanitarian assistance during the peace implementation period. Instead, the SRSG, DHA, and UNDP headquarters chose a senior former UNDP official with peacekeeping experience, who would be able to focus full-time on humanitarian coordination, to run UNOHAC. This decision dealt a setback to the principle of continuity in UN oversight through the office of the UN resident coordinator, and the resident coordinator himself (who had only recently arrived in Maputo) felt personally humiliated.

The decisions that produced these outcomes were made very rapidly after the peace agreement was signed, without adequate consideration of their possible effect or sufficient understanding of the situation on the ground. The specifications for the mission were developed in late October 1992, in a matter of days, leaving little time for planning and discussions with the relevant actors. For example, UN agencies did not yet appreciate the implications that creating an SRSG might have for UN leadership in the field. Although the Department of Political Affairs had been involved in the Rome negotiations, other UN agencies and departments were brought into the process at a very late stage. UNOHAC was set up after consultation with all agencies in Maputo. These agreed on the overall structure and the participation of key agencies through seconded staff. The initial proposals for UNOHAC did not stipulate whether it would be integrated into the peacekeeping operation or who would head it. These decisions were left to the SRSG, who firmly stated that he would not have allowed UNOHAC to remain outside ONUMOZ.[32]

Although UNOHAC was created to coordinate humanitarian assistance, it was not responsible for coordinating all peace implementation assistance. The Rome donors conference of December 1992 declared that UNOHAC should "serve as the follow-up coordinating mechanism to ensure efficient, transparent and flexible programming and should provide overall coordination of United Nations agencies' operations" relating to refugee return and reintegration of war-affected populations. UNDP was ultimately given responsibility for coordinating the technical assistance

associated with preparing for the elections.[33] Moreover, a series of disagreements—among the donors, between donors and UNOHAC, and
between the donors and the government—resulted in the active involvement of bilateral donors and the UNDP in planning and oversight of reintegration programs for ex-combatants.

As in the case of Angola during the same period, the creation of field
offices improved the UN's ability to conduct needs assessments, establish
priorities, and coordinate the delivery of assistance to those in need.[34] In
each of Mozambique's ten provinces, UNOHAC established Provincial
Humanitarian Assistance Committees. These enabled representatives of the
government and Renamo to work productively with the humanitarian
community. The committees were particularly useful in gaining information on previously inaccessible areas that had been under Renamo's control
and in distributing this data to humanitarian actors. They also helped build
mutual confidence between the two formerly warring parties.

In the sphere of refugee return and resettlement, UNHCR acted with
considerable autonomy. Although UNHCR was unprepared at the time of
the peace agreement, it established a network of suboffices in areas with
high returnee populations. These offices had funds for Quick Impact Projects (QIPs), enabling UNHCR to disburse $87 million for these purposes
between 1993 and 1996. However, UNHCR staff did not create a technical unit until January 1995, limiting its ability to develop and review
appropriate projects. In addition, the agency declined to engage in technical collaboration or joint planning for reintegration with either UNOHAC
or UNDP. Not until 1995, when repatriation was about to end, did UNHCR
sign a Memorandum of Understanding with UNDP. This lack of collaboration stands in contrast to the experience in Cambodia and Central America, where UNHCR and UNDP worked from the outset on integrated,
multisectoral reintegration programs.

Donors also discussed assistance for peace implementation in a number of ad hoc coordination groups. The Aid for Democracy group, which
had originated in meetings of ambassadors interested in supporting
Mozambique's democratization process, evolved into a working group in
which donors discussed, among other subjects, how to organize the electoral process. Although the EU initially presided, UNDP began chairing
these meetings in early 1993. The group created a series of committees.
One, the Electoral Subgroup, met fortnightly and then weekly as the elections approached. In mid-1993, after rejecting UNOHAC's reintegration
plan, the donors created another subgroup to advance ex-combatant reintegration. Under the leadership of the Netherlands and Norway, this subgroup developed the single largest ex-combatant reintegration program, the
Reintegration Support Scheme (RSS). In addition, the Like-Minded Group
of donors met weekly.

Each of these groups consisted only of donors. UNDP was responsible for coordination between the Aid for Democracy group and the government. On the electoral process, UNDP coordinated with the Technical Secretariat for Electoral Administration (STAE) and the ONUMOZ Electoral Unit. These three bodies effectively developed the electoral plan that was discussed in cabinet but did not require cabinet approval. The plan also had the full approval of the donor community. UNOHAC was responsible for coordinating with CORE on demobilization and reintegration. While UNOHAC staff felt that they had a good collaboration with the government and Renamo, it was subsequently recognized that UNOHAC's work "could have benefitted from informal donor working groups to develop joint programs and consensus."[35] Admittedly, it might have been difficult to achieve such consensus in view of the very different approaches to the content of reintegration programs on the part of UNOHAC and some of the major donors, but serious efforts were not made to bridge these differences.

The donor community, although fairly small and in close contact professionally and socially, contributed to the lack of cohesion. Often, excellent personal communications between staff from different organizations did not translate into institutional collaboration. As will be discussed in the following section, programs for mine clearance and ex-combatant reintegration were particularly contentious. Had UNOHAC been a more successful facilitator, some of these problems might well have been overcome. It is surely no accident that two of the more successful collaborative programs were overseen by UNDP, whose resident representative, Eric de Mul, was given high marks regarding transparency and facilitation. Some donors thought that the World Bank, whose resident representative throughout most of the peace implementation period, Roberto Chavez, was also highly regarded, should have played a more central role in ex-combatant reintegration.[36] At the time, however, it would have been extremely difficult for the Bank's resident mission to take on this issue, because the Bank was only beginning to involve itself in demobilization and reintegration activities.

Pledge Gap Versus Implementation and Conceptual Gaps

Available evidence suggests that Mozambique did suffer from a "pledge-disbursement gap" between 1988 and 1991 for assistance provided through the Consultative Group process. In some years, the difference between CG pledges and subsequent disbursements reached 30 percent. After 1992, however, the gap for CG pledges narrowed considerably.[37] That the potential for overpledging at Consultative Group meetings remained is underscored by the comment of a World Bank official familiar with the CG process since 1993. According to this official, the Bank staff routinely "ignored" pledges made at these gatherings, concentrating instead on the firm commitments that emerged in the weeks following the meetings.

With regard to pledges of assistance for peace implementation activities, the data indicate that, with a lag of a year or two, there were no significant gaps between pledges and disbursements. Table 5.3 summarizes the peace implementation program against which donors pledged in December 1992, and Table 5.4 outlines the initial pledges generated, classed by country or organization. Table 5.5 provides information on commitments by program for all major peace implementation activities.

The funds for peace implementation were primarily coordinated and tracked by UNOHAC. However, UNDP also supervised a number of extremely important programs: electoral assistance, the Reintegration Support Scheme for demobilized soldiers, and land mine removal (both initially and post-ONUMOZ). In addition, the special representative's office coordinated the Renamo trust fund and the all-party electoral trust fund. Consistent, conscious "overpledging" does not seem to have been a problem for the majority of Mozambique's development partners. Only Italy appears to have regularly pledged more than it intended to deliver and to have been extremely slow in disbursing its assistance.

Many of the lags in delivering assistance for peace implementation resulted from political delays in the peace process. For example, documents prepared for the CG meeting of December 1993 indicate that of $290 million pledged at the Rome donor meeting for peace implementation activities during 1993, nearly 75 percent had to be carried over to 1994. More than half of this carryover represented assistance for demobilization and the electoral process, both of which had been postponed because of political disagreements between Renamo and Frelimo—as well as Renamo's lack of preparation to participate effectively in the peace process.

Such delays in the peace process increased the likelihood that donors, constrained by one-year budget cycles, might not be able to carry over to the next year the funds they had pledged for specific purposes. Still, most pledges for peace implementation programs were eventually honored. In some cases, problems in other African countries worked to Mozambique's advantage. When Switzerland suspended its development programs in Rwanda following the April 1994 genocide, the Swiss Development Cooperation increased significantly its contribution to Mozambique's Reintegration Support Scheme (RSS) program.

The RSS program, administered by UNDP, became the most successful reinsertion program for demobilized soldiers in Mozambique. Still, it was nearly derailed by concerns at UNDP headquarters about whether UNDP should accept responsibility for a multiyear project for which only the first year's outlays were guaranteed—and nothing more than pledges existed for the second phase. The UNDP resident representative had to argue strenuously to persuade New York to take a chance on the program.

In general, the "pledge-disbursement gap" posed a far smaller problem for Mozambique than did both an "implementation gap" and a "conceptual

Table 5.5   External Support for Peace Implementation Activities (U.S.$)

Sector/Area of Support	Total Needs	Total Obligated Funds
Emergency Relief (1993–1994)		
Relief food	85,821,900	74,764,188
Food aid logistics	67,151,169	46,736,658
Non-food relief items	23,411,925	9,015,753
Transport of vulnerable groups	2,770,000	2,492,692
Natural disasters—Cyclone Nadia	2,347,780	1,944,954
Subtotal	181,502,774	134,954,245
Repatriation Operation[a]		
UNOHAC period (1993–1994)	41,862,339	19,590,475
UNHCR projected (1995–1996)	n.a.	2,089,039
Subtotal	41,862,339	21,679,514
Reintegration		
Agriculture (1993–1994)	128,185,314	68,247,363
Health (1993–1994)	64,100,000	31,722,260
Water and sanitation (1993–1994)	27,835,000	17,712,450
Roads and bridges (1993–1994)	34,600,000	38,191,000
Education (1993–1994)	13,025,000	5,063,284
Multisectoral programs (1993–1994)	38,987,000	21,275,035
UNHCR projected (1995–1996)	n.a.	35,358,415
Subtotal	306,732,314	217,569,807
Mine clearance (1993–1994)	31,617,535	28,170,349
Institutional support (1993–1994)	18,023,000	10,260,934
Demobilization (1993–1994)		
Food	7,916,808	8,400,000
Non-food items (tents, bedding, etc.)	3,161,500	2,326,534
Health care	3,976,022	3,056,168
Water supply	753,000	850,000
Registration	300,000	179,000
Technical unit	1,312,747	2,921,000
Subtotal[b]	17,420,077	17,732,702
Ex-combatant reinsertion (1993–1996)		
Social reintegration	477,800	395,000
Vulnerable groups	1,525,000	351,000
Home transport	12,222,344	11,580,000
Civilian clothing	2,721,687	3,036,000
Government demobilization subsidy[c]	22,470,000	10,259,000
Reintegration Support Scheme	22,527,580	35,500,000
Information and referral service	4,219,000	7,865,000
Vegetable/tool kits	n.a.	1,888,000
Food-for-home ration	n.a.	8,600,000
Subtotal	66,163,411	79,474,000
Ex-combatant reintegration (1994–1996)		
Occupational skills development/training	14,965,000	4,400,000
Provincial fund-IOM	5,500,000	5,000,000
Provincial fund-GTZ		6,340,000
Subtotal	20,465,000	15,740,000
Electoral process (1993–1994)		
Electoral structures	9,030,000	9,030,000
Equipment and materials	23,738,000	23,738,000
Transport facilities	17,351,000	17,351,000
Civic education	3,574,000	3,574,000

(continues)

Table 5.5 continued

Sector/Area of Support	Total Needs	Total Obligated Funds
Training	4,561,000	4,561,000
Technical assistance	6,215,000	6,215,000
All-party trust fund	n.a.	1,880,000
Subtotal	64,469,000	66,349,000
Renamo trust fund (1993–1994)	n.a.	13,600,000
Total[c]	748,255,450	589,790,551

Sources: UNOHAC, *Consolidated Humanitarian Assistance Programme, 1992–1994 Final Report,* pp. 84–87; Financial Report of UNOHAC (to adjust for double-counting in *Final Report*); UNDP/DDSMS, *Elections in the Peace Process in Mozambique,* p. 53; Barnes, "Reintegration Programmes for Demobilised Soldiers in Mozambique," Annex 1, (Financial Support for Reintegration of DS); UNHCR, "Final Report: QIPs" (June 20, 1996).

Notes: a. Direct cost inside Mozambique for repatriation of refugees only. Support for refugee resettlement and reintegration included under Reintegration.

b. Includes $11 million from the assessed contribution to ONUMOZ. Excludes values of services provided by peacekeeping troops.

c. Government subsidy denominated in meticais; difference between need and obligated amount in U.S. dollars due to inflation.

gap." In brief, donors tended to fund programs they felt were good investments; they were disinclined to fund projects they believed to be poorly conceived or executed.

Implementation gap. The mine action program offers an excellent example of a poorly executed program that alienated donors and caused them to develop parallel projects. On December 31, 1992, the Supervisory and Monitoring Commission approved a list of twenty-eight roads in the central provinces as priorities for mine clearance. Donors responded rapidly, providing $7.5 million to the DHA trust fund to supplement another $18.5 million in the ONUMOZ budget. However, disagreements and delays hindered further elaboration and implementation of this program, first by UNOHAC and then by UNDP. The UNOHAC director, following the ceasefire commission views, determined that a comprehensive national plan should be put in place before de-mining could begin. But the formulation of this program was delayed severely by Renamo's withdrawal in March 1993 from the work of all the peace accord commissions. This effectively halted peace implementation activities for six months. At that point, the SRSG could have avoided further delays by transferring mine clearance from the commission on humanitarian grounds. He chose not to do so.

At the same time, UN efforts to start work on the twenty-eight priority roads were complicated by a combination of UNDP's internal procedures; bureaucratic disagreements between the UN, UNDP, and the UN Office for Project Services (UNOPS, the executing agency); and complaints by the

United States that no U.S. firm had made the short list. An entire year passed before the secretary-general's office intervened, ordering UNDP/ UNOPS to award the road contract. By this point, the Dutch and Swedish governments had requested the return of their contributions to the UN de-mining trust fund. Consequently, most de-mining activities carried out dur-ing the two-year peace implementation period were funded directly by bilateral contributions. Indeed, the UN's national mine survey got under way only in February 1994—some eight months after it was supposed to have been completed—because UNDP was unable to approve funding rapidly for the $200,000 project. Similarly, UNDP procurement rules delayed the establishment of the training center for de-miners, even though Dutch trainers were available from mid-1993. As a result, the UN did not field mine clearance teams until October 1994, two years after the signing of the GPA.

Although conceptual disagreements and personality conflicts con-tributed to problems with UNDP's mine action program, the donors' frus-trations with the de-mining effort and their decisions to bypass the UN program were largely driven by UN bureaucratic constraints.[38] When the UNDP finally awarded the contract to clear the priority roads in mid-1994, DHA requested that UNDP return the remaining funds to support an Accelerated De-mining Program (ADP) that would build up Mozam-bique's national capacities. This DHA program, staffed by New Zealand technical officers, is now a UNDP project and continues to carry out mine clearance activities in the southern and central parts of Mozambique.

In contrast to the problems associated with de-mining programs, the donors were extremely pleased with the development and coordination of electoral assistance. Once the details of the electoral process were agreed on, UNDP prepared a matrix for the donors, pairing actors with specific tasks that each had agreed to implement and/or fund. Thanks to a high degree of transparency and an agreed-upon plan of action, trust fund resources could be used flexibly, according to need, and the donors were enthusiastic about UNDP's coordination efforts. The UNDP resident rep-resentative held regular meetings to update the donors on progress. These consultations proved critical in an environment characterized by rampant rumors. Because the donors were so well informed, they were able to reas-sure a suspicious and insecure Renamo leadership and to reduce tensions between Renamo and the government.[39]

The budget for the electoral process was also developed in a transpar-ent manner, identifying "expenditure packages" that reflected the central components of the electoral process or key equipment and material requirements. It was anticipated that this would facilitate donor financing and clarify where gaps and duplication of effort existed. Funding modali-ties were also highly flexible. Donors provided resources in three different ways: cost sharing, trust funds, and parallel financing. The government provided slightly more than 8 percent of the electoral costs. The contributors to the trust fund included Canada, Finland, Italy, the Netherlands, Norway, and the United States. In addition, Denmark, Portugal, Spain, Sweden, the UK, and UNDP contributed resources via cost-sharing arrangements; and Austria, Canada, the European Union (EU), France, Italy, and Portugal provided parallel financing.[40] The technical and financial support provided by external donors for national elections is summarized in Figure 5.1.

Conceptual gaps. The numerous problems associated with developing reintegration activities for ex-combatants during 1993 were primarily the result of conceptual disagreements.[41] Initially, donors were highly skeptical of the need for special programs targeted exclusively at demobilized soldiers in a country where one-third of the population had been displaced and few people (if any) had escaped the effects of war. Although the donors subsequently reversed course and came to support targeted programs, they also rejected many of the programs proposed by UNOHAC and the government.

In particular, donors disagreed with UNOHAC and the Mozambican parties about whether to focus on long-term programs or on relatively short-term programs that might buy time for the peace process by supporting demobilized soldiers for a year or two. Some donors were also reluctant to increase the burden on the country's weak administrative structure (although the strongest proponent of this view, the United States, also had an ideological objection to giving the government a role in implementing programs).

At the June 1993 follow-up donors meeting in Maputo, UNOHAC argued that CORE's mandate under the GPA implied a special status and treatment for demobilized soldiers.[42] It simultaneously presented a Consolidated Humanitarian Appeal that included $23.5 million for ex-combatant training, job creation, and job placement. UNOHAC, preferring programs consistent with longer-term, sustainable development objectives, worked according to a three-year time frame. Its proposed program envisioned a major role for the Mozambican government:

> It must be squarely stated: the responsibility for developing reintegration programmes rests with the Government of Mozambique, as it commands the bulk of employment and training assets on offer, even when supported by outside financing. Accordingly it has been UNOHAC's policy to look to the Government for leadership in the matter of reintegration and to maximize the role and involvement of Mozambican institutions, public and private, in such programmes. In UNOHAC's view, it would be counterproductive to take any action that might be interpreted as diluting the

Figure 5.1   External Support for National Elections

The GPA stated that a National Election Commission (CNE) should be established to organize and manage the election process. Though the Commission was to be set up by government, one-third of its members were to be appointed by Renamo. The peace agreement also anticipated that the elections could not take place without international support. Protocol VII of the GPA requested that the Italian government convene a donor conference to discuss financing the electoral process, emergency programs, and programs for the reintegration of refugees, internationally displaced persons, and demobilized soldiers.

The conference was held in Rome on December 15–16, 1992. At that time, the estimated budget for the organization of the elections was $76.9 million (including $10 million for contingencies). The conference called on the United Nations to be the coordinator of technical assistance to the electoral process and requested that the secretary-general facilitate the receipt of contributions to the electoral process—including support to political parties—through the UN.

It was evident from the start that substantial technical assistance would be required for the CNE and the STAE (Technical Secretariat for Electoral Administration) to operate at the national, provincial, district, and local levels. UNDP immediately set up a flexible technical assistance project that could be revised as the process evolved and the specific needs became clearer. The European Union initially chaired donor meetings, but once the UNDP project was approved in May 1993, the UNDP resident representative assumed leadership of the coordination of assistance to the elections. The Aid for Democracy donor group—which consisted of representatives of seventeen donors—focused on defining the needs and obtaining the necessary support for the elections. Initially meeting monthly, this group convened more and more frequently as the elections approached.

A number of factors contributed to the relatively high cost of the Mozambican elections. One was substantial mistrust between the government and Renamo, which meant that UN volunteers were assigned to all 128 districts. UN personnel were placed at the district level to ensure impartiality. The very thorough, but costly, photo ID electoral registration cards also raised the cost of the elections. However, it should be understood that these costs built confidence in the process.

Three funding modalities for international financial support to the elections were agreed upon to accommodate the varying requirements of donor governments and/or organizations and, at the same, offer flexibility, operationality, and response capacity to gaps and needs as they emerged. These included the UNDP trust fund; cost sharing; and parallel financing.

The cost-sharing modality financed the UNDP project that provided all technical assistance to the election process and some of the costs for telecommunications equipment, aircraft leasing, and civic education materials. The UNDP trust fund financed a range of components including equipment, transport, civic education, training, and some support for the electoral structures themselves. The parallel financing mode was developed to ensure that those donors, especially the EU, that were unable to fund through UN mechanisms were nonetheless part of a coherent, approved program. Total international community financing was $59.1 million; the government of Mozambique paid salaries and provided offices valued at $5.4 million.

Government's responsibility in this regard. The Ministry of Labor should be officially recognized as the implementing agency for CORE-related programmes, making decisions on technical assistance requirements, and rule on other forms of external support.[43]

Initially, the government was especially interested in developing credit programs targeted at demobilized officers. It pushed these programs strongly, including in conversations with the under-secretary-general for humanitarian affairs, Jan Eliasson. Nonetheless, UNOHAC did not support these narrowly targeted credit programs.

Although the June 1993 meeting resulted in some pledges, a significant gap remained between the amount requested and the amount pledged, especially for the reintegration of demobilized soldiers. This experience generated considerable animosity between UNOHAC and much of the donor community. Clearly, the donors were still not ready to approve programs that targeted the reintegration of ex-combatants. They particularly opposed credit programs, which had a poor track record in Mozambique.[44]

However, as disturbances by soldiers awaiting demobilization began to escalate in July–August 1993, the donors began to consider special programs more attractive. In part, they recognized that the area-based reintegration programs for returning refugees and the internally displaced could not absorb all of the approximately 90,000 soldiers eligible for demobilization benefits. Nonetheless, donors felt that a UNOHAC proposal of October 1993—which would have provided vegetable and tool kits on departure from assembly areas, training, occupational kits-and-credit programs, employment, referring and counseling services for the demobilized—was not sufficient. Fearing a disruption of the peace process and unhappy with UNOHAC's proposals, the Like-Minded Group—led by the Netherlands and Norway—developed the Reintegration Support Scheme (described in Figure 5.2). While all of the longer-term programs UNOHAC proposed in October 1993 were eventually implemented to some degree, most of the nearly $95 million donors provided to reintegrate demobilized soldiers was allocated to reinsertion programs that lasted a maximum of two years, and in most cases less (see Table 5.5).

Although tensions and disagreements with donors diminished significantly during 1994, these events had significantly compromised UNOHAC's ability to act as coordinator of ex-combatant reintegration. As a result, the projects that donors developed never functioned as a coherent program. This was true both for the different categories of projects—Reintegration Support Scheme, Information and Referral Service (IRS), Provincial Fund, Occupational Skills Development (OSD)—and within sectors. The RSS was implemented by UNDP, which contracted with the Banco Popular de Desenvolvimento (BPD) to actually make the payments to demobilized soldiers. The IRS was implemented by the International Organization for Migration (IOM). There were two Provincial Fund projects, one implemented by IOM and the second by the German Agency for Technical Cooperation (GTZ).

Training was perhaps the most fragmented sector. The OSD, managed by the International Labour Organization (ILO), competed with similar

Figure 5.2   Demobilization and Reintegration in Mozambique

The demobilization of soldiers and their reintegration into civilian life was an essential part of the Mozambican peace process. The General Peace Agreement called for a cease-fire, separation of forces, the movement of the soldiers into assembly areas, disarmament, the set up of a smaller unified army, the demobilization of the remaining troops, and the development of programs for their economic and social reintegration.

Political constraints tied to the peace process and institutional rivalries within the donor community delayed planning for reintegration programs until late 1993 and the actual demobilization process until January 1994. Initially donors were not willing to finance special programs for the demobilized soldiers (DS), preferring them to be included within overall reintegration programs. It was only after the DS in preassembly and assembly stage began to demonstrate their capacity and propensity for violence that the SRSG could convince the donor community that investments in cash payment schemes and other entitlements were necessary and worthwhile for the entire peace process. The thirty-six-month program that was eventually approved by the Reintegration Commission (CORE) included support during three interdependent but overlapping phases: demobilization, reinsertion, reintegration. In all, the various programs benefited 92,881 demobilized soldiers from the government forces (70,902 veterans, or 77 percent) and Renamo (21,979 veterans, or 23 percent), and cost $95 million.

Demobilization involved only a few programs to prepare the DS for civilian life—for example, the Information and Social Reintegration Project and Demobilization and Reintegration of Vulnerable Groups. Less than 1 percent of the funds ($750,000) for the total reintegration program was expended in this phase.

Reinsertion support constituted 80 percent of the funds allocated to targeted programs for the DS. This included a range of material benefits for all DS including civilian clothing, transport to their chosen destination, a seed-and-tool kit, a two-week food-for-home ration, and a three-month ration at their destination. The government paid salaries for six months ($10.4 million). This was supplemented by the Reintegration Support Scheme (RSS), which provided a critical financial safety net for each DS. Over eighteen months, each DS received a cash subsidy based on actual salary levels, except for privates, who received twice their monthly salary. The Information and Referral Service (IRS) implemented at the provincial level provided information and assistance to DS regarding entitlements and other training and employment opportunities.

The CORE approved two programs to support more substantive *reintegration* in the medium and longer term. The Occupational Skills Development Project (OSD) provided vocational and entrepreneurial training to facilitate self-employment. A Provincial Fund (PF) was established in all ten provinces to provide grants to small community-based projects that would provide temporary or permanent employment to DS or their families to ease their reintegration into their communities. These programs received $15.3 million or 16 percent of the total funds.

An important characteristic of the Mozambique approach was the recognition that demobilized soldiers should receive entitlements and have access to opportunities. Entitlements are critical because they guarantee that all soldiers, regardless of political affiliation, educational level, rank, or district of origin, receive similar benefits. In Mozambique, these entitlements—especially the cash payments by government and the international community—were seen as a major contributing factor to political and military stabilization. In studies carried out by UNDP in early 1997 (three years after demobilization), only 14 percent of the DS stated that they were without work. Since only 8 percent of the veterans benefited from training opportunities and 28 percent had access to Provincial Funds for small projects, the entitlements were critical for keeping the peace.

programs funded by the Danish, Italian, Portuguese, and South African governments. Because the government of Mozambique was unwilling to allow CORE to be involved with donor programs developed outside the framework of CORE, it was extremely difficult to coordinate the various initiatives. As a result, different programs provided trainees with quite different levels of benefits.[45] In addition, the various programs competed among themselves, so that—for a short time—field staff from two different agencies involved in implementing training programs were forbidden to speak with each other without prior approval from their supervisors in Maputo. The implementing agencies were also afflicted by a variety of internal problems that hampered program execution. Problems such as these encouraged some donors to transfer funds donated to the UNOHAC trust fund to the UNDP trust fund for the RSS.[46]

Peace Consolidation

The peace process formally came to an end in October 1994, with the country's first multiparty elections. Balloting for the presidency and the national legislature occurred October 27–29. Results were announced on November 19, and the SRSG formally declared the elections to have been "free and fair." The Security Council agreed to extend ONUMOZ's mandate until the new government was installed in Maputo or until December 15—whichever came first. President Joaquim Chissano was inaugurated on December 9, 1994, officially terminating the ONUMOZ mandate. SRSG Aldo Ajello left Maputo on December 13, and the military component of the peacekeeping mission drew down very rapidly.

Although UNOHAC was to have terminated its activities one week after the elections, DHA persuaded the mission that a transition period was desirable, particularly for staff in provincial offices implementing ongoing programs. Provincial staff continued working until November 30, and the Maputo office of UNOHAC closed at the end of December. By the end of January 1995, the entire UN mission had been liquidated.

Although the abrupt departure of the peacekeeping mission may have seemed desirable to headquarters in New York—as well as to the Mozambique government, which had chafed under the restrictions on its sovereignty inherent in such an operation—it risked undermining the consolidation of a fragile peace. It also complicated efforts to track expenditures for peace-related activities (see Table 5.6).

UNOHAC's ongoing projects were transferred to UNDP's newly established Reconstruction and Rehabilitation Unit. This unit did not, however, develop a conceptual view of how peace consolidation might proceed and the role that donors could play; nor did it attempt to coordinate

Table 5.6 Mozambique External Financing: Pledges and Disbursements 1995–1998 (U.S.$ millions)

Year	Total	Food Aid-Market	Food Aid-Emergency	Balance of Payments	Investment	Seeds	Demining	Demobilization/ Reintegraton	Resettlement	Refugees	Debt	Others
1995												
Pledged/Disbursed	1082.0	21.3	138.4	200.4	359.6	2.6	1.5	45.7	9.4	37.1	187.0	78.7
Grants	851.0	21.3	138.4	112.1	217.8	2.6	1.5	45.7	9.4	37.1	187.0	78.7
Bilateral	661.0	9.9	25.6	102.4	193.1	1.4	1.5	21.5	9.4	36.9	187.0	72.1
Multilateral	42.4	11.3	6.2	9.7	13.7	1.2						0.2
UN system	148.5		106.6		11.1			24.2		0.2		6.4
Credits	230.0			88.3	141.7							
Bilateral	11.5				11.5							
Multilateral	218.5			88.3	130.2							
1996												
Pledged	968.7	11.1	45.2	195.7	582.3	0.5	2.1	26.4	11.5	21.0	10.0	62.7
Grants	652.1	11.1	45.2	117.3	290.9	0.5	2.1	26.4	11.5	21.1	10.0	62.7
Bilateral	523.8	11.1	16.3	98.2	290.9	0.5	2.1	10.0	11.5	20.7	10.0	52.3
Multilateral	65.9			19.1	44.0							2.8
UN system	62.2		28.9		9.2			16.4		0.3		7.5
Credits	316.0			78.5	238.2							
Bilateral	24.1			0.7	23.4							
Multilateral	292.6			77.8	214.8							
Disbursed	977.7	22.4	29.3	193.1	491.7	0.7	5.8	34.3	3.0	17.2	59.3	120.4
Grants	677.2	22.4	29.3	65.3	319.2	0.7	5.8	34.3	3.0	17.2	59.3	120.4
Bilateral	565.3	17.8	13.8	64.7	283.6	0.7	5.8	11.9	116.8	17.2	59.3	87.5
Multilateral	62.5	4.5		0.5	26.1	6.8						24.4
UN system	49.3		15.5		9.3			15.6		0.4		8.5
Credits	300.4			127.8	172.6							
Bilateral	17.7				17.7							
Multilateral	282.8			127.8	154.9							

(continues)

Table 5.6 continued

Year	Total	Food Aid-Market	Food Aid-Emergency	Balance of Payments	Investment	Seeds	Demining	Demobilization/ Reintegraton	Resettlement	Refugees	Debt	Others
1997												
Pledged	1106.6	11.8	24.2	218.1	678.1	0.05	13.4	8.5	7.5	18.7	15.9	109.8
Grants	757.4	11.8	24.2	148.4	398.6	0.05	13.4	8.5	7.5	18.7	15.9	109.8
Bilateral	594.6	11.8	17.1	115.8	332.3	0.05	9.4	4.8	7.5	16.8	15.9	62.7
Multilateral	123.6			32.5	53.7		0.04	3.0				34.2
UN system	39.1		7.1		12.5		4.0	0.6		1.9		12.9
Credits	349.2			69.68	279.5							
Bilateral	53.6	0.3	53.3									
Multilateral	295.6			69.4	226.2							
Private												
Disbursed	814.3	12.1	17.9	188.7	419.1	0.002	8.7	6.2	3.8	15.8	32.8	108.8
Grants	543.8	12.1	17.9	114.4	222.9	0.002	8.7	6.2	3.8	15.8	32.8	108.8
Bilateral	443.1	12.1	10.8	82.3	187.4	0.002	8.7	4.7	3.8	15.7	32.8	84.5
Multilateral	74.4			32.1	26.8			1.5				13.9
UN system	26.2		7.1		8.7			0.004		0.1		10.3
Credits	270.4			74.2	196.2							
Bilateral	45.9			0.3	45.7							
Multilateral	224.4			73.9	150.4							
Private	5.0				5.0							
1998												
Pledged	993.7	14.2	31.5	179.1	545.1		17.1	4.5	6.4	16.1	49.5	129.8
Grants	659.6	14.2	31.5	100.0	290.2		17.1	4.5	6.4	16.1	49.5	129.8
Bilateral	522.6	14.2	26.7	63.2	244.0		12.4	1.7	6.4	15.1	49.5	89.1
Multilateral	99.8			36.8	35.9			2.4				24.6
UN system	37.2		4.8		10.2		4.6	0.3		0.9		16.1
Credits	334.0			79.1	254.9							
Bilateral	26.1				26.1							
Multilateral	307.8			79.1	228.7							
Private												

Source: Ministry of Planning and Finance, Maputo, September 16, 1998.

donors. Rather, it focused on providing administrative support to UNDP projects, including mine clearance, the OSD, the RSS, and DHA trust fund projects inherited by UNDP. Donor coordination was left in the hands of the World Bank, operating through the Consultative Group process. Neither the World Bank nor any other organization attempted to map the needs of peace consolidation.

Despite the lack of a comprehensive framework, important peace consolidation issues were not completely ignored. Some were taken up through the Consultative Group process, although less frequently with each passing year. The government and donors discussed ways to nurture the fragile democratization process inaugurated by the country's first multiparty elections, to strengthen public sector accountability and transparency, to enhance civilian management of the security forces, and to support the civilian police. Recognizing Mozambique's special status as a country recovering from a devastating civil war, donors have tended to hold the country to a somewhat more relaxed standard of macroeconomic performance.

Donors have played important roles in peace consolidation—for example, by stimulating the development of donor-government working groups on public finance and governance issues, by attempting to temper IMF rigidity on macroeconomic benchmarks during 1995, by funding police reform, and by helping to strengthen critical aspects of governance.

The first postelection CG meeting, scheduled for December 1994, was postponed until March 1995. This delay resulted largely from demands by the U.S. and British ambassadors that it not be held until the new government was in place and could identify its expenditure priorities. The two ambassadors were particularly eager to see a sharp and rapid reduction in military expenditure and an increase in social expenditure. Most of Mozambique's other development partners, although favoring the redirection of public spending away from wartime priorities, were not as insistent on the rapid reduction in military spending. They were, however, generally supportive of the notion that the government should clarify its priorities.

Consequently, the donors worked with the government to establish donor-government working groups for budget and governance issues. Ministers and vice-ministers met with donors to identify priority issues and to discuss them in a results-oriented manner designed to empower the Mozambican participants. As a result, the CG meeting of March 1995 was the first at which the government of Mozambique took primary responsibility for preparing the discussion documents, and the donors received the government budget prior to the meeting. The working groups became an institutionalized form of donor-government consultation and helped Mozambique become, in the 1997 words of the World Bank country director, "one of the few countries in Africa where financial sector reform is taking hold."[47]

Discussions at the March 1995 CG meeting were wider ranging than in previous years. The topics covered ran from fiscal and monetary policies through issues of privatization and poverty to questions of governance and improved donor-government relations. The breadth of discussion reflected the government's own orientation, the requirements of peace consolidation, and the changing nature of the dialogue between donors and their development cooperation partners. Specific peace consolidation issues included strengthening parliamentary institutions, guaranteeing freedom of the press, supporting the police and judicial systems, engaging in progressive decentralization, improving financial accountability, and reducing corruption.[48] Some donors, notably the United States, sought to place conditionalities on the government and to elaborate specific benchmarks for progress in these areas. Most donors, however, agreed with the Danish representative who argued, "This is not the time (in the area of political processes) for rigid conditionalities." Nonetheless, the donors sent a clear message that they expected to see improvements in governance by the time of the next CG meeting.[49]

The donors also stressed the importance of macroeconomic stability. The Bank's Mozambique country director described this as "an absolute prerequisite" for foreign assistance in her closing statement to the 1995 CG meeting.[50] Still, most of Mozambique's donors demonstrated their flexibility on this issue six months later, when the IMF proposed terminating its Enhanced Structural Adjustment Facility (ESAF) arrangement with Maputo—because the government had increased the minimum wage and resisted budgetary cuts that the IMF thought necessary to meet agreed inflation targets. A number of Mozambique's major donors balked at the IMF proposal. Representatives of Canada, the European Union, Finland, the Netherlands, Switzerland, UNDP, and the United States sent a letter to the Fund, arguing that any additional budgetary cuts to meet ESAF targets would seriously constrain prospects for growth—and endanger sustainable peace in Mozambique. Rather than budget cuts, these donors called for increased public investment.[51] In the end, the minimum wage increase stood, and the government complied with most of the conditions of the ESAF arrangement, with delays.

The most important outcome of the controversy was that the IMF and Mozambique established a more equal working relationship. The government had begun to take ownership for reconstruction and was able to negotiate from a position of greater strength. Because the government had adopted a responsible economic policy, it ultimately commanded the respect of bilateral donors and the Bretton Woods institutions.

Governance issues, especially concerns about corruption and decentralization, remained on the CG agenda during 1996 and 1997. At the 1997 CG meeting, the World Bank country director for Mozambique recognized that the government had "gone some way" toward addressing these

concerns.[52] Positive steps had included decentralization of public administration; approval of the legal framework for local elections; and (proposed)
anti-corruption legislation, including the Government Ethics Bill and the
High Authority Against Corruption Bill. During the 1997 meeting, donors
and the government discussed the holding of municipal elections and the
need for the government to make "anti-corruption a reality, by creating the
necessary institutions, and by taking rapid action in pending cases."[53]

The concern on the part of Mozambique's development partners that
particular peace consolidation issues be addressed has been important in
encouraging the government to take action in those areas. The fact that
these efforts have occurred without the development of a mutually agreed
upon framework for peace consolidation means, however, that some
important issues have been ignored or dealt with in a fragmented manner.
The reorientation of government expenditure from the security sector to
development priorities is a case in point.

Despite the legitimate concern about reorienting government expenditures away from wartime priorities, none of the donors appeared to be
aware of one of the fundamental preconditions for sustained reductions in
security expenditure: the strengthening of the institutional and human
capacities needed to manage and monitor reform of the security sector,
including the creation of security forces accountable to an elected civilian
government and supported by transparent financing instruments. Had
donors helped the government to develop a *comprehensive* needs framework for peace consolidation, this gap would have been identified.

As it happened, training of the armed forces and police began
extremely slowly. Some Mozambican nationals have received scholarships
to take higher degrees in security and peace studies, and donors have occasionally funded seminars for senior political and military leaders on civil-
military relations and the role of the military in democratic societies.
There has, however, been no systematic effort by the government, donors,
or international NGOs to upgrade the civil institutions that oversee the
country's security forces.[54] Without strengthening these institutions, it will
prove difficult to create a relatively transparent security sector that is
accountable to elected civilian officials or civil society organizations capable of fulfilling the monitoring function that is so important in democratic
societies.

The Mozambique experience demonstrates that when donors and government work together in a collaborative spirit, important changes can
occur. It also demonstrates that the Consultative Group process can
address important peace consolidation issues and gain government support
for them. A country like Mozambique, which was confronted with a triple
transition and extremely limited resources, faces extremely difficult
choices in prioritizing the issues it will deal with at any given time. It is

important, therefore, that all issues pertaining to the consolidation of peace—without which the development effort in any country faces possible disruption—be on the table when priorities are determined.

Conclusion

One of the clear lessons to emerge from studies of support for peace implementation and postconflict peace building is that these undertakings are a hybrid of emergency and development work. Because they involve a host of activities not traditionally part of the mandates of either relief or development agencies, they require institutional and personal flexibility. They also require political astuteness on the part of agency staff and an ability to work collaboratively with institutions possessing significantly different cultures and priorities. These requirements were not well or widely understood in 1993 and 1994. As a result, the development and relief agencies working in Mozambique were often not well equipped to deal with the realities of war-to-peace transitions—whether in terms of funding mechanisms, personnel, institutional procedures, or program content.

Nonetheless, peace implementation enjoyed significant external support in Mozambique. The donors understood that peace was critical to the country's long-term economic and social development and were willing to invest resources to help the peace process succeed. They engaged in creative funding strategies that enabled them to find ways around restrictions on support for demobilized soldiers and other aspects of peace implementation. Although donors frequently bypassed the government, developed their own programs, and were extremely sensitive to institutional turf issues, they also provided critical assistance that enabled hundreds of thousands of war-affected Mozambicans to begin to rebuild their lives.

For the most part, the donors delivered what they promised. The problems that arose were due primarily to delays in the peace process, disagreements over program content, and concerns about implementation. Consequently, donors developed and funded programs that differed from those that the government or Renamo would have formulated had they been fully in control. Still, one cannot say that these programs were necessarily less effective because they reflected donor concerns. The government, for example, never really liked the RSS program, and it would have preferred programs targeted at the officer corps. In fact, the RSS turned out to be one of the more effective and successful peace implementation programs.

Macroeconomic policy did not proceed in a vacuum: it was partly shaped by the needs of the peace process. Still, it remains an open question whether peace implementation and traditional economic concerns would have coexisted as well as they did if the donors had not been as generous in providing additional support for peace implementation. Mozambique also benefited from an extremely loyal donor community that was willing at a critical moment to voice its disagreement with the IMF and worked hard to strengthen the capacity of the Ministry of Finance and Planning and other key government agencies involved in economic management.

Most of all, Mozambique benefited from a generalized war-weariness. Neither side in the conflict could prevail by force, and neither side was willing to return to war when the peace process ran into difficulties, despite some tense moments. Many other countries, including several whose experiences are discussed in this book, have not been so fortunate.

Mozambique's experience demonstrates that a country that is ready for peace will benefit from external support, even if that support is not delivered in the most effective manner. It will benefit even more if peace implementation activities are fully integrated into the overall economic program, if external actors work together to help implement the peace accord rather than protecting institutional turf, if donors work closely with national actors in developing and implementing programs, and if all parties understand that peace implementation is the first step on the road to peace consolidation.

Notes

1. These fifteen years of war had been preceded by a ten-year war of independence from Portugal between 1964 and 1974. The war between Renamo (known as the MNR in its early years) and the government is frequently divided into two periods. The first, 1976–1979, coincided with Rhodesia's creation of and support for Renamo. The second, 1981–1992, saw Renamo become an important player in South Africa's efforts to destabilize supporters of the African National Congress.

2. A not insignificant portion of this aid was intended to help Mozambique prosecute the war against the Mozambique National Resistance that lasted for most of the 1976–1992 period. For example, a good deal of the assistance received from the former Soviet Union and its Warsaw Treaty Organization allies was intended to be used for military purposes, and much of it took the form of loans rather than grants. It has been estimated that as of January 1, 1991, Mozambique owed the former Soviet Union some 650 million rubles. *Moscow News,* cited in Fituni, "Russia's Arms Sales," p. 5.

3. Mozambique incurred a significant financial cost by closing the border. Some $500 million in transit revenues were foregone over four years. The government reportedly anticipated receiving compensatory aid from Western countries, but this was not forthcoming. See Dos Santos, Honwana, and de Brito, "Enhancing Security and Development," p. 12, footnote 8. See also Christian Michelsen Institute with Nordic Consulting Group, *Evaluation,* p. 35.

4. Malawi also allowed Renamo to operate from its territory.

5. On the creation and development of Renamo, see Abrahamsson and Nilsson, *Mozambique;* Simpson, "Foreign and Domestic Factors"; Vines, *Renamo;* and

Geffray, *La Cause des Armes.* See also Dos Santos, Honwana, and de Brito, "Enhancing Security and Development," p. 10, and Christian Michelsen Institute with Nordic Consulting Group, *Evaluation,* p. 36.

6. Internally generated economic weaknesses were compounded by a number of external economic factors, such as significantly increased oil prices and rising interest rates. See Christian Michelsen Institute with Nordic Consulting Group, *Evaluation,* p. 36.

7. In an effort to end the war, the government also concluded the Nkomati Accord with South Africa in 1984. This deprived the ANC's armed wing, Umkhonto we Sizwe, of the use of Mozambique's territory, but it did not succeed in cutting off all assistance to Renamo, and the war continued. See, for example, Ohlson and Stedman with Davies, *The New Is Not Yet Born,* pp. 99–101.

8. Landau, *Rebuilding the Mozambique Economy,* pp. 5, 52. Growth rates in 1986, 1987, and 1988 were 2.0 percent, 4.0 percent, and 5.5 percent, respectively. As this review of World Bank activities in Mozambique demonstrates, early reforms were quite limited. Rather than focusing on privatization of publicly owned firms and financial institutions, the Bank sought to improve the efficiency of these entities by supporting the government's Economic Action Program through the first rehabilitation credit. This approach proved to be not very cost-effective. See Landau, chap. 3, pp. 9–14. Between 1985 and 1990, Mozambique received $390 million from the Bank. Eighty percent was allocated to economic reforms, and 53 percent took the form of balance of payments support.

9. Christian Michelsen Institute with Nordic Consulting Group, *Evaluation,* p. 38.

10. Ibid., p. 45.

11. This strategy had been developed over the course of 1991 by an interministerial commission.

12. The only direct contribution of the Bank to peace implementation was the use of $500,000 left over from an education project to fund training and job creation efforts for demobilized soldiers through the German government's technical assistance agency, GTZ. For a description of the way in which the return of peace shaped one of the bilateral donor's aid program, see Christian Michelsen Institute with Nordic Consulting Group, *Evaluation,* pp. 27–32.

13. Christian Michelsen Institute with Nordic Consulting Group, *Evaluation,* p. 47. Internal quotation from "Chairman's Closing Statement," Mozambique Consultative Group Meeting, December 1991.

14. UNDP never asked the operational agencies if they had candidates for the position of head of the emergency unit. This contrasts with the case of Angola where, following the resumption of hostilities in 1992, a qualified senior staff member from WFP was seconded to become head of DHA's field operations. In February 1992, shortly after the creation of the Department of Humanitarian Affairs, UNDP had sent a mission to Mozambique, headed by Michael Priestly, a senior adviser to the UNDP administrator with extensive experience in emergency situations. Priestly advised UNDP to transform UNSCERO into a UN coordination unit, with staff seconded from UN agencies. This recommendation was not accepted, and a new director of the UNDP Emergency Unit with no emergency experience was named by UNDP. For more detail, see Barnes, *Humanitarian Aid Coordination,* pp. 16–17.

15. This was in contrast to the Consolidated Inter-Agency Appeals, which grouped proposed projects by agency under thematic headings and where agency programs and priorities appeared to predominate.

16. Although Renamo had attempted to capitalize on its anticommunist rhetoric to gain Western support in the early 1980s, it failed—primarily because its roots were so clearly in the white Rhodesian and South African military forces. Even the United States government, which had initially supported UNITA against the socialist-oriented MPLA in Angola, never endorsed Renamo in its fight against the Mozambican state. In fact, starting in 1981, the United States inaugurated a policy of "constructive engagement" in the conflicts that bedeviled southern Africa and began to urge South Africa to abandon its destabilization policy. The architect of this policy, Assistant Secretary of State for African Affairs Chester Crocker, argued that destabilization was too costly and would ultimately prove to be unsuccessful in guaranteeing South Africa's security. Specifically with regard to Mozambique, USAID began providing assistance in 1984. In 1988, the U.S. Department of State released a report, known as the Gersonny Report after its author Robert Gersonny, that documented Renamo's brutality and human rights abuses, such as kidnapping civilians (including children) to serve as soldiers and forcing a taxation system in rebel-controlled areas to sustain Renamo's war effort. See Barnes, "The Humanitarian Factor."

17. If force is required to create space for the emergence of propeace actors, and the international community is unwilling to employ that force (as in Angola), external actors will have a limited ability to nurture peace and avoid a relapse into conflict.

18. The total cost of the UN peace mission over thirty months was $1.1 billion. Humanitarian/peace implementation assistance totaled $617 million, and the direct costs of ONUMOZ were $565 million. See Barnes, "Peacekeeping in Mozambique."

19. See, for example, Hanlon, *Mozambique.*

20. In Sierra Leone, for example, the IMF conditioned assistance in 1996/1997 on the newly elected civilian government's willingness to eliminate the rice ration for the armed forces as well as to keep expenditures below an agreed ceiling. See Zack-Williams, "Sierra Leone," pp. 151–152. While the distribution of rice rations to the armed forces was not free of corruption, and the rice did not always reach its intended destination, the withdrawal of the subsidy was clearly seen by at least some members of the Armed Forces of the Republic of Sierra Leone as a concrete manifestation of the reduced status that civilian rule would bring for members of the military. The reduced rice ration has been cited as one of the immediate causes of the May 25, 1997, coup d'état by junior officers that temporarily ousted the elected government—the effects of which continued to be felt into 1999. World Bank staff attempted to draw the attention of their management to the IMF's conditions because they correctly foresaw the political problems that cutting the rice could produce, but Bank management was unwilling to take up this issue with the IMF. As a result of the agreement on expenditure targets, the Sierra Leone government sought to renegotiate its contract with Executive Outcomes (EO), the private security firm hired by the previous military government to bolster security against the rebel force, the Revolutionary United Front. This led to EO's withdrawal from Sierra Leone, placing the government and civilian population at greatly increased risk.

As Chapter 4 in this volume describes, governments of postconflict countries can use the adjustment process and the Bretton Woods institutions as an excuse for not allocating domestic resources to peace implementation activities. In such a case, it is important for the Bank and the Fund to be in close communication with the external actors most closely involved with peace implementation to ensure that they do not unwittingly contribute to a failure of the peace process.

21. United Nations, *The United Nations and Mozambique,* pp. 146–147.

22. UNDP transferred the UNSCERO/UNDP resident representative one week before the signing of the GPA. There was much criticism of this decision at the time from donors and government, since this individual was the UN official with the most contact with Renamo and the chair of the Humanitarian Assistance Committee, which had Renamo participation prior to the signing of the GPA. One can only speculate that if the UNSCERO/UNDP resident representative had not been moved, he would have been the logical choice to head up UNOHAC, in view of his experience. In that case, much of the ensuing conflict over peace implementation issues might well have been avoided.

23. *General Peace Agreement,* cited in Document 12, United Nations, *The United Nations and Mozambique,* pp. 116–119.

24. See World Bank, "Strategy and Program," pp. 32–33. The costs associated with resettling refugees and the internally displaced were not included in Mozambique's national budget. Costs associated with elections and demobilization were included in the budget because they required the expenditure of local funds as well as external financing. See "From Emergency to Sustainable Development," p. 30, para. 96. This latter document grew out of a World Bank study prepared by what was known as "the Vision Mission" to identify key issues for the transition to peace as well as to assist in the development of longer-term, strategic thinking on development objectives.

25. "From Emergency to Sustainable Development," p. 3.

26. "Letter Dated 30 December 1992," S/25044, January 4, 1993, Document 28, in United Nations, *The United Nations and Mozambique,* pp. 159–170, provides a summary of the proceedings in Rome and reproduces the document presented by the government of Mozambique and Renamo outlining assistance requirements.

27. The $61 million excluded the lion's share of the costs of establishing and running the assembly areas for combatants, which was covered by ONUMOZ through the assessed budget, as well as a $22.5 million demobilization benefit to be paid by the government of Mozambique to all demobilized soldiers. See "Letter Dated 30 December 1992," S/25044, January 4, 1993, Document 28, in United Nations, *The United Nations and Mozambique,* p. 162.

28. It must be remembered, however, that the programs against which donors pledged were altered several times over the course of the peace implementation period, and the sums shown in Table 5.3 are only indicative.

29. "Letter Dated 30 December 1992," S/25044, January 4, 1993, Document 28, in United Nations, *The United Nations and Mozambique,* pp. 160–161. See also Christian Michelsen Institute with Nordic Consulting Group, *Evaluation,* p. 67.

30. UNOHAC ultimately had twenty-four professional staff in Maputo and the ten provinces. Eighteen of these were seconded by the European Union, the International Organization on Migration (IOM), Switzerland, Swedrelief, UNDP, UNHCR, UNICEF, USAID, WFP, and WHO. One purpose of secondment, in addition to reducing the charge on the ONUMOZ budget, was to increase coordination and collaboration between ONUMOZ and these other agencies, which, for the most part, did not occur. See Barnes, *Humanitarian Aid,* p. 23, for information on the structure of UNOHAC.

31. Barnes, *Humanitarian Aid,* pp. 22–23. As a "lessons learned" study of UNHCR's reintegration activities in Mozambique noted, the decision to integrate humanitarian coordination (i.e., UNOHAC) into the peacekeeping mission "made sense." Nonetheless, it "alienated UN agencies on the ground . . . [and constituted] a missed opportunity to build on gained wisdom and negatively loaded the inter-agency

relationship within UNOHAC. But . . . UN agencies . . . could have given more of a benefit of the doubt to UNOHAC." UNHCR, "Mozambique," p. 10. See also the section below on "Conceptual Gaps."

32. The question of the location of the unit coordinating humanitarian assistance for peace implementation has been a contentious matter in a number of peace implementation environments. In Angola, for example, the SRSG (the late Maître Alioune Blondin Beye) decided that the humanitarian coordination unit, UCAH, would not colocate with the peacekeeping mission. This decision was based essentially on Beye's belief that raising voluntary funding for humanitarian activities would be considerably more difficult if UCAH were physically located at UNAVEM III headquarters, because of the perception among donors and NGOs that UNAVEM was a "military" operation and thus off-limits to humanitarian actors. Nonetheless, the director of UCAH reported to the SRSG and attended the SRSG's weekly meetings for heads of departments. See Ball and Campbell, *Complex Crisis,* pp. 15–19.

Similarly, despite the strong criticisms of UNOHAC as part of the peacekeeping mission made by Dennis Jett while he was U.S. ambassador in Mozambique, in correspondence to Sam Barnes (July 27, 1997) he subsequently reflected, "Regarding the humanitarian aspect of the PKO, I think everything should be under the control and responsibility of the Special Rep of the Secretary General. Some tend to see humanitarian action as something that is good under any circumstances and that has to be divorced from political influences. I think the military and political impacts of humanitarian assistance are inescapable and need to be factored in."

33. "Letter Dated 30 December 1992," S/25044, January 4, 1993, Document 28, in United Nations, *The United Nations and Mozambique,* pp. 160–161.

34. Barnes, *Humanitarian Aid,* p. 24. On Angola, see Ball and Campbell, *Complex Crisis,* pp. 27–29.

35. Barnes, *Humanitarian Aid,* p. 26.

36. In January 1994, Swiss Development Cooperation's resident representative, Gregor Binkert, commented to his predecessor that "looking at the experience with UNOHAC, I only wish that the World Bank would have been in charge of the reintegration component. UNOHAC has simply wasted a full year, thereby jeopardizing peace and the political stability of this country. But also the bilateral donors prefer to continue with their own little projects; strategic thinking *and acting* is very scarce around here. I am looking at a big Black Hole opening up in front of me." Binkert, Letter to Jürg Frieden. Interestingly, World Bank Resident Representative Chavez was so highly regarded by the Like-Minded Group donors that he attended many of their meetings.

37. World Bank, "Strategy and Program," pp. 31–32.

38. Eaton, Horwood, and Niland, *The Development of Indigenous Mine Action Capacities,* pp. 32–33; Barnes, *Humanitarian Aid,* pp. 25–25; Christian Michelsen Institute with Nordic Consulting Group, *Evaluation,* pp. 78–79.

39. Similarly, the donors were so pleased with the management of the RSS program that it was oversubscribed, and an additional lump sum payment to each demobilized soldier was made at the end of the program.

40. Details of assistance to the electoral process are found in UNDP/DDSMS, *Elections.*

41. On the development of the reintegration programs, see Barnes, *Humanitarian Aid,* pp. 25–26; Barnes, "Reintegration Programmes," pp. 6–11; Ball, "Mid-Term Evaluation"; Creative Associates International, Inc., *The Information and Referral Service;* and Christian Michelsen Institute with Nordic Consulting Group, *Evaluation,* pp. 67–75.

42. At much the same time, the World Bank was developing the argument that demobilized soldiers constitute a "specially disadvantaged group," which required some degree of targeted assistance to provide them with a social safety net while they readjusted to civilian life. See, Colletta and Ball, "War to Peace Transition."

43. UNOHAC, "Comments on the USAID Paper on the Reintegration of Demobilized Soldiers." See also Barnes, "Reintegration Programmes," pp. 6–8.

44. UNOHAC had proposed a $20 million kits-and-credit program to assist 10,000 demobilized soldiers to become self-employed. Only Italy pledged a small amount of money for this project. The arguments raised against credit schemes were that they would take an extremely long time to come on line, and past experience indicated that it was highly likely that the ex-combatants would view the credits as entitlements that did not need to be repaid. See Ball, "Mid-Term Evaluation," p. 68.

45. Ball, "Mid-Term Evaluation," p. 29.

46. Barnes, "Reintegration Programmes," describes the reintegration programs for demobilized soldiers and analyzes their degree of success.

47. Pomerantz, "Chairman's Opening Statement," para. 3.

48. República de Moçambique, "Establishing," pp. 11–15; Marshall, "Mozambique."

49. Marshall, "Mozambique," p. 3.

50. Christian Michelsen Institute with Nordic Consulting Group, *Evaluation,* p. 49.

51. Ibid., pp. 48–49; *Economist,* "The IMF in Africa."

52. Pomerantz, "Chairman's Opening Statement."

53. Pomerantz, "Chairman's Opening Statement," para. 16.

54. Civilian management of the security sector—particularly the military components of the security sector—remains a significant stepchild of development policy. Only Britain has a policy that specifically outlines how its development agency (DFID) can support reforms aimed at strengthening the capacity of civil institutions and civilians to manage and monitor the armed forces. See Department for International Development, "Poverty and the Security Sector. Policy Statement" (1999). This report can be accessed through the DFID website www.dfid.gov.uk. For a description of the components of comprehensive security sector reform, see Ball, *Spreading Good Practices.*

6

The Palestinian Territories

Rex Brynen, Hisham Awartani
& Clare Woodcraft

IN JUNE 1967, ISRAELI FORCES OCCUPIED EAST JERUSALEM, the West Bank of the Jordan River, and the Gaza Strip, the only portions of the original British mandate of Palestine that had remained under Arab control following the establishment of Israel in 1948. More than a quarter century of military occupation followed.

On September 13, 1993, Palestine Liberation Organization (PLO) leader Yasir Arafat, Israeli prime minister Yitzhak Rabin, and U.S. President Bill Clinton met in Washington to sign an Israeli-Palestinian Declaration of Principles. The agreement itself was the product of months of secret, Norwegian-mediated negotiations in Oslo. In it, the two parties at the core of the Arab-Israeli conflict agreed that "it is time to put an end to decades of confrontation and conflict, recognize their mutual legitimate and political rights, and strive to live in peaceful coexistence and mutual dignity and security to achieve a just, lasting and comprehensive peace settlement."[1] To do so, they committed themselves to a series of principles, to various interim measures (including partial Israeli territorial withdrawal and limited Palestinian self-government), and to eventual negotiations on the so-called final status issues: Jerusalem, refugees, settlements, security arrangements, and borders.

On October 1, representatives of some forty-three countries met in Washington "to support the historic political breakthrough in the Middle East through a broad-based multilateral effort to mobilize resources to promote reconstruction and development in the West Bank and Gaza."[2] A total of $2.1 billion in aid was pledged to this end for the period 1994–1998. It was, said the president of the World Bank, an "unprecedented opportunity: to open the door to development and to invest in peace."[3] Certainly, the Palestinians anticipated such a "peace dividend": one opinion survey in June 1994 found that more than a third felt that the peace process would improve their economic situation, while only one in seven expressed fear that conditions would worsen.[4]

Five years later, the aid effort appeared to have had little effect, measured against the standards of a healthy peace process or sustainable development. In November 1995, Prime Minister Yitzhak Rabin was assassinated by an Israeli extremist opposed to the peace process. In May 1996, his successor, Labor Party leader Shimon Peres, lost to a Likud coalition headed by Benjamin Netanyahu, in part because of a series of bombings by Palestinian rejectionists. The new hard-line government was critical of the Oslo process and reluctant to withdraw from additional Palestinian territories. Instead, it intensified Jewish settlement activity in the Occupied Territories despite widespread international condemnation.

The economic picture was no brighter. After the disbursement of some $1.5 billion in international aid, more than two-thirds of Palestinians expressed the view that the peace process itself had harmed the economy.[5] Periodic Israeli closure of the West Bank and Gaza cost hundreds of millions of dollars in lost employment and exports, undercutting development efforts. Between 1992 and 1996, real per capita gross national product (GNP) fell by 36 percent in the West Bank and 34 percent in Gaza.[6]

In addition to the costs of closure, the Palestinian Authority (PA) and local nongovernmental organizations (NGOs) frequently complained about the tardiness or inappropriateness of much donor assistance. So too did ordinary Palestinians: few believed that foreign aid primarily benefited either the general population (17 percent) or the neediest sectors within it (11 percent).[7] Problems of inefficiency and corruption within the PA itself further clouded the picture.

Thus, political setbacks and economic restrictions combined to create a situation very different from the one that donors had initially imagined. At a donor meeting in December 1997, the World Bank noted:

> Many of you were here at the first [Consultative Group] for the West Bank and Gaza in December 1993. The atmosphere then was very different. There was a sense of anticipation. We were quite confident that Palestinian economic skills would at last flourish; that sustained growth was feasible; and that a sound economy would make a major contribution to peace.
>
> That was almost exactly four years ago. Where do we find ourselves today?
>
> Clearly, not where we expected to be. Far from witnessing a renaissance of the Palestinian economy, we have lived through an extended crisis—punctuated by terrorist acts and severe economic decline. Palestinian real per capita incomes have fallen by a quarter. Unemployment has risen from less than ten percent to over twenty percent today, with peaks of fifty percent in Gaza in times of tight border closure. The number of Palestinians living in poverty, using a benchmark of $650 per annum, has

risen to more than twenty-five percent of the population, and over a third in Gaza.

Private investment, far from increasing, has collapsed. Estimates suggest that about $1 billion was invested in 1993, and that this fell to a mere $250 million by 1996—truly sobering when you recall that Palestinian economic strategy has always been based on vigorous private sector growth.

To put it bluntly: we expected the economic program to succeed, and to strengthen the political process. Instead, political conflict has undermined the Palestinian economy and blunted the efforts of donors.[8]

This study examines the performance of international donors in Palestine during the first five years of the international aid effort, 1993–1998.[9] It focuses on the *mobilization of assistance* for Palestine; the *organization and coordination of aid*, including attempts to apply donor conditionality; the *record of aid delivery*, including factors shaping the speed of disbursement; and the sectoral *allocation of assistance* by international donors. Finally, the study identifies the *lessons to be learned* from donor experiences, suggesting that these have relevance for other, comparable cases of transitional assistance.

Mobilizing Assistance

From the initial $2.1 billion mobilized at the Washington donor conference of October 1993, international pledges grew to more than $4.2 billion by November 1998. The European Union (EU) emerged as the largest donor, followed by the United States, Germany, Japan, Saudi Arabia, the World Bank, Norway, Italy, and the Netherlands (see Table 6.1). Approximately one-quarter of this total amount has taken the form of hard or soft loans rather than outright grants. Furthermore, a portion of aid has been "tied." Although loans, tied aid, and commodity assistance were undoubtedly less common in Palestine than in "ordinary" cases of development assistance, they could limit the utility of some of the aid offered.

Was this level of donor support adequate to the challenges facing the West Bank and Gaza? Not surprisingly, different views emerged. In announcing the initial Washington pledging conference, U.S. secretary of state Warren Christopher suggested that donors needed to raise some $3 billion over ten years. He based this figure on a six-volume World Bank study, *Developing the Occupied Territories: An Investment in Peace,* published in September 1993. The Bank estimated the West Bank and Gaza's medium term (1994–1998) financing requirements to be $2.5 billion; since a portion of this would be met by private capital inflows, donors would need to mobilize $1.35 billion for medium-term public sector investments

Table 6.1   Donor Assistance to the West Bank/Gaza, 1993–1998
             (as of November 1998)

Country/Organization	Assistance (U.S.$)
Algeria	10,000,000
Arab Fund	150,000,000
Argentina	1,368,000
Australia	13,010,000
Austria	25,350,000
Belgium	39,080,000
Brunei	6,000,000
Canada	43,568,000
China	15,935,000
Czech Republic	2,718,000
Denmark	50,131,000
Egypt	17,210,000
European Investment Bank (EIB)	300,000,000
European Union	421,580,000
Finland	13,904,000
France	80,549,000
Germany	355,422,000
Greece	28,231,000
Iceland	1,300,000
India	2,000,000
Indonesia	2,000,000
International Finance Corporation (IFC)	70,000,000
Ireland	7,074,000
Israel	102,000,000
Italy	156,837,000
Japan	312,023,000
Jordan	20,211,000
Korea, Republic of	15,000,000
Kuwait	25,000,000
Luxembourg	11,500,000
Netherlands	154,166,000
Norway	244,021,000
Portugal	825,000
Qatar	3,000,000
Romania	2,880,000
Russia	4,778,000
Saudi Arabia	208,000,000
Spain	147,152,000
Sweden	95,774,000
Switzerland	90,316,000
Turkey	54,971,000
UN Development Programme	12,000,000
United Arab Emirates	25,000,000
United Kingdom	128,656,000
United States	500,000,000
World Bank	228,700,000
World Food Programme	9,334,000
Total	$4,208,574,000

Source: MOPIC, December 1998 (unpublished document).

and $85 million for technical assistance. The Palestinian territories would need another $1.6 billion in public investment in the longer term (1999–2003). Subsequently, Bank estimates for external donor assistance for the five-year transitional period were increased to $2.4 billion to include the costs of institution building and current expenses.[10] Given these estimated requirements, donor mobilization appeared fully adequate.

Prior to Oslo, the PLO had drawn up its own assessment of economic needs, the *Programme for Development of the Palestinian National Economy for the Years 1994–2000*. This called for some $14.4 billion in investments over seven years.[11] Despite its longer time frame and expectation that 60 percent of investments would come from the private sector, the PLO plan proposed an annual level of assistance twice as large as the Bank envisioned. To justify this amount, the Palestinians noted that Israel itself was receiving some $3.7 billion per year in U.S. economic and military assistance (and had received some $50 billion since 1979).

In broader perspective, annual Palestinian aid receipts since 1993 (around $240 per capita) have been below the roughly $380 per capita received by Bosnia, but well above the $60–80 per capita received during peace-building periods in El Salvador, Somalia, Mozambique, and Haiti, and approximately twice the $130 per capita received by postgenocide Rwanda. Indeed, on a per capita basis, Palestine receives perhaps the third or fourth highest level of aid in the world, and almost ten times the average for developing countries as a whole. This disparity clearly reflects the perceived strategic value and political salience of the Arab-Israeli conflict. Indeed, some donor agencies required special authority to provide "transitional" development assistance to Palestine, which might not have qualified for aid on the basis of need alone.

Burden Sharing

If one examines measures of what might be termed the relative generosity of donors, imbalances are apparent.[12] Among Western donors, Norway stands out as the most generous, devoting around 0.021 percent of its GNP to the Palestinian territories. The United States (0.0014 percent of GNP), by contrast, fares poorly by this indicator, despite its preeminent position in the peace process. In general, more geographically distant states (the United States, Japan, Canada, Australia) have shown much less commitment than have European countries, especially when additional EU multilateral contributions (0.0009 percent of EU GNP) are taken into account. Among European states, the so-called Like-Minded Countries (Norway, the Netherlands, Sweden, and Denmark) have made a particularly strong contribution, ranging from 0.0070 to 0.0090 percent of GNP—that is, around five to seven times the relative burden assumed by the United States.

Measured relative to the size of their economies, Arab donor states generally rank well ahead of their Western counterparts, even more so when the pledges of the Arab League's Arab Fund for Economic and Social Development are included. Indeed, on this basis even low-income Egypt (0.0081 percent) and low-middle-income Jordan (0.0698 percent) mobilized a greater proportion of GNP than most developed economies. Israel's own rate of aid mobilization (0.0194 percent of GNP) has approximated that of the most generous European donors, but behind that of several regional states including Jordan.

The substantial variation in donor generosity underscores the need to examine a range of factors affecting aid mobilization. Certainly, realpolitik or commercial interest provides part of the explanation. EU assistance, for example, can be seen as part of its broader Euro-Mediterranean policy, which has clearly been driven by political and economic concerns. However, realpolitik does not provide a full explanation, as indicated by high levels of Nordic mobilization and low levels of U.S. mobilization. In the former case, broad political and societal support for foreign assistance has played a significant role, although Norwegian aid is also motivated by that country's role in the negotiation of the Oslo agreement. By contrast, the low U.S. response has reflected domestic political resistance to foreign aid and the unusual concentration of U.S. official development assistance (ODA) on a limited number of states (notably Israel and Egypt).

Such variations in rates of aid mobilization can have important political implications for relations among donors. Where significant imbalances exist, disputes over aid leadership and distribution of the financial burden can inhibit the development of effective mechanisms of donor coordination. Interestingly, however, such disagreements have not significantly increased the propensity of donors to "free ride"—that is, to restrict contributions in the expectation that others would assume the financial costs of the peace process. On the contrary, the initial pledging period actually saw substantial pledge escalation between the United States and the EU as each sought to enhance its political position in the peace process. Donor conferences themselves provided another spur, as did ministerial-level meetings and visits by donor ministers or heads of government to the region. In all of these cases, donors clearly preferred to have some new project or initiative—an "announceable"—to bring to the table.

Competition among donors also created confusion about what had actually been pledged, and sparked false expectations in Palestine. Donors often announced the same project in several different forums, making it difficult to distinguish "new" money from "old."[13] In order to establish *who* had promised *what,* the World Bank and later the Palestinian Ministry of Planning and International Cooperation (MOPIC) issued regular reports on donor pledges and commitments. Although different donor accounting systems and slow donor reporting hampered their accuracy, these reports—together with the five-year pledging period—proved very useful in tracking donor assistance.

Organizing Assistance

The assistance program for the West Bank and Gaza has been complex, involving more than forty countries, over two dozen UN and other multilateral agencies, a score of Palestinian ministries, and hundreds of Palestinian and international NGOs. An array of equally complex coordinating mechanisms has emerged since 1993 to harmonize the activities of these actors.

The Architecture of Donor Coordination

At the outset, two major structures were established to provide some overall external direction to the aid effort: the Ad Hoc Liaison Committee (AHLC) and the Consultative Group (CG). The AHLC is a high-level political group of key donors, charged with providing overall direction to the international aid effort. The CG is a World Bank mechanism used to coordinate donor programs and to win support (and funding) for assistance programs. In addition, a special, ministerial-level Conference on Economic Assistance to the Palestinian People was held in January 1996 to give added impetus to the recently signed Palestinian-Israeli Interim Agreement.

Within this overall structure, donors and the Palestinians have created a number of substructures (Figure 6.1). During the initial implementation of the Gaza-Jericho agreement in spring 1994, a Coordinating Committee for Assistance to the Palestinian Police (aptly named COPP) was established, with Norway acting as chair, to secure and coordinate donor pledges of police funds and equipment. In November 1994, the AHLC decided to establish a Local Aid Coordination Committee (LACC) in the territories, which would facilitate coordination on the ground among the major aid agencies and with the PA. The LACC, cochaired by Norway (as AHLC chair), the World Bank, and the Office of the United Nations Special Coordinator in the Occupied Territories (UNSCO), gathers thirty local donor representatives for monthly meetings. The LACC has established twelve thematic sectoral working groups (SWGs), each with one or more PA ministry as "gavel holder," a donor as "shepherd," and a United Nations agency as "secretariat." Through 1997–1999, a number of further revisions to the structure of the SWGs were adopted.

In November 1994, AHLC also decided to establish a Joint Liaison Committee (JLC), consisting of the LACC cochairs and the Palestinian

Figure 6.1   The Architecture of Donor Coordination

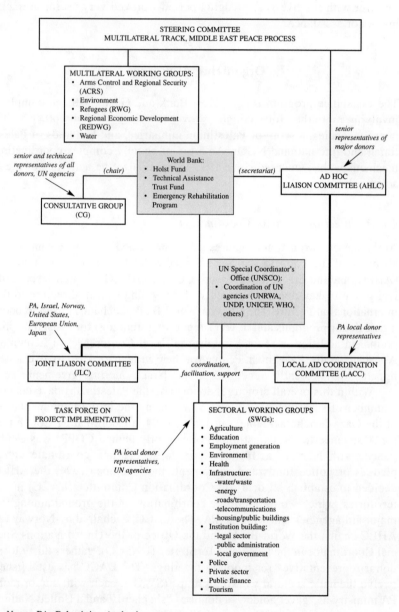

Notes: PA: Palestinian Authority.
UNDP: United Nations Development Programme.
UNICEF: United Nations Children's Fund.
UNRWA: United Nations Relief and Works Agency.
WHO: World Health Organization.

Authority (chair), to deal with significant obstacles to the prompt and effective delivery of assistance, as well as to review Palestinian budgetary performance, revenue generation, and priorities for technical assistance. The United States, the EU, Japan, and Israel subsequently joined the JLC. However, its effectiveness was constrained by the breakdown in Israeli-Palestinian relations after the Israeli elections of May 1996.

On the Palestinian side, the initial counterpart to donor coordination mechanisms was the Palestinian Economic Council for Development and Reconstruction (PECDAR), established in 1994 to track donor assistance, to channel aid into specific projects, and (generally) to manage the PA's relations with the donor community. Later, most of these roles were assumed by MOPIC and the Ministry of Finance. Line ministries, the office of the president, and municipal governments also played important roles in the aid process.

Leading the Effort

In the immediate aftermath of Oslo, the United States and the European Union competed vigorously to assume the leading role in the donor effort. Washington considered U.S. leadership essential, reasoning that no other actor enjoyed America's leverage over the Israelis and Palestinians. It also regarded the complex decisionmaking process within the EU and European Commission frustrating and cumbersome.

For their part, most European countries considered it unfair for the United States to insist on a dominant political role while Europe shouldered the primary financial burden for the peace process. Initially, they also wished to see the coordination of international assistance occur within the framework of the multilateral Regional Economic Development Working Group (REDWG), a component of the Madrid peace process "gaveled" by the EU. The EU was more likely to favor a substantial Palestinian role in the aid process. European countries viewed their relations with the Middle East as more evenhanded than that of the United States, which was seen to have a chronic pro-Israeli tilt. Within the EU, the perceived need to chart a distinctive European path in the Middle East varies among member states. France was particularly critical of Washington, whereas Great Britain was generally more willing to support U.S. initiatives.

These tensions manifested themselves in a variety of ways. As noted earlier, competition produced some escalation in aid pledges before the October 1993 aid conference, with the U.S. pledge growing from $250 million to $500 million and the EU commitment rising to ECU 500 million (or about $600 million).

Less positively, U.S.-EU competition engendered disputes over the structure of the aid process. Shortly before the Washington conference, the European Commission expressed the "view that the Community, as the main financial contributor, should seek to play a central role in [donor] coordination."[14] Not surprisingly, Washington preferred a structure in which the U.S. role was preeminent. It also favored a leading role for the World Bank in donor coordination and mobilization. The EU, by contrast, tended to see the Bank as a U.S. proxy. In the end, the structure that emerged was that of the AHLC, formally established in November 1993 to provide overall political guidance for the aid process. Reflecting European concerns, the AHLC was formally linked to the Steering Committee of the multilaterals, with its membership consisting of the United States, Russia, the European Union, Japan, Canada, Saudi Arabia, and Norway. The PA, Israel, Egypt, Jordan, and Tunisia became associate members. All decisions within the AHLC were to be taken by consensus. The World Bank was assigned responsibility for acting as secretariat, and the UN was admitted as an associate member only after lengthy debate and a Norwegian-brokered compromise. In an effort to address competing U.S. and EU ambitions, Norway was eventually assigned the role of AHLC chair.

By the time of the November 1994 meeting of the AHLC, major U.S.-EU conflict over leadership of the aid effort had faded. Even the venue of the AHLC (formal meetings in Europe, and "informal" meetings in Washington) reflected a symbolic effort to assuage European concerns. In practice, the United States assumed the leading role in the committee, preparing the groundwork for each meeting in consultation with other leading members.

However, irritants continued to arise. With total EU assistance (including bilateral programs) representing almost half of all donor support—compared to the U.S. contribution of around 14 percent—Europeans generally felt that they should acquire a larger political role in the peace process. The perception that Washington's unilateralism and pro-Israeli stance sometimes endangered either the aid effort or the broader peace process reinforced this position. In 1998, a European Commission report advised the European Parliament that "if the international assistance effort is to be renewed, it must be redefined. It is clear that the basic shareholder should be the key coordinator."[15] A subsequent round of discussions among the major donors proved inconclusive.

The International Financial Institutions

Case studies of other war-to-peace transitions have often been critical of international financial institutions (IFIs), accusing them of undercutting peace building through a rigid application of harsh (and politically destabilizing) economic medicine.[16] In the West Bank and Gaza, however, the World Bank and International Monetary Fund (IMF) have both played roles that are generally constructive—although not without shortcomings.

The World Bank assumed a particularly important role in coordinating aid as AHLC secretariat, chair of the Consultative Group, cosecretariat of the LACC and JLC, and cosecretariat of four of the SWGs. The Bank has helped to assess local economic conditions and to formulate (in association with the PA) broad development priorities. Bank officials presented the first scheme for donor priorities, the Emergency Assistance Program for the Occupied Territories (EAP), at the first Consultative Group meeting in December 1993. Later, the Bank played an important role in the development of various Palestinian development plans.

The Bank has also helped to design and administer multilateral donor programs aimed at key Palestinian needs. Soon after the Oslo accords it began to manage two quick-disbursing facilities, the Technical Assistance Trust Fund (TATF) and the Johan Jürgen Holst Peace Trust Fund (or Holst Fund). The TATF received some $23 million from twelve donors through 1994 to assist in the development of nascent Palestinian technical and administrative infrastructures. The Holst Fund supported the start-up and recurrent costs of the Palestinian Authority, providing some $246 million over the period 1994–1997.[17] In addition, the World Bank Group put in place more than a dozen other development programs, disbursing approximately $119 million in Bank loans and $67 million in donor cofinancing by mid-1998.

Early on, the Bank received heavy criticism for moving too slowly. Whereas the Holst Fund moved funds quickly, the TATF was held up initially by wrangling between the Bank and PECDAR. The Bank's Emergency Rehabilitation Project (ERP) was especially slow, with only $2 million in Bank funds and none of the $31 million received from donors being disbursed in 1994.[18] As one Bank official admitted in late 1994, "The program, from any objective evaluation, is a failure . . . little has happened on the ground . . . the money that has been disbursed has not shown much to the people. . . . Like it or not, [the Bank] is viewed as the leaders of this program. If we sit and do not react we will ultimately be blamed. More than this, the peace process will fail."[19] An internal assessment identified a series of Bank and donor assumptions that had proved unrealistic: that progress in political negotiations would be steady; that a well-functioning PA administration would be rapidly established; that the private sector would impart a vital development impetus; that the PA would become financially viable (and not need budgetary support) by the end of 1994; that donor commitments would be more timely; and that donors would speed assistance by delivering it under a World Bank umbrella with pooled resources, cofinancing arrangements, and simplified procedures. These expectations had not been met. Instead, negotiations generally took longer than anticipated; the Bank found itself entangled in Palestinian turf battles, particularly between PECDAR and MOPIC; the private sector remained moribund; Palestinian budgetary needs stayed high; and donor coordination and implementation lagged, with few donors opting for the umbrella of a single program and joint cofinancing with the Bank. For their part, Palestinian officials complained not only about the pace of Bank and donor programs but also about the Bank's "inflexibility" and its failure to empower Palestinian institutions. The Bank "did not help build Palestinian capacity, but replaced it."[20]

In order to speed responsiveness, the Bank made a series of internal institutional reforms. At headquarters, the office dealing with the territories was effectively upgraded to country division status. More important, authority over the program was moved out of headquarters and to the Bank's resident representative in the field, Odin Knudsen (later, Joseph Saba). This move faced significant initial resistance within the Bank, representing as it did a major departure from past practice. Meanwhile, the PA continued to complain about the lack of Palestinian input in Bank operations.

Ironically, when the Bank did demonstrate greater responsiveness, it created other difficulties. This occurred most notably in spring/summer 1996, when the Bank, following urgent appeals by Arafat, used the Holst Fund to support an emergency job creation program implemented through PECDAR. A number of donors (notably from the United States, Norway, and UNSCO) complained that the Bank was merely financing unsustainable make-work projects, that it was diverting precious (and difficult-to-raise) Holst Fund money, and that it had inadequately consulted with donors. The Bank refuted all of these charges. Some U.S. officials seemed most perturbed by a multilateral agency showing independent initiative ("activism" and "politicization," as one U.S. State Department official put it), and not necessarily by the job creation itself.

Devolution of authority into the field strengthened the Bank's ability to implement its own programs and to play a broader role in the donor effort. Over time, the importance of some Bank functions declined: the MOPIC took over preparation of the regular donor matrices, and budgetary support through the Holst Fund became less important by 1997–1998. However, the Bank continued to play a critical role in various multidonor projects, in support for PA policy planning, and in facilitating both high-level (AHLC, CG) and local coordination activities. In one 1997 survey of donor officials, conducted by the Center for Palestine Research and Studies (CPRS), 38 percent rated the World Bank's performance as "positive," and only 9 percent rated it as "negative." Both PA officials and Palestinian NGOs offered a more mixed assessment, with 30 percent rating it as "negative."[21]

Although the IMF's role in Palestine has been less central than the Bank's, the Fund has been very successful in providing oversight and advice to the Palestinian Authority on its fiscal affairs since late 1994.

While the recurrent costs of the PA proved larger than donors had first anticipated, and concerns about PA expenditures have remained, the IMF has helped to establish an effective revenue-collection system and a reasonable system of cost control.[22] Indeed, some PA officials—chafing under expenditure restrictions—complain of excessively close relations between the Ministry of Finance and the IMF. Finally, the Fund's periodic monitoring reports and other analyses have become a useful tool for donors, not only in reporting on Palestinian budgetary measures, but more broadly in providing information on the current situation and facilitating future donor planning.

UN Coordination

Within the UN system, the secretary-general first responded to the challenge of the Oslo agreement by appointing a task force to report on current and potential UN efforts. Subsequently, in June 1994, Norwegian scholar-turned-diplomat Terje Rød Larsen was appointed the first United Nations special coordinator in the Occupied Territories. His office, UNSCO, was given a mandate to facilitate coordination among UN programs, represent the UN in donor meetings, maintain contact with local NGOs, support the Declaration of Principles (as requested by the parties), and represent the secretary-general in the multilateral working groups.

Coordinating the UN system, however, was more easily said than done. In 1993, three UN agencies were present on the ground: the United Nations Relief and Works Agency (UNRWA), the United Nations Development Programme (UNDP), and the United Nations Children's Fund (UNICEF). Of these, the four-decade-old refugee agency UNRWA was by far the largest, and indeed the largest single employer within the entire UN system.

By 1997, the number of UN agencies with a presence in the territories surged to twenty-five, fifteen of which maintained field offices. One negative result was the rise of substantial turf wars, exacerbated by the fact that (as one staffer put it) "there are probably more senior UN officials per square kilometer in Gaza than anywhere outside New York."[23] UNRWA, as the largest and most senior UN actor in the field, felt that it should be the senior partner in any UN development effort. So did the UNDP, which had often assumed the coordinating role in other countries. Many officials at both were critical of what they saw as UNSCO's ineffectiveness. Given its lack of both line authority and budgetary control, there was very little that UNSCO could do other than to "urge" UN agencies to cooperate more effectively.

UNSCO succeeded in producing a series of documents—starting with *Putting Peace to Work* (1995–1996) and thereafter the UN's *Programme of*

Cooperation in the West Bank and Gaza Strip—that combined project listings, proposals, priorities, and sector analyses. These documents helped to give greater cohesion to UN efforts, as did the establishment of a UN compound headed by UNSCO, which provided space and support in Gaza for many of the smaller UN programs.

UNSCO was also tasked with assisting donor coordination more broadly in its capacity as cochair of the LACC, cosecretariat of the LACC and JLC, and secretariat of some of the SWGs. Its effectiveness was constrained, however, by limited staff resources and technical capacity. Moreover, UNSCO's initial extremely good working relationship with the World Bank deteriorated; UNSCO officials privately accused the Bank of being slow and showing poor political judgment; Bank officials accused Larsen of grandstanding. For a period in 1996, two camps composed of the World Bank and PECDAR (on the one hand), and UNSCO, UNRWA, and UNDP (on the other) became for a time virtual competitors in the business of emergency job creation.

Finally, UNSCO's effectiveness in aid coordination benefited from Larsen's considerable political skills, which had been in evidence in the original Oslo peace talks and in subsequent negotiations. Exploiting his dynamism, media savvy, personal ties to senior Israeli (Labor) and Palestinian leaders, and close working relationship with the United States, Larsen encouraged and cajoled donors, Israel, and the PA alike, both privately and publicly, to respond to the urgent situation on the ground. Donors generally held him in high regard, increasing his effectiveness as a fund-raiser for UN programs and giving him somewhat greater powers of suasion within the UN system.

Larsen resigned his position in October 1996, being succeeded temporarily by Peter Hansen, the UNRWA commissioner-general, and eventually by Chinmaya Gharekhan in February 1997. With these changes, UNSCO's role in donor mobilization and coordination weakened somewhat. By late 1996, donor programs in the West Bank/Gaza were quite mature, and there was less possibility of mobilizing substantial new funds. Moreover, MOPIC had emerged as an entity with considerable capacities. Most important, the return of Likud to power in Israel (and the consequent rise in Palestinian-Israeli tensions) limited the influence of both Larsen and his successors. UNSCO continued to undertake quieter but nonetheless important work, supporting the LACC and SWGs and (beginning in autumn of 1996) issuing a series of very useful reports on economic trends that brought home to policymakers the economic deterioration in the territories.

The Effectiveness of Coordination

Some have criticized the aid coordination structure that developed to support donor assistance in the West Bank and Gaza as excessively complex and unwieldy. In practice, however, it is difficult to see what other architecture might be more effective. On the one hand, donor coordination required meetings of senior policymakers and technical experts from the donor community (hence the Consultative Group); at the same time, the CG was clearly too large a group to discuss overall donor policy, which was pursued more effectively in a smaller setting involving the principal donors and regional actors (the AHLC). Although the United States might have preferred a less multilateral framework, it could not (given that it constituted only a fraction of total donor pledges) have insisted on anything else. Moreover, the inclusive character of the Consultative Group (in particular) undoubtedly facilitated the mobilization of additional pledges after the initial donor meeting in October 1993.

At the same time, it soon became clear that the AHLC and CG were not sufficient, since neither could provide the frequency of meetings or detailed follow-up that would be necessary at the project level. Donors and the PA needed local structures of coordination.

Given Palestinian institutional weaknesses, it was only natural that the World Bank, UNSCO, and the IMF would assume key roles in facilitating this. Similarly, the need to organize myriad UN agencies on the ground made UNSCO important, quite apart from its value as a general support to the LACC/SWGs and its role (particularly under Larsen) as a political facilitator.

That the complex architecture that emerged after 1993 was necessary, however, does not automatically mean that it was as effective as its architects had hoped. One survey of donor officials, PA officials, and local NGOs found that opinions on donor coordination were mixed, with a slightly larger portion holding negative perceptions.[24]

With regard to high-level coordination, some aid officials expressed dismay that AHLC meetings focused on political issues rather than on aid design and coordination, and that the (theoretically, more technical) Consultative Group meetings were similarly dominated by foreign ministries and political symbolism. Palestinian officials often expressed frustration at the difficulty they encountered in converting general pledges of support for Palestinian public investment programs made at CG meetings into concrete commitments to specific projects.

Locally, participants found that raising issues in the JLC was not necessarily the same as resolving them, since appropriate political will or follow-up by Israeli, Palestinian, and donor bureaucracies was often lacking. The LACC provided a useful forum for raising broad issues of concern, and at times donor criticism of the Israelis and Palestinians could be quite pointed. Still, some officials bemoaned the lack of real dialogue on development issues.

The performance of the various sectoral working groups and subgroups was uneven, varying with the complexity of the sector being addressed and the degree of energy and initiative shown both by the (donor) shepherd and the (PA) gavel-holder. Moreover, most donors in most sectors continued to pursue their programs bilaterally, using the SWGs to share information on their activities rather than to coordinate future plans. The technical weakness of some SWG secretariats was also a hindrance.

As discussed later, the institutional weaknesses of the PA presented donors with a dilemma: when the coordination structures were being established and the PA was still weak, it seemed expeditious to assign the leading role to donors and international agencies. Later, however, this lack of Palestinian "ownership" over the coordination of its own aid proved a point of friction and even inefficiency.

In broader perspective—and despite such criticisms—the situation in Palestine may still be much better than in many other cases of transitional assistance. If donor coordination has been less than some have hoped for, it has still been better than many had feared.

Conditionality

In many cases of international peace building, a degree of formal or informal conditionality has been imposed on assistance in order to encourage parties to abide by agreements and undertake the measures necessary for reconstruction.[25] In the Palestinian case, donor concern over a variety of issues—transparency, accountability, and institution building on the Palestinian side, and concern over impediments to Palestinian development on the Israeli side—resulted in the Tripartite Action Plan on Revenues, Expenditures and Donor Funding for the Palestinian Authority (TAP) of April 1995. The TAP, signed by the PA, Israel, and Norway (in its capacity as chair of the AHLC), contained a series of specific commitments. The Palestinian Authority agreed to improve its domestic revenue-collection systems; restrain civil service hiring; clarify the division of responsibilities among the main PA economic institutions; establish regulatory frameworks and commercial codes; and make efforts to eliminate donor support for start-up costs by the end of 1996. Israel undertook to cooperate with the PA in establishing a functioning tax system; facilitate the transfer of goods between the West Bank and Gaza and between the territories and neighboring countries; and finalize negotiations on industrial zones and on construction of a port for Gaza. Donors promised to extend budgetary support and police funding through 1995; support quick-disbursement job creation programs; and provide preferential trade access. They also warned that "their own continuing efforts would be contingent upon performance by Palestinians and Israelis in implementing the steps described in this action plan." The AHLC and IMF, in conjunction with the JLC and LACC, were to monitor implementation of the agreement.[26]

The TAP was subsequently revised in January 1996. These revisions included new Palestinian commitments to abide by budgetary targets, to strengthen fiscal expenditure management and budgetary controls, to consolidate revenue accounts, to establish a commission on public administration, and to identify clearly development priorities. Israel undertook to "remove measures which have proven impediments to the achievement of sustained economic growth in the West Bank and Gaza Strip" (while recognizing Israel's obligation to provide for the "security of its citizens"), and particularly to facilitate movement to and from Gaza (and between it and the West Bank). Finally, donors agreed to deliver promptly their outstanding pledges, to support the PA's medium-term economic strategy, and to provide budgetary support to the PA (on the understanding that "this would not continue beyond 1996").[27]

The TAP provided a useful mechanism to signal donor concerns, focus PA (and Israeli) attention on specific issues, and monitor specific actions taken or not taken. Still, however, many of its provisions went unfulfilled. The PA continued to delay civil service reform and the consolidation of accounts, although it dealt with other tax and transparency issues more effectively. Israel continued to impose periodic closure on the territories in the name of "security." Negotiations over "safe passage," the Gaza port, and industrial estates all dragged on without resolution.

Much of the reason for this was the donors' lack of leverage—or, perhaps, lack of willingness to exercise leverage. At a time when the Palestinian economy was in sharp decline, donors were generally unwilling to halt assistance to the territories, for fear of further damaging the peace process. In particular, support for Palestinian recurrent budget expenditures continued longer than most donors would have wished.

Instead of direct conditionality, a more diffuse linkage tended to occur: the inefficiency of a particular ministry might deter donor support for its projects, and reports of corruption and administrative inefficiency tended to sap already reluctant donor support for recurrent costs. Such indirect and uncoordinated linkages, however, generally failed to elicit desired changes from the PA. This was particularly true when Palestinian behavior was driven by strong local political imperatives.

With regard to Israeli policy (arguably the largest single reason for Palestinian economic decline), donors had even less leverage and were unwilling to use what leverage they had. At one point, the EU suggested that the TAP include a compensation clause, whereby Israel would assume the costs of closure; this proposal went nowhere in the face of Israeli and U.S. opposition. In the words of Swedish foreign minister Lena Hjelm-Wallen, "Any economic pressure on Israel will be rejected by the Americans, and this makes the exercise of economic pressure somewhat difficult."[28]

Delivering Assistance

As the Palestinian Authority assumed control of Gaza and Jericho in the summer of 1994, it soon became apparent that, despite the large and public pledges made in Washington in October 1993, donor funds would be slow to arrive. The first and most immediate priority was to secure support for start-up and recurrent costs, as well as for funding and equipment for the police. At the November 1994 meeting of the AHLC, the Norwegian chair warned that the reconstruction program too was proceeding slowly, with disbursements predicted to fall 40 percent below the targets set by the World Bank.[29] The Palestinian Authority complained that delays were "an attempt to politically pressure us, to make us accept conditions."[30] In the end, donors committed some $820 million against specific projects in 1994 and actually disbursed $524 million, or 66.4 percent of commitments (see Table 6.2).[31] While this record was much better than anticipated, much of the delivery occurred in the final quarter of the year, amid mounting criticism of the slow pace of aid delivery.

Such criticism of the pace of assistance was, in part, politically motivated. By criticizing donors, the PA diverted attention from its own shortcomings and exerted pressure for accelerated disbursements. Donors replied that support for Palestinian recurrent costs, transmitted through the Holst Fund, was delivered in a timely fashion and indeed represented a large share of 1994–1995 disbursements. In the case of investment and rehabilitation projects, however, planning and engineering cycles could be compressed only so much. Still, it was clear that the aid was much slower arriving than anyone would have wished.

By the end of 1995, donors argued that they had turned the corner. In October of that year, Terje Larsen noted, "[In 1994] I called the donor effort a failure . . . but now donors are moving speedily."[32] In fact, in 1995, 1996, and 1997 the level of disbursements did not rise, nor did the gap between commitments and disbursements substantially narrow. Perhaps more important than the annual disbursement figures, however, was the fact that an aid pipeline had now been established, consisting of an array

Table 6.2   Aid Commitments and Disbursements

	Committed (U.S.$ millions)	Disbursed (U.S.$ millions)	Disbursed (% commitments)
1994	789.2	523.8	66.4
1995	604.7	415.5	68.7
1996	855.9	557.3	65.1
1997	657.3	464.9	70.7

of projects in the preparatory, planning, implementation, and wind-down phases. Unlike the initial, cash-starved period in 1994, this ensured a relatively smooth and constant flow of donor resources. Moreover, improvements in Palestinian revenue generation meant that the PA was increasingly less dependent on donors for immediate budgetary support, although it did continue to rely on external sources for virtually all public investments. As of March 1998 (85 percent of the way through the 1994–1998 pledging period), 84.6 percent of pledges had been committed by donors against specific projects, and 54.5 percent had already been disbursed.[33] While the PA might have hoped for even higher rates of delivery, by international standards—and especially by the standards of peace-building operations elsewhere—such results seem acceptable. Palestinian complaints of a slow donor response did not stop, but they did become more muted. They were also increasingly aimed at the failure of donors to fund specific programs and priorities.

Structural Constraints

There were several reasons for the slow start of the aid program as well as for subsequent delays. Some of these were structural in character, associated with the immediate political and economic context within which development and donor assistance programs have operated. Many were attributable to legacies of the Israeli occupation, which had left an underdeveloped infrastructure, heavy economic dependence, and a weak and fragmented public sector. In addition, donor programs faced particular constraints associated with both the absorptive capacity of the territories and the responsiveness of the private sector. Finally, a variety of constraints (and needs) were associated with the various political agreements that have characterized the interim period of the peace process.

Absorptive capacity. Clearly, donor assistance to the West Bank and Gaza, representing around 12 percent of Palestinian GNP, has pushed the upper margins of the absorptive capacity of the Palestinian economy. The promise of both development assistance and private sector investment caused land prices to skyrocket in some areas (notably in Gaza and Ramallah) and caused price increases in some construction materials. More serious still—at least in the initial years of the aid program—were bottlenecks arising from the limited technical and physical capacities of the local construction sector, the underdevelopment of the financial services sector, weaknesses in local infrastructure, and other constraints.

A number of efforts were made to break these bottlenecks. The World Bank, for example, designed its Emergency Rehabilitation Project (ERP I) around smaller projects. Although well suited to the capacities of the construction sector, the projects proved too scattered to attract the interest of larger regional and international contractors, who might otherwise have become engaged. The second Emergency Rehabilitation Project (ERP II) addressed this in part by emphasizing labor-intensive activities that not only required physical plant, but also addressed the growing need for local employment generation. A parallel approach, evident in the World Bank's Municipal Infrastructure Rehabilitation Project, was to combine subprojects into larger packages to attract international consultants and contractors if serious local capacity constraints arose.

Of course, donors could have designed projects that incorporated the lead time required to raise the capacity and technical expertise of local contractors. Yet, here and elsewhere in the assistance effort, donors faced a trade-off: should they design programs to maximize long-term capacity building even if this delayed implementation; or should they stress timely implementation even if this failed to build local capacity?

The Palestinian private sector. From the outset, donor assistance programs assumed that substantial private sector investment (spurred by the peace process and by an inflow of expatriate investment capital) would play a major role in sustaining economic growth in the territories. In practice, investment flows were disappointing. Although a few substantial Palestinian holding companies were active and real estate speculation was extensive, Palestinian expatriate investment failed to reach hoped-for levels. On the contrary, total investment in the Palestinian economy fell from around 19 percent of GDP in 1993 to 10–11 percent by 1997, with the vast bulk (85 percent) of this investment in residential housing and very little (less than 5 percent) in capital equipment and machinery.[34]

Several factors accounted for this. Most important, political and economic uncertainty increased the already high degree of risk of investment in the West Bank and Gaza. Even expatriate Palestinian investors proved wary of risking capital in this environment. Broader private sector growth was also hampered by the weaknesses of local infrastructure in transportation, communication, and energy. The legal and regulatory context—based on a complicated amalgam of Turkish, British, Jordanian, Egyptian, Israeli, and PA regulations—"is far from ideal, characterized by numerous regulatory hurdles and a lack of legal transparency which increases the burden, risk, and confusion involved in doing business."[35] Potential investors also cited concerns regarding corruption, threats to the free movement of goods and people, limits on the transferability of capital, and an underdeveloped financial services sector. Finally, it was not evident that the West Bank and Gaza offered comparative economic advantages for foreign investment, given competition from Israel and Jordan.

Not all of these constraints, of course, were purely structural. Many were also bound up with politics and policy decisions. Business often complained that high rates of taxation, the PA's interventionist policies, and the proliferation of semipublic, semiprivate monopolies all deterred investment and undercut entrepreneurship.

In order to redress the lack of private sector investment, the PA held high-profile meetings with Palestinian entrepreneurs. In April 1995, it announced a Palestinian Investment Law offering tax exemptions of up to five years, but the law was criticized as unclear, inadequate, and outmoded.[36] The PA also made initial efforts to regularize commercial codes.

The donor community was also slow to respond to these problems. In many cases the donors' export credit and investment guarantee agencies cited investment risks as a justification for not supporting projects in the territories, thus essentially negating any meaningful contribution they might have made to economic revitalization. Belatedly, in March 1997, the International Finance Corporation (IFC) began lending operations in the territories, and the Multilateral Investment Guarantee Agency (MIGA) established an Investment Guarantee Fund. The latter, however, was ill suited to the challenge of periodic closure. Other donor programs have also sought to inject greater flexibility into the local financial services sector, whether through microenterprise schemes, capacity building in the banking sector, or attempts to encourage the emergence of local mortgage lending.

The interim agreements. Donor assistance during this period took place against a complex backdrop of a series of interim Palestinian-Israeli agreements: the September 1993 Declaration of Principles, which first established the PA in Gaza and the West Bank city of Jericho; the May 1994 Gaza-Jericho agreement and associated Paris protocols on economic relations; the "early empowerment agreements" of 1994 and 1995, which transferred policy areas to the PA; the Palestinian-Israeli Interim Agreement (Oslo II) of September 1995, which expanded Palestinian autonomy in the West Bank; and the largely unimplemented Wye Memorandum of October 1998. These defined both the extent of economic authority available to the PA and the political space within which donor programs must operate.

The interim nature of these agreements naturally inhibited long-term planning. Moreover, each agreement produced specific needs and imperatives, such as the establishment of the administrative structures of the PA and the expansion of the Authority into an increasing number of policy areas. The various agreements also altered the geographic area under Palestinian control and the PA's revenue base. The specific provisions of the Oslo II agreement, for example, allowed the PA to manage the main sectors of the economy (such as health, education, the tax system) but gave it only partial control over instruments and strategies (for example, over the type of fiscal instruments or the choice of external economic relations).

These agreements also created a complex and unwieldy patchwork quilt of territorial arrangements, with declining Palestinian governmental authority from one zone to the next.

Furthermore, the customs union model adopted under the Paris protocols and subsequent Interim Agreement proved to have a number of weaknesses. These include the loss of PA customs revenues on goods purchased through Israeli intermediaries; the loss of policy independence arising from a linkage to Israeli trade policy; constrained access to the Israeli market due to closure; and practical constraints on the PA's trade access to other countries.[37] This increased the risk associated with Palestinian enterprise and created a pattern of trade discrimination in favor of Israeli concerns, aggravating the problems of Israeli intermediaries, dependence, and tax leakage.

Israeli Constraints

The existing structural constraints on aid implementation were compounded by obstacles arising directly or indirectly from Israeli actions. Indeed, many donors (and even some Israeli diplomats) observed that Israeli policies were the single most important constraint on Palestinian economic development.

Some of these obstacles arose from the legacies of ongoing Israeli occupation, the constraints imposed by the various interim agreements, and the slow pace of the peace process itself. However, two other aspects of Israeli policy merit further attention. The most important has been closure, which has had devastating effects on the territories and, at times, has severely hampered development assistance. In addition, a number of bureaucratic or politically motivated obstacles have often inhibited development.

Closure. Throughout the occupation, Israel often used checkpoints and local curfews as means of social control, particularly after the eruption of the Palestinian uprising in December 1987. From March 1993, permits were required for Palestinians to enter Jerusalem or Israel, and permanent checkpoints were established to enforce this. With the advent of Palestinian self-government (and its associated territorial autonomy in much of Gaza and major population centers in the West Bank), restrictions became more severe. Moreover, two additional measures were periodically adopted by Israel: *general closure*, which restricted all movement into and out of PA-controlled areas; and *internal closure*, which prevented movement between population centers within the West Bank.[38] Data compiled by the United Nations shows the use of closure increasing steadily so that by 1996–1997, this meant that the West Bank and Gaza were closed for more than one-quarter of all regular commercial days.[39]

The impact of closure was devastating. Palestinian workers were cut off from work (and wages) in Israel, compounding a longer-term substitution of Palestinian with foreign labor. The average number of Palestinians working in Israel fell from about 100,000 workers in the early 1990s, to around 32,000 in 1995 and 23,000 in 1996,[40] before rising to 38,000 in 1997. Closure halted or restricted imports and exports and had serious effects on the public sector: trade interruptions and declining domestic sales reduced fiscal revenues, while closure increased demands on social services and state employment—thus compounding the budgetary problems of the PA.

One source estimates that between 1994 and 1996, Palestinian employment losses due to closure totaled $685 million, with a further $1,809 million in trade-related costs.[41] Another estimate by UNSCO puts the costs of closure at some $4–6 million per day during severe closure, or between $864 million and $1.3 billion during 1994–1996.[42] By either calculation, the costs of closure represent between 7 percent and 15 percent of Palestinian GNP—roughly equal to the $1.4 billion disbursed by the entire international donor community over the same period.

Closure had an equally profound impact on donor programs. The hardship it imposed forced donors to sponsor emergency job creation programs and to inject assistance rapidly into the territories. Projects were disrupted by interruptions in both the flow of building materials and the mobility of project personnel (especially locally engaged Palestinian staff). In the longer term, it was impossible for both donors and the PA to envisage a strategy of sustainable development in an environment characterized by the periodic (and unpredictable) interruption of trade, uncertain Palestinian access to external markets, and severely corroded private sector confidence.

Donors repeatedly criticized the use of closure, noting that it was "counterproductive to security concerns by undermining the key cornerstone on which the donor community participates in the peace process" and reminding Israel that "the responsibility for Palestinian welfare does not rest with donors alone."[43] Successive UN special coordinators were particularly outspoken in this regard, and UNSCO issued detailed assessments of both the general impact of closure and specific incidents.[44] The Tripartite Action Plan called upon Israel to facilitate the movement of goods and persons to and from the West Bank and Gaza. However, U.S. officials rejected the notion of pressuring Israel on closure, much to the chagrin of other donors (and many of their colleagues in the U.S. Agency for International Development [USAID]). Instead, the United States tried to work around these obstacles by providing equipment and procedures to facilitate the inspection of trucks leaving Gaza, close diplomatic monitoring of closure, and support for border industrial zones that would enable Palestinians to work without entering Israel.

The Israeli government too sought mechanisms for lessening the economic impact of closure, including the idea of industrial estates. In December 1997, Israel announced that it would issue some 30,000 "closure-proof" labor passes to Palestinians considered a low security risk. In 1998, the number of closure days dropped significantly. However, Israel retained closure as a policy instrument.

Other impediments. Other Israeli policies also had negative effects on aid implementation in the territories. In the CPRS survey, not one donor described Israel's role as positive, and 39 percent described it as "obstructive" and 27 percent as "very obstructive." Not surprisingly, PA officials took an even dimmer view: 29 percent described Israeli actions as "obstructive" and 69 percent as "very obstructive."[45]

One impediment was the initially slow pace of Israeli tax clearances to the Palestinian Authority under the terms of the Gaza-Jericho agreement. Subsequently, in August and September 1997, Israel temporarily withheld customs and excise clearances as a way of exerting pressure on the PA. Given that these receipts account for more than 60 percent of the PA budget, this step posed a serious threat to political stability; it was widely criticized by the donor community.

In addition, both donors and the PA have complained about the sclerotic rate of some Israeli customs procedures, which can leave imported materials languishing on Israeli docksides for weeks or months. Ever-present Israeli concerns about security tied up some goods even longer. Storage costs (payable by the donors or the PA) thus mounted, sometimes exceeding the value of the shipment. Palestinians also had problems in securing the visas and other documents required for foreign experts working on development projects, in receiving value-added tax (VAT) rebates, and in agreeing with Israel over product standards.

Many such impediments arose from inefficiencies within the Israeli bureaucracy or from problems of interagency coordination; other obstacles were created by right-wing customs and other officials hostile to the peace process. Still other delays, however, clearly reflected official policy. A case in point was the water sector, one of the (contentious) areas reserved for final status negotiations. While the interim agreements authorized the PA to develop additional water resources, those projects that might increase water production (rather than improve distribution) seemed to encounter particularly frequent obstacles.

The establishment of the JLC—which allowed both donors and the PA to raise such irritants directly with senior Israeli officials and in so doing also flag them for the attention of AHLC—eased these problems somewhat. Subsequently, the JLC established a Task Force on Project Implementation to follow up on reports. However, another bureaucratic factor often stymied its effectiveness: while delays were usually associated with the actions (or lack thereof) of the Israeli defense forces, the ministry of finance, or port and customs officials, it was the Israeli foreign ministry that was represented in the JLC. Both aid officials and Israeli diplomats expressed periodic frustration at this bureaucratic disconnection.

Moreover, whatever goodwill existed largely evaporated after Israel's change of government in May 1996. Cooperation and facilitation mechanisms languished, and some of the coordination mechanisms established under the architecture of both the interim agreements and the AHLC/ LACC stopped meeting.

Palestinian Constraints

Structural and Israeli constraints on aid implementation, while substantial, explain only part of the difficulty in transforming aid pledges into concrete projects. Palestinian factors also slowed the delivery of assistance, with many donors (and Palestinian NGOs) critical of the PA's ability to identify projects, to prepare proposals, to coordinate with donors, and to manage projects in a financially transparent manner.[46]

Most donors failed to anticipate the lack of Palestinian preparedness and the associated institutional growing pains of the PA. Following its assumption of control in Gaza and Jericho, the PA had to staff ministries; acquire the necessary office space, equipment, and other supports; delineate bureaucratic responsibilities; establish coordination and communication mechanisms; reform legal and regulatory systems; and set national priorities—all essentially from scratch. This has presented a task more daunting than that confronting some war-torn societies, where the skeleton of a bureaucratic structure might already be in place. On the other hand, the PA did have the advantage of a relatively highly educated population and access to considerable technical skills in the diaspora. As in other cases, external assistance was a significant local political resource, and its delivery had profound local political ramifications. Aid, institution building, and the political consolidation of the PA proved to be inextricably bound, further complicating an already complex environment.

Technical expertise. Some of the problems the Palestinian Authority encountered in handling assistance stemmed from shortages in human resources. Although the PA did inherit some of the structure of the former civil administration (notably in the education sector), it lacked both trained senior management and technical experts in many policy areas. Even when these skills existed, many expatriate Palestinian professionals in the Palestinian diaspora were understandably reluctant (or could not afford) to uproot and work under difficult conditions in the territories. Compounding human resource weaknesses, appointments to administrative and technical units within the PA were often driven by political favoritism and nepotism.

To build human capital in Palestine, donors established a Technical Assistance Trust Fund. To tap diaspora skills, the UNDP's Transfer of Knowledge Through Expatriate Nationals (TOKTEN) program provided short-term support for Palestinian expatriates working with the PA; later, the World Bank established a Palestinian Expatriate Professional Fund. However, such programs encountered problems due to differentials in pay and status between locals and expatriates. All told, donors committed roughly $547 million to technical assistance by March 1998, representing around 17 percent of all commitments.[47]

Institutional effectiveness. The institutional constraints experienced by the PA, like the human resource constraints, have stemmed in part from inexperience and the challenges of assembling the bureaucracy of a protostate. Compounding these obstacles, the senior leadership (and Arafat in particular) seemed unwilling to create meaningful administrative structures or to clarify decisionmaking authority. This inhibited economic policymaking. Moreover, the PA failed, at least initially, to establish the fairly demanding mechanisms of accountability and transparency that donor agencies required, slowing the disbursement of assistance significantly.

Emerging bureaucratic structures in Palestine soon became personal and political power bases, enmeshed in competition with each other and with preexisting NGOs. One important example was the Palestinian Economic Development and Reconstruction Authority (PEDRA), later renamed the Palestinian Economic Council for Development and Reconstruction (PECDAR). PECDAR was established in October 1993 to be the primary (but transitional) conduit for foreign assistance. However, donors were uncomfortable with a variety of aspects of PECDAR, including the predominance of political rather than technical personnel, unclear lines of authority, and a lack of solid auditing mechanisms. Such disputes delayed the initiation of programs and the conclusion of a World Bank agreement with the PLO/PA. It took more than six months of pressure from the Norwegian chair of the AHLC, bilateral diplomatic representations, a diplomatic démarche by donors, and final negotiations with the World Bank to persuade Arafat, the PLO Executive Committee, and the PA to approve revised bylaws for PECDAR in mid-May 1994.

The subsequent establishment of separate PA economic and line ministries raised further questions about PECDAR's future role and the locus of economic authority. Personal and institutional rivalries between PECDAR and the Ministry of Planning and International Cooperation accentuated these problems. In the end, MOPIC emerged as the official intermediary between donors and the PA. The PA also attempted to designate the Ministry of Finance as the central agency for receiving donor funds.

Meanwhile, some Palestinian line ministries, municipalities, and agencies continued to approach donors on an individual basis, rather than operating through MOPIC or any other centralized mechanism. Some donors complained about this. Most, however, continued to pursue the path of least resistance, arranging whatever projects seemed easiest with whatever level or branch of Palestinian authority or society seemed most amenable—a practice that one senior PECDAR official described as "signature shopping." Some donor officials responded by citing the need to disburse funds expeditiously. The effect, however, was that donors committed their assistance in those sectors where Palestinian counterpart institutions were strong (for example, education or health), rather than those where institutional capacity or competence was weak (for example, agriculture or tourism). This pattern, of course, exacerbated uneven institutional development and hindered effective economic planning.

In addition to the economic policy and line ministries, the Office of the President retained a role in a great many projects and economic decisions. Surrounding the president, a bevy of advisers and shady hangers-on, all claiming some influence, authority, or *wasta* (intermediation), often further clouded economic accountability. Although this problem diminished as PA ministries developed, donors also expressed concern about the existence of funds outside the control of the Ministry of Finance and under the apparent direct control of Arafat. Most notable has been the approximately $100 million per year in petroleum excise taxes collected by Israel and paid to a numbered Bank Leumi account. Although the PA has repeatedly pledged (in the TAP and elsewhere) to consolidate all accounts, by the end of 1998 it had yet to take this step.

Finally, institutional development within the PA was characterized by the rapid (and, in the view of most donors, excessive) growth of the Palestinian bureaucracy. Between October 1994 and late 1997, public sector employment more than doubled, from some 35,000 employees (including 12,000 members of the security services) to more than 81,000 (including around 37,000 members of the security services), representing some 16 percent of the labor force.[48]

Corruption. Donor concerns about Palestinian transparency and accountability, which had been a real drag on the initial implementation of aid programs, resurfaced in 1996 with reports of growing corruption. These reports alleged that aid funds were being mishandled within ministries, that officials enjoyed excessive perks at public expense, that favoritism and kickbacks influenced contracting decisions, and that some PA officials (and ministries) enjoyed excessively close connections with private sector companies. Perhaps the most obvious manifestation of corruption, however, was the rise of semiprivate, semipublic monopolies. These controlled the import trade in a number of sectors (fuel, cement, gravel, cigarettes, flour, steel, building materials), typically in conjunction with an exclusive external (usually Israeli) supplier and one of the PA's myriad security agencies. Some estimates suggested that twenty-seven or more such monopolies were operating in the territories by 1997.[49] These arrangements in turn spawned an expanding array of second-generation commercial activities—legal enterprises established with the proceeds of murkier business operations.

In May 1996, the PA's own Public Monitoring Department (PMD) issued a report detailing some $329 million in forgone revenues and irregular or excessive expenditures by PA ministries and official bodies.[50] In a statement presented to an informal AHLC meeting in Washington, D.C., PA representatives explained that many of the items cited as forgone revenues in fact reflected deliberate policy decisions rather than evidence of wrongdoing.[51] Arafat subsequently appointed a special commission to examine the question of corruption, while a special committee of the Palestinian Legislative Council (PLC) issued a follow-up report detailing alleged abuses in a number of PA ministries.[52] Neither report, however, addressed the problem of semiofficial monopolies, the operations of Arafat's office, or the role of the security services. In July 1997, the PLC adopted a resolution calling for the entire PA cabinet to be replaced. However, the corruption issue was partially sidelined by the continued uncertainty of the peace process. The PLC effectively closed its file on the 1997 PMD report without having taken any effective action, and a token cabinet reshuffle in 1998 had little impact on good governance.

It remains difficult to get a sense of the true scope and effect of corruption within the PA. Certainly, public perceptions of corruption have grown, from 49 percent identifying it as a problem in September 1996 to 61 percent by March 1998.[53] The PLC investigation, although weak in several respects, brought greater attention to the issue. A variety of political and media dynamics also amplified attention to corruption, which was seized upon by local opponents of the PA, the international media, the Israeli government (under Netanyahu, but not Labor), and by external critics of the aid program (notably in the United States).

Some corrupt activities—most notably the operation of the monopolies—combine elements of an extortion racket and an inefficient and extralegal system of taxation, with some funds lining private pockets but a substantial share financing the off-the-books expenses of the PA. Indeed, two of the largest companies involved in such activities have close links to Arafat's office. On balance, though, official corruption appears to be less widespread in Palestine than in neighboring Egypt, Lebanon, or Syria, and less severe than in Cambodia, Haiti, and a number of other postconflict countries. Certainly, there are no other countries in the Arab world where reports as critical of the government as those produced by the PMD and PLC would be publicly released.

On the other hand, it is clear that corruption *has* adversely affected development in a number of ways. The monopolies tended to inhibit private sector development and to distort market prices. Corruption within the PA also introduced policy distortions and eroded confidence in public institutions.[54] Externally, press reports of corruption threatened political support for assistance (and particularly budgetary support) in donor countries.

Political imperatives. In evaluating the nature and effects of Palestinian institutional constraints, one needs to bear in mind the political context in which aid is being implemented. For the Palestinian Authority, the receipt and expenditure of aid has been closely tied not only to the developmental needs of the West Bank and Gaza, but to two additional (and not always complementary) imperatives: political consolidation of the PA, and the need to strengthen the PA vis-à-vis Israel.

With regard to the *internal politics,* aid, public investment, and public employment provided an opportunity to reward supporters and buttress political constituencies. This approach to public policy—hardly unique to the PA—was reinforced by Arafat's neopatrimonial style of political management, which emphasizes personalism and patronage at the expense of long-term institution building.[55] In short, much PA decisionmaking has been driven not by concerns over economic efficiency or sustainability, but by considerations of political consolidation.

Viewed in this light, the growth of public sector employment becomes understandable. As Muhammad Dahlan (head of PA "Preventative Security" in Gaza) explained: "I cannot tell a prisoner who has spent 15 years in jail that I have no job for him."[56] The employment of otherwise unemployed former intifada-era street activists has secured loyalty to Arafat's Fateh organization and coopted others away from the opposition and potential troublemaking. Discussing patronage at a more senior level, one PECDAR official observed: "If someone has put in thirty years, you can't throw them away, even if they might be less efficient than a new university graduate. Palestinians who have struggled know how to protect the peace process—it is they who are politically reliable."[57]

Political patronage by the PA has included not only public sector employment, but also specific projects. Thus, Arafat has been careful to preserve some discretionary funds, whether through the petroleum excise account or through revenues raised by the monopolies, to lavish on supporters. The PA too has generally encouraged donors to channel support through the PA rather than through alternate (NGO) channels, thus allowing the Authority to claim appropriate political credit.

Political consolidation underpins many of the rivalries and divisions apparent within PA administrative structures. Encouraging competition between subordinates is a hallmark of neopatrimonial political management, serving both to inhibit the emergence of rival power centers and to strengthen the position of the leader. Unclear lines of administrative authority serve a similar purpose, allowing a leader to reallocate responsibilities among subordinates and enhancing the primacy of political loyalty and personal relationships over institutional structures and bureaucratic procedures. The rivalry between MOPIC and PECDAR has all the hallmarks of such a situation.

Corruption can also be seen as having, at least in part, political roots.[58] As a political reward, it has the advantage of being wholly or partly self-financing. It is also easily withdrawn from clients when political circumstances dictate, or leveled as a charge against excessively ambitious or politically suspect subordinates—as the leader cloaks himself or herself in the mantle of feigned moral outrage.

Faced with these problems, donors have devoted growing resources to institution building and public sector reform. Similarly, the TAP included various public sector reforms. Many such initiatives have seemed naive, however, treating the issue as one of technical competence rather than recognizing the political roots of the problem. Despite donor admonishments that reform would bring greater cost-effectiveness, there was little incentive for change. From Arafat's perspective, the existing system helped to sustain remarkably stable support despite political stalemate and economic decline. Indeed, with a personal approval rate averaging over 70 percent through 1996–1997 (compared to 48 percent for the legislature), Arafat probably suspected that he had a firmer grip on the task of political management than did either his domestic critics or the donors.[59]

With regard to *external politics,* the PA has not surprisingly attempted to use foreign assistance to strengthen its position in negotiations with Israel. As a PECDAR official noted early in the process, "In the first phase, our economic planning is completely determined by political reasoning. . . . We have to be professional from a political point of view, not an economic point of view."[60]

The issue of Jerusalem provides one example. The PA has made a continual effort to maximize its presence and connection to the city. The initial formation of PECDAR was delayed, for instance, by its charter's initial reference to the city as its headquarters. Later, the PECDAR offices (and the West Bank offices of MOPIC) were deliberately sited on the very edge of the city, virtually a "stone's throw" from an Israeli checkpoint. In September 1994, a CG meeting collapsed when the PA included Jerusalem projects among its proposals to donors. There has been a constant game of cat and mouse between the PA and Israel over the presence of PA-linked offices in East Jerusalem and periodic Israeli threats or measures against these.

The Palestinians have used large infrastructure projects to buttress their negotiating position. Both the proposed Gaza port and the completed

Gaza airport were driven by political as well as economic logic: they have been intended to reduce Palestinian dependence on Israel and to enhance the symbolism of Palestinian protosovereignty. Similarly, Palestinians justify their emphasis on road construction (which constitutes almost one-quarter of all infrastructure investments under the 1998–2000 Palestinian Development Program) on transportation grounds, but an unspoken motive may also be to consolidate territorial control and block the expansion of Israeli settlements.

Donor Constraints

Donors too were responsible for a significant share of delays and other weaknesses in the delivery of assistance. Palestinian officials and NGOs reported substantial dissatisfaction with projects that donors prioritized, their slowness in processing proposals, and their delay in fulfilling commitments.[61] At the same time, Palestinian appraisals of particular donors varied significantly.[62] Comparative rates of donor aid implementation (Table 6.3) suggest that these differing appraisals may be warranted.[63]

Since all donors had to confront a common economic and political setting in the territories, similar various challenges posed by Palestinian

Table 6.3 Proportion of Pledges Disbursed (selected donors, to September 1997)

Donor	Aid Disbursement (% of pledges, including Holst Fund)	Aid Disbursement (% of pledges, excluding Holst Fund)
Russia	95	95
Norway	94	93
Switzerland	91	89
Japan	87	86
Denmark	80	79
Canada	80	73
European Union	71	71
Saudi Arabia	60	51
US (USAID+OPIC)	54	50
World Bank	47	47
Sweden	42	35
Italy	33	25
Israel	14	0
Turkey	7	7
EIB	0	0
Average	50	47

Source: MOPIC, *Quarterly Monitoring Report,* November 28, 1997.
Notes: EIB: European Investment Bank.
OPIC: Oversees Private Investment Corporation.
USAID: U.S. Agency for International Development.

politics and institutions, and the same impact of closure and other Israeli actions, these factors cannot explain variations in donor performance. At least in part, therefore, such variation reflects the particularities of different donor programs.

Institutional responsiveness. One significant constraint on rapid aid disbursement has been the institutional structure and internal dynamics of aid agencies themselves. One EU aid official recounts how, when asked by Brussels to report on the extent to which Palestinian factors were limiting the aid effort, he declined to do so—arguing that donor limitations had been at least as important, and perhaps more so.[64] And, though it might be argued that the multilateral EU faces particularly intense bureaucratic constraints, other donors face institutional obstacles of their own.

Of course, one should not underestimate the institutional challenge of expanding donor aid programs rapidly, from around $200 million per year at the start of the decade to three or four times that amount after 1993. New staff had to be hired and new projects identified. Since most aid agencies had an existing "stable" of projects and contacts, the initial reaction was to do more of the same rather than to rethink aid priorities.

Yet, doing more of the same could be problematic. Many earlier aid programs had been heavily dependent on small NGO projects and could not easily be scaled up. Before Oslo, for example, U.S. aid had been channeled largely through U.S. private voluntary organizations rather than administered directly. The dramatic expansion of U.S. programs for the territories forced USAID to expand its infrastructure on the ground, generating bureaucratic and political struggles over issues like staffing levels, location (East Jerusalem versus Tel Aviv), and line authority.

Gradually, donors began to develop new and larger aid programs. However, these projects were generally subject to complex and time-consuming bureaucratic processes—entailing lengthy procedures for planning, proposal, assessment, and procurement. In part, such hurdles responded to a decade of criticism that Western development agencies funded wasteful or inappropriate aid programs. As a result, donors were intent on spending funds carefully, in support of long-term development. However, these same attitudes and processes often proved poorly suited to the political realities of peace building in Palestine, which required the rapid delivery of assistance in such a way as to strengthen the ongoing diplomatic process. Furthermore, many initial donor agency assumptions were "very facile," underestimating the political and economic difficulties that lay ahead.[65] Through 1994–1995 these difficulties expressed themselves in a clash between the realpolitik of foreign ministry officials and the commitment of their aid counterparts to sustainable development. In the case of the U.S. assistance program, State Department officials often complained about the slowness and inappropriateness of USAID programs in the territories, while many USAID officials complained that they were being diverted from real, sustainable development: "How do you plan, develop, and do something of quality if you are under [constant political] pressure?"[66]

The delivery of international assistance was also complicated by legal restrictions. Japan, for example, was bound by domestic legislation that limited assistance to international organizations and recognized states (thus excluding the Palestinian Authority). The Japanese thus delivered most of their aid through multilateral agencies (notably UNDP, UNRWA, and the World Bank–administered TATF and Holst Fund). The World Bank too faced administrative complications, since the PA was not a member state, and the Oslo agreement gave the PLO responsibility for Palestinian external relations. As a result, the World Bank signed its agreement with PECDAR, a PA institution established under a mandate from the PLO Executive Committee.

Support for the Palestinian police was particularly problematic since restrictions prevented many aid agencies from providing direct assistance. Although donors held meetings on the police in Oslo in December 1993 and in Cairo in March 1994, they pledged only $2 million in support by the second meeting.[67] Both the Bank and UNDP declined to assume the role of transferring (and, in a sense, bureaucratically "laundering") donor support for police salaries. Eventually, UNRWA assumed the role from late 1994 until mid-1995, after receiving special authorization from the UN General Assembly.[68] Later, the mandate of the Holst Fund broadened, and the PA began to collect significant tax revenues, obviating the need for this mechanism.

Of the various institutional factors shaping donor responsiveness, one key element has been the local presence of agencies, including sufficient field staff. Smaller donors have often found themselves unable, because of personnel shortages, to pursue project opportunities or to participate fully in consultative and donor coordination mechanisms. Perhaps even more serious, overworked field staff are less likely to show the initiative or to assume the additional responsibilities required in peace-building situations, where the developmental context is fluid and uncertain and where local (in this case, Palestinian) counterpart agencies may not be in a position to fully assume their project responsibilities. Still, the number of aid personnel may be less critical than the quality of those assigned to the field. In challenging environments like the West Bank and Gaza, idiosyncratic factors can have a substantial impact on the success of aid programs. The effectiveness of both the Bank and UNSCO, for example, rested to a substantial degree on the skills of Odin Knudsen, Terje Larsen, and their successors.

Finally, donor efficiency was strongly correlated with willingness to delegate decisionmaking authority and autonomy. Because of its complex, dynamic nature, peace-building assistance cannot easily be directed from headquarters; local officials need the authority to act on their own initiative. The devolution of World Bank authority to the resident representative in Gaza proved a great success; other agencies (like UNDP and USAID) permitted their field directors to utilize accelerated procurement procedures. As a Bank official later noted: "As donors it took us time to adapt our procedures to such a fluid environment. Had we created an effective local coordination forum at the beginning, rather than waiting until 1995, we could have adjusted much faster. We should have decentralized our management into the field sooner than we did."[69]

Sectors and channels of assistance. Variations in aid disbursement across donors have reflected not only varying degrees of institutional responsiveness and local presence, but also the sectors chosen by different donors. Support disbursed through the Holst Fund could be moved extremely quickly, with the transfer from donor to the World Bank to the Palestinian Authority taking as little as a few weeks. Support for multilateral programs through the Bank, the UNDP, and other agencies were also relatively quick and painless for donors (although it might take rather longer for the project to start on the ground). In the early years, small and medium-sized donors that lacked an established bilateral program frequently exploited these channels. Sectoral aid involving high proportions of technical assistance was often easy to move, and both humanitarian relief and short-term emergency employment programs were structured deliberately for rapid disbursement. NGOs, by their very nature, were eager to accept donor money quickly, although the process of supporting many small NGO projects tended to demand large donor staff resources relative to the amounts disbursed.

Assistance in other areas was much slower, usually by virtue of the inherent scale, technical complexity, and political complications of projects in particular sectors. This was particularly true of large infrastructure projects. Thus, while an overall average of 64 percent of all committed funds had been disbursed by donors as of March 1998, there was substantial variation across sectors: 98 percent of committed funds for democratic development had been disbursed, but only 55 percent of those in the water/sanitation sector, 50 percent of those in the energy sector, and 25 percent of those in the transportation sector. Similar variation could be found across the various types of assistance: by March 1998, donors had disbursed 92 percent of transitional and budget support commitments, 79 percent of funds for NGOs, and 64 percent of technical assistance commitments—but only 54 percent of public investment.[70]

Loans, risk insurance, and export and investment guarantees usually proved the most difficult component of aid programs to deliver. It soon became clear that, amid the political uncertainty and periodic economic closure, few projects in the territories were sound enough to meet the banking standards that ordinarily determined lending practice. The United States allocated $125 million of its support to the Overseas Private Investment Corporation (OPIC), but by December 1995 only one project (a Gaza-based concrete factory) had received investment guarantees. The subsequent failure of that investment hardly encouraged greater OPIC risk taking. Similarly, the EU allocated approximately half of its assistance through the European Investment Bank ($300 million), but by September 1997 only 30 percent of this had been committed—and none disbursed. Overall, loan commitments by all donors were disbursed at less than one-third the rate of grants.

Domestic politics. In many donor countries, internal politics has also helped to shape or constrain assistance to the Palestinians. In the CPRS survey, 60 percent of Palestinian NGOs and 75 percent of PA officials perceived this to be a significant problem. An even greater proportion of both groups of respondents (84 percent and 92 percent, respectively) regarded the internal politics of the United States, in particular, as problematic.[71]

In the United States, the issue was affected by strong congressional support for Israel, suspicion of the Palestinian Authority, and a generally less-than-friendly attitude to both foreign aid and multilateralism. The U.S. Congress passed the PLO Commitments Compliance Act of 1993 and the Middle East Peace Facilitation Acts (MEPFA) of 1994 and 1995, each of which required the State Department to certify periodically the Palestinian compliance with the Oslo agreement (and other conditions).[72] Some members of Congress, encouraged by right-wing pro-Israeli lobby groups, sought to tighten restrictions still further. In August 1997, the MEPFA were allowed to expire without renewal. For the State Department and USAID, battles with Congress over aid to the Palestinians were a constant political headache, one aggravated by the change of Israeli government in May 1996. Under Labor, the Israeli embassy and most pro-Israeli lobby groups had supported U.S. assistance to the Palestinians; this was no longer the case once Netanyahu assumed power.

At other times, the impact of donor domestic politics on donor programs could be less direct. In late 1995 and early 1996, the congressional legislation necessary for U.S. assistance to the West Bank and Gaza was delayed not only by certain members of Congress opposed to aid to the Palestinians, but also by unrelated legislative battles over issues ranging from abortion to the reorganization of the State Department. Congressional hostility to foreign aid encouraged institutional caution with USAID, undoubtedly affecting its Palestinian programming. Donor agencies in other countries, faced with declining budgets, the possibility of legislative criticism, and potential investigation by the press or the government auditor's office, had grown similarly cautious.

Allocating Assistance

As of June 1998, a total of $3.6 billion (of $4.1 billion pledged) had been committed by donors against specific projects, and $2.5 billion of this amount had been disbursed against specific projects. Although efforts to track donor commitments and disbursements are hampered by methodological and data limitations, nonetheless some general patterns are evident.

Sectoral Distribution

A sectoral analysis of aid disbursements over the period 1994–1997 (Figure 6.2) shows a peaking and then a decline in support for social services (primarily health and education); a decline followed by a rise in support for state building (primarily institution building and police); and an increase in support for infrastructure (notably in water/sanitation, transportation, and energy).[73] These shifts were to be expected, given the initial start-up costs of the Palestinian Authority and its gradual institutionalization, the delays involved in larger infrastructure projects, and the initial ease of channeling funds through the functional social service ministries. Direct support for the productive sectors of the economy (including agriculture, industrial development, and private sector support) remained surprisingly low, although growing realization of the importance of private sector activity renewed donor attention to this area in 1997. Geographically, an analysis of SWG sectors undertaken by UNSCO in 1996 suggested that 50 percent of donor commitments (excluding public finance and police) were directed to the West Bank and Gaza, 29 percent to Gaza alone, and 18 percent to the West Bank alone (with the designation of 3 percent "unspecified").[74] Given that almost 60 percent of Palestinians reside in the West Bank (excluding East Jerusalem), this would appear to signal a disproportionate share of resources going to Gaza. However, this concentration is largely explained by the initial costs of establishing PA authority in Gaza, as well as the higher degree of social need there.

The following section discusses four different sectors and types of assistance. It focuses on the diversion of donor resources into emergency job creation, the low attention given to the agricultural sector, the provision of technical assistance, and support for NGOs. While far from the totality of the assistance effort, these areas illustrate a number of important

Figure 6.2   Sectoral Allocation of Assistance (U.S.$ thousands)

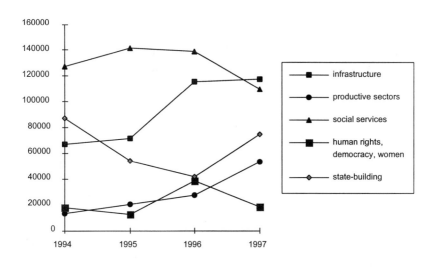

points about the allocation of donor assistance within the West Bank and Gaza.

Emergency job creation. The forerunner of emergency job creation schemes was a number of earlier employment-generation programs in the territories, operated by UNRWA, Save the Children Federation, and others.[75] In late 1994, UNDP launched a "Gaza cleanup" program, driven largely by the political need to show immediate tangible benefits in the territories following the establishment of the PA. Other similar campaigns were launched in conjunction with the employment-generation SWG.

Following the bombings of February–March 1996 and the subsequent prolonged closures, PECDAR implemented two additional and much larger emergency job creation schemes, one sponsored by the World Bank and the other by UNDP. UNRWA also expanded its employment-generation programs, providing up to 52,500 full-time equivalent jobs at their peak in summer 1996.[76] Programs with the heaviest labor input generally involved the lowest level of permanent asset creation (and vice versa). Consequently, many "second phase" employment programs put greater emphasis on asset creation.

Emergency job creation programs were short-term and temporary responses to the fundamental problem of enduring Palestinian unemployment and the economic and political shocks of periodic closure. Given the circumstances, donors had little alternative in 1996–1997 but to divert resources from sustainable development projects to emergency employment schemes. In the longer term, donor programs needed to reconcile the goals of job creation and longer-term productive investment.

Agriculture.   Whereas donors channeled resources unexpectedly into emergency job creation, they largely ignored the agricultural sector. Although agriculture accounts for approximately one-fifth of Palestinian employment, trade, and gross domestic product (GDP), it had received only 1.5 percent of donor commitments and 1 percent of disbursements ($24.8 million) by the third quarter of 1997.[77]

Part of this reluctance reflected political considerations. The agricultural sector, being bound up with issues of land and water consumption, is a potentially sensitive one. Israeli authorities discouraged development of this sector by limiting water usage. Moreover, much agricultural land fell within areas beyond the administrative control of the PA.

From an economic standpoint, the World Bank's assessment of 1993 emphasized the uncertain competitiveness of this sector. The Bank called on donors to spend some $46 million in this area, representing around 3.8 percent of overall commitments.[78]

The lack of donor enthusiasm for this sector was compounded both by the apparent lack of interest of the Palestinian Authority and by the morass of bureaucratic politics. The first PA cabinet did not have a minister of agriculture. When one was appointed, he often complained (prior to resigning in 1998) that he was unable to fire corrupt or incompetent senior staff.[79]

Technical assistance.   Technical assistance, or the transfer of knowledge (often from external experts), is an essential tool for building capacity in developing countries. It is also often a form of tied aid, in which funds flow back to consultants and technical experts in the donor country.

Palestinian officials frequently complained about technical assistance and, in particular, about the excessive volume and low quality that donors have provided. In many cases, the external experts provided cannot speak Arabic, have had a poor understanding of local conditions (and politics), and produce reports that languish on shelves. Moreover, foreign experts are almost invariably paid at rates several times greater than those of their Palestinian counterparts, creating additional tensions. Initiatives such as the UNDP's TOKTEN program and the World Bank's Palestinian Expatriate Professional Fund attempted to make greater use of expatriate Palestinian expertise, but these programs still faced the dilemma of offering high financial incentives to attract expertise while ensuring their smooth integration into local institutions where salaries were substantially lower.

Poor donor coordination (or competition) also created problems. Palestinian agencies might be offered multiple technical experts from different sources, each providing contradictory advice or training. Palestinian officials reported substantial frustration when donors supplied experts instead of the required equipment or financial resources—particularly when local expertise was available but other resources were not. There was also a widespread perception that donors linked aid priorities to their ability to insert their own national technical experts into a project.

None of this criticism is to suggest, of course, that technical assistance is unimportant: as one UNDP official noted, "All the negative things [said] about technical assistance are true—but they still need technical assistance."[80] However, donors clearly also needed to pay greater attention to when and where it was really required, and in what form it could best be provided.

NGO support. The refocusing of post-Oslo international aid efforts toward the newly established Palestinian Authority squeezed both Palestinian NGOs, of which some 850–1,200 operate in the West Bank and Gaza, and international NGOs, of which approximately 200 are active.[81] In the early 1990s, the NGO sector received approximately $170–240 million from the PLO and international donors and were, in the absence of a state apparatus, responsible for a significant portion of the health, education, and social welfare sector, as well as development. As a consequence of the Gulf War and (later) of the redirection of aid funds to the PA after 1993, this amount fell to roughly $60–90 million by the middle of the decade.

There were several reasons for this trend. First many development projects were simply too large for Palestinian NGOs to bid on or participate in effectively. Second, while NGOs are often cost-effective and disburse funds "on the ground" more quickly than other channels, donors sometimes find them more difficult to deal with, especially given both the smaller size of grants and the considerable staff time required to oversee their activities. NGOs have shown poor coordination among themselves and were unable to find a formula for representation within the donor coordination framework. Furthermore, the overriding political imperative of aid was to strengthen the PA (and thus the peace process). In the eyes of some foreign ministry staff, NGOs did not figure prominently in this process.

At the same time, the PA attempted (with some success) to bring Palestinian NGOs under its control. The PA's initial *Draft Law Concerning Charitable Societies, Social Bodies and Private Institutions* envisaged an extensive system of state registration and supervision, apparently based on the most restrictive elements of Egyptian and Jordanian NGO law. NGO, donor, and PLC criticism, as well as bureaucratic infighting among Palestinian ministries, led to marked improvements in the proposed law. Such PA efforts to subordinate the NGO sector were, in part, a natural process of extending state authority into various social policy sectors. However, they also represented efforts to strengthen the PA's political sway.

In addition to the PA, NGOs also faced more subtle pressures from donors. Since donors rarely support the recurrent costs of core NGO programs, NGOs have been forced to fund their regular activities and operating costs through special project grants. Accordingly, many Palestinian NGOs tailor their appeals to the thematic priorities of funders, less out of conviction than from the imperatives of fund-raising.

Given the cost-effectiveness, flexibility, and innovation of the Palestinian NGO sector, as well as its broader contribution to a pluralistic Palestinian society, its weakening is a source of concern. Indeed, the World Bank, historically rather removed from NGO activity, itself proposed creating a Palestinian NGO project to supplement existing funding sources.

The proposal soon faced serious challenges. The PA was unenthusiastic about an independent pipeline of resources to local NGOs; local NGOs were concerned about the possible role of the Bank and PA in allocating grants; and Palestinians questioned how the fund would deal with NGOs based in Jerusalem. Moreover, a host of new NGO coordinating groups suddenly appeared in the territories, some closely tied to the PA and others clearly hoping to get a piece of any new funds. For their part, many donors were unwilling to contribute to an anonymous fund when they could gain greater political profile by directly financing NGOs. However, the proposal eventually received approval from the PA, NGOs, and donors. It was launched in 1997 with $14.6 million in financial support from the World Bank, Italy (which earmarked its contribution for Italian NGOs), and Saudi Arabia.[82]

Agenda Setting

The preceding analysis examined the sectoral allocation of donor assistance in Palestine and underlined some of its implications. But do these patterns of assistance best meet the needs of the West Bank and Gaza? Have disbursed funds been used in an optimal fashion, to promote peace building and lay the foundations for sustainable development? By what criteria can the "relevance" of donor assistance be measured?

Clearly, assessing the relevance of assistance is inherently more ambiguous and subjective than either assessing aid pledges or examining the speed with which these are implemented. Reflecting this subjectivity, Palestinian officials, donors, and analysts disagree on priorities. These differences often reflect the bureaucratic position of the observer, the technical expertise of the specialist, and the ideological orientation of the analyst. Thus, NGOs frequently bemoan the decline of support given to the NGO sector;[83] the Palestinian Authority objects that "donor assistance has been diverted from [public] investment"[84]; the private sector and international financial institutions emphasize the need to "rely on the private sector as much as possible"[85]; UN agencies underscore their "comparative advantage . . . as a principal development partner"[86]; and the Palestinian left complains that the private sector and the World Bank are "following the dictates of the new imperialist policy in the Arab homeland."[87] Similarly, water specialists tend to emphasize the importance of water, municipalities stress the need for local public works, and so forth. Such differences of view, to the extent that they inform potentially conflicting policies, can have deleterious effects on international peace building.

One way of getting at such issues is to examine the process of agenda setting and the extent to which agreed sets of developmental and peace-building priorities emerge and are accepted by concerned actors. In the case of the Palestinian territories, both the PLO and the World Bank had examined possible aid priorities prior to the Oslo agreement. Subsequently, at the time of the 1993 Washington donors conference, the World Bank was entrusted with producing a basic blueprint for Palestinian social and economic needs.

The result was the Emergency Assistance Program. This envisaged $1.2 billion in donor support over three years (1994–1996) in the form of public investments ($600 million), private sector support ($300 million), start-up expenditures ($225 million), and technical assistance ($75 million). The budgetary gap between PA tax revenues and expenditures was forecast to be only $158 million in 1994 and $40 million in 1995, with the PA to become self-sustaining (of recurrent costs) by 1996.

In practice, some sectoral needs proved greater than first estimated, and the PA's need for budgetary support substantially exceeded the World Bank's projections. All told, donors disbursed around $500 million for transitional and start-up costs through 1994–1997 (including $246 million through the Holst Fund), approximately twice the level that had been initially anticipated. The provision of budget support, although fundamental to the survival of the PA (and hence to the peace process), was very unpopular with most development agencies, which saw it as nonproductive expenditure. The growth of the Palestinian public sector, and later reports of corruption and financial mismanagement, dampened donor enthusiasm still further. "Some argue that we compromised the development program by diverting so much to budget support," the World Bank later noted. "Obviously those grant resources are now unavailable for investment—but what choice was there? In 1994 and 1995, Palestinian recurrent expenditure far exceeded revenues."[88]

Moreover, the imposition of closure in the spring of 1996 made it imperative to disburse funds rapidly for emergency job creation; this was a "stop-gap initiative, intended to alleviate economic hardship and lessen the risk of destabilizing social unrest."[89]

Even apart from the unanticipated need to fund recurrent costs and emergency employment generation, there is little evidence that donors utilized the EAP as a yardstick for directing their aid. As of November 1996, some areas had received disbursements substantially greater than the EAP targets (education, 343 percent; health 161 percent), whereas others had received only a portion of the amounts suggested in the EAP (power, 10 percent; agriculture, 6 percent; support to private sector and industry, 0 percent).[90]

The first medium-term economic strategy put forward by the Palestinian Authority was the $550 million Core Investment Program, which the PA presented at the October 1995 CG meeting and at the January 1996 ministerial donor conference. Although nominally presented to donors by MOPIC, the program was in fact assembled largely by the World Bank and UNSCO, with input from key donors (notably the United States). Some 60 percent of the program was directed to physical infrastructure and 30 percent to social services, with the remainder supporting industrial zone infrastructure and legal reform.

PA institutions, led by MOPIC, played a larger role in the development of the Palestinian Public Investment Program (PPIP) for 1997, proposed to donors at the November 1996 CG meeting. This listed (but did not fully describe) some 309 projects totaling $1.3 billion, of which infrastructure represented 42 percent, social services 34 percent, private sector support 16 percent, and institution building and legal reform 8 percent.

The PPIP was supplanted in turn by a more ambitious and integrated Palestine Development Plan (PDP), intended to be a rolling three-year planning exercise. The 1998–2000 version, endorsed by the PA in July 1997 and presented to donors at a CG meeting in December 1997, envisaged total investments of $3.4 billion. Of this, $0.7 billion was already committed by donors, and $0.2 billion was to be provided by the PA; the PA requested $2.5 billion in additional support from donors.[91] Reflecting a concern that inadequate attention has been directed toward establishing the basis for future economic growth, the program placed heavy emphasis on the development of economic infrastructure. Yet again, some sectors were more successful than others in attracting investment. Whereas 91 percent of the democratic development subsector and 22.1 percent of the human resources sector had already been funded by the time the plan was finalized, only 10.3 percent of the infrastructure sector had received the desired donor commitments. A revised and expanded PDP, covering the period 1999–2003 and calling for $6 billion in investments, was presented to donors in February 1999. This placed even heavier emphasis on infrastructure.

As is evident from both the World Bank's EAP and the PA's PPIP and PDP, agenda setting has been far more complex than simply identifying sectoral "needs" or "priorities" based on abstract technical criteria. One survey of PA officials noted that "democracy," "human rights," and "gender" had been relatively overfunded by donors, whereas "economic development," "physical infrastructure," and "agriculture" had been underfunded.[92] Respondents considered "Palestinian preferences" (along with the "sectoral expertise of donors") as relatively unimportant in shaping donor aid programs. Except for the World Bank's EAP, most aid coordination mechanisms (UNSCO and the LACC) were not seen as important in agenda setting. The most important determinants in the targeting of international assistance were, Palestinians believed, "donors' desire for enhanced political profile," "the economic interests of donors," and "the World Bank," followed by "domestic lobby groups," "the desire to produce immediate local benefits," and "the desire to politically strengthen the Palestinian Authority."

It can be argued that such a view overstates the rationality of donor programs. As with any large bureaucracy, donor decisions have in large part been driven by institutional and idiosyncratic factors, as well as by a substantial degree of serendipity: the need to move money out of a budget before the end of a financial year, the appearance of fleeting project opportunities, the outcome of particular meetings or high-level contacts, or the sectoral preferences of senior aid officials. Asked to explain the emergence of water as an area of concentration for USAID, for example, one U.S. official simply noted that "a couple of the people who managed the program were water resource people."[93] Similarly, the development of the World Bank's innovative Palestinian NGO project was largely driven by the Bank's dynamic principal country officer, who himself came from an NGO background.

Yet, with this important caveat firmly in mind, it is nonetheless clear that donor agenda setting has been driven by political and economic calculations. As one World Bank spokesperson noted, "If we are honest, we have to admit we still place too much emphasis on visibility and commercial self-interest, which interferes with cooperation among ourselves and with our Palestinian colleagues."[94] Yet donors themselves work in an environment in which the general sustainability of assistance depends on demonstrating to their governments and publics that aid serves their national interest, whether in terms of advancing foreign policy, securing new trade and investment opportunities, or upholding a broader set of values. Of course, the relative mix of motives varies from donor to donor. USAID often appears particularly eager to justify aid in terms of U.S. interests. By contrast, there is much greater public support for aid in the Nordic countries, as well as less tying of assistance to national procurements.

The result of all this can be emphasis on sectors with trade or investment potential, the tying of assistance (including the provision of donor technical assistance), emphasis on projects with high political visibility or trendy themes (such as democratization), while less "glamorous" sectors (such as agriculture) are ignored. One manifestation of this tendency is the "showcase" project driven overwhelmingly by political rationales. At times, the results can be spectacularly expensive and unsuccessful: the USAID-funded Karameh Towers housing project, or the EU-funded Gaza European Hospital are cases in point.[95] Other cases have been more ambiguous: Norway's provision of $10 million (through UNDP) for neighborhood improvements, green spaces, and children's playgrounds in Gaza, for example, certainly did not fall within the confines of traditional development programming and was criticized by some as a cosmetic, nonproductive make-work scheme. Yet the parks it created did provide a symbolic public indicator of the changed atmosphere brought on by self-rule and the peace process.

As donors note, the mismatches that occur between donor and Palestinian priorities can also be a function of weak internal agenda setting by the Palestinian Authority. Weak PA direction allows donors to propose a multiplicity of programs and projects without prioritization. Although the PA has gradually improved its agenda setting (most recently in the form of the PDP), the development agenda still resembles a "wish list" of various PA ministries rather than a cohesive and integrated national plan.

The complex process of both donor and PA agenda setting occurs against the backdrop of the perceived political needs of the peace process, most notably the need to stabilize the Palestinian Authority. Perhaps the clearest evidence is donor support for the Holst Fund through 1994–1996, as well as support for emergency job creation in 1996–1997. Neither of these activities fitted into the traditional framework of development assistance; indeed, most aid agencies would ordinarily have viewed these as wasteful or ineffective expenditures that encouraged dependency rather than sustainable growth. In the West Bank and Gaza, however, the imperative of political and social stability prevailed. Institutionally, this tended to reflect the triumph of foreign ministry officials over their aid agency colleagues, particularly in the early, politically crucial years of the program.

As the assistance program has continued, however, a modus vivendi appears to have developed: despite periodic irritations, tensions, and lack of coordination, both the PA and donors seem to have settled upon a course with which all were fairly comfortable. While the expected economic "peace dividend" has failed to materialize for most Palestinians, it is no longer possible to blame either the donors or the PA for this. Instead, the greatest reasons for failure lie with external economic shocks and the general decline of the peace process itself.

Conclusion

International assistance to Palestine stands out as one of the largest and most complex cases of post–Cold War economic peace building. It is, moreover, a process that is still under way, with an end result that it is unclear. In November 1998, donors pledged some $3.3 billion for the next five years of assistance to the West Bank and Gaza. In May 1999, Israel faced new elections. That same month, the peace process timetable established under the Oslo agreement expired.

Certainly, the steady deterioration of the peace process under Likud and the broader decline of the Palestinian economy in the 1990s underscore that development assistance can neither create peace in the absence of political will among all of the local parties nor single-handedly create prosperity in the face of multiple economic shocks and structural constraints.

Yet, this having been said, the increase in post-1993 international assistance has played an important and perhaps critical role. Without such aid, Palestinian GNP would have declined a further 7 to 8 percent.[96] It is unlikely that the Palestinian Authority could have established itself as a functional bureaucratic entity without outside support. The provision of such assistance has undoubtedly strengthened the political stability of the PA, whether by buttressing policy performance or permitting political patronage.

From the point of view of the international community and other countries undergoing war-to-peace transition, the Palestinian case holds out a number of important lessons. These concern all aspects of the aid process: the mobilization of assistance; the organization and coordination of such assistance; the timely delivery of aid; and its effective allocation and implementation.

Mobilizing Assistance

The Palestinian case underscores that there presently exists no agreed mechanism for burden sharing among donors. In fact, it is doubtful that such a mechanism is possible across different cases of transitional assistance. Instead, donor commitment is a function of political, strategic, and economic interests, as well as the size, structure, and objectives of their foreign aid program. The Nordics (or Like-Minded Group) donors stand out as particularly generous among Western countries, whereas the United States provides a surprisingly small share of assistance in view of its economic size and global leadership.

This difference affects not only the total amounts mobilized by donors toward peace building; in addition, *inequitable burden sharing among donors can inhibit donor coordination,* by creating tensions over "leadership" of the aid effort. Although these tensions have been managed effectively for most of the period since 1993, they have surfaced periodically between the United States and the EU, occasionally hampering the effectiveness of donor coordination mechanisms.

Another lesson to arise from the Palestinian case is that *close monitoring and periodic donor meetings help to ensure donor compliance with aid pledges,* by providing an opportunity for a periodic "status report" or "reality check" by the donor community. The mere fact of having to attend such meetings creates pressures to mobilize and disburse funds. With regard to assistance to the Palestinians, effective tracking of aid (first by the AHLC/World Bank, later by MOPIC), coupled with a clear five-year pledge period, facilitated measurement, monitoring, and comparison of donor pledges. This mechanism is much more effective in Palestine than in many other cases of transitional assistance, where data are lacking and where the pressures on donors to deliver are correspondingly reduced. MOPIC's reporting compares favorably with aid management in many nontransitional developing countries, and it represents a substantial achievement given the size and complexity of the donor effort.

A third observation with regard to the mobilization of assistance is that *"pledge inflation" can generate excessive local expectations.* Certainly, the Palestinians initially expected more assistance, more quickly delivered, and more directly and flexibly allocated. While pledge inflation was limited by the existence of fairly effective reporting mechanisms, it did nonetheless create political tensions and suspicions when Palestinians perceived that promises went unfulfilled. This said, it should be noted that unrealistic expectations were fed not only by donors (anxious to maximize the political "bang" for their financial "buck"), but also by the PA, which sometimes overrepresented aid pledges or blamed donors for its own shortcomings.

Organizing Assistance

The Palestinian case spawned a host of donor coordination mechanisms beyond the traditional donor Consultative Group. These included the AHLC, JLC, LACC, and SWGs, as well as the coordinating roles assumed by the World Bank, UNSCO, and MOPIC. The effectiveness of these mechanisms has been mixed.

On the positive side, The Palestinian experience suggests that *coordination mechanisms need to be created at both top/external and local/sectoral levels.* High-level coordination (the AHLC and CG) is important to provide some overall sense of direction and to address fundamental constraints. Conversely, local meetings (the LACC and SWGs) have the advantage of involving those local aid officials who actually know what is happening on the ground (as opposed to the sometimes less-informed diplomats and senior aid officials who may attend high-level meetings). The Palestinian experience also suggests that *both inclusive and exclusive coordination mechanisms are useful.* Inclusive mechanisms—such as the

CG or LACC—give all donors some sense of participation in the process and allow a broad airing of analyses and views. More limited groups— such as the AHLC or JLC—bring the key actors together in smaller forums more suited to effective decisionmaking.

On the negative side, it is not clear that coordinating mechanisms in Palestine provided the recipients with *sufficient influence in the coordination process,* notwithstanding donor development rhetoric about host country "ownership." There were, of course, some good reasons for this: donors found it more expeditious to act unilaterally than to await the development of Palestinian capacity in aid management. But there were less noble factors at work too, and the entire coordinating structure was probably too slow to react and accommodate the growth of Palestinian institutional capacity. Moreover, it is important that host country weaknesses do not become an excuse for circumvention; instead, donors must *enhance the recipient's capacity to participate in, manage, and learn from coordination meetings.*

Part of the responsibility for coordination lies with the recipient. At times, the PA could have done more to report back on, and systematically learn from, donor meetings. Moreover, poor coordination and turf wars within the PA—notably between PECDAR and MOPIC—have hampered interaction with donors as well as effective internal PA policymaking. Competition between local NGOs and the PA has been another unfortunate feature of aid management, with some Palestinian officials clearly favoring tighter controls on NGO activity.

Another problem is the unfortunate *tendency of donor coordination meetings to become information-sharing meetings,* rather than structures for planning/coordination or venues for real sustained dialogue on developmental directions and obstacles. This pattern emerges from the framework for meetings and from competition or unilateralism among donors.

Of course, the *quality of donor coordination mechanisms depends a great deal on both the quality of the coordinators and on the political context* within which coordination takes place. Both the World Bank and UNSCO have been moderately successful, but they have also demonstrated shortcomings. Initially slow to respond, the Bank enhanced its responsiveness by devolving authority into the field. UNSCO suffered both from a lack of any meaningful line authority over the UN agencies it was meant to "coordinate" and from its small size and weight relative to UNRWA and UNDP. Both cases demonstrated that key individuals can be hugely important in aid coordination. The success (or failure) of agencies and offices has often been a product of who occupies senior positions, just as the success or failure of particular projects has often been shaped by the characteristics of key project personnel.

Finally, it is clear that, in Palestine, *donor conditionality has generally proven ineffectual.* Some conditionality might have blunted the PA's tendency to take a domineering role in local economy through expanding bureaucracy and semipublic monopolies, but the donors typically saw the Palestinians as too vulnerable to be punished for noncompliance. Moreover, there is a potential contradiction between conditionality and host country ownership of the development process.

Conversely, Israeli actions—a major factor in the weakness of the Palestinian economy—have not been subject to sanction or conditionality because the Israeli position is too strong. The latter, of course, can be viewed as failure of political will, notably in the continuing pro-Israeli tilt in U.S. Middle East policy. One should be careful in drawing too many general conclusions from this case, however. In less sensitive regions and less salient transitions, donors might well wield conditionality with greater frequency and to greater effect.

Delivering Assistance

Analytically, the case of the West Bank and Gaza illustrates the methodological problems involved in tracking disbursements and suggests the difficulty of comparing the delivery of assistance across cases. In general, however, it can be concluded that (despite a slow start) *the record in Palestine is comparatively good.* By the end of 1998, a very large portion of 1994–1998 aid had been disbursed or committed.

One reason for this was the *Holst Fund,* which proved to be *an extremely effective mechanism* for disbursing funds to the PA in a timely fashion and for supporting the critical task of building Palestinian institutions. Indeed, it is a mechanism that deserves emulation in other comparable cases. This success is in some ways ironic, since the Holst Fund was generally unpopular among donor officials, who would have preferred to support visible long-term development projects rather than less visible short-term budget support. While the Holst Fund was effectively wound down in 1997–1998, it is important that the mechanism be kept in place to respond to any (presently unforeseen) short-term emergency financing requirements.

Conversely, other mechanisms have been less successful. *Loans and investment guarantees have proven particularly ineffectual,* especially when granted through agencies (OPIC, the European Investment Bank, IFC) whose regulations and operating procedures are ill suited to the unstable and time-sensitive imperatives of peace building. While some such funds are probably better than none, such support should not be seen as a substitute for much more useful and effective grant and soft loan assistance; they can, in fact, aggravate the problem of unmet host country expectations.

With regard to factors that have slowed or otherwise constrained the delivery of assistance, *Israeli policies stand out as having a particularly negative effect.* Closure has been the most evident and costly of these, but other actions have also had a debilitating effect on the flow of assistance.

It is also evident that *problems of Palestinian institution building have also slowed the delivery of assistance.* Some of these obstacles were perhaps unavoidable, given the nature of the transition; others might have been averted. Still, it is important to understand the political dynamics (such as the neopatrimonial strategies of political management) that may underlie Palestinian weaknesses. A lesson of this case is that *for transitional assistance, the context is always inherently political.* Donors cannot and should not be naive. Rather they should try to understand and anticipate such factors and help to *foster the process of institution and capacity building,* even when activities go outside the traditional job descriptions of aid agencies and officials. Indeed, responding effectively to the complexities of host country politics and to the weaknesses of host country institutions is a fundamental element of effective reconstruction and peace building.

As important as Israeli and Palestinian constraints have been, it is also clear that donors at times have slowed the delivery of assistance. *Institutional factors within donor agencies are very important* in determining and delivering but are generally underexamined by analysts. Moreover, *idiosyncratic factors—specifically the quality of local presence—are extremely important.* Finally, *domestic politics within donor countries can have effects on the timely and effective delivery of donor assistance.* This effect varies from donor to donor, and probably from case to case. However, the United States seems peculiarly vulnerable to such dynamics, which may raise larger questions about the U.S. capacity to undertake economic peace building.

Allocating Assistance

The experience of the West Bank and Gaza demonstrates that a variety of factors shape the allocation of donor assistance, with the desire for high political profile and the economic interest of donors ranking high among these. While this may be unavoidable, donors must maintain focus on *the fundamentals of transitional assistance: political stabilization and economic reconstruction/development.* Given the uncertain environment that they face, donors must build flexibility into their programs and even then expect the unexpected. Here too, the development of effective field staff with appropriate decisionmaking authority is essential.

The Palestinian case also underscores *the importance of collaborative donor/recipient agenda setting.* In particular, donor assistance must aim to develop the agenda-setting capacity of host countries. Without it, donor efforts become even more uncoordinated, not to mention mismatched to local needs and circumstances.

There has been substantial criticism of the short-term nature of much international assistance to Palestine, with its focus on budget support and emergency employment generation rather than long-term productive investment. This study, however, suggests that both the Holst Fund and emergency employment measures were politically necessary stopgaps. At the same time, the study teaches that technical assistance needs to be more carefully provided. At present, the provision of such assistance has been donor driven and often ill suited to local circumstances.

As the political and economic situation stabilizes, more resources should be directed toward investment. Unfortunately, stabilization of the situation is largely beyond the control of donors (or, for that matter, the PA in present circumstances). Moreover, the provision of foreign aid is only part of the picture: a vibrant private sector has a fundamental role to play in Palestinian sustainable development. Current conditions—some of them self-inflicted by the PA, many of them imposed by factors beyond Palestinian control—render this very difficult.

Notes

We wish to thank the very many persons who contributed to this study, whether through interviews or other forms of assistance. This includes current and former officials of the Palestinian Ministry of Economy, the Ministry of Planning and International Cooperation, and PECDAR; Canada, Denmark, Finland, Japan, Norway, the European Union, South Africa, Sweden, Switzerland, Turkey, the United States, and other countries; the UN Secretariat, UNDP, UNRWA, UNSCO, the IMF, and the World Bank; and various Palestinian and international NGOs. We would also like to thank our respective institutions for their support and encouragement: McGill University/*Palestinian Development InfoNet;* the Center for Palestine Research and Studies; and the Palestinian Economists Association/ *Palestine Economic Pulse.* Support was also received from the Social Sciences and Humanities Research Council of Canada (SSHRC), the Fonds FCAR, and the United States Institute of Peace for earlier phases of the work.

Portions of this study are drawn from Rex Brynen, *A Very Political Economy,* and from the Center for Palestine Research and Studies (team leader, Hisham Awartani); CPRS, *Prevailing Perceptions on Aid Management.*

1. For full text of the agreement, see the *Journal of Palestine Studies* 23, no. 1 (autumn 1993), pp. 116–121; or from the Israel Information Service at www.israel-mfa.gov.il/peace/dop.html.

2. Conference to Support Middle East Peace, *Cosponsors' Summary.*

3. Preston, "The International Effort to Invest in Peace."

4. CPRS, *Public Opinion Polls,* no. 10, June 10, 1994, and no. 16, March 16–18, 1995.

5. Jerusalem Media and Communications Center (JMCC) public opinion survey, *Palestine Report,* April 11, 1997, p. 7; Palestinian Authority, MOPIC, *Quarterly Monitoring Report,* June 1997, table 1.

6. UNSCO, *Quarterly Report,* April 1997, tables 3, 5.

7. JMCC public opinion survey, *Palestine Report,* April 25, 1997, pp. 8–9.

8. World Bank, *The Donor Experience and the Way Ahead.*

9. For fuller discussion of the context of Palestinian development, see Diwan and Shaban, *Development Under Adversity?;* World Bank, *Developing the Occupied Territories;* Roy, *The Gaza Strip;* Brynen, *A Very Political Economy.*

10. Preston, "The International Effort to Invest in Peace"; World Bank, *Developing the Occupied Territories,* vol. 1, pp. 24–25; Bouhabib, "The World Bank and International Aid to Palestine," p. 65.

11. PLO, *Programme for Development of the Palestinian National Economy,* pp. 38, 41. The figure of $14.4 billion is adjusted to 1994 prices, including contingencies.

12. For a more detailed presentation of these statistics and the basis for their calculation, see Brynen, *A Very Political Economy.*

13. Such pledge inflation occurred at the special ministerial-level Conference on Economic Assistance to the Palestinian People, held in Paris in January 1996. This meeting announced pledges of some $1,365 million, consisting of $865 million for the Palestinian Public Investment Plan (PPIP) and $500 million in unspent commitments yet to be disbursed in the next fifteen months. In practice, the two sums overlapped considerably, with some of the "undisbursed funds" already committed to the PPIP. However, both donors and Arafat encouraged this sleight of hand, believing that a total exceeding $1 billion would bolster the PA on the eve of the elections for the Palestinian Legislative Council. By the end of 1996, actual donor disbursements totaled only $528 million.

14. Commission of the European Communities, *EC Support for the Middle East Peace Process,* p. 3.

15. Commission of the European Communities, *The Role of the European Union.*

16. Carbonnier, *Conflict, Postwar Rebuilding and the Economy,* pp. 33–36.

17. World Bank, *Holst Peace Fund Status Statement,* November 21, 1997.

18. World Bank, *West Bank/Gaza Update,* June 1998.

19. Comments by World Bank official, November 1994.

20. This paragraph based on interviews with a number of World Bank officials, June 1995, June 1996, July 1997; with U.S. State Department officials, June 1996; and with PECDAR officials, January 1995, July 1996; Balaj, Diwan, and Philippe, "External Assistance to the Palestinians."

21. CPRS, *Prevailing Perceptions on Aid Management,* p. 18. The survey questioned thirty-four donor officials (including international organization staff), eighty-two officials from local NGOs, and seventy-four officials from the PA.

22. Interview with IMF official, June 1996.

23. United Nations, *Programme of Cooperation in the West Bank and Gaza Strip, 1998–99;* interview with UN official, June 1995.

24. CPRS, *Prevailing Perceptions on Aid Management,* pp. 11–12.

25. For a broader discussion of "peace conditionality," see Boyce, "External Assistance to the Peace Process in El Salvador"; Ball, *Pressing for Peace.*

26. Text of this version of the *Tripartite Action Plan* in *Journal of Palestine Studies* 24, no. 4 (summer 1995).

27. *Tripartite Action Plan,* January 1996.

28. Interviewed in *al-Quds al-'Arabi,* April 3, 1998.

29. *Chairman's Summing-Up,* Third Meeting of the Ad Hoc Liaison Committee, November 1994.

30. Yasir Arafat in *Reuters World Report,* November 15, 1994.

31. MOPIC, *Quarterly Monitoring Report,* December 31, 1997.

32. *Reuters World Report,* October 26, 1995.

33. MOPIC, *Quarterly Monitoring Report,* March 31, 1998.

34. Roberts, "The Prospects for the Palestinian Economy."

35. IPCRI, *The Legal Structure for Foreign Investment in the West Bank and Gaza Strip,* introduction.

36. For a detailed critique, see Findler, "Foreign Private Investment in Palestine."

37. For a fuller discussion, see Diwan and Shaban, *Development Under Adversity?*

38. This discussion of closure relies heavily on UNSCO, *Quarterly Report* (April 1997), and Diwan and Shaban, *Development Under Adversity?*

39. UNSCO and World Bank, *Closure on the West Bank and Gaza;* UNSCO, *Quarterly Report,* October 1997, table 21.

40. Data drawn from UNSCO, *Quarterly Report,* October 1996, p. 12; UNSCO, *Quarterly Report,* April 1997, table 22; UNSCO, *Quarterly Report,* October 1997, table 1.

41. Diwan and Shaban, *Development Under Adversity?* table 3.1.

42. MOPIC, *Quarterly Monitoring Report,* June 5, 1997; UNSCO and World Bank, *Closure on the West Bank and Gaza.*

43. LACC, *Co-chairs' Summary.*

44. On-line versions of some of these can be found at the UNSCO website, http://www.arts.mcgill.ca/mepp/unsco/unfront.html.

45. CPRS, *Prevailing Perceptions on Aid Management,* p. 17.

46. In the CPRS survey, 38 percent of donors had a negative view of PA project identification/prioritization, 49 percent of donors (and 42 percent of PA officials) had a negative view of intra-PA coordination, and 34 percent of donors (and 42 percent of PA officials) had a negative view of PA financial transparency. CPRS, *Prevailing Perceptions on Aid Management,* pp. 12–13.

47. Calculated from MOPIC, *Quarterly Monitoring Report,* March 31, 1998. Comparison of MOPIC data with known projects, however, suggests that this may overestimate the amount of technical assistance.

48. Diwan and Shaban, *Development Under Adversity?;* PA, Ministry of Finance, *Report on Fiscal Developments in April–September 1997,* p. 5; UNSCO, *Quarterly Report,* October 4, 1997, p. 9.

49. *Ha-Aretz,* April 4, 1997. Some estimates (*Palestine Report,* May 30, 1997) suggest that these monopolies earn $200 million or more per year—although these estimates seem extremely high given the total volume of trade.

50. PA, Public Monitoring Department, *First Annual Report 1996.*

51. For example, public land had been sold for $72 million less than its market value to encourage private development; $45.5 million in customs had not been collected on the property of returnees to facilitate their reintegration into the territories; $44 million in electrical bills were uncollected due to poverty in the territories. PA, *Statement by the Palestinian Delegation on the Internal Audit Report of 23 May 1996.*

52. PLC, *Report of the Special Committee.*

53. Center for Palestine Research and Studies poll results, archived at http://www.cprs-palestine.org/polls/97/poll30a.html#corrupt; summary of March 1998 poll conducted by CPRS, on *PALDEV Digest,* March 19–26, 1998. Similarly, some 45 percent of donors (and 75 percent of local NGOs) expressed the view that there has been a "very strong" or "strong" misuse of funds by the PA. CPRS, *Prevailing*

Perceptions on Aid Management, p. 23. "Misuse of funds" in this survey need not apply solely to corruption, however.

54. In a November 1997 CPRS poll, 61 percent of respondents held that the PA acted in accordance with public interests.

55. Brynen, "Neopatrimonial Dimensions of Palestinian Politics."

56. *al-Quds al-'Arabi* (London), April 25, 1997, p. 4 (via Foreign Broadcast Information Service/World News Connection).

57. Interview with PECDAR official, July 1996.

58. It is also encouraged by other characteristics of war-to-peace transitions: the influx of external resources, the uncertainty of transition arrangements, and the weakness of existing institutions. For a further general discussion of peace building and the "politics of getting," see Brynen, *A Very Political Economy,* chap. 1.

59. Averages calculated from those evaluating performance as "good" or "very good" in polls conducted by the CPRS in September 1996, December 1996, April 1997, June 1997, September 1997, and December 1997.

60. Samir Hulayla, interviewed in *Middle East Report* 186 (January–February 1994), pp. 7–8.

61. In the CPRS survey, 50 percent of PA officials (but only 14 percent of donors) had a negative view of donor prioritization; 51 percent of PA officials (and 14 percent of donors) had a negative view of donor expediency; and 55 percent of PA officials (but only 9 percent of donors) had a negative view of donor fulfillment of commitments. CPRS, *Prevailing Perceptions on Aid Management,* pp. 10–11.

62. In the case of the EU, 50 percent of PA officials rated EU performance as "positive" and 12 percent as "negative," and in the case of UNDP, 45 percent rated it "positive" and 12 percent "negative." With regard to USAID, however, only 12 percent rated its performance as "positive," while 43 percent rated it "negative." CPRS, *Prevailing Perceptions on Aid Management,* p. 18. The fourth institution studied by CPRS, the World Bank, placed between UNDP and USAID in the eyes of PA officials.

63. MOPIC, *Quarterly Monitoring Report,* November 28, 1997.

64. Interview, February 1997.

65. Interview with senior World Bank official, January 1995.

66. Interviews with USAID officials, December 1994, July 1995, January 1998.

67. This discussion draws heavily on Lia, *Implementing Peace.*

68. UNGAR 49/21B of 1994 on "Financing of the Palestinian Police Force."

69. World Bank, *The Donor Experience and the Way Ahead.*

70. Calculated from MOPIC, *Quarterly Monitoring Report,* March 31, 1998.

71. CPRS, *Prevailing Perceptions on Aid Management,* p. 16. The question is worded so that it might refer to both domestic politics and foreign policy.

72. PLO Commitments Compliance Act of 1993 (Public Law 101-246), the Middle East Peace Facilitation Acts of 1994 (Public Law 103-246), and the Middle East Peace Facilitation Act of 1995 (Public Law 104-107). The text of the State Department's periodic certifications can be found in the documents section of the *Journal of Palestine Studies.*

73. In this figure, "infrastructure" includes energy, housing, waste, telecommunications, transportation, and water; "social services" includes education, health, rehabilitation of detainees/returnees, and humanitarian assistance; "productive sectors" includes agriculture, industrial development, tourism, and private sector development; "state building" includes police, legal affairs, and institution building. MOPIC's "undefined" and "multiple sectors" are not included. Disbursement data

for 1994–1996 are drawn from MOPIC, *Quarterly Monitoring Report*, November 28, 1997; disbursement data for 1997 are drawn from MOPIC, *Quarterly Monitoring Report*, March 31, 1998.

74. LACC, *Partners in Peace*, p. 13.

75. For further analysis (from which this discussion draws heavily), see Al-Botmeh and Sayre, *Employment Generation Schemes;* and UNSCO, *Emergency Employment Generation Schemes*.

76. AHLC, *The Employment Generation Program in the West Bank and Gaza*.

77. MOPIC, *Quarterly Monitoring Report*, November 28, 1997.

78. World Bank, *Developing the Occupied Territories*, vol. 4: *Agriculture;* World Bank, *Emergency Assistance Program for the Occupied Territories*.

79. *Palestine Report*, August 21, 1997; *Palestine Report*, October 22, 1997.

80. Interview with UNDP official, July 1997.

81. World Bank and UNDP estimates.

82. Interviews with World Bank officials; World Bank, *Palestinian NGO Project*, December 1997.

83. For example, Zaucker, *Toward Middle East Peace and Development*.

84. PA, *Presentation to the Fifth Meeting of the Consultative Group*.

85. Hanna, "What Economic System for Palestine?"

86. UNSCO, *United Nations Programme of Cooperation 1998–99*, p. 3.

87. Samara, "The World Bank's Policy in the Palestinian Self-Rule Areas," p. 15.

88. World Bank, *The Donor Experience and the Way Ahead;* World Bank, *Holst Peace Fund Status Statement*, November 21, 1997.

89. AHLC, *The Employment Generation Program in the West Bank and Gaza*, p. 1.

90. AHLC, *Matrix of Donors' Assistance to the West Bank and Gaza*, November 1996.

91. PA, *Palestinian Development Plan 1998–2000*.

92. Survey conducted by Hisham Awartani, Center for Palestine Research and Studies, late 1997.

93. Interview with senior USAID official, June 1996.

94. World Bank, *The Donor Experience and the Way Ahead*.

95. In the case of Karameh Towers in Gaza, the average price of a four-bedroom flat—U.S.$30,000—was extremely high given an average per capita income of $1,200 and the declared intention of constructing housing for low-income families. Gaza European Hospital is a sophisticated and ambitious project to provide a center for primary and secondary health care in the southern Gaza Strip. However, it has proven expensive, ill planned, and poorly sited; and it is not clear that the PA will be able to sustain its substantial recurrent costs. For a fuller discussion, see Brynen, *A Very Political Economy*.

96. With thanks to Salem Ajluni of UNSCO for a quick back-of-an-envelope (or in this case, e-mail) estimate, April 11, 1998.

7

South Africa

Michael Bratton & Chris Landsberg

THE COMPLEX REGIME TRANSITION THAT OCCURRED IN SOUTH Africa in the early 1990s had at least three dimensions: a political transition to democracy, an economic transition to a global marketplace, and a military transition to peace. These elements unfolded each to a different extent and each at its own pace. The route was blazed by a political compromise that culminated in South Africa's first popular elections in April 1994. This successful political transition was followed by a much more tentative set of economic reforms in which the newly elected government sought to balance imperatives of market liberalization with urgent demands for social justice. Amid the euphoria of reconciliation and reform, supporters of the new South Africa hoped that they had seen the last of the brutal violence associated with apartheid. Yet it soon became clear that this bitter legacy could not be wished away; all too soon, resurgent violence in the form of crime began to threaten progress on the political and economic fronts.

The international community embraced the South African transition and, in the process, helped to shape it. As this chapter shows, aid relationships evolved gradually, encompassing the South African government only after a legitimate democracy had been installed. Seeking to avoid dependence on external resources, the new South African government exercised control over its relations with donors by emphasizing bilateral rather than multilateral ties. The levels and composition of official development cooperation are documented below, along with estimates of the extent to which aid pledges were actually committed and disbursed after 1994. We find that, although gaps do exist in the delivery of aid, these are not unusually large and will probably be closed by most donors in the fullness of time. Of greater concern are long delays in the implementation of projects administered by state and nongovernmental organizations (NGOs) within the country. In their rush to associate themselves with a political success

259

story, international donors deposited more aid resources on South Africa than could be used well.

South Africa's Triple Transition

The main protagonists in South Africa's complex transition—Nelson Mandela's African National Congress (ANC) and the National Party (NP) government of F. W. de Klerk—focused principally on political objectives.[1] Whereas the ANC sought to secure majority rule on the basis of a universal franchise within a unitary state, opposition parties hoped for veto power in some kind of group-based, even federal, arrangement. Ultimately, no side obtained all that it wanted, settling instead for an interim power-sharing pact. The negotiated agreement that emerged in 1993 from the multiparty negotiating forum provided for an interim constitution, elections in 1994, and a Government of National Unity until 1999.[2] In practice, plans for an attenuated transition were quickly bypassed by events. With the withdrawal of the National Party from the government in 1996 and the introduction of a permanent and very liberal constitution in 1997, South Africa accelerated its entry into an era of competitive multiparty democracy.[3]

As the country moved away from authoritarian rule, attention turned to the parallel passage from a command economy to free markets. South Africa already possessed a thoroughly mixed economy in which the most sophisticated private sector on the African continent stood alongside a protectionist state. Against this model, the ANC favored, at least until the early 1990s, the nationalization of banks, mines, and industries. Neither of these precedents adequately predicted what was to follow. By 1996, the ANC-led government adopted a self-imposed structural adjustment program known as Growth, Employment, and Redistribution (GEAR), which sought to generate jobs through foreign private investment. This dramatic conversion to neoliberal economics can be attributed to several factors: guarantees of property rights embedded in the pact with South Africa's white middle classes; pressures for government deregulation pushed by trading partners, potential investors, and aid donors; and the reentry of South Africa into the world economy at a time of intense competition for scarce investment capital. The extent of economic liberalization was constrained constantly, however, by pressures within the ANC alliance for the redistribution of assets, incomes, and services.

Whereas economic reform lagged behind political events, the effort to establish social peace was intimately intertwined with the transition to democracy. South Africa's political evolution is often described as miraculous because it ended in compromise rather than bloodshed. But these alternative outcomes were always connected. The parties to the pact were driven to the bargaining table in good part by a violent cycle of state repression and armed resistance that threatened repeatedly to escalate out of control. The apartheid government and the liberation movements both resorted to tactics of terror, intimidation, and vigilantism. Low-intensity warfare that verged on civil war broke out mainly within urban townships (especially on the East Rand) and a few rural areas (especially KwaZulu-Natal).[4] Because the civil war was not all consuming, cessation of hostilities was never the prime object of negotiations; instead, the shift from war to peace was ancillary to the main political project of transferring power into black hands. As such, we will argue, the ramifications of armed conflict were never fully taken into account.

An Exceptional Transition?

While distinctive, the South African experience was not unique. When compared cross-nationally, it can be seen to share both similarities and differences with other cases of complex transition, including those addressed in this book.

In the sense that political transitions also began before economic reforms elsewhere (e.g., Bosnia and Herzegovina, Cambodia, and the Palestinian territories), South Africa reflects a generic tendency for complex transitions to be led by political initiatives. There are few cases in the contemporary world—like the People's Republic of China—in which economics remain in command of transition processes, with market reforms preceding political liberalization. The closest example in this book is El Salvador, where donor-led initiatives for economic stabilization and adjustment were introduced well before political negotiations brought an end to the civil war. Whenever mass enfranchisement comes first, however, newly elected governments must be acutely attuned to the possible electoral consequences of economic choices. Unlike the Chinese Communist Party, the ANC in South Africa has little leeway to force the pace of marketization; instead, it has to attend constantly to balancing and managing the needs of its majority political constituency.

But compared to, say, Russia, the challenges of economic transition in South Africa were far less daunting. Most basic institutions—like capital markets, a private banking system, and contract law—were already firmly in place. And compared to countries like Bosnia, Cambodia, and Mozambique, the purpose of political agreement was less to terminate an encompassing civil war than to enfranchise a previously excluded population. For this reason, South Africa did not face the postwar challenge of jump-starting a devastated national economy or rebuilding shattered physical infrastructure; rather, it possessed a network of production, communications, and service institutions that was the envy of Africa.

Important, however, is that the South African government also inherited a majority population that had been severely deprived of job opportunities and basic services. These problems seemed to require a long-term strategy of socioeconomic development rather than an emergency plan for postconflict reconstruction. Because its civil war had been episodic and parochial, South Africa seemed to have fewer needs for reconstruction assistance—that form of aid that bridges the divide between emergency relief and development assistance—than other countries transiting from war to peace. However, this interpretation tended to overlook the special needs of the "lost generation" of youngsters who had left school to join the antiapartheid struggle. Many young people—not only the 11,000 returning ex-combatants of the ANC's armed wing—had learned to use weapons as a means of survival in the context of "war-like gangs."[5] Estimates of the number of South African youths and adults lacking basic literacy and numeracy ranged from about 10 to 15 million. In this regard, the social profile of the South African poor resembled that of a country like Mozambique or Cambodia more closely than many observers were ready to acknowledge. Far from being poised to leapfrog onto a trajectory of sustained development, South Africa first had to "reconstruct" those parts of its population that had been most brutalized and deprived under apartheid.

Similarly, South Africa's extensive state apparatus, which was designed for bureaucratic control and military repression, was not well suited to the tasks of either reconstruction or development. In one sense, South Africa possessed a strong state that had the capacity to deliver an array of sophisticated "First World" services to the white segment of the population. Viewed from the perspective of the country's own black majority, however, the state was weak because it lacked political legitimacy. Before 1994, nonwhite South Africans roundly rejected the institutions of government they encountered in their daily lives, especially security agencies like the police and the local government structures responsible for delivering basic services. Indeed, at the height of the country's internal conflict in the mid-1980s, political activists succeeded in turning many urban townships and rural "homelands" into ungovernable "no-go" zones. Thus, the prospects for the entire transition—especially the transitions to peace and prosperity—came to depend on the rehabilitation of the local-level institutions of the South African state.

The Evolution of Assistance

International development assistance began to flow into South Africa well before the 1994 political transition. At first, modest amounts of aid were directed to resistance organizations and victims of apartheid as part of a

coordinated campaign to bring down the old regime. Once political negotiations began on the country's future, larger amounts of assistance were
quickly disbursed in order to encourage a peaceful transfer of power.
Finally, the election of a government of national unity signaled the onset
of large-scale, longer-term bilateral programs of official development cooperation with the South African government.

Pretransition Assistance (Before 1990)

On the receiving end of opprobrium against apartheid, the white-ruled
Republic of South Africa became an international pariah. From the 1960s
onward, the United Nations led a global campaign to isolate South Africa
that was backed by the Organization of African Unity (OAU), the Non-
Aligned Movement (NAM), and, later, the Southern African Development
Co-ordination Conference (SADCC).[6] Among Western countries, the Scandinavian people and their governments, along with counterparts in Canada
and New Zealand, took the hardest line toward Pretoria. Together with the
African states, they were the first to join arms, oil, athletic, cultural, academic, and trade boycotts designed to punish and ostracize the South
African government. As diplomatic ties were cut with the white minority
regime, the African national liberation movements came to be seen as the
authentic representatives of the people of South Africa.

Responding to rising violence within the country, Pretoria cracked
down in June 1986, arresting hundreds of antiapartheid activists and ban-
ning organs of the mass democratic movement under a state of emergency.
This intensified level of repression could not be ignored, even by South
Africa's traditional allies. While President Ronald Reagan and Prime Minister Margaret Thatcher continued to resist the imposition of sanctions,
international public opinion turned against them. A so-called Eminent Persons Group of senior Commonwealth politicians traveled to South Africa
in January 1986 to propose a negotiated settlement to the apartheid crisis.
When the South African Defense Force responded with cross-border raids
on alleged ANC bases in Botswana, Zambia, and Zimbabwe, the British
prime minister could no longer prevent the Commonwealth from imposing
punitive measures. In Washington, the U.S. president was forced to impose
limited sanctions against South Africa in an attempt to forestall wider
actions proposed by Congress. Yet, in October 1986, Congress overrode a
presidential veto to pass the Comprehensive Anti-Apartheid Act, which,
among other things, prohibited a range of South African imports and
banned new investments and bank loans.

Employing carrots as well as sticks, the international community held
out the prospect that the South African government could end its diplomatic isolation and receive international financial assistance by entering

into good faith negotiations with its adversaries. This would require an end to the state of emergency and the release of Nelson Mandela and other political prisoners, the abolition of proscriptions on political organizations, and, ultimately, the establishment of a nonracial democracy. Pressure for a negotiated settlement was not placed exclusively on Pretoria. In January 1987, U.S. secretary of state George Schultz met ANC president Oliver Tambo in Washington to discuss preconditions for negotiations. By this time, sanctions had turned South Africa into an international outcast; it had diplomatic relations with only twenty-three states, compared with the ANC's twenty-six representative offices worldwide.[7]

Under these conditions, international development assistance was directed exclusively to the victims of apartheid. The emphasis was humanitarian, on aiding people rather than an illegitimate government.[8] Much pretransition aid was spent outside the country in the form of transfers to the exiled liberation movements or through a worldwide airlift of black South African students to overseas educational institutions. The United Nations, proclaiming "a special responsibility towards the oppressed people of South Africa," operated a trust fund for education and training and made a point of inviting liberation movement representatives to conferences and seminars.[9] In 1980, the United States established the U.S.–South Africa Leadership Exchange Program to build capacity for democratization, expanding this program after 1986. The Scandinavian countries and the Commonwealth helped neighboring African states that had been destabilized by the South African military—for example, by supporting SADCC. Solidarity was extended to South African political prisoners, refugees, and their families through private contributions to the International Defense and Aid Fund for Southern Africa.[10] Such funds proliferated globally during the 1980s and were well subscribed.

Within South Africa, aid flowed to NGOs and community-based organizations (CBOs) that ran grassroots development projects. Sweden—which between 1970 and 1993 contributed more than $400 million to the antiapartheid cause—actively backed the trade union movement and groups providing legal assistance.[11] The United Kingdom provided an estimated 50 million rand (R) between 1979 and 1990, especially through community groups.[12] Other donors (including the United States, the European Community [EC], Germany, Denmark, Norway, and Canada) promoted civil society as a popular alternative to the state, often through the medium of churches and political foundations. Among the favored South African recipients were apex organizations like the South African Council of Churches, the South African Bishops Conference, and the Kagiso Trust. Impressed with the vibrancy of NGOs and CBOs, donors devised creative aid programs that featured flexibility and consultation rather than red tape. Given the disturbed conditions in the country, donors were even willing to turn a blind eye to "struggle accounting," whereby recipients could not always fully document where funds had been spent.

Assistance for Transition (1990–1994)

Combined pressures at home and abroad ultimately created a political opening in South Africa. Beset with economic recession, an ungovernable population, and international isolation, President F. W. de Klerk, on February 2, 1990, announced the release of Nelson Mandela and the normalization of political activity. The four-year transition that followed involved a series of landmark elite pacts: a political pact to share power in a government of national unity; an economic pact to guarantee property rights and civil service pensions; and a military pact to extend amnesty to individuals who confessed to politically motivated atrocities. While these deals were struck largely as a result of the self-interested calculations of South African actors, international interventions—including promises by Western donors of development assistance—played a part in nudging negotiations forward.

The Conference on a Democratic South Africa (CODESA) and its successor forums, which ultimately produced a transitional executive authority, an interim constitution, and an agreement on open elections, was accompanied by increased foreign involvement in South Africa's domestic affairs.[13] Western governments helped to ensure their own preferred outcomes by dispensing diplomatic recognition, suspending sanctions, and pledging aid flows as rewards for negotiated compromises. The National Party and the South African business community saw considerable advantage in normalizing diplomatic and trade ties. The ANC and its allies in the labor movement and community organizations welcomed the prospect of foreign aid to help in the delivery of housing, water, education, and health services.

Thus gradually began Pretoria's international rehabilitation.[14] De Klerk was invited to visit ten European countries and the United States during 1990, where he was praised for his political courage and urged to stay a reformist course. Sanctions began to crumble as erstwhile foes in the Low Countries, Scandinavia, and the Commonwealth urged a restoration of trade ties. The international community retained some punitive levers, however: Sweden, Japan, and the United States left some trade restrictions in place even as they lifted others. Once CODESA got under way, Denmark, the only country in the European Community still favoring sanctions, agreed to allow the EC to lift them. Sweden moved swiftly to help the ANC and other political parties in preparing position papers for CODESA and, once an election date had been agreed, in gearing up for the 1994 elections.

An instructive case of international pressure was the referendum of March 1992, when whites were asked to vote for or against the political reform process.[15] Western governments combined threats of new punishments for a "no" verdict and promises of economic rewards for a "yes" vote.[16] The clear message was that only a vote for reform would allow South Africa to reenter the international community and attract the support necessary for economic growth. Another example was the interim constitution, whose technical content was influenced by visiting legal specialists and CODESA study tours of democratic countries with plural societies— all organized under quick-disbursing aid grants. The result was an "eclectic document" that drew not only on the South African experience, but also on ideas derived from German, U.S., Swiss, British, and Indian sources.[17]

The assassination of South African Communist Party (SACP) secretary-general Chris Hani in April 1993 was a turning point for foreign involvement in South Africa's democratization. This event, and the disturbances that followed, forcibly reminded the international community of the volatility of the South African situation. Foreign well-wishers feared that the whole process would come unstuck in a flurry of violence. As early as 1992, the UN had urged the ANC to suspend its mass mobilization campaign and return to the negotiating table. When Mandela and de Klerk together visited Philadelphia to receive the Liberty Award in 1993, U.S. president Bill Clinton held out the prospect of a major aid package to bolster the South African economy in return for firm dates for establishing a transitional executive council and for holding an election. In a further effort to keep the process of compromise alive, Western powers stated that they expected any new government to abide by all the agreements reached at the negotiating forums.[18]

Once it became clear that the parties to the South African conflict were truly committed to change, donors began to make major pledges of aid. An important milestone was Clinton's announcement of the South African Democratic Support Act of 1993, which promised some $600 million for activities leading up to and following a founding election.[19] At about the same time, the Federal Republic of Germany launched a program for official development cooperation with the South African government focusing on vocational education, rural development, and the promotion of small business enterprises. By 1993, official flows of foreign aid to South Africa had jumped to $307 million.[20] The European Union (EU) was by far the biggest donor at the time, followed by the United States, Germany, Sweden, and the United Kingdom. Most assistance went into education, human rights, housing, and community development, and almost all was channeled through NGOs.[21]

As elections approached, donors began to switch their assistance from civil society to the state, adding grants to governmental units to accompany their portfolios of NGO grants. Different donors moved various distances along this route. The Canadian International Development Agency (CIDA) swung wholeheartedly into government-to-government relations, arguing that supporting NGOs usurped not only government's functions but also its legitimacy. By contrast the U.S. Agency for International Development (USAID) contended that a plural civil society, including policy advocacy NGOs, was vital to democracy. In a final bid to ensure a successful transition, international donors pumped quick-disbursing funds into the historic elections of April 27, 1994, financing both the Independent Electoral Commission and the voter education activities of numerous NGOs. Donors also supported a huge contingent of international election observers, whose measured endorsement of the chaotic elections as "substantially free" (without saying they were fully fair) was instrumental in granting the new government an international stamp of approval.[22]

The Reconstruction and Development Program (circa 1994)

The new Government of National Unity (GNU) soon announced its development strategy. Called the Reconstruction and Development Program (RDP), a draft was issued as an election manifesto in early 1994 and in a more polished form as a government white paper in November of the same year. The RDP aimed at nothing less than the eradication of the inequalities of apartheid. It became the framework not only for government policy but also for the allocation of aid.

Because the ANC developed the principles for the RDP prior to coming to power, the program reflected the redistributive goals that enjoyed strong support among the ANC's partners, namely the trade union confederation and the Communist Party.[23] The RDP had emerged from a series of party policy conferences in the early 1980s, some held with UN assistance. In September 1991, UN Secretary-General Pérez de Cuéllar had endorsed measures to redress social and economic imbalances in South Africa, particularly in the areas of housing, education, employment, and health.[24] UN agencies had organized planning meetings on educational needs in Paris in June 1991, on socioeconomic problems in Windhoek in May 1992, and on sustainable economic growth in London in January 1994.[25] At the same time, the World Bank initiated studies on various sectors of the South African economy and began a program to train South Africans in the fundamentals of economic policy analysis and development management.

In contrast to other cases of complex transition, an international pledging conference aimed at addressing the country's reconstruction and development needs comprehensively was never held for South Africa. Before 1994, the South African government did not enjoy the diplomatic legitimacy to host or participate in such a high-profile event. The closest analogue was a donor gathering sponsored by the ANC in Arusha, Tanzania, in July 1992. Its purpose was to review policy proposals (including many that were ultimately included in the RDP) on the eve of the ANC's presumed assumption of power.[26] The donors who attended included the Nordic countries, the United States, and Canada, as well as many EC members like Britain, France, and Germany. Although pledges were not invited, the Arusha conference enabled donors to begin planning.

The Reconstruction and Development Program started out as a five-year plan to cover the years 1994–1999. Its goals included the construction of a million new homes; clean water, sanitation, and health care for all; redistribution of 30 percent of the country's farmland; a ten-year compulsory education cycle; and a public works program to create jobs.[27] President Mandela referred to the RDP as a vision of a "people-centered society."[28] This ambitious agenda understandably aroused great expectations among the poor.

Symbolically, given the country's massive deficit of decent and affordable homes, the RDP was announced through the Ministry of Housing. The program itself, however, was administered by a new, free-standing coordinating office, headed by its own cabinet minister.[29] Line ministries responsible for various technical development tasks (like housing, water, health, and education) were required to contribute 5 percent of their annual budgets to the RDP office. They then reapplied for funds to undertake projects in their areas of responsibility, after which the RDP office would redistribute resources to government implementing agencies.

The RDP became the vehicle through which donor assistance was channeled to South Africa. The government's own resources and donor contributions were comingled in an RDP Fund from which individual programs and projects were financed. The government set the pace by committing R 7.2 billion (U.S.$2.4 billion) over three years from its own National Revenue Account.[30] International donors were requested to direct all development assistance through the RDP Fund and, because the government was intent on avoiding a debt trap, to provide grants rather than loans.

From RDP to GEAR

For reasons that will be discussed later, the RDP office was closed in March 1996, and its functions and budget were distributed to other units of government. Thereafter, the office of the deputy president assumed responsibility for economic policy planning and for programs on disability, gender, and children. The treasury took over the RDP Fund, whose fiscal balance stood at R 7.5 billion at the time of the March 1996 budget.[31] Government spokespersons insisted that the RDP itself had not been terminated; instead the purpose of the reorganization was to ensure that the

RDP was not reduced to "a ghetto function" but became the focus of all government spending.[32]

Repackaged as a "national growth and development strategy," the revised RDP paved the way for a June 1996 macroeconomic policy document titled "Growth, Employment and Redistribution."[33] The thrust of GEAR was consistent with that of the international financial institutions, foreign investors, and the local business community insofar as it emphasized job creation through private investment.[34] It aimed to create a competitive platform for export-led growth, an annual GDP growth rate of at least 6 percent, a fiscally responsible public budget, a more flexible labor market, and the privatization or streamlining of public agencies. GEAR gave recognition to the reality that a growth strategy driven by public expenditure was unsustainable in a modern global economy based on mobile capital. Although the government denied that it had changed direction, describing GEAR as the strategy to reach goals defined in the RDP policy framework, it was hard to avoid the impression that social redistribution had been downgraded.

Objectives of Development Cooperation

To raise funds for the RDP, President Mandela made a round of visits to Europe and North America during 1994 and early 1995. Welcomed as a hero, he was able to attract "significant but not overwhelming" pledges of development cooperation.[35]

In lending support, donors had several goals: to identify themselves with Mandela's policy of racial reconciliation; to help stabilize a new multiparty democracy; to contribute to social redistribution in the aftermath of apartheid; and to endorse economic reforms that could serve as an example for the rest of Africa.[36] In their own words, donors wanted to help consolidate "a broadly based, economically sustainable democracy" upon which rested "great hopes for the entire continent."[37] Donor officials also candidly reminded the South African government that development cooperation would serve mutual interests and that Western countries sought strong allies and reliable trading partners.

Realistically, multiple challenges lay ahead if South Africa were to succeed in simultaneously restoring economic growth, reforming the state, and reaching the poor. The agenda for change called for nothing short of a "transformation"—to use the favored terminology of the ANC—of the political, economic, and social institutions inherited from the past. In this enormous task, donors recognized that South Africa possessed substantial human capacity in comparison to other African countries. But "the essence was to unlock these resources in order to support the policies of the new Government and indeed, to assist in the development of new policies."[38]

As such, the South African government and the donor community alike came to regard donor funds as a key resource for leveraging a reallocation of government priorities and spending away from old patterns.

The goodwill of the international community for the South African experiment was evidenced by donor willingness to extend official development assistance (ODA) to a middle-income country that did not, technically speaking, qualify for any aid at all. Moreover, large development cooperation programs were launched at precisely a time when donors were experiencing fiscal austerity at home. Indeed, the Swedish government greatly expanded aid to South Africa while seeking domestically to reduce its own recurrent welfare obligations. Germany did the same, even though restrictions were placed on its global development budget as a result of the high costs of its own national reunification. And the Clinton administration took on major new aid commitments to South Africa while simultaneously trying to "downsize" USAID and to balance the federal budget. The subjective impulse of Western governments to associate themselves with one of the twentieth century's great stories of human emancipation overcame these objective limitations. For a five-year period beginning in 1994, South Africa became a darling of the donor community.

The Structure of Development Cooperation

Pledge Levels

As shown in Table 7.1, South Africa's main international donors pledged about $4.7 billion in development cooperation aid for the five-year period from 1994 to 1999. This estimated total includes ODA grants, loans to the South African government, and direct grants to NGOs.[39] Table 7.1 does not include the contributions of several (generally smaller) bilateral donors for whom data were unavailable.[40] For the same reason, the multilateral agencies of the United Nations system with programs in South Africa are also excluded, as are flows from private foundations.[41] Taking into account all thirty or so official bilateral and multilateral donors active in South Africa between 1994 and 1999, the total amount of ODA pledged was probably more than $6 billion.

This amount represents a significant increase over previous aid levels. Donors clearly intended to expand their assistance programs significantly after the 1994 changeover. An annual average of about $1.2 billion in post-transition pledges up to 1999 represents a fourfold increase over the peak ODA disbursement rate of about $300 million per year during the late transition years.[42] A good part of the promised expansion involved the addition of concessional loans to existing grant portfolios; for the 1994–1999

Table 7.1 South Africa: Pledges of Aid by Donor Countries, 1994–1999

Donor Country	Pledge Period	Donor Currency	Type of Cooperation (in donor currency, millions)			Total Pledge	
			ODA Grants[a]	Loans	NGO Grants	in Donor Currency (millions)	in U.S.$ millions[b]
EU	1994–1999	ECU	740.0	675.0	0.0	1,415.0	1,774.1
United States	1994–1999	U.S.$	768.1	211.9	0.0	980.0	980.0
Japan	1994–1997	U.S.$	40.0	500.0	10.0	550.0	550.0
United Kingdom	1995–1999	£	250.0	0.0	0.0	250.0	421.6
Germany	1994–1998	DM	269.6	80.0	19.0	368.6	239.2
Sweden	1995–1999	SKr	1,150.0	0.0	135.0	1,285.0	186.9
Denmark	1995–1999	DKr	850.0	0.0	200.0	1,050.0	178.2
Netherlands	1995–1999	f	100.0	0.0	100.0	200.0	115.7
Norway	1995–1999	Nkr	400.0	0.0	200.0	600.0	94.0
Canada	1995–1999	Can$	67.1	0.0	17.7	84.8	61.7
Australia	1995–1999	A$	14.5	0.0	44.7	59.2	46.8
Switzerland	1995–1998	SwF	21.0	0.0	26.0	47.0	35.0
Ireland	1994–1999	£Ir	13.1	0.0	0.0	13.1	21.9
Finland	1996–2000	Fmk	52.0	0.0	7.5	59.5	12.9
New Zealand	1996–1999	$NZ	3.3	0.0	0.0	3.3	2.3
All donors							4,720.3

Source: Government of South Africa, Department of Finance, Annual Consultation (AC) Minutes, 1995–1998. Where available, data are total pledges reported in aggregate by the donor. Where aggregate figures were unavailable, totals were estimated by summing indicative allocations for individual projects.

Notes: a. Unless otherwise indicated, official development assistance (ODA) grant figures may include indirect grants to NGO and private sector entities.
b. Exchange rate calculated at January 2, 1997, i.e., the midpoint of the 1994–1999 pledge period. All figures are rounded.

period, loans amounted to $1.6 billion, or about one-third (33.9 percent) of the total amounts pledged.

To place aid pledges in perspective, it must be remembered that South Africa possesses an unusual capacity to finance development programs from domestic savings. Moreover, its creditworthy government can borrow money from local and international financial markets if it so chooses.[43] Thus, foreign aid constitutes less than 2 percent of the government budget and under 0.2 percent of GNP. These extraordinarily low figures suggest that the international community has relatively little political leverage in determining the content and terms of aid spending. This interpretation is offset, however, by the preemption of 90 percent of South Africa's public budget by recurrent costs, including civil service salaries (some 43 percent of the total budget) and public debt repayment (some 20 percent).[44] Thus, aid transfers become more strategically important when viewed in relation to the 10 percent of the budget that remains available for capital investments. In this regard, estimated pledges of aid totaling $6 billion represent more than twice the amount (R 12.5 billion over five years) earmarked by the South African government as its own contribution to the RDP.[45]

The size of donor programs varied considerably within these omnibus levels. As Table 7.1 suggests, donors to South Africa can be classified into three categories: those with large programs (with total pledges of reconstruction aid of over $500 million), those with medium-sized programs (between $100 million and $500 million), and those with small programs (under $100 million). The three large donors—the European Union, the United States, and Japan—together accounted for a full 70 percent of the total pledges documented here. These donors were also the principal source of loan funds. By contrast, the seven small donors collectively provided less than 6 percent of total anticipated flows. This pattern of tight aid concentration represents an extension of trends that were evident even before the transition. In 1993, the three largest donors (then the European Community, the United States, and Sweden) together accounted for some 62 percent of total flows.[46] After 1994, ever larger amounts of aid were funneled through a few major channels, even as numerous new donors entered South Africa officially for the first time.

The European Union (previously the European Community) has consistently been South Africa's largest donor, accounting single-handedly for about one-third of aid flows both before and after 1994. In October 1994, an EU delegation signed a cooperation agreement with the South African government to establish a European Program for Reconstruction and Development (EPRD). Its overall objective was to "redress the inequalities inherited from the system of apartheid," especially in rural areas where poverty and inequality were concentrated.[47] Initially, the EPRD covered a three-year planning period (1994–1996), for which the EU pledged a sum of ECU 365 million in gradually increasing annual increments; the amount was "indicative" and was supposed to "have the necessary flexibility to respond to changing needs."[48] The EU later expanded its "financial envelope" by adding annual supplements of about ECU 125 million.[49] In addition, the EU admitted South Africa to its General System of Preferences (GSP), mainly with respect to industrial products. The two sides also signed a landmark cooperation agreement in October 1995, opening the way for up to ECU 675 million in loans.

As for the United States, the "Clinton pledge" was programmed as a "transitional package" of assistance over three years, 1994–1996. Recognizing the importance of opening the U.S. market, President Clinton designated South Africa a beneficiary country under the GSP, allowing the entry of more than 4,000 products into the United States.[50] In September 1994, the South African government entered its first bilateral agreement with USAID, involving $9 million for the administration of justice and $39 million for lowcost housing. Soon thereafter, the two sides reached agreements to launch the Peace Corps in South Africa and to provide technical assistance for rural development, school nutrition, electrification, and water supplies. In total, USAID envisaged spending approximately $559 million in grants by the end of 1996, to which it added a further $209 million for 1997 through 1999. Quite apart from loan funds totaling more than $200 million, these promises of ODA exceeded the original Clinton pledge.

In July 1994, the government of Japan pledged $550 million over three years, thereby becoming South Africa's third largest donor. The Japanese package had two components: a grant of $50 million, with the remainder in loans. The grant was distributed between financial assistance to the government ($30 million) and to NGOs ($10 million) on the one hand, and technical assistance ($10 million) on the other. The loan package consisted of $250 million on concessional terms from the Overseas Economic Cooperation Fund and $250 million in export-import bank guarantees.[51] In addition, Japan promised South Africa $500 million in trade assurances. More so than other foreign donors, Japan reserved the right to determine how its money was to be spent and who would benefit.

Finally, most European countries established major bilateral assistance programs. In July 1994, Britain unveiled a £120 million support package to South Africa, along with export credit facilities.[52] The German government expanded development aid to South Africa to DM 110 million for 1994–1995 and doubled technical assistance through German Catholic and Protestant churches, political foundations, and NGOs. Each Scandinavian government made announcements of its own: Sweden committed SKr 220 million, mainly for democracy and human rights; Norway promised Nkr 300 million for education, the environment, and black business development; and the Danish government pledged a DKr 430 million grant for these fields and for the prevention of violence.[53] The Netherlands, Switzerland, and Finland also made pledges.[54]

Since many of the smaller and medium-sized donors planned their aid on a year-to-year basis, total pledges can be discerned only in retrospect. Nevertheless, the early annual pledges made in 1994 or 1995 constitute a benchmark for subsequent infusions. Because smaller donors started from a low base, their programs often expanded very rapidly. Thus, the Irish government's bilateral docket rose sixfold, from £Ir 0.4 million in 1994 to £Ir 3.0 million in 1997. A favored approach for smaller donors was to offer technical assistance and overseas study in areas of comparative advantage, as the Australians did in water management and public service reform.

South Africa's links with the Bretton Woods institutions remained quite modest. After 1994, the new government entered only one new agreement with the International Monetary Fund (IMF)—for a $4 million loan for drought relief, which was fully paid off by the end of 1998—although it continued to service debts to that institution incurred by previous administrations. The World Bank provided South Africa with funds totaling $102 million for reducing poverty, improving public sector management, and developing the private sector.[55] The African Development Bank promised to spend about $150 million over five years through South African companies involved in developmental activities.[56] South Africa's limited entanglements with the multilateral financial institutions can be traced to the relatively high price of their capital and the availability of more attractive loan rates from commercial banks within the country. But broader considerations were also at play: the suspension of IMF and World Bank loans to the previous government in the mid-1980s, the ANC's distrust as a liberation movement of the established institutions of global capitalism, and the new government's genuine aversion to debt.

Quite apart from the size of contributions, donors differed in the importance they attached to South Africa. Table 7.2 records their aid pledges to Pretoria as a share of each donor's net global aid expenditure in 1994. It reveals that, of all bilateral donors, the United Kingdom devoted the largest share of its total 1994 aid flows to South Africa (2.64 percent), no doubt as a means of reinforcing long-standing political and economic ties originating from the colonial era. The United States also assigned an above-average share (2.21 percent) of its dwindling global aid effort to restoring ties with a strategic African country whose racial history and consumer culture evoked echoes of its own. In recognition of a sense of "struggle" solidarity, the Scandinavian donors also granted South Africa a high profile in their assistance portfolios (an average 2.09 percent).[57] For all these donors, South Africa was far and away the largest bilateral assistance program that they planned for sub-Saharan Africa in the late 1990s. By contrast, Japan, Germany, and most Commonwealth countries made a below-average effort and did not grant special treatment to South Africa.

Table 7.2   South Africa: Share of Global ODA, 1994 (U.S.$ millions)

Donor Country	ODA Pledge to South Africa 1994–1999	Mean Annual ODA Pledges 1994–1999	Global Net ODA 1994[a]	South Africa's ODA Share (%)[b]
United Kingdom	421.6	84.3	3,197	2.64
Denmark	178.2	35.6	1,446	2.46
United States	980.0	196.0	9,927	2.21
Sweden	186.9	37.4	1,819	2.06
Norway	94.0	18.8	1,137	1.65
Netherlands	115.7	23.1	2,517	0.92
Finland	12.9	2.6	290	0.90
Australia	46.8	9.4	1,091	0.86
Japan	550.0	110.0	13,239	0.83
Switzerland	35.0	7.0	982	0.71
Germany	239.2	47.8	6,818	0.70
Canada	61.7	12.3	2,250	0.55
New Zealand	2.30	0.5	110	0.46
All donors	2,924.3	584.8	44,823	1.41

Source: Government of South Africa, Department of Finance, Annual Consultation (AC) minutes, 1995–1998.

Notes: a. The figures in this column were obtained from the Organization for Economic Cooperation and Development, "Overseas Development Assistance, 1950–1996" (OECD, Development Assistance Committee, www.oecd.org).

b. Mean annual official development assistance (ODA) pledges to South Africa are as a percentage of global net ODA, 1994.

The Sectoral Distribution of Aid

As pledge levels rose, so the composition of aid changed. This section examines three ways in which the structure of international cooperation evolved after April 1994: by development sector, by geographic area, and by institutional channel (that is, whether governmental or nongovernmental).

Development sectors. The Reconstruction and Development Program reshaped the composition of aid. Donors, keen to associate themselves publicly with the new government's development priorities, embraced the RDP strategy, and added major new elements to the sectoral mix of assistance. For example, the European Union and South Africa agreed that the EU would focus on assisting basic social services (which would absorb up to 60 percent of transfers), private sector development (up to 20 percent), good governance (up to 20 percent), and southern Africa regional cooperation (up to 5 percent).[58] Similarly, USAID established new strategic objectives in governance and civil society, basic and tertiary education, private sector development, housing, and health; USAID assured the South African government that it had "refocus(ed) its entire program toward the RDP."[59]

Other donors supported government efforts to revise public policy in selected sectors. After 1994, almost every government line ministry moved to repeal outdated laws and to replace these with forward-looking legislation. Donors saw in this remarkable outburst of policymaking an opportunity both to signal support for progressive change and to press their own agendas for policy reform. They commonly backed the white paper process, by which ministries engaged expert consultants and held public hearings to develop official policy recommendations. For example, Norway supported white papers on local government and on fisheries, Denmark on biodiversity and land and water policy, and Australia and Canada on broadcasting. Sweden, for its part, backed a Presidential Review Commission on civil service reform. Interestingly, the larger donors were reticent to openly engage in public policy dialogue, perhaps out of a concern that they would be accused of exerting heavy-handed conditionality.

Because donors took the RDP as their landmark, an orthodoxy emerged about South Africa's priority needs. To the extent that data are available, Table 7.3 lists the main sectors of assistance.[60] It indicates that donors were active in the following six sectors, in order of importance: education (primary, secondary, and tertiary); democracy and governance (including human rights and public administration); agriculture (including water development and natural resource management); business development (especially for small, medium-scale, and microenterprises); health (notably primary and preventative care); and housing (including related infrastructure). Indeed, donor programs were cut from similar cloth. Their tendency to converge on shared priorities was reinforced by choices of common program themes, such as black empowerment, advancement of women, and environmental protection—and often all of the above.

To be sure, some donors had idiosyncratic interests. The Danes created a free-standing fund for environmental protection alongside their aid program, and the Swedes assumed almost single-handed responsibility for arts and culture. Moreover, small donors did not always try to cover all major sectors, as illustrated by Switzerland's preference to stand aside from support for agriculture and business development.

Most important, the large donors had different priorities across sectors. The EU and United States continued to emphasize education, making this sector the leading recipient of aid in South Africa both before and after 1994. Indeed, given the large size of the total EU and U.S. portfolios, the weighted mean proportion of total flows into the education sector is 35.1 percent. By contrast, both Sweden and the United Kingdom allocated the largest chunks of their spending (44.7 percent and 34.8 percent, respectively) for democracy and governance. Meanwhile, Norway, Denmark, and the United States took the lead on business development (ranging from 19.5 percent to 46.7 percent of their respective programs). The major

**Table 7.3   South Africa: Sectoral Distribution of Aid, 1994–1998
(as percentage of selected donor programs[a])**

Donor Country	Education	Democracy/ Governance	Agriculture/ Rural Development	Business Development	Health	Housing	Other
European Union	43.8	11.4	17.5	2.8	10.9	6.7	6.8
United States	33.2	6.6	0.0	19.5	27.2	13.5	0.0
Sweden	21.6	44.7	0.0	6.2	0.0	27.5	0.0
United Kingdom	19.6	34.8	30.6	1.7	9.5	0.2	2.1
Denmark	18.2	27.3	18.2	36.4	0.0	0.0	0.0
Norway	8.7	16.0	14.3	46.7	2.4	11.9	0.0
Switzerland	16.5	18.2	0.0	0.0	0.0	65.3	0.0
All donors (unweighted means[b])	23.1	22.7	11.5	16.2	7.1	17.9	1.3
All donors (weighted means[c])	35.1	15.6	13.6	11.6	10.9	8.0	5.2

Source: Calculated from Department of Finance, International Development Cooperation (IDC) unit, various Annual Bilateral Consultations, 1994–1998.

Notes: a. Sectoral distribution data are not systematically available for all countries. Data are percentages of actual financial commitments by selected donors, 1994–1999, except Denmark, for which data are pledges.

b. Caution: unweighted means do not take into account the relative size of donor programs.

c. Weighted means are corrected to reflect the relative size of donor programs.

thrust of assistance following the transition was in building institutional capacity, both within organs of government (for example, through public administration training) and in the private sector (especially for emergent black businesses). Indeed, democratic governance and business development were among the fastest-growing sectors of aid activity after 1994, with education shrinking in its share of overall flows even as it grew in real terms.

Thus did the international donor community underscore its concern for the consolidation of South Africa's political and economic transitions. What is less clear is whether adequate donor resources were devoted to sustaining the third element in the triple transition: the passage from war to peace.

High levels of social spending in education and housing helped to sustain peace indirectly. Still, while some donors (e.g., the Netherlands and Germany) emphasized vocational education and skills training for the "lost generation" of former political activists, viable institutional models did not exist to reliably deliver training, let alone jobs. At the same time, few donors were willing to invest heavily in strengthening security institutions, no doubt because these organs had been central to the repressive apparatus of the apartheid state.

The Scandinavian Group and Like-Minded countries were most creative in breaking this donor resistance: Denmark focused directly on the prevention of violence, largely through NGOs but also with support to the state correctional services; Sweden assisted the reform of the South African Police Service (SAPS) through human rights training and other initiatives; and the Netherlands helped establish a civilian Secretariat for Safety and Security. The United Nations Development Programme (UNDP) supported research on crime and policing.[61] Other major donors, however, steered clear of the security sector. USAID, for example, was prohibited by congressional statute from supporting any law enforcement activities. Hence, the U.S. government provided only small amounts of security sector support through alternate channels like its Drug Enforcement Agency and Federal Bureau of Investigation. In our view, support for the peace transition remains an underfunded area of endeavor.

Geographic spread. In terms of real distribution, aid before 1994 had flowed mainly into urban and periurban areas, where civic organizations and self-help NGOs had been most active. The rural parts of the country were underserved, in good part because they were governed by "Bantustan" administrations that were unrecognized by the international community. With the end of apartheid and the reintegration of former "homelands" into a unified South Africa, the government sought to bring development to the most impoverished rural regions. The government acknowledged, however, that "RDP objectives cannot be addressed simultaneously for the whole country unless the RDP Core Cabinet Committee prioritizes geographical areas."[62] Accordingly, Nelson Mandela designated high-profile Presidential Lead Projects that focused on delivering basic social services to pockets of deprivation within each province. The Department of Finance reminded donors that three provinces—Gauteng, KwaZulu-Natal, and Western Cape— were relatively wealthy and that efforts should be concentrated in areas experiencing "serious resource and capacity constraints."[63] In response, some donors chose geographic program foci: the Germans and the Norwegians focused on Mpumalanga Province, the New Zealanders on the Eastern Cape Province, and the Swedish on the Northern Cape.

Institutional channels. The institutional distribution of aid also underwent a sea change. Before the 1994 elections, assistance programs to South Africa were highly decentralized because they were carried out by hundreds of CBOs and NGOs working at the grassroots level. With the advent of majority rule, an opportunity arose for donor governments to expand diplomatic relations with South Africa and to negotiate bilateral aid agreements. The European Union undertook that henceforth all its funding for basic social services would be delivered through government ministries and that funding for other sectors would be divided equally between the central government and "agents of decentralized cooperation," including provincial and local governments.[64] The United States, having entered into "close consultation with technical departments at central and provincial levels," adjusted its allocation to the government from virtually nil in 1993 to an estimated 50 percent in 1998.[65] Starting from a similarly low base, Sweden allocated 26 percent of its 1996 ODA contribution to the government followed by 44 percent in 1997, in part by launching its first program of support for public administration in South Africa.[66]

Donors did not abandon the voluntary sector. Switzerland aimed for a fifty-fifty split between government and NGOs, and Norway's program was made up of three equal parts: one-third each to the public, private, and voluntary sectors.[67] In addition, international grant funds to government departments like the Ministry of Justice (for human rights promotion) and the Ministry of Health (for HIV/AIDS awareness) were regularly subcontracted to NGO implementing agencies. The South African government assured the donors that it "strongly support[ed] a vibrant and independent NGO sector" and expressed "appreciation for the dual approach . . . particularly using NGOs where government had experienced problems in absorbing funds."[68] Nevertheless, there is no gainsaying the fact that NGOs saw their overall levels and their relative share of development cooperation fall after 1994. Funds were reallocated on two fronts: to the development initiatives of central, provincial, and local governments, and to the private sector for programs to promote trade, investment, and small business.

Above all, NGOs bore the brunt of efforts to consolidate and rationalize aid. As donors increased their pledges, so they focused on fewer areas of cooperation. Without rejecting the principle of pluralism, they aimed to reduce the array of directly supported grassroots projects in favor of a smaller number of umbrella organizations. Indeed, both donors and the government came to share an interest in centralized aid programs. The government wished to augment the public budget and to deploy increased levels of resources to address problems of reconstruction and development. Donors wished to reduce administrative complexity in expanded aid programs by eliminating excess contact points and management units. While continuing to recognize that civil society had an important role in development, emerging cooperation programs featured a larger role for government entities and a smaller one for NGOs.

The Architecture of Cooperation

From the outset, the South African government sought to occupy the driver's seat in its relations with international donors. It did so by setting out clear priorities for development cooperation, first under the RDP and later under GEAR, to which assistance programs were supposed to adhere. In reality, the government had little difficulty in bringing donors along since, in broad terms, the donor community embraced the new government's development vision and priorities.

At the same time, the South African authorities insisted on coordinating donor programs themselves, first in the RDP office and later through the International Development Cooperation (IDC) unit of the Department of Finance (DOF). Whenever donor resources were involved, this office was responsible for strategic planning and review. Because the host government rather than donors took the lead, a bilateral architecture emerged for the management of development cooperation in South Africa. The government introduced procedures to consult individual donors on a one-to-one basis and according to its own time schedule. The South Africans thereby were able to establish more official control over aid than governments in other transitional situations, where assistance has tended to flow through coordinated donor groups and multilateral channels.

The precedents for a bilateral architecture derived from the ANC's history. In the pretransition period, almost all assistance to the ANC-in-exile and to NGOs in the internal mass democratic movement had originated from bilateral sources. There was little, if any, donor coordination except that which the ANC could impose by remote control from abroad. Even after an ANC-led government assumed power, it did not seek to convene the members of the international financial community to make pledges against a shopping list of aid requests. The government explicitly wished to avoid consortia like the Consultative Groups (CGs), held regularly in Paris for the least developed countries, in which donors club together to recommend policy adjustments in return for the extension and restructuring of debt. Because South Africa was quite well placed to cover its outstanding foreign obligations,[69] a senior official in the Ministry of Finance could afford to dismiss CGs as "begging-bowl excursions."[70]

Binational commissions. In a clear expression of its preference for bilateralism, the South African government established Binational Commissions (BNCs) with several of its key partners: the United States, Germany, China, and India. These institutions restored and expanded relationships severed during South Africa's long era of diplomatic isolation. The BNCs enabled officials from each country to interact regularly at the highest levels of government, to promote vital interests, and to map out areas of cooperation, including aid priorities.

The decision to form a South Africa–United States Binational Commission was made by Presidents Clinton and Mandela during the latter's state visit to Washington in 1994.[71] The fact that the United States maintains BNCs with only three other countries—Russia, Egypt, and Mexico—symbolizes the geopolitical importance that U.S. officials attach to South

Africa and the southern Africa region. Established in March 1995, the South Africa–United States BNC is cochaired by the South African deputy president and the U.S. vice president, who meet for private dialogue and a plenary session every six months with the venue alternating between countries. This BNC also provides a valuable forum for resolving policy differences—for example, on South African arms sales abroad or military crises in sub-Saharan Africa. Much of the work is conducted through specialist committees—on science and technology, the environment, human resource development, energy, and business development—which set the policy parameters for subsequent aid programs.

Annual bilateral consultations. The South African government holds annual consultations on development cooperation with each of the bilateral donors. The South African delegations to these talks are headed by the director of the DOF's IDC unit; donor delegations are headed by a relevant ambassador, aid director, or senior home office aid official.[72] Delegations number between three and fifty persons, depending on the size and complexity of the cooperation program (see Table 7.4). The first annual consultation took place with the Netherlands in March 1995. New Zealand, by contrast, entered the arrangement as late as April 1997. For some countries (such as Sweden and Denmark), consultations occur on a precise annual cycle; with other countries (like the UK and Australia), meetings have been fewer and less regular.

Apart from ensuring that donor plans are consistent with national priorities, the South African government has cited several purposes for annual consultations: "to review the progress of ongoing programmes . . . to find joint solutions to problems encountered . . . to firm up [annual] programming exercises . . . [and] to explore ideas on the future directions of development cooperation."[73] Because the participants include government officials from functional ministries charged with implementing aid projects, the consultations offer an opportunity to make sure that all actors are operating along agreed-upon lines. In practice, they have enabled mutual learning, with government and donors figuring out how to inaugurate and operate foreign-funded development programs in the South African setting.

While the formal agenda of these consultations allows only for the consideration of ODA projects, in practice the meetings also perform a diplomatic function, reminding the partners of related political, NGO, and private sector ties. For example, Germany has used the annual meeting to advertise its trading and investment leadership. Likewise, Sweden followed one official consultation by briefing NGO partners, reassuring them that the Swedish International Development Agency (SIDA) would not close its funding window for NGOs, and advising them to tender for South African government development programs.[74] As a management tool to assess

Table 7.4   South Africa: Size of Government and Donor Delegations at Annual Consultations, 1997–1998

Donor Country	Dates of Consultations	South African Delegation	Donor Delegation	Total Attendance	Staff-Program Ratio
Australia	March 30, 1998	5	15	20	1 to 3
Canada	October 29, 1998	8	6	14	1 to 10
Denmark	September 17–18, 1997	44	9	53	1 to 20
European Union	March 25–26, 1998	52	13	65	1 to 137
Finland	October 21, 1997	15	3	18	1 to 4
Germany	November 5–7, 1997	24	21	45	1 to 11
Ireland	October 28, 1997	14	3	17	1 to 7
New Zealand	June 19, 1997	8	5	13	1 to 0.5
Norway	May 13–16, 1997	16	6	22	1 to 16
Sweden	November 19–20, 1997	45	13	58	1 to 14
Switzerland	September 22, 1997	10	5	15	1 to 7
United Kingdom	February 11, 1998	24	13	37	1 to 32
United States	April 15, 1998	39	29	68	1 to 34
All donors (means)		23.4	10.8	34.2	1 to 23

Source: Calculated from Department of Finance, International Development Cooperation (IDC) unit, various Annual Bilateral Consultations, 1994–1998.

Note: The staff-program ratio is calculated as follows: the donor delegation is used as a proxy measure for a donor's field staff; aid pledges are used as a proxy for the size of the donor's program in South Africa.

progress throughout the year, the proceedings are minuted. The relationship between parties remains flexible, however, since "the minutes can be amended from time to time by mutual agreement; they do not bind the parties for the entire period."[75]

Because the South African government deals with donors individually, substantial problems of aid coordination fall at its own doorstep. The DOF is officially responsible for the macromanagement of development assistance programs, whereas line departments run particular projects at the microlevel, including financial reporting.[76] Because its IDC unit is small and understaffed—with a complement of just six professionals—the DOF is unable to monitor the flow of donor resources reliably or to view aid from a strategic, policy perspective. In the view of several aid officials interviewed for this study, too many important decisions on the deployment of aid resources are devolved to departments, or even to consultants. Nor has the IDC managed to avoid duplication. As shown above, donor strategies in South Africa are remarkably similar, clustered as they are around common sectors and themes. Yet the DOF has never used the annual bilateral consultations to instruct any donor to reallocate its funds because a similar project in the same sector was already under way. And because the annual bilateral consultations do not cover nonofficial flows to the voluntary sector, the IDC has done little more than lament that, "with regard to NGOs, there [is] much overlapping in activities."[77]

Tacitly acknowledging a need for coordination, the Government of National Unity announced in late 1995 that it planned to convene in South Africa its own donor "consultative group" called the South African International Development Forum.[78] At first, donors welcomed this initiative, but when the forum failed to meet, they expressed concern that such "attempts to improve the coordination of development efforts seem to have come to a halt."[79] Other donors advocated the designation of an official, not only in each government department but (more crucially) also at the provincial level, to ensure that various donor efforts did not clash. The South African delegation responded that, although departmental contact persons were in place and were fulfilling their roles, the process of aid management was still very new and "much learning is taking place."[80]

In the absence of any formal mechanisms for aid coordination, donors in South Africa relate to one another on an ad hoc basis. The smaller donors, who are keen to identify neglected niches, are most eager to share information with others. Larger donors are less flexible but have sometimes intervened to help break policy logjams or to build support for high-profile projects: for example, the United Kingdom offered to assist in facilitating the South African government's management of Japanese aid, and Sweden called for multilateral contributions to the civil service review commission.[81] In their most concerted effort, almost all donors presented a united front in urging the South African government to enact legislation governing the flow of development cooperation funds. At almost every annual bilateral consultation, they raise the need for streamlined procedures for aid commitment and disbursement and, as detailed below, were ultimately successful in inducing the government to amend the RDP Fund Act.[82]

The Cooperation Process

Do donors fulfill their pledges? Does aid reach intended beneficiaries? These crucial questions are best answered by breaking down the development cooperation process into its component stages: from pledges to commitments, from commitments to disbursements, and from disbursements to implementation. At each stage, we analyze the extent to which gaps have emerged between what was promised and what was actually delivered.

From pledges to commitments. In committing resources, the bilateral parties sign agreements in which they take on legal, financial, and administrative responsibilities for given programs or projects. The South African government and its international partners have established a reputable track record in converting indicative pledges into firm financial commitments. Table 7.5 shows that by May 1998, a "typical" donor had committed some 72.3 percent of pledged assistance.

Table 7.5 South Africa: Commitments and Disbursements of Official Development Assistance, 1994–1998

Donor Country	Commitment Period	Commitments in Donor Currency[a] (millions)	Commitments as % of Pledges[a]	Disbursements (through 5/98) in Donor Currency	Disbursements as % of Commitment
Finland	n.a.	Fmk 50.5	97.1	50.5	100.0
Netherlands	1995–1997	f 60.0	60	60.0	100.0
France	1993–1998	F 196.5	n.a.	161.5	82.1
Sweden	1995–1998	SKr 331.9	28.9	269.3	81.1
Denmark	1994–1998	DKr 750.0	88.2	542.0	72.3
United States	1994–1998	U.S.$ 531.6	69.2	377.9	71.1
Japan	1994–1997	U.S.$ 50.0	100.0[b]	35.0	70.0
Norway	1995–1999	Nkr 570.0	95.0[b]	330.0	57.9
United Kingdom	n.a.	£ 209.7	83.9	76.0	36.2
Germany	1992–1997	DM 132.8	49.3	44.1	33.2
European Union	1995–1997	ECU 379.6	51.3	49.6	13.1
China	n.a.	U.S.$ 25.0	n.a.	0.0	0.0
All donors (unweighted means[c])			72.3		59.8
All donors (weighted means[d])			63.8		47.0
All donors, except European Union (weighted means[d])			77.6		66.6

Source: Government of South Africa, *Progress Reports on Commitments and Disbursements of Donor Funds*, May 14, 1998.
Notes: a. See Table 7.1. Includes only official grants to government; all loans excluded.
b. Includes grants to NGOs.
c. Caution: unweighted means do not reflect the relative sizes of donor programs.
d. Weighted means are corrected to reflect the relative sizes of donor programs.

This finding, however, must be qualified in several respects. First, commitment rates (i.e., commitments as a percentage of pledges) vary across donors. Whereas, for example, 100 percent of Japanese grants were committed, the equivalent figure for Sweden was just 28.9 percent, a difference that calls for explanation. Second, there is no such thing as a "typical" donor in South Africa because bilateral aid programs come in various sizes, making it necessary to correct any unweighted average of commitment rates. Once corrected, the weighted mean for aid commitments in South Africa falls to a less impressive 63.7 percent. Third, we must recall that one donor—the European Union—has an extraordinarily large program that is almost twice the size of the next largest donor and which alone amounts to 37.5 percent of total aid pledges. Precisely because this huge program has a low commitment rate (51.3 percent), it plays an inordinately heavy role in depressing the weighted mean. We therefore contend that a weighted mean for all donors except the EU is the most valid summary measure of aid performance in South Africa. This figure, presented in the bottom line of Table 7.5, reveals that some 77.6 percent of aid pledges were converted into firm financial commitments by May 1998.

The experience of turning pledges into commitments has been quite smooth for some donors, rockier for others. For example, after encountering initial difficulty in activating bilateral agreements during 1995, the United States was able to conclude fourteen such agreements by September 1996. A critical role in this process was played by the director and staff of the DOF's IDC unit, who facilitated signing ceremonies before the end of the U.S. financial year.[83] By September 1997, the head of the Danish aid delegation was able to report that "planning and programming within the prioritized areas had by-and-large been completed" and that there were "no funds uncommitted or unutilized" from programs that had begun in 1994.[84] In Denmark's case, commitments appear to have been accelerated by the signing of a general framework agreement covering the donor's entire development program, a device that cut through some of the red tape involved in obtaining government approvals on a project-by-project basis.

Other donors expressed frustration with the commitment process. By November 1997, fully three years after starting aid negotiations with the new government, the German aid delegation reported that only two technical assistance project agreements had been signed, while nine others were still pending.[85] The delegation head warned that legal uncertainties would arise and financial commitments would lapse if implementing agreements were not concluded soon. In practice, at least eighteen German-funded projects began implementation *before* official agreements were signed.[86] And in several cases (involving commitments to build housing for farm workers and to help restructure local government), funds were reprogrammed to other purposes because the government had not completed its sectoral white papers.[87]

Ironically, Sweden's "Rapid Response Fund," designed for quick development impact, bogged down. Every year from 1996 onward, SIDA was forced to carry forward uncommitted funds—sometimes amounting to as much as half of its planned annual assistance—into the next financial year.[88] Disappointed in long delays in developing new programs for 1998 and beyond, the head of the Swedish delegation stated that Sweden might have to reconsider its support to the education sector.[89] Similarly, the UK delegation complained about provincial governments, noting that "donors are not in a position to police recipients with respect to adhering to the guidelines, particularly in signing agreements."[90]

At the root of the problem was the fact that South Africa, whose government had long been shunned by the international community, was ill equipped to deal with a sudden influx of foreign aid. Because it lacked enabling legislation to govern development cooperation, the government fell back on constitutional rules or cumbersome administrative procedures for managing new flows. The interim constitution stipulated that only the president could sign international agreements, including letters of aid commitment. And because national ministers were the only government officials allowed to submit a presidential minute, all international agreements had to go through a minister to the president. Moreover, Parliament had to ratify any agreement that required new or amended legislation or that placed an unbudgeted financial burden on the state.

Predictably, a bottleneck occurred in the office of the president, not least because of the multiple competing demands on the time of an overworked President Mandela. Aid agreements also required the concurrence of implementing ministries; especially for integrated projects, this was a complex quest. Government and donors alike were unclear on the division of responsibility between traditional line ministries, the new provincial governments, and the overarching RDP office. Donors sometimes found themselves negotiating with officials who had neither the experience nor the authority to enter into aid agreements.

Despite such teething problems, a wide gap did not emerge between pledges and commitments. Because donors were dedicated to underwriting South Africa's experiment in multiracial reconciliation, they followed through on aid pledges even in the face of fiscal austerity at home and delays in the field. The South African government, for its part, helped most major donors deliver on their pledges, even if this necessitated a last-minute scramble to commit funds before the expiry of donor budget deadlines. Through a mutual learning process, donors and government modified their expectations and procedures. The process of adaptation probably led donors that committed funds on a rolling annual cycle or a multiyear horizon to scale back later pledges. The main reason for a pledge gap in May 1998—amounting to about one-quarter of total pledged aid—was that initial pledge periods had not yet run their course. There is good reason to believe that the remaining commitment gap will have been further closed by the end of 1999, around the time that the first round of donor pledges expire.

From commitments to disbursements. The disbursement of aid—that is, action by donors to release advance payments, to deliver goods and services directly, or to reimburse invoiced expenditures—has proven more of a challenge. In the brief period since 1994, a wider gap has opened up between commitments and disbursements than that documented between pledges and commitments.

Table 7.5 displays disbursement rates (i.e., disbursements as a percentage of commitments) in May 1998. The unweighted average disbursement rate for all donors was 59.8 percent (or a weighted 47.0 percent). The latter figure can be interpreted to mean that, when the size of donor commitments is taken into account, less than half of committed aid resources had actually been transferred to implementing agencies. Even more than before, however, average figures are distorted by the European Union, whose large program and low disbursement rate (just 13.1 percent) are statistical outliers. Thus, we prefer again to use a weighted mean for all donors except the EU, which reveals a somewhat more respectable disbursement rate of 66.6 percent.

Problems of disbursement arose principally as a result of elaborate procedures introduced by the South African government for administering the RDP. The government announced in 1995 that all grant aid should be deposited in the RDP Fund; from there it would be paid into the state's general Revenue Fund; Parliament would then allocate amounts to departments or provinces; and these implementing agencies would call on the RDP office to release payments on a reimbursement basis. Donors were admonished in the strictest terms to avoid direct transfers to implementing agencies. Early annual consultations between donors and the DOF were replete with queries about the correct procedures for disbursement and with complaints that the government's own departments and provinces did not understand official RDP requirements. In practice, therefore, several donors simply opted to administer aid funds directly themselves or, ignoring RDP rules, to contract local providers on their own.[91]

Moreover, in the absence of enabling legislation, aid disbursements were subject to the existing laws of the land. Among other conditions, these laws required that project contracts could be tendered only to indigenous suppliers who used locally sourced materials; in addition, value-added tax (VAT) was payable on all aid transactions. Without exception, aid donors opposed these requirements.

Finally, committed funds were sometimes blocked from disbursement by new procedures for project development and approval. From 1995 onward, the Special Cabinet Committee for the RDP set spending priorities for the RDP Fund and was supposed to approve all project proposals and business plans that had been developed by national line ministries or provinces. An RDP Programme Steering Committee was charged to "implement" the approved projects. The government warned the donor community not to try to expedite this process—for example, by drafting proposals or plans on behalf of government agencies. Yet donors soon began to signal concern at the slow pace at which such documents were forthcoming.[92] One warned that it could not "keep committed funds on its books unproductively much longer" and reminded the government that resources "lost through logistical delays cannot be rolled over."[93]

From disbursements to implementation. The South African government and its international partners obtained some success, but also encountered setbacks, in putting the RDP into effect. The government set ambitious targets, such as the construction of a million houses by the year 2000, and designated 1995 as the "year of delivery."[94] In fact, only 10,000 houses were built that year with state-funded subsidies.[95] By 1998, a new National Housing Corporation claimed to have "construction underway" for 60 percent of the target.[96] A national health system brought citizens free primary health care through a network of local clinics, and a feeding scheme was introduced for children of single and unemployed mothers.[97] Generally speaking, however, the delivery of planned benefits fell behind schedule in all sectors except rural water supply and electrification.

In South Africa, the responsibility for implementing aid-funded development activities was divided between various levels and units of government. The RDP office (and its successor IDC unit) was designed to manage and coordinate aid flows; functional ministries took charge of aid programs in each sector; and line departments, provincial governments, local authorities, and NGOs were responsible for actual project implementation. Thus, progress required that various parties interact regularly from the outset.

In the early days, a major obstacle to effective delivery was the RDP office itself. It inserted a centralized layer of bureaucracy into the policy implementation process, bottling up development funds.[98] From both donor and public perspectives, the RDP office fell short as a development guide and facilitator. At the same time, the weaknesses of newly established provincial and local government structures became apparent. With their inexperienced personnel and inadequate budgets, these institutions found it impossible to meet highly politicized demands for the immediate delivery of services. Local government was especially hamstrung by the refusal of many residents of the vast urban townships to pay for services provided.[99] The disbursement of donor funds was undercut by a "culture of nonpayment," as citizens withheld local matching contributions out of an amalgam of entitlement, opportunism, protest, and genuine inability to pay.

Donor experiences in the implementation of aid-funded projects can be illustrated with reference to the European Union. The Department of Health was the first government institution to enter into an agreement with the EU, through a program to raise AIDS awareness and to secure equality for HIV-infected persons. Soon thereafter, the EU agreed to provide the Ministry of Education with equipment, books, and training to historically disadvantaged (i.e., formerly black) universities and *technikons* (vocational colleges). The implementation of both these founding projects was delayed by "institutional capacity constraints and personnel changes" and by complications arising from allegedly corrupt practices. The education project was required to absorb a transfer of bursary funds from a defunct NGO (the Kagiso Trust) whose resources had been mismanaged; and the health project became embroiled in a scandal in which official tendering procedures may have been bypassed in the award of funding for the production of an anti-AIDS musical (*Sarafina II*). Both projects had to be redesigned and their end dates extended.[100]

The EU's experience reinforced perceptions that whereas some central government ministries were well managed, others were not. For example, EU-funded projects through the Ministry of Water Affairs for water reticulation projects in the Eastern Cape started promptly and remained on schedule for completion in 1999. Other EU initiatives that unfolded as planned included a Ministry of Justice project designed to enable NGOs to promote and protect human rights and to support the Truth and Reconciliation Commission's investigation unit. By contrast, other projects stalled. An EU-funded land reform project took off slowly, in part because it was a pilot effort that required the establishment of district offices in the Department of Land Affairs. And one of the EU's largest projects, a $30 million program through the Ministry of Housing intended to underwrite the construction of shelter in the Cato Manor settlement in Durban, ran aground on conflicting land claims and power struggles among local project leaders.

Because implementation is ongoing, firm patterns in the activation of aid-funded development projects are hard to discern. Nevertheless, one can infer a couple of suggestive hypotheses from disbursement data. First, project implementation appears to proceed more effectively in sectors where the main task is to build human or institutional capacity and more slowly in sectors that require the delivery of material goods and services. By way of illustration, Table 7.6 shows that selected donors have attained a higher disbursement rate in the democracy and governance sector (58.9 percent) than in the agriculture sector (9.5 percent).

Second, implementation appears to proceed more effectively through governmental institutions than through NGOs. Table 7.7 shows disbursement rates of 91.2 percent and 66.9 percent for these respective institutional channels. While interesting, this counterintuitive finding should be treated with caution. It is based on data that were available for only one donor (Norway) and may not hold generally. Still, the finding does challenge the conventional wisdom that civil society is always a more effective channel for delivering development benefits. (We discuss this issue in greater detail in a subsequent section.)

Midcourse corrections. To its credit, the South African government sought to address implementation problems as they arose. The president's decision in March 1996 to close the RDP office offers a good example.

Too often, RDP funds could not be spent because the RDP minister lacked the authority to tell line ministries how to allocate their budgets and

Table 7.6   South Africa: Disbursements of Official Development Assistance by Sector, 1994–1998

Sector	Disbursement (as % of commitments)
Democracy and governance	58.9
Health	56.2
Education	49.4
Business development	48.9
Housing	35.2
Other	17.0
Agriculture and rural development	9.5

Source: Based on available commitment and disbursement data for selected donors: European Union, United States, Sweden, Norway, and Switzerland. Available data for all other donors are insufficiently complete to allow disaggregation by sector.

Table 7.7   South Africa: Disbursements of Norwegian Aid by Institutional Channel

Sector	Disbursement via Government Ministry (% of commitments)	Disbursement via NGO (% of commitments)
Education	100.0	65.9
Democracy and governance	98.1	94.7
Housing	100.0	40.6
Business development	83.5	33.5
Agriculture and rural development	16.3	0
Health	100.0	100.0
All Sectors	91.2	66.9

Source: Annual Bilateral Consultations, SA-Norway, November 1997.

because the RDP system required cumbersome procedures of double accounting. The shutdown of the RDP was essentially an exercise in efficiency that removed a redundant layer of bureaucracy. Some observers saw the reorganization in more political terms, noting that it granted greater powers to the deputy president and the minister of finance. Was the closure a political power play? Was Thabo Mbeki beginning to assume the mantle of de facto prime minister? We interpret the demise of the RDP office in more mundane terms, as an administrative decision driven by a quest to improve program performance.

By late 1997, the departments of finance, foreign affairs, and the presidency introduced legislation into the South African Parliament to streamline the aid commitment and disbursement processes. The new legislation took the form of amendments to the RDP Fund Act. It addressed comprehensively several concerns that donors had expressed. Henceforth, technical assistance agreements could be signed directly with implementing agencies without prior presidential approval; donor resources could be transferred directly from the RDP Fund to implementing agencies, bypassing the State's general revenue account; donor regulations, rather than South African ones, would apply to contract tenders; and taxes would not be charged on aid expenditures. In return, donors would disburse aid in advance, rather than waiting for implementing agencies to submit claims for reimbursement.

Finally, beginning with its March 1998 budget, the South African government embarked on significant budgetary reform by introducing a three-year rolling expenditure plan known as the Medium-Term Expenditure Framework (MTEF). By means of the MTEF, the Ministry of Finance aimed "to direct expenditure to priority services, achieve more efficient planning and management, achieve more credible and open government, and provide a framework for assessing policy proposals and for linking them with costs."[101] The MTEF promised to bring about what the RDP had failed to do—that is, break the inertia embedded in inherited budgets and recast departmental and provincial spending priorities along developmental lines. Another potential benefit was the MTEF's promise to reduce the rollover of unspent funds.

Even the most frustrated donors expressed approval for these midcourse corrections. In March 1998, the EU noted (perhaps overoptimistically) that "the concerns expressed for slow implementation of projects . . . have been largely dealt with."[102] The German delegation claimed that outstanding institutional problems with delivering low-cost housing had been "settled."[103]

Interpreting Delays

The above account suggests that unwieldy procedures on the part of the South African government were largely to blame for delays in the release of aid. In this section, we broaden this interpretation to include other, related factors. Obstacles also emanated from donors' own procedures, from their occasional conflicts with government, and from a gradual demobilization of civil society. Above all, delays in implementing aid projects arose from weaknesses in the capacity of South African institutions, especially those of the state.

Cumbersome donor procedures. The administrative performance of every large donor was problematic, each in its own way. While most donors labeled their aid programs after 1994 as "transitional" or "reconstruction" assistance, only the donors with small- and medium-sized programs were sufficiently flexible to introduce mechanisms for quick disbursement. Large donors like the EU and Japan continued to use standard operating procedures that were better suited to long-term development assistance.

The EU's complications stand out. An evaluation report on its South Africa program bluntly described the European Commission as "a slow, bureaucratic organization, which took too long to approve projects and process payments."[104] For example, a major program to support the strengthening of the national Parliament was held up for at least two years, because EU headquarters in Brussels was tardy in releasing approved funds. Unlike other donors who retrieved undisbursed grant funds at the end of each financial year, the EU had a liberal rollover policy that reduced incentives to put money to work quickly.[105] Blockages resulted mainly from the centralized nature of the EU aid operation, which consisted of a relatively small field office and the referral of routine project approvals to Brussels, where too many organizations and levels of the commission (with overlapping responsibilities, incomplete information, and inadequate coordination) became involved. Delays were especially likely if EU member governments intervened to ensure consideration of their own national institutions for implementation contracts.

Although the United States had a stronger disbursement record, USAID lost flexibility after 1994. Formerly known among its South African NGO clients as a sympathetic and responsive donor, the agency came to be criticized for the inaccessibility of its Pretoria-based staff, the complexity of Washington's application and reporting requirements, and delays in the procurement of goods and services.[106] For instance, more than two years elapsed between the 1994 announcement of a USAID project to support linkages between U.S. and South African universities and the actual award of the first grant monies. One source of problems was an aid budget that expanded much faster than the organization's field staff. To address the shortage of locally hired personnel, the agency took bids from private contractors to manage projects, a process that often added a year or more to the start of projects. Moreover, the highly visible U.S. aid program attracted a wide array of stakeholders in South Africa and Washington, D.C.; these individuals and groups exerted demands on the program from both the left and the right of the political spectrum. Such crosscutting political pressures combined to make USAID staff extremely cautious.

Small and medium-sized donors were more nimble at moving money. Norway had a record of rapid commitments, the Netherlands of rapid disbursements, and Finland of both (see Table 7.5). Indeed, donors from Scandinavia and the Low Countries were given high marks by their local partners, not only for speedy release of funds, but for involving South Africans in project and program planning.[107]

The relative size of donor programs is the single most important factor in explaining the timeliness of aid delivery in South Africa. This record can be expressed as an actual "yield" on grant pledges, calculated as commitment rate multiplied by disbursement rate. Table 7.8 presents in summary form the relevant yield data for ten major donors. As can be seen, a strong inverse relationship exists between the amount of grant funds that a donor pledged to the government and the subsequent yield in the form of disbursed funds.[108] Statistically, this association is particularly strong and highly significant when the variables are treated as ranked data.[109] We conclude that the larger a donor's program, the harder it was to launch.

Two qualifications are necessary. The first concerns the size and duration of projects. Small projects that were planned to begin and end early were obviously much more likely to get under way than projects with longer time horizons. Thus, even large donors sought to get a few manageable projects "up and running." A second consideration was the size of the donor's field staff, a factor that helps us understand the difference in the pledge yield records of the two largest donors. While both the EU and the United States were short-staffed, the EU was more so; indeed, it had the least favorable staff-program ratio of any donor (see Table 7.4). Thus, the United States was more effective than the EU at dispensing aid in South Africa in part because it had personnel available on the ground.[110]

Donor-government disputes. We noted earlier that adaptive policy learning has characterized donor-government relations in South Africa. Sometimes, however, disagreements emerged over the terms of aid. For example, disputes erupted between the EU and the government in both the health and education sectors, with the former charging that the latter went back on commitments to fund key programs.[111]

A major case of hiccups also accompanied Japan's pledge to provide loans and trade guarantees. Due to exchange rate risks and the price of forward cover, the landed cost of these yen-denominated facilities was only marginally cheaper than loans on the domestic market. The South Africans therefore indicated that unless the terms of loans were made more conces-

Table 7.8 South Africa: Actual Yields of Pledged Aid, May 1998

Donor Country	Grant Pledge (U.S.$ millions)[a]	Grant Pledge (rank)	Staff Size (rank)[b]	Commitment (rank)[c]	Disbursement (rank)[c]	Yield (rank)	Yield (%)[d]
Finland	11.3	10	8	2	1	1	97.1
Japan	50.0	9	.	1	6	2	70.0
Norway	94.0	8	7	3	7	5	55.0
Netherlands	100.0	7	.	7	1	4	60.0
Denmark	144.2	6	6	4	4	3	63.8
Sweden	174.9	5	3	9	9	9	23.4
Germany	167.3	4	2	10	3	8	16.4
United Kingdom	421.6	3	3	5	8	7	30.4
United States	768.1	2	1	6	5	6	49.2
European Union	927.8	1	3	8	10	10	6.7
All donors (unweighted average)							43.2
All donors (weighted average)							29.9
All Donors, without European Union (weighted average)							51.7

Notes: a. Figures from Table 7.1.
b. Figures from Table 7.4.
c. Figures from Table 7.5.
d. Yield = commitment rate x disbursement rate (see Table 7.5).

sional, the government would have difficulty using them. As the South African rand began to depreciate rapidly against major world currencies in the second quarter of 1998, the government became even more reluctant to draw on these lines of credit. If one were to include loan figures, Japan's performance in committing resources is among the worst of all donors.

The employment of foreign technical assistants was another source of irritation between government and donors. The South African authorities contended correctly that technical expertise already existed within the country and that indigenous consultants were familiar with local conditions. While several donor programs were delayed over this issue, tensions were most explicit with respect to German aid, a large portion of which was made up of technical assistance resources.[112] Germany's mediocre commitment and disbursement record is largely a function of this donor's requirements for the use of expatriates.

South Africa's relations with the United States became strained over democracy and governance. Before and after the political transition, the Americans consistently emphasized the strengthening of civil society as the centerpiece of open and accountable government. Their aid program included grants to independent watchdog organizations, like the Institute for Democracy South Africa (IDASA) and the South African Institute for Race Relations (SAIRR), that have challenged aspects of the government's record on delivering services, protecting minority rights, and combating nepotism and corruption. Revealing sensitivity to criticism, the South African delegation expressed concern "that these NGO programs are not subject to regular discussions with relevant government counterparts regarding initiatives undertaken and objectives pursued."[113] Although few major program changes resulted, the government's public call for a review of all USAID programs in the period preceding U.S. president Bill Clinton's visit to South Africa in March 1998 was unsettling to the bilateral relationship.

In general, though, donor-government relations have not been upset by disagreements over economic policy. As the South African government has adopted its own neoliberal economic strategy, it has met most of the policy conditions on which Western donors might be tempted to insist.[114] Thus, the South African case does not feature the foot-dragging of a government reluctant to agree to unwelcome policy changes and uncommitted to implementing them in practice. Nevertheless, the South African government has staked out a leadership position among African and Commonwealth countries against the general principle of aid conditionality as a tool of foreign policy. It uses its current favored position in international affairs and its preeminence among African countries to criticize interference in the rights of small sovereign states to make their own policy decisions. South Africa also calls for increases in concessional aid—if not for itself, then for the continent as a whole.

Given historically close (or at least neutral) relations with the ANC, certain European donors have found it somewhat easier to raise contentious issues with the South African government. The Swedish delegation has called for "clear central policies related to Government's relationships with NGOs involved in development work," and the Swiss reminded their hosts bluntly that "sometimes NGOs might challenge and criticize government . . . [and that] this different role was important and part of a democratic society."[115] The Danish delegation expressed concern that political violence in KwaZulu-Natal and the high national incidence of crime continued to threaten the country's stability.[116] And, in an apparently coordinated effort, several European delegations observed that "corruption has far-reaching negative impacts on resource management and development cooperation" and urged the government to join them in rooting out this growing problem in South Africa.[117]

The demobilization of civil society. The South African case suggests that, despite civil society's importance to the consolidation of democracy and development, voluntary organizations actually play reduced roles following complex transitions. While South African NGOs and community-based organizations had been major political and economic actors before 1994, their representative and delivery functions were largely usurped by political parties during the transition and by government ministries thereafter. The rise of civil society in South Africa has been followed, if not by a fall, then at least by a stumble. For brevity's sake, we illustrate this claim with reference to just two attributes of voluntary organizations: institutional capacity and political autonomy. Donors helped undermine both.

The capacity of the voluntary organizations in South Africa to achieve their objectives has declined since 1994. First, having achieved the supreme goal of majority rule, many nonstate actors wondered what to do next. Some NGOs simply folded up their tents, while others sought to reorient their organizations to novel challenges of policy advocacy, civic education, or the monitoring of governmental performance. Second, the sector lost many of its most talented leaders, who were attracted to leadership opportunities in the public and private sectors. Third, a general decline in the spirit of voluntarism had a negative impact on NGO capacity. During the "struggle" years, untold numbers of South Africans quietly made heroic personal sacrifices; now, former activists are preoccupied with issues of employment, income, and family welfare and are no longer willing to bear the costs of permanent political mobilization.

Fourth, and most relevant here, NGOs encountered a funding crisis as donor resources, previously lavished on resistance organizations, were redirected to a legitimate government. A 1995 survey of forty-one NGOs showed an average 40 percent drop in foreign funds and yawning budget deficits.[118] By 1998, about sixty adult literacy and basic education centers closed their doors as donor resources dwindled. Many NGOs were forced to retrench staff; others complained that the constant need to raise funds steals valuable time from project work.[119] Nor was the government likely to fill the gap left by donors: its March 1998 budget offered just R 50 million of start-up funding to its own NGO-funding conduit, a mere fraction of what NGOs had requested.[120]

As civil society lost capacity, so its autonomy eroded. Perhaps hoping to mimic the labor movement's integration into the governing ANC coalition, NGOs sought to develop a cozy corporatist relationship with the state. For example, a South African NGO Coalition (SANGOCO) was formed to draft legislation for registering and regulating voluntary associations, to encourage policy advocacy, and to seek government funding. The National Economic Development and Labor Council (NEDLAC), which serves as a consultative forum for business, labor, and government, added a fourth chamber to represent civil society. The government proposed a National Development Agency (NDA), located in the office of the deputy president, to oversee the distribution of donor and government funds to NGOs.[121] Finally, the best-organized NGOs have become private contractors specializing in the delivery of public services to areas of the country and sections of the population that the authorities cannot easily reach.[122]

None of these developments necessarily means that civil society has been captured and subordinated by the state. The relationship between NGOs and the state remains fluid and negotiable and, on many development issues including poverty alleviation, NGOs act as a pressure group to the left of government. But already, government-NGO partnerships have begun to undermine the pluralism and independence of the voluntary sector. Donors who have encouraged such corporatist arrangements (as when the United Nations Development Programme [UNDP] and SIDA underwrote the costs of designing the NDA) have surely strengthened the hand of the state.[123]

At the same time, many citizens seem reluctant to take responsibility for development. As noted earlier, South African civil society is still pervaded by a culture of resistance that originated in the rent and service charge boycotts launched by the mass democratic movement against apartheid township boards. Since 1994, government agencies have found it difficult to collect service fees and tax payments, not only in squatter settlements but also, increasingly, in upscale white suburbs. Officials estimate that one-third of individuals default on their income tax, that one-third of companies evade VAT, and that total unpaid taxes together amount to some R 15 billion annually.[124] Campaigns to promote more responsible citizenship, like the ANC's *masakhane* (let's work together) campaign to encourage voluntary payments of service fees, have to date induced little positive response.

Even more important, civility in society is being displaced by crime. The crime wave that began in the early 1980s peaked during the years of political transition. By 1997, the frequency of some serious offenses (murder, aggravated theft, robbery of businesses) began to wane, but others (especially assault, residential burglary, and rape) continued to climb.[125] Evidence is mounting that former combatants from the apartheid conflict—both old regime security forces and liberation movement guerrillas—are using war skills to pursue careers in crime.[126] Because South Africans of all races lack confidence in the capacity of the police to prevent offenses or punish wrongdoers (see next section), citizens have increasingly taken the law into their own hands. The responses vary across social groups: in wealthy communities, citizens retreat behind the protection of a burgeoning private security industry; in less fortunate communities, people are more likely to resort to vigilante action.[127] Significantly, fear of crime is more prevalent among blacks than whites.[128]

The crime wave has direct implications for reconstruction and development. It undercuts employment to the extent that it discourages foreign investors from establishing or expanding businesses. It drives professionals with essential development skills to leave the country. And it counteracts the government's efforts to extend basic services to neglected areas. For example, government programs to bring electricity and telephones to poor communities are continually disrupted by illegal hookups or the theft of newly installed cables. The costs of implementing housing and infrastructure projects in urban townships rose by an estimated 30 percent as contractors slapped on surcharges to pay for security.[129] The national commissioner of police has described crime as the biggest single threat to South Africa's new democracy. In the words of a political leader, "Crime is the soft underbelly of the Reconstruction and Development Program."[130]

Weak state capacity. If society is becoming less "civil," then the task of consolidating peace, prosperity, and democracy will fall even more heavily on the state. But do state institutions possess the necessary capacities?

Given South Africa's complex constitutional structure—which features national, provincial, and local tiers, each with their own functions, as well as numerous quasi-independent oversight bodies—the problem of building state capacity is not a simple one. Generally speaking, the state apparatus tends to perform less well as one moves from well-established institutions at the political center to new and untested structures in the locality. Moreover, capacity building is complicated by the fact that the ANC is seeking to deliver an expanded range of services even as it radically revises the structure and composition of the state. This juggling act has been aptly likened to "moving the furniture into a new house before you have finished building it."[131]

At the political center, the government is trying simultaneously to "downsize" a bloated public bureaucracy and to make it more racially representative. Some central government ministries became virtually paralyzed as inexperienced new recruits and intransigent old-order functionaries struggled over what to do and how to carry out these reforms.

The problematic quest for public management capacity can be illustrated with reference to the Ministry of Education and the Ministry of Justice, entities that have received large infusions of foreign assistance. The Ministry of Education soon became overwhelmed with the tasks of raising student enrollments while maintaining academic standards at primary, secondary, and tertiary levels across an uneven and segregated educational system. More so than in any other sector, a chasm opened up in education between policy rhetoric and actual performance. Instead of gaining access to "education for all," schoolchildren found themselves in schools that were short of trained teachers and educational materials; the worst-hit schools even lacked basic sanitary facilities. Absenteeism, strikes, and violence plagued many former black institutions.[132] In one province, 103 percent of the education budget was spent on salaries despite national recommendations that personnel costs should not exceed 85 percent.[133] The crisis in education was encapsulated in the Ministry of Education's announcement that in 1997 only 47 percent of eligible pupils passed the secondary school matriculation exam, the lowest rate ever.[134]

As intimated earlier, the state's police and criminal justice systems also performed badly. The Ministry of Safety and Security operates a hierarchical policing structure in which local station commanders report directly to a national commissioner in Pretoria. Because police officers have little incentive to respond to community needs—and are sometimes corrupted by racism or collusion with criminals—they are distrusted by the general public. The Ministry of Justice has exacerbated this negative image by failing to prosecute offenders vigorously. The problems are manifold: prosecutors are inexperienced and overworked; witnesses are inadequately protected; hearings are needlessly postponed; and many badly prepared cases are thrown out of court because of poor communication between detectives and prosecutors. As in the Ministry of Education, poor implementation of public policy in the Ministry of Justice can be traced in good part to middle managers who lack either motivation or experience or who are starved of operating resources.

Below the national level, South Africa's constitution stipulates an expanded range of functions for nine newly defined provincial governments. Together, provincial and local governments manage fully 57 percent of total government expenditures, including the bulk of developmental transfers in key areas such as health, education, and social welfare. Yet provincial governments also find themselves in a quandary due to the

RDP's emphasis on geographical redistribution. Whereas the richer provinces face shrinking budgets and cannot service all their programs, the poorer provinces are receiving more money but do not have the institutional capacity to use it to good effect. Despite pressing social needs, provincial authorities have routinely rolled over unspent funds. The government estimated that up to R 10 million were recycled in the 1997 fiscal year, with greater amounts expected for 1998. Moreover, building a coherent set of government accounts in a context of a new system of national and provincial administration has been one of the DOF's more intractable problems. At present, arrangements to control the financial flow of donor and government funds from the central government to the provinces is extremely weak, creating opportunities for corruption.[135] Quantifying the implementation gap is difficult in a context where RDP projects are ongoing and provincial authorities have few mechanisms to monitor progress.

At the grassroots level, some 850 local government authorities are overloaded with multiple responsibilities for (among other things) water, sanitation, electricity, roads, and refuse services. In March 1997, the minister for local government said that about one out of three local authorities lacked adequate discretionary funds to deliver basic services at an acceptable level, with one out of eight possessing insufficient cash reserves to cover monthly obligations. In the absence of reliable statistical and accounting systems, most nonurban local authorities cannot even characterize their financial positions with any accuracy.[136] A white paper on local government, issued in March 1998, recommended the closure of bankrupt units and their absorption into viable neighboring jurisdictions. While these local government problems manifest themselves as financial difficulties, they clearly run far deeper; the entire arena is a volatile mix of conflicting and unresolved political claims inherited from the apartheid past.

Beyond Aid?

What about the future? Because South Africa is a middle-income country, donors have regarded aid as a temporary measure. From the outset, they planned to reduce aid, or to phase it out entirely, and to replace it with other political and business "partnerships." In a partnership, so goes the rhetoric, "development cooperation does not try to do things *for* developing countries and their people, but *with* them . . . local actors should progressively take the lead while external partners back their efforts to assume greater responsibility for their own development."[137]

Exit strategies. Almost all of South Africa's donors proposed exit strategies, though these plans did not always pan out exactly as intended. Some saw 1999 as a watershed year, during which power-sharing arrangements would expire, a second round of elections would be held, and Nelson Mandela would step down from the presidency. Thus, 1999 would end conclusively the process of political transition. At first glance, this looked like a good time to leave.

In 1998, the Norwegian government was still publicly committed to withdrawing its bilateral aid presence by 1999.[138] Initially, the Danish government planned to follow suit, but by 1997 it pledged a further $20 million and extended its timetable for a further three years.[139] The Swedish government's aid mandate runs through the year 2003, but it too plans to review its program in the wake of the 1999 elections; if this review confirms South Africa's progress, SIDA will continue to wind down, boosting and extending assistance only if democracy is deemed to be unraveling.[140] Other donors remain committed to a phased withdrawal. Ireland anticipates concluding its ten-year aid operation by 2004, after which South Africa will have to depend on its own resources.[141] The United States also has an explicit exit strategy; it has reduced its 1999 commitment by one-third from 1998 levels, and it plans to close the USAID mission in Pretoria in 2005.[142]

The aid representatives of other countries, like the United Kingdom, state that they will remain in South Africa. The Labour government of Prime Minister Tony Blair has reorganized its aid establishment into a Department for International Development (DFID), which intends to offer more resources and longer-term commitments to help eliminate poverty. Following OECD (Organization for Economic Cooperation and Development) guidelines, DFID draws a distinction between aid and (government, NGO, and private) "partnerships." In evaluating such programs, emphasis will be placed on development outcomes, as measured against precise targets, rather than on aid contributions.[143]

In reality, all major donors are likely to retain some kind of reduced presence in South Africa for the foreseeable future. The Norwegians are negotiating an extension to their exit plans, and the Americans are exploring possibilities for endowing selected NGOs to take over priority development activities. Donors are agreed that any 1999 termination date now looks terribly premature. While the transition to democracy is essentially complete, work remains to be done in consolidating fragile new political institutions. And major needs remain in completing both the economic and (especially) the peace transitions. Still, donors would clearly like to change the nature of their assistance, a subject to which we now turn.

From aid to trade. Since the end of the Cold War, international relations have been marked by the erosion of state sovereignty and the globalization of commercial markets. Under these circumstances, Western governments expect aid to be gradually supplanted by trade and investment, especially in "emerging markets" like South Africa.

This was the leitmotif of U.S. president Bill Clinton's extensive tour of Africa in early 1998, which included a four-day state visit to South Africa. At every stop he underlined the U.S. desire to transform lopsided donor-recipient relations into mutually beneficial exchanges between economic equals.[144] The United States is not alone among South Africa's partners in defining a new strategy of cooperation that downgrades aid in favor of the aggressive promotion of commercial links. The German government has argued that a booming South African economy can do far more to alleviate poverty than aid ever could; this attitude underpins Germany's program to create an enabling policy environment for commercial exchanges and for the promotion of local and foreign entrepreneurs.[145] Similarly, the Danish government aims to supplement traditional aid programs with direct business-to-business ties between Danish and South African companies.[146] As president of EU, finally, the United Kingdom declared its commitment to working for an early establishment of a South Africa–EU free trade pact.[147]

For most donors, South Africa is either their largest partner in Africa or their fastest-growing African market. Certainly this is the case for long-standing commercial associates like the United Kingdom and the United States, but it is increasingly true for others, too. Trade between Australia and South Africa, for example, doubled between 1994 and 1996 alone.[148] And the benefits run both ways: South Africa's trade deficit with Switzerland is dropping sharply as it sells more gold ingots in this prime market.[149]

But Pretoria has expressed mixed feelings about the proposed shift from aid to trade. President Mandela at first reacted sharply to the Clinton administration's Africa Growth and Opportunities Act (AGOA), a free trade initiative that expands U.S. trade preferences for African exports, provides loan guarantees for U.S. investors in Africa, and promises debt relief.[150] His objection centered on political conditions that would disqualify South Africa from U.S. preferences if it continued to trade with Iran, Iraq, and Libya—countries the United States regards as rogue regimes. The public airing of such policy disagreements can be read as an indication that the bilateral relationship between the United States and South Africa is maturing into a partnership on an equal footing. Speaking as a continental leader, Mandela has also called for an increase in aid to poorer African countries;[151] in response, Clinton pledged to restore U.S. assistance to Africa to earlier levels. Putting a positive spin on this revised U.S. position, a senior U.S. official remarked that "it was South Africa that reminded us of the tremendous need and benefits of these twins [aid and trade] and of the contribution that foreign assistance makes helping to create the enabling environment for increased trade." Deputy President Mbeki later announced that AGOA now had South African support.[152]

The private sector. With aid on the wane, South Africa's private sector will be called upon to assume a larger role in development financing. Since

1994, many established business houses have expanded their corporate social investments (CSI). Like donors, the private sector climbed on the RDP bandwagon: in the words of the chief executive of the Council of South African Bankers, "We can't imagine what would happen if the RDP is a failure," echoing the sentiments of a well-known industrialist who had said of the majority population, "If they don't eat, we don't sleep."[153]

The origins of CSI in South Africa date back to the pretransition period when North American- and European-based multinational corporations were challenged about their social responsibilities and, in reaction, sought to comply with codes of business conduct like the Sullivan principles and EC corporate directives. CSI was on the agenda too when forward-looking South African business executives sought out the ANC in exile in order to prepare for a postapartheid environment. More recently, CSI has come to be seen as a means to make good on affirmative action and black economic empowerment in South Africa's white-dominated corporate world.

Since 1994, a group of local companies has formed the Southern Africa Grantmakers' Association (SAGA) to share information on philanthropy. SAGA encourages its members to commit 1 percent of after-tax profits to CSI.[154] Several companies have joined forces to establish the Joint Education Trust (JET). With a startup budget of R 500 million, JET aims to upgrade the quality of teaching in the formal education system, advance adult basic education, and improve education and job prospects for unemployed youth.[155] Other companies have launched education or social welfare initiatives that benefit existing or prospective employees, although whether these go beyond narrow corporate self-interest to broader social impact is still unclear.

Along the same lines, South African companies have taken a special interest in the crime conundrum. A lobby group calling itself Business Against Crime (BAC) has helped to set the policy agenda in a sector where government is widely perceived to be ineffective. Rather than criticizing the government, however, BAC has sought to play a "partnership" role—for example, by arranging for a no-nonsense businessman to be seconded to government as the architect of a national crime prevention strategy. The business community has also become a resource provider, in one instance donating laptop computers and cellular telephones to community police posts. But again, the coverage of such initiatives is uneven at best.

With the closure of the RDP office in 1996 and a looming economic recession in 1998, the private sector may lose some of its appetite for CSI. Unlike in donor countries, the laws of South Africa do not offer tax incentives for corporate donations. SANGOCO, the national NGO coalition, has lobbied parliament, the bureaucracy, and the national tax commission for tax breaks that would enable companies and wealthy individuals to deduct charitable contributions to NGOs. So far, these efforts have been in vain.

South Africa as a regional power. South Africa is the dominant power of the southern Africa region. It boasts the largest, most diverse, and most advanced economy on the continent, with a gross domestic product three times that of Nigeria or Egypt.[156] Backed by public policies that encourage export-led growth and a sophisticated financial infrastructure, South African companies are making significant inroads into the economies of neighboring states.[157] South Africa has naturally assumed leadership of the finance and investment portfolio of the Southern Africa Development Community (SADC) and been charged by member states to design a free trade zone and development fund for the region.

At the same time, South Africa has staked a claim to continental leadership, by campaigning, for example, for the IMF and World Bank to pay greater attention to Africa's needs for debt forgiveness and market access. It has used annual consultations with bilateral donors to urge the West to move ahead on its Highly Indebted Poor Country Initiative by extending debt relief to thirty African countries.[158] South Africa has also attempted to exert political influence abroad, intervening in support of human rights in Nigeria and the peaceful resolution of conflict in the Democratic Republic of Congo, actions that have engendered Western support. In the vision of the country's likely next president, South Africa is a catalyst in the sub-Saharan region, not only for democratization, but also for a comprehensive "African Renaissance."

As international donors look beyond old models of aid, they see new opportunities in this vision. Many of South Africa's external partners are reconceptualizing development cooperation on a regional basis, with South African institutions playing leadership, coordinating, or intermediary roles. South Africa has begun to explore regional initiatives in trade, investment, peacekeeping, democracy, and governance with Sweden, Switzerland, Germany, Denmark, Canada, the United Kingdom, and the United States (among others).[159] A note of caution was sounded by a Norwegian official, speaking on behalf of the Nordic countries, who reminded the government that some neighboring states resent the penetration of their economies by South African companies and SADC's trade imbalance with South Africa.[160] Nor do other regional leaders automatically accept South Africa's political ascendancy, as illustrated by Robert Mugabe of Zimbabwe's rejection of Mandela's peace initiatives in Congo. Any regional aid strategy will have to offset such reactions.

Conclusion

In countries undergoing complex transitions, the long-term challenge is to consolidate and build upon gains made in democracy, prosperity, and peace. In countries like South Africa, where the transition was led by political processes, the health of the new democracy has come to hinge on subsequent economic and social developments. The effective provision of mass benefits is particularly important in South Africa, because the new electorate is drawn disproportionately from segments of the population that remain severely disadvantaged. As the country approached a second round of open elections in 1999, the campaign centered on the performance of the ANC-led government in delivering jobs, services, and security. While the ANC was easily reelected,[161] many voters continue to reject its market-friendly strategy, and some have even begun to question the developmental effectiveness of democracy.[162]

The onus for delivering social and economic benefits falls not only on the state, however, but also on its partners in the development enterprise. These include both international donor agencies (who help to mobilize resources) and NGOs (who help to implement development programs). Both these sets of partners have been actively involved in policymaking under South Africa's new dispensation. Indeed, the immediate posttransition period in South Africa was a productive interlude of progressive reform, during which popular policies were enacted for almost every development sector. But amid the welter of promising policy papers, the nagging question remains: are the state and its partners effective enough to ensure proper implementation?

Achievements and Gaps

This study has focused on the first links in the long chain of development cooperation that stretches from donor to ultimate beneficiary. We have reviewed pledges of aid by international donors and the subsequent commitment and disbursement of resources to South African development agencies. The study has shown that by May 1998, and excluding the European Union, the South African government had received about one-half of the official development assistance originally pledged to it by international donors (see Table 7.8). In monetary terms, this yield (commitments multiplied by disbursements) amounted to an estimated $2.4 billion over four years, double the average annual volume of disbursed aid to South Africa before May 1994.[163]

Is the glass of development cooperation therefore half empty or half full? There are several reasons to view the South African case in a positive light. First, aid pledges are broad targets set by politicians to signal diplomatic support; as such, they should be interpreted loosely as little more than statements of intent. Yet, within four years (and again excepting the EU), South Africa's donors had already converted three-quarters of total promises into firm financial commitments. This suggests that donors were well on their way to fully following through on pledges. Second, according to standards broadly accepted within the donor community, commitments of ODA (rather than pledges) are the relevant benchmark against which aid performance should be measured. By these standards, donors (the EU again excepted) can be seen to have disbursed rapidly two-thirds of the grants to which they had officially committed themselves. These figures represent estimable achievements, especially when one considers that the pledge period will last through 1999, by which time commitment and disbursement rates are likely to have risen further.

Yet major concerns remain. In general, the Western powers were so eager to demonstrate political support for the South African "miracle" that they hastily pledged more aid money than could easily be managed. Administrative bottlenecks arose at both the donor and recipient ends. The programs of the large donors were often too ambitious, inflexible, or bureaucratized to immediately alleviate pressing social needs. Thus, the capacity of large donors to disburse resources often lagged behind the readiness of some of South Africa's better-organized government and NGO agencies to proceed with program implementation. The case of the EU— whose abysmal disbursement record pulls South Africa's overall aid yield level down below 30 percent—requires further investigation and correction. By contrast, small- or medium-scale donors who could move money rapidly were frustrated by the limited capacity of other South African partners to absorb it. In these cases, it was donors who scaled back their annual pledges and commitments to better match the perceived pace at which aid funds could be fruitfully applied.

We have found that gaps in delivery tend to widen as one moves along the cooperation chain. Notably, the disbursement gap (one-third of commitments) is greater than the commitment gap (one-quarter of pledges). This study has devoted only passing attention to the later phases, especially program expenditure and the delivery of goods and services. In part, this is because the South African transition is too recent to have generated concrete results. Nonetheless, one cannot ignore the fact that the disparity between disbursements and implementation is the widest gap of all, even though we cannot yet quantify its size precisely.

We conclude that implementation delays are due principally to deep deficits of institutional capacity within the country itself. Capacity concerns have various dimensions—human, financial, and organizational—and they arise at several levels of the state and society. Civil servants, old and new, have little experience in serving poor communities. Too much public funding is tied up in bureaucratic overheads. And frontline delivery agencies— especially local government and the security services—have been discredited by their associations with the old regime and require rebuilding from the ground up. Even South Africa's once vibrant civil society has not fully reoriented itself from the tasks of political liberation to those of socioeconomic development. For these reasons, the gap between disbursed resources and program implementation remains the weakest link in the development cooperation chain.

Policy Lessons

The South African case points to policy lessons that are relevant to aiding reconstruction and development in similar settings. For ease of presentation, these will be listed in point form.

• To gain influence over the size, terms, and composition of aid flows, a host government must: (1) enjoy international diplomatic goodwill as a result of a successful political transition, (2) limit aid to a relatively small proportion of government revenues, and (3) conduct aid negotiations principally through bilateral channels.

• To commit and disburse pledged aid quickly, international donors must: (1) package aid into small programs and projects, (2) avoid rigid terms or explicit policy conditions, and (3) employ adequate field staff to oversee aid delivery.

• The coordination of aid flows is enhanced if donors voluntarily adhere to policy priorities identified by the host government. By the same token, care must be taken that an emerging policy orthodoxy does not neglect important sectors, including the public safety and security sector.

• Governments that claim authority to coordinate aid must ensure that they develop sufficient capacity to (1) monitor aid flows, (2) identify areas of duplication, and (3) convene donor consultative forums.

• Donors should not expect NGOs to become effective developmental agents at a time when international support is being redirected to the government. For their part, governments should resist trying to coordinate nongovernmental development initiatives or to supervise the distribution of funding in civil society.

• Donors and governments should collaborate on policy reform, particularly to make development benefits more accessible to neglected populations. But investments in policy formulation must be complemented by adequate resources for implementation.

• Delivering basic services to poor populations requires local institutional capacity. Donors and governments should continue to emphasize the development of viable financial and management systems for local institutions of all types, but especially for representative local government.

Comparative Reflections

Finally, the South African case casts light on the dynamics of complex transitions. The various dimensions of "triple transitions" do not unfold according to a common schedule and, in turn, unsynchronized initiatives create distinctive sequences of change in different countries.

Within a couple of years of South Africa's founding election in April 1994—and certainly by the time its liberal constitution came into effect in February 1997 accompanied by broad acceptance from all ideological quarters—a political transition to democracy can be deemed to have been completed.[164] The remaining challenge of building a supportive political culture for the country's impressive formal array of democratic institutions can be regarded as an issue mainly of democratic consolidation. The same cannot be said for other transiting entities like Cambodia, Bosnia and Herzegovina, and the Palestinian territories, where the legitimacy of constitutional rules—even the boundaries of the state—remain in dispute.

By contrast, the transition to a market economy in South Africa is incomplete. Indeed, the neoliberal direction of economic change charted by the South African government's GEAR strategy was contested vigorously by public opinion and within the high reaches of the ruling alliance. By 1998, South Africa's "emerging market" economy had been battered by investment and currency crises in Asia and stood on the brink of recession, raising more questions about the consequences of market reforms. But, unlike in Russia, the economic crisis was not so severe as to threaten to bring down the government. Economic reformers in South Africa retained the upper hand in policy debates and decisions. Whatever the ultimate outcome, however, the economic transition in South Africa is already destined to be far more extended and uncertain than the political transition.

But the most intractable aspect of South Africa's triple transition is the achievement of social peace. The brutality of the apartheid regime—revealed vividly in public hearings before South Africa's Truth and Reconciliation Commission—has spawned a lasting legacy of violence. This heritage was revealed in the excesses of apartheid and liberation politics before 1990 and in turf struggles between local party leaders during the transition period; since 1994, it has been manifest in extraordinarily high levels of criminal and social violence. Even as government authorities seek to develop innovative strategies to root out crime, new forms emerge in the guise of international syndicates and terrorist gangs. South Africa has lagged behind places like El Salvador and Mozambique, where considerable resources were devoted to demobilizing and redeploying combatants into productive roles in economy and society. In this regard—and again in contrast to El Salvador, Bosnia and Herzegovina, and the Palestinian territories—South Africa has suffered from a reluctance on the part of the international donor community to engage problems of safety and security with anything like the volume of attention and resources that they deserve. As such, the incomplete peace transition remains the Achilles' heel of South Africa's political "miracle."

Not only are complex transitions unsynchronized but, in part, they may even be inherently contradictory. Gains along one dimension of transition may undermine progress along another. Because democratization raises demands for accountability in the use of state power, it loosens institutional controls over society. Because market reform requires structural adjustments in order to achieve long-term economic gains, it imposes short-term costs on some of society's most vulnerable members. In these ways—not only in South Africa, but in the other transiting countries considered in this book—political and economic liberalization may inhibit the attainment of social peace. International aid donors should sharpen their analyses of such interactions. Only when we better understand the dynamics of complex transitions will we be able to predict the ramifications of external interventions and effectively direct aid to the places where it will do the most good.

Notes

The authors thank Claude Kabemba, Claire Kruger, and Nicholas Bratton for help in identifying and analyzing source materials.
1. See Friedman, *The Long Journey,* and Friedman, "South Africa," p. 1165.
2. Ibid.
3. See Friedman, "No Easy Stroll to Dominance."
4. Steven Holtzman classifies South Africa as a country with only "some" conflict areas as a means of distinguishing it from countries with "major conflicts"; see his "Post-Conflict Reconstruction." Terry Karl disagrees, regarding South Africa as a case of "war transition"; see her "War Transitions."
5. Thompson, *A History of South Africa,* pp. 256–257. A definitive source is Wilson and Ramphele, "Children in South Africa."
6. Landsberg, "Exporting Peace?"
7. Geldenhuys, *Isolated States,* p. 162.
8. See Landsberg, "Directing from the Stalls?"
9. United Nations, *The United Nations and Apartheid,* p. 48.
10. Ibid., p. 83.
11. Government of Sweden, *Sweden's Development Cooperation with South Africa.*
12. Overseas Development Administration, *British Aid to South Africa.*
13. Ibid.
14. Ibid.
15. Geldenhuys, "The Foreign Factor in South Africa's 1992 Referendum," p. 45.
16. Kabemba, "Political and Economic Implications of the Reincorporation of South Africa into SADC."
17. Thompson, *A History of South Africa,* p. 250.
18. Landsberg, "Directing from the Stalls?" pp. 285–287.
19. USAID, *USAID/South Africa Briefing Book,* p. 2.
20. UNDP, *Development Cooperation Report for South Africa, 1993,* p. 5.
21. Ibid., p. 8.

22. Johnson and Schlemmer, *Launching Democracy in South Africa,* pp. 326–332.

23. The RDP was coauthored by Congress of South African Trade Unions, the South African Communist Party, the South African National Civics Association, the National Education Coordinating Committee, and, of course, the ANC. It was extensively "workshopped," critiqued, and redrafted.

24. United Nations, *The United Nations and Apartheid,* p. 127.

25. In addition, Canada's International Development Research Center (IDRC) underwrote preparations by the Congress Alliance's macroeconomic research group to develop a macroeconomic growth strategy.

26. See Landsberg and de Coning, "From 'Tar Baby' to Transition."

27. African National Congress, *The Reconstruction and Development Programme.* See also *A Basic Guide to the Reconstruction and Development Programme* (gopher://gopher.anc.org.za). For commentary, see Simkins, "Problems of Reconstruction," and Adelzadeh and Padayachee, "The RDP White Paper," p. 5.

28. *South Africa Yearbook, 1995,* p. 54.

29. Ibid.

30. *The RDP (Reconstruction and Development) Monitor* 2, no. 2 (October 1995).

31. Ibid.

32. Ibid.

33. Government of South Africa, *Growth, Employment and Redistribution.* For a detailed assessment of GEAR, see *Indicator South Africa,* 14, no. 3 (spring 1997).

34. South Africa Foundation, *Growth for All.* For commentary on the influence of international and domestic investors on economic policy, see Habib and Padayachee, "South Africa."

35. Thompson, *A History of South Africa,* p. 263. Promises of official development assistance were more readily forthcoming than offers from private investors, who "remained cautious."

36. Shaw, "The Bloody Backdrop."

37. The quotations are drawn from statements made by the heads of the U.S. and German delegations to annual bilateral consultations with the South African government in April 1998 (p. 2) and November 1997 (annex 3), respectively. Hereafter, annual bilateral consultations with the South African government will be designated in these endnotes as "AC" and identified by the name of the country and the date of the consultation, followed by the page and annex number.

38. AC, SA-Denmark, 9/97, p. 2.

39. In some cases, the figures for ODA grants include indirect grants to NGOs and private sector organizations that were channeled through government departments. The figures are estimates because the researchers were unable to locate a definitive list of aggregate pledges. Figures provided by the government of South Africa's Department of Finance did not cover all countries and focused mainly on commitments and disbursements (i.e., not pledges). The United Nations Development Programme (UNDP) had yet to produce a comprehensive Development Cooperation Report for the years after 1993, though such a compilation was about to be commissioned at the time of writing.

40. Including Belgium, China, the Flemish government, France, Greece, Italy, the Kuwait Fund, and Spain.

41. That is, the International Labour Organization (ILO), UNFPA, UNCTAD, and the World Bank.

42. The total value of ODA disbursed in South Africa was U.S.$295.3 million in 1992 and $306.8 million in 1993. See UNDP, *Development Cooperation Report for South Africa.*

43. Interview, World Bank country representative in South Africa, March 21, 1998.

44. "Business Report: Budget Special '98," *Independent Newspapers* (Johannesburg), March 12, 1998, p. 12. See also South African Institute of Race Relations, *South Africa Survey, 1996/1997,* p. 697.

45. R 12.5 billion = U.S.$2.7 billion in January 1997.

46. UNDP, *Development Cooperation Report for South Africa,* p. 7.

47. AC, SA-EU, 5/97, p. 1.

48. Ibid., p. 2.

49. Government of South Africa, *Multi-Annual Indicative Programme*, p. 2.

50. Interview, director, IDC, March 13, 1998.

51. Ibid.

52. Government of South Africa, *Progress Report on Commitments and Disbursements of Donor Funds.*

53. Ibid.

54. Ibid.; see also annual consultation minutes for each country.

55. This amount consisted of a $24.5 million IBRD loan to government, $19.6 million in grants to various public agencies, $20.8 million in Multilateral Investment Guarantee Agency (MIGA) loan guarantees, and $37.8 million in International Finance Corporation (IFC) equity investments for South African companies. See Department of Finance, International Development Finance Unit, "World Bank and Commonwealth Operational Programme in South Africa," mimeo, September 1998.

56. Interview, director, IDC, March 13, 1998.

57. South Africa had "by far the largest programme" of Danish assistance to countries defined by DANIDA as "in transition" (AC, SA-Denmark, 9/95, p. 2).

58. AC, SA-EU, 8/96, p. 10.

59. AC, SA-US, 10/95, pp. 4–5.

60. The data in Table 7.3 are incomplete in several major respects: (1) they refer to financial commitments since no sectoral breakdown is available for pledges; (2) many donors do not provide sectoral breakdowns for commitments; and (3) donors do not include all projects in their status reports, hence some commitments are excluded from the calculations. Thus, these figures are rough orders of magnitude rather than precise measurements and should be treated with caution.

61. Institute for Security Studies (Midrand), "Issue Areas for Future Funding."

62. AC, SA-US, 10/95, p. 5.

63. AC, SA-Norway, 11/97, p. 7.

64. AC, SA-EU, 5/97, p. 10.

65. AC, SA-US, 10/95, p. 5; 11/96, p. 4; 4/98, p. 4.

66. AC, SA-Sweden, 11/97, annex 4.

67. AC, SA-Norway, 11/97, p. 4; AC, SA-Switzerland, 11/97, p. 5.

68. AC, SA-UK, 3/96, p. 3; AC, SA-Switzerland, 11/97, p. 5.

69. See *South Africa Yearbook, 1997.* The ratio of foreign debt to total export earnings declined from 126.1 percent in 1985 to 93.8 percent in 1995. Interest payments on foreign debt equaled no more than 6.4 percent of total export earnings in 1996.

70. Interview, director, IDC, March 13, 1998.

71. USIA (United States Information Agency), "US-South Africa Binational Commission Fact Sheet." See also "Executive Deputy President Thabo Mbeki to Host US Vice President Al Gore for the Fifth Meeting of the SA-US Binational Commission," Pretoria, Office of the Executive Deputy President, February 18, 1998. On the SA-German Binational Commission, see Friedman, "Give Us the Tools," especially pp. 3–4.

72. Somewhat exceptionally, the deputy minister of finance "opened" the first annual consultations with Norway in 1996.

73. AC, SA-EU, 3/98, p. 1.

74. AC, SA-Germany, 11/97, annex 3; AC, SA-Sweden, 11/96, annex 4.

75. AC, SA-UK, 3/96, p. 3.

76. AC, SA-Sweden, 11/96, p. 5.

77. AC, SA-Denmark, 9/95, p. 3.

78. AC, SA-US, 10/95, p. 3.

79. AC, SA-Sweden, 11/96, p. 4.

80. AC, SA-Canada, 10/95, p. 5.

81. AC, SA-UK, 3/96, p. 7; AC, SA-Sweden, 11/96, p. 7.

82. The Swedish International Development Agency (SIDA) went so far as to provide technical and financial assistance for this purpose (AC, 11/97, p. 4).

83. AC, SA-US, 10/95, p. 3; 11/96, p. 8.

84. AC, SA-Denmark, 9/97, p. 4.

85. AC, SA-Germany, 11/97, p. 11.

86. Ibid., annex 5.

87. AC, SA-Germany, 6/96, p. 4; 10/96, p. 9.

88. AC, SA-Sweden, 11/96, p. 3; 11/97, p. 2.

89. Ibid., 11/97, p. 3.

90. AC, SA-UK, 3/96, p. 4.

91. For example, AC, SA-UK, 3/96, p. 5. Concerns were also expressed about the questionable legal status of the many projects where procedures had not been followed (e.g., where funds had been deposited in free-standing bank accounts) and about the capability of government auditors to track donor funds, especially after they had been mixed with general revenues.

92. Ibid., p. 3.

93. AC, SA-Canada, 9/96, p. 3; 11/97, p. 4.

94. *RDP Monitor* 2, no. 2 (October 1995).

95. Ibid.

96. "Ministry Gets 'Realistic' About Housing Targets," *The Sunday Independent*, September 27, 1998, p. 9.

97. *RDP Monitor* 3, no. 11 (August 1997).

98. *RDP Monitor* 2, no. 2 (October 1995).

99. Ibid.

100. AC, SA-EU, 4/98, pp. 6, 13.

101. "Opening Statement: South Africa," AC, SA-Germany, 11/97, annex 2.

102. AC, SA-EU, 3/98, p. 1.

103. AC, SA-Germany, 6/97, p. 2.

104. European Union, "Special Report No. 7/98," p. 96.

105. The Danes and the Canadians, among others, required quick disbursement; warnings that undisbursed funds could be lost seem to have propelled the cooperation process forward. The Americans, for their part, advised that South African government efforts to change agreed-upon sectoral priorities (for example to introduce a new line of funding for agriculture) could result in the reallocation of unspent funds to partners other than South Africa.

106. Based on remarks of NGO leaders at a ten-year retrospective program review, USAID/South Africa, Pretoria, November 4, 1997.

107. For example, South African NGOs cited the programs of the Swedish International Development Agency as "an ideal model which NGOs wish other donors would follow" (AC, SA-Sweden, 11/96, annex 4).

108. Pearson's r = -.582, significance = .07.

109. Spearman's r = -.830, significance = .003.

110. It should be noted, however, that relatively favorable staff sizes were not enough to ensure good yield rates for Sweden and Germany.

111. Letter from the deputy minister of finance to the ambassador, EU Delegation, May 2, 1997.

112. AC, SA-Germany, 6/97, 11/97.

113. AC, SA-US, 4/98, p. 6. The United States replied that "90 percent of [its] nonbilateral program is directly supportive of government priorities and programs" (p. 4).

114. For example, "IMF Report Finds SA Economy's Fundamentals Solid," *Business Day* (Johannesburg), July 7, 1998.

115. AC, SA-Switzerland, 9/97, p. 4.

116. AC, SA-Denmark, 9/96, p. 4; 9/97, p. 3.

117. AC, SA-EU, 3/98, p. 4; AC, SA-Germany, 11/97, p. 13.

118. James and Caliguire, "Renewing Civil Society," p. 63. See also Community Agency for Social inquiry, *Tango in the Dark*.

119. "Too Little, Too Late for NGOs?" *Mail and Guardian*, September 18–24, 1998, p. 36.

120. *The Sunday Independent* (Johannesburg), March 15, 1998.

121. Advisory Committee, Office of the Executive Deputy President, *Structural Relationships Between Government and Civil Society Organizations*. The forerunner of the NDA was an interim body, formed March 1996, known as the Transitional National Development Trust (TNDT). The TNDT administered a fund of R 120 million that was jointly contributed by the EU and the South African government, 68 percent of which was disbursed by November 1997. See Habib and Taylor, "South Africa."

122. For useful discussion of these and related issues, see Humphries and Reitzes, eds., *Civil Society After Apartheid*.

123. Indeed, the recommended model for the NDA as a statutory board seems to have been derived from Sweden, following a SIDA-funded study tour there. See Advisory Committee, *Structural Relationships,* p. 23.

124. *The Sunday Independent* (Johannesburg), September 6, 1998, p. 7, quoting sources in the South African Revenue Service and (the Katz) Tax Commission.

125. Shaw, "Of Crime and Country," pp. 1–5.

126. Friedman, "Not Just Order But Democracy Threatened."

127. This paragraph is based on Mark Shaw's excellent "South Africa: Crime in Transition."

128. In Johannesburg, 58 percent of whites and 67 percent of blacks feel unsafe in their neighborhoods at night. The relevant figures for Cape Town are 20 percent and 50 percent, respectively. Institute for Security Studies, *Victim Surveys*.

129. Estimates provided by Business Against Crime as reported in *The Mercury* (Durban), March 30, 1998.

130. Shaw, "Of Crime and Country," p. 157.

131. Interview, mayor of Durban, August 19, 1998.

132. "Inadequate Security in Public Schools."

133. Zafar, "An Analysis of the Education Crisis in KwaZulu-Natal," p. 4.

134. Education Foundation, *EduSource Data News,* p. 1.

135. "Public Service Corruption Has Devoured 21bn," *Business Day* (Johannesburg), August 6, 1998.

136. "The Collection of Local Government Statistics in South Africa," AC, SA-Switzerland, 9/97, annex 2.

137. OECD/DAC, *Shaping the 21st Century,* p. 13.

138. AC, SA-Norway, 11/97, p. 4.

139. Interview, DANIDA, March 1998.

140. Interview, SIDA, March 1998.

141. AC, SA-Ireland, 12/96, pp. 3–4.

142. AC, SA-US, 4/98, p. 3. Against an indicative allocation of $72.6 million for 1998, U.S. assistance was set to decline to U.S.$50 million in 1999: "a clear indication of a rapidly declining funding curve."

143. AC, SA-UK, 2/98, pp. 2, 12. For targets see also OECD/DAC, *Shaping the 21st Century,* p. 2.

144. "Clinton Punts a US Partnership with SA," *Business Day,* March 27, 1998.

145. AC, SA-Germany, 10/96, p. 24.

146. AC, SA-Denmark, 11/97, p. 4.

147. AC, SA-UK, 2/98, p. 2.

148. AC, SA-Australia, 3/98, p. 2.

149. AC, SA-Switzerland, 9/97, p. 3.

150. "Mandela's Advice Shocks U.S. Officials," *The Independent on Saturday,* March 28, 1998.

151. "Mandela Champions Cause of Poor Nations," *Business Day,* May 20, 1998.

152. "Mbeki Broadly Supports Africa Bill," *Business Day,* August 28, 1998.

153. Both quotations are from Simkins, "Problems of Reconstruction," p. 84.

154. Alperson, *Foundations for a New Democracy,* p. 9.

155. Including Liberty Life, Anglo-American, Gencor JCI, Shell, Southern Life, and Standard Bank. Ibid., p. 6.

156. *South Africa at a Glance, 1997–98,* p. 64.

157. Kornegay and Landsberg, "Phaphama iAfrica," p. 4.

158. AC, SA-Germany, 11/97, annex 2; Sweden, 11/97, p. 2; UK, 2/98, p. 1.

159. AC, SA-Sweden, 11/96, p. 2; Switzerland, 9/97, p. 6; Germany, 10/96, p. 24; Canada, 11/97, p. 5; UK, 3/96, p. 3; US, 11/96, p. 8.

160. "Regional Slant to Norway's Aid for SA," *Business Day,* July 15, 1998.

161. For example, Friedman, "Next Poll to Gauge Democracy's Support"; Mattes, "Votes Available."

162. Mattes and Thiel, "The Prospects for Democratic Consolidation in South Africa."

163. Annual bilateral disbursements averaged about $300 million per annum in 1992 and 1993 and about $600 million between May 1994 and May 1998.

164. Juan Linz and Alfred Stepan consider a transition to democracy to be complete when the state eliminates competing claims to its authority and major political interests agree on core constitutional procedures. See their *Problems of Democratic Transition and Consolidation,* p. 3.

8

Bosnia and Herzegovina

Zlatko Hertić, Amela Šapčanin
& Susan L. Woodward

IN THE SIX YEARS FOLLOWING THE START OF BOSNIA AND Herzegovina's war of independence in 1992, financial assistance to the country surpassed $5 billion in multilateral pledges alone.[1] These included eight multilateral pledging conferences, three other voluntary arrangements, and two wartime precursors of subsequent multilateral peace implementation programs. The pledges had three goals: reconstruction of war damage, consolidation of cease-fire agreements and the implementation of a peace accord, and the transition to a market economy. This study examines their objectives, programs, sectoral allocation, coordination structure, and the methodological difficulties of assessing delivery and implementation.

In comparative context, the Bosnian case is a positive story of international interest, commitment, and delivery. The fact that it represents what donors can do when political will is present makes its experience, both good and bad, of particular importance for future cases. The timing of this study intersects the peace process and the reconstruction effort in mid-course—and when the transition process toward democracy and markets had only just begun. This makes its findings necessarily tentative. Significant obstacles to drawing definitive conclusions also exist in the quality and variety of available data: the existence of three official, contradictory databases; inconsistent and incomplete reporting; and deliberate donor efforts to conceal pledge gaps. The differences in these sources are so great, in fact, that estimates of the actual delivery and implementation of aid differed by more than $1 billion. As a result of the difficulties this causes in evaluating pledged aid, we call upon the donor community to improve the accountability and transparency of its aid through reforms that could include standardizing the definition and reporting of actual aid flows.

The provisional explanations offered here for apparent gaps and delays between aid pledged and that actually delivered and implemented distinguish between donors and recipients. On the donor side are problems in the coordination mechanisms, implementation capacity, and use of political conditionality in the allocation of aid. On the recipient side, continuing political disagreements about the goal of the peace accord, its cumbersome decisionmaking procedures, and insufficient transparency and accountability on the use of aid take prominence.

Country Context

Bosnia and Herzegovina was one of five independent states created out of the dissolution of the Socialist Federal Republic of Yugoslavia. According to the prewar census, the Bosnian population in 1991 was 4,366,000, inhabiting a country of 51,129 square kilometers (about one and a half times the size of Belgium). A multinational republic—some would say a "mini-Yugoslavia"—Bosnia was home to three constitutionally recognized national communities: Bosniacs, members of the Muslim community, were 43.7 percent of the population in 1991; Serbs, belonging to the Serbian Orthodox Church, were 31.4 percent; and Croats, of the Roman Catholic Church, were 17.3 percent. The remaining 7.6 percent of the prewar population declared their national identity as Yugoslav or another (minority) nationality.

Following its declaration of independence in March 1992, Bosnia and Herzegovina was engulfed in a four-year-long war launched by the opponents of its independence. These included segments of the Croat and Serb populations, remnants of the Yugoslav army, and Bosnia's two neighbors—Croatia on the north and west and Serbia on the east—who intervened to support the Bosnian-Croat and Bosnian-Serb armies in the country. More than one-half of the population of Bosnia and Herzegovina either lost their lives, were injured, were internally displaced, or took refuge abroad. According to initial World Bank estimates, productive capacity destroyed by the war was valued at $15–20 billion.[2] Bosnian government authorities estimate the overall war damage, including loss of personal property, at $50–70 billion. Industrial production fell by 90 percent from the prewar level, unemployment reached 90 percent, and 90 percent of the population relied on international humanitarian assistance for survival. Trade and supply infrastructure and relationships were in many cases completely severed, and access to credits dissolved. The government's budget depended on humanitarian, in-kind assistance or on goods financed by foreign aid, remittances, and the direct financial intervention of foreign governments.

The war also interrupted a process of transition from an open but socialist economic system (dominated by aging defense-oriented industries) to a market economy oriented toward exports. As a result of the economic crisis of the 1980s affecting all of Yugoslavia, Bosnia was already one of the poorer Yugoslav republics. The war accelerated its decline. In

1990, Bosnia's gross domestic product (GDP) was $10.633 billion, or $2,429 per capita. By the time the Dayton-Paris accords were signed in December 1995, GDP had fallen 80 percent to $2.1 billion (or $500 per capita in 1997).

There were some bright spots, however. The Bosnian economy, like that of Yugoslavia generally, had been far more open, market oriented, and diversified than that of other socialist countries. More than half of its exports had been sold to Western markets for hard currency. Moreover, Bosnia possessed a highly educated labor force, strong capacities in civil engineering, and a vigorous entrepreneurial class that produced complex goods such as aircraft and machine tools. More than half of output and employment was generated by the industrial sector, including energy, machinery, electrical equipment, textiles, leather, footwear, and raw materials (such as wood, coal, and bauxite). Almost 500 Bosnian engineering and construction companies operated abroad before the war, generating roughly 7 percent of GDP.

Programs of multilateral economic assistance to Bosnia and Herzegovina were organized initially in conjunction with international efforts to negotiate a peace from September 1992 to November 1995; subsequently, to cement several local ceasefires; and, ultimately, to support a comprehensive peace agreement, the Dayton General Framework Agreement for Peace (GFAP). These various aid initiatives have addressed three pressing challenges: the ongoing humanitarian emergency in Bosnia; the reconstruction of the nation's tattered infrastructure;[3] and Bosnia's economic transition from a socialist system to a market economy.

The Dayton Peace Agreement

Most of the recovery aid to Bosnia and Herzegovina has been delivered in the context of the Dayton GFAP. This framework was designed to force formerly warring leaders to cooperate in creating the political and economic institutions of a newly sovereign, independent state under terms being implemented by international authorities. Unfortunately, all three of the warring parties were dissatisfied with major elements of the accord and regarded it as little more than a cease-fire. (Indeed, two of the parties—the Bosnian Serbs and the Bosnian Croats—were represented at the Dayton negotiations by neighboring states.) The difficult work of forming a postwar government began only after national elections in September 1996. Continuing political disagreements left the country without a central bank, a common currency, a telecommunications and postal sector, and other key institutions of an economy until early 1998.

To secure the tenuous peace in Bosnia, the international community assembled an Implementation Force (IFOR), composed of troops from thirty-six countries and led by NATO, to implement the military terms of the Dayton agreement. Authorized initially for only twelve months, IFOR was extended another eighteen months and renamed the Stabilization Force (SFOR). In June 1998, NATO extended SFOR's mandate indefinitely. Meanwhile, an international civilian presence took nearly a year to be fully organized. Over the next two years, it gained increasing authority from the international community to make local decisions in the face of continuing disagreements among the parties, using largely economic instruments as leverage.

The Washington[4] and Dayton accords created a decentralized governmental structure for Bosnia and Herzegovina, which was divided into a Bosniac and Bosnian Croat Federation and the Serb Republic (Republika Srpska), with the two linked by a central state government. The Federation, covering 51 percent of the territory of Bosnia and Herzegovina, is subdivided into ten cantons. Six are essentially Bosniac, two are Croat, and two are mixed. Each canton is subdivided into municipal governments. This intermediary unit (the canton) does not exist in Republika Srpska, which retains the administrative structure of former Yugoslavia, with local units called communeš (opštine), or counties.

The Dayton constitution aimed to retain one unified—albeit very weak—state by granting maximal autonomy to the two entities, thus avoiding partition by calling upon parties to participate in a highly decentralized relationship. The *state government* retains exclusive responsibility for foreign policy; customs policy; monetary policy; immigration and asylum policies; air traffic control; payment of international financial obligations (incurred with the consent of both entities); enforcement of state-level legislation; and interentity transport, communications, and energy infrastructure. Decisionmaking power is shared between a three-member presidency (each representing one ethnic group) and the Council of Ministers. Lacking an independent source of revenue, the Bosnian state finances its activities entirely from transfers from the two entities, proportionally: two-thirds from the Federation, and one-third from the Republika Srpska.

The *entity governments* have exclusive responsibility in their territories over defense; internal affairs (including police); environmental policies; economic and social sector policies (such as agriculture, industry, education, and health); refugees and displaced persons; reconstruction programs; and justice, tax, and customs administration. To carry out these responsibilities, each entity controls the customs duties and excise taxes collected in its territory.[5]

Peace Implementation Structure

The Dayton peace agreement also established a structure for international community involvement in its implementation at the military, political, and economic level. The North Atlantic Treaty Organization (NATO) was entrusted with leading the implementation of the military aspects of the peace agreement. At the political level, a six-nation contact group (France, Germany, Russia, the United States, the United Kingdom, and—since 1996—Italy) continues to assert overall international leadership on the settlement.

More broadly, a large group of states, international organizations, and agencies met in London on December 8–9, 1995, to create a Peace Implementation Council (PIC) that would oversee implementation of the Dayton accords. Between annual conferences of the entire PIC membership, decisions on peace implementation are taken by the PIC Steering Board, composed of representatives of the G8 countries, the presidency of the European Union, the European Commission, and the Organization of the Islamic Conference (OIC). With the agreement of the United Nations Security Council,[6] the PIC Steering Board designates a High Representative (HR) to oversee the Bosnian parties' compliance with the peace accords, to coordinate the activities of all civilian international organizations and agencies, to report periodically to the international community, and to be final arbiter and interpreter of the civilian implementation of the peace agreement.[7]

Finally, the Dayton peace agreement was made contingent on a major international effort to reconstruct Bosnia and Herzegovina. The World Bank and the European Commission of the European Union (EU) have taken the lead in this undertaking, which has involved an array of bilateral and multilateral donors, nongovernmental organizations (NGOs), and implementing agencies. A complicated structure of coordination has emerged to help harmonize and reconcile the activities of various actors possessing different mandates and objectives.

The Donor Conferences and Associated Multilateral Assistance Mechanisms

The vast share of multilateral assistance to support postconflict reconstruction and economic transition in Bosnia and Herzegovina has been organized by the World Bank through a series of periodic pledging conferences. The Bank architects of this program held their first planning meeting with Bosnian officials in Warsaw in January 1995.[8] The following October, the Bank used an informal donor meeting to generate support and recommendations for Bosnian reconstruction. The first formal pledging conference occurred in Brussels on December 21–22, 1995, when donors were asked to support a four-year, $5.1 billion Priority Reconstruction and Recovery Program (PRRP), prepared by the government of Bosnia and Herzegovina with the aid of the World Bank, the EC, and the European Bank for Reconstruction and Development (EBRD).

The PRRP, by far the largest donor effort to reconstruct Bosnia, built on two preceding multilateral programs to support partial cease-fire agreements in the country. In June 1994, donors had pledged $95 million for the Action Plan to Restore Public Services in Sarajevo. Similarly, the European Union Administration of Mostar, June 1994–June 1996, was supported by reconstruction assistance from the EU budget in the amount of ECU 144 million (approximately $162 million). In addition, beginning in 1992, United Nations humanitarian agencies—including the UN High Commissioner for Refugees (UNHCR), World Food Programme (WFP), International Organization on Migration (IOM), Food and Agriculture Organization (FAO), World Health Organization (WHO), and others—had mobilized significant funds through annual UN Consolidated Inter-Agency Appeals (or CAPs). Pledging conferences have also been utilized to support various peace implementation activities.

Restoring Life to Sarajevo[9]

On March 4, 1994, the UN Security Council adopted Resolution 900, mandating a restoration of essential public services in Sarajevo, as a first multilateral effort to address Bosnian recovery and to take advantage of a cease-fire agreement for the city. William Eagleton, former head of the United Nations Relief and Works Agency (UNRWA), was appointed senior civilian official with the task of drafting and supervising the implementation of the program's action plan. At a Coordination Conference in Vienna on May 24–25, 1994, Eagleton presented this plan to more than thirty potential donor countries and many UN agencies and NGOs, appealing for contributions to an international trust fund, which had been set up for this purpose. Based on the work of a joint U.S.-UK team that visited the city in March 1994 and close cooperation with both the Bosnian government and the Bosnian Serbs, the action plan provided a comprehensive overview of needs, priorities, and costs in fourteen essential sectors: electricity, water, gas, solid waste disposal, public transport, airport, railways, roads and bridges, telecommunications, public health, education, housing and heating, urbanism, and essential production.

Although focusing on emergency aid, the Sarajevo Action Plan was intended to be a starting point (and model) for the long-term reconstruction of the entire country. In its design and in the problems it confronted, it foreshadowed the subsequent effort led by the World Bank and the EU. The donors envisioned two stages: during the first (emergency) phase, they would exploit the cease-fire and "weapons exclusion zone" around Sarajevo to repair the city's infrastructure; during the second (transition) phase, they hoped to use the city's recovery as an incentive for peace. At Vienna, Eagleton presented a request for $253 million to finance the emergency phase and another $278 million for the transition phase. While acknowledging that donor fatigue would make it difficult to achieve these figures, Eagleton argued that "Sarajevo is a symbol and many people are interested in it, including in those parts of the world that have not contributed to some of the humanitarian programs."

At a pledging conference in New York in June 1994, twenty-seven donor states pledged $95 million for the Action Plan, including more than $20 million for the UN Trust Fund. Of those pledged funds, $18.1 million were deposited in the Trust Fund, with some $3.2 million that remained outstanding. That is, the pledges were less than requested for the first phase by $158 million, and the gap in delivery of aid pledged was $76.9 million.

Special Coordinator Eagleton opened an office in Sarajevo and began to coordinate a restoration program through "action groups" reporting to a committee that included Sarajevo authorities. Regular meetings of the coordination committee brought together government and municipal officials and donor representatives, as well as UN agencies and NGOs actively involved in emergency reconstruction. Participants gained awareness of the need for strong donor coordination, for maintaining dialogue among concerned parties, for creating a focal point to assist agencies in designating priorities, and for involving local authorities who would eventually assume responsibility for the initiative.

Despite rapid initial progress, the Sarajevo initiative was undermined by a deteriorating security situation and the Bosnian Serbs' rejection of a peace plan proposed by the Contact Group in July 1994. Air and land routes into the city were blocked for extended periods, and water and electricity supplies were subject to protracted interruptions. These factors, which persisted until the signing of the Dayton agreement, rather than a shortage of funds, were the main obstacle to implementing the Action Plan.[10]

The special coordinator continued to mobilize donor resources and technical expertise to address the most immediate emergency problems stemming from the continued siege of the city.

Implementation accelerated significantly after the Dayton peace accords, when a large-scale international reconstruction effort for the country began. The responsibilities of the special coordinator were quickly transferred to the Office of the Special Representative of the Secretary-General (SRSG) and Coordinator of the United Nations Mission in Bosnia and Herzegovina (UNMIBH). As of April 15, 1996, nearly $100 million had been made available for 285 projects. Nations contributing troops to the UN effort provided an additional $30 million in in-kind aid, mainly for emergency repairs to utilities installations, roads, and bridges. Another large part of the Action Plan was also financed through bilateral agreements.

The final report of the special coordinator emphasizes the importance of effective financial control mechanisms and accountability to facilitate faster disbursement of funds for the urgent needs of such programs. To meet these needs, a small unit was established in UNMIBH to manage the Trust Fund and to provide regular information on its activities.

The European Union Administration of Mostar

The European Union Administration of Mostar (EUAM) emerged following the Washington Agreement of March 1994, which created a federation between the Bosnian government (Bosniac) and Bosnian Croat forces. Having lost out to the United States in a competition for the coordinator's position in Sarajevo, the European Union took similar responsibility for the second largest city of the Bosnian Federation. The EU appointed Hans Koschnick, former mayor of Bremen, as chief administrator in Mostar. Koschnick insisted on sufficient resources—contributed from the EU budget rather than individually allocated by the member states—and demanded the authority to spend these funds as he saw fit. The EUAM began operations in July 1994 for a planned mandate of two years. Its design and objective—to cement the cease-fire and reconciliation between the two parties through economic reconstruction—foreshadowed the programs that would follow the Dayton accords.

Mostar was a city divided by the war into Croat (West Mostar) and Bosniac (East Mostar) parts. Its eastern side was much more thoroughly destroyed by artillery shells and mortar attacks than was Sarajevo. The EU viewed reconstruction simultaneously as a task of peace building within the federation and a major step toward ending the wider war. [11]

Crucial to the effectiveness of this effort was delegation of authority to the field—a lesson ignored in the subsequent EU assistance programs in support of the Dayton accords. The administrator in Mostar had full powers to make decisions related to reconstruction, including management and procurement. Of a total EUAM budget of ECU 144 million (approximately $162 million), some 90 percent was spent for reconstruction. Project activities covered most sectors, including housing, administrative buildings, hospitals, water supply, waste management, and the repair of bridges. The EUAM directed DM 86 million (about $53 million) to an Investment Support Program (ISP) to support large public companies and to a Small Enterprise Program (SEP), which supported 399 projects and created 800 jobs in its two years.

The principle guiding EUAM assistance was a belief that reconstruction would directly contribute to peace by creating joint projects and fostering political cooperation. Every project was expected either to further the goal of reconciliation or to sustain the viability of the city or, preferably, both. But the goal of reconstruction also meant that money would be spent according to need. Thus, for example, 90 percent of the housing budget went to Mostar East, where most of the housing damage was, while the majority of funds for water and electricity was spent in Mostar West, where the major facilities were located. Moreover, Bosnian Croat hard-liners, who opposed reintegration and who had independent economic ties to neighboring Croatia, including direct budgetary support from the Croatian government, chose to accept the aid but to obstruct the political process. The fact that approximately 60 percent was spent in East Mostar and 40 percent in West Mostar, for example, led them to accuse Koschnick of a percentage principle favoring Bosniacs. Koschnick's efforts to counteract the nationalist position were constrained by the EU's two-year time limit, by the lack of international cooperation in pressuring Croatia, and by the blatant lack of political support from donor capitals at critical moments of political decision.[12]

Municipal elections on June 30, 1996, were intended to crown the results of this assistance effort. Instead, Bosnian Croat hard-liners in West Mostar refused to accept the results, which handed over control of the city council to the opposing Bosniac-Serb coalition. The response of the EU administrators was to threaten an end to their presence and financial support of Mostar, but the ultimatum came too late in the aid program. EUAM had already spent more than $160 million, and the EU had pledged only a further $5 million, hardly an incentive to separatist hard-liners who had obtained significant resources without cooperating politically and who would welcome EUAM's withdrawal as a recognition of the de facto division of Mostar.

Five years after the Washington Agreement, Mostar remained divided, but the EUAM could claim some success in guaranteeing the viability of East Mostar and placing its population in a position of approximate equality in political dialogue with West Mostar. As one of the members of the EU team recollects, "The primary success [of the EUAM] was to provide some normalcy to the city's citizenry and to keep the political debate on the table and not on the confrontation line. If we had not had the money, we probably would not have had even that much success."[13]

Humanitarian Assistance:
The UN Consolidated Inter-Agency Appeals Process

On December 3, 1991, several agencies of the United Nations, including UNHCR, WFP, UNICEF (United Nations Children's Fund), and WHO, issued a joint appeal for funds to address the escalating conflict in the former Yugoslavia. Soon thereafter, other UN and international agencies, NGOs, and governments joined in what would become one of the largest humanitarian operations of the decade.

The role of the UN humanitarian effort changed dramatically with the peace agreement and shift from wartime relief to peace building. In particular, Annex 7 of the Dayton accords entrusted to UNHCR the lead role in the repatriation of refugees and the right to return home of internally displaced persons (IDPs). The 1996 CAP requested $823 million for Bosnia, Croatia, and Yugoslavia, of which $500.97 million was allocated for Bosnia and Herzegovina to finance the activities of UNHCR ($197 million) and WFP ($194 million) as well as UNICEF, WHO, FAO, the United Nations Development Programme (UNDP), the United Nations Educational, Scientific, and Cultural Organization (UNESCO), the United Nations High Commissioner for Human Rights (UNHCHR), United Nations Volunteers (UNV), IOM, and the Department of Humanitarian Affairs (DHA). Although carryover funds from 1995 allowed the target for Bosnia to shrink to $423 million, the 1996 CAP collected only 50 percent of its target. This forced UNHCR to revise its planning figures for Bosnia and Herzegovina to approximately $156 million and to abandon plans to expand its shelter project for repatriation.

The UN's assistance strategy for 1997 was formulated in a more positive environment. Relations among countries in the region had begun to normalize, and the international community had replaced its initial, twelve-month commitment with an additional eigteenth-month "stabilization period" that included a continuing military presence. The humanitarian community now concentrated on programs for the return, repatriation, and reintegration of IDPs and refugees, on assistance to the most vulnerable population groups, and on the phaseout of relief during the stabilization period by promoting sustainability and the smooth transfer of responsibility to local authorities. UN agencies also sought to enhance coordination among themselves in areas of reconstruction, employment, and human rights.

The CAP for 1997 estimated Bosnia's requirements at $372.5 million—more than two-thirds of the budget for the whole region.[14] (UNHCR's portion was $125.3 million and WFP's was $109.2 million.) As of February 3, 1998, 94 percent of CAP requirements had been met through contributions.[15] The 1998 CAP for Bosnia requested another $263.3 million (with $87 million to cover UNHCR needs). Reflecting the change in needs and in aid policy, these programs focused not only on relief but also on durable solutions for refugees and IDPs, capacity-building activities, and rehabilitation, while the UNDP assistance assumed the lead (up from $12 million in 1997 to $89.9 million in 1998), and the WFP and IOM declined, respectively, to $30.6 million and to $13.6 million.[16]

The Priority Reconstruction and Recovery Program

The primary, multilateral, postconflict reconstruction and transition initiative for Bosnia and Herzegovina has been the PRRP. Organized by the World Bank, in coordination with the Bosnian government and other major donors such as the European Commission and EBRD, its planning had begun as early as January 1995, ten months before the Dayton negotiations. Meeting in Warsaw in the spring of 1995 with the representatives of the government in Sarajevo, the World Bank architects of this project began to generate support and recommendations for Bosnian reconstruction officially at an informal donor meeting in October 1995, using the opportunity of the annual World Bank and International Monetary Fund (IMF) meeting in Washington. An assessment of war damages and transition costs produced a three-to-four-year multisectoral program of $5.1 billion—the PRRP (see Table 8.1).[17] Its key objectives were to initiate a broad-based rehabilitation process that would jump-start economic recovery and growth, strengthen government institutions, and support transition to a market economy.

The first formal pledging conference, held in Brussels on December 21–22, 1995, was charged with financing the PRRP's most urgent needs.[18] The meeting designated the World Bank and the EU as lead agencies and outlined basic principles for donor coordination. Fifty countries and twenty-seven international organizations pledged $615 million, *exceeding the conference's target of $518 million by $97 million.* The Brussels meeting was succeeded by a Sectoral Technical meeting in Paris in January 1996 and a donor information conference in Sarajevo in March 1996. A second pledging conference took place in Brussels on April 12–13, 1996. Fifty-two countries and twenty international organizations pledged another $1.23 billion, *exceeding the conference's target of $1.2 billion by $30 million.*[19]

Table 8.1   **External Financing Requirements for the Priority Reconstruction and Recovery Program (U.S.$ millions)**

Sector	Revised Priority Reconstruction and Recovery Program	Firm Commitments 1996–1997	1998 Sector Allocations/ Requirements
Agriculture	260	126	40
Education	275	173	45
Employment generation	225	109	50
Energy	789	456	170
Heating and natural gas	166	90	30
Electric power and coal	623	366	140
Fiscal and social support	712	339	196
Health	340	172	50
Housing	710	451	148
Industry and finance	593	344	97
Land mine clearance	170	74	32
Telecommunications	134	40	50
Transport	542	308	70
Water and waste management	350	171	68
Subtotal		2,763	1,016
Support to peace implementation		243	
Security			72
Total	5,100	3,006	1,088

Source: European Commission and World Bank, "Bosnia and Herzegovina."

On January 9–10, 1997, the World Bank and the EU organized a second donor information conference to provide the international community an update on reconstruction needs for 1997. And on July 23, 1997, after substantial delays, the World Bank and the EU sponsored a third pledging conference in Brussels, attended by forty-eight countries and thirty international organizations. This gathering emphasized the need to move gradually from reconstruction to sustainable recovery and growth through institution building and policy reforms. The conference mobilized $1.1 billion, *failing to reach the conference's target of $1.4 billion, short $300 million.*[20]

A fourth Brussels pledging conference was held on May 7–8, 1998, after a number of delays and uncertainty about the date, due to the precondition that an agreement with the IMF be negotiated and approved by the Council of Ministers. The most feasible target for 1998 was estimated at $1 billion, of which $520 million would be used to reintegrate refugees and displaced persons. The conference mobilized $1.25 billion, *thus exceeding the conference's target by $250 million.* Of this amount, $867.3 million was allocated to reconstruction, $228.8 million to balance of payments support, and $140.5 million to peace implementation activities. [21]

Peace Implementation Activities and Democratic Transition

Most donor activity has focused on reviving Bosnia's economy. Architects of the PRRP admitted much later that the program should have included funds for peace implementation activities from the start, but when they added this category to the request in 1998, they did so reluctantly, fearing a reduction in donor support for priority infrastructure.[22] Nonetheless, other pledging conferences and voluntary appeals have sought funding for important postconflict and transition initiatives, such as police reform, election supervision and monitoring, independent mass media, democratization, human rights promotion and monitoring, and military training and modernization.

The United Nations
International Police Task Force and Police Reform

The International Police Task Force (IPTF) was established by the Dayton agreement within the framework of the UNMIBH to monitor police force activities on human rights practices and to restructure and reform the civilian police. Together the IPTF and the two entity governments designed a police restructuring plan and convened a donor conference at Dublin on September 30–October 2, 1996, to request $106 million over two years. Later requests were made at subsequent Brussels conferences. Donors have also channeled cash and equipment through a UN trust fund for the Police Assistance Program as well as directly to the IPTF or entity governments.

By mid-1998, total pledges amounted to an estimated $61.5 million, or *$43 million less than requested at donor conferences.* The United States alone had pledged some $30 million, but $15 million of this was blocked by the Lautenberg legislation, which prohibited aid to the Republika Srpska.[23] Neither the $10 million pledged by the EU nor the $17 million for the UN Trust Fund had been delivered. IPTF officials assessed the value of the trust fund mechanism as limited because of difficulties in gaining access to its monies, donor restrictions on disbursement, and cumbersome preparation of cost plans.[24]

Peace Implementation Activities:
Human Rights, Media, Democratization, Arms Control

Donors had allocated an estimated $200–250 million in aid to peace implementation activities as of December 1997. They pledged an additional $140.5 million at the fourth donor conference in May 1998. The largest sums have been devoted to the development of independent, local media through support for an Open Broadcast Network (OBN). The EU, USA, Sweden, and Japan granted an initial $10.2 million to OBN, with additional contributions made by Canada, the Czech Republic, Germany, Great Britain, Ireland, the Netherlands, and the Soros Open Society Fund, and a second pledging phase of $6 million. In late 1997, an international trust for OBN was set up to attract corporate investment and to manage the project as a business concern. Other pledged aid has gone to support human rights projects such as human rights observers, the International Criminal Tribunal for the former Yugoslavia (ICTY), and the human rights office within the Office of the High Representative (OHR).

Primary financing for democratization and elections support, however, has not come from pledging conferences but from a core budget of the Organization for Security and Cooperation in Europe (OSCE), the primary implementing agency in this field.[25] Some of its activities are fully funded, such as its democratization projects, the Human Rights Chamber, and the international ombudsperson, but commitments lagged for others, such as the organization of state, entity, and municipal elections and related activities (including out-of-country voting, the maintenance of a radio network, media monitoring, and activities related to the Armaments Reduction Agreement).[26] The OSCE also established a Fund for Voluntary Contributions to support the OSCE Action for Peace, Democracy, and Stability in Bosnia and Herzegovina. By February 13, 1998, pledges of voluntary contributions, confirmed in writing, were about $34 million, with a *delivery gap outstanding of $4.7 million.*

The Donor Conference for Brčko

The mechanism of a pledging conference was also used to obtain resources and discuss strategies for the strategically located town of Brčko, placed under temporary international administration pending an arbitration decision on its final status that the peace negotiations could not resolve. On November 4–5, 1997, representatives of more than twenty countries and ten international organizations met in Brčko and focused on three areas: reconstruction of municipal infrastructure, development of small business and microcredit, and creation of second-destination housing for displaced Serbs occupying homes of potential returnees. The first commitments of aid were announced on April 8, 1998, when the EC pledged more than DM 12 million (about $7.5 million) to facilitate the return of refugees and IDPs to the city.[27]

Military Assistance: The "Train and Equip" Program

The donor community used another pledging conference to raise funds to equip and train the joint army of the Bosniac and Bosnian Croat Federation. The Dayton negotiators made the commitment to the Bosniac leadership to win their support for the accords and to seal the agreement with a military balance between the armies of the two entities and a deterrent against the Bosnian Serb army. An assessment of needs commissioned by the U.S. Department of Defense proposed a budget of $740–860 million in equipment; this amount was later reduced to $570–670 million.[28] At a multilateral meeting in Ankara, the United States pledged $100 million in used, refurbished equipment,[29] and Turkey pledged $2 million in training assistance; but the anticipated aid from other Islamic countries did not materialize. After a follow-up mission by Clinton administration official Mack McLarty, Kuwait, Saudi Arabia, and the United Arab Emirates contributed $100 million. Subsequent contributions by Malaysia and Brunei brought the total pledged to $155 million, nearly all of which—some $152 million—was delivered. The estimated value of the Train and Equip program is $400 million (cash, equipment, and training provisions), but its pledges and expenditures are not included in the databases on aid to Bosnia.

Assessing the Gap: Methodological Issues

Of the approximately $5 billion pledged in humanitarian, peace implementation, and postconflict reconstruction assistance to Bosnia and Herzegovina, the overwhelming preponderance, an estimated $4.2 billion, has been pledged at the four Brussels pledging conferences to support the PRRP. From the outset, both donors and the Bosnian government stressed the need for transparency in tracking the commitment, allocation, and disbursement of pledged funds—and the importance of accountability to constituencies in donor countries and to the recipient, Bosnia and Herzegovina, as well.

While there is general agreement as to the amounts pledged at the Brussels meetings, there are major difficulties in identifying actual commitments and disbursements. No assessment of pledging gaps can be made without analyzing the availability and quality of data and evaluating related accounting practices. One of the main challenges in tracking aid flows to Bosnia and Herzegovina is the existence of several, often inconsistent databases. Such discrepancies, and the lack of uniform reporting guidelines, make it nearly impossible to determine the exact amount of aid currently implemented (whether defined as the firm allocation by sector or by actual indicators of delivery—disbursement, expenditure, or stage of completion).

Databases on Donor Activities in Bosnia and Herzegovina

We analyzed three primary sources of data: (1) the Donor Data Base (DDB), maintained by the World Bank and EC, (2) the Reconstruction Contract Module (RCM) and Project Information Monitoring System (PIMS), maintained by the International Management Group (IMG), and (3) Bosnian authorities' databases. A number of other offices, agencies, and Project Implementation Units (PIUs) maintain database modules on activities within a specific sector, which are not analyzed here. Because these sources of information vary in their purpose and design and their comparison reveals significant discrepancies in estimates of total aid flows, any assessment requires a comparison of the methodologies of data collection and classification each employs.

Donor Data Base. The DDB, maintained by the World Bank in conjunction with the European Commission and in cooperation with the authorities of Bosnia and Herzegovina, records all types of donor funds, based on donor information as the sole source of data.[30] Its purpose is to provide the donor community with a general financial overview of all the funds it has pledged, committed, disbursed, and expended toward Bosnian reconstruction and rehabilitation.

Nonetheless, the semiannual World Bank and EC reports recognize certain deficiencies in the process of collecting data and advise that figures should be taken as best estimates. To gauge better the amounts actually spent on projects (i.e., "funds expended"), donors were asked to provide estimates of the unused portions of such advances. Approximately 15 percent of the overall disbursement figures are based on such estimates. The last published report, dated December 1997,[31] provided figures on aggregate delivery of donor aid (see Table 8.2).

The database records flows according to several accounting benchmarks: amounts pledged, amounts committed, amounts transferred to international

Table 8.2 Status Report to the Donor Community from the European Commission and the World Bank, December 1998[a]

Donor	Total Pledges 1996	1997	1998	1996–1998	Total Commitments[b] 1996	1997	1998	1996–1998	Transfers to International Agency Trust Funds[c]	Under Implementation	Disbursed[d]	Funds Expended
Albania	0.02	—	—	0.02	0.02	—	—	0.02	—	0.02	0.02	0.02
Australia	1.13	—	—	1.13	1.13	—	—	1.13	—	1.13	1.13	1.13
Austria	11.50	8.40	8.00	27.90	25.08	7.99	10.41	43.48	1.1	43.49	38.51	36.51
Belgium	7.57	2.80	2.70	13.07	6.52	0.99	2.76	10.27	—	7.43	5.39	5.39
Brunei	2.00	—	—	2.00	18.70	4.42	0.00	23.12	—	19.47	19.47	19.47
Bulgaria	0.01	—	—	0.01	0.03	0.00	0.00	0.03	—	0.03	0.03	0.03
Canada	25.44	14.60	11.40	51.44	23.27	16.21	13.15	52.63	7.0	50.00	44.08	44.08
Croatia	0.50	10.60	—	11.10	14.29	10.61	0.00	24.90	—	22.87	14.29	14.14
Czech Republic	6.00	0.50	0.70	7.20	6.42	0.55	0.00	6.97	—	6.33	6.33	6.33
Denmark	5.10	10.60	4.40	20.10	9.63	8.94	—	15.57	—	14.11	12.90	11.82
Egypt	1.00	2.60	1.00	4.60	1.03	3.33	4.17	8.53	—	5.41	1.37	1.37
Estonia	0.07	0.10	0.10	0.17	0.07	—	0.01	0.08	—	0.07	0.07	0.07
Finland	5.00	5.50	6.00	16.50	8.94	10.54	—	19.47	—	15.27	10.47	9.55
Federal Republic of Yugoslavia	10.00	10.00	10.00	30.00	11.70	10.00	2.40	24.10	—	24.10	14.10	14.10
F. Y. R. Macedonia	0.10	—	—	0.10	0.10	0.05	—	0.15	—	0.16	0.16	0.16
France	9.29	10.14	12.50	31.93	13.19	3.81	—	17.00	—	15.23	15.23	11.48
Germany	39.25	12.20	25.80	77.25	55.00	25.20	26.13	106.33	—	97.78	88.07	88.07
Greece	7.00	10.00	8.00	25.00	7.00	9.95	8.00	24.95	—	16.95	16.95	16.95
Hungary	1.00	—	—	1.00	1.00	—	0.45	1.45	—	1.45	1.45	1.45
Iceland	1.60	—	—	1.60	0.85	—	0.75	1.60	0.9	0.85	0.65	0.65
Indonesia	2.10	—	—	2.10	2.08	1.00	—	3.08	—	3.06	3.06	3.08
Ireland	6.00	2.00	2.00	10.00	6.20	3.01	2.57	11.78	1.4	11.43	11.08	11.08
Italy[e]	63.65	34.80	15.60	114.05	67.09	37.01	8.98	113.08	48.4	51.09	44.30	44.30
Japan	136.70	130.00	120.00	386.70	100.67	106.11	78.83	285.61	92.7	115.49	114.32	89.29

(continues)

Table 8.2 continued

Donor	Total Pledges				Total Commitments[b]				Transfers to International Agency Trust Funds[c]	Under Implementation	Disbursed[d]	Funds Expended
	1996	1997	1998	1996–1998	1996	1997	1998	1996–1998				
Jordan	1.37	—	—	1.37	—	1.37	—	1.37	—	1.23	—	—
Kuwait	35.00	12.70	—	47.70	21.15	26.40	—	47.55	—	1.15	—	—
Latvia	0.09	—	—	0.09	0.11	—	—	0.11	—	0.11	0.11	0.11
Lithuania	0.07	—	0.10	0.17	0.07	—	0.07	0.14	—	0.07	0.07	0.07
Luxembourg	3.23	2.80	1.50	7.53	2.50	2.33	3.27	8.10	0.8	7.32	7.08	7.08
Malaysia	12.00	12.30	—	24.30	12.00	14.94	0.27	27.21	—	14.97	13.41	13.41
Netherlands[e]	100.02	75.00	70.00	245.02	106.56	100.96	77.57	285.19	154.0	235.77	202.20	202.2
Norway[e]	40.76	27.00	45.00	112.76	42.63	38.54	26.82	107.79	11.5	78.29	78.29	74.05
Poland	2.90	—	—	2.90	2.90	—	3.00	5.90	—	5.85	—	—
Portugal	1.00	—	—	1.00	—	—	—	0.00	—	—	—	—
Qatar	5.00	—	2.00	7.00	5.00	4.31	—	9.31	—	7.84	3.80	3.80
Republic of Korea	1.00	0.80	—	1.80	1.00	0.80	0.35	2.15	—	1.80	1.80	1.80
Romania	0.21	—	—	0.21	2.09	6.56	—	8.65	—	8.65	8.65	8.65
Russia	50.00	—	—	50.00	—	—	—	0.00	—	—	—	—
San Marino	0.14	—	—	0.14	0.23	—	—	0.23	—	0.23	0.23	0.23
Saudi Arabia	50.00	25.00	—	75.00	43.00	32.00	0.00	75.00	—	40.40	37.42	37.42
Slovakia	1.50	1.50	—	3.00	1.50	1.50	—	3.00	—	1.50	1.50	1.50
Slovenia	2.89	3.00	3.00	8.69	3.70	2.27	13.00	18.97	—	15.39	13.42	13.42
Spain	17.50	21.20	7.00	45.70	16.46	21.01	3.02	40.49	2.1	10.92	19.92	19.92
Sweden	30.40	25.00	46.20	101.60	36.88	28.01	27.90	92.79	3.1	82.07	75.69	75.69
Switzerland[e]	33.50	35.30	36.04	104.84	36.56	34.19	58.62	129.37	15.5	127.16	110.24	110.24
Turkey	26.50	—	20.00	46.50	12.20	—	67.80	80.00	—	12.70	12.70	12.70
United Kingdom	39.70	27.50	17.53	84.73	57.75	26.69	—	84.44	6.4	81.01	65.47	65.47
United States	281.70	242.10	242.75	756.55	294.67	260.36	202.77	757.80	2.8	687.08	592.47	592.47

(continues)

Table 8.2 continued

Donor	Total Pledges				Total Commitments[b]				Transfers to International Agency Trust Funds[c]	Under Implementation	Disbursed[d]	Funds Expended
	1996	1997	1998	1996–1998	1996	1997	1998	1996–1998				
International Institutions												
CE Soc. Dev. Fund	5.00	—	1.50	6.50	6.50	—	—	6.50	—	2.00	2.00	2.00
EB RD	80.21	—	—	80.21	35.57	61.40	—	96.97	—	47.35	19.36	19.36
European Commission	367.10	306.10	—	1,007.10	452.29	267.43	307.06	1,026.78	—	856.69	517.09	517.10
IsDB	15.00	—	1.10	16.10	19.00	—	1.26	20.26	—	19.00	14.28	14.28
ICRC[f]	1.50	—	—	1.50	1.50	—	—	1.50	—	1.50	1.50	1.50
IFAD	7.30	—	—	7.30	7.32	14.00	—	21.32	—	7.32	6.72	6.72
IFC	0.00	—	—	0.00	0.00	6.81	22.07	28.88	—	11.94	11.94	11.94
IMF	0.00	—	80.73	80.73	—	—	80.60	80.60	—	80.60	33.00	33.00
OIC	3.00	—	—	3.00	3.00	—	—	3.00	—	3.00	3.00	3.00
Soros Foundation	5.00	—	—	5.00	5.96	—	—	5.96	—	0.61	0.26	0.26
UNDP[f]	2.00	—	—	2.00	8.99	4.68	1.42	15.09	—	15.09	12.33	12.33
WHO[f]	1.18	—	—	1.18	1.88	—	—	1.88	—	1.88	1.88	1.88
World Bank	330.00	160.00	100.00	590.00	357.60	165.00	91.00	613.60	—	477.83	458.88	454.83
Totals[g]	1,895.80	1,242.04	1,235.56	4,374.40	1,978.58	1,381.28	1,146.37	4,506.23	347.6	3,478.58	2,791.16	2,751.94

Source: World Bank and EU, *Donor Data Base Report* (Washington, D.C.: World Bank, 1998).

Notes: a. Information on commitments and status of implementation as of December 31, 1998 is not available for the following countries/institutions: Albania, Australia, Brunei, Bulgaria, Council of Europe, Czech Republic, Denmark, F.Y.R. Macedonia, Finland, France, ICRC, Kuwait, Latvia, Lithuania, Norway, OIC, Poland, Portugal, San Marino, Soros Foundation, Spain, Slovakia, United Kingdom, and WHO.

b. Includes both indicative and firm commitments and reflects, where applicable, retroactive adjustments reported by donors.

c. Several donors have transferred part of their contributions to trust funds administered by international agencies, including international financial institutions. This column shows the amounts actually transferred by these donors. Donors who have placed grant funds to Bosnia and Herzegovina in a trust fund with the World Bank include: Austria US$1.1 million; Canada US$4.5 million; Iceland US$0.9 million; Italy US$46.4 million; Japan US$48.6 million (as part of a US$50 million contribution Japan transferred to a World Bank administered trust fund for postconflict countries; Luxembourg US$0.5 million; the Netherlands US$154.0 million; Norway US$7.8 million; Sweden US$ 3.1 million; Switzerland US$13.6 million; the United Kingdom US$6.4 million. These funds are considered to be under implementation or disbursed once actual work contracts are under way or payments made.

d. Included an estimated total of US$39.2 million in advance for future payments to suppliers; this amount has been subtracted to reach "funds expended."

e. Donors who contribute to resolution of arrears with IBRD are as follows: Italy US$15 million; the Netherlands US$6.5 million; Norway US$1.5 million; Switzerland US$2 million. These amounts are not included in the reconstruction pledges shown.

f. ICRC, UNDP, and WHO implement various programs on behalf of bilateral donors, in addition to carrying out programs funded by pledges made at donors' conferences. Uncommitted pledges totaling US$356.0 million are not included. Total commitments plus uncommitted pledges add up to more than the 1996–1998 pledged amounts

g. Uncommitted pledges totaling US$356.0 million are not included. Total commitments plus uncommitted pledges add up to more than the 1996–1998 pledged amounts because several donors have committed funds over and above their total 1996–1998 pledges in order to continue ongoing activities.

agency trust funds, amounts under implementation, amounts disbursed, and amounts expended. Implementation is measured according to financial benchmarks rather than impact.[32]

RCM and PIMS. The Reconstruction Contract Module tracks the implementation of aid projects in Bosnia and Herzegovina. Maintained by the IMG,[33] under the auspices of the Economic Task Force (ETF)[34] and with technical support from the World Bank, it records data provided by the implementing agencies themselves and only after final contracts have been signed.[35] This procedure is designed to prevent the inclusion of projects that may later be canceled, as well as to provide current, detailed information on all funds spent directly on concrete projects and programs in the country.

However, the database requires an extensive level of information on actual contracts that many donors were often not willing to provide or in some cases were unable to provide. This is often the case with NGOs whose accounting practices are not uniform. "A huge trade-off was made between the quality of data and willingness of donors to provide such information," said one of the officials involved in the early stages of its design. Early attempts to merge the World Bank/EC database (as a database that monitors aggregates) and the RCM module (which focuses on the final implementation stage) never materialized. In mid-1997, IMG took over the database from its original sponsor, the World Bank. In 1998, a number of changes were made to make it more of an economic database. The aim is an instrument that would eventually provide a comprehensive overview of all ongoing and completed and income-generating projects in Bosnia and Herzegovina and enable a better assessment of the viability and sustainability effects of the programs. In mid-1998, it contained data on about 2,000 contracts in "nonreconstruction" sectors totaling DM 1 billion ($620 million):[36] agriculture, industry and industrial finance (including all major credit lines), finance and trade, external debt service, government institution building, social support, peace implementation activities, and land mine clearing.

The Project Information Monitoring System collects detailed data only on infrastructure projects currently in preparation, under way, or completed. It covers the following sectors of "reconstruction": education, energy, health, housing, telecommunications, transport, water, and sanitation. Information for the PIMS is gathered regionally by IMG field offices and nationally by IMG's sector units. Updates are supposed to be provided monthly to the IMG Sarajevo office, where the final version of the global PIMS database is produced.

In combination, the RCM and PIMS figures yield the data shown in Table 8.3.

Table 8.3   RCM Plus PIMS, August 1998

In Millions of Currency Units	Completed 1995 and before	Completed 1996	Completed 1997	Completed 1998	Ongoing	Total
1. RCM	0	277.75	128.81	3.92	477.16	937.64
2. PIMS	32.36	441.30	660.13	49.57	1,094.23	2,477.58
Total DM 1+2	32.36	719.05	788.94	303.49	1,571.39	3,415.22
Total 1 + 2 in U.S.$ millions (DM 1.62: $1)	$22.58	$477.83	$455.01	$168.14	$870.58	$2,109.20

Source: OHR, *Economic Task Force Secretariat,* 1998.

The viability of IMG's databases and the accuracy of the group's reporting (in terms of the extent to which the data capture the actual flow of funds) have frequently been contested. One frequent criticism is that IMG data capture no more than 60 to 65 percent of the actual flow of funds and that IMG is not properly staffed for such an ambitious effort. Nonetheless, the Office of the High Representative and its Economic Task Force secretariat rely primarily on this source in the publication of monthly newsletters on general economic developments, progress in reconstruction, and contract information.[37]

The Bosnian authorities as a source. The Department for Reconstruction of the Foreign Ministry maintains a database that relies on information from donors, implementing agencies, government institutions, and World Bank reports.[38] The strength of this database rests on its coverage of bilateral channels of aid, which are tracked up to the implementation stage. This is helpful in examining the performance of countries that prefer bilateral aid commitments to pledging within multilateral contexts. For example, many Islamic countries prefer to implement their aid in coordination with Bosnian agencies and maintain a good reporting relationship with the government.

However, the overall quality of the information in this database has come into question, partly because donors often neglect requests for information from the Bosnian government. The EC has been particularly reluctant to provide information in the early stages. Many donors, particularly the larger ones, had not provided data by the end of 1998 for that year's update report. Local deficiencies have also complicated the task of obtaining accurate figures.

At the entity levels, both the Federation government and a reconstruction cabinet of the Serb entity have committed themselves to collect data to monitor the delivery of aid to their respective entities. However, resistance from Republika Srpska authorities and incomplete Federation data have made it difficult to verify implementation figures for the entity level.

Because they rely upon a variety of data sources and adopt various approaches to defining and classifying this information, both state and entity state level figures should also be considered as best estimates.

Explaining Differences in
Financial Figures Among the Databases

The need to maintain different databases to improve monitoring of aid delivery by enhancing transparency has been fully recognized by all major players in the reconstruction effort. But the differences in coverage and in data collection methods, the overall lack of uniform accounting practices, the multiplication of effort, and even instances of organizational rivalry do raise questions. Many implementing organizations complain that the multiple requests for data represent an added burden of time and money on their operation, because reports requested often need to be tailored to the specific database format and information required. (Their resistance can be illustrated by the fact that as of October 1998, reliable data for a 1998 progress report were not yet available.) The differences in database designs and purposes and in the success of data collection impede quantitative comparisons among them as well as any global assessment of aid delivery. The following findings illustrate the complexity of this effort, much beyond mere quantitative discrepancies.

Different definitions being used. The general problem is the difference in what is counted as "under implementation" or "completed" and which stages of contracts and their figures are included and which are not. For example, the RCM utilizes categories such as "in implementation" for signed contracts only; "completed" for contracts completed only; and "unspecified" for contracts that are either completed or in implementation but for which the status could not be determined due to incomplete information. In contrast, the DDB utilizes "under implementation" for firmly committed funds for which contracts have been tendered, signed, or completed; "funds expended" for (1) fiscal/balance of payments support, (2) actual expenditures made against works, goods, and service contracts, and (3) value of assistance delivered in-kind; and "disbursed" for funds (1) transferred to a Bosnian account or disbursement agency in Bosnia and Herzegovina, (2) funds expended, and (3) advance payments to implementing agencies. Since these categories in the DDB are generally broader in definition, the total financial aggregate presented in the DDB is higher than that in the

RCM. For example, a large part of the funds "disbursed" in the DDB will not appear in the RCM because the actual work or final transfers to beneficiaries have not begun.

Time lags and project cycle. Definitional differences create time lags in the entry of data. For example, a project in the tendering phase is entered in the DDB as "under implementation," but it is not included at all in the RCM. In addition, the project cycle is longer for larger and nonemergency projects; thus, as reconstruction assistance moves into later phases, the disbursement of new tranches will take longer.

Different sources of data, methods of collection, and regularity of update. The collection process for the DDB is considerably less complex and time consuming than that for the RCM or PIMS. DDB works with only fifty-nine sources, which is the total number of donors that have committed funds for Bosnia and Herzegovina, and is updated semiannually. RCM works with hundreds of sources, namely, implementing agencies that work directly in the field and are the only source able to provide data on actual progress and payments that are made on an almost daily basis with a high degree of accuracy and detail. However, due to the complexity of the data collection process (insufficient staff, extent of the detail required, varying accounting systems among organizations, in particular the NGOs), at any given moment the total value of projects in the DDB would be higher than in the RCM. This poses a serious challenge to the ability of the RCM to keep up-to-date. Finally, the RCM depends on the willingness of its many sources to provide such detailed information. As a result, not all contracts may get reported to the RCM.

Operating costs. The DDB by definition keeps data on the grand total of funds that are committed by donor countries to Bosnia and Herzegovina. However, a portion of the total is not necessarily spent on concrete programs or projects, but used to cover the operating costs of the reconstruction and rehabilitation effort. This includes, for example, the administrative budgets of agencies, including salaries for international staff, operating costs of implementing agencies, or administrative costs for Bosnia and Herzegovina–related activities in home countries. Estimates of how much has been spent so far on these indirect expenses as a proportion of the pledged total for Bosnia and Herzegovina are hard to get. No more than a fraction of these "indirect" donor funds are recorded by the RCM, because they are in most cases not directly related to one single project or contract. They also are not reported to the database staff in Bosnia and Herzegovina.

Home services. Research reveals that donors occasionally require external expertise to prepare and implement projects, particularly for larger projects. Often these services are contracted with companies from the donor country. As the cost of these services for projects in Bosnia and Herzegovina are actual expenses for the donor, these amounts will be reported by the donor to the DDB, while they remain invisible and unrecorded by the RCM, because in many cases such contracts are made outside Bosnia and Herzegovina.

Donor contribution for SFOR-implemented projects. Finally, donor states also contributing troops to the NATO-led Stabilization Force channeled part of their pledges to support reconstruction activities conducted by their troops, such as bridge reconstruction, road repair, school building, and hospital rehabilitation. The databases are not clear how such important contributions by the military are treated.

The Muddy Definition of "Assistance"

In the end, any assessment of the actual extent and quality of aid pledged, delivered, and implemented will depend on how "assistance" is defined. The public character and peer pressure of pledging conferences pushes donors to pad their pledges or to avoid specifying projects so as to retain flexibility in expenditures (or to include expenditures not normally considered part of an aid package). Double counting or muddying the distinction among aid delivered for humanitarian assistance, reconstruction, peace implementation, and economic transition also occurs.

In the Bosnian case, pledges have included commercial loans (EBRD, Turkey, Iran) and an IMF standby arrangement;[39] in-kind assistance, often valued at much higher prices than commercial goods or local products and delivered at the expense of the recipient country; technical assistance, which the recipient did not always request or appear to need (a preliminary estimate of $120 million in mid-1998); tied aid, an obligation to purchase goods originating from the country that has pledged funds calculated under less competitive prices; and contributions to international organizations in the peace operation (such as to UNHCR programs, the OHR, ICTY, or OSCE, and to IFOR/SFOR troops).[40] Duplication and repetition of pledges across various donor conferences and emergency appeals[41] have also obscured the overlap in categories of humanitarian, reconstruction, peace implementation, and transition assistance. Also troubling is a lack of reliable NGO data,[42] considering their role as one of the main channels for delivering humanitarian assistance and implementing reconstruction and peace-building projects. One effect of the above double counting is that the financing gaps are probably much greater than the current databases suggest.

The Record of Implementation

With some notable exceptions, the commitment of aid pledged by donors to the reconstruction of Bosnia and Herzegovina is an impressive record when compared to other cases in this book.[43] Implementation has been less successful than this record would suggest, with substantial delays occurring as a result of the state structure created by the peace agreement; the need for donors to create implementation capacity and ongoing disagreements over coordination and policy; and the politics of aid aimed at implementing a peace agreement on the part of both the donor community and the recipient governments.

Dayton Agreement—Decentralized Structure

The Dayton agreement mandated an unusually decentralized political system for Bosnia and Herzegovina, handing most powers to its two entities and creating a very weak common government. In the economic sphere, the state enjoys clear authority only over monetary policy, foreign trade, customs policy, debt servicing, and interentity transport, energy, and communication. Lacking any substantial, independent sources of budgetary revenue, the state depends fully on contributions from the two entities. Moreover, the three Bosnian communities have continued to hold divergent interpretations of the Dayton agreement. The Bosniacs have pressed consistently for a strong state, whereas the Croats and Serbs have held out for maximal decentralization to the entities or even (in the Federation) to the cantons. This conflict played out in the construction of the new state, including the institutions necessary for the absorption of aid.

Thus, for example, obstruction from Bosnian Croat and Serb parties delayed critical decisions on the creation of a common currency and central bank as well as the implementation of major aid projects. The unwillingness of the entities to pay regularly their share of the state budget also jeopardized the central government's efforts to service its foreign debt. This complicated and delayed implementation of pledges from the international financial institutions (IFIs), as the regular servicing of the pre-war debt was the precondition for their implementation. It also hindered the effectiveness of the central institutions as the payment of salaries to the central administration has been irregular. With the future of the Bosnian state uncertain, donors feared difficulty in mobilizing new pledges before skeptical parliaments and began in the spring of 1997 to pressure for more determined implementation of the peace agreement. The six major powers overseeing the process within the Contact Group responded by strengthening the powers of the High Representative to arbitrate and even impose decisions on the authorities when they were unable to do so themselves.[44]

This step was not universally welcomed, however, for some donors feared that this would undermine the sense of Bosnian "ownership" that they considered essential to lasting peace and economic reform.

Donor Coordination

Given the size and complexity of the PRRP and the large number of donors helping to implement it, success would seem to require close aid coordination among the donors and with the government. Coordination was indeed a preoccupation during 1995–1996 of the largest donors: the World Bank, the EC, the G7 countries, and the Netherlands. Their deliberations produced an elaborate and evolving structure to coordinate assistance to Bosnia and Herzegovina.

At first, donors reached consensus only on the lead role of the World Bank and the EC in convening pledging conferences. They continued to disagree profoundly on the mechanisms of aid coordination. The World Bank, supported by most of the G7 countries, the Netherlands, and the government of Bosnia and Herzegovina, proposed periodic meetings to mobilize financial support; creation of an external "aid coordination board" (designated by the donor community); and appointment of a small, highly professional "reconstruction task force," to be located in Bosnia and Herzegovina. The World Bank also sought to include Islamic donors in the aid coordination mechanism, in recognition of the country's large Muslim population and in the hope of spreading the costs of Bosnian recovery.

Meanwhile, the United States, the leading diplomatic actor in the peace negotiations, drafted its own three-tiered coordination mechanism: a political Steering Board of the Peace Implementation Council (first tier), to be chaired by the High Representative as the link between that external political guidance and operational responsibility for implementation of the peace agreement (second tier), and an Economic Task Force (third tier) composed of representatives of the World Bank and IMF, EC, EBRD, bilateral donor agencies, NGOs, and UN agencies to communicate and coordinate activities in the field. The World Bank expressed considerable concern about the U.S.-proposed "superstructure," which would give the High Representative a significant role in coordinating reconstruction. The Bank's Articles of Agreement stipulate that only its board of directors can guide its lending operations. In addition, World Bank officials were sensitive to the prospect that the High Representative, the United States, and other donors would try to apply "political conditionality" to the disbursement of aid. Such a strategy would not only delay the reconstruction program, but it would also enmesh the Bank in the consideration of "political" criteria outside the economic mandate also set forth in its Articles of Agreement.

This conflict between the lead agencies responsible for mobilizing donor resources (primarily the World Bank) and the lead diplomatic actors responsible for implementing the peace agreement (primarily the United States government and the High Representative) was resolved when the impending elections for the first nationwide government, in September 1996, led to general concern about the effect on voters of delays in assistance and its "peace dividend" (primarily jobs). Asserting their political role in the peace process and donors' goal of political progress, the United States and the OHR won the day, obtaining their preferred aid coordination structure and the principle that international assistance be used as an instrument for implementing the peace agreement. Nonetheless, the donor conferences—including both pledging and informational meetings—also served as an effective framework for the donors and the Bosnian government to share knowledge, to identify and prioritize needs, to mobilize resources, to plan joint projects, and to implement new policies. Within the context of these conferences, donors convened the economic task force, chaired jointly by the World Bank and the EC; briefed the High Representative (who had no direct role in donor coordination); and created sector task forces to exchange information and collaborate in particular spheres of recovery. The standard World Bank/government management structure, the PIUs staffed by locals, also have been adopted.

Today, the main instruments for donor coordination are the PIC Steering Board, the ETF, and the sector task forces. The Steering Board, chaired by the High Representative, gives guidance for the implementation of the peace agreement, which includes the reconstruction of Bosnia and Herzegovina. The ETF, also chaired by the High Representative, coordinates the operational aspects of economic reconstruction as well as discussing the economic policy and other measures being jointly recommended to the Bosnian state, Federation, and Republika Srpska authorities.[45]

The issue of membership in both the PIC Steering Board and the ETF has been controversial, leading to disagreements between the OHR and some bilateral donors and NGOs. It is unclear why, for example, the World Bank has never been invited to serve as a member of the PIC Steering Board, nor even to participate as an observer when reconstruction issues are discussed; this seems particularly odd given that the other major aid player, the European Union, is a member. Likewise, the composition of the ETF has caused friction. The United States[46] has been present at all of its meetings, whereas other major donors like Japan and the Netherlands were not regularly invited. In reaction to their protests, some bilateral donors have been invited to attend ETF meetings as observers. However, the NGO community continues to question why its only representative at these meetings is the IMG, and also why the EBRD, although very slow in its delivery of pledges, has been granted full membership. Hasan Muratović, a former Bosnian prime minister, speculates that the OHR designed the PIC board to skirt a World Bank role in donor coordination—and thus to permit the use of political conditionality.[47]

These decisions on membership were particularly significant in the case of Islamic donors. Thanks to good coordination between the Bosnian government and the World Bank, Muslim donors made a strong showing at the first and second donor pledging conferences, accounting for 15 percent of total pledges. At its ministerial meeting in September 1995, the Organization of Islamic Countries formed the Assistance Mobilization Group for Bosnia and Herzegovina (AMG/OIC), composed of fifteen leading Islamic donors who meet three to four times a year. At its meeting in Sarajevo on March 15, 1996, the AMG/OIC asked the High Representative to admit one of its members as a permanent member of ETF.[48] The OHR failed even to reply to this request. In response, Islamic donors have reduced their contributions to the multilateral aid program. At the third donors' conference held in Brussels on July 23, 1997, AMG/OIC countries contributed only 6 percent of the total amount pledged, and their contribution was even smaller at the fourth donor conference in May 1998.

Finally, the third tier in the current donor coordination mechanism are eleven operational, sector task forces. Unlike the ETF, which consists solely of international actors, these bodies include Bosnian representation. The chair of each varies according to sector. IMG chairs separate task forces on power, coal mining, housing, transport, and water and waste management. The U.S. Agency for International Development (USAID) manages one on industry, and Britain's Overseas Development Association (ODA, now the Department for International Development [DFID]) chairs another on natural gas and district heating. The International Labour Organization (ILO) chairs a task force on employment and training issues; UNESCO, on education and cultural activities; WHO, on public health and the social safety net; and UNMIBH, on de-mining. Finally, the World Bank and the IMF cochair a task force on economic policy. Collectively, the task forces have reduced contradictions, duplication, and overlap among donor activities, but their overall success in full implementation of coordinated programs on the ground has been limited.

The World Bank and the EC have taken the lead in drafting the guidelines and program for Bosnian reconstruction and in procuring and coordinating external resources for the recovery effort. Coordination between the World Bank and the Bosnian government has been very close. In contrast, Bosnian authorities express much dissatisfaction with the performance of the EC in aid coordination. UN agencies are heavily involved in the sector task forces, and UNHCR, in partnership with SFOR and the International Center for Migration Policy Development (ICMPD), provides the donor community with information on potential returnees and physical conditions in their hometowns and villages.[49] Although about $200–300 million (or

10–15 percent of reconstruction funds) are being implemented by 400 NGOs operating in Bosnia and Herzegovina (three-quarters of them exclusively within the Federation), they have not participated substantially in the task forces and have little interaction with the government. In some cases, local authorities are completely unaware of NGO activities.

The Bosnian government has also played an important role in donor coordination. At the second pledging conference in April 1996, donors recommended that it establish a mechanism to facilitate the exchange of timely and valuable information with the donor community, with funds specified for the purpose from the Netherlands, the World Bank, the EC, Japan, and UNDP. Two months earlier, in mid-February 1996, the government created a Reconstruction Cabinet, composed of fifteen members of the state and entity governments and chaired by the prime minister, to help manage the PRRP. This structure and that of the World Bank and European Commission worked very closely to prepare all donor meetings, including the first donor information conference in Sarajevo in March 1996, while the Bosnian government alone has coordinated the activities of several major bilateral donors.

Nonetheless, the government's overall coordination mechanism has been severely hampered by political quarrels over the state's structure. Ministers from Republika Srpska opted not to participate in the donor meetings prior to the September elections, and the international community treated the wartime government (primarily Bosniacs by 1995)—which the Serbs refused to acknowledge as legitimate—as its interlocutor until then. In the meantime, the Federation established its own coordination board and cabinet minister for reconstruction, and Republika Srpska established an aid coordination unit within the economic ministry. Immediately after the elections, the High Representative abolished the transitional government before new structures were in place and provided no alternative to fill the void while quarrels over its formation played out. The government of Republika Srpska has never joined the state-level coordination structure, and efforts to coordinate aid within the Serb entity have been hampered by weak governmental capacity and geographic dislocation of ministries between two competing centers, Pale and Banja Luka. Likewise, coordination within the Federation government has suffered from a lack of consensus and confidence between Bosniacs and Croats on many issues.[50] Even after state institutions were established in February 1997, state-level coordination of reconstruction remained nonexistent.

Implementation Capacity: Donors

The postconflict reconstruction of Bosnia and Herzegovina is notable for the quick response by the donor community. The World Bank played a particularly productive role, beginning dialogue with the government in January 1995, long before the cease-fire and the Dayton negotiations. The Bank also established an early field presence, opening a Resident Mission shortly after the Dayton agreement, staffing it well, and delegating many operational authorities from its headquarters in Washington, aimed at decentralizing the program's implementation. The Bank simplified and streamlined procedures (especially in the area of procurement) and accelerated the execution of projects. The Netherlands also helped jump-start the recovery effort by providing special funds to prepare projects and (even earlier) by extending a bridging loan to clear Bosnia's arrears to the IMF. This step enabled Bosnia and Herzegovina to join the Fund, a precondition of World Bank membership.

The record was not uniform, however. The other leading donor, the European Union, reversed its innovations in the EUAM, which had streamlined procedures, delegated operational authority to the field, and decentralized procurement processes. Although the EU opened an office in Sarajevo even before the World Bank, its approach to Dayton implementation reverted to standard procedures for planning, approval, and procurement, which were extremely cumbersome and slow. It also reverted to centralized operations in Brussels, delaying the delivery of funds and the implementation of projects and engendering criticism from many sides, not least from the Bosnian authorities. Despite appeals from the Bosnian government that it cofinance World Bank projects (in underfunded areas like energy and education[51]), the EU clung to bilateral channels, arguing that it had doubts about the transparency and effectiveness of the Bosnian government's implementation structure.

The EC did, however, attempt to adjust. In late 1996, in light of difficulties encountered in the import supply programs and the extended procedures for aid disbursement, the EC concluded that it would not be able to spend the funds budgeted for 1996. It responded by reallocating some funds from emergency supplies to long-term reconstruction projects; extending the deadlines of other projects by twenty-four months; and channeling other projects through the World Bank programs. These adjustments, however, slowed disbursement for 1997 and added confusion to the aid program by tying pledged budget lines to the EU fiscal year, which differed from Bosnia's. By the spring of 1998, the criticism of EC delays was so great that the EC changed its approach to implementation. Apparently using the USAID approach as a model, it began to channel funds and implementation through NGOs in the field and to shift from large-scale, long-term infrastructure projects to smaller projects that could be delivered rapidly. This new approach did not reduce costs, however, and it generated new criticisms from Bosnian authorities dissatisfied with the role of NGOs in the recovery effort.

Implementation delays characterized other donors as well. While the UNHCR was considered very efficient by Bosnian authorities, they viewed UNDP and the United Nations Industrial Development Organization (UNIDO) as very slow. The EBRD established a field presence, but its management apparently considered political risks too high to begin serious involvement in the country. The OHR, as primary coordinator, required six months to one year after the Dayton signing to set up shop and establish field offices, while its key role in the U.S.-initiated coordinating structure did not begin until nine months into the Dayton implementation.

Among bilateral donors, the Netherlands was particularly quick to deliver on its aid commitments by cofinancing World Bank projects. USAID was also able to move quickly in implementation by adapting its internal mechanisms to give field officers greater autonomy. Germany, Austria, the Nordic countries, Great Britain, Malaysia, Switzerland, and Saudi Arabia also have strong aid implementation records. In contrast, Bosnian authorities have expressed concern with slow and complicated mechanisms for delivery of aid from Japan and Italy. Other major donors, like Turkey, have implemented very small amounts of pledged commitments; still others have not fulfilled their pledges at all (Russia, Iran, Kuwait, and Romania).

Disagreements about the proper coordination structure also influenced implementation. In particular, many donors were reluctant to use the PIU structure preferred by the World Bank and the Bosnian government for implementing PRRP sectoral projects. Many of them preferred to use their own implementation structure, while others judged the government's implementation capacity to be weak (or suspected corruption). Some, like the European Union, preferred to bypass the Bank/government structures in order to apply political conditionality more directly.[52] The Bank countered that the PIUs accelerated the pace of implementation of the PRRP significantly, while reducing operational costs because of the lower compensation scale for local staff.

Staffing issues also directly affect implementation, and they demonstrate in particular the close relation between the implementation capacity of donors and that of the recipient government. The number of foreign consultants engaged in Bosnia and Herzegovina has been very large, as has the amount of technical assistance extended. While the number of employees of most of the international agencies has been stable, the OHR increased its size from 300 in 1997 to 700 in 1998. These consultants, irrespective of quality, and international staff are paid out of pledged aid, reducing thereby the monies for local employment. Equally if not more hazardous to the long-term quality of implementation is the competition between local authorities and international agencies for staff; the best-trained staff naturally gravitate toward the higher salaries paid by international agencies—

about 10,000 local staff in 1998—leaving local authorities who cannot pay such salaries with older and less-qualified applicants.

Absorption and Implementation Capacity—Recipients

Explanations for Bosnian contributions to delays and gaps in the delivery of pledged funds tend to focus on the lack of local capacity (particularly structures of implementation and human capital) and on corruption. Closer analysis suggests, however, that local capacity is stronger than generally asserted, but recognized only belatedly by donors, and that the issue of corruption is far more complicated and political than portrayed by media exposés. Far more significant complications have arisen from political disagreements among the Bosnian parties, between the parties and the donors, and over the structure of the Dayton-defined constitution.

Economic indicators of success were clearly visible within a few years of the Dayton signing, at least in most parts of the Federation entity. Economic growth increased by 50 percent in 1996, before slowing to 30 percent in 1997, and 20 percent in 1998. Much of this growth, obviously, reflects the large influx of external assistance.[53] The current account deficit in 1998, $1.2 billion, was largely covered by foreign aid. Major roads, railways, bridges, and airports had been repaired, and electric power production had been restored. Unemployment fell from 90 percent to around 40 percent. The Croat areas of the Federation, which escaped the worst war damage, achieved the highest level of recovery.

In the Republika Srpska, by contrast, economic improvement was visible only in selected areas. GDP per capita lagged seriously, reaching in 1998 less than a quarter of the Federation's figure for 1996. Not until the first quarter of 1997 did growth suggest the beginnings of a modest recovery, and Republika Srpska's absorptive capacity remains far behind that of the Federation. The transition to a market economy was even slower.[54]

Judging from the Federation's performance, there is reason to think that Bosnia and Herzegovina possesses a relatively high capacity to absorb economic aid. World Bank officials evaluate project implementation as "good" and praise the government's role in coordinating donors and conferences. With a disbursement ratio of Bank-funded or Bank-managed projects well above 60 percent, the country is a success story among International Development Association (IDA) recipients.

Political problems and ambiguities arising from the Dayton agreement, however, did cause reconstruction and economic reform in many areas to lag well behind schedule. Because donors depended on functioning state institutions, the delays in forming a government at the state level until February 1997, continuing delays in the creation of a common administration, and lack of cooperation between the entities directly slowed the delivery of assistance. Regular contacts between entity governments began only in mid-1998, although economic relations then took priority. The lack of consensus and confidence between Bosniacs and Croats in the Federation led to the maintenance, and growth, of parallel administrative arrangements while Croats refused to dismantle institutions that were illegal according to the Dayton accords.[55] Weak administrative capacity in the Republika Srpska was exacerbated by the geographical dispersal of ministries and by profound political disagreement over aid policies and cooperation with the Dayton accords and international officials between a moderate Western part and an uncooperative Eastern part.

The complex Dayton constitution encouraged decisionmaking gridlock, and the very fact of annual elections, encouraged by the international community to obtain new leaders who would cooperate with the Dayton accords, put a political drag on the policy reforms that donors considered essential to sustainability but that politicians knew would be politically unpopular. Similarly, the parties' different legal interpretations of the peace agreement, such as over the legal status of public enterprises, delayed projects and economic reforms, while reducing donor contributions in critical areas such as railways and telecommunications. Disagreements about the responsibilities of different levels of government delayed the creation of mechanisms to regulate privatization and the disbursement of $100 million from the World Bank to support economic reforms, public finance management, and privatization.

In addition to these causes of delay, early postwar politics led ethnic criteria to dominate over need assessments in the distribution of international assistance. Depriving poorer areas, or ones that were more affected by the war but that had less political influence within their own ethnic groups, of needed aid created significant gaps in project completion and in distribution countrywide. Noncooperation directly affected the mobilization of pledges, as in the requirement that legislation indispensable to an IMF standby agreement be approved first. Agreement on five loans requested by the IMF (the quick-start package) was reached only after seven months of negotiations. Since the approval of this package was a condition for convening the third donor conference, the conference was postponed from February until July 1997. That conference fell short of its financial target by $300 million. The cost of refusal to cooperate can be illustrated as well with a water project in Goražde (Federation entity). Pledges of $5 million by Saudi Arabia and Malaysia were allocated to build a water system because the neighboring Čajniće (in Republika Srpska) would not agree to joint use of existing facilities. Despite intervention by the OHR, Serb intransigence won out; finances were redirected from a revolving fund set up to restart industry, thus creating a financing gap in that sector in order to ensure a permanent and regular water supply to Goražde.

The Dayton constitution also permitted endless obstruction of the whole recovery process. Legally, approval of all loans required consensus of the three-person presidency and ratification by Parliament (and by the Council of Ministers in the case of grants). Using the complex levels of jurisdiction and procedures for approval to block initiatives, the Bosnian Serbs and Bosnian Croats conditioned approval of foreign aid on their communities' receipt of certain percentages of assistance. The consequences can be seen clearly between 1996—before the Dayton institutions were formed, when sixteen World Bank projects were approved—and fiscal year 1997, when only eight projects were approved and the process took much longer.[56] Some donors responded to these delays by postponing or abandoning the implementation of their pledges.[57] Others reacted to the multiethnic-signature system by shifting attention to local authorities, thus weakening government ownership over reconstruction coordination. Even where state-level policy decisions are made, the constitutional arrangements give jurisdiction over implementation to the entities, which often have opposing views on the same subject—particularly regarding trade and fiscal issues.

Especially damaging to reconstruction was the failure for more than two years after Dayton of both government and donors to establish an effective mechanism for land mine clearance, because it postponed a number of infrastructure projects as well as creating gaps in the implementation of pledges.[58] The lack of coordination, effort, and funding for de-mining activities in areas of refugee return remains a major concern.

Political Conditionality

At least as important in explaining delays in the delivery of pledged aid is the use of multilateral economic assistance as an instrument to achieve the political objectives of the Dayton peace agreement. For donors these goals center primarily on the restoration of a single, multiethnic Bosnia and Herzegovina through the execution of the specific annexes of the peace accord, particularly those concerning the repatriation of refugees; the right to return to prewar homes of IDPs and refugees; and full cooperation with the International Criminal Tribunal for the former Yugoslavia.[59] To these were added, in 1997–1998, the creation, for the protection of returnees, of multiethnic police forces at the local level.

Apart from the economic conditionality that always accompanies loans from the international financial institutions, donors emphasized during the Dayton negotiations and at the first London conference on civilian implementation in December 1996 that they intended to employ political conditionality. Recognizing that the future of economic development in Bosnia and Herzegovina required international support, the PIC proclaimed that such support will be forthcoming during the consolidation period on condition that the authorities in Bosnia and Herzegovina comply fully with the provisions of the peace agreement, as well as the commitments on economic development, established at this conference.[60] The principle has been repeated at all pledging conferences and PIC meetings. The Sintra meeting of the PIC Steering Board on May 30, 1997, chose to intensify international commitment to the principle ("that international assistance with economic reconstruction should be conditioned upon full compliance with the Peace Agreement").[61] At the PIC meeting in Bonn, on December 10, 1997, and in Madrid, on December 16–17, 1998, the council chose to "remind" the authorities in Bosnia and Herzegovina that economic assistance by the international community remains strictly conditional upon compliance with the peace agreement and subsequent obligations.[62] The primary tool of this commitment has been the ETF, where the High Representative could provide donors with a framework for political conditionality. The High Representative has also used the occasion of donors' pledging conferences to request assistance in conditioning economic aid.[63]

The primary result of political conditionality was to prevent reconstruction aid to Republika Srpska, which received only 2 percent of total assistance in 1996 and hardly more in 1997. At first, the international community refused to lift its wartime economic sanctions on Bosnian Serbs until they fulfilled the terms of the demilitarization Annex 1-A in October 1996. Their economic isolation continued, however, when they refused to attend the first donor conference as part of the Bosnian government delegation, as required by the High Representative, before elections had created a postwar government. By 1997, the cause was their hindrances to the return of refugees and IDPs and to the apprehension of indicted war criminals. When the extraordinary Republika Srpska parliamentary elections of November 1997 brought a change of power to a prime minister who declared commitment to the Dayton accords, the international community reversed its course. Donors, including the United States, began to provide a significant amount of reconstruction aid to the western part of Republika Srpska, but not to the eastern half or to individual communities accused of harboring indicted war criminals.[64] From 1995–1997, Republika Srpska had received only DM 113 million out of DM 1.5 billion spent in Bosnia and Herzegovina. In the first six months of 1998, Republika Srpska received DM 400 million of the DM 2.1 billion of ongoing or completed projects.[65]

Political conditionality: donors' inconsistencies. Nonetheless, applying the principle of political conditionality was less simple than declaring it. Disagreements among donors about the principle itself slowed the delivery of pledged funds. In the first year of Dayton's implementation, many of the quarrels over coordination structures and policy authority between the

OHR, the EC, and the United States, on the one hand, and the World Bank, on the other, reflected different attitudes toward political conditionality. World Bank opposition went beyond the prohibitions of its charter to the negative effects on economic reconstruction if projects were to be stopped and started at will (often not practically possible, in any event). In addition, the EC applied its own set of political conditions independent of the Dayton accords, covering human rights practices, independent media, and a commitment to democracy, according to the criteria it applied to all countries of the region (called its "regional approach") for access to autonomous trade preferences, Phare aid, and eventual opening of contractual negotiations with the EU.

Disagreements on the principle also led many donors to channel more of their pledged aid away from multilateral and toward bilateral programs. This was the case both for donors who preferred stronger use of political conditionality, such as the United States and the EC, and those who were uneasy about conditioned aid and preferred economic rationales alone, such as Great Britain, Japan, Canada, Spain, Germany, and France.[66] By allowing donors to rely on their own variable interpretations of compliance with the GFAP, however, increased bilateralism not only sent conflicting messages to the Bosnian parties but also reduced coordination, with attendant delays in implementation. Some donors even provided reconstruction aid in the guise of humanitarian assistance, which is generally not conditioned, to avoid the requirement of political conditionality.

Donors showed considerable inconsistency in applying political conditionality. While they withheld aid when Republika Srpska refused to cooperate on refugee return and the ICTY, the majority of donors (except the United States and the Netherlands) delivered assistance unconditionally on the other side of the interentity boundary line in 1996, even though the Bosnian Croat community failed to cooperate on indicted war criminals or refugee return. Moreover, the Bosnian Croats did not lose any aid when their delegation failed to appear at the fourth donor conference, in May 1998. Similarly, in November 1997, the international community channeled aid to the western part of Republika Srpska, in support of President Plavsić and the moderates who backed her, even though there had been few results on indicted war criminals or the return home of refugees and IDPs in areas where they would be the minority.[67]

The conflict between political conditionality and the goal of economic assistance did lead donors to change tactics in some cases. To facilitate refugee return, for example, the UNHCR and the United States launched an Open Cities initiative, encouraging municipalities to declare publicly their willingness to allow the return of minority refugees—whereupon they would be rewarded directly with foreign assistance. This change in policy from a "black list" to a "white list" uses positive rather than negative incentives as a form of aid conditionality closer to proponents of peace conditionality and more acceptable to those donors concerned about the economic distortions of withholding aid. This initiative reflected a more general trend among donors, including the EC with its new Obnova program,[68] to have more control over beneficiaries by going to localities, adapting their procedures to be able to negotiate municipal aid agreements. But municipal leaders were not necessarily more accountable than national leaders, and the rapid turnover of most foreigners, usually on six-month contracts, meant that local politicians who failed to gain aid in one period could simply wait out their departure and try again rather than alter behavior. To counteract this lack of accountability over time, the OHR began in late 1998 to devise a separate database for donors and international officials that would record all official relations with a municipality and create a picture of compliance or noncompliance.

Even the World Bank was pressured to subordinate its reconstruction program to the political goals of the Dayton implementers. Its forestry project waited eight months for board approval because the U.S. representative objected that the project could benefit some indicted war criminals who controlled the wood sector industry in Republika Srpska. In December 1997, approval of a $17 million, major reconstruction assistance program for Republika Srpska was delayed and reduced when NGOs and several major donors protested the inclusion of assistance to Foča, a town in eastern Republika Srpska where several indicted war criminals reside.

Economic conditionality. Economic conditionality has also been applied to aid by the IMF and World Bank; for example, a key precondition for reconstruction assistance was the prior negotiation and implementation of an IMF standby arrangement. While most donors supported the principle of economic conditionality, early disputes over when to move from food donations to fees that would initiate cost-recovery principles were particularly intense. Despite unusually low requirements for the IMF standby, Bosnian authorities and some key donors accused the IMF of being insufficiently flexible in its insistence on a normal standby (credit under commercial terms) instead of a highly concessional Enhanced Structural Adjustment Facility (ESAF), for which it was eligible—a policy that added another cause of significant delay in the delivery of pledges.

Corruption and Transparency

The failure of pledged aid to show visible results on the ground also led to charges (and countercharges) of corruption in the use of funds. These allegations, which have gained substantial media attention both in Bosnia and internationally, have constituted a primary justification for donor delays in aid delivery. The strongest accusations came from the British foreign minister, Robin Cook, in his capacity as revolving president of the European Union, during his visit to the country in August 1997. High Representative Bildt also made public allegations on several occasions. While these charges have generated substantial media attention, their timing and the fact that the loudest voices represent the EC suggest that these allegations may have in part been intended to deflect criticism away from donors for their slowness in delivering on pledges.

The issue of corruption is more complex than it first appears, and that includes the politics of donors.[69] Neither the independent Bosnian parliamentary commission, established shortly after the visit of Foreign Minister Cook, nor international audits have found any large evidence to support these charges. The World Bank has several times announced publicly[70] that there is no corruption in Bank-financed projects, meaning that aid officials have known at all times exactly where the money is. Alija Izetbegović, chair of the state collective presidency, observed repeatedly that donor assistance could hardly be subject to Bosnian government corruption because almost 70 percent of the total assistance is implemented by foreign organizations. These are usually managed by nationals of the donor countries themselves and rarely transfer actual funds to government accounts.[71] It is true that Bosnian authorities have more freedom with bilateral assistance (such as that coming from Islamic countries), but these donors have not complained. And while some cases of highly publicized scandal may have justified attention, donor efforts to circumvent quarrels at the center by working directly with municipalities may, some suggest, have increased the incidence of corruption—particularly the classic kind, such as kickbacks in construction contracts and informal accounting methods in local banks.

Because allegations of corruption from the donor side, whether true or not, can tighten scrutiny to the point of harming the ability to mobilize future funds and risking the loss of pledged funds, the subject must be handled carefully. The charges raise several issues. One is the need for better data on the actual aid effort on the ground so as to counter wild accusations spread through the mass media. World Bank officials promote the PIU structure as not only speeding implementation but also avoiding a cycle of accusations between government and donors; but it also reduces the opportunity to apply political conditionality. The OHR has formed an Anti-Fraud Unit (AFU) to assist the authorities in identifying illegal activities and helping to draft anticorruption legislation.[72] The World Bank and the Bosnian government have established a joint Procurement and Auditing Unit to monitor the World Bank's projects. Moreover, the Bosnian authorities have invited an international NGO, Transparency International, to help them in fighting fraud and corruption. But the issue of accountability applies to donors as well as the recipient. The solution to unsubstantiated accusations is better monitoring, prompt correction of potential delays that may occur in delivery, and precise identification of the source of impediments to delivery.

A second issue is the nature of corruption itself in the transition from war to peace and from a collapsed socialist state to an only partially institutionalized, functioning democratic state and an entirely new system of accounting and economic organization. As the head of the OHR unit on corruption argues, this is a structural problem far more than individual cases of the misuse of funds or private enrichment. Corruption is therefore a matter of political reform and systemic transformation, developing the restraints and enforcement powers of a democratic state, including the clear separation between a professional civil service and political authorities. A "global strategy" devised by the unit in the fall of 1998 was presented to the PIC meeting at Madrid in December 1998. At the same time, individual temptation is in part an artifact of the international approach to peace in Bosnia and Herzegovina. By committing the international presence in a series of short-time segments, a year or eighteen months at a time, combined with an infusion of aid in quantities never before seen in the country, donors encourage individuals who must think long term about providing for families and friends to take advantage while the monies are available.

To the extent that economic corruption is acknowledged on all sides, moreover, the misuse has far less to do with foreign aid than with domestic revenues. The serious lack of transparency with respect to collecting and spending customs and tax revenues is due in part to the underdevelopment of the fiscal system and in part to the political contest arising from the Dayton accords over the proper jurisdiction of economic authority.[73] In Republika Srpska, for example, most of the revenues collected in 1996 (before election of the first postwar government) were not deposited to the budget accounts. Since the establishment of a new government in November 1997, however, the performance of Republika Srpska has been better than that of the Federation, where the lack of political agreement and parallel customs and tax administrations have allowed both the Bosniacs and Bosnian Croats to misuse revenues.[74] Throughout Bosnia and Herzegovina, corruption and evasion of taxes and customs increased dramatically in 1996–1998. As the Dayton agreement did not regulate the control of state borders, the possibilities for smuggling are widespread.[75] At the same time, the OHR, SFOR, IPTF, and some donors helped to establish and continue to tolerate several illegal open marketplaces at the interentity boundary line as a success indicator of their goal of freedom of movement throughout the country and, in bringing people from both entities into regular trading contact, of reconciliation and reintegration. They thus refuse repeated government efforts to close them down because no taxes are paid. Moreover, the international (both civilian and military) employers of approximately 10,000 Bosnian citizens do not pay the local income taxes due the government. Nonetheless, such corruption in taxes and trade does hit at the heart of aid policy, which is intended to be only a temporary substitute for domestic resources.[76]

Other Factors Contributing to Delays in Pledged Assistance

While the factors contributing to delays in the delivery and implementation of aid in the Bosnian case have parallels in other cases, there are significant particularities of the case that cannot be ignored, especially those arising from the breakup of its former state.

Foreign Debt

Bosnia's prewar debt, valued at $630 million in 1996, represents a heavy financial burden on a war-torn economy. Although the World Bank reprogrammed the debt in 1996, the arrangement, in the view of the Bosnian government, will not enable the country to repay it without significant IDA assistance after the year 2000. For example, the country is obliged to repay around $200 million in interest arrears accrued during the war. The result of the debt, in fact, is an overall positive net transfer of aid from the Bank to the country that is almost insignificant (around $50 million), leading the government to consider the $670 million already committed for reconstruction as insufficient.[77] Similarly, the government considers the agreement with Paris Club creditors finally concluded in 1998 to be based on overly optimistic economic projections presented by the IMF and a resulting 67 percent debt reduction instead of 80 percent.[78]

In addition, government ownership over foreign debt management will be very weak for some time. Due to late payments to the World Bank, the country lost an interest waiver and around $2 million. The decentralized structure of the Dayton constitution, which also affects debt management, enabled some of the parties to "blackmail" each other and the IFIs by conditioning their approval of regular repayments of the prewar debt on donors' readiness to invest in certain projects, to the benefit of one national group and areas with no war damage. As such repayments are a condition for new investment, the IFIs chose a pragmatic approach and conceded to these demands for ethnonational criteria in place of assessed need and war damage.

Foreign Trade

According to the Dayton constitution, formal trade relations with other countries are the sole prerogative of the state government. Nonetheless, the government of Republika Srpska and the Croat part of the Federation Customs Administration have been granted preferential trade treatment by neighboring Yugoslavia and Croatia, respectively. Although these are in violation of the State Customs Law adopted in 1998, and the Madrid PIC final document requests both entities to abolish these practices immediately,[79] no action has resulted. The entity budgets continue to lose significant customs revenues, and substantial amounts of international assistance in the form of trade ends up in the coffers of Croatia or Yugoslavia. The resulting sizable imports from these neighboring countries also hinder the transition and sustainability sought by donors by creating unfair competition for domestic production and slowing growth in employment.[80] By significantly decreasing the country's ability to service its foreign debt, it could also complicate delivery of IFI assistance.

External Shocks

While delays in aid delivery cannot be attributed directly to events over which donors and the government have no immediate influence, three external influences indirectly burden the aid process in significant ways. Most directly is the pressure from some European countries, mainly Germany, to send refugees back home to Bosnia in an uncontrolled fashion and before conditions in the political and security environment and in housing reconstruction are ready. Yet donors' assessment of progress on peace implementation, on which they based decisions about continuing assistance, focused particularly on refugee return. Simultaneously, judgments on economic transition took little account of the additional economic burden on public expenditures of additional pensioners and unemployed from returning refugees.[81] Second, the global financial crisis began to threaten the mobilization and delivery of the last stage of pledges for the PRRP in 1998.[82] And third, the peace process and economic transition cannot be isolated from the other parts of the former Yugoslavia and their resolution. Yet the peace negotiators and the donors, with some exceptions, prefer to treat Bosnia independently, within the bounds of sovereignty. Moreover, continuing instability in the neighborhood, such as the war that began in the Serbian province of Kosovo in the spring of 1998, creates competing demands for donors' aid, probable delays in delivering on existing pledges, and further delays in normalization that could attract foreign investment and the transition from aid to sustainability.[83]

Conclusion and Lessons to Be Learned

Timing of the Effort, Early Planning, and Political Importance of a Case

One of the most important lessons of the Bosnian experience is the importance of early planning and involvement of multilateral organizations. Partial cease-fires, around Sarajevo in February 1994 and in the Federation after March 1994, made it possible for donors to consider assistance and to begin planning long before the peace accords. The Sarajevo restoration effort provided an early, systematic assessment of conditions and needs and a comprehensive view of reconstruction. Early planning in late 1994 and early 1995 by the World Bank enabled a speedy mobilization of donors and assistance, particularly in the first year after the accords. Early funding of project preparation, made possible by contributions from the Netherlands, was indispensable. So too was the streamlining of normal Bank procedures and an early and strong field presence with discretion over implementation, including procurement.

Behind this speed in mobilizing funds, however, was firm political support by the most relevant international actors. As one Bank official noted, this provided the Bank with additional "wind in the back" in the crucial first year. The critical role of Dutch loans to clear arrears with the IMF demonstrates the need for a standing international instrument for other cases, along the lines of other specialized funds for postconflict circumstances that have been created at the World Bank and elsewhere.

Political and Security Framework

At the same time, reconstruction assistance cannot meet the financing needs of the country, nor can it lead to economic recovery, without the prior establishment of a necessary minimum political framework for institutional cooperation within the country. As Nicole Ball writes in a recent study of the Bosnian program, Bosnia and Herzegovina thus reinforces a lesson that has been observed in previous peace processes, namely, that economic reconstruction cannot occur in a political vacuum. Some degree of political normalization is essential for economic recovery.[84]

The political and security framework is also essential to sustain donor interest. Throughout the reconstruction effort following the Dayton agreement, donors stressed refugee return as their priority goal. Yet, while economic assistance is crucial for the successful reintegration of refugees, it had little influence on the decision of people to return to their place of origin.[85] Surveys conducted by the Commission for Real Property Claims of Displaced Persons and Refugees (CRPC) indicate that security guarantees from local authorities and the return of former neighbors ranked much higher on the scale of importance (47 percent) for returns to areas where they would be in the minority than did prospects for job opportunities (16 percent) or housing reconstruction (12 percent). The fact that 93 percent of 1997 returns were to areas where they would be in the majority, with only 10,000 "minority returns" that year, seemed to be reinforcing "donor fatigue" in 1998.

A further critical element of the political framework is the peace agreement itself. Ambiguities in the Dayton agreement contributed significantly to delays in the realization and mobilization of pledges. The result was to create new powers for the High Representative responsible for coordinating international activities in Bosnia and Herzegovina that would permit him to intervene and impose an interim or arbitration decision when the decisionmaking procedures of the peace agreement allowed the parties to stall or even avoid making decisions on their own. But these powers did not dissolve the hindrances built into the agreement itself or work toward local ownership of the process.

Donor Conferences

Donor conferences are clearly the main instruments for mobilizing support for the reconstruction effort. Their timing is often used as an incentive to build consensus within the country or to accelerate the reconstruction effort in general. Among their many benefits were centralization of the lobbying effort by the Bosnian government, identification of priorities, and setting up of coordination structures and channels for information exchange. The first meeting of the two entity governments, for example, occurred at a donor conference. The coordination at donor conferences may help—although not fully resolve—the extent of overlap of donor efforts on the ground and the overfunding of areas with high "media visibility" for home consumption of donor publics. In the Bosnian experience, this mechanism was of huge importance in mobilizing large amounts of assistance, which was forthcoming in some cases as a result of perceived peer pressure. The size of the pledge becomes in some cases almost a matter of prestige.

On the other side of the story lies the danger that expectations are raised unnaturally, particularly in the recipient country, with respect to the speed and actual value of aid that follows. Verbal pledges are made before they are approved by legislatures. Between a pledge and the release and expenditure of funds on the ground and the result in a visible impact in the country, much time may elapse. The structure of such legislative procedures in donor countries can also dilute pledges in the process—and in certain cases, even fail to produce any aid at all. The long time between a pledge and a commitment alone suggests that to be effective, pledging conferences should be held early in the year, when the construction season is dormant and planning can begin. Optimal scheduling is not possible, however, if the timing of conferences is itself an instrument of conditionality used by donors to gain leverage over parties' behavior in implementation of a peace agreement or prescribed elements of an economic transition.

Triple Transition

Economic reconstruction does not occur in a vacuum, and donors had three separate objectives in giving aid: supporting the transition from humanitarian emergency to reconstruction, from war to peace, and from socialism to a market economy in a manner that permitted sustainable recovery. Assessing donor preferences and gaps among types of aid is difficult, however, because countries report their aid in global form, not always distinguishing strictly between aid and nonaid expenditures, rarely distinguishing between funds for reconstruction and funds for market transition and economic reform, and using peace implementation as a residual category for all expenditures not explicitly "economic" (lumping assistance to the IPTF, UNHCR, the ICTY, and NGOs together). In practical terms, many activities often overlap, so the donor's intentions are difficult to discern. But this also reflects the fact that donors often perceive all instruments of the "triple transition" as proceeding in parallel in the postconflict situation.

Sequencing does matter, however, in the efficiency and effectiveness of the transition process. Yet the organizational basis for aid programs, in which each implementing organization has its own mandate and specialization and its jealously guarded autonomy, makes it nearly impossible for donors to confer and agree on a strategy for transition. Their choice of priorities and pace, despite the creation of task forces for coordination, was driven far more by politics in their home countries and institutions, by organizational mandates, and by the preference for *visible* contributions in place of institutional development or political reform. Donor interests in repatriating Bosnian refugees placed overwhelming priority on housing construction. Despite rhetorical emphasis on the contribution of employment to peace, employment creation lagged.

Despite recognition that they had not paid enough attention in the early stages to the political aspects of the transition, World Bank officials, along with the EU, IMF, and EBRD, continued to place priority and resources on infrastructural reconstruction and orthodox approaches to economic transition. But even then, the policy reforms—such as in banking, property rights, long-term supply and payments frameworks, cost recovery, and taxation—were continually delayed, with direct consequences for delays in assistance. And the special needs of peace building were not addressed except by efforts to speed procedures, decentralize operations (to the country and then later within the country), and use aid as a weapon to enforce the peace agreement.

Donor quarrels over the best structures for coordination dominated over genuine disagreements about aid strategy and policy. Those quarrels over strategy and aid priorities led donors to defect from multilateral programs to bilateral aid; deadlock at the state level led donors to municipalities; and difficulties in implementation (on both donor and recipient sides) led to more channeling of aid through foreign NGOs. Participation matters: donors want a say over how monies are spent, and the recipients are far more likely to "misuse" funds if they are not included in decisions. Although disagreements about the use of political conditionality continue, the control over funds for political influence was sufficiently strong to delay most assistance to an entire half of the country for more than two years and to introduce specific delays in pledges and interruptions in programs throughout the period analyzed here. Changes in strategy for the use of aid and in programs that would meet the needs of postconflict conditions have received minimal attention.

Accountability and Transparency

Accountability is an important concern in the effectiveness of aid pledges, both for the donor community and for the recipient country and target beneficiaries. In his remarks at the donors information conference in Brussels on January 9, 1997, Carl Bildt, then the High Representative for Bosnia and Herzegovina, stressed: "We need to have honest numbers and more rapid efforts if we are to be successful. There is always a tendency towards creative accounting when it comes to governments making pledges. But such attempts backfire sooner or later. We should no longer tolerate such attempts but make certain that we have honest figures and honest commitments."[86]

Economists working in the field operation in Bosnia and Herzegovina stress the difficulty of quantifying the pledge gap because definitions vary among the databases, operating costs (often very large) are not specified, updates are infrequent, and inaccuracies or duplication in the databases cannot be easily checked because they are not readily accessible to the public. Despite their rhetorical emphasis on transparency, donors and IFIs do not commit monies for monitoring. The assessment of gaps between pledges and delivery is seriously hampered by the quality and nature of the data. At least three major (and two lesser) databases exist; data within them are only estimates; and unclear reporting guidelines create doubts, inconsistencies, and overlaps in the data.

Therefore, one proposal for consideration and discussion with the major participants involved in this process would be to recognize the need for improved tracking of actual aid delivery figures on the ground and for strengthened cooperation to avoid a duplication of effort. In effect, both donors and the recipient government need to create proper and uniform accounting practices. This would help measure the impact of assistance on the target country, and show the use of funds for operating costs in delivering aid, for the implementing agencies, for technical assistance, and so forth. Another proposal, made by OHR in Sarajevo, is to publish the data on the internet or to merge various databases into a sort of "live database" module that would be accessible to all agencies involved. Particularly because of the large number of donors and the frequent turnover in field personnel, such a publicly open database could reduce duplication, be an incentive to donors to provide information regularly, and provide a check on the progress of projects and the need for correction. The best check against corruption, the misappropriation of funds, or wasted aid is a policy of transparency and consistency in the reporting of both donors and recipient countries.

Implementation

Finally, much of the pledge gap in Bosnia and Herzegovina reflected delays in delivery and implementation, not nonfeasance or default. Causes of these delays could be found on both the donor side, where inexperience created heavy start-up costs, and the recipient side, where host-government procedures were woefully underdeveloped. Delay was exacerbated by the decisionmaking procedures of the peace agreement itself, by the dominant role of political conditionality in the use of aid, and by the complex coordination problems of so large an operation as the "Dayton" mission.

Notes

1. This is less than one-tenth of the total spent by the international community in Bosnia since 1992, estimates of which vary from $49 billion to $70 billion over those seven years, 1992–1998, largely for the presence of international organizations on the ground, particularly the stationing of military forces to assist the peace after the peace accord was signed in November 1995.

2. World Bank (Central Europe Department) and European Bank for Reconstruction and Development, "Bosnia and Herzegovina."

3. The war had damaged or destroyed most of the country's bridges; large sections of its electric power grid; several hundred miles of roads, railways, and telecommunications networks; and more than half of the housing stock, schools, health facilities, and commercial buildings. The conflict had also left an estimated half a million land mines (mostly uncharted) throughout the country.

4. The Washington Agreement—ending a year of fighting between the Bosniacs and hard-line Croats who had set up a parastate, "Herzeg Bosnia," with support

from Croatia proper—was signed in March 1994 as a result of U.S. diplomatic initiative. It created a Federation of Bosnia and Herzegovina, which was to include all areas of Bosnia and Herzegovina outside Serb control, and set up a "confederal" link with Croatia.

5. At a lower level, the canton governments in the Federation are responsible for all other matters not granted explicitly to the Federation government. These include education, culture, housing, public services, local land use, and social transfer expenditures. To finance these activities, the cantons are given ownership of sales, income, and property taxes, as well as the fees charged for public services. The municipal governments are granted "self-rule on local matters," including those delegated to them by the canton. But when the majority population of the municipality is different from that of the canton in which it is located, the cantonal government is obliged to grant that municipality self-rule on all normally cantonal responsibilities.

6. UN Security Council Resolution 1031.

7. Dayton peace agreement, annex 10.

8. Held at the Bank's resident mission in Warsaw for reasons of security, this was a working-level meeting between the Bank's country officer and country economist and three Bosnian officials from the ministry of foreign affairs and the Central Bank, and it followed months of planning by the Bosnia and Herzegovina Working Group at headquarters working closely with the Bank's executive director for Bosnia, from the Netherlands.

9. United Nations, UN SG General Reports to the Security Council, *Status of Implementation of the Plan of Action as of 15 April 1996;* Action Plan for Sarajevo; and newspaper interviews with Thomas Eagleton.

10. UN Doc S/1996/381, May 28, 1996.

11. See Koschnick and Schneider, *Brücke über die Neretva.*

12. One such occasion was Germany's rejection (as a result of Croatian pressure) of Koschnick's plan for a unified central district in Mostar at the March 1996 PIC meeting in Rome.

13. Interview by Amela Šapčanin.

14. United Nations, Consolidated Inter-Agency Appeal for Bosnia and Herzegovina, Croatia, Federal Republic of Yugoslavia, Former Yugoslav Republic of Macedonia, January–December 1997 (New York and Geneva: United Nations Department of Humanitarian Affairs, November 1996).

15. UNHCR Funding Overview 1997.

16. United Nations Consolidated Inter-Agency Appeal for Bosnia and Herzegovina, Croatia, Federal Republic of Yugoslavia, Former Yugoslav Republic of Macedonia, January–December 1998 (New York and Geneva: United Nations Department of Humanitarian Affairs, November 1997).

17. European Commission World Bank, "Bosnia and Herzegovina—The Priority Reconstruction Program."

18. These included rehabilitation of transport and gas; agriculture and key infrastructure, telecommunications, social sectors, and mine clearance equipment; recurrent support for education and health; support to key government institutions; establishment of a social fund; provision of working capital to jump-start production in small and medium enterprises; and reserves for a central bank. "Chairman's Conclusions," First Donors Conference on the Reconstruction of Bosnia and Herzegovina.

19. The objectives of the PRRP included rehabilitation of key infrastructure and social sectors to jump-start production and ensure improved access to basic

services and housing to facilitate the return of displaced persons and refugees; implementation of projects in support of employment generation and demobilization of soldiers; strengthening of key government institutions and establishment of basic economic institutions of the two entities and the state, including a new central bank, as called for under the Dayton-Paris peace agreement; continuation of efforts toward macroeconomic stabilization; and implementation of the de-mining project as an important prerequisite for physical implementation of other projects. "Chairman's Conclusions," Second Donor Conference on the Reconstruction of Bosnia and Herzegovina.

20. Priority areas included programs to facilitate refugee return (including housing, jobs, and basic social services); continued reconstruction of war-devastated infrastructure (including energy, transport, and telecommunications); rehabilitation of social sectors; employment creation through private and financial sector development; and institution building and policy reforms to facilitate the country's transition to a market economy. "Chairman's Conclusions," Third Donor Conference on the Reconstruction of Bosnia and Herzegovina.

21. Official results as of June 3, 1998, obtained by request from the World Bank.

22. Interviews by Susan Woodward.

23. Senator Frank Lautenberg (DNJ) sponsored the War Crimes Prosecution Facilitation Act of 1997 (S804, May 23, 1997), which restricts U.S. bilateral assistance and instructs the U.S. executive director to the international financial institutions (specified as the IMF, IBRD, IDA, IFC, MIGA, and EBRD) to oppose and vote against any aid or grants to countries, entities, or cantons providing sanctuary to indicted war criminals who are sought for prosecution before the International Criminal Tribunal for the Former Yugoslavia (can be seen on website http:// Thomas.LOC.gov); it was incorporated into the Foreign Operations Appropriations Act for 1998, Section 573 of HR 2159, and became law on November 12, 1997.

24. See David Kriskovich, *Restructuring Progress in Bosnia/Herzegovina.*

25. "General Information—Budget," from OSCE website (www.osceprag.cz/ info/budget/budget97.htm).

26. OSCE Report on Voluntary Contributions, February 13, 1998.

27. This is a part of a DM 126 million (approximately $78 million) commitment from the European Commission awarded in seventeen contracts to NGOs to facilitate the return of refugees and displaced persons to Bosnia and Herzegovina.

28. Woehrel, "Bosnia: U.S.-Led Train-and-Equip Program," p. CRS-2.

29. The goods provided under this "draw-down authority" were later discovered to be worth only $85 million, leaving $15 million in draw-down that would be used for ammunition, spare parts, and reconditioning of other excess defense articles. Balkan Institute, "Arm-and-Train: A Status Report."

30. Nedeljko Despotović, Minister in the Federation government in charge of reconstruction, has often expressed his dissatisfaction with the implementation and disbursement figures as provided by the donors, charging that they are often inflated and do not reflect the reality on the ground (interview by Zlatko Hurtić).

31. Due to difficulties in obtaining the data on the 1998 progress report from a number of larger donors, a more recent update was not available at the time of this study.

32. According to World Bank definitions, (1) a *pledge* is an expression of intent to mobilize funds for which an approximate sum is indicated; (2) a *firm commitment* is a pledge that has been (a) approved by a national legislative body or multilateral board and (b) allocated to a specific sectoral program or project; (3)

amounts *under implementation* are those firmly committed funds for which contracts have been tendered, signed, or completed; (4) *disbursed funds* are those transferred to an account in the name of a Bosnian agency or a disbursement agency (foreign or local) in Bosnia and include expenditures made against works, goods, and service contracts and for fiscal or balance of payments support (in-kind assistance is considered disbursed once provided); (5) *funds expended* represent (a) actual expenditures made against works, goods, and service contracts, (b) the value of assistance delivered in kind, and (c) fiscal or balance of payment support; the definition of funds expended does not include advances made to implementing agencies for future payments to suppliers. European Commission and World Bank, "Bosnia and Herzegovina—Implementation of Priority Reconstruction Program."

33. IMG, an intergovernmental organization focused on the infrastructure reconstruction and recovery of Bosnia and Herzegovina, was officially established at the London Conference on the Former Yugoslavia in August 1993. In November 1994, it became an autonomous organization with a managing board that determines the organization's strategy and budget and contracts technical experts. IMG's main function remains the assessment of war damage of infrastructure and needs assessment in energy transmission and distribution, housing, school and medical equipment, transport, telecommunications, water supply and waste management, irrigation, etc.

34. The Economic Task Force was established within the OHR and is chaired by the High Representative. It consists of the World Bank, the IMF, the European Commission, the IMG, and the EBRD.

35. In the RCM database, a contract is defined as a signed agreement between the implementing agency and the final supplier of the work, goods, or services.

36. The distinction between reconstruction and nonreconstruction sectors is found in the monthly newsletter of the Economic Task Force Secretariat, OHR, vol. 1, no. 5, July 1998, although it is not quite clear why this division among the sectors was made.

37. These newsletters can also be viewed on http:\\www.ohr.int.

38. The categories applied in the collection process include: amounts *indicated*—potential amount pledged but no signed implementation documents exist; amounts *confirmed*—participating amounts as indicated by the signed documents of implementation or other confirmed documents; amounts *in implementation*—participating amounts for which contracts have been signed, the procurement is under way, tenders have been published, work is in progress, or work is completed; amounts *unallocated*—unspecified sources of information for potential pledge amounts; and *totals*—amounts indicated, confirmed, and in implementation according to an earlier report from 1996 Bulletin of the Department for Reconstruction, Ministry of Foreign Affairs.

39. The amount of the IMF loan to the government of Bosnia and Herzegovina was included in the overall pledging figures at the fourth donors conference, under the balance of payments support category. It is questionable whether this should be classified as reconstruction assistance.

40. Even Sweden, a large aid donor, for example, counts "disbursements" to UNESCO as a part of its "Balkan effort," even though those expenditures are not in Bosnia; others include the salaries of seconded diplomats or SFOR soldiers, or the computers and cars used by OHR staff (interviews with OHR staff by Susan Woodward).

41. This was the case particularly with the first donor conference in Brussels, which did include, under the amounts pledged at the time, some portions of funds that had been previously put to use for the ongoing activities under various NGO

or UN programs prior to the signing of the peace accords, but also the fourth donor conference in 1998. Staff present in May 1998 report that it was impossible to tell at the conference itself what was being pledged, "repledged," or "reallocated," and that in the final $5.1 billion program, some aid had been pledged two and three times over (interviews by Susan Woodward in Sarajevo).

42. For example, NGOs tend to record programs, not projects—for instance, the purchase of 20 tons of wheat flour or books would be recorded but not contributions to specific projects or villages; their bookkeeping procedures are different from those of the IMG or World Bank (interviews by Susan Woodward).

43. World Bank, *The World Bank's Experience with Post-conflict Reconstruction,* vol. 2.

44. These powers were discussed at a meeting of the Peace Implementation Conference at Sintra, Portugal, in May 1997, and were agreed on definitively in the official conclusions of its meeting at Bonn, Germany, in December 1997 (hence the label the "Bonn Powers" of the High Representative). According to the Dayton agreement, the three wartime currencies were to be replaced by a single currency for the entire country. Because it did not establish the currency's design, however, disagreements (mainly between Bosniacs who preferred a single design for the currency and Serbs who insisted on different designs for the Federation and the Republika Srpska) went on for about a year until the High Representative, in spring 1998, finally made the decision himself. This significantly delayed approval of the IMF standby arrangement and the World Bank's adjustment operation, as well as the holding of the fourth pledging conference for Bosnia and Herzegovina.

45. OHR, "OHR and Reconstruction."

46. The special envoy of the president of the United States, Richard Sklar, succeeded by Claude Ganz, was deputy chairman of the ETF.

47. Interview with Zlatko Hurtić.

48. "Chairman's Conclusions," AMG/OIC meeting, March 15, 1996.

49. The Refugee Return Task Force (RRTF) is placed within the OHR and chaired by one of the High Representative's deputies. Other members of the RRTF are the European Commission Humanitarian Office (ECHO), the World Bank, and the IMG. In addition, IFAD plays an important role in the agricultural sector, through cofinancing, development, and coordination activities with the World Bank.

50. Many times the Croat (or Bosniac) deputy minister did not have information about the activities of his Bosniac (or Croat) minister.

51. The EC also failed to deliver already committed funds for the operational costs of the PIU for the Bank's forestry project.

52. The EC's failure to provide already committed funds for the operational costs of the PIU, for example, by delaying the implementation of the Bank's forestry project.

53. European Commission and World Bank, "Bosnia and Herzegovina—The Priority Reconstruction Program.

54. OHR RRTF Report, December 1997.

55. Many times, the Croat or Bosniac deputy minister would not have information about the activities of a Bosniac or Croat counterpart.

56. Three of the World Bank projects (Education II, IGA, and Essential Hospital Aid) were on hold for five months to be approved by the presidency because the Bosnian Croat and Bosnian Serb members were not satisfied with the amount of assistance allocated to the Croat-controlled area in the Federation and to Republika Srpska. It took an additional two months for these projects to be ratified by the National Assembly before implementation could start.

57. The reconstruction grant assistance of Poland was on hold for some six months before it was approved by the Council of Ministers. Similarly, the U.S. government decided to withdraw the concessional credit in food to Bosnia and Herzegovina because the Croat side refused to approve the operation on the grounds that it was scheduled to be implemented at the state level, not at the entity level, as they preferred.

58. The Council of Ministers signed a Memorandum of Understanding and Agreed Principles for De-mining only on October 30, 1997, to become effective after January 1, 1998. Entity governments were obliged to set up their own Mine Action Centers by March 31, 1998. OHR, "Bosnia and Herzegovina 1998: Self-sustaining Structures: Conclusions," Bonn Peace Implementation Conference, December 10, 1997 (document of OHR, Sarajevo, on website http://www.ohr.int/docu/d971210a.htm#07), pp. 15–16.

59. "Conclusions of the Peace Implementation Conference," London, December 8–9, 1995.

60. The London Peace Implementation Conference, December 4–5, 1996, documents.

61. In particular, "The Steering Board supported the High Representative's recommendation to deny new economic assistance to municipalities continuing to tolerate indicted persons working in a public capacity and would follow this up." "Summary of Points in the Sintra Declaration: 30 May 1997," OHR Fax, May 30, 1997.

62. OHR, "Bosnia and Herzegovina 1998: Self-sustaining Structures: Conclusions" (see note 58).

63. Statement by the High Representative, the Donor Conference for Bosnia and Herzegovina, Brussels, July 10, 1997.

64. In December 1997, the World Bank was supposed to approve a major project for Republika Srpska called Reconstruction Assistance to Republika Srpska ($17 million). Originally, the project was to include assistance to Foča, a town in the eastern part of Republika Srpska, where several indicted war criminals continue to reside without hindrance. As a result of objections from NGOs and several major donors, the Foča project was removed.

65. Much of this increase, from DM 28 million in the first six months of 1996 and 1997 to DM 400 million in 1998, was largely spent, however, on cross-entity projects, not in Republika Srpska alone. The increase showed up only by mid-1998, despite the change in November 1997, however, because the process of lifting the High Representative ban on Republika Srpska, of decisionmaking, tendering, starting a project, government decisionmaking within the RS, and the donor conference all took more than six months to yield aid (interviews at the OHR with Susan Woodward). In other words, this discrepancy in aid between the two entities reflects the consequences of political conditionality, delays in implementation, and the consequences of political decisions on the part of the Republika Srpska government in Pale (until late 1997), which paid the price in aid forgone for their refusal to participate in the first donor conference and then to sign aid agreements through the Sarajevo government because they were, in their view, fighting a contest over sovereignty. Weighing the relative consequences of each is difficult to do. The complex domestic politics of conditionality—for example, in the United States—and its effect on programs of multilateral institutions is a separate subject in itself.

66. Legislation in the United States enhanced its political use of aid; for example, the Lautenberg law. Among other major donors, the Netherlands also has been consistent in conditioning its reconstruction assistance on the apprehension of indicted war criminals and the return of refugees.

67. Similarly, in 1998, the OHR and major donors organized a conference in Sarajevo to establish the principles for refugee return to large cities; when the conference declaration did not show any results in Sarajevo by August, economic assistance was withheld only from the Bosniac authorities.

68. *Obnova* is the Bosnian word for reconstruction or renewal. The program was established to enable the EC to work with local authorities and reward particular regions or localities in an entity without rewarding those who did not meet political conditions. This was accompanied by significant decentralization of EC operations, beginning effectively in August 1998.

69. There is some evidence that the EU may well have trumped up charges of corruption in Mostar in order to revoke the special fast procedure for adopting projects in the post-Dayton environment, replacing it with political conditionality. The High Representative, also, had few tools over the parties except economic resources, and in the campaign against the World Bank's opposition to political use of reconstruction aid, he is said to have used charges of corruption.

70. Rory O'Sullivan, resident representative of the World Bank in Sarajevo, in his statement at the donor information meeting (Brussels, January 10, 1997), even remarked that the level of corruption in Bosnia and Herzegovina may be less than in any other European country.

71. Izetbegović invited the OHR and donors to form a joint commission to investigate charges against possible corruption in the implementation of donor pledges. Only the United States, however, expressed a wish to be directly involved in its work.

72. See Section VII, paragraph 4, "Corruption and Diversion of Funds," in Conclusions to Bonn meeting of the PIC, December 10, 1997, pp. 12–13.

73. The European Commission's Customs and Fiscal Assistance Office (CAFAO) did an extensive investigation in Bosnia and Herzegovina and issued a report that accused both entity governments of a lack of transparency in the collection and expenditure of public revenues.

74. The vast corruption within the tax administration led former prime minister, Hasan Muratović, to initiate abolition of the customs as a revenue source and their replacement with a sales tax.

75. The EU-financed office for customs monitoring in Bosnia and Herzegovina (CAFAO) has reported several times that there are over 400 ways to enter the country illegally, while there are only thirty border crossings and those have hardly any controls. This led the 1998 PIC meeting at Madrid to request in its final document that the entities and the state form special police units for the country's border crossings. At the same time, Federation prime minister Edhem Bićakčić has publicly accused members of the NATO-led military forces (SFOR) of smuggling cigarettes into the country and of selling at illegal open markets.

76. Several donors told Bosnian authorities that the implementation of "their taxpayers' money" would be dramatically slowed down unless the country established a more effective system in the collection and use of "its own taxpayers' money."

77. Mirsad Kurtović, minister for foreign trade and economy, interviewed by Zlatko Hurtić.

78. The request for 80 percent was made by Neven Tomić, cochair of the Bosnia and Herzegovina Council of Ministers, during the first round of negotiations with the Paris Club (July 1998), by contesting the relevance of the IMF projections.

79. High Representative Carlos Westendorp, in a letter to both entities in December 1998, requested that both start implementing the State Customs Law. As

of February 1999, the Republika Srpska government had refused. The Federation prime minister did issue an order to the Federation Customs Administration to begin implementation, but this was rejected by the Croat part of the Federation government, which, unlike the Bosniac part, continued to apply preferential trade treatment to goods imported from Croatia. Both Serb and Croat governments, because of their control over the borders, can use preferential trade treatment to smuggle goods and thus resist abolishing it.

80. According to the entities' statistical bureaus, imports from the Federal Republic of Yugoslavia and the Republic of Croatia to Bosnia and Herzegovina in 1998 amounted to DM 1.2 billion, while exports were less than DM 200 million.

81. In an interview with Zlatko Hurtić, Rasim Kadić, minister for refugees and social affairs in the Federation government, noted that around 200,000 refugees, mainly from Germany, were forced to return to Bosnia in 1997–1998.

82. For example, there are serious signs that Japan and Malaysia will not be able to realize their pledges due to the current financial crisis.

83. In 1998, some of the larger donors, such as the EU and Canada, announced plans to redirect Bosnian aid funds to Kosovo should the crisis continue. By early 1999, senior German official Hans Koschnick warned that 25 percent of the EU assistance intended for Bosnia and Herzegovina may be reallocated to reconstruction in Kosovo (Reuters, February 16, 1999). In addition, refugees from Kosovo began to flood into Bosnia in the summer of 1998—some 20,000 by August—adding directly to the burden of humanitarian assistance in Bosnia.

84. Ball, "Lessons for International Actors," p. 23.

85. Reconstruction and Return Task Force, "An Action Plan in Support of the Return of Refugees."

86. OHR, "Statement of High Representative," January 9, 1997.

9

Beyond Good Intentions: External Assistance and Peace Building

James K. Boyce

EXTERNAL ASSISTANCE HAS POLITICAL AS WELL AS ECONOMIC impacts: aid affects not only the size of the economic pie and how it is sliced, but also the balance of power among competing actors and the rules of the game by which they compete. In postconflict societies, particularly those where the conflict ends in a negotiated settlement rather than a winner-take-all victory, the political impacts of aid can help to decide whether the peace endures or war resumes.

The "good intentions" of this book's title refer to an explicitly political aim: the building of peace. To be sure, external assistance in postconflict settings has less noble motivations, too—among them, geopolitical rivalries and commercial interests. Yet the consolidation of peace certainly ranks high among the objectives of most donors in postconflict settings, and most citizens in the donor countries probably agree that it should be the overriding goal.

Translating this objective into practice is not a straightforward matter, as the essays in this volume make clear. Aid is not like water, which sprayed on the flames or embers of conflict invariably helps to extinguish them. Indeed, it can be more like oil. Appropriate aid can diminish the risks of conflict, but inappropriate aid can fuel it. External assistance can support a country's adjustment toward peace, but it can also impede that adjustment if it deepens the fault lines of conflict, or if it tilts power balances in favor of those still willing to return to war.

The net impact of aid depends, first, on whether the donors truly make peace building their overriding objective and, second, on how effectively their assistance serves this goal. The focus of this book is primarily on the latter issue. Yet the case studies reveal that one reason for the shortcomings of postconflict assistance is the tension between peace building and other donor objectives.[1] In this chapter, I draw some lessons as to how donors can—if they choose to do so—get the most "non-bang for the buck."[2]

Beyond "How Much?"

The pledges of aid analyzed in this book are direct responses to negotiated peace accords. In all except the South African case, international donor conferences were convened within a few months—a few days in the case of Bosnia—of the signing of an accord (see Table 9.1). Aid pledges provided not only ex post international backing for the peace processes, but also ex ante carrots. The prospect of an external peace dividend was among the inducements for the warring parties to negotiate an end to the conflict.

The South African case differs in that the struggle between the apartheid regime and the opposition led by the African National Congress (ANC) culminated in neither an internationally brokered accord nor a donor conference. Nevertheless, South Africa too fits into the aid-as-reward-and-incentive scheme. During the apartheid years, the country was subject to wide-ranging international sanctions; after the watershed April 1994 election, the ANC-led national unity government became, in the words of Bratton and Landsberg, in Chapter 7 of this volume, "a darling of the donor community."

Just as the signing of an accord does not guarantee peace, so pledges do not guarantee the delivery of aid. Peace implementation can falter, and wars can reignite. Angola is a recent case in point. Promises of aid likewise can evaporate with changes in the political climates of recipient and donor countries.

The initial impetus for this volume was the recognition that postconflict pledges of aid do not always materialize in full and a concern that chronic gaps between pledges and disbursements may jeopardize the

Table 9.1 Peace Accords and Donor Conferences

Country	Accord Signed	Initial Donor Conference
Cambodia	October 1991, Paris	June 1992, Tokyo
El Salvador	January 1992, Mexico	March 1992, Washington
Mozambique	October 1992, Rome	December 1992, Rome
Palestine	September 1993, Oslo	October 1993, Washington
Bosnia	December 1995, Paris	December 1995, Brussels

consolidation of peace. The case studies illuminate the extent of such shortfalls and the reasons for them. But they also reveal that the amount of aid is not the only measure of how effectively aid contributes to peace building—nor is it necessarily the most important indicator.

The sums pledged at donor conferences send important signals, but the numbers are not sacred. Rather they reflect a rough balance in donors' calculations between supply and demand—that is, between their available resources and initial assessments of postconflict needs. The latter are often biased downward by optimistic assumptions, and the former are sometimes biased upward by donor wishes to be seen as wielders of big carrots. When commitments subsequently fall short of pledges, or disbursements fall short of commitments, this may or may not be cause for dismay. As Forman and Patrick remark in Chapter 1 of this volume, "in some cases a gap might even be good, if it means that less money is wasted than would have been the case otherwise." Indeed, "wasted" money—in the sense of zero effect on the peace-building objective—is not the worst-case scenario, because ill-conceived aid can have a negative effect.

To move beyond good intentions, aid donors must consider the full range of effects their assistance will have on the peace process. This is not only a question of *how much* aid is delivered, but also of (1) *what types* of aid are given? (2) *to whom?* and (3) *with what conditions* attached?

Aid: What Types?

"If your only tool is a hammer," an old adage goes, "every problem looks like a nail." The toolkit international donors bring to postconflict transitions was not designed for peace building. The expertise of the donor agencies—in emergency relief, infrastructure projects, macroeconomic policy, and so on—is relevant to many of the tasks at hand. But the architecture of peace also requires new tools and new uses of familiar ones.

Peace Priorities Versus Donor Priorities

The case studies repeatedly document mismatches between the priorities of peace implementation and the priorities of the donors. Immediate peace-building priorities typically include the demobilization of ex-combatants, the establishment of public security forces under civilian control, the reform of the justice system, and the creation of new democratic institutions. Longer-run priorities include pursuing a path of economic growth that reduces social tensions rather than exacerbating them, and fostering an inclusive political environment. Faced with these challenges, donors all too often have simply pursued business as usual. To cite a few examples:

• In El Salvador, the donors directed the bulk of their postwar assistance to physical infrastructure, such as roads and electricity, rather than to high-priority peace needs such as the National Civilian Police and the land transfer program for ex-combatants. This resulted in "large financing gaps in the programs more critical for the peace process" (this volume, Chapter 4).

• In the Palestinian territories, donor priorities included "showcase" projects like the Gaza European Hospital and the USAID-funded Karameh Towers housing project, "driven overwhelmingly by political rationales" (this volume, Chapter 6). The operative political rationale in these instances was flagpole value, not peace building.

• In Bosnia, donors again put disproportionate emphasis on infrastructure as opposed to peace implementation. Even as recognition of this bias grew, the multilateral donors "continued to place priority and resources on infrastructural reconstruction and orthodox approaches to economic transition" (this volume, Chapter 8). Meanwhile, several European bilateral agencies placed "overwhelming priority on housing reconstruction" to expedite the repatriation of refugees from the donor countries; in so doing, they have returned refugees not to their original places of residence, but rather to new locations where they form part of a postwar ethnic majority, thereby helping to consolidate the results of "ethnic cleansing."[3]

• In Mozambique, "none of the donors appear to be aware of one of the fundamental preconditions for sustained reductions in security expenditure: the strengthening of the institutional and human capacities needed to manage and monitor reform of the security sector, including the creation of security forces accountable to an elected civilian government and supported by transparent financing instruments" (this volume, Chapter 5). Once again, the need to promote civilian control of security forces was neglected.

In part, these disjunctions between donor priorities and peace priorities reflect the institutional inertia of aid agencies, which have yet to adapt fully to the special circumstances of postconflict transitions. The hammer-and-nail syndrome is reinforced by biases in favor of aid tied to imports from the donor country; by the quest for political visibility, which leads to overfunding in some sectors and underfunding in others; and by donor reluctance to finance recurrent expenditures, an issue to which I return below.

The Short Run and the Long Haul

In the long run, John Maynard Keynes famously observed, we are all dead. Where the peace is fragile, one cannot ignore the risk that many people can die in the very short run, too. There are compelling reasons for donors to accept peace maintenance as a top priority and to incorporate this constraint into their allocation decisions. Yet if short-run priorities are allowed to dominate completely the long-run requirements of peace building, the final outcome can be no less tragic.

Donors confront several tensions between the short-run and long-run demands of peace building:

• *Timely implementation versus capacity building.* Some postconflict needs are so pressing that donors cannot wait to build local capacity to address them: the necessary expertise and materials must be imported. Nevertheless, donors generally pay at least lip service to the long-run goals of building local institutions, training local personnel, and stimulating the local economy. In practice, much aid is disbursed in the intermediate time frame between short-run emergencies and an ever receding long run. Even beyond the emergency phase, donors often defer capacity building in favor of quick results. Peou and Yamada (this volume, Chapter 3) note that when donors attempted "Khmerization" policies in Cambodia, one result was a slowdown in disbursements. Yet the need for capacity building is greatest precisely where it is most lacking.

• *Current expenditure versus investment.* A similar dilemma arises in allocating donor resources between current expenditures and investment. In Palestine, budget support through the Holst Fund was crucial in allowing the Palestinian Authority to meet its payroll, and emergency job creation projects provided at least some cushion against the debilitating economic effects of the Israeli border closures. In effect, these expenditures purchased short-run political stability. But they did so at an opportunity cost in terms of investment in long-run development. There is some scope for easing this trade-off over time: in the case of budget support, by making aid conditional on progress in domestic resource mobilization; in the case of job programs, by designing labor-intensive projects to build useful infrastructure.

• *Elite pacification versus egalitarian growth.* Finally, donors often face a trade-off in the distribution of the benefits of aid between political elites and the population at large. In the short run, the commitment, or at least acquiescence, of political elites to the peace process can be enhanced by offering them a generous slice of the peace dividend. Yet such efforts to pacify the elite can run counter to the inclusive pattern of economic growth needed to consolidate peace in the long run. The trade-off is particularly steep where elite payoffs do not take the form of one-off lump sums (as in the Renamo trust fund in Mozambique), but rather of rights to future income streams. In Palestine, for example, de jure and de facto monopolies provide financial glue for "neopatrimonial" political order, but at the same time they deter private investment.[4] In Bosnia, formerly state-owned enterprises, such as the aluminum factory in Mostar, have been effectively privatized into the hands of nationalist leaders who seek to perpetuate ethnic divisions. In Cambodia, the plundering of the country's forests by politically connected individuals and military officers is eroding the livelihood security of a desperately impoverished population. Such predation by the powerful—too often tolerated, if not encouraged, by donors in the name of political expediency—corrodes the long-run prospects for a lasting peace.

These trade-offs and the resulting dilemmas cannot be wished away. Rather than either-or choices, donors must keep an eye on both the short run and the long haul. The fact that capacity building, investment, and egalitarian growth are long-run goals does not mean that steps toward them can be deferred to another day, because the long run is simply the cumulative result of short-run decisions.

Aid: To Whom?

"If you are designing a project for a seismic zone," a World Bank official remarks, "you need to take account of the risk of earthquakes."[5] In the social seismic zones of postconflict countries, the distribution of the benefits of aid has special importance. To speak of "aid to postconflict countries" is to use shorthand that obscures the fact that aid flows not to countries as a whole, but rather to specific groups and individuals. Any influx of external resources invariably affects the distribution of income, wealth, and power in the recipient country. The distributional effects of aid can ease social tensions or deepen them, reinforce the peace process or undermine it.

Balances of Power

The donor-as-fireman metaphor implies that spraying more aid on a conflict necessarily improves the prospects for peace. The earthquake metaphor is more apposite: it recognizes that peace building often rests on fragile balances of power within and between the parties to the conflict. Aid can tilt these balances toward peace or war.

Even seemingly benign types of aid can undermine the peace process if channeled to malign hands. After the Dayton peace agreement, for example, some donors channeled food and humanitarian relief through local Red Cross branches controlled by hard-line Bosnian Croat nationalists. The hard-liners withheld aid to ethnic "minorities" (some of whom were the majority in their communities before the war) who attempted to return to their former homes. At the same time, they used aid as a weapon to discourage Croats who were displaced from other parts of Bosnia, and now living in these municipalities, from returning to *their* former homes: the displaced Croats were told they would receive aid only if they registered to vote in their new place of residence; if they exercised their right under the Dayton accords to register in their former communities—thereby signaling an intention to return—they were denied relief.[6]

The parties to the conflict are generally quite aware of the political weight of postconflict aid. During the United Nations Transitional Authority in Cambodia, for example, Funcinpec and the Khmer Rouge "viewed any aid disbursed to [the Hun Sen–controlled state of] Cambodia as bolstering their enemy's political legitimacy" (this volume, Chapter 3). For this reason, they effectively blocked a World Bank emergency loan for government budget support.[7] Similarly, Bosnian Serb and Croat leaders have blocked approval of World Bank loans while bargaining over their shares of the proceeds (this volume, Chapter 8).

The balancing act facing the donors is especially delicate when the peace accord results primarily not from an internal stalemate, as in El Salvador or Mozambique, but rather from external pressure, as in Cambodia or Bosnia. Even in the relatively auspicious circumstances of the former countries, however, donors must devote serious attention and resources to "nurturing political will" for peace building (this volume, Chapter 5).

In the short run, this means using aid to tilt power balances in favor of peace *within* each of the contending parties (which often remain divided between opponents and proponents of the negotiated settlement) and to maintain the balance *between* the parties on which the peace process rests. El Salvador provides an example of the latter:

> The United Nations, the international donor community, and (equally, if at times more ambiguously) the United States played key roles in maintaining the balance between a government newly possessed of its "monopoly of armed force" and not always disposed to comply with agreements that could threaten its future hold on power and a civilian (and newly civilianized) opposition weary of war and eager to put the past behind them. (This volume, Chapter 4)

Over time, as peaceful contests for power become established as the new norm, the balance of forces among the contending parties can and will shift. Yet the "to whom" question is important from a longer-run perspective, as well. The consolidation of peace requires inclusive economic growth and an inclusive political environment. Both dimensions of inclusion are related: a more equal distribution of income and wealth fosters a more equal distribution of power, and vice versa.

Democratization and Peace Building

In its broadest sense, "democracy" refers to an equitable distribution of power—an objective for which free and fair elections are necessary but not sufficient. Democratization in this sense is a crucial element of peace building: it not only opens the space for nonviolent political competition, but also helps to sustain the balanced distribution of power that underpins the peace process. Democratization offers the only assurance that no actor will become so powerful as to be able to resort to violence with impunity, nor that any will become so desperate as to do so as the only alternative to abject subjugation.

External assistance actors can support democratization in three main ways. First, as discussed above, donors can directly help to finance the strengthening of democratic institutions, including the reform of police forces and the judiciary and the establishment of new institutions for the protection of human rights, civilian control over public security forces, and free and fair elections. Second, as discussed in the next section, donors can condition their assistance on the mobilization of domestic resources for these purposes. Finally, they can seek to ensure that the economic gains from their assistance are distributed so as to reduce, rather than widen, inequalities of wealth and power.

The inequalities that cast a shadow over the prospects for peace include not only vertical disparities of class but also horizontal divisions of race, ethnicity, religion, and region. The latter cleavages frequently define the contours of violent conflict, and economic policies that exacerbate them have been identified as an important underlying cause of civil wars.[8] The political economy of conflict demonstrates the folly of neglecting distributional concerns in the single-minded pursuit of economic growth: a preoccupation with how to bake a bigger pie is dysfunctional when conflicts over how it is to be sliced threaten to smash the pie.

Two instruments can help aid donors to incorporate these concerns into policy analysis and project appraisal. The first is the use of "distributional weights" in cost-benefit analysis. These put greater value on every dollar of benefit (or cost) to the poor than to the rich, on the premise that dollars are worth more to those who have fewer of them. Methodologies for this purpose are well developed, yet rarely applied.

A second instrument, still in its infancy, is conflict-risk impact assessment.[9] This examines how prospective policies or projects would affect the risk of conflict in social seismic zones. Like environmental impact assessment, conflict-risk impact assessment is bound to be an imperfect art. It will take time to hone this tool, and complete precision is likely to prove an elusive goal. The learning curve may be long and its slope uncertain, but these are not reasons to shirk from climbing it.

Aid: With What Conditions?

External assistance rarely is given without conditions. Postconflict assistance is no exception. The pledges of aid that were the starting point for this volume were themselves conditional on the signing of a peace accord (or, in South Africa, the transition to majority rule). If the overriding objective of the donors is peace building, then the conditions placed on subsequent delivery of aid must be assessed first and foremost in terms of their impact on this goal. Some conventional conditions may prove to be counterproductive, while other, unconventional conditions may help to advance the peace process.

Conventional Macroeconomic Conditionality

Among the most important conventional conditions pressed by aid donors—in particular, by the international financial institutions—are those relating to macroeconomic policy. The short-run goal is macroeconomic stabilization: fiscal and monetary discipline to curtail inflation and stabilize exchange rates. The long-run goal is adjustment, or changes in the structure of the economy, including the relative sizes of the tradeable and nontradeable sectors and of the public and private sectors. Short-run stabilization is mainly the province of the International Monetary Fund (IMF); longer-run adjustment is mainly that of the World Bank and the regional development banks.

Formal conditionality is embodied in performance criteria, which tie disbursements to the attainment of specific targets. For example, the IMF often requires a borrower government to cut its budget deficit to a stated percentage of GDP before successive tranches of an IMF loan can be disbursed. But conditionality is also conveyed in the informal policy dialogue between donor and recipient. Whether formal or informal, conditionality makes aid contingent on specified actions on the part of the recipient.

Whatever the wisdom of the conventional macroeconomic conditions—a matter of considerable debate—in postconflict transitions their efficacy must be viewed through the special lens of the peace process. Insofar as macroeconomic conditions clash with peace-building objectives, there is a compelling case for modifying the former.

Following the UN Transitional Authority in Cambodia (UNTAC) period, for example, the IMF and World Bank pressed the new coalition government to downsize the Cambodian civil service by 20 percent. A senior UN official in Phnom Penh explains:

> The IMF just applied a standard ratio: your population is 11 million, so the size of your civil service should be x. But the historical circumstances here are almost unique. In 1979 Cambodia was a wasteland: it had no civil service, no banking, no money, and 90 per cent of the intelligentsia was dead. The new government had to put together a system, starting from nothing. They paid people in rice to teach. The fact that these people were not trained is not their fault. You can't tell them, "Now you're useless," and throw them on the scrap heap. It's not decent, and it's not possible politically.[10]

In practice, the coalition government expanded public employment by around 15 percent to accommodate job seekers from the erstwhile opposition. A subsequent World Bank evaluation concluded: "The installation of a reduction process early in the life of the coalition arrangement—which was based on *raising* the size of the civil service in order to absorb large numbers of the incoming parties' functionaries—was never politically realistic."[11]

To reduce the budget deficit, the Cambodian government instead curtailed nonsalary expenditures. "The outcome was 'remarkable progress' on the macroeconomic balances," the evaluation dryly observes, "combined with continued erosion of non-maintained infrastructure and of health, education and other services." In effect, these social expenditures were relegated "to the status of *de facto* policy residuals."[12]

Similar tensions emerged in Mozambique. In 1995, the IMF and the World Bank pressed for fiscal and monetary contraction, terming macroeconomic stabilization an "absolute prerequisite." Other donors feared that this orthodox prescription jeopardized the long-term goals of economic recovery and political stabilization. Reportedly at the initiative of the United States ambassador, several of these donors took the "unprecedented step" of writing to the IMF to voice this concern.[13]

Proponents of macroeconomic discipline rightly argue that rampant inflation can undermine political stability as well as economic recovery, and that inflation often hits the real incomes of the poor especially hard. These are indeed compelling reasons to control inflation. But policymakers do not face an all-or-nothing choice between inflexibility and hyperinflation. Fiscal and monetary stringency is always a matter of degree.

Similar to the short-run trade-off between inflation and unemployment portrayed in macroeconomics textbooks, a trade-off can exist between the size of the government budget deficit on the one hand, and the social tensions triggered by inadequate public expenditures on the other. This is depicted in Figure 9.1. Within a certain range, increases in the government budget deficit can reduce social tensions by financing peace-related expenditures.[14] Beyond some point, labeled *B* in the figure, this effect is overtaken by the adverse economic and political impacts of profligate spending and high inflation. When officials at the international financial institutions maintain that the relaxation of fiscal discipline would undermine the peace process, they are assuming that the country is on the *BC* portion of the curve. When others advocate relaxation of budget-deficit targets to support the peace process—like the signatories of the donors' letter in Mozambique—they are assuming that the country instead lies on the *AB* segment.

Similar trade-offs may exist between other conventional macroeconomic aims and peace-building objectives. For example, "structural adjustment" programs often push for trade liberalization and the privatization of

Figure 9.1   Budget Deficits and Social Tensions

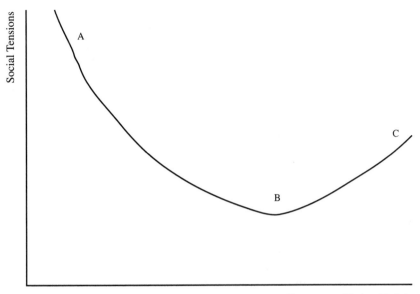

Government Budget Deficit

state-owned enterprises. If trade liberalization leads to an influx of cheap agricultural imports, and this undermines the livelihoods of peasant producers, the resulting risks to equity and stability must be weighed against the presumed benefits.[15] If privatization in practice amounts to what the Russians call "grabitization,"[16] the resulting increases in the concentration of wealth and power can undermine peace building, particularly if the individuals who appropriate state-owned assets are hostile to the full implementation of the peace accords.

Peace Conditionality

The special circumstances of postconflict transitions not only mean that conventional macroeconomic conditionality must be reconsidered in light of its impacts on peace building, but also raise the possibility that formal performance criteria and informal policy dialogue can be used to encourage the implementation of peace accords and the consolidation of peace processes. Elsewhere I have termed this "peace conditionality."[17] This unconventional form of conditionality is founded on the initial link between the peace accord and aid pledges: peace conditionality translates this grand bargain between the international community and the warring parties into a series of minibargains, which link disbursements to specific peace-building measures.

In terms of the curve in Figure 9.1, peace conditionality is a way to *shift* the curve downward, as opposed to moving along it. That is, peace conditionality aims to reduce social tensions and risks to the peace process at any given level of deficit spending. In terms of fiscal policy, peace conditionality may address the level and composition of public expenditures and revenues, rather than just the balance between them. Peace conditionality can also address a range of nonfiscal policies.

Level of expenditure and revenue. Government budget deficits can be reduced either by cutting expenditures or by raising revenues. In their zeal to trim deficits, the international financial institutions often have given insufficient attention to the *level* of public expenditure and revenue at which balance is attained. Many postconflict countries—El Salvador, Guatemala, Cambodia, and Bosnia are examples—have exceedingly low levels of both revenue and expenditure. In the absence of countervailing incentives, including conditionality, there is a danger that aid will relax the need for governments to raise revenue: external resources will then "crowd out" domestic resource mobilization rather than encouraging it. But aid is "intended to be only a temporary substitute for domestic resources" (this volume, Chapter 8). If so, increased revenue is often necessary to sustain peace-related programs.[18]

Composition of expenditure and revenue. In addition to their level, the composition of government expenditure and revenue can have critical impacts on peace building. High priorities for public expenditure include the new democratic institutions and health, education, and poverty-reduction programs. Other items not only rank lower on the scale of priorities but in some cases may even be "negative priorities" in the sense that they are inimical to the peace process. Some military expenditures are a case in point.[19] Yet governments may be reluctant both to cut "unproductive" expenditures and to finance new programs to which they agreed only under the duress of conflict. In the case of El Salvador, the Nordic donors raised this issue early in the peace process, calling on the World Bank to apply conditionality to the composition of expenditures (see this volume, Chapter 4). The international financial institutions chose not to confront the issue, defining it as a political question outside their limited economic purview.[20]

In Guatemala, the international financial institutions have been more willing to recognize the fiscal implications of peace building. The Guatemalan peace accords, formally concluded in December 1996, include annual targets for increases in tax revenues and in public expenditure for health, education, and housing: the ratios of each of these to GDP are mandated to rise by 50 percent by the year 2000. The international financial institutions have supported these targets: when IMF managing director Michel Camdessus visited Guatemala in May 1997, he announced that the key condition for an IMF standby agreement would be the government's compliance with the fiscal provisions of the peace accords it had already signed.[21] The language of the Guatemalan accords is more vague, however, with respect to the composition of revenues—how the tax target is to be met—specifying only that taxation should be "globally progressive." The incidence of taxation is important not only because it affects the distribution of after-tax income, but also because it can decisively influence the political sustainability of tax increases in a context of democratization.[22] So far the donors have shown little inclination, however, to bring their full weight to bear on behalf of more progressive taxes.

Other policies. The scope for peace conditionality extends beyond fiscal policies. In Bosnia, as Hurtić, Šapčanin, and Woodward (this volume, Chapter 8) observe, hard-line nationalists often have chosen "to accept the aid but to obstruct the political process." In response, the donors at times have exercised "political conditionality," sometimes with a measure of success. Conditionality was used to persuade Bosnian Serb leaders to participate in the country's collective presidency in 1996; it helped to precipitate a political thaw in Bosnia's Serb Republic in the following year; and at the local level, some donors, including the Office of the United Nations High Commissioner for Refugees, have experimented with conditionality as a tool to encourage municipal authorities to welcome minority returns.[23] The withholding of international financial institution loans to Croatia in 1997, orchestrated by the United States, played a central role in the Tudjman government's decision to hand over indicted war crimes suspects to the Hague tribunal. While the priority issues for peace conditionality vary from time to time and from place to place, the basic principle is the same: external assistance is tied to specific actions by recipients to secure peace-building objectives.

The Political Economy of Peace Building

External assistance actors are often reluctant to acknowledge the political implications of their aid. At the international financial institutions, whose boards of directors include representatives of the borrower governments, deniability often verges on denial. The World Bank's *Articles of Agreement,* for example, specify that the Bank will make loans "with due attention to considerations of economy and efficiency and without regard to

political or other non-economic influences or considerations."[24] Yet "economy and efficiency" can seldom be neatly divorced from "political considerations." The two spheres typically intersect, and perhaps nowhere is
that intersection larger than in countries emerging from civil war.

Figure 9.2 depicts a range of possibilities. At one extreme is Figure
9.2(a), a hypothetical world where there is no overlap whatsoever between
the economic and the political. Reality is better depicted by Figure 9.2(b),
where the two spheres intersect. In postconflict countries, the overlap is
likely to be larger, as shown in Figure 9.2(c). Indeed, in some places the
situation may more closely approximate Figure 9.2(d), where the economic is merely a subset of the political.

Given the overlap between economics and politics, the exclusionary
clause in the World Bank's charter can be read in either of two ways: as
excluding all political considerations regardless of their economic importance, or as ruling out only those political considerations that are economically irrelevant. In postconflict settings, the absurdity of the first reading
is particularly apparent.

External assistance for peace building will not be universally welcomed in postconflict countries, particularly if rather than writing a blank
check, the donors seriously address the questions raised above. Recipient
governments naturally prefer aid that is highly fungible, that flows through
their hands and theirs alone, and that comes with no strings attached. Some
will object to peace conditionality, in particular, claiming it is an affront to
national sovereignty.[25] Yet aid inevitably alters the room for maneuver of
domestic political actors and the power balances among them, whether or
not conditions are attached. In this sense, it is external assistance itself—
not the presence or absence of conditions—that compromises "national
sovereignty."

**Figure 9.2 Mandated Considerations and Nonconsiderations for the International
Financial Institutions**

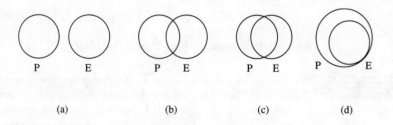

Notes: P = Political and other noneconomic considerations.
E = Considerations of economy and efficiency.

For donors and recipients alike, the central issue is not *whether* aid will have political impacts, but *what* these will be. To help to build peace, it is not enough for donors to fulfill their aid pledges: they must also reshape their policies and practices to serve this aim. The donors must be prepared to direct aid to high-priority peace-related needs, rather than pursuing business as usual. They must weigh carefully the effects of aid on the distribution of income, wealth, and power and incorporate these effects into their decisionmaking calculus. They must reorient conditionality to support peace building by modifying conventional policy prescriptions and by using aid to encourage domestic actors to close gaps between their own pledges and performance. If the donors' commitment to peace building is to extend beyond good intentions, not only the quantity of aid will count, but also these qualities.

Notes

Research for this chapter was partially supported by grants from the John D. and Catherine T. MacArthur Foundation and the United States Institute of Peace. The views expressed are the author's alone.

1. For a classic account of the diverse motivations for external assistance, see Griffin and Enos, "Foreign Assistance." For an assessment of the impact of conflicting donor motivations on "second-generation" political conditionality, see Hook, "Building Democracy." For more on the role of political will in postconflict assistance, see Boyce, *Peace Conditionality*.

2. The phrase is Michael Brown's; see his "Internal Conflict and International Action," p. 625.

3. International Crisis Group, "Hollow Promise?"

4. The fragility of the peace process and border closures have also been major deterrents to private investment. See Brynen, "Neopatrimonial Dimensions of Palestinian Politics," and Kanaan, "Uncertainty Deters Private Investment."

5. Personal interview, Washington, D.C., December 1997.

6. Personal interviews with NGO fieldworkers in Bosnia, June 1998; see also International Crisis Group, "Hollow Promise?" Similar manipulation was reportedly common in Bosnia's Serb Republic; see Kumar, *Divide and Fall?* pp. 123–124.

7. See Doyle, *UN Peacekeeping in Cambodia*, p. 51, and World Bank, *The World Bank's Experience*, vol. 5, p. 23.

8. Stewart, "The Root Causes of Conflict: Some Conclusions."

9. For discussions, see Reinicke, "Can International Financial Institutions Prevent Violence?" and Bush, "A Measure of Peace."

10. Personal interview, Phnom Penh, November 1998.

11. World Bank, *The World Bank's Experience*, vol. 5, p. 29; emphasis in the original.

12. Ibid., pp. 15, 34.

13. Christian Michelsen Institute, *Evaluation of Norwegian Assistance*, p. 49. Also see Ball and Barnes, Chapter 5 in this volume.

14. See Boyce, "External Resource Mobilization," and Boyce and Pastor, "Aid for Peace," for further discussion of this trade-off.

15. Such impacts will be particularly severe where the real exchange rate has appreciated due to inflows of aid and/or remittances from expatriated workers. El Salvador is a case in point; for discussion, see Acevedo, "Structural Adjustment."

16. Wedel, *Collision and Collusion*, p. 133.

17. See Boyce, "External Resource Mobilization," and *Peace Conditionality*; Boyce and Pastor, "Aid for Peace"; and World Bank, *The World Bank's Experience*, vol. 1.

18. In the case of El Salvador, which (along with Guatemala and Haiti) has one of the lowest ratios of tax revenues to GDP in the Western Hemisphere, a World Bank evaluation reports that some Bank staff now agree that "the Bretton Woods institutions should have pushed harder at the outset on tax effort." World Bank, *The World Bank's Experience*, vol. 3, p. 41.

19. "Military" spending can refer to a broad range of activities, however, some of which may be important for peace building. Examples include demobilization programs, land mine clearance, and the establishment of public security forces under civilian control. More generally, it is important to disaggregate the broad expenditure categories in terms of their impact on peace building. For example, not all spending under the headings of health and education addresses high-priority peace-building needs.

20. For further discussion, see Boyce, "External Resource Mobilization." An ex post World Bank evaluation concurs: "If tax effort and the pattern of public expenditures have a direct bearing on postconflict reconstruction, as they did in El Salvador, it is legitimate to include these parameters in the conditionality agenda." World Bank, *The World Bank's Experience*, vol. 3, p. 51.

21. Ruiz Calderón, "Camdessus."

22. For further discussion of the Guatemalan case, see Jonas, *Of Centaurs and Doves;* and Boyce, *Peace Conditionality*.

23. Boyce and Pastor, "Aid for Peace."

24. International Bank for Reconstruction and Development, *Articles of Agreement*, Art. III, Sec. 5(b).

25. The ANC-led South African government, for example, has opposed "the general principle of aid conditionality as a tool of foreign policy." See Bratton and Landsberg, Chapter 7 in this volume. Yet the ANC opposed unconditional aid to South Africa in the apartheid era. The distinction hinges on *what* foreign policy objectives conditionality supports.

Acronyms

ACC	Administrative Committee on Coordination (UN)
ACRS	Arms Control and Regional Security (Palestine)
ADB	Asian Development Bank
ADP	Accelerated De-mining Program (Mozambique)
AFU	Anti-Fraud Unit (UN)
AGOA	Africa Growth and Opportunities Act
AHLC	Ad Hoc Liaison Committee (Palestine)
AMG/OIC	Assistance Mobilization Group for Bosnia and Herzegovina/Organization of Islamic Countries
ANC	African National Congress
ARENA	National Republican Alliance (El Salvador)
ASEAN	Association of Southeast Asian Nations
BAC	Business Against Crime (South Africa)
BNC	Binational Commission (South Africa)
BPD	Banco Popular de Desenvolvimento (Mozambique)
CABEI	Central American Bank for Economic Integration
CAFAO	Customs and Fiscal Assistance Office (EC)
CAP	Consolidated Inter-Agency Appeal (UN)
CBO	community-based organization
CCC	Cooperation Committee for Cambodia
CCF	Cease-Fire Commission (Mozambique)
CCFADM	Joint Commission for the Formation of the Mozambican Defense Force
CDC	Council for the Development of Cambodia
CENE	National Executive Commission on the Emergency (Mozambique)
CERE	Commission on Reintegration (Mozambique)
CG	Consultative Group
CGDK	Coalition Government of Democratic Kampuchea

CGM	Consultative Group meeting
CIDA	Canadian International Development Agency
CIREFCA	International Conference on Central American Refugees
CISAC	Center for International Security and Cooperation
CMAC	Cambodian Mine Action Center
CNE	National Election Commission (Mozambique)
CODESA	Conference on a Democratic South Africa
CONARA	National Commission for the Restoration of Areas (El Salvador)
COPAZ	National Commission for the Consolidation of Peace (El Salvador)
COPP	Coordinating Committee for Assistance to the Palestinian Police
CORE	Commission on Reintegration (Mozambique)
CPE	Provincial Emergency Commission (Mozambique)
CPP	Cambodian People's Party
CPRS	Center for Palestine Research and Studies
CRDB	Cambodian Rehabilitation and Development Board
CRPC	Commission for Real Property Claims of Displaced Persons and Refugees
CSC	Supervisory and Monitoring Commission (Mozambique)
CSI	corporate social investment
DAC	Development Assistance Committee
DCG	Donor Consultative Group
DDB	Donor Data Base (World Bank/EC)
DESA	Drought Appeal for Southern Africa
DFAIT	Department of Foreign Affairs and International Trade (Canada)
DFID	Department for International Development (formerly ODA-UK)
DHA	Department of Humanitarian Affairs (UN)
DOF	Department of Finance (South Africa)
DPA	Department of Political Affairs (UN)
DPKO	Department of Peacekeeping Operations (UN)
DS	demobilized soldier
EAP	Emergency Assistance Program (for the Occupied Territories)
EBRD	European Bank for Reconstruction and Development
EC	European Community
ECAP	Expanded Consolidated Inter-Agency Appeal (UN)
ECHO	European Commission Humanitarian Office
ECOSOC	Economic and Social Council (UN)
EIB	European Investment Bank

EO	Executive Outcomes
EOG	Emergency Operations Group (Mozambique)
EPRD	European Program for Reconstruction and Development
ERD	Emergency Response Division (UNDP)
ERP	Emergency Rehabilitation Project (World Bank)
ESAF	Enhanced Structural Adjustment Facility (IMF)
ETF	Economic Task Force
EU	European Union
EUAM	European Union Administration of Mostar
FAO	Food and Agriculture Organization
FMLN	Farabundo Martí National Liberation Front
Frelimo	Mozambique Liberation Front
FSTC	free-standing technical cooperation
GDP	gross domestic product
GEAR	Growth, Employment, and Redistribution plan (South Africa)
GFAP	General Framework Agreement for Peace (B&H)
GNP	gross national product
GNU	Government of National Unity (South Africa)
GOES	Government of El Salvador
GPA	General Peace Agreement (Mozambique)
GRF	Global Post-Conflict Reconstruction Fund
GSP	General System of Preferences (European Union)
GTZ	German Agency for Technical Cooperation
HIPC	Highly Indebted Poor Countries
HR	High Representative (B&H)
IACS	In-Country Aid Coordination System (Cambodia)
IASC	Inter-Agency Standing Committee (UN)
IBRD	International Bank for Reconstruction and Development
ICMPD	International Center for Migration Policy Development
ICORC	International Committee on the Reconstruction of Cambodia
ICRC	International Committee of the Red Cross
ICTY	International Criminal Tribunal for the Former Yugoslavia
IDA	International Development Association
IDASA	Institute for a Democratic South Africa
IDB	Inter-American Development Bank
IDC	International Development Cooperation
IDP	internally displaced person
IFAD	International Fund for Agricultural Development
IFC	International Finance Corporation
IFI	international financial institution

IFOR	Implementation Force (B&H)
ILO	International Labour Organization
IMF	International Monetary Fund
IMG	International Management Group
IOM	International Organization on Migration
IPA	International Peace Academy
IPTF	International Police Task Force
IRS	Information and Referral Service (Mozambique)
IsDB	Islamic Development Bank
ISP	Investment Support Program (B&H)
ITC	investment-related technical cooperation
JET	Joint Education Trust (South Africa)
JIU	Joint Inspection Unit (UN)
JLC	Joint Liaison Committee (Palestine)
JMCC	Jerusalem Media and Communications Center
KPNLF	Khmer People's National Liberation Front
LACC	Local Aid Coordination Committee (Palestine)
LAN	local area network
MEA	Municipalities in Action (El Salvador)
MEPFA	Middle East Peace Facilitation Acts
MIGA	Multilateral Investment Guarantee Agency
MINUGUA	United Nations Mission for the Verification of Human Rights in Guatemala
MOPIC	Ministry of Planning and International Cooperation (Palestine)
MTEF	Medium-Term Expenditure Framework (South Africa)
NAM	Non-Aligned Movement (South Africa)
NATO	North Atlantic Treaty Organization
NCRD	National Committee for Rehabilitation and Development (Cambodia)
NDA	National Development Agency
NEDLAC	National Economic Development and Labor Council (South Africa)
NGO	nongovernmental organization
NP	National Party (South Africa)
NPIMS	National Public Investment Management System (Cambodia)
NPRDC	National Program to Rehabilitate and Develop Cambodia
NRP	National Reconstruction Plan (El Salvador)
OAU	Organization of African Unity
OBN	Open Broadcast Network (B&H)
OCHA	Office for the Coordination of Humanitarian Affairs (UN)

ODA	official development assistance
ODA	Overseas Development Association (now DFID-UK)
OECD	Organization for Economic Cooperation and Development
OED	Operations Evaluation Department (World Bank)
OHR	Office of the High Representative (B&N)
OIC	Organization of the Islamic Conference
ONUMOZ	United Nations Operation in Mozambique
ONUSAL	United Nations Observer Mission in El Salvador
OPIC	Overseas Private Investment Corporation
OSCE	Organization for Security and Cooperation in Europe
OSD	Occupational Skills Development Project (Mozambique)
OTI	Office of Transition Initiatives (U.S.)
PA	Palestinian Authority
PAE	Economic Action Program (Mozambique)
PCU	Post-Conflict Unit (World Bank)
PDP	Palestinian Development Plan
PECDAR	Palestinian Economic Council for Development and Reconstruction
PEDRA	Palestinian Economic Development and Reconstruction Authority
PERC	European Rehabilitation Program in Cambodia
PF	Provincial Fund (Mozambique)
PIC	Peace Implementation Council (B&H)
PIMS	Project Information Monitoring System
PIN	Peace Implementation Network
PIP	Public Investment Program
PIU	Project Implementation Unit (World Bank)
PLC	Palestinian Legislative Council
PLO	Palestine Liberation Organization
PMD	Public Monitoring Department (Palestine)
PMU	Project Management Unit (Cambodia)
PPIP	Palestinian Public Investment Program
PRASAC	Rehabilitation and Support Program for the Agricultural Sector of Cambodia
PRE	Economic Rehabilitation Program (Mozambique)
PRK	People's Republic of Kampuchea
PRN	National Reconstruction Plan (Mozambique)
PRODERE	Programme for Displaced Persons, Refugees and Returnees (UNDP)
PRRP	Priority Reconstruction and Recovery Program (B&H)
QIP	Quick Impact Project (UN)
RC/HC	Resident Coordinator/Humanitarian Coordinator (UN)

RCM	Reconstruction Contract Module
RDP	Reconstruction and Development Program (South Africa)
REDWG	Regional Economic Development Working Group (Palestine)
Renamo	Mozambique National Resistance
RRTF	Refugee Return Task Force
RS	Republika Srpska
RSS	Reintegration Support Scheme (Mozambique)
RTs	roundtables
RWG	refugee working group (Palestine)
SACP	South African Communist Party
SADC	Southern Africa Development Community
SADCC	Southern African Development Co-ordination Conference
SAGA	Southern Africa Grantmakers' Association
SAIRR	South African Institute for Race Relations
SAL	structural adjustment loan
SANGOCO	South African NGO Coalition
SAPS	South African Police Service
SEDP	Socioeconomic Development Plan (Cambodia)
SEP	Small Enterprise Program (B&H)
SFOR	Stabilization Force (B&H)
SIDA	Swedish International Development Agency
SNC	Supreme National Council (Cambodia)
SOC	State of Cambodia
SRN	Secretariat for National Reconstruction (El Salvador)
SRSG	Special Representative of the Secretary-General, Office of the (UN)
STAE	Technical Secretariat for Electoral Administration
STF	Systemic Transformation Facility (IMF)
SWG	sectoral working group (Palestine)
TAP	Tripartite Action Plan (on Revenues, Expenditures and Donor Funding for the Palestinian Authority)
TATF	Technical Assistance Trust Fund (World Bank/Palestine)
TNDT	Transitional National Development Trust (South Africa)
TOKTEN	Transfer of Knowledge Through Expatriate Nationals
TRAC	Target for Resource Assignments from the Core (UNDP)
UNBRO	United Nations Border Relief Operation
UNDP	United Nations Development Programme
UNEP	United Nations Environment Programme
UNESCO	United Nations Educational, Scientific, and Cultural Organization

UNHCHR	United Nations High Commissioner for Human Rights, Office of the
UNHCR	United Nations High Commissioner for Refugees, Office of the
UNICEF	United Nations Children's Fund
UNIDO	United Nations Industrial Development Organization
UNMIBH	United Nations Mission in Bosnia and Herzegovina
UNMOT	United Nations Mission of Observers in Tajikistan
UNOHAC	United Nations Office of Humanitarian Assistance Coordination
UNOPS	United Nations Office for Project Services
UNRISD	United Nations Research Institute for Social Development
UNRWA	United Nations Relief and Works Agency
UNSCERO	United Nations Special Coordinator for Emergency Relief Operations
UNSCO	United Nations Special Coordinator in the Occupied Territories, Office of the
UNTAC	United Nations Transitional Authority in Cambodia
UNV	United Nations Volunteers
USAID	United States Agency for International Development
USIA	United States Information Agency
VAT	value-added tax
WFP	World Food Programme
WHO	World Health Organization
ZANU	Zimbabwean African National Union
ZAPLA	Zimbabwean African National Liberation Army

Bibliography

Abrahamsson, Hans, and Anders Nilsson. *Mozambique: The Troubled Transition from Socialist Construction to Free Market Capitalism,* trans. Mary Dally (London: Zed Books, 1995).

Acevedo, Carlos. "Structural Adjustment, the Agricultural Sector, and the Peace Process," in James K. Boyce, ed., *Economic Policy for Building Peace: The Lessons of El Salvador* (Boulder: Lynne Rienner, 1996).

ADB (Asian Development Bank) et. al. *Cambodia: Short-Term Needs,* August 1993.

———. *Cambodia: Socio-Economic Situation and Immediate Needs,* May 1992.

Adelzadeh, Azghar, and Vishnu Padayachee. "The RDP White Paper: Reconstruction of a Development Vision," *Transformation* 25, no. 5 (1994).

Advisory Committee, Office of the Executive Deputy President. *Structural Relationships Between Government and Civil Society Organizations,* March 1997.

African National Congress. *The Reconstruction and Development Programme: A Policy Framework* (Johannesburg: Umanyano Publications, 1994).

AHLC (Ad Hoc Liaison Committee). *The Employment Generation Program in the West Bank and Gaza* (September 5, 1996).

———. *Matrix of Donors' Assistance to the West Bank and Gaza* (various years).

Ajello, Aldo. "The Coordination of Humanitarian Assistance in Mozambique in the Context of the United Nations Peace-keeping Operation," manuscript, New York, April 24, 1996.

al-Botmeh, Samieh, and Edward Sayre. *Employment Generation Schemes in the West Bank and Gaza Strip* (Jerusalem: MAS, November 1996).

Alperson, Myra. *Foundations for a New Democracy: Corporate Social Investment in South Africa* (Johannesburg: Ravan Press, 1995).

Arafat, Yasir. Interview in *Reuters World Report* (November 15, 1994).

Balaj, Barbara, Ishac Diwan, and Bernard Philippe. "External Assistance to the Palestinians: What Went Wrong?" unpublished manuscript.

Balkan Institute. "Arm-and-Train: A Status Report," *Military Watch* 2, no. 11 (May 29, 1997).

Ball, Nicole. "The Challenge of Rebuilding War-Torn Societies," in Chester A. Crocker, Fen Osler Hampson, and Pamela Aall, eds., *Managing Global Chaos: Sources of and Responses to International Conflict* (Washington, D.C.: USIP, 1996).

———. "Lessons for International Actors," draft of an article to be published in a volume on the Bosnian settlement, Jane Sharp, ed., January 20, 1998.

————. "Mid-Term Evaluation: Demobilization and Reintegration Support Project (656–0235), Mozambique," prepared for U.S. Agency for International Development/Maputo (Washington, D.C.: Overseas Development Council, August 3, 1995).

————. *Pressing for Peace: Can Aid Induce Reform?* ODC Policy Essay 6 (Washington, D.C.: Overseas Development Council, 1992).

————. *Spreading Good Practices in Security Sector Reform*, Saferworld Report (London: Saferworld, December 1998).

Ball, Nicole, and Kathleen Campbell. *Complex Crisis and Complex Peace: Humanitarian Coordination in Angola* (New York: UN Office for the Coordination of Humanitarian Affairs, March 1998).

Ball, Nicole, with Tammy Halevy. *Making Peace Work: The Role of the International Development Community* (Washington, D.C.: ODC, 1996).

Barnes, Sam. *Humanitarian Aid Coordination During War and Peace in Mozambique: 1985–1995,* Studies on Emergencies and Disaster Relief, Report no. 7 (Uppsala: Nordiska Afrikainstitutet in cooperation with Swedish International Development Agency, 1998).

————. "The Humanitarian Factor in the Mozambique Peace Negotiations: 1990–1992," in Stephen Chan and Moises Venancio with Chris Alden and Sam Barnes, eds., *War and Peace in Mozambique* (London: Macmillan, 1998).

————. "Peacekeeping in Mozambique," in Oliver Furley and Roy May, eds., *Peacekeeping in Africa* (London: Ashgate Publishing, 1998).

————. "Reintegration Programmes for Demobilised Soldiers in Mozambique," prepared for UNDP/RSS, Maputo, March 1997.

"Bending the Rules," *The Economist* (June 28, 1997).

Benson, Charlotte. *The Changing Role of NGOs in the Provision of Relief and Rehabilitation Assistance: Case Study 2—Cambodia/Thailand* (London: Overseas Development Institute, Regent's College, Working Paper 75, November 1993).

Bertram, Eva. "Reinventing Governments: The Promise and Perils of United Nations Peacebuilding," *Journal of Conflict Resolution* 39, no. 3 (September 1995): 387–418.

Binkert, Gregor. Letter to Jürg Frieden, World Bank, January 26, 1994.

Blustein, Paul. "A Loan Amid the Ruins: World Bank Shifts Aid to Rebuilding War-Torn Countries," *Washington Post* (February 13, 1996).

Bouhabib, Abdullah. "The World Bank and International Aid to Palestine," *Journal of Palestine Studies* 23, no. 2 (winter 1994).

Boyce, James K. "Adjustment Towards Peace: An Introduction," *World Development* 23, no. 12 (1995): 2067–2077.

————. "External Assistance to the Peace Process in El Salvador," *World Development* 23, no. 12 (1995): 2101–2116.

————. "External Resource Mobilization," in James K. Boyce, ed., *Economic Policy for Building Peace: The Lessons of El Salvador* (Boulder: Lynne Rienner, 1996).

————. *Peace Conditionality: External Assistance and Post-Conflict Transitions* (forthcoming, 2000).

Boyce, James K., and Manuel Pastor, Jr. "Aid for Peace: Can International Financial Institutions Help Prevent Conflict?" *World Policy Journal* 15, no. 2 (Summer 1998): 42–49.

Broder, John M. "Clinton Declares Most War Cleanup Is Europe's Task," *New York Times* (June 1, 1999).

Brown, Michael E., "Internal Conflict and International Action," in Michael E. Brown, ed., *The International Dimensions of Internal Conflict* (Cambridge: MIT Press, 1996).

———. "Internal Conflict: Causes and Implications," in Michael E. Brown, ed., *The International Dimensions of Internal Conflict* (Cambridge: MIT Press, 1996).

Brynen, Rex. "Neopatrimonial Dimensions of Palestinian Politics," *Journal of Palestine Studies* 25, no. 1 (Autumn 1995): 23–36.

———. *A Very Political Economy: Peacebuilding and Foreign Aid in Palestine* (forthcoming).

Bush, Kenneth. "A Measure of Peace: Peace and Conflict Impact Assessment of Development Projects in Conflict Zones" (Ottawa: International Development Research Centre, March 1998).

Carbonnier, Gilles. *Conflict, Postwar Rebuilding and the Economy: A Critical Review of the Literature,* War-Torn Societies Project Occasional Paper no. 2 (Geneva: UNRISD, 1998).

Carnegie Commission. *Preventing Deadly Conflict* (New York: Carnegie Commission, 1997).

Carothers, Thomas, and Juan Alberto Fuentes. "La Cooperación Internacional en Guatemala," report prepared for the Institute for Democracy and Electoral Assistance, typescript, Guatemala City, June 1998.

Carter Center. *1997–1998 State of World Conflict Report* (Atlanta: Carter Center, 1998).

CDC/CRDB. *Development Cooperation Report (1997/98), Main Report* (Phnom Penh: CDC/CRDB, June 1998).

———. *Development Cooperation Report (1996/97), Main Report* (Phnom Penh: CDC/CRDB, May 1997).

———. *Development Cooperation Report (1995/96), Main Report* (Phnom Penh: CDC/CRDB, May 1996).

———. *Development Cooperation Report (1994/95)* (Phhom Penh, May 1995).

Center on International Cooperation (NYU). "Meeting Essential Needs in Societies Emerging from Conflict," paper prepared for the Donor Roundtable on Bridging the Gap Between Humanitarian Assistance and Long-Term Development (June 1999).

"Chairman's Conclusions." First Donor Conference on the Reconstruction of Bosnia and Herzegovina, Brussels: December 20–21, 1995.

"Chairman's Conclusions." Second Donor Conference on the Reconstruction of Bosnia and Herzegovina," Brussels, April 12–13, 1996.

"Chairman's Conclusions." Third Donor Conference on the Reconstruction of Bosnia and Herzegovina," Brussels, July 23, 1997.

Chanda, Nayan. "Indochina," in Anthony Lake et al., eds., *After the Wars* (Washington, D.C.: Overseas Development Council, 1990).

Cholmondeley, Hugh. "The Role of the UN System in Response to Crisis and Recovery—A Strategic Approach," report for the Consultative Committee on Program and Operational Questions (CCPOQ), March 3–7, 1997.

Chopra, Jarat. "Introducing Peace-Maintenance," *Global Governance* 4, no. 1 (Jan.–March 1998): 1–18.

Chote, Robert. "Finally, Relief in Sight: The IMF and the World Bank Plan to Ease the Debt Burdens of Poor Countries Emerging from Conflict," *Financial Times* (September 9, 1998).

Christian Michelsen Institute with Nordic Consulting Group. *Evaluation of Norwegian Assistance to Peace, Reconciliation and Rehabilitation in Mozambique,* UD Evaluation Report 4.97 (Oslo: Ministry of Foreign Affairs, 1997).

Cohen, Roger "An Agreement on Debt Relief for Poor Lands," *New York Times,* June 19, 1999.

Colletta, Nat J., and Nicole Ball. "War to Peace Transition in Uganda," *Finance and Development* 30, no. 2 (June 1993): 36–39.

Collier, David. "The Comparative Method: Two Decades of Change," in Dankwart Rustow and Kenneth Paul, eds., *Comparative Political Dynamics* (New York: Harper Collins, 1991), pp. 7–31.

Commission of the European Communities. *EC Support for the Middle East Peace Process,* Communication from the Commission to the Council and the European Parliament, Brussels, September 29, 1993.

———. *The Role of the European Union in the Middle East Peace Process and its Future Assistance,* Document IP/98/37, January 16, 1998, archived at http://europa.eu.int.

Community Agency for Social Enquiry (CASE). *Tango in the Dark: Government and Voluntary Sector Partnerships in the New South Africa* (Johannesburg: CASE, 1996).

Conference to Support Middle East Peace. *Cosponsors' Summary,* October 1, 1993.

Consultative Group. *Statements* (various years).

Cortright, David, and George A. Lopez. "Carrots, Sticks, and Cooperation: Economic Tools of Statecraft," in Barnett R. Rubin, ed., *Cases and Strategies for Preventive Action* (New York: Council on Foreign Relations and Twentieth Century Fund, 1998).

Costa, Gino. "La Reforma Policial en El Salvador," paper presented at the forum on the International Community and Police Reform in Central America and Haiti, Johns Hopkins S.A.I.S., Washington, D.C., November 3–4, 1994.

CPRS (Center for Palestine Research and Studies). *Prevailing Perceptions on Aid Management,* Research Reports Series 9 (Nablus: CPRS, December 1997).

———. *Public Opinion Polls* (various years), archived at http://www.cprs-palestine.org/polls/.

Creative Associations International, Inc. *The Information and Referral Service and Provincial Fund (IRS/PF) for the Reintegration of Demobilised Soldiers in Mozambique: Internal Review of Activities: Final Report* (Washington, DC: Creative Associates, February 1996).

"Debt Rhetoric Has to Face Reality Test," *Financial Times,* June 21, 1999.

Dempsey, Judy. "Palestinian Aid Faces Obstacle Course," *Financial Times* (June 6, 1997).

Department for International Development (DFID). "Poverty and the Security Sector. Policy Statement," www.dfid.gov.uk (1999).

De Soto, Alvaro, and Graciana del Castillo. "Obstacles to Peacebuilding," *Foreign Affairs* 94 (spring 1994): 69–93.

Development Associates. *Evaluation of the Peace and National Recovery Project (519–0394),* final report submitted to USAID, January 1994.

DFAIT (Department of Foreign Affairs and International Trade). "Canada's Peacebuilding Initiative," www.dfait-maeci.gc.ca/peacebuilding.

Diwan, Ishac, and Radwan A. Shaban, eds. *Development Under Adversity? The Palestinian Economy in Transition* (Washington, D.C.: World Bank, 1999).

Donini, Antonio. *The Politics of Mercy: UN Coordination in Afghanistan, Mozambique, and Rwanda,* Occasional Paper, Thomas J. Watson Institute, 1997.

Dos Santos, Elisa, João Honwana, and Miguel de Brito. "Enhancing Security and Development in Mozambique," unpublished report to the Overseas Development Council, Washington, D.C., Maputo, 1996.

Doyle, Michael W. *UN Peacekeeping in Cambodia: UNTAC's Civil Mandate* (Boulder: Lynne Rienner, 1995).

Drachman, Steven S. "The War in Cambodia and the Case for Judicial Enforcement of Human Rights Conditions on Foreign Aid," *Columbia Journal of Transnational Law* 30, no. 3 (1992): 661–695.

Duffield, Mark. "Complex Emergencies and the Crisis of Developmentalism," *IDS Bulletin* 25, no. 4 (October 1994).

Ear, Sophal. "Cambodia and the 'Washington Consensus,'" *Crossroads: An Interdisciplinary Journal of Southeast Asian Studies* 11, no.2 (1997): 73–97.

Eaton, Robert, Chris Horwood, and Norah Niland, *The Development of Indigenous Mine Action Capacities: Study Report* (New York: United Nations Department of Humanitarian Affairs, ca. 1998).

Economist (U.S. edition), "The IMF in Africa, Affray," (October 28, 1995).

Economist Intelligence Unit. *EIU Country Report: Mozambique* (second quarter, 1993).

Education Foundation (Johannesburg). *EduSource Data News* 20 (March 1998).

European Commission. "Linking Relief, Rehabilitation, and Development (LRRD)," communication from the Commission to the Council and the European Parliament, Brussels, March 28, 1996.

European Commission and World Bank, "Bosnia and Herzegovina—Implementation of Priority Reconstruction Program: Status Report to the Donor Community," November 1997.

———. "Bosnia and Herzegovina—The Priority Reconstruction Program: The Achievements and 1998 Needs," April 1998.

European Union. "Special Report No. 7/98 in Respect of the European Community Development Aid Programme regarding South Africa (1986–1996)," *Official Journal of the European Communities* 41 (July 1998): 96.

Fagen, Patricia Weiss. "El Salvador: Lessons in Peace Consolidation," in Tom Farer, ed., *Beyond Sovereignty: Collectively Defending Democracy in the Americas* (Baltimore: Johns Hopkins University Press, 1996).

Fahlen, Marika. "Post-Conflict Reconstruction: The Need for a New Global Financial Mechanism," UNHCR note for discussion, February 8, 1996.

Findler, David. "Foreign Private Investment in Palestine: An Analysis of the Law on the Encouragement of Investment in Palestine," *Fordham International Law Journal* 19, no. 2 (December 1995).

Fituni, Leonid L. "Russia's Arms Sales to Africa: Past, Present and Future," *CSIS Africa Notes* 140 (September 1992).

Foley, Michael W. "Laying the Groundwork: The Struggle for Civil Society in El Salvador," *Journal of Interamerican Studies and World Affairs* 31, no. 1 (spring 1996).

Foley, Michael W., and Franzi Miguel Hasbún, with Luis Córdova. *ONG's, Desarrollo y Democracia en El Salvador,* research report, Fundación para la Gestión Social, San Salvador, December 1995.

Foley, Michael W., et al. *Land, Peace and Participation: The Development of Post-War Agricultural Policy in El Salvador and the Role of the World Bank,* Occasional Paper Series, Washington Office on Latin America, Washington, D.C., June 1997.

Friedman, Steven. "Give Us the Tools: South African Development Needs and SA-German Cooperation" (Johannesburg: Centre for Policy Studies, 1998).

———. *The Long Journey, South Africa's Quest for a Negotiated Settlement* (Johannesburg: Ravan Press, 1993).

————. "Next Poll to Gauge Democracy's Support," *Business Day* (April 20, 1998).
————. "No Easy Stroll to Dominance: Party Dominance, Opposition and Civil Society in South Africa," *Towards Democracy* (fourth quarter, 1996).
————. "Not Just Order But Democracy Threatened," *Business Day* (January 26, 1998).
————. "South Africa," in Seymour Martin Lipset, ed., *Encyclopedia of Democracy* (London: Routledge, 1995).
"From Emergency to Sustainable Development." Prepared by the World Bank in consultation with the Government of Mozambique, Consultative Group meeting, Paris, December 1993.
GAO (General Accounting Office). *Aid to El Salvador: Slow Progress in Developing a National Civilian Police,* GAO/NSIAD-92-338 (Washington, D.C.: United States General Accounting Office, September 1992).
————. *El Salvador: Status of Reconstruction Activities One Year After the Peace Agreement,* draft statement of Harold J. Johnson, director, International Affairs Issues, United States General Accounting Office, before the Subcommittee on Western Hemisphere Affairs, Committee on Foreign Affairs, House of Representatives, March 23, 1993.
Garten, Jeffrey E. *The Big Ten: The Big Emerging Markets and How They Will Change Our Lives* (New York: Basic Books, 1998).
Geffray, Christian. *La Cause des Armes au Mozambique: Anthropologie d'une Guerre Civile* (Paris: Karthala, 1990).
Geldenhuys, Deon. "The Foreign Factor in South Africa's 1992 Referendum," *Politikon* 9, no. 3 (December 1992).
————. *Isolated States: A Comparative Analysis* (Johannesburg: Jonathan Ball Publishers, 1990).
General Peace Agreement for Mozambique. Rome, October 4, 1992.
George, Alexander, and Timothy J. McKeown. "Case Studies and Theories of Organizational Decision-Making," *Advances in Information Processing in Organizations* 2 (1985): 21–58.
GOES (Government of El Salvador). *Los Acuerdos de Paz en El Salvador: Informe de Cumplimiento al 30 de Abril de 1996,* San Salvador, 1996.
Government of Cambodia. *National Programme to Rehabilitate and Develop Cambodia,* Phnom Penh, February 1994.
Government of Italy. "Letter Dated December 30, 1992, Transmitting the Conclusions of the Donors Conference for Mozambique, Held in Rome on December 15–16, 1992," Document 28, in *The United Nations and Mozambique, 1992–1995* (New York: United Nations, 1995).
Government of South Africa. Annual Consultation Minutes, 1995–1998 (Department of Finance).
————. *Growth, Employment and Redistribution: A Macro-Economic Strategy for South Africa* (Pretoria: Department of Finance, 1996).
————. *Multi-Annual Indicative Programme: Framework for Cooperation between the Republic of South Africa and the European Community* (Pretoria: Department of Finance, May 1997).
————. *Progress Report on Commitments and Disbursements of Donor Funds* (Pretoria: Department of Finance, May 14, 1998).
Government of Sweden. *Sweden's Development Cooperation with South Africa* (Pretoria: Embassy of Sweden, 1996).
Graham, Carol. *Safety Nets, Politics, and the Poor* (Washington: Brookings Institution Press, 1994).

Griffin, Keith B., and John L. Enos. "Foreign Assistance: Objectives and Conse-
quences," *Economic Development and Cultural Change* 18, no. 3 (1970): 313–327.
Grube, Douglas I. "Donors in Disarray: Prospects for External Assistance to Cam-
bodia," Special Report of Cambodia Development Resource Institute, Phnom
Penh, April 1998.
Ha-Aretz. (Various issues).
Habib, Adam, and Vishnu Padayachee, "South Africa: Power, Politics and Eco-
nomic Policy in the Transition to Democracy," *Tiers Monde* (forthcoming).
Habib, Adam, and Rupert Taylor. "South Africa: Anti-Apartheid NGOs in Transi-
tion," *Voluntas* (forthcoming, 1999).
Hanlon, Joseph. *Mozambique: Who Calls the Shots?* (London: James Currey, 1991).
———. *Peace Without Profit: How the IMF Blocks Rebuilding in Mozambique*
(Oxford: Heineman, 1996).
Hanna, Nagy. "What Economic System for Palestine?" paper presented to the confer-
ence "Management of the Palestinian Economy," Nablus, December 13, 1995.
Hedges, Chris. "Leaders in Bosnia Are Said to Steal up to $1 Billion," *New York
Times,* August 17, 1999.
Heininger, Janet E. "Cambodia: Relief, Repatriation, and Rehabilitation," in Eric
A. Belgrad and Nitza Nachmias, eds., *The Politics of International Humani-
tarian Aid Operations* (London: Praeger, 1997).
"Help for a Self-Helper," *Washington Post* (September 2, 1997).
Hewison, Kevin, Richard Robison, and Garry Rodan, eds. *Southeast Asia in the
1990s: Authoritarianism, Democracy and Capitalism* (St. Leonards, Australia:
Allen and Unwin, 1993).
Hjelm-Wallen, Lena. Interview in *al-Quds al-'Arabi* (April 3, 1998).
Holtzman, Steven. "Post-Conflict Reconstruction," Work in Progress Paper, World
Bank, 1995.
Hook, Steven. "Building Democracy Through Foreign Aid: The Limitations of
United States Political Conditionalities, 1992–96," *Democratization* 5, no. 3
(Autumn 1998): 156–180.
Hovi, Jon. *Games, Threats, and Treaties: Understanding Commitments in Interna-
tional Relations* (Washington: Pinter, 1998).
Humphries, Richard, and Maxine Reitzes, eds. *Civil Society After Apartheid*
(Johannesburg: Centre for Policy Studies, 1995).
IMF (International Monetary Fund). "Adaptations of IMF Policies and Proce-
dures," *IMF Survey,* September 1996.
———. *Annual Report,* 1996.
———. "A Macroeconomic Framework for Assistance to Post-Conflict Countries,"
1996.
"Inadequate Security in Public Schools: Coordinating a Response." *Briefing,* Inde-
pendent Projects Trust, Public Information Service, Durban, March 6, 1998,
pp. 1–6.
Indicator South Africa 14, no. 3 (spring 1997).
Institute for Security Studies (ISS). "Issue Areas for Future Funding," manuscript
(Midrand, South Africa: ISS, May 1998).
———. *Victim Surveys* (Midrand, South Africa: ISS, 1998).
International Bank for Reconstruction and Development. "Consultative Group for
Mozambique: Paris, May 15–16, 1997, Chairman's Report of Proceedings,"
CG97-29, Washington, D.C.: July 24, 1997.
———. "Mozambique: Policy Framework Paper, 1997–1999," SecM97-386, Wash-
ington, D.C., May 15, 1997.

International Crisis Group, "Going Nowhere Fast: Refugees and Internally Displaced Persons in Bosnia," Sarajevo, April 30, 1997, available on the web at: http://www.intl-crisis-group.org.
———. "Hollow Promise? Return of Bosnian Serb Displaced Persons to Drvar, Bosansko Grahavo and Glamoc," Sarajevo, January 19, 1998.
International Republican Institute and National Democratic Institute for International Affairs. *The Continuing Crisis in Cambodia: Obstacles to Democratic Elections,* Washington, D.C.: January 30, 1998.
Intrac. *Differing Approaches to Development Assistance in Cambodia: NGOs and the European Commission,* Phnom Penh, August 1996.
IPCRI (Israel-Palestine Center for Research and Information). *The Legal Structure for Foreign Investment in the West Bank and Gaza Strip,* Commercial Law Report Series 1, October 1994.
James, Wilmot, and Daria Caliguire. "Renewing Civil Society," *Journal of Democracy* 7, no. 1 (1996).
Johnson, R.W., and Lawrence Schlemmer, eds. *Launching Democracy in South Africa: The First Open Election, April 1994* (New Haven: Yale University Press, 1996).
Joint Evaluation of Emergency Assistance to Rwanda. *The International Response to Conflict and Genocide: Lessons from the Rwanda Experience* (4 vols.). *Study 4: Rebuilding Post-War Rwanda* (Copenhagen: Steering Committee of the Joint Evaluation of Emergency Assistance to Rwanda, 1996).
Jonas, Susanne. *Of Centaurs and Doves: Guatemala's Peace Process* (Boulder: Westview, 1999).
Kabemba, Claude. "Political and Economic Implications of the Reincorporation of South Africa into SADC," master's thesis, University of Witwatersrand, 1996.
Kanaan, Oussama. "Uncertainty Deters Private Investment in the West Bank and Gaza Strip," *Finance and Development* 35, no. 2 (1998): 34–37.
Karl, Terry Lynn. "El Salvador's Negotiated Revolution," *Foreign Affairs* 71, no. 2 (1992).
———. "War Transitions: Ending Armed Conflict and Starting Democracy in 'Uncivil' Societies," draft paper, 1999.
Kato, Elisabeth Uphoff, "Quick Impacts, Slow Rehabilitation in Cambodia," in Michael W. Doyle, Ian Johnstone, and Robert C. Orr, eds., *Keeping the Peace: Multidimensional UN Operations in Cambodia and El Salvador* (Cambridge: Cambridge University Press, 1997).
Kornegay, Francis, and Chris Landsberg. "Phaphama iAfrica: The African Renaissance and Corporate South Africa," *African Security Review* 7, no. 4 (1998).
Koschnick, Hans, and Jens Schneider. *Brücke über die Neretva: Der Wiederaufbau von Mostar* (Munich: Deutscher Taschenbuch Verlag, 1995).
Krasner, Stephen D. *International Regimes* (Ithaca: Cornell University Press, 1983).
Kriskovich, David (deputy commissioner, IPTF). *Restructuring Progress in Bosnia/Herzegovina,* prepared for seminar on security sector reform in Bosnia and Herzegovina, National Defense University, June 12, 1997.
Kumar, Krishna. "The Nature and Focus of International Assistance for Rebuilding War-Torn Societies," in Krishna Kumar, ed., *Rebuilding Societies after Civil War: Critical Roles for International Assistance* (Boulder: Lynne Rienner, 1997).
Kumar, Krishna, et al. *The International Response to Conflict and Genocide: Lessons from the Rwanda Experience. Study 4: Rebuilding Post-War Rwanda*

(Copenhagen: Steering Committee of the Joint Evaluation of Emergency Assistance to Rwanda, March 1996).

Kumar, Radha. *Divide and Fall? Bosnia in the Annals of Partition* (London: Verso, 1997).

LACC (Local Aid Coordination Committee). *Co-chairs' Summary,* September 8, 1997, archived at http://www.arts.mcgill.ca/mepp/unsco/lacc970908.html.

———. *Partners in Peace,* July 1996, archived at http://www.arts.mcgill.ca/mepp/unsco/unfront.html.

Lake, Anthony, ed. *After the Wars: Reconstruction in Afghanistan, Indochina, Central America, Southern Africa, and the Horn of Africa* (New Brunswick, N.J.: Transaction Publishers, 1990).

Landau, Luis. *Rebuilding the Mozambique Economy: Country Assistance Review* (Washington, D.C.: World Bank, 1998).

Landsberg, Chris. "Directing from the Stalls? The International Community and the South African Negotiating Forum," in Steven Friedman and Doreen Atkinson, eds., *The Small Miracle: South Africa's Negotiated Settlement* (Johannesburg: Ravan Press, 1994), pp. 276–300.

———. "Exporting Peace? The UN and South Africa," Centre for Policy Studies (Johannesburg), International Relations Series 7, 2 (1994).

Landsberg, Chris, and Cedric de Coning. "From 'Tar Baby' to Transition: Four Decades of US Foreign Policy Towards South Africa," *CPS PIA* 18, no. 6 (March 1995).

Lawrence, Stewart. *Postwar El Salvador: Funding for Peace?* draft GAO report, manuscript, April 1, 1992.

Lia, Brynjar. *Implementing Peace: The Oslo Peace Accord and International Assistance to the Enhancement of Security,* Forsvarets Forskningsinstitutt (Norwegian Defence Research Establishment), FFI/RAPPORT-98/01711.

Linz, Juan, and Alfred Stepan. *Problems of Democratic Transition and Consolidation* (Baltimore: Johns Hopkins University Press, 1996).

Lumsdaine, David Halloran. *Moral Vision in International Politics: The Foreign Aid Regime, 1949–1989* (Princeton: Princeton University Press, 1993).

Macrae, Joanna. "Linking Relief, Rehabilitation, and Development," *RRN Newsletter* (June 1996).

Management Systems International. *Assistance to the Transition from War to Peace: Evaluation of USAID/El Salvador's Special Strategic Objective (Project No. 519-0394),* Washington, D.C.: August 1996.

Marshall, Katherine. "Emerging from Conflict: What Roles for the International Development Finance Institutions?" Development Discussion Paper No. 587, Harvard Institute for International Development, June 1997.

———. "Mozambique Consultative Group Meeting, Chair's Closing Statement," Paris, March 14–15, 1995.

Mattes, Robert. "Votes Available: Anyone Want Them?" manuscript, Institute for Democracy in South Africa, September 1998.

Mattes, Robert, and Herman Thiel. "The Prospects for Democratic Consolidation in South Africa," *Journal of Democracy* 9, no. 1 (1998): 95–108.

McAndrew, John. *Aid Infusions, Aid Illusions: Bilateral and Multilateral Emergency and Development Assistance to Cambodia, 1992–1995* (Phnom Penh: CDRI, January 1996).

MIPLAN, *Consolidating the Peace Through National Reconstruction and Poverty Alleviation,* report to the Consultative Group Meeting, Paris, April 1, 1993 (San Salvador, 1993).

————. *Economic and Social Program, 1989–1994,* report to the first Consultative Group Meeting, Paris, May 15–16, 1991 (San Salvador, 1991).

————. *Financiamiento Contratado y en Proceso de Negociación con la Comunidad Internacional para la Ejecución del Plan de Reconstrucción Nacional (PRN),* San Salvador, February 1993.

————. *Financiamiento Contratado y en Proceso de Negociación con la Comunidad Internacional para la Ejecución del Plan de Reconstrucción Nacional (PRN),* San Salvador, May 1993.

————. *Financiamiento Contratado y en Proceso de Negociación con la Comunidad Internacional para la Ejecución del Plan de Reconstrucción Nacional (PRN),* San Salvador, August 1993.

————. *Financiamiento Contratado y en Proceso de Negociación con la Comunidad Internacional para la Ejecución del Plan de Reconstrucción Nacional (PRN),* San Salvador, September 1993.

————. *Financiamiento Contratado y en Proceso de Negociación con la Comunidad Internacional para la Ejecución del Plan de Reconstrucción Nacional (PRN),* San Salvador, May 1994.

————. *Financiamiento Contratado y en Proceso de Negociación con la Comunidad Internacional para la Ejecución del Plan de Reconstrucción Nacional (PRN),* San Salvador, July 1995.

————. *Financing Needs to Conclude the Peace Agreements,* report to the Consultative Group meeting, Paris, June 22, 1995, San Salvador, 1995.

————. *Los Grupos Consultivos, sus Ofrecimientos y Aportes para El Salvador,* San Salvador, November, 1995.

————. *Memoria de Labores 1991–1992,* San Salvador, 1992

————. *Memoria de Labores 1993–1994,* San Salvador, May 1994.

————. *National Reconstruction Plan, Preliminary Version,* San Salvador, September, 1991.

————. *National Reconstruction Plan, Revised Version,* San Salvador, November, 1991.

————. *National Reconstruction Plan,* report to the Consultative Group meeting, Washington, March 23, 1992, San Salvador, 1992.

————. *Resumen Promesas de Ayuda del Grupo Consultivo en Washington,* San Salvador, 1992.

MIPLAN-SRN-FMLN. *Actas de Reuniones Sostenidas Entre MIPLAN, Secretaría de Reconstrucción Nacional y Comisión Nacional de Reconstrucción del FMLN entre el 17 de Febrero y el 12 de Marzo de 1992,* San Salvador, March 17, 1992.

MOPIC. *Quarterly Monitoring Report* (various dates).

Moscow News. 48 (1991).

Muscat, Robert. "Conflict and Reconstruction: Roles for the World Bank" (Washington, D.C.: World Bank, 1995).

Mysliwiec, Eva L. "Cambodia: NGOs in Transition," in Peter Utting, ed., *Between Hope and Insecurity: The Social Consequences of the Cambodian Peace Process* (Geneva: UN Research Institute for Social Development, 1994).

————. *Punishing the Poor: The International Isolation of Kampuchea* (Oxford: Oxfam, 1988).

Natsios, Andrew S. *US Foreign Policy and the Four Horsemen of the Apocalypse: Humanitarian Relief in Complex Emergencies* (Westport, Conn: Praeger, 1997).

Nordic Statement. CG meeting of El Salvador, April 1, 1993.

OECD (Organization for Economic Cooperation and Development). *Geographical Distribution of Financial Flows to Aid Recipients 1999,* www.oecd.org/dac/.

OECD/DAC (Organization for Economic Cooperation and Development, Development Assistance Committee). *Conflict, Peace, and Development Cooperation on the Threshold of the 21st Century* (Paris: OECD, 1997).
———. *Shaping the 21st Century: The Contribution of Development Cooperation* (Paris: OECD, May 1996).
Ogata, Sadako, and James D. Wolfensohn. "The Transition to Peace in War-Torn Societies: Some Personal Observations," background paper to multidonor roundtable, January 15, 1999.
Ohlson, Thomas, and Stephen John Stedman, with Robert Davies. *The New Is Not Yet Born: Conflict Resolution in Southern Africa* (Washington, D.C.: The Brookings Institution, 1994).
OHR (Office of the High Representative). "Bosnia and Herzegovina 1998: Self-Sustaining Structures: Conclusions," Bonn Peace Implementation Conference, December 10, 1997, http://www.ohr.int/docu/d971210a.htm#07, pp. 15–16.
———. *Economic Task Force Secretariat,* vol. 1, 1998, various issues, Sarajevo.
———. Monthly Newsletter of the Economic Task Force Secretariat, http:\\www.ohr.int.
———. "OHR and Reconstruction," January 16, 1997.
———. "Statement of High Representative," Brussels Donor Information Conference, January 9, 1997.
Overseas Development Administration. *British Aid to South Africa* (London: Overseas Development Administration, March 1995).
Oxfam. "Oxfam International Submission to the Heavily Indebted Poor Country (HIPC) Debt Review," April 1999.
PA (Palestinian Authority). *First Annual Report 1996,* Public Monitoring Department, Gaza, May 1997.
———. *Palestinian Development Plan 1998–2000: Project List and Annexes,* December 1997.
———. *Presentation to the Fifth Meeting of the Consultative Group [for the] West Bank and Gaza Strip,* Paris, December 14–15, 1997.
———. *Quarterly Monitoring Report of Donor Assistance,* Ministry of Planning and International Cooperation, various dates.
———. *Report on Fiscal Developments in April–September 1997 and Outlook for the Remainder of 1997,* Ministry of Finance, October 31, 1997.
———. *Statement by the Palestinian Delegation on the Internal Audit Report of 23 May 1996,* presented to the Ad Hoc Liason Committee, June 5, 1997.
PALDEV Digest. (Various issues).
Palestine Report. (Various issues).
Paris, Roland. "Peacebuilding and the Limits of Liberal Internationalism," *International Security* 22, no. 2 (fall 1997): 54–89.
Pastor, Manuel, and James K. Boyce. "El Salvador: Economic Disparities, External Intervention, and Civil Conflict," in E. Wayne Nafziger, Frances Stewart, and Raimo Vayrynen, eds., *Weak States and Vulnerable Economies: Humanitarian Emergencies in the Third World* (Oxford: Oxford University Press, 1999).
Peace Implementation Network. *Command from the Saddle: Managing United Nations Peace-Building Missions,* Fafo Report 266 (Oslo: Fafo Institute for Applied Social Science, 1999).
Pearl, Daniel. "Continental Divide," *Wall Street Journal* (August 22, 1997).
Peou, Sorpong. "Cambodia: A New Glimpse of Hope?" *Southeast Asian Affairs 1997:* 83–103.

———. "The Cambodian Elections of 1998: Liberal Democracy in the Making?" *Contemporary Southeast Asia* 20, no. 3 (December 1998): 279–297.

———. *Conflict Neutralization in the Cambodia War: From Battlefield to Ballotbox* (Kuala Lumpur, Singapore, and New York: Oxford University Press, 1997).

———. *Foreign Intervention and Anti-Democratic Regimes in Cambodia: Towards Illiberal Democracy?* (forthcoming).

———. "Hun Sen's Preemptive Coup: Causes and Consequences," *Southeast Asian Affairs 1998:* 86–102.

PLC (Palestinian Legislative Council). *Report of the Special Committee of the Palestinian Legislative Council on the Report of the Head of General Control Office, First Annual Report 1996* (in Arabic).

PLO (Palestine Liberation Organization). Department of Economic Affairs and Planning, *Programme for Development of the Palestinian National Economy for the Years 1994–2000: Executive Summary* (Tunis: PLO, July 1993).

Pomerantz, Phyllis (Country Director for Mozambique, Africa Region, World Bank). "Chairman's Closing Statement," Mozambique Consultative Group meeting, Paris, May 15–16, 1997.

———. "Chairman's Opening Statement," Mozambique Consultative Group meeting, Paris, May 15–16, 1997.

Popkin, Margaret, et al. *Justice Delayed: The Slow Pace of Judicial Reform in El Salvador* (Washington, D.C.: Washington Office on Latin America/Hemisphere Initiatives, December 1994).

Preston, Lewis. "The International Effort to Invest in Peace in the Occupied Territories, and the Role of the World Bank," Conference to Support Middle East Peace, October 1, 1993.

Przeworski, Adam, and Fernando Limongi. "Modernization: Theories and Facts," *World Politics* 49 (January 1997): 155–183.

RDP (Reconstruction and Development) Monitor.

Reconstruction and Return Task Force. "An Action Plan in Support of the Return of Refugees and Displaced Persons in Bosnia and Herzegovina," March 1998.

Reindorp, Nicola. "Towards an Assistance Strategy for Rwanda," consultant's report for UNDP, July 1998.

Reinicke, Wolfgang H. "Can International Financial Institutions Prevent Internal Violence? The Sources of Ethno-National Conflict in Transitional Societies," in A. and A. H. Chayes, eds., *Preventing Conflict in the Post-Communist World* (Washington, D.C.: Brookings Institution, 1996).

Renner, Michael. *Budgeting for Disarmament: The Costs of War and Peace,* Worldwatch Paper 122, Washington, D.C., November 1994.

República de Moçambique. "Establishing the Basis for Economic and Social Development: Key Policies," report prepared for the Consultative Group meeting for Mozambique, Paris, March 1995.

República de Moçambique, Ministry of Planning and Finance. Poverty Alleviation Unit. "The Poverty Reduction Strategy for Mozambique," prepared for the Consultative Group meeting for Mozambique, Paris, March 1995.

Roberts, Adam, and Benedict Kingsbury, eds. *United Nations, Divided World* (Oxford: Clarendon Press, 1993).

Roberts, Nigel. "The Prospects for the Palestinian Economy," paper presented to the conference on Resolving the Palestinian Refugee Problem: What Role for the International Community? University of Warwick, UK, March 23–24, 1998, archived at http://www.arts.mcgill.ca/mepp/prrn/prwarrob.html.

Rosa, Herman. *AID y las Transformaciones Globales en El Salvador* (Managua: CRIES, 1993).

————. *El Banco Mundial y el Futuro del Ajuste Estructural en El Salvador,* Boletín PRISMA 3–4, San Salvador, November–December 1993.

Rother, Larry. "As Leaders Bicker, Haiti Stagnates and Its People Fret," *New York Times* (July 17, 1998).

Rothkopf, David J. *The Price of Peace: Emergency Economic Intervention and U.S. Foreign Policy* (Washington: Carnegie Endowment for International Peace, 1998).

Roy, Sara. *The Gaza Strip: The Political Economy of Dedevelopment* (Washington, D.C.: Institute for Palestine Studies, 1995).

Ruiz Calderón, Juan Carlos. "Camdessus: La condición para Certificar la Economía es Cumplir con los Acuerdos de Paz," *Siglo Veintiuno* (Guatemala City, May 27, 1997).

Samara, Adel. "The World Bank's Policy in the Palestinian Self-Rule Areas: Economic Restructuring and People's Re-Education," *News from Within* 11, no. 10 (October 1995).

Seelye, Katharine Q. "Crisis in the Balkans: The Reconstruction; Allies Seek a Way to Promote Prosperity in Restive Balkans," *Washington Post* (April 21, 1999).

Segovia, Alexander. "Domestic Resource Mobilization," in James K. Boyce, ed., *Economic Policy for Building Peace: The Lessons of El Salvador* (Boulder: Lynne Rienner, 1996).

Shaw, Mark. "The Bloody Backdrop: Negotiating Violence," in Steven Friedman and Doreen Atkinson, eds., *The Small Miracle, South Africa's Negotiated Settlement* (Johannesburg: Ravan Press, 1994), pp. 182–203.

————. "Of Crime and Country: Reported Crime Trends in South Africa and Future Scenarios," *Crime Index* 2, no. 3 (1998): 1-5.

————. "South Africa: Crime in Transition," unpublished manuscript, Institute for Security Studies, Midrand, South Africa, 1997.

Simkins, Charles. "Problems of Reconstruction," *Journal of Democracy* 7, no. 1 (January 1996): 82–95.

Simpson, Mark. "Foreign and Domestic Factors in the Transformation of Frelimo," *Journal of Modern African Studies* 31, no. 2 (1993).

South Africa at a Glance, 1997–98. (Johannesburg: Editors Incorporated SA, 1998).

South Africa Foundation. *Growth for All: An Economic Strategy for South Africa* (Johannesburg: SAF, February 1996).

South Africa Yearbook, 1995. (Pretoria: South African Communications Service, 1995).

South Africa Yearbook, 1997. (Pretoria: South African Communications Service, 1997).

South African Institute for Race Relations (SAIRR). *South Africa Survey, 1996/1997* (Johannesburg, SAIRR, 1997).

Spence, Jack, et al. *Chapultepec: Five Years Later: El Salvador's Political Reality and Uncertain Future* (Cambridge, Mass.: Hemisphere Initiatives, January 16, 1997).

Speth, James Gustave. "Linking Relief to Development: Lessons and Perspectives," background paper to multidonor roundtable, January 15, 1999.

Stahler-Sholk, Richard. "El Salvador's Negotiated Transition: From Low-Intensity Conflict to Low-Intensity Democracy," *Journal of InterAmerican Studies and World Affairs* (spring 1996).

Stanley, William, et al. *Protectors or Perpetrators? The Institutional Crisis of the Salvadoran Civilian Police* (Washington, D.C.: Washington Office on Latin America/Hemisphere Initiatives, January 1996).

Stedman, Stephen John. "Negotiation and Mediation in Internal Conflict," in Michael E. Brown, ed., *The International Dimensions of Internal Conflict* (Cambridge: MIT Press, 1996).

Stewart, Frances. "The Root Causes of Conflict: Some Conclusions," in E. Wayne Nafziger, Frances Stewart, and Raimo Vayrynen, eds., *The Origins of Humanitarian Emergencies: War and Displacement in Developing Countries* (Oxford: Oxford University Press, 1999).

Stokke, Olav, ed. *Aid and Political Conditionality* (London: Frank Cass, 1995).

Swedish Ministry of Foreign Affairs, "Mobilization and Allocation of Resources for Post-Conflict Assistance and Identification of Appropriate Modalities for Implementation," note for discussion by the DAC Task Force on Conflict, Peace, and Development Cooperation, January 9–10, 1997.

Swedish Statement. CG Meeting on El Salvador, April 1, 1993.

Than, Mya. "Rehabilitation and Economic Reconstruction in Cambodia," *Contemporary Southeast Asia* 14, no. 3 (December 1992), 269–286.

Thompson, Leonard. *A History of South Africa* (New Haven: Yale University Press, 1995).

Tripartite Action Plan on Revenues, Expenditures and Donor Funding for the Palestinian Authority. (Various dates).

UNDP (United Nations Development Programme). *Apoyando a Nuevos Protagonistas en la Agricultura Salvadoreña: Programa de Capacitación para Excombatientes del FMLN* (San Salvador: UNDP/El Salvador, December 1993).

———. *Comprehensive Paper on Cambodia,* March 20, 1992.

———. *Development Cooperation Report for South Africa, 1993* (Johannesburg: UNDP, 1993).

———. *Final Progress Report. Emergency Programme for Persons in Process of Demobilization in El Salvador* (San Salvador, UNDP/Regional Bureau for Latin America and the Caribbean, February 1993).

———. *Human Development Report 1996* (New York: Oxford University Press, 1996).

———. *Human Development Report 1998* (New York: Oxford University Press, 1998).

———. *Programa de Apoyo a la Reinserción Económica de Lideres y Mandos Medios del FMLN (Proyectors ELS/93/006 y ELS/93/012)* (San Salvador: UNDP/El Salvador, March 1993).

———. *Report on UNDP Activities and Coordination Related to the Peace Process in El Salvador* (San Salvador: UNDP/El Salvador, December 15, 1992).

———. *Technical and Financial Cooperation with El Salvador, as Reported by Donors (1992–1997)* (El Salvador: UNDP/El Salvador, July 1997).

UNDP/DDSMS (United Nations Development Programme and United Nations Department for Development Support and Management Services). *Elections in the Peace Process in Mozambique: Record of an Experience* (New York: United Nations, 1996).

UNDP/ERD (United Nations Development Program/Emergency Response Division). "Building Bridges Between Relief and Development: A Compendium of the UNDP Record in Crisis Countries," www.undp.org/~erdweb/bridges.htm.

———. "Informal Briefing Note on Strategic Frameworks," December 1997.

———. "One-Page Rationale for Expanded Consolidated Inter-Agency Appeals" (undated).

———."TRAC 1.1.3 Crisis Committee Approvals," December 17, 1997.

———."Working for Solutions to Crisis: The Development Response," December 1998.

UNDP (United Nations Development Programme), Rwanda Mission. "Linking Relief to Development," June 1998.

UNHCR (United Nations High Commissioner for Refugees). "Final Report: QIPs," Maputo, UNHCR, June 20, 1996.

———. "Mozambique: An Account from a Lessons Learned Seminar on Reintegration," Geneva, June 24–25, 1996.

UNHCR (United Nations High Commissioner for Refugees) and World Bank. "Roundtable on the Gap Between Humanitarian Assistance and Long-Term Development," summary of multidonor Brookings Institution meeting, January 15, 1999.

UNICEF (United Nations Children's Fund). "Summary of UNICEF Program of Cooperation in Cambodia: 1992–1995," unpublished report, Tokyo, ICORC II, March 1994.

United Nations. "Africa: Secretary-General's Report to the United Nations Security Council," April 16, 1998.

———. "Comments of the Secretary-General and the ACC on the Report of the Joint Inspection Unit," July 30, 1998.

———. "Draft Strategic Framework for International Assistance in Afghanistan," Report of the Inter-Agency Mission to Islamabad and Afghanistan, September 19–October 15, 1997.

———. An Inventory of Post-Conflict Peace-Building Activities (New York: United Nations, 1996).

———. Programme of Cooperation in the West Bank and Gaza Strip, 1998–99 (Gaza: UNSCO, 1997), archived at http://www.arts.mcgill.ca/mepp/unsco/unfront.html.

———. "Report of the Secretary-General," July 16, 1997.

———. Report of the United Nations Fact-Finding Mission on Present Structures and Practices of Administration in Cambodia: 24 April–9 May 1990 (New York: United Nations, June 1990).

———. "Second Report to the Secretary-General on the Work of the Special Coordinator for Economic and Social Development," December 1996.

———. "The Secretary-General's Statement to the Special Meeting of the General Assembly on Reform," July 16, 1997, www.un.org/reform/track2/htm.

———. Supplement to An Agenda for Peace (New York: United Nations, January 3, 1995).

———. The United Nations and Apartheid, 1948–1994 (New York: UN Department of Public Information, 1994).

———. The United Nations and Mozambique, 1992–1995 (New York: UN Department of Public Information, 1995).

———. Working with NGOs: United Nations System Operational Partnerships with Non-Governmental Organizations (draft), Joint Inspection Unit report, December 1992.

United Nations, Deputy Secretary-General. "Draft Generic Guidelines for a Strategic Framework Approach for Response to and Recovery from Crisis," October 27, 1998.

———. "Strategic Framework for Afghanistan," June 23, 1998.

United Nations, DHA (Department of Humanitarian Affairs). "Afghanistan: Coordination in a Fragmented State" (New York and Geneva: United Nations, December 1996).

———. Consolidated Inter-Agency Appeal for Bosnia and Herzegovina, Croatia, Federal Republic of Yugoslavia, Former Yugoslav Republic of Macedonia, January–December 1997 (New York and Geneva: United Nations, November 1996).

————. Consolidated Inter-Agency Appeal for Bosnia and Herzegovina, Croatia, Federal Republic of Yugoslavia, Former Yugoslav Republic of Macedonia, January–December 1998 (New York and Geneva: United Nations, November 1997).

————. *Humanitarian Report 1997* (New York: United Nations, 1997).

United Nations, DHA-UNDP. "Building Bridges Between Relief and Development," Final Report of DHA-UNDP Workshop, United Nations Staff College, Turin, Italy, June, 1997.

United Nations, ECOSOC. "Strengthening of the Coordination of Emergency Humanitarian Assistance of the United Nations: Report of the Secretary-General," June 12, 1998.

United Nations, General Assembly. *Assistance for the Reconstruction and Development of El Salvador,* Report of the Secretary-General, Report A/52/433, October 8, 1997.

————. *La Situación en Centroamérica: Procedimientos para Establecer la Paz Firme y Duradera, y Progreso para la Configuración de una Región de Paz, Libertad, Democracia y Desarrollo: Evaluación del Proceso de Paz en El Salvador,* Report of the Secretary-General, A/51/917, July 1, 1997.

————. "Strengthening of the Coordination of Emergency Humanitarian Assistance of the United Nations," GA Resolution 51, February 10, 1997.

————. *Strengthening of the Coordination of Humanitarian and Disaster Relief Assistance of the United Nations, Including Special Economic Assistance: Special Economic Assistance to Individual Countries or Regions: Assistance for the Reconstruction and Development of El Salvador,* Report of the Secretary-General to the United Nations General Assembly, A/52/433, October 8, 1997.

United Nations, Joint Inspection Unit. "Coordination at Headquarters and Field Level Between the United Nations Agencies Involved in Peace-Building: An Assessment of Possibilities," September 1997.

United Nations, OCHA (Office for the Coordination of Humanitarian Affairs). "Relations Between Representatives of the Emergency Relief Coordinator and Special Representatives of the Secretary-General," note for guidance, January 19, 1999.

————. "A Simple Guide to Strategic Frameworks," October 1998.

United Nations, Security Council. *Further Report of the Secretary-General on the United Nations Observer Mission in El Salvador,* United Nations Security Council S/26790, November 23, 1993.

United Nations, UN SG General Reports to the Security Council. *Status of Implementation of the Plan of Action as of 15 April 1996.*

UNOHAC (United Nations Operation in Mozambique, Office of Humanitarian Assistance Coordination). "Comments on the USAID Paper on the Reintegration of Demobilized Soldiers," mimeograph, Maputo, ca. October 1993.

————. *Consolidated Humanitarian Assistance Programme, 1992–1994, Final Report* (New York: United Nations Department for Humanitarian Affairs, December 1994).

UNSCERO (United Nations Special Coordinator for Emergency Relief Operations). *Closing Reports,* Maputo, UNSCERO, 1987–1993.

UNSCO (United Nations Special Coordinator in the Occupied Territories). *Emergency Employment Generation Schemes,* August 1996.

———. *Quarterly Report: Economic and Social Conditions in the West Bank and Gaza Strip* (various dates), archived at http://www.arts.mcgill.ca/mepp/unsco/unqr.html.

———. *United Nations Programme of Cooperation for the West Bank and Gaza, 1998–99* (Gaza: UNSCO, 1997).

UNSCO (United Nations Special Coordinator in the Occupied Territories) and World Bank. *Closure on the West Bank and Gaza: Fact Sheet,* October 6, 1997.

UNTAC (United Nations Transitional Authority in Cambodia). *Rehabilitation and Development in Cambodia: Achievements and Strategies,* report prepared for Donors Review Meeting, Phnom Penh, February 25, 1993.

Urabe. *Statement by the Japanese Representative at the Consultative Group Meeting for El Salvador,* March 23, 1992.

USAID (United States Agency for International Development). *After the War Is Over What Comes Next? Promoting Democracy, Human Rights, and Reintegration in Post-Conflict Societies* (Washington, D.C.: USAID, May 1997).

———. *From Bullets to Ballots: Electoral Assistance to Post-Conflict Societies* (Washington, D.C.: USAID, 1997).

———. *USAID/South Africa Briefing Book* (Pretoria: USAID, 1995).

USAID/El Salvador (United States Agency for International Development/El Salvador). *Action Plan FY1992–1993* (San Salvador: USAID, February 1991).

———. *El Salvador, FY1990–1994 Country Development Strategy Statement* (San Salvador: USAID, June 1989).

———. *The First Three Years of the Peace and National Recovery Project (519-0394): Lessons Learned* (San Salvador: USAID, October 1994).

———. *FY 1993 ESF: Economic and Democratic Reform Program,* Program Assistance Approval Document (San Salvador: USAID, 1993).

———. *FY 1994 ESF: Modernization of the State,* Program Assistance Approval Document (San Salvador: USAID/El Salvador, July 29, 1994).

———. *Sustainable Development and Democracy in El Salvador, 1997–2002* (San Salvador: USAID, March 1996).

USAID/OTI (United States Agency for International Development/Office of Transition Initiatives). "Operational Challenges in Post-Conflict Societies," USAID Workshop, October 28–29, 1997.

USIA (United States Information Agency). "US-South Africa Binational Commission Fact Sheet" (Washington, D.C., USIA, 1997).

Vines, Alex. *Renamo: Terrorism in Mozambique* (London: James Currey, 1991).

Wedel, Janine R. *Collision and Collusion: The Strange Case of Western Aid to Eastern Europe, 1989–1998* (New York: St. Martin's, 1998).

Wilson, Francis, and Mamphela Ramphele. "Children in South Africa," in *Children on the Front Line* (New York: UNICEF, 1987).

Woehrel, Steven. "Bosnia: U.S.-Led Train-and-Equip Program," *CRS Report for Congress,* December 13, 1996.

WOLA (Washington Office on Latin America). *Reluctant Reforms: The Cristiani Government and the International Community in the Process of Salvadoran Post-War Reconstruction* (Washington, D.C.: WOLA, 1993).

Wood, Bernard. "Lessons and Guidance for Donors: Key Points from the Development Assistance Committee's Guidelines on Conflict, Peace, and Development Cooperation," (Paris: OECD, fall 1997).

Wood, Elizabeth. "The Peace Accords and Post War Reconstruction," in James Boyce, ed., *Economic Policy for Building Peace: The Lessons of El Salvador* (Boulder: Lynne Rienner, 1996).

World Bank. "Conflict Prevention and Post-Conflict Reconstruction: Perspectives and Prospects" (Washington, D.C.: World Bank, August 1998).

————. *Consultative Group for El Salvador, Paris, April 1, 1993: Chairman's Report of Proceedings* (Washington, D.C.: IBRD, October 29, 1993).

————. *Consultative Group for El Salvador, Paris, May 15 and 16, 1991: Chairman's Report of Proceedings* (Washington, D.C.: IBRD, August 2, 1991).

————. *Developing the Occupied Territories: An Investment in Peace* (six vols.) (Washington, D.C.: World Bank, September 1993).

————. *The Donor Experience and the Way Ahead*, statement to the Fifth Consultative Group Meeting for the West Bank and Gaza, December 14–15, 1997.

————. *El Salvador: Competitiveness Enhancement Technical Assistance Project*, Project Identification Document, May 29, 1995.

————. *El Salvador: Public Sector Modernization Project*, Project Identification Document, October 1995.

————. *El Salvador: Updating Economic Memorandum*, Report No. 4054-ES (Washington, D.C.: IBRD, January 21, 1983).

————. *Emergency Assistance Program for the Occupied Territories* (Washington, D.C.: World Bank, 1994).

————. *Holst Peace Fund Status Statement* (various dates).

————. News release no. 92/LAC (Washington, D.C., IBRD, 1993).

————. *Palestinian NGO Project: Discussion Paper*, April 1, 1997, archived at http://www.arts.mcgill.ca/mepp/pdin/docs/wbngos2.html.

————. "Partnership for Development: Proposed Actions for the World Bank," May 20, 1998.

————. *Post-Conflict Reconstruction: The Role of the World Bank* (Washington, D.C.: World Bank, 1998).

————. "Strategy and Program for Managing the Transition to National Reconstruction," prepared for the meeting of the Consultative Group for Mozambique, November 1992.

————. *West Bank/Gaza Update* (various dates), archived at http://www.palecon.org.

————. *The World Bank's Experience with Post-conflict Reconstruction, Vol. 1: Synthesis Report*, Report No. 17769 (May 4, 1998).

————. *The World Bank's Experience with Post-conflict Reconstruction, Vol. 2: Bosnia and Herzegovina Case Study*, Report No. 17769 (May 4, 1998).

————. *The World Bank's Experience with Post-conflict Reconstruction, Vol. 3: El Salvador Case Study*, Report No. 17769 (May 4, 1998).

————. *The World Bank's Experience with Post-conflict Reconstruction, Vol. 5: Desk Reviews of Cambodia, Eritrea, Haiti, Lebanon, Rwanda, and Sri Lanka*, Report No. 17769 (May 4, 1998).

————. *World Development Report 1997* (Washington, D.C.: World Bank, 1997).

World Bank (Central Europe Department) and European Bank for Reconstruction and Development. "Bosnia and Herzegovina: Priority for Recovery and Growth," Discussion Paper, December 8, 1995.

World Bank and European Union, *Donor Data Base Report* (Washington, D.C.: World Bank, 1997).

Zack-Williams, Alfred B. "Sierra Leone: The Political Economy of Civil War, 1991-98," *Third World Quarterly* 20, no. 1 (1999).

Zafar, Samiera. "An Analysis of the Education Crisis in KwaZulu-Natal," *Education Monitor* (Durban, Education Policy Unit, University of Natal) 9, no. 1 (March 1998).

Zartman, I. William. "Dynamics and Constraints in Negotiations in Internal Conflicts," in I. William Zartman, ed., *Elusive Peace: Negotiating an End to Civil Wars* (Washington, D.C.: Brookings Institution, 1995).

Zaucker, Joachim, with Andrew Griffel and Peter Gubser. *Toward Middle East Peace and Development: International Assistance to the Palestinians and the Role of NGOs During the Transition to Civil Society* (Washington, D.C.: InterAction, December 1995).

The Contributors

Hisham Awartani is professor of economics at An-Najah University in Nablus (Palestine) and head of the Economics Department at the Center for Palestine Research and Studies. He was a member in the steering committee of the Harvard University project on Economics of Transition after Peace and served as member in the Palestinian negotiating team on economic relations with Israel. He has published numerous papers on facets of the Palestinian economy and is the author of *The Economy of the West Bank and Gaza Strip, 1967–1993*.

Nicole Ball is a fellow at the Overseas Development Council in Washington, D.C. Her recent publications include *Complex Crisis and Complex Peace: Humanitarian Coordination in Angola* (with Kathleen Campbell); *Spreading Good Practices in Security Sector Reform;* and *Managing Conflict: Lessons From the South African Peace Committees* (with Chris Spies).

Sam Barnes is currently a Bunting fellow at Harvard's Radcliffe Institute for Advanced Study, where she is conducting research on the topic of postconflict peace consolidation. A specialist in social and economic rehabilitation in postconflict societies, she has worked for the United Nations in Mozambique, Liberia, Angola, Somalia, Tajikistan, and Bosnia. Her most recent publications include *Humanitarian Aid Coordination During War and Peace in Mozambique: 1985–1995* and *NGOs in Peacekeeping Operations*.

James K. Boyce is professor of economics at the University of Massachusetts, Amherst. He is the editor of *Economic Policy for Building Peace: The Lessons of El Salvador*, an outcome of the Adjustment Toward Peace project that he directed on behalf of the United Nations Development Programme.

411

Michael Bratton is professor of political science and African studies at Michigan State University. His most recent coauthored book is *Democratic Experiments in Africa: Regime Transitions in Comparative Perspective.* He spent 1998 as a Visiting Fulbright Senior Scholar at the Universities of Natal and Durban-Westville in South Africa.

Rex Brynen is associate professor of political science at McGill University in Montreal. He is author of *A Very Political Economy: Peacebuilding and Foreign Aid in Palestine,* and author or (co)editor of five other books on Middle East politics.

Michael Foley is associate professor of politics at The Catholic University of America in Washington, D.C. He has published on grassroots politics in Latin America and on the role of civil society organizations in the peace process and postconflict development issues in El Salvador. He is also the author, with Bob Edwards, of numerous articles on social capital and civil society. Foley is currently writing a book on the insurgencies in southern Mexico in the 1990s and their roots in the crisis in rural development in that country.

Shepard Forman is founder and director of the Center on International Cooperation at New York University. Previously, he was director of the Ford Foundation's international affairs programs (1991–1996) and human rights and governance programs (1981–1991). He is author of *Diagnosing America: Anthropology and Public Engagement* and coeditor, with Romita Ghosh, of *Promoting Reproductive Health: Investing in Health for Development.*

Zlatko Hurtić is assistant to the executive director of the World Bank. He was previously employed by the Ministry of Foreign Affairs of Bosnia and Herzegovina, most recently as assistant minister and head of the Department for Reconstruction and Economic Recovery.

Chris Landsberg is deputy director of the Centre for Policy Studies, an independent policy research center based in Johannesburg. He was a former Rhodes Scholar at Christ Church, Oxford, and a Hamburg Fellow at Stanford. Landsberg has published widely on South Africa's foreign policy, and Africa's international relations and the international dimensions of democratization. He is presently working on a manuscript: *The Diplomacy of Transition: The International Community and South Africa's Triple Transition, 1994–1999.*

Stewart Patrick is research associate at the Center on International Cooperation at New York University. He holds a doctorate in international relations from Oxford University and has been a research fellow in foreign policy studies at the Brookings Institution and a guest scholar at the Norwegian Nobel Institute. He is currently writing a book titled *America's Quest for an Open World: Multilateralism and the U.S. National Interest.*

Sorpong Peou is associate professor of political science, Sophia University, Tokyo. Formerly, he was a fellow at the Institute of Southeast Asian Studies (Singapore). He is the author of *Conflict Neutralization in the Cambodia War: From Battlefield to Ballot-Box* and *Foreign Intervention and Regime Change in Cambodia.*

Herman Rosa is the director of PRISMA (Programa Salvadoreño de Investigación sobre Desarrollo y Medio Ambiente), a policy-oriented research center based in San Salvador. He has published a number of articles linking environmental, social, and economic issues in El Salvador and has also studied the role of external donor agencies and financial institutions in El Salvador since the 1980s. He is the author of *AID y las transformaciones globales en El Salvador.*

Amela Šapčanin currently works as a management associate with Citibank, N.A (Global Emerging Markets). She served in the foreign service of Bosnia and Herzegovina (1993–1996) and worked on several projects as a research associate and consultant with the World Bank in Washington, D.C., and has coauthored several case studies on microfinance in the Middle East and North Africa.

Clare Woodcraft is currently the banking and finance associate editor at *Middle East Economic Survey*, Cyprus. She was formerly the managing editor of the Palestinian Economic Pulse based in Ramallah, the West Bank, where she participated in numerous economic/development research projects on Palestine.

Susan L. Woodward is a senior research fellow at the Centre for Defence Studies, King's College, University of London. She has been a senior fellow at the Brookings Institution in Washington (1990–1999), and a professor of political science at Yale University, Williams College, Mount Holyoke College, and Northwestern University. She has served as head of the analysis and assessment unit in the office of the Special Representative of the Secretary General for UNPROFOR, as well as special advisor to the head of the OSCE Mission to Bosnia and Herzegovina. She is the author of *Balkan Tragedy: Chaos and Dissolution after the Cold War* and *Socialist Unemployment: The Political Economy of Yugoslavia, 1945–1990.*

Kenji Yamada is a chief researcher at the International Development Center of Japan, a private, nonprofit think tank specializing in international development policy. He has conducted a number of study projects on development and aid policy, including military expenditures in developing countries, participatory development, global environmental problems, and socioeconomic development in Cambodia. He has taught at Waseda University since 1994.

Index

Absorption of aid: in Bosnia and Herzegovina, 27, 345–347; in Cambodia, 81–86; incapacity, 11; in the Palestinian territories, 223–224; in South Africa, 298–300, 306

Accountability, 16; among recipients, 58–59; in Bosnia and Herzegovina, 329, 358–359; in the Palestinian territories, 24, 231; tracking aid delivery, 56–58

Acts of Congress: Comprehensive Anti-Apartheid Act of *1986,* 263; Foreign Operations Appropriations Act of *1998,* 361*n23;* Middle East Peace Facilitation Acts of *1993,* 239; PLO Commitments Compliance Act of *1993,* 239; South African Democratic Support Act of *1993,* 266; War Crimes Prosecution Facilitation Act of *1997,* 327, 361*n23,* 364*n66*

ADB. *See* Asia Development Bank

Ad Hoc Liaison Committee (AHLC): delivery of aid, 222; establishment of, 211; EU-U.S. conflict in, 214; failure of, 219, 229; reform of PECDAR, 230; Tripartite Action Plan monitoring by, 220; value as coordinator of, 250, 251

Administrative capacity, 83–84, 99

African Development Bank, 8, 274

African National Congress (ANC): anti-apartheid struggle, 368; bases in the frontline countries, 161; bilateral aid, 280; conditionality of aid, 382*n25;* corporate social investment, 303; elections, 305; European ties with, 296; *masakhane* campaign, 297; political objectives of, 260; Reconstruction and Development Program, 267; view of aid, 265

Agency for International Development (USAID), 46; in Bosnia and Herzegovina, 341, 343–344; in Cambodia, 100; downsizing of, 270; in El Salvador, 118–121, 135, 136–138, 147, 157*n78;* in Mozambique, 201*n30;* in the Palestinian territories, 227, 236–237, 247, 248; in South Africa, 178, 273, 275, 292–293, 295, 301

AHLC. *See* Ad Hoc Liaison Committee

Aid: decentralized nature of, 13–15; defining need for, 172–173; definition, 337; distributional effects of, 372–379; domestic politics and, 14, 40–41, 96–97; donor-driven, 37; double counting, 41; fatigue, 11; inappropriate, 367; need for flexibility in, 197; objectives for, 11; for peace, 110*n110,* 367; political consequences of, 262–265, 367, 372–381; tracking flows of, 57–58, 172–174; types, 99, 369–372

Aid for Democracy Group, 181, 182, 188

Ajello, Aldo, 174, 177, 179, 191

ANC. *See* African National Congress

415

About the Book

THIS COMPARATIVE STUDY IS CONCERNED WITH THE CAUSES—
and consequences—of failures to fulfill pledges of aid to postconflict
societies.

In each of six case studies—Bosnia, Cambodia, El Salvador, Mozambique, Palestine, and South Africa—the coauthors (including one scholar
from a donor state and one from a recipient) first establish the sources,
composition, and objectives of pledged aid and examine aid conditionality,
delivery, and coordination. They then trace aid absorption, benefits, and
impact on peace building and economic recovery. Finally, they assess the
causes, consequences, and lessons of pledge gaps: What explains shortfalls
in aid delivery? What social, economic, and political difficulties have
ensued? And what does the experience suggest for future multilateral
efforts at transition assistance? Good intentions notwithstanding, it is clear
that recurrent delays and failures in aid follow-through can threaten vulnerable polities whose collapse would endanger regional peace and security.

Shepard Forman is founder and director of the Center on International
Cooperation (CIC) at New York University. Previously, he was director of
the Ford Foundation's International Affairs Programs (1991–1996) and
Human Rights and Governance programs (1981–1991). His most recent
publication is *Diagnosing America: Anthropology and Public Engagement*.
Stewart Patrick is research associate at CIC; he has also been research
fellow in foreign policy at the Brookings Institution and guest scholar at
the Norwegian Nobel Institute. He is currently writing a book on multilateralism and U.S. foreign policy.